# FILM

# FILM

## A Modern Art

Aaron Sultanik

CORNWALL BOOKS
NEW YORK • LONDON • TORONTO

Cornwall Books
440 Forsgate Drive
Cranbury, NJ 08512

Cornwall Books
25 Sicilian Avenue
London WC1A 2QH, England

Cornwall Books
2133 Royal Windsor Drive
Unit 1
Mississauga, Ontario
Canada L5J 1K5

The paper used in this publication meets the minimum requirements of the
American National Standard for Permanence of Paper for Printed Library
Materials Z39.48-1984.

**Library of Congress Cataloging in Publication Data**

Sultanik, Aaron, 1949–
    Film, a modern art.

    Bibliography: p.
    Includes index.
    1. Moving-picture plays—History and criticism.
I. Title.
PN1995.S79    1985       791.43'75       82-48693
ISBN 0-8453-4752-7 (alk. paper)

Printed in the United States of America

To
Johnnie Cole Kelly,
Light of my Life

# Contents

# Acknowledgments

The loving support of my parents, Kalman and Bronia Sultanik, throughout the many years of research and revision that went into this work is indelibly imprinted on my memory.

I would also like to thank Donald Richie, who opened the film archives of The Museum of Modern Art to my studies.

# Introduction

*Film: A Modern Art* is a three-part survey of the medium of motion pictures—first, as it evolves within a network of ideas and artistic experimentation unique to modern culture; second, as an art form which has created a unifying narrative legacy; and third, as a contemporary stylistic phenomenon. There have been numerous interpretations of film, from studies of its wide ranging sociological impact to historical accounts that identify the figure of the director as the guiding force in its triumphs and disasters. One commonly experienced aspect of the film experience is its ability to capture the ebb and flow of nature, and perhaps more significantly, that of consciousness. Film can be the most scientific of media through its documentarian presentation of reality; it can also simulate the dynamic of conscious and subconscious sensation through its autonomous rhythms and settings. Whether in its reproduction of the physically interconnecting, objective sphere of man, nature, and history, or in its penetration of the mentally imaginary, subjective realm of a character's inner fears and dreams, the multifaceted techniques of the medium inspire eclectic styles of filmmaking and an equally eclectic mass of moviegoers.

The "idea" of film art—interpreting the film experience in terms of its aesthetic congruity—seems, at best, a precarious endeavor. Few will argue that there have been good, perhaps great films; but the nexus of the film experience has been as a popular, populist art, attracting an audience which requires no special education or enlightenment to enjoy its moving pictures. Yet one of the reasons film art remains one of the most intriguing of propositions is the discovery of original compounds of art that have resulted from film's immediate social extension as an entertainment medium and from its dramatic origin in traditional themes and myths. An inquiry into the art of the movies, owing to the diverse role of film in the twentieth century, is considerably different from a critical analysis of classic literature and the arts. The story of the movies cannot be explained simply through the sublime moments of film art; our study of film art entails an appreciation of the combative and often creative interplay involving social mores, big business financing, technological progress, and artistic vision throughout the history of motion pictures.

*Film: A Modern Art* is divided into three sections—"Mind, Modernism, and the Movies," "The Varieties of the Film Experience," and "The Contemporary Cinema." "Mind, Modernism, and the Movies" is a study of the intellectual

13

currents that preceded and paralleled the course of film history. Before reviewing the seminal films and filmmakers that have made the film experience one of
thought and style, an attempt is made to pinpoint the intellectual parameters
which established a mode of inquiry and style of exposition for the modern age.
Modernism is the linking, cognitive thread for those philosophers and artists
who gave new meaning to basic constructs of thought and style. By first
approaching modernism as a unique conceptual and sensory framework, an
establishing shot of the inner world of nineteenth-century thought is presented;
by then identifying modernism as a new style or development in the arts, a more
intimate, detailed image of the artistic experimentation of the last decades of the
nineteenth century and the first decades of the twentieth century is developed;
when the movies are then turned to as a conclusive manifestation of modernism,
this close-up view will result in a comprehensive picture of its varied social and
artistic meanings.

The first three chapters of "Mind, Modernism, and the Movies" are devoted
to the origins of modernism, first among philosophers and critics in Europe,
then among leading intellectual and artistic voices in America, and concluding
with a general formulation of modernism through examples of its leading expo-
nents in America and Europe. The next five chapters review major developments
in the art of film, beginning with the documentarian tendencies in the shorts of
Edison and the Lumières; the archetypal experiments and innovations of
Georges Méliès, R. W. Paul, and Edwin S. Porter; and the critical narrative
punctuation of D. W. Griffith. The chapters on the silent film conclude with
studies of key German and Russian films and the abstractions of the French
avant-grade. The underlying realism of the sound film is exemplified through
the nationalism of Russian filmmakers, the naturalism of Jean Renoir, and the
transition, first in comedy from silent-film slapstick to the theatrical, verbal
panache of Ernst Lubitsch, and second in the crime film from the psychological
exercises in terror by Fritz Lang to the melodramatic conventions essayed in the
English cinema by Alfred Hitchcock. The postwar period begins with the Italian humanist cinema and ends with examples of revolt and retrenchment in the
American film of the sixties and seventies.

I have included two concluding chapters on film acting and film criticism in
"Mind, Modernism, and the Movies." The one on acting was incorporated
because of the hegemony of narrative cinema among the film capitals of the
world and the role of the film actor as the primary vehicle for film's numerous
experiments in classic and modern stylizations. The crafts of cinematography,
cutting, and composition could have equally merited independent sections. But
as they support the art of the actor—our focus in narrative cinema—I felt that
they were adequately summarized in the previous chapters, while the art of the
film actor demands special consideration because of our penetration of a film
through his presence. The chapter on film criticism offers a brief review of
several trends in the popular and academic resonance of the movies.

In "The Varieties of the Film Experience," an extended survey of film history, the most popular story formulas of the major filmmaking countries are

assembled into seven distinct types of narrative. As an eclectic art film has borrowed not only themes and myths from Western literature and art, but also the techniques and genres of representation in the literature and art of the past. The recurrent paradox of the film experience—utilizing the most modern of instruments while adapting traditional, often outdated stories and myths— confounds the critic undertaking a straightforward record of its artistic achievments. An industry and art like filmmaking derives its appeal from satisfying a heterogeneous audience; the idea of imposing an artistic chronology on its commercial interests appears to abstract the very impetus of filmmaking. Yet by first acknowledging the paradox of movie modernism—its dependence on modern technology to reexamine the meaning of classic literature and art—this dualism can best be appreciated by an examination of the most enduring film narratives.

The model that I have adopted, interpreting film history through developments in the epic, comedy, crime, fantasy, religious, documentary, and avant-garde film, attempts both a generic and classic evaluation of film history— generic in that these story genres have continued to attract filmmakers and their audience as the most popular forms of film narrative, classic in that the breakdown of an art into distinct narrative models underscores the influence of classic literature and art on film and the film under consideration as the most inclusive method of writing a critical history. The other critical options in undertaking a film history—chronological, national, individual—appear to have significant shortcomings for the stylistic congruity that I seek. The chronological summary in chapters 4 through 7 of "Mind, Modernism, and the Movies" encompasses different types of films and diverse national and individual influences. It was incorporated into this first part because it provided a necessary stylistic abstract by which one could measure the validity of modernism in film history. But in "The Varieties of the Film Experience" the reader is presented with a historical analysis of various story genres with the purpose of learning their individual meaning—how different films and filmmakers have reinterpreted the proposed story model. A chronological review assimilates numerous types of films and styles; our critical method offers a sharper, more exacting stylistic history.

A history through studies of individual countries or moviemakers can prove even more fragmentary. The cultural and social factors that influence a film can be discussed in the narrative context that I propose; but a discussion of a movie as an example or symbol of social history, while fulfilled through a national survey, is not my objective. The interpretation of film history through individual, transcendent voices shows a tendency to romanticize history and to see the individual figure and the vagaries of his personal life as primary influences in the making of a film; in an art constituted of numerous personalities and disciplines, the dangers of this method are increased. A film's style can be traced to any one of a number of factors, from that of its social origins and commercial pressures to the craftsmen perfecting its final form. The emphasis that I place on narrative rather than on director or star is more sensitive to the eclectic disciplines that comprise the making of a film and to an understanding of the film narrative itself as the objective end result of filmmaking.

"The Contemporary Cinema" may seem, at first, an unnecessary addition to a survey of film history. Several important issues, however, with far-reaching social and stylistic consequences justify a separate account of major developments in postwar American and foreign film circles: the end of World War II; the rise of television as a new rival to the movies; the final Supreme Court ruling against monopolization of movie distribution by the major studios; the Congressional investigations into Communist sympathizers in the film community; the academic acceptance of film studies; and the parallel change in film journals by a generation of film critics with a new awareness of the continuity of the past, and their prominence among the new voices of filmmaking in Italy, France, England, and America. Yet several, if not all, of these occurrences were previously manifest in film history: World War I enabled American producers to gain significant control and prestige as the entrepreneurs of the film world; radio was an antecedent of television in American society; the courts had entertained arguments against movie monopolization since the "patent war" at the turn of the century; outcries against movie pornography accompanied the filming of a kiss in 1895, and more fervent demands for censorship grew as the movies increased in length and popularity; film had attracted serious attention from the time of Griffith's *The Birth of a Nation*, and its academic sanctification in the fifties was only a long overdue recognition of its education of moviegoers throughout the world. There are numerous stylistic subdivisions that one can superimpose upon a reading of the silent and sound film, but as the adventures in film stylization of the fifties, sixties, and seventies operate within a considerably different social context, our approach seems less arbitrary.

The reason for the studies of the French and Italian cinema through the films of their major directors, with concluding chapters on general trends in the French and Italian cinema, was created out of necessity more than anything else. Since most of my moviegoing was in New York City's repertory film theaters and The Museum of Modern Art, I have been limited by the politics and pragmatics of film distribution and by the difficulties in achieving universal film libraries. As this book is being sent to the printers, a major film retrospective is underway at The Museum of Modern Art—a festival of French films from the early sound period to the appearance of the New Wave. Though few if any masterpieces have surfaced, this retrospective allows us to better understand the appeal of movies in France while increasing our knowledge of their craftsmen and actors. A survey of the artistry of Truffaut, Resnais, Godard, Chabrol, and that of their most long-standing partners in production and acting fulfills a similar function. Their successes and failures, like those of their most accomplished contemporaries in the American cinema, become a record of personal, national, and international history; whereas their films provide the filmgoer with an insight into the upper echelons of filmmaking, the retrospective of the more conventional French movie fare at The Museum of Modern Art offers a detailed picture of the French film industry and the degree of similarity it shares with the archetypes and clichés of movie production throughout the major filmmaking countries.

The films of Luis Buñuel, Orson Welles, and Ingmar Bergman have been separated because of their role as independents in film production, though both Buñuel and Bergman established significant relationships with filmmaking industries in Mexico and Sweden. The inclusion of Japanese cinema needs no defense, other than mentioning that I was able to include a modest review of its newer faces and films largely due to the creative, continuous programming of the Japan Society in New York. If only all nations were so well-served abroad.

The final chapter in "The Contemporary Cinema" examines the role of the avant-garde in the movies of the seventies, particularly in the West German film renaissance, and the influences of technology on film. The technical mastery of moving pictures gave birth to the most powerful art of the twentieth century; as technology assumes a life independent of its artistic uses, one's estimate of present and possible film styles must begin and end with an understanding of the consonances and dissonances that exist between film as technology and film as art.

# FILM

Let us now make another simile, to illustrate the condition of the knowing subject according to Kant. The knowing subject becomes rather like a spectator who sits in a cinema and watches the moving picture appearing on the screen before him. Similarly the observer of nature, or of the world in general, sees before him a living pageant of color, sound and other qualities. However, according to Kant, the projector that throws the picture on the screen is not something existing outside the spectator, but it is his own mind, using a film upon which outside impressions have been impressed. The screen itself is not outside the spectator, but it is his own consciousness, on which the film made by the recording apparatus of his own mind is projected. So that everything— the show, the projector, the screen—all, except impressions on the film— exists only in the mind of the spectator, and there is nothing outside it, save the things in themselves, unknowable in their own nature.

—G. N. G. Orsini, *Coleridge and German Idealism*

# Mind,
# Modernism, and the Movies

# 1

# The Evolution of Modernism (i)

We are products of the modern imagination. Our education of children, our choices for elective office, our styles of dress, the movies we see—all are expressions of our modernism. A concept like modern culture is juxtaposed to a classic idea of culture while a modernist in art is clearly distinguished from a classicist. Yet for all the freedom which the term exhibits in our vocabulary, it is apparent that modernism undergoes a wide variety of modifications, assuming nuances of meaning peculiar to each phenomenon it describes. One striking aspect of the term is its constant change of resonance; because of the continuous experimentation surrounding the evolution of modernism, the most recently acclaimed modernist often reclassifies his predecessor as old-fashioned, perhaps even a classicist.

The idea of modernism is further complicated by the variety of intellectual prophets and social movements that have been identified as precursors of the modern. One commonly cited point of origin is Francis Bacon and his scientifically experimental theory of knowledge; other familiar examples include the ethical radicalism of Rousseau and Montesquieu's comparative method of analyzing legal institutions. Literary historians, musicologists, and art critics have selected from an equally diverse group of figures in determining the origins of modernism. The internal inflection of the poet's fantasies in Wordsworth's *The Prelude*, the sudden explosions of sound in Berlioz's program music, and Cézanne's telescopic penetration of the figurative textures of nature and their distillation into encompassing volumes of cones, spheres, and cylinders have found their supporters among the disciples of modernism. A potential solution to the many interpretations of the origin and meaning of modernism can be found by first proposing a definition of modernism that can illuminate the concepts and styles that prefigured the film medium. If the mastery of motion pictures was not an isolated technological achievement but part of a profound reorganization in the way the world is perceived, it is essential to see how the intellectual and art world of the nineteenth century anticipated the self-perpetuating sensory power of the movies. One can undertake a study of the film medium through a review of nineteenth-century photography and motion picture camera technology, but I believe that an inquiry into film will be immeasurably enhanced by understanding how the technological triumph of the movies was paralleled in various critical theories and styles. Modern culture, in the framework of this study, entails an approach to man and nature that is underscored in the organic, dynamic continuity of motion pictures.

One term that appears almost interchangeable with a discussion of the revolutionary or modern aspects of nineteenth-century art is "romanticism." But there are several problems implicit in equating modernism with romanticism. The more general one involves our awareness that romanticism—as a challenge to the classic standards of harmony and symmetry through its advocacy of the artist's intuition and emotions—can be discovered in different periods of history and hence loses its singular relevance in our study of the movies and modern culture. Yet unless one undertakes a historical review of the arts by analyzing the possible ebb and flow of classicism and romanticism, it is a problem that can be partially resolved as the meaning of romanticism in nineteenth-century aesthetics and art is confronted.

A second problem concerning the correlation of modernism and romanticism is that the numerous expressions of romanticism among philosophers and artists of the nineteenth century make it impossible to avoid oversimplifying the term's meaning. This problem is not unique to our study but is inherent in language itself; in art and literary criticism terms like "classicism" and "romanticism" invariably reveal nuances that they did not originally possess. Romanticism must then be approached in a piecemeal manner by tracing its development in nineteenth-century philosophy and art as an entirely original conceptual framework. Although aspects of romanticism can be uncovered in the art and philosophy of different periods, it will be unraveled expressly through the imagination of the nineteenth century. Our intention is to formulate a cohesive interpretation of romanticism that can elucidate the impact of modernism and its significance in the evolution of the film medium.

One of the crucial tests faced by the Enlightenment was the articulation of a social and moral philosophy that recognized the individual's ability for social development and self-awareness. Cartesian philosophy established the primacy of man's rational faculty, a cornerstone in the social and epistemological methodology of the Enlightenment. The idealization of the individual achieves its initial social flowering in the revolutions in France and America and in their controversies and legislation concerning the role of the state and the relative equality and perfectibility of their citizens. In the field of aesthetics the romantic idealism of German philosophy is fundamental to the Enlightenment's appreciation of the individual and his perception of art and nature.

Our starting point is Kant's *The Critique of Judgment*. Kant's classic critiques are concerned with the origin and nature of our thoughts and feelings, and their potential synthesis in leading the individual to a more certifiable level of self-consciousness and a more proximate sense of a superior, eternal design in nature. In *The Critique of Judgment*, Kant approaches the faculty of judgment as a mediating influence between the faculty of reason—from which our self-consciousness arises—and that of understanding—which attempts to discover the nature of the outside world. Art—as the object of our faculty of judgment—presents the individual with a representation of beauty. According to Kant, the artistic process, because of its innate formal design and underlying intellectual unity, involves a synthetic unification of the faculties of reason and understanding in that of judgment. The work of art is interpreted as a reflection of the dynamics of self-consciousness through the parallel process of intellectual self-awareness in both oneself and the work of art; the work of art also mirrors the nature of one's understanding of the outside world through the microcosmic, mimetic, evolutionary form common to both the work of art and nature. By seeing both the dynamics of self-consciousness and evolutionary form manifested in a work of art, Kant was able to provide a more securely rational basis for man's apprehension of a divine, cosmic order. By turning to aesthetics to elaborate his teleological argument, Kant modified the more radical aesthetic formulations of poet-seers such as Schiller by characterizing the feeling of pleasure resulting from the perception of the symbolic strategies of the artist as a unification of all of the individual's faculties of a priori determination. In his response to the empirical skepticism of Hume, Kant, although still maintaining the individual's inability to grasp the noumenon—the substratum, the eternal core of nature—sees the artist's creation leading to a more acute self-consciousness and a greater understanding of God.

Kant's examination of artistic form and the elevating quality surrounding its perception is, however, only a prelude to his consideration of the sublime. The sensation of sublimity, according to Kant, differs from that received in contemplation of art because it engages the individual with an idea dissociated from the finite forms of art—the individual recognizes a power that cannot be fathomed by the human mind. For Kant the sublime, through its negation of external forms and its absorption of the individual into the breadth of the cosmos, instills in man a more profound expression of his harmony with God.

Kant's moral and intellectual triumph involves the repudiation of the atomism of both the Ionian founders of Greek philosophy and of the seventeenth- and eighteenth-century empiricists. Whereas an original materialist like Epicurus avoided attributing a moral power to the design of nature, the empiricists of the Enlightenment attempted to nullify idealism by seeing the mind and its moral absolutes as a product of the sensations of nature. Kant did not so much refute the materialism of the early Greek philosophers or the rationalist doubts of the empiricists as he elevated his inquiry into the intellectual dynamics of the mind into a search for its moral affirmation in art and nature. He inverted Plato's argument against the inclusion of the poet-painter into a utopian republic by ascribing not deception but enlightenment to the artist. Kant saw the work of art as an ideal form; the artist as genius brings one to the boundary of the finite—through the manifold properties of the work of art—and the infinite—through the activating principles of creation and consciousness underlying his work. Art exists as the clearest, most tangible testimony to man's affinity with God. It is left to the Kantian principle of sublimity to cross the final chasm between what the mind can understand of the machinations of the universe and what it can ultimately sense of its own place in the cosmos and of the supreme force of God.

Among Kant's immediate successors, Schelling attempted a more self-confident interpretation of the powers of the mind and its correspondence to nature by envisaging a parallel process of evolution occurring in both the mind and nature. For Schelling the work of art, by unifying our conscious and subconscious faculties, results in the apprehension of the sublime. Kant's classical, conservative conception of the artist as a quasi-independent instrument of the aesthetic bounty of nature and Schelling's more radical, subjective viewpoint, in which the artist seems to mirror the creative resources of nature, were two of the key sources for one of the earliest and most emblematic of romantic theories of aesthetics: Coleridge's *Biographia Literaria*.

Coleridge, like Schelling, examined the relationship between sensation and thought, their role in art and in the perception of the sublime. Although he refused to accept the shades of deism in Schelling's philosophy, remaining firm in his religious conviction of a moral, Kantian foundation in the perception of the infinite, Coleridge too believed in the work of art as microcosm, which, by duplicating the evolution in nature, unifies one's conscious powers of thought and subconscious levels of sensation. His discussion, for example, of Wordsworth's psychologically accented poetry as reflecting the process of evolution in the vegetable world leads to a recognition of the self-referential unity of the work of art and the transcendent powers of the mind of the artist. Writing some one hundred and fifty years later and spanning the field of modern poetry from Wordsworth through Valéry, Geoffrey Hartman confirms the pertinence of Coleridge's romantic, cognitive, aesthetic doctrine.

> Aesthetic and perfect knowledge have for their object the wakeful body, namely the body in the exercise of a continuous primary act of knowledge, that of perception. In perception knowledge is truly act.... Nature, the body, and human consciousness—that is the only text.[1]

Implicit in Coleridge's rationalization of a subjective, transcendent theory of aesthetics is the premise that intuition or the feelings of the individual are the catalyst for one's ideals of truth and beauty. Whereas nature was previously conceived as a mechanical superstructure with its predetermined, irrevocable laws of operation, it is now approached as a mirror to the individual's thoughts and emotions. A large part of English romantic peotry in the first half of the nineteenth century can be seen as a realization of Coleridge's defense and development of German romantic idealism in which the poet's pursuit of the sublime reflects the dynamics of creation in the mind and nature. While the social and moral philosophers of the Enlighenment advanced the principle of freedom and equality, the aesthetic imprint of German philosophy and English poetry lies in their recognition of the individual's ability to challenge the objective idealism of art. In place of the objectivity of the artist's vision and that of nature, a subjective, dynamic sense of man and nature is championed. It results in a gradual, unequivocal rejection of the aesthetics of the eighteenth century, as evident in Keat's distaste for Boileau's strict, metric forms as it is in the manner that Delacroix's strident colors displace David's serene neoclassicism.

Coleridge was one of the first to articulate this romantic ethos, but he did not fully pursue its radical implications. For if Keats and Delacroix threatened the lyric uniformity and chromatic symmetry of the prevailing classical idiom, it was only in the latter part of the nineteenth century that romanticism revealed its complete departure from the rules and ideals of classicism. Stéphane Mallarmé and John Ruskin were keenly aware of the new standards of truth and beauty in the arts; yet they assumed a different moral stance in discussing the modern style. Mallarmé, among other French romantic poets, inferred the dynamic, organic potential of a poem as a modern substitute for its previous mechanical contrivedness.

> The pure work implies the elocutory disappearance of the poet who abandons the initiative to words mobilized by the shock of their inequality; they light one another up with mutual reflections like a virtual trail of fire upon precious stones, replacing the breathing perceptible in the old lyrical blast or the enthusiastic personal direction of the phrase.[2]

A critical premise in Mallarmé's theory is the displacement of the objective reality of nature; a poetic method is devised that reflects the cognitive and visual ellipsis underlying the artist's apprehension of reality. A poem is not a passive vehicle for an idea or symbol but achieves its ideas and symbols through the interaction—typographically, phonemically, textually—between its words. Mallarmé's criticism, then, not only serves as an expression of symbolism, but in his disavowal of the linear, sequential structure of a poem in favor of a dynamic one, in advocating the transiency of nature and in one's apprehension and recreation of nature he provides a valuable insight into the genesis of modern poetry.

There is a similar thesis at work in Ruskin's studies of modern poets and painters. Like Mallarmé he understood that the revolution in literature and the fine arts sought to establish an entirely original meaning concerning the relationship between the artist and nature; but unlike Mallarmé Ruskin's analysis of the pathetic fallacy expressed his profound distance from the new, modern voice in poetry and painting. Ruskin realized that owing to the artist's increasing subjectivity, the image of the poet-painter no longer represented the forms and figures distinguished by the naked eye. The artist has rejected a picture of nature as an objective reality with its timeless substance while embracing one that allows him to capture the mutability or flux of nature. The modern poem or painting, as defined by Mallarmé and Ruskin, demands special consideration of the dynamics of perception and creation, of those raw fragments of poetic and pictorial form that constitute the fully realized poem and painting. In substituting a subjective attitude about nature for its previously respected objective ideals, the artist has imbued nature with the vagaries and confluences that characterize his own cognitive and visual faculties. To Mallarmé this initiated an art of adventurous creativity; to Ruskin it was a sign of man's loss of faith.

In his biography of Cézanne, Vollard recounts that when expressing his disapproval of a popular artist, Cézanne would describe the painter as "realistic." Cézanne's opposition to realism, however singular his use of the term, is another example of the modernist's rejection of the verisimilitude of art. Impressionism was comprised of numerous painters and styles and was only one of several modern movements in painting of the late nineteenth century, but I think it fair to deduce certain commonly held principles in the art world of that epoch. Foremost was the abstraction of the three-dimensional stability of man and nature through the breakdown of their corporeal, figurative unity and the suggestion of their more fluid, tenuous makeup through the interplay of the objective properties of light, line, color, and volume with the painter's eye. The artist was concerned with questioning the nature of perception and organic evolution; it resulted, for example, in the subdivision of an object or scene into thousands of fragments in Seurat's pointillism and in the evocative treatment of color that Manet discovered in the Spanish masters and that possessed a greater spatial autonomy in his own work and in that of Gauguin. By acknowledging the independence of his vision and the idea of nature as inherently dynamic, the impressionist painter responded with much more freedom in looking at the world by selecting color solutions and methods of pictorial unity that captured the kinetically determinate elements in one's vision and in the evolution of nature. The impressionists theorized that the potential for afterimage would augment the painter's ability to convey the sensory evolution underlying both nature and perception. M. E. Chevreul's celebrated study of the harmony and contrast of colors can be read as a scientific corollary to the color experiments of several impressionists and to the prevailing artistic concern with an empirical, psychological approach to the interplay of form and vision. The sharper, richer hues of the impressionists and postimpressionists, their creative rearrangements of the laws of perspective, whether in Degas's fruitful studies of photographic displacement in long shot and close-up or in Pissarro's pioneering experiments with light as the unifying, organizational principle in looking at nature, enabled the artist to picture a scene in a manner distinct from that of the naked eye and in a style that photography, during this period, could not duplicate.

One of the earliest analogies made between the arts and film occurred in Debussy's review of Strauss's *Ein Heldenleben* in which he compared Strauss's rhythmic dissonances to the dynamic format of the movies. Strauss's tone poems, like the music of Berlioz and Liszt, can also be interpreted as part of the modern aesthetic in that they challenge the harmonic cohesiveness of the sonata form. Igor Stravinsky was not especially happy with Pierre Boulez's choice of Berlioz as the inspiration for Stravinsky's revolutionary ballet scores, and Robert Craft has shown that Stravinsky's allegiance to the exploding sonorities and divergent rhythms in Russian music of the late nineteenth century was tempered by his affinity with the vertical and horizontal equilibrium of the eighteenth- and nineteenth-century classicists. Yet both Debussy and Boulez grasped an important aspect of musical modernism. The program music of Berlioz, Liszt, and Strauss was a major departure from the orthodoxies of the sonata because of a radical degree of chromaticism that stripped the music of its linear, harmonic unity in favor of a more melodically discontinuous style. Their use of digressive musical motifs, their tendency to continually modify metronomical markings, and their allegiance to the spirit if not the letter of romantic literature contributed to what Alfred Einstein summarized as the revolutionary change in the "sound" of nineteenth-century music. The classic fugues and symphonies of Bach and Beethoven were predicated on the precise, mathematical underpinnings of polyphony, harmony, and counterpoint; the music of Berlioz, Liszt, and Strauss eschewed the underlying harmonic geometry of the baroque and classical musical idiom, and experimented instead with a melodic line that generated a variety of contrapuntal rhythms.

The poetics of a Mallarmé or Debussy connote a significant change in the intent and perception of the nineteeth-century art world. Furthermore, the displacement of previously established models of verisimilitude and consonance by a vision of sight and sound more faithful to dynamic modalities reverberated in the philosophy of the nineteenth century. Hegel's phenomenology was a representative philosophic expression of the belief in nature as a self-perfecting mechanism; social positivists throughout Europe applied his ontological model to the social perfectibility of man and the state. Henri Bergson, one of the foremost disciples of the scientific and moral positivism of the nineteenth century, established a parallel between the temporal, sequential character of the mind and nature and the dynamic method of the movies. He first reformulated the Enlightenment and the Hegelian ideal of "becoming" as the paramount force in both nature and human action:

> A conduct that is truly our own, on the contrary, is that of a will which does not try to counterfeit intellect, and which, remaining itself—that is to say, evolving—ripens gradually into acts which the intellect will be able to resolve indefinitely into intelligible elements without ever reaching its goal. The free act is incommensurable with the idea, and its "rationality" must be defined by this very incommensurability, which admits the discovery of as much intelligibility within it as we will. Such is the character of our own evolution; and such also, without doubt, that of the evolution of life.[3]

If one then considers the dynamic continuity in Bergson's idea of the will and nature in conjuction with the images in a Mallarmé poem, an impressionist painting, and the melodic digressions in the program music of the romantics, there appears to be an undeniable parallel between the philosopher's conceptual schema and that of the artist. Both the philosopher and the artist challenge the belief in a fixed, predetermined universe. In philosophy this development implies a radical departure from the scientific and moral absolutes that had remained current throughout the Enlightenment; in art it constitutes a rejection of the codified formalism in the poetry of the Augustan period, in French neo-classicism, and in the sonata style.

Bergson eventually identifies the infant film medium as the quintessential expression of evolution as a continuous process.

> The cinematographical method is therefore the only practical method, since it consists in making the general character of knowledge form itself on that of action, while expecting that the detail of each act should depend in its turn on that of knowledge. In order that action may always be enlightened, intelligence must always be present in it; but intelligence, in order thus to accompany the progress of activity and ensure its direction, must begin by adopting its rhythm.[4]

Bergson's three-part equation of nature, the mind, and the movies rests on his abstraction of the uniquely phenomenological nature of the silent film. His interpretation, which will have special relevance in the Russian theory of montage, remains of primary importance to our inquiry because Bergson proposes that the medium of motion pictures should not be interpreted simply in terms of chemical and mechanical experiments, but as one example, perhaps the most formidable one, of the revolution encompassed in the term "modernism."

In beginning our study of the movies with a brief review of the extensive experimentation in the art world of the nineteenth century, several antecedents to the cinematic method and style have been underlined. We have also learned how the evolution of modernism, which grew out of the metaphysical assumptions in German romantic philosophy, led Bergson to identify the cinema as a paradigm of both cognitive and natural evolution.

---

1. Geoffrey H. Hartman, *The Unmediated Vision* (New Haven: Yale University Press, 1954), pp. 152, 153, 155.

2. Stéphane Mallarmé, *Selected Prose Poems, Essays, and Letters* (Baltimore: Johns Hopkins University Press, 1956).

3. Henri Bergson, *Creative Evolution*, trans. Arthur Mitchell, p. 54. Copyright 1911, 1939 by Holt, Rinehart and Winston. Reprinted by permission of Holt, Rinehart and Winston, Publishers.

4. Ibid., p. 333.

# 2
# The Evolution of Modernism (ii)

Movements such as romanticism, symbolism, and impressionism grew out of an arduous intellectual struggle that measured new theories of man and nature against the vibrancy of the past. American society, however, confronted the impetus of modernism—socially, culturally, and artistically—in a completely different manner. Born of the Enlightenment, America was envisioned as an arcadia in which visions of man reborn and Rousseau's noble savage abounded. Political theorists in America were fully aware of their monumental task in establishing a nation founded on the principles of reason, liberty, and equality. Although their intellectual legacy was European, there was a concerted effort among leaders, philosophers, and artists to create a uniquely American vision. Despite the absence of homogeneity among the ideas that were tested, there was a widespread belief that America represented a golden opportunity to incorporate the ideals of the Enlightenment to a degree impossible in Europe.

The first evidence of America's artistic identity—the paintings of John Singleton Copley and Benjamin West—celebrated a classical formalism and grandeur embedded in the heroes and mythology of the war of independence. Their predecessors, suffering from a dearth of art academies and patronage, had labored in a primitive style with little understanding of the human form other than as an execution of cubes suspended in flat space. Prerevolutionary portraiture, even in the flowering of Flexner's "Patroon Painters," existed in an ethereal, transparent cosmology, a disquieting compromise between the religious scope of medieval art and the warmth and naturalism of the Dutch school. As American artists became more self-assured in technique and theme, they infused the unity of man and nature with a humanism unalterably affixed to its theistic origin. Our artists fell in love with the harmonies of society and nature because they existed as the most poignant expression of the design and force of God. The arcadia that European philosophers and artists had originally imagined became an integral part of the American sensibility. The "luminism" that Edgar Richardson discusses as the decisive technical and moral force in nineteenth-century American art, evidenced in still life and portraiture as well as nature studies, would play a major role in the treatment of light, man, and nature in the American film.

The awe and reverence of nature that interpenetrate the Hudson River School prominently figure in the poetry of Bryant. It permeates Cooper's *The Leatherstocking Tales* through his extended psychological descriptions of the anima of nature and his idealized portraits of Hawkeye and Chingachgook. Emerson's celebrated "The American Scholar" had called for America's political and cultural leaders to give form to the singular spirit of political freedom and natural beauty that had contributed to the founding of America; this symbol of the individual in a land of undaunted beauty was one example of how Americans began to idealize their country: America was coming of age in an image of self-innocence, most vividly through the pristine splendor of its land and heroes.

Yet this incipient ideal of purity was considerably modified by the nature of the century in which America matured. Although Bryant and Cooper imagined America existing in a timeless orb in which a vision of an uncorrupted individual and landscape was celebrated, the deistic scope of nineteenth-century American attitudes in politics and the arts was transformed if not uprooted by extreme social and economic changes. Upon landing in America, Charles Dickens was quick to note the unsettling nature of this young republic; when he returned some twenty years later, Dickens struck a similar theme of bewilderment at the facility with which the society had changed:

> Also, to declare how astounded I have been by the amazing changes I have seen around me on every side—changes moral, changes physical, changes in the amount of land subdued and peopled, changes in the rise of vast new cities, changes in the growth of older cities almost out of recognition, changes in the graces and amenities of life, changes in the Press, without whose advancement no advancement can take place anywhere.[1]

Mark Twain and Charles Dudley Warner presented a more pessimistic vision in *The Gilded Age*, suggesting that there was little room for the idealism cherished in an earlier age. Emerson's high-minded optimism, for which Carlyle reproved him, seemed to suffer near irreparable damage in the course of America's growth as an industrial and political force. In transforming the American wilderness into an American empire, its leaders and artists discovered that the ideals of the Enlightenment, an essential foundation in the mythology of the Hudson River School, of Bryant and of Cooper, could not exist as absolutes, but would be mitigated by the single most dominant effect of American democracy—the ability, or more precisely, the exigence of change at each level of society. There arose a less unified approach to the mythologizing of America; the idealized vision of the painters and writers of the first half of the nineteenth century was replaced by a more eclectic cultural ideal, one that reflected the diversity of its people and institutions. Although the genteel tradition of New England society functioned as an archetype of American literature, Mencken credits folklorists like Twain and Warner, rather than a more stately writer like Lowell, with creating the first signs of an indigenous literary voice.

Because of the accelerating nature of America's social expansion, this variable of change—whether it is characterized by the term "industrialization" or by Turner's " western thesis" and his concept of the unexplored spaces of the West as a wellspring of democratic ideals—existed as the most vital force in American society. Lewis Mumford reviews its impact on the country's leaders and mores:

> The expansion that Emerson had hoped for had indeed taken place; but its dominant effect was on the utilitarian plane. Charles Francis Adams, who had served in the battlefields, now took command of railroads and stock-yards: in him, the old Adams tradition of public service was limited to the little town of Quincy, and to such work as he did in later years on the Metro-politan Park Board of Boston. Mark Twain wasted endless time and energy that should have gone into his own education, trying to make a fortune out of various inventions that took his fancy; while Henry Adams, typical of those who could make no connections with the crass outward scene, after surveying the politics of Washington at close range, took refuge in the South Seas, in Japan, in Europe, in the Middle Ages, one of that large group of disoriented and bewildered Americans, Henry James, Raphael Pumpelly, William Story, Ambrose Bierce, Bret Harte, who could find no sufficient nourishment in the soil where their roots spread, and who had even before the Civil War begun to wander uneasily about Europe—grateful for the contemplative mood it promoted, the one luxury that reckless kings of commerce could not buy, could not afford to cultivate, could not import.... Make no doubt of it: those who stayed behind needed either a double thickness of skin, or they needed the narrow convictions and the faith in the immediate activities of the country that the industrialist exhibited.[2]

Industrialization resulted in a feeling of estrangement if not desperation among American artists, leading Henry James, upon his return to America in the first decade of the twentieth century, to characterize the architectural aes-thetic of the Eastern seaboard as "formidable foreground." But it would be wrong to define its force as wholly negative in sustaining the ideals that had originally nurtured American society. Tocqueville was the first to warn against isolating any one principle other than the love of equality and its accompanying dynamic thread. Although America was initially shaped by Calvinism—which in turn was modified by the Enlightenment's emphasis on reason, scientific inquiry, and self-improvement—the nineteenth century, the first period in which Americans would test the validity of their principles in a social and intel-lectual history uniquely their own, exposed the problems surrounding the accommodation of these principles. Even Perry Miller, the great biographer of the intellectual psychodrama of America's "errand into the wilderness," was not successful in discounting Tocqueville's realization that no one idea can re-sist the intrinsic inclination for change that characterizes both Americans and their democratic institutions. While admitting the cogency of Tocqueville's phi-losophic equation of democracy and the seemingly unparalleled acceptance of change among Americans and their institutions, an attempt must be made to better understand this climate for expansion and experimentation. The term "enlightenment" or even a concept like equality allows for a variety of inter-pretations; one must undertake then a more concrete understanding of the interaction between America's profoundly religious heritage and the radical industrial and scientific temperament of the nineteenth century.

During the first decades of the nineteenth century, the religious revival questioned the influence and direction of America's social maturation; a feeling was manifest that the country's successful social and scientific endeavors were leading to a weakening of its religious mission. Jacob Bigelow's *Elements of Technology* was among the first of many expressions of the prevalent social concern over the apparent friction between moral and spiritual values and the progress spearheaded by politicians, financiers, and scientists. In *The Rise of American Philosophy*, Bruce Kuklick discloses that this progressive orientation led political, educational, and scientific scholars to adapt the Darwinian thesis of evolutionary survival to the development of the legal code. In proposing an analogy between animal instinct and human reason, they incorporated elements of Berkeleyan and Kantian idealism to explain how the mind is guided by the principle of moral absolutism in substantiating its dependence on everyday experience. In the writings of Charles Peirce and William James there appears an inevitable moral and rationalist defense of the numerous social and intellectual forces that had reshaped nineteenth-century America. Characterized as an "epistemological realist," Peirce's original formulation of pragmatism and its subsequent development by James rest on their belief that whatever truth an individual maintains must be tested and proven through everyday experience. Peirce defined pragmatism as "the scholastic doctrine of realism," whereas James argued that moral and spiritual truths, like those of the scientific community, can and must be proven through their utilitarian value. Their rationalizations enabled Americans to see how technological progress could serve as the theological source of American beliefs. One can find aspects of pragmatism in Franklin's "common sensisms" and in Emerson's more romantic declaration that the ideal should permeate daily life. But it is only in Peirce and James that the final step was made in America's acceptance of a basic axiom of the Enlightenment: the shaping of a society on rational, scientific, empirical truths.

This pragmatist doctrine was reflected in the arts primarily in two ways. First was the predominantly nontheoretical orientation of American artists who matured during a period of social and cultural expansion; second, and perhaps more important, is that with this emphasis on experience artists would be encouraged to accept the most subjective, untested stylistic theory with the least hesitation. If the preeminent aspect of modernism is its rejection of the objective idealism of art and its displacement by a theory of man and nature as independent, organic entities, then America would prove the exemplary nation in the evolution of modernism because of the fluid, practical nature of its institutions and beliefs. While there is an overriding element of scientific positivism in the writings of Peirce and James, their philosophy can be interpreted as a defense of the aesthetic of American artists in the way Copley and Cooper assimilated and exemplified the very real figures, events, and forms around them. Pragmatism can also be discovered in the more radical experiments of Poe and Ives; their modernist approach to image making and a sound continuum reflects the freedom of the artist to divorce himself from the existing classical ideal. Romantic philosophy had stressed the feelings of the individual and the idea that nature was no longer seen as constant and mechanical but as continuous and organic. Pragmatism, although more valid as a rationalization of the practicality of spiritual truths and the spirituality of scientific truths, contains an implicit defense of modernism in that the modern artist relies on a self-construed structure instead of a prescribed code of truth and beauty.

The daring of Poe's essays or Ives's theory of musical composition are noteworthy examples of the experimental nature of the American art scene. They show American artists more easily embracing modernism than their European contemporaries, similar to the way America's founding fathers had implemented the ideals of the Enlightenment with less resistance than political leaders in Europe.

"Thought," for Poe, is the activity by which man most closely resembles God. Ergo the most puissant man is he whose mental processes most closely resemble, in their operation if not in their scope, those of the deity. Such a "thinker" is nowhere to be found in Poe's poems, where the protagonists are without exception suffering, passive beings. But if his theory of poetry denied him the creation of such a personage in verse, nothing need keep Poe from such exercise of "thought" in his own criticism. He is indeed just such a "thinker" in his "Philosophy of Composition," a master-creator working out the details of his preconceived plan, observing himself in the act of conceiving, choosing, shaping, succeeding. And, as Eliot has said, because of this self-awareness, Poe pointed the way to the symbolist poets, the way to their self-consciousness as artists: Maker, not merely Finders.[3]

Daniel Hoffman shrewdly evaluates the reasons for Poe's emphasis on the origins of poetic form and on the nature of its sensory and cognitive unity. Whereas the impressionists disrupt the verisimilitude of nature by studying the effect of light and color on man's perception of nature, Poe, like Coleridge and Mallarmé, plays a major role in the poetic revolution of the nineteenth century by a defense of the self-referential quality of a poem and the poet as its supreme arbiter.

Poe's literary output is one example of the willingness of American artists to test new styles and ideas, a phenomenon that is magnified in Charles Ives's musical modernism. From the time of the revolution America's musical societies had a distinctly European identity; Ives was the first major composer who in his sensitivity to the sensibility of his literary antecedents and to the idealism of his country's political doctrines, sought a musical form that led him to break away from the canons of European classicism. Ives's *Concord Sonata*—in which the melodic textures disrupt the triadic unity of the sonata—is one vibrant example of the increasing independence and isolation of the poet's vision. The diatonic differentiation, basic to the contrapuntal progression and uniformity of the sonata, is swept aside by the chromatic tonality of Ives's composition. The polytonal musical forms that infiltrate his music can also be interpreted as an expression of nationalism if one characterizes as American

Ives's desire to discover his country's diverse heritage through his eclectic musical modernism—the solitary notes of meditation of New England's poets transcribed through the expressionism of the *Concord Sonata*, or the expansive outbursts of the sounds of a crowd, generated through the intermixing of numerous hymns in the last movement of his Fourth Symphony. Paul Rosenfeld elaborated this theme in discussing the thematic and musical identity of Ives's songs:

> But out of that miscellaneousness, extreme for all the visibility of the personal thread in the intensely disparate fabrics, an idea greets us: the idea that all things possessing breath of their own, no matter how dissimilarly and to what differing degrees, are ultimately consonant. That is good Americanism, and the postscript but re-expresses that feeling and that idea in the maxim, "Everything from a mule to an oak, which nature has given life, has a right to that life; whether they (its values) be approved by a human mind or seen with a human eye, is no concern of that right." And when the prose runs: "I have not written a book for money, for fame, for love, for kindlings. I have merely cleaned house. All that is left is on the clotheslines," we merely recognize anew the American speaking with the spirit of the Artist.[4]

While American society was testing the ideals of the Enlightenment with an immediacy and authority impossible in Europe, several major nineteenth-century American artistic formulations extended the romantic, invariably modern orientation of the arts. America's intellectual heritage was not only influenced by this artistic freedom, but in contributing to modern culture, America found its intellectual foundations originating in the idea of modernism. Henry James looked askance at America's "age of energy," its lack of respect for enduring values and institutions, while Gertrude Stein welcomed the opportunity to explore the potentialities of a new metaphysic and aesthetic, as *The Making of Americans* exuberantly documents. Whether one sides with James's conservative cultural ideal or Stein's more adventurous one, it was just such an unsettled, explosive society in which film, as an exemplary modern form, would evolve.

---

1. Charles Dickens, *Martin Chuzzlewit* (New York: Dodd, Mead & Co., 1945), p. 751.
2. Lewis Mumford, *The Brown Decades* (New York: Dover Publications, 1971), pp. 7 and 8. Copyright © 1931, 1959, 1977 by Lewis Mumford.
3. Daniel Hoffman, *Poe Poe Poe Poe Poe Poe Poe* (New York: Doubleday, 1972), p. 96. Copyright © 1972 by Daniel Hoffman. Used by permission.
4. Paul Rosenfeld, *Musical Impression: Selections from Paul Rosenfeld's Criticism*, ed. Herbert A. Leibowitz (New York: Hill and Wang, 1969), p. 246.

# 3

# The Evolution of Modernism (iii)

The modern aesthetic in literature, painting, and music was one vital expression of the revolutionary nature of nineteenth-century intellectual history. As artists began to experiment with techniques and styles that challenged the objective idealism of nature, an invention like the movie camera would assume a dual if not paradoxical role, exemplifying the methods of the modernists while adopting a style of dramatic, pictorial realism.

By reflecting the dynamic progression and spatial inclusivity of the movie camera, the increasingly organic, psychological perspective of modern artists would prove a most alienating experience in its reconstruction of reality. But to accept the movie's dynamic method of presenting reality as a paradigm of modernism without an appreciation of how each art form transcribes a dynamic schema leads to a transparent, doctrinaire interpretation of modernism. The futurist movement in painting, which used color and objects for their mobile properties, was one of the earliest and most conspicuous examples of the impact of film and technology on the arts. Futurists attempted a literal duplication of film dynamics and were justly criticized by Wyndham Lewis as "a sensational and sentimental mixture of the aesthete of 1890 and the realist of 1870."

Lewis understood that a modern aesthetic did not simply mean showing objects in a kinetic instead of static condition, but that it first required questioning the implications of a dynamic apprehension of reality. Modernism entails not only the discovery of themes and forms germane to a newly created technological reality, but also the documentation of their effect on one's thought and senses. It is partially expressed by Delaunay in his studies of the Eiffel Tower and in Marin's drawings of the Woolworth Building. Delaunay retains a quasi-futurist perspective in which the three-dimensional reality of the Eiffel Tower is only modestly abstracted into a vertically interconnected, dynamic projectile. The spaces that are left open or disconnected or that are rendered by opaque smudges exist as a visual parallel to the continuous material extension of the tower in space. Delaunay's calligraphic compression represents a visual-cognitive gestalt of the individual's impression of space as the interaction between a dynamic form and its changing structural identity in the mind's eye. In his succeeding orphism style, Delaunay earned recognition as one of the first modern painters to undertake a thorough abstraction of pictorial form; yet the more literal nature of Delaunay's earlier futurist exercises lacked the trenchant experimentation in the interchange between cognition and visualization that characterized the art of the cubist painters.

Marin's early experimental drawings of New York cityscapes reveal a similar inclination for futurist improvisation. He attempts a more bold, albeit less successful reading of the futurist doctrine than appeared in Delaunay's study of the Eiffel Tower. In his sketch of the Woolworth Building the background image of the building possesses fewer of its objective properties than Delaunay's Tower. It is a dominant spiraling form, a gravitational vortex that encompasses the viewer's attention. The foreground figures of the pedestrians are treated as part of a blurry, disconnected horizon. The lack of refinement in suggesting the envelopment of the horizontal by the vertical—the absence of any central axis to lead the eye into the extending space of the Woolworth Building—can be assuaged by one's appreciation of Marin's growing interest in the textures of form and their pictorial evolution into the "hatching" style which he would perfect in his later works.

Notwithstanding the inadequacies of futurism as reflected in the drawings of Delaunay and Marin, its artists are in the vanguard of modernists involved in dissecting the process of visualization in painting, in recording the gestation of thought in literature, and in developing a tone row that would accommodate the multiple melodic and rhythmic variations in the chromaticism of late nineteenth-century music. Modernism was an aesthetic revolution, and in a most uncompromising way a metaphysical one, leading Wittgenstein to claim that his studies in linguistics entailed an investigation into the origin and structure of cognition: "Does not my study of sign language correspond to the study of the processes of thought, which philosophers have always taken as so essential for the philosophy of logic?"[1]

Freud's theory of the unconscious had challenged the rational, mechanistic foundation of Cartesian philosophy and the social positivism of the Enlightenment. Original literary creations such as Gertrude Stein's Melanctha or James Joyce's Stephen Dedalus can be read then as parallels to Freud's studies of the psychology of the subconscious through their internalization of thought and physical reality. The stream of consciousness of Stein and Joyce, among many others, originates in the individual's psyche, making for a highly complex literary style that has little in common with the probing social commentary and piecemeal character delineation that flourished in the nineteenth-century novel. Authors like James and Tolstoy had presented a picture of society in which man and nature possess a historical authenticity and in which the moral dilemma is enunciated by the author himself or through the novel's objective treatment of the protagonist's destiny; the oblique format of the modern novel, however, derives from the protagonist's mnemonic response to sensation. Whereas Freud had alerted philosophers to ambiguous, subconscious levels of thought and feeling, stream-of-consciousness stylists reject the verisimilitude of characterization, action, and nature in the nineteenth-century novel. The social and intellectual parameters of James and Tolstoy—their exacting, progressive studies of the moral and physical fabric of society, and their masterly character portraits—are reidentified in the creations of Stein and Joyce through the protagonists' inner thoughts, creating a far more subjective, mutable picture of man and society. The resonance of a particular scene is expressed in terms of the characters' internal faculties, subordinating the social and physical coordinates of time and space to the subjective reconstructions of the mind.

If the writer then draws our attention from what is said to what is thought, from conscious to subconscious, from an objective, unifying picture of the individual and nature to the implosive, sensory configurations of the mind, the painter explores the invisible instead of the visible, the changing, fleeting, cognitive and visual interplay of mind and eye in place of the unified, idealized image of man and nature that was first codified in the Renaissance. Daniel-Henry Kahnweiler, the noted art dealer and a brilliant critič of modern art, elaborates several of the aesthetic concerns of the modern artist:

> The nature of the new painting is clearly characterized as representational as well as structural: representational in that it tries to reproduce the formal beauty of things; structural in its attempt to grasp the meaning of this formal beauty in painting.... This new language has given painting an unprecedented freedom. It is no longer bound to the more or less verisimilar optic image which describes the object from a single viewpoint. It can, in order to give a thorough representation of the object's primary characteristics, depict them as stereometric drawing on the plane, or, through several representations of the same object, can provide an analytical study of that object which the spectator then fuses into one again in his mind.[2]

Kahnweiler's analytic essay, although primarily concerned with cubism, can be read as a defense of the dynamic, visually internal, evolutionary orientation of modern artists. The romantic aesthetic of the nineteenth century encouraged an exploration of the fragments of light, line, color, and volume that constitute the fully realized form. The spatial coherence of Western art had reached a breaking point with impressionist and expressionist painters who initiated the idea that the elements that distinguish a form and the changing, dynamic interaction of these elements were more important than maintaining a static, uniform realism. But it is not only a matter of admitting the technical daring of nineteenth-century art; one must also consider the pertinent changes in the painter's iconography. The church, the aristocracy, and, more recently, the bourgeoisie had largely controlled the mythology of the artist; the art world of the late nineteenth century, with its emphasis on the subjective, psychological nature of man's vision, led the artist to reexamine his role in society; the growing independence of the artist from society originated in the subjective, relativistic approach to image making in the aesthetic of the major art movements at the turn of the century. The romantic impulse enabled artists to substitute their own feelings about a person or place for the basic beliefs manifest in the "adaptations" of scripture or in the idealized portraits of the aristocracy and

bourgeoisie. The following statement by Malevich explains how the internalization of the painter's imagination brought about an interpretation of the raw,
basic substance of the image in a manner not unlike previous depictions of the
ideals of Greek and Christian mythology:

> No more "likeness of reality," no idealistic images—nothing but a desert!...
> Suprematism is the rediscovery of pure art which, in the course of time, has
> become obscured by the accumulation of "things." It appears to me that, for
> the critics and the public, the painting of Raphael, Rubens, Rembrandt, etc.
> has become nothing more than a *conglomeration* of countless "things," which
> conceal its true value—the feeling which gave rise to it. The virtuosity of the
> objective representation is the only thing admired.... The black square on
> the white field was the first form in which non-objective feeling came to be
> expressed. The square = feeling, the white field = the void beyond this
> feeling.[3]

What then are the values most relevant to the modern painter? Two terms
which permeate modern art and that will reappear in our study of the film
medium are "multiple perspective" and "organic dynamic." Whereas central
perspective defines one of the major achievements of the Renaissance in accom-
modating the idea of transcendence and the spatial incongruity of the medieval
world to its scientific and humanist doctrine, the term "multiple perspective"
characterizes the cubistic approach to an object from numerous points of view;
the Renaissance axiom of the spatial verisimilitude underlying the individual's
perception of nature is replaced by a study of the interaction between the artist's
apprehension of the image and the image's dynamic properties. In "reading"
the cubists' canvases, newly found theories of visual construction result in the
assimilation of arcane, often disruptive visual emblems that reflect the artist's
liberation from the ideals of verisimilitude and the icons of physical and spiritual beauty that have inspired Western art.

The term "organic dynamic" is fundamental to the interests of the abstract,
nonfigurative school of painting and will have special meaning in our review of
the Russian silent film. It denotes the artist's conceptualization of the invisible
world of matter as a living form whose structural relationships fulfill a similar
function to the icons of Greco-Christian mythology. A world that can only be
seen under a microscope is incorporated into modern art by the abstract painter's belief that his major concern is to dissect the internal makeup of the image.
The abstract artist's emphasis on primary forms and colors is his way of discovering the world anew: this quest for scientific and cognitive authenticity
among plastic artists is, however, the most reductionist and subjective of experiments and has contributed to the public's estrangement from modern art. R. H.
Wilenski compared the artist to the biologist who in studying nature searches
for quintessential forms among animals and plants:

> It is by such studies that the modern sculptors have arrived at the concept of
> the universal analogy of form, the concept of all human, animal and vegetable
> forms as different manifestations of common principles of architecture, of

which the geometric forms in their infinity of relations are all symbols; and at the concept of the meaning of geometric relation as the symbolisation of this universal analogy of form.[4]

The uses of primitivism, especially in the works of Constantin Brancusi and Henry Moore, further illuminate the radical metaphysics of modern art. Moore characterized Brancusi's achievement as "distilling the classic excrescence," which is similar to the Bauhaus ideal of "less is more." Moore's championing Brancusi's studies of crystalline, archetypal forms in the human and animal world appears to acknowledge the irrelevance of classic techniques and themes in modern art. Moore's style, in a far more uncompromising manner than Brancusi's, exemplifies this classic-modern schism; Moore is a primitive involved with the gestation of form in nature, whereas Brancusi's aesthetic results in a sublimely realized art of formal elegance. The primitivism of Moore, with its rough-hewn figures, takes the viewer through a landscape that might have existed during the Paleolithic Age or, more glumly, that awaits the survivors of the final holocaust. It is a world in which human and animal forms have yet to fully evolve: Moore forces the public to respond to his creations, not as finished forms contiguous with the mimetic, didactic values of Western art, but as unfinished, evolving shapes that challenge one's textbook definition of art. If the geometric impulse in much of modern art retains a sense of visual symmetry through its scientific reconstruction of man's vision, Moore's abrogated, amorphous organisms incorporate formlessness instead of form as the ultimate content of the modern style. Moore's primitivism distills the aesthetic reductivism of modern art by examining the evolution of form in figures that have yet to reach a discernible completed shape.

While Picasso continued to work from the expressive human form, rejoicing in his last erotic sketchbooks in the interplay between the subjective, vertiginous lines of the abstractionists and the objectified, sexual instincts of man, Kandinsky's nonfigurative approach has proven to be the most resonant visual aesthetic in the postwar art world. A similar analogy can be drawn in the respective theories and music of Arnold Schönberg and Igor Stravinsky. Modernism in music is generally seen as beginning with Schönberg's theories and compositions; after extending the expansive chromaticism of nineteenth-century music to the dangerous boundary separating music and sound, he formulates the tone row as the unifying format to encompass the pantonality that had obliterated the usefulness of the eight-tone scale. Schönberg's rejection of the interval and the exclusion of any thematic recapitulation in his later compositions represent the decisive stylistic formula of musical modernists, especially when one considers that Stravinsky, though not originally subscribing to the abstraction of the Second Viennese School, found his neoclassicism leading him to adopt their technique in his last works.

A second intriguing aspect of twentieth-century music, and one that will reverberate throughout our study of the cinema, is the way a modern art form like jazz, while consigned to the ranks of low art, is a technical prototype of modernism. This is most apparent in its stressing the live, improvisational aspects of a performance. Although there are significant differences among jazz stylists in the freedom given members of the group to play off the melody, an integral part of the jazz performance lies in the immediately experienced solo, which, while incorporating the original time frame and melody, allows the different soloists to introduce a variety of conflicting beats and melodies. Similar to the fauvists, the cubists, and even the abstract expressionists who occasionally retain the imprint of a recognizable form, the "hot jazz" stylists of the first decades of the twentieth century begin with a basic melody out of which the improvisations build. A major development in modern jazz, first manifest in the rhythmic flourishes of bebop and leading to the radical improvisations of virtuosos such as Lester Young and Charlie Parker, finds the melodic line disappearing because of the musician's desire to define the complete structural autonomy of his solo. Whereas painters like Albers, Newman, and Stella evoke the symbolic nature of the square, circle, and other geometric configurations, jazz modernists remove the "classical" element of their vocabulary in experimenting with the raw fragments of notes at the most extreme pitch and rhythm. Like the abstract organisms in paintings by Kandinsky and Klee or the musical entropies of Webern, the fleeting rhythms of modern jazz performers take the improvisational roots of jazz to its most radical, subjective level by refusing to integrate any previously heard musical passage in their variations.

The emphasis on subconscious processes of thought in stream of consciousness; the abstract expressionist's belief in the spiritual identity of primitive, nonfigurative forms; and the rhythmic and melodic fragmentation implicit in twentieth-century music underscore the profound repercussions in the aesthetics of the nineteenth century. The modernists' acute degree of subjectivity and their interest in the elusive, microscopic variants of the art experience—in both the mind of the audience and in the dynamics of their creations—originate in the romanticists' championing of intuition and in their approach to nature as an organic form; it has led artists to question the dynamics of sensation and to their replacing the fixed, congruent outlines of a thought, image, or sound with an investigation into their dynamic organization. Since the modern writer, painter, and composer are concerned with the evolution of thought, vision, and sound rather than the fully realized thought, image, or melody, their aesthetic proves more experimental, disparate, tentative. The impatience that so much of the public has shown with modern art is to a large degree an expression of its refusal to admit the metaphysical as well as aesthetic dimensions of modern art. If one adheres to a classic definition of art, much that has been achieved under the rubric of modernism would not gain acceptance as art. The romantic artist originally sustained many of the ideals and icons of Western art; the modern artist, however, owing to a legacy of emotionalism, an increasing disregard for a homogeneous reality or form, and a greater interest in the ephemeral clusters of sensation and sound, has been forced to reexamine the basic constituents of the art experience. If metaphysics is distinguished from aesthetics in that the former is concerned with the nature of man and society and the latter with an expression of the most sublime forms, figures, and events of his world, then modernism is as much a metaphysical revolution as an aesthetic one.

The origins of modernism are numerous; one art form, however, that seems to underline America's greater affinity with the modernist ethic is the dance. A significant portion of modern dance choreography consists of ideas and forms relating to the American experience. In George Balanchine's *Who Cares?*, the idiosyncratic American energy and frivolity of George Gershwin's music is complemented by a romantic vitality that spices the clichés of American popular dance with the more self-conscious extravagance of classical ballet. In Jerome Robbins's impressionistic punctuation of classical music, for example, in *Dances at a Gathering*, he gives his dancers a more reflective, spontaneous, dramatic presence. His stage tableaux rarely settle into static, conventional pictures of grace and beauty but are redrawn by the casual movements of a dancer off to the side or by the sudden rush of the surrounding dancers into the central stage action. The dance becomes a meditation, superimposing the dynamic improvisations of the dancers on the folk sources of the music and dance.

The recurrent juxtaposition of classical and modern in the work of Balanchine and Robbins—the inclination of Balanchine to reconfirm the classical origin of his fluid, geometric variations and of Robbins to highlight the kinetic elasticity of his dancers—finds a natural wellspring for a regeneration of the dance in the more athletic figure of the modern American dancer and his identity as a repertory of classical formalism and abstract experimentation.

To try to imagine how the world is perceived and ordered was largely the concern of Jean Piaget; yet it is also the legacy of modernism. The cumulative force of art in the twentieth century—the subjective nature of perception and the dynamic expansion of an image or note that had previously sustained an empathetic objectivity through the pictorial uniformity of three-dimensional space or the harmonic symmetry of the eight-tone scale—has brought art to the edge of a cognitive and spatial abyss. If the splitting of the atom represents the most impressive and frightening achievement of science in the twentieth century, our modernists have explored the paradox of this discovery through their atomistic implosion of perception and form, awakening us to the myriad qualites that determine our ideals of truth and beauty while suggesting a mysterious core of cognition and creation that we are forever at the mercy of.

1. Ludwig Wittgenstein, *The Blue and Brown Books* (Oxford: Basil Blackwell, 1958).

2. Daniel-Henry Kahnweiler, *The Rise of Cubism*, trans. Henry Aronson (New York: Wittenborn Art Books, 1949), pp. 1, 12.

3. Kasimir Malevich, *The Non-Objective World*, trans. Howard Dearstyne (Chicago: Paul Theobald & Co. Publishers, 1959), pp. 68, 74, 76.

4. R. H. Wilenski, *The Meaning of Modern Sculpture* (London: Faber & Faber, 1932), p. 159.

# 4

# The Art of the Silent Film (i)

The late nineteenth century experienced an almost universal fascination with the mastery of motion pictures. The conclusive chronophotographic experiments of Eadweard Muybridge showing a horse's four feet simultaneously off the ground, in which the electric bell shutter devised by John D. Isaacs synchronized the successive exposures to the horse's movement, revealed an aspect of the cinema's visual comprehensiveness that would play a significant role throughout the course of film history. By testing the vulnerability of the naked eye their experiments suggested that the inevitable mastery of motion pictures would continually challenge the individual's perception of the natural world. Muybridge and Isaacs had exposed the duplicity of man's visual faculty; it was left to the Lumière brothers, Méliès, Porter, and other film pioneers to explore the extent of this rift in the visual dynamic of man and machine.

Among the sundry events drawn from everyday society that were featured in the first movie shorts, none caused as much excitement as the arrival of a train in a station:

> As all over the world in that year—in London at the Royal Polytechnic Institute, in New York at Koster and Bial's Music Hall, in Spain and in Sweden —Lumière's approaching train brought screams of terror from the more impressionable members of the audience.[1]

The uproar surrounding the exhibition of the train's arrival has been treated as one of the celebrated footnotes in film history, but little effort has been made to inquire into the reasons for the pandemonium brought about by the Lumières' short. What should interest any student of the movies is not simply understanding the sociology of the first film shorts but the technical and aesthetic factors that govern film's "reproduction" of the natural world and the viewer's perception of the action. The outstanding question that must be resolved in the Lumières' short does not concern the nature of the images being recorded, but how the camera's apprehension of the train's arrival distorts one's perception of this everyday occurrence.

In the Lumières' short the camera captures the forward motion of the train as it enters the station. Had the audience observed the train's arrival from a position which did not isolate its forward motion, viewing instead a medium shot of the tracks with the camera situated at the center of the platform, some excitement might have resulted, but no one would have left his seat, and film enthusiasts would be without a most fascinating short in beginning a study of film aesthetics. In the medium shot that I propose there is a conventional reproduction of the people and objects at a train station. But because of the positioning of the camera in the Lumières' short, audiences were unsure of the permanence of the natural world on film; the camera has negated whatever visual safeguards one relies on when standing near the edge of a platform. We may move back a few paces but we will not run away from an oncoming train because we are aware of the track extensions on which the train will continue its entrance into the station. The Lumières' short, then, does not simply reproduce the train's arrival in a station, but condenses this action from a singular point of view. The camera is not a passive observer of nature but functions as the organizer of the spectator's apprehension of reality.

Film historians have postulated a dialectical interpretation of film history in the work of the Lumières and Méliès, but one need look no further than the shorts of the Lumières with their commonplace, documentary footage to discover the element of disproportion that Méliès would explore in a more exuberant manner. Instead of characterizing the nature of the film medium as dialectic, the Lumières' short leads one to first acknowledge its autonomy. Whether the images are drawn from the natural world, as in the Lumières, or from contrived, studio effects, as in Méliès, the film medium rejects the temporal and spatial conventions that its audience utilizes in the perception of nature.

The comic, disruptive impact of the film image upon audiences experiencing the movies for the first time is brilliantly exploited in two films, *The Magic Box*, a genteel, historical biography of movie pioneer William Friese-Greene, and Jean-Luc Godard's ironic fable, *Les Carabiniers*. In *The Magic Box* Robert Donat as the inventor, after realizing that his machine records movement, rushes out into the street trying to find someone to witness his startling discovery. He stumbles across a policeman played by Laurence Olivier, and Donat brings Olivier to his home to view the film. When the "show" is over, Olivier walks to the screen, moves it aside, and looks for the people projected from Friese-Greene's magic box. Like Olivier's policeman, film audiences at the turn of the century found the reproduction of the natural world fragmented, distorted, and oftentimes ludicrous. They had yet to realize that the figures and actions on the screen were not part of the external world but were animated by the magic box and the whims of the cameraman, designer, and cutter. In Godard's *Les Carabiniers* one of the dumbwitted protagonists enters a movie house where he sees a woman taking a bath. He innocently walks around, searching for the most revealing angle of her naked figure, and finally in frustration tears down the screen. Like Olivier's policeman he too cannot understand that the people and objects on the screen are not part of the natural world but inhabit a space that demands a conceptual and visual framework different from the one utilized in everyday society.

The public response to the Lumières' short of the train's arrival in a station and the similar reflex action of disquietude that greeted R. W. Paul's short of the motion of sea waves intimate the incongruity between man's perception of reality and that of the camera. Georges Méliès explored the medium's idiosyncratic potential through his pictorial inventiveness in tales of adventure and the unknown. Unlike the Lumières, who set out to record daily life, Méliès confined himself to the studio where his imaginative backdrops accentuated the illusory potential of the film image. His technical innovations are extensions of his talents as a stage designer. Although his shorts show no camera movement or any sense of dramatic punctuation through editing, his unequivocal delight in bringing his theatrical fabrications to life makes him the pioneer of film fantasy. Whether his shorts concern the allure of an Arabian palace, life on the moon, or a trek across the North Pole, Méliès exploited the medium's sympathy for exotic, mysterious, wholly imaginary worlds. The performances in his shorts are awkward, and the fanciful design, augmented by his inventive use of trick effects, presents a surfeit of graphic splendor and satire; but in pursuing the medium's facility for conjuring the inert or invisible, Méliès led audiences to rethink the power of this infant medium.

The apparently limitless fluency of the cinema in challenging one's perception of man and nature was also developed in the work of Edwin Porter. In *The Dream of a Rarebit Fiend*, Porter, like Méliès, draws from the medium's arsenal of special effects to depict the dreamer's fantasies. Porter's *The Life of an American Fireman*, like his more acclaimed *The Great Train Robbery*, is an original experiment in crosscutting, building up the tension between two separate events in space by juxtaposing them within the context of a fire and train robbery. Crosscutting, like the double exposure of the face of the fireman's wife or the close-up of the outlaw shooting at the camera, functions as one of several important devices used by the director to grammatically and dramatically shape his picture of reality. With their playful experimentation and innocent spoofing of the audience's visual and dramatic expectations, the shorts of Méliès and Porter find these filmmakers attracted not so much to the reproduction of the natural world as to its reconstruction. Their numerous primitive effects begin to distinguish the medium's independence from the rules that govern the individual's interaction with nature.

Another aspect of the medium's increasing technical and artistic self-awareness is uncovered in Wladyslaw Starewicz's *The Cameraman's Revenge*. Starewicz's short, an animated cartoon of modeled insect and animal figures, concerns a married couple of ants whose gestures are more studied and deliberate than those of the actors in the Méliès and Porter productions. The husband is engaged in an adulterous affair, and when he finds his wife carrying on with a friend, he furiously admonishes her. A neighbor, jealous of the husband, shows the wife a film in which the husband's deceptions are exposed, and the film ends with her lambasting the husband. The original value of *The Cameraman's Revenge* lies in Starewicz's recognizing the cinema's anthropomorphic potential, presenting the animal world as if he were recording the vicissitudes of a human couple. It would prove the nexus of the Disney empire, with various animal figures moving and speaking in a lifelike manner. Not only does the cinema radically fragment one's perception of man and nature, but it humanizes the animal world with the same fluency with which it dehumanizes human actors.

Although several English shorts produced by Cecil Hepworth utilize cross-cutting and a "chase" finale in the manner of Porter's work, the European cinema favored a more static, theatrically oriented style of film production. *Don Juan's Wedding* is one of the first of countless examples of a silent film that fails to use its techniques other than to passively record a theatrical performance. This has evolved into one of the major attributes of the medium—the preservation and in some cases the enhancement of a play, dance, or opera on film. But in *Don Juan's Wedding* the director's insensitivity to the camera placement or to any type of dramatic punctuation through the editing underlines the film's static theatricality. In *The Assassination of the Duke de Guise* one again notes the constricted use of space, which, like Porter's *Uncle Tom's Cabin*, results in self-parody because there is no cinematic experimentation to modify the performers' overly expressive gestures. *Queen Elizabeth* with Sarah Bernhardt is another exercise in stilted expressiveness, marked by Bernhardt's stationary performance and theatrical mannerisms. It is a piece of antique theater history and even more antiquated filmmaking.

The Italian cinema is credited with having made a significant breakthrough in the narrative cogency of the silent film. The major differences between the aforementioned theatrical works and Italian films like *Lydia* and *La donna nuda* lie in two areas. First, the works are not theatrical in origin, leading to the second major development, the lack of dependence on scenic backdrops and the static use of space in the previously cited films. But these early Italian films seem, at best, a compromise between theater and film. The drama in *Lydia* is not as convoluted as the French productions, and there is one striking sequence in which a woman enters a cab with the following shot showing her arrival, but this imaginative use of film time and space is overshadowed by melodramatic playacting and lethargic camerawork. *La donna nuda* does not rely on the theatrically conceived backdrops that proved so cumbersome in French films, but the tediousness of the script creates little tension between the theatrics of the story and acting and their viability on film.

One of the purposes of the chapters on the evolution of modernism was to explain the immersion of American society in the social and artistic application of technology because of the absence of long-standing cultural orthodoxies. The scientific revolution of the nineteenth century that included the perfection of the moving image was embraced with greater fervor in America because this young nation found itself coming of age at a time when the modern ethic in the arts and sciences was achieving its maximum expressiveness. Other factors need to be considered in evaluating the impact of science and technology in America and Europe, but I think it fair to conclude that Americans were less resistant to the profound metaphysical and aesthetic implications of the arts and sciences of the late nineteenth century. Can one argue, then, that Americans would prove more gifted, natural filmmakers, at least during the first decades of the twentieth century than their European contemporaries? Or should one conclude that since Europeans brought a more diverse, complex set of attitudes to the movies, they would prove more intelligent filmmakers? But in reviewing the original film experiments of the American and European cinema there should be little controversy in admitting that the primitive American cinema, reaching its aesthetic fruition in the shorts and first features of D. W. Griffith, was more sensitive to the dynamics of film than contemporary efforts in the European cinema.

Griffith's first works, like those of Mack Sennett, are remembered for their helter-skelter action and the use of a chase format to resolve the story line. This would be reason enough to consign both Griffith and Sennett to the rank of primitive, with slight interest to anyone other than the historian. While Sennett's major contribution was adapting the antic rhetoric of the vaudeville stage to the equally antic formulas of the movie short, Griffith almost single-handedly took a crude, explosive medium and created a discernible film syntax in the three major areas of filmmaking—camerawork, cutting, and composition. The critical challenge that Griffith met in his work in over four hundred shorts was in his stylizing the film drama in a manner wholly independent of the laws governing one's perception of nature. He was attracted to the idea that the camera could envision the most sublime vistas and, hence, was more inclined to conceive his stories in a poetic manner rather than a novelistic one. An outstanding quality of his work in feature films is the graphic, pictorial intensity of his settings, and one is struck in his earliest efforts by his sensitivity to the grandeur of nature, whether the setting is a New England hamlet or a primeval society. His keen photographic eye leads the viewer to see his first shorts as studies of natural archetypes in which his romantic leads—boyish heroes and nymphets—function as symbols of innocence and idealism. Griffith is not simply interested in resolving some archaic Victorian melodrama but in revealing the resonance of the human form in the most pristine settings. His vision is similar to that of a photographer in that he searches for the most expressive, poignant gesture, but as a filmmaker he recognizes that his stylistic congruity rests on how long he chooses to isolate a particular feature or action and its meaning within the story. Yet it is not only Griffith's appreciation for rustic settings and types that characterize his shorts, but also his interest in imbuing his settings and characters with a vibrancy they lack in the theater or a photograph. His shorts are marked by an expressiveness that, although possible in the theater or a photographer's studio, creates a unique narrative and emotional cogency on film. His experiments with the use of lighting, for example, diminish the filmmaker's reliance on natural sunlight and assert a more dramatic, symbolic motif in the narrative complexity of the infant film medium. His creative partnership with cinematographer Billy Bitzer in shorts such as *The Unchanging Sea* and *The Painted Lady* and in the embryonic, trial runs of *The Avenging Conscience* and *Intolerance* in *The House of Darkness* and *A Man's Genesis* leads to the refinement of the medium's pictorial origins. Characters and settings are not presented within a theatrical proscenium but derive their authenticity from their expressiveness as poetic symbols—the image of Linda Arvidson endlessly awaiting the return of her husband from the sea in *The Unchanging Sea*; the extended, intensive, emotional close-ups of Blanche Sweet in *The Painted Lady*; the penumbra of isolation and madness, atmospherically rendered in *The House of Darkness*; and the atavistic symbols of evil and bestiality in *A Man's Genesis*.

The penetrating lighting and increasing variety of camera angles used to establish the expressiveness of a character or situation advanced the plasticity and dramatics of the film short. Griffith's experiments with crosscutting and the chase finale would also elaborate their original appeal in the work of Hepworth and Porter. The use of a chase to end their films enabled them to resolve the most amorphous of plots while drawing attention to the cinema's ability to fragment and rearrange two separate spaces and actions. By cutting between a fire and the fire fighters and between the train robbers and their pursuers, Porter crystallized the suspense in his two stories while upseting the perfunctory linear development of a story on film. Whereas Griffith expanded the spatial permanence of a film from his scenic, archetypal vistas to his impassioned close-ups, his use of crosscutting and the chase show a degree of control in their cadence and exposition lacking in earlier treatments. One not only thinks of the popular and surprisingly buoyant treatment of the chase and the plight of the trapped maiden in *The Lonedale Operator*, but of the pinpoint, symbolic details in the social criticism of *A Corner in Wheat* and *The Usurer*. The cutting in *A Corner in Wheat* delineates an epic, objective point of view through the parallel exposition of the harvesting of the wheat, the mercilessness of the rich, and the sufferings of the workers. In *The Usurer* the metaphors are more personal and emotional, intercutting between the corrupt capitalist and the anguish and death inspired by his indifference. Though too sympathetic to Griffith's dramatic fervor, the notes compiled by Ron Mottram and Tom Gunning for the seminal retrospective of Griffith's Biograph years at The Museum of Modern Art perceptively argue that these shorts are not merely forerunners of Griffith's great experiments in feature-length narrative, but are exciting, empathetic, trenchant works of art.

While Griffith undertook to infuse the film medium with the visual splendor of romantic painters and photographers and the vivid detail of the social realists of the nineteenth century, comedy proved the most popular of film genres. The comic thrust of the movies, alongside the medium's facility to animate supernatural figures and settings, was its most natural and greatest resource. Comedy seemed, at first, a basic component of the silent-film experience because of filmmakers' inability to adapt to the absence of sound and to the ensuing emphasis on the dynamic, pantomimic expressiveness of the characters and actions. Considering the numerous examples of physical distortion and visual displacement in the first film shorts, silent-film comedy offered the clowns of vaudeville theater another means to punctuate man's foibles and physical incongruity. But the idea that the comic potential of the film medium is its greatest attribute is not based on the awkwardness of the figures and actions in the shorts distributed by the Lumières and Edison at the turn of the century.

The inherently dispossessing nature of the silent film led to Griffith's experimentation in determining how long to hold on a single expression or gesture and to his discovery of the proper editing schema for telling his story. The cadence of a silent film is one of its salient features, and when critics disdainfully write about Griffith's Victorian morality, they are usually referring to the quaint, facile poetry he used to introduce a scene or to the intertitles used in place of the dialogue.

Although Max Linder is credited with creating the first comic protagonist on film, a gentleman outsider whose physical dexterity was expanded by Chaplin, one must turn to Sennett and the American film to see how and why comedy flourished during the silent era. There are several classic features of Sennett's comedies, the most noteworthy being the accentuated speed of his films, the extravagant explosions of physical chaos, and his fascination with various forms of motion like cars and trains. The preponderance of speeding cars and trains, like his repertory of social caricatures and their involvement in destructive acts, denotes a dizzying, prehistoric world over which man has little control. Making people and objects go faster than they normally would, like the humanization of the animal world in Starewicz's *The Cameraman's Revenge*, alerted film audiences during the first decades of the century to expect the unexpected. It appears, then, that comedy evolved as the first major film genre because of the element of disproportion and self-parody that was visible in both dramatic and documentary shorts. It is also important to recognize the omnipresence of the the the chase in Sennett and in Griffith. In Sennett the chase is not as dramatically distinct as in Griffith's films: there is a sustained element of frenzy and pandemonium from his films' inception; the exaggerated chase finale seems a logical resolution of the preceding physical mayhem. Time and space in a Sennett-produced comedy have little if any meaning; each physical object exists only as part of the comedian's improvisational arsenal, whether to be attacked or adapted into his wrecking plans. Slapstick, at least during the silent-film era, is the way of the world.

Slapstick was a natural, albeit primitive response to technology and the increasing uniformity of manners and morals among America's social classes. Sennett was the folk spirit of silent-film comedy, who with his co-writers and performers, found a natural extension of the vaudeville stage on film. The stylistic undercurrents of his satyrlike shorts, containing equal amounts of savagery and sexuality, functioned as dramatic counterpoints in the work of film's two greatest comic artists. Both Chaplin and Keaton graduated from vaudeville into Sennett's troupe where they continued to polish their distinct comedy skills. In Sennett's cloud-cuckoo country the zaniness is based on the principle of a speeded-up universe—people and objects moving faster and faster until the world around them has collapsed. When first working for Sennett, Chaplin observed that he found the routines too fast and that what intrigued him and contributed to his departure from Sennett's troupe was a desire to slow down the action and establish an element of incongruity out of what appeared an endless roller coaster ride of crazines. Keaton would approach this problem in a more schematic manner, and his fascination with the dynamics of various technologies would remain a central motif in his feature-length films.

Chaplin, however, is a more detached observer of vaudeville buffoonery; with the appearance of the character of the tramp, a sense of aesthetic distance is created for the audience. Chaplin's tramp—part con man, part gallant, part naïf, part nihilist—functions as a dramatic foil to the chaotic turn of events. He does not, like Ben Turpin and his cross-eyed stupor, personify the anarchic action; and, unlike Keaton in his first shorts for Sennett, he does not become another anonymous example of slapstick razzle-dazzle. Instead his ill-fitting, worn-out clothes and his miraculous exhibitions of gracefulness suggest a note of rueful asymmetry. The tramp challenges the destructive imprint of slapstick with a more acutely poetic note of ridicule by conceiving a massage as an invitation to wrestle or by inspecting a damaged clock as if it were a medical examiner's cadaver. An absurd situation is resolved through a more pointed and poetically absurd reaction: he brings order to his world through a disingenuous approach to the madness around him.

While Chaplin satirizes the primitive spirit of slapstick humor, Keaton takes the elements of speed and chaos at the heart of Sennett's work and fulfills their most accelerating, destructive potential. Because of the radical style of kinetics that marks each aspect of his films—from the characters' constant running about to the perpetual state of motion in the world surrounding them—there is no distinct chase finale in his films. *Cops*, his most celebrated short, exemplifies this principle: the chase that begins the film with one man in pursuit of Keaton leads to his being pursued by the entire community. Thus, within a period of less than twenty-five years, the chase, first used by Hepworth and Porter to develop and resolve the story line while suggesting film's ability to convey a spatial and temporal intercontinuity, has become increasingly effective because of Keaton's realization that an extremely rapid narrative can be utilized from the film's inception. It was not only a critical turning point in the evolution of the comedy film in that Sennett's idea of making things go faster reached its apotheosis in Keaton's work, but it also proved essential to the conceptualization of montage by both Russian filmmakers and the French avant-garde.

---

1. Jay Leyda, *Kino* (London; Winchester, Mass.: Allen & Unwin, 1960), p. 20.

# 5
# The Art of the Silent Film (ii)

The natural tendency of the silent screen to abstract human motion and emotion, in addition to its facility to visualize the most exotic figures and settings created an underlying problem for filmmakers. Directors were faced with interpreting reality in the manner man apprehends everyday society, while making their fantasies genuinely removed from the appearance of the visible world. Two films that examplify this problem are Chaplin's *Shoulder Arms* and Victor Sjöström's *The Phantom Carriage*.

Chaplin was forced to change the ending of his film, awakening in boot camp to find that the honors he has won belong to the dream life of a private in the army. The film is a satire on the road to glory in which Charlie's impersonations, from a German officer to a tree, enable him to outwit his adversaries. To then identify the tramp's idiosyncratic military maneuvers as part of a dream is plausible because the action is clearly implausible. Chaplin is not interested in detailing the physical hardships of war but in undercutting its ideals of valor. The action lacks the slightest realistic element; though the drama is no more fanciful than his other silent films, one does not feel that the cogency of *Shoulder Arms* has been invalidated by identifying the story as a dream.

But the dream from which Sjöström awakens near the end of *The Phantom Carriage* is not supported by a similar thread of irrationality. Like other Scandinavian films released during the second decade of the century. *The Phantom Carriage* is a literate, expressive film; while it avoids the cluttered, boxed-in effect of previously cited European films, the film lacks Griffith's dramatic, lyric expansiveness. The story concerns Sjöström as a wayward husband who is escorted by Death in observing the effects of his callous behavior. Unlike Chaplin's reconstruction of the road-to-glory saga, Sjöström's staging does not imbue his somnabulist's journey through the town with a distinct, dreamlike undercurrent. The stylistic paradox implicit in *The Phantom Carriage* is central to the language of the silent film—how to utilize the awesome visualizing powers of the movies to recreate the evolution of daily life or, if the story demands it, how to stylistically fashion and sustain a dream or fantasy. One of the reasons numerous filmmakers during the silent era identified their stories as dreams was that it seemed simpler to distort than to treat an action and character in a manner similar to their appearance and evolution in the visible world. The undeniable aura of mystery of the silent film invites a suspension of the laws governing reality. Yet it is critical to determine the effectiveness with which a director differentiates a fantasy from everyday society. One country whose entire silent-film legacy seems to respond to this artistic challenge is Germany.

The strength of the American cinema as the first important national cinema grew out of its democratic social fabric which inclined audiences to the irreverent, energetic style of slapstick comedy. The German cinema, however, developed in a different sociological and artistic environment. While the optimism surrounding America's industrial progress was translated by Sennett and his stars into a vision of breathtaking speed and carefree violence, the German film heightens the note of anomaly and fantasy surrounding one's initial response to the silent-film image. This is not to slight Lubitsch's historical epics or Lang's expert Mabuse crime films. But the original interest in fantasy and horror stories, astutely documented by Lotte Eisner, finds German filmmakers drawn to the illusory, foreboding qualities of the silent-film experience in exploring the depression and rancor in postwar German society. Films like *The Cabinet of Dr. Caligari*, *The Golem*, and *Waxworks* conceptualize a world of madmen and demons. Their most telling effect is the use of a nonrealist visual design, incorporating elements of Gothic and baroque art, art nouveau, and abstraction, to establish a parallel between the theme of terror and anguish and the distorted, constricted appearance of the towns and homes. Murnau's *Nosferatu* is an important exception; although the baroque design is a natural complement to the ghoulish plot, it is a film that derives a large part of its intensity from the compressed script and cutting. The story unfolds with many more shots and in a much more abrupt fashion than these other German films; its dynamic editing, more so than its design, isolates the motifs of unrest and dread. However, it is not only the work of the cinematographer and art director that distinguishes the fantasy in exemplary films such as *The Cabinet of Dr. Caligari*, *The Golem*, or *Waxworks*. The acting, whether manifest in the performers' heightened facial gestures or densely emotive movements, is a further representation of the sense of the abnormal and the supernatural that possesses the characters and pervades their society.

Other examples of the art of the German film—*The Last Laugh*, *The Joyless Street*, *Variety*, and Lang's studies of a criminal conspiracy: *Dr. Mabuse the Gambler*, *Spies*, *The Testament of Dr. Mabuse*, *M*—are among the most congruent and dramatic examples of expressionism in twentieth-century art. I use the term "expressionism" rather than "realism" because of the films' psychological stylization of reality and their emphasis on haunted characters and periods in which the social order is in chaos. In *The Last Laugh* it is the moving camera that denotes the theme of dehumanization surrounding the life of Emil Jannings's hotel doorman. Each person and action is introduced and assimilated through the moving camera; Jannings's pitiful tragedy lies in his inability to work as quickly as his younger replacement. Because the personal touches that he brings to his job are no longer desired, he is then relegated to the lower depths of the high-class hotel. *The Joyless Street* and *Variety* are more personal studies of a moral abyss and personal redemption. The working-class district and the circus environment in the two films are seen from a highly personal point of view that focuses on the erotic underpinnings of the two stories. In *The Joyless Street* it is the destructive chemistry of poverty and greed that threatens Greta Garbo; in *Variety* it is Jannings's trapeze high-wire act that personifies the jealousy that torments him and leads to his killing his partner. The graphic intensity of the two films is not meant to enhance the comprehensiveness of the real world on film, but to reveal its pernicious, psychological impact on the protagonists' behavior.

*M*, Lang's early sound-film classic, is perhaps the last chapter of German film expressionism. In his earlier, more elaborate crime films, Lang's camera continually opens and closes on unsettling dramatic tableaux; the hierarchical structure and erotic design of the nightclub in *Dr. Mabuse the Gambler* are examples of the nightmarish contours of an expressionist style. The most devious technique in *M* is the intercutting between the police and the underworld as they plan to corner Peter Lorre's child murderer. Lang also occasionally uses an overhead shot that pictures the town as an enclosed, claustrophobic setting, an effect that also questions the prevalence of studio locations in German film production. Whether the demon is Dr. Caligari or Dracula, Dr. Mabuse or, as Siegfried Kracauer has shown, Adolf Hitler, the idea of a world gone mad, of a society marked by disturbing figures and configurations characterizes the vision of German filmmakers who turned to the silent film to undertake a richly detailed, symbolic history of their precarious, violent social history. In the process they mastered the medium's affinity with psychological dramatization and established the foundations for the fantasy and crime films.

During the silent-film era both the American and German film industries utilized a number of narrative forms and styles in responding to the medium's enormous resources. In France and Russia, however, two countries with completely different cultural legacies, the former experiencing an artistic cornucopia and the latter facing the challenge of using the movies to unify its people after a revolution, one aspect of the medium—its rhythmically dynamic organization of time and space—became the decisive technique.

The French film derived its identity from the avant-garde; numerous painters, writers, and theorists joined with the fledging film community in advancing the absurdist nature of the movies. Although there has been a considerable abridgment of film history in this section, I do not think it unfair to characterize the French silent film through the work of the avant-garde and to pass over, momentarily, Abel Gance, perhaps the single most creative figure in the French silent film. But even if the avant-garde is isolated as the crucial voice in the French cinema during the period following World War I, one must admit the variety of theories and techniques supported during these years. One group was influenced by the surrealist-dadaist doctrine that film should function as a visualization of the unconscious, of bizarre, often murderous fantasies. Buñuel's first efforts, *L'Age d'Or* and *An Andalusian Dog*, and Cocteau's *The Blood of a Poet* underscore the artists' freedom in visualizing their most arcane, symbolic fantasies. The second group, in which the work of Hans Richter, Man Ray, and Fernand Léger stands out, correlates the cinema's power of abstraction with their original experiments in various modern styles of painting. In both cases there is an absence of any realistic or narrative element; their work emphasizes either the surrealist's belief in the erotic, anarchic design of the subconscious or the then prevailing interest of modern painters in the kinetic makeup and interconnectedness of sensation and nature.

The limitations of the avant-garde film aesthetic result from its restrictive experiments in exposing the inadequacies of the naked eye through the infinite number of abstract or absurdist variations possible only in a film. In Man Ray's emblematic *Emak Bakia* his rayograph technique, in which materials are placed directly on the sensitized film and recorded without the use of a camera, centers the viewer's interest in a chemically plastic interaction. There is a pronounced element of self-indulgence in these films, whether in the form of the countless "symbols" in the two films by Buñuel and Dali or in their parodying the audience's construction of reality. This is not to overlook the genuinely comic, lyric, and expressionist qualities of directors associated with the avant-garde, like René Clair, Jean Vigo, and Dimitri Kirsanov. What gives their films a dimension lacking in a prototypical avant-garde short like *La Marche des machines* is a complementary dramatic element that allows one to consider their work against similar experiments in comedy, documentary, and suspense. That Jean Renoir, the most revered figure in the French cinema, should have rejected the premise of the avant-garde in *Nana* and his first sound films suggests the ephemeral nature of this experimental, theoretically limited film style.

This interest in editing nuances, whether to simulate a dream or to abstract the viability of man and nature in a film, brings us to a problem first raised in Porter's shorts. By crosscutting between the fire and the advance of the fire engine, Porter experimented with the medium's condensation of time and space. The abbreviated cuts in the last scenes in *The Life of an American Fireman* placed the kinetics of the medium in the service of the suspense; it would be left to future directors like Griffith to introduce a greater variety of rhythmic and editing variations to enhance the audience's appreciation of the story's dramatic components. In the French avant-garde, both in Buñuel's proposed equation of the film image and the unconscious, and in the abstractions of filmmakers trained as painters, the kinetics of film were being used in a didactic manner. The viewer would be shocked by the nature and discontinuity of the images of Buñuel and Dali or be forced to admit the fragmentation underlying the appearance of man and nature on film. In the Russian silent film, however, the dynamics of montage are adapted in a narrative context, providing the most comprehensive and radical example of a kinetic universe.

Montage is a style of editing based on the schematic arrangement and progression of the film images. This highly specialized editing style was most cogently articulated in the films and essays of Eisenstein and Pudovkin. In Eisenstein's films the editing establishes a juxtaposition between two antipodal images, a form of Marxist dialectic which Eisenstein termed a "collision of ideas." In

Pudovkin's films the chronological aspect of the editing is emphasized, with each shot treated as a piecemeal link in the story line. Eisenstein's editing scheme is dynamic, Pudovkin's, linear; yet for all the literature about the development of montage in the Russian silent film, little interest has been shown in exploring the relationship between a montage-oriented cinema and the social environment or in explaining montage as the unifying technique in the structure of a film.

The enormous potential of the movies to educate a young nation was immediately recognized by Lenin and the Russian film community. It is especially important to remember in the case of the Russian cinema, as is true to a lesser degree of the American film, that the film medium, owing to the revolution, would have a forcefulness it had yet to possess in any country during the first decades of the twentieth century. Their movies can be labeled "propaganda," but it is propaganda of a most complex nature, encompassing an idea of history, philosophy, and aesthetics that transcends the more peremptory definition of the nonfiction film. In America there was a natural attraction for the medium because the country had embraced industrialization as both an intellectual force and social reality. In Russia, the revolution had brought filmmakers into the cultural limelight and provided them with a unified audience hoping to better understand their recent victory.

Why, then, did Russian filmmakers turn to montage as the most concise way of idealizing their past and unifying their audience? The answer does not lie so much in either the poverty-ridden nature of Russian film technology or the overrated editing experiments undertaken by Lev Kuleshov as in the stylistic correlation between the socialist ideals of the revolution and the dynamism of the silent film.

Since the overthrow of the tsar and the victory of the proletariat existed as the overwhelming social legacy of the new nation, filmmakers sought a technique that would best exemplify this conflict. Montage, or the accentuated dynamic and dialectic thrust of their films, was not simply manifested in the dramatically explosive endings of *Strike, Mother, The Battleship Potemkin, The End of St. Petersburg*, and *October*; it permeated Russian filmmakers' interpretation of the constant, volatile energy of a populace in arms against its rulers. Montage became a cinematic realization of both Hegel's analysis of history as a self-perpetuating, self-perfecting, activating force and the materialist bias of Marxist philosophy by dramatizing the struggle of the proletariat against the tsarist regime through "material correlatives." Russian filmmakers established a structural-ideological parallel between Marx's historical abstraction of thesis-antithesis and a stylization of the film narrative as a series of juxtaposed or interrelated images. The progressive economic schema of socialist historians was based on the dynamic, impersonal thrust of history and the identification of its underlying materialist scope. To then adapt this historical polemic in a film narrative, each person, object, and dramatic subplot is assimilated into the montage framework, thus representing the dialectical nature of history and the dynamic, thesis-antithesis makeup of the workers' struggle. Whereas the speed of the

American comedy films, particularly in the work of Buster Keaton, expresses America's comic attitude toward technology, the montage style of the Russian film celebrates the ideological undercurrents of the revolution.

Eisenstein and Pudovkin utilize this equation as the structural and thematic basis of their films. In *October* Kerensky's entry into the tsar's chamber develops through a montage of a mechanical peacock revealing its plumage; his character is then personalized by cutting to a clay figurine of Napoleon. In *Mother*, after a title is introduced—"Justice is sure, swift, merciful"—Pudovkin cuts to three judges antipodal to the title; they are not treated as characters with a distinct psychological makeup, but as animate objects who are part of the visual dialectic of oppressor and oppressed. One of the judges is drawing a horse, a second looks at his watch hidden between law books, while the presiding magistrate is characterized by cutting from his face to a bust of the tsar. Not only are the characters delineated through their material coordinates in a brief visual association, but inanimate objects as well are incorporated into this dynamic visual schema. The single most famous sequence in the Russian cinema and perhaps in all of film history—the Odessa Steps sequence—features the animation of a stone lion, signifying the uprising of the people while intensifying the suspense and carnage. One might argue that it is only during the most dramatic moments—the Odessa Steps sequence, the stock market sequence in *The End of St. Petersburg*, the rise of the Mongols in *Storm over Asia*, the storming of the palace in *October*—that montage as a dynamic, materialist aesthetic is most vividly realized. Yet in considering the unique opportunity enjoyed by Russian filmmakers for adapting this new, immensely popular and powerful medium to advance their political ideology, it is critical to see how in propounding a Marxist dialectic, each character, subplot, and image contributes to the viewer's understanding of the kinetically all-inclusive nature of the war between rich and poor. These films climax at a fast pace, but from their inception they have utilized the dramatic components as part of a dynamic, dialectic schema. The underlying kinetic scope of the Russian silent film identifies the encompassing nature of the revolution and the collective identity of the proletariat. Montage thus became exemplary of Hegel's dynamic idea of history and of Bergson's theory of continuous time through the constant interplay of people and objects. Although ideally suited to convey the historical and temporal variables of Hegel and Bergson, the Russian montage stylizations fail to offer a distinct humanistic resolution. This is most dramatically revealed in Alexander Dovzhenko's *Earth* and most comically in Dziga Vertov's *Man with a Movie Camera*.

Dovzhenko was the one major Russian filmmaker who was not drawn to the immediacy of montage. His films are antithetical to those of the montage dialecticians who employ a technique that duplicates Marx's dialectical concept of history by emphasizing the continuous nature of time and the collective nature of the revolution. While both *Zvenigora* and *Arsenal* concern an uprising that is not unlike those in the films of Eisenstein and Pudovkin, Dovzhenko's films focus on the visually breathtaking aesthetics of revolt and destruction. Their temporal and spatial chronology is not unified or sequential in the manner of

Eisenstein or Pudovkin; his temporal schema is discontinuous, moving from one crescendo effect to the next, a tone poem of blood and violence. Unlike the films of Eisenstein or Pudovkin, Dovzhenko's first efforts experiment with a style of pictorial plasticity that calls more attention to the image itself than to the ongoing historical conflict. *Zvenigora* finds Dovzhenko's unstructured yet intuitive film eye providing some of the richest examples of a resplendent, animistic countryside and the visual autonomy of the human form in the silent film. Images are not juxtaposed to one another; Dovzhenko is more interested in exploring the plastic virtues of his countryside and characters, an approach that is augmented by his frequent use of slow motion. There is a paramount belief in the raw, corporeal beauty of man and nature that reaches its dramatic and aesthetic fruition in *Earth*. In *Earth*, the last masterpiece of the Russian silent film, Dovzhenko strives for a mood of tranquillity and the sublime; his continuous dissolves on man and nature create a unified image of the grandeur of the Russian people and countryside. But during the last sequence he introduces a montage framework, crosscutting between the grief-stricken bride and the funeral of her murdered lover. The technique is antipodal to Dovzhenko's films because it distorts the spatial unity of man and nature that his film has so profoundly detailed. Montage expressively documented the dynamic, abstracted nature of the revolution, but the final scene in *Earth* shows its incongruity in personalizing a film's theme and characters. With the coming of the sound film this problem would be magnified.

Dziga Vertov's *Man with a Movie Camera* follows daily activity around Moscow's streets in an ironic exploitation of montage and the general trickery practiced by filmmakers. Unlike the more linear *Berlin—Symphony of a Big City* which also uses a montage framework, *Man with a Movie Camera* emphasizes the fluency with which a moving camera, dynamic editing, and multifaceted imagery capture the kaleidoscopic structure of daily life. Whereas Eisenstein's theory of montage parallels both the evolutionary nature of Bergson's concept of time and that of Marx's historical dialectic, Vertov's film, shorn of any historical or dramatic motif, finds montage an ideal form for capturing the dynamic continuity of history and our perception of it. As an example of the collective sweep of daily life, Vertov's film fulfills the allure of the movies for the viewers of Lumière's first shorts or Olivier's policeman in *The Magic Box*.

The fundamental principle of montage, whether in the work of Eisenstein, Pudovkin, or Vertov, is that it creates a spatial and temporal relativity about man and his surrounding world. In their films there is no individual protagonist because it is the collective, dynamic makeup of history that is stressed. It is a much greater problem for Eisenstein and Pudovkin than a documentarian like Vertov because some form of dramatic resolution must be manifest in their films. In their silent films, which are largely concerned with the overthrow of the tsarist regime, montage was used as a stylistic corollary to a materialistic interpretation of history and the kinetic nature of revolution. But in their early sound films, which are primarily concerned with honoring the heroes of the past and a stable, permanent society, montage was no longer a viable technique.

Montage also plays an integral role in cartoons. E. H. Gombrich has defined the cartoon as a mixture of metaphor and convention. The metaphor lies in the kinetic nature of cartoons, in which the exaggerated movement and the constant mutability of the characters and settings find the montage formulas of the Russians applied to the animal world; the convention consists of the narrative and dramatic resources of the cartoonists, ironically adapted in Starewicz's *The Cameraman's Revenge* and for which Disney became famous. One of the antecedents of the cartoon, the zoetrope, with its figures painted on slides, was in itself a precursor of the movies, but because of the secondary role of the camera in animation, several graphic artists, such as Len Lye and Norman McLaren, have chosen to draw their images directly on the film stock.

The dynamic nature of montage was applied by the French avant-garde and Russian filmmakers as the most expressive technique for duplicating the kinetic nature of our vision, the absurdity of our dreams, and the dialectical schema of revolution. Yet its similar effectiveness in cartoons suggests that montage, like the film medium itself, contains a Pandora's box of paradoxes.

# 6
# The Art of the Sound Film (i)

The technical mastery of sound radically changed the nature of the film experience. During the silent era filmmakers, in a very short period of time, had discovered a variety of ways to inject new life into narrative forms like epic, comedy, crime, and fantasy. More important, the original experiments of Méliès, Porter, and Griffith took a crude mechanism for filming reality and brought about a major reevaluation in the way we see the world. What at first were fragmentary distortions of everyday society evolved into highly stylized, contemporary portraits of history. With the mastery of sound, the medium lost its sympathy for the fantastic, for the dreamlike, and for the duplication of the dynamics of evolution in nature and history. With the addition of sound, film's previous distance from the aesthetics of verisimilitude was negated. Sound forced the camera angles and lighting keys of the cinematographer, the dynamics of the editor, and the designs of the art director to conform to the visual conventions in use in everyday life. The plastic, symbolic expressiveness of the individual image, or the rapid succession of images favored by certain comedic moviemakers, the French avant-garde, and the Russian film community could no longer function as texts in themselves. The text would now be heard as well, forcing filmmakers to rethink their conception of the image as it supports our primary social level of communication in dialogue. Poetry had become prose.

This is not to say that the silent film offers a richer artistic potential than the sound film. A good many if not the majority of silent films sorely miss the element of sound, existing in fact as mute dramas in which the viewer attempts to follow the actors' lip movements. For the more creative figures in the silent film the absence of sound led to a more ambitious use of filmmaking techniques, in some cases as a substitute for the "missing speech" and in others as a redefinition of the natural world and one's perception of it. Yet one of the "prose" elements of a sound film is that it contains the poetic levels of meaning of a silent film—the ability to integrate sound or the absence of it as one feature of the medium's representation of physical reality. Silence is golden, but silence exists as one aspect of a pluristic sound universe.

The musical forms that accompanied the silent film have led to several misjudgments about the aesthetics of the nontalking film. They concern the musical phrasing of the solo piano player whose accompaniment is regarded as a stylistic equivalent to the visual sequence. This is not to dismiss the fun-filled, music-hall trappings of the silent film, but merely to call attention to an obvious but overlooked phenomenon in the screening of silent films. Similar to the way the genteel, often lachrymose titles are cited as proof of the naiveté and facile formulas of the silent film, the quaint, melodramatic musical punctuation of the solo piano player often obscures the cogency of a film passage. The function of the silent-film accompanist is to provide a transparent form of musical notation to underscore the dramatic mood for the audience. Of course it was not always the piano player who with his musical shorthand attempted to enliven the intensity of a scene. The dramatic potential of the music was fully exploited by producers during the twenties, with numerous symphonic poems expanding a film's dramatic expressiveness. Ben Hall offers one example of a truly inspired social and musical absurdity.

The organ in the Atlanta Fox may not have been equipped for panic, but there was one make of theatre instrument that came close. This was the "Symphonic Registrator" organ built by Marr & Colton. Above the usual row of stop tabs controlling the standard ranks of the organ (Tibia, Vox Humana, Flute, Strings, etc.) there was an additional row of tabs. Each of these was marked by a spot of color—violet, blue, green, red, pink, yellow, orange—and these were inscribed with a catalogue of emotions and situations that would make the most brazen scenario writer blush for shame: "Love (Mother);" "Love (Passion);" "Love (Romantic);" "Quietitude;" "Jealousy" (green spot); "Suspense" (blue); "Happiness;" "Hate;" "Mysterious" (gray); "Gruesome" (black); "Pathetic;" "Riot" (red)—to list only a few.[1]

Because of the absence of sound the music presents an aural mimesis of the film story. It is then necessary to emphasize the stylistic autonomy of the silent film because of the diffusive quality of both the soloist's musical melodramas and the classic textures of the symphonic orchestra. This is especially important when one recognizes the natural inclination to interpret the silent-film image as a mimetic or thematic equivalent to the music. There is less controversy surrounding the possible interdependence of music and image during the sound era because with the verisimilitude of a sound film, the music functions as one component of the film's dramatic reality, compressing, undercutting, or elaborating the visual sequence. Although there are considerable artistic differences between the music of Max Steiner and Sergei Prokofiev, both Louis B. Mayer and Sergei Eisenstein are looking for "mood music," Mayer to sweeten his already saccharine treatments and Eisenstein to celebrate his "ultimate reality."

The appearance of the sound film clarifies another feature of the movies, one that is usually dismissed as a necessary evil. It concerns the commercial application of the medium and the control exercised by movie producers. But what is often overlooked is that the producer is simply the most tangible proof of the commercial and technological foundations of the medium; one of the lessons of the Anderson-Richie *The Japanese Film* is that the producer as ogre is a universal phenomenon. Film was originally an outgrowth of experiments in photography, and technical innovations do not stop for one's aesthetic convenience with either the silent or sound film but lead to, among other recent developments, the electronic currents of television. To then deny the loss of the silent film as commercial exploitation is myopia of a very advanced degree. Art has never existed in a vacuum, and although it may be easier to reconcile one's romantic notion of the artist with the princely ideal of patronage than with the pernicious hierarchy of film production, the similarities between the role of the filmmaker and that of artists in past cultures have been documented well enough, and the low esteem in which film craftsmen have been held has improved considerably. The techniques of filmmaking cannot be separated from their artistic possibilities. Just as the silent film offers dramatic alternatives not available to the photographer, the sound film, with its complete reproduction of the natural world, stands as the logical extension of the silent film. If the silent film, in the case of both the Lumières and Méliès, exemplified physical autonomy, the predominant attribute of the sound film appears to be that of verisimilitude since the medium possesses the one feature whose absence had encouraged the diverse stylizations of the silent era.

The first major conceptualization of a sound-film continuum occurred in Russia. Eisenstein saw the mastery of sound as inspiring an "ultimate reality":

> THE DREAM of a sound-film has come true.... ONLY A CONTRAPUNTAL USE OF sound in relation to the visual montage piece will afford a new potentiality of montage development and perfection.... THE FIRST EXPERIMENTAL WORK WITH SOUND MUST BE DIRECTED ALONG THE LINE OF ITS DISTINCT NON-SYNCHRONIZATION WITH THE VISUAL IMAGES.... This new technical discovery is not an accidental moment in film history, but an organic way out of a whole series of impasses that have seemed hopeless to the cultured cinematic avant-garde.[2]

Eisenstein correctly notes that a nonsynchronous use of sound enhances the dramatic tension, but in the major Russian productions of the thirties the manipulation of sound through the dialogue and music does not play a supportive role, but the dominant one. The major task facing the Russian film industry was the utilization of a sound film to idealize the transcendent nature of Russian solidarity and history. During the silent era, montage became their most expressive technique in expounding a dialectic interpretation of the war between oppressor and oppressed. The continuous, evolving nature of montage established a fundamental equation between a collective, materialist interpretation of history and the temporal and spatial relativity of people and objects in a densely rhythmic film style: montage proved the most effective, resonant manner by which to duplicate the dynamics of revolution. With the appearance of sound the Russian cinema undertook a radical transformation of stylistic priorities, substituting the dynamic scope of montage with its impersonal interpretation of history for a static picture of nature, celebrating the permanency of the land and a pantheon of individual heroes in a manner first suggested by Dovzhenko's *Earth*. It is the first case of nationalism in film history and one of the most problematic.

The underlying problem in films like *Chapayev* and the "Maxim Trilogy" does not lie in their abandoning a dynamic film style but in their subordinating the various dimensions of moviemaking to what Eisenstein labeled the "ultimate reality." Similar to their specialized historical application of montage, Russian filmmakers interpreted "ultimate reality" to mean the nationalistic potential unique to the realistic dimensions of a sound film. In their silent films the editing established the dynamic, dialectical nature of their microscopically conceived class uprisings; their sound films would then extend this theme through idealized pictures of Russian solidarity in realistic settings. But unlike the masterly compositions of Griffith, Lang, and Dovzhenko, the pictorial style of *Chapayev* and the "Maxim Trilogy" derives from the literal, straightforward, didactic nationalism of the drama. The Russian sound-film epics cannot incorporate the poetic elements in the films of Griffith, Lang, and Dovzhenko because of their overriding socialist imprint. This platitudinous approach results in scenes such as the young Maxim berating the police in *The Return of Maxim*, a film no less stilted and dramatically stereotyped than Mickey Rooney's Andy Hardy epics. In *Chapayev* there is a seduction by a machine gun, a primitive equation between love and revolution, while a large part of the film consists of songs which portray the Russian people as a group of overzealous boy scouts.

The "Gorky Trilogy," perhaps the most representative of the Russian epics of the thirties, is more humanistic than *Chapayev*, but it lacks the complex, iconographic style of Eisenstein's sound films. *The Childhood of Maxim Gorky* is almost wholly restricted to the home where the hero is raised, a setting marked by its poverty and the grim squabbles among the child's relatives. The camerawork has little visibility; director Mark Donskoy relies on a series of perfunctory sharp cuts when the family begins one of its many quarrels. This is characteristic of the Russian film industry's attempt to find a cinematic equivalent for the realistic novel of the nineteenth century, but the actors' theatrical mannerisms and the lack of nuance in detailing the effects of poverty make for a passive example of social realism. In the second and third parts of the "Maxim Trilogy"—*The Return of Maxim* and *The Vyborg Side*—Maxim finds romance and then takes part in the revolution. The films employ a crude form of psychology and mythmaking that is devoid of the slightest dramatic subtlety, showing the gung ho Maxim as a wholly contrived archetype of social consciousness. In *Sons and Mothers*, one of the more intelligent studies of the clash between an individual and history on film, one not only finds richer gradations to the acting and plot, but the inquiring camera eye captures Lenin's moral evolution against the background of his aristocratic upbringing. On the evidence of the handful of Russian films distributed in America during the 1970s, it seems that the rigid censorship placed on moviemaking in Russia is softening and that with films like *Sons and Mothers* or *An Unfinished Piece for Player Piano* the Russian film has shed the poetics of mummification that tragically undercut one of the richest of all silent-film legacies.

Because of its pronounced didactic identity in the newly formed proletariat culture, the Russian cinema provides the most striking example of the retrogressive elements of the sound film. Other examples of the dramatic uses of the sound film—the styles of Ernst Lubitsch, Alfred Hitchcock, Jean Renoir—are unusually evocative in suggesting the decisive changes in the major narrative forms of the silent film.

Comedy was, arguably, the most diverse and successful of American film genres. The raucous, absurdist temperament of vaudeville comedians was naturally drawn to a medium whose irreverent, solipsistic treatment of man and nature was apparent in the first shorts of Méliès and Porter. Silent-film comedy is not only a testament to an art form that has all but disappeared, but it also enabled artists like Chaplin and Keaton to discover new ways of shaping the anarchic scope of vaudeville humor. The development of slapstick in the sound film will never rival the transcendent mischief and grace of silent-film clowns because the sound film, with its naturalistic components, presents a protagonist who cannot exploit the intuitive symbolism in appearance and gesture of his. pantomimic predecessors. With the mastery of a sound-film continuum, the primeval, presocial rumblings of silent-film slapstick, with its physical chaos and prevailing irrationality, are replaced by a dialectic of naturalism and the dynamics of speech—from the elegance and bourgeois esprit of Ernst Lubitsch and the idiosyncracies of rural speech and behavior in Preston Sturges, to the theatrical conceits of Sacha Guitry and the more plaintive voice of the common man in the films of Marcel Pagnol.

Among comedy film directors, Lubitsch remains the best example of the singular modifications in comedy from the kinetic, pantomimic style of silent-film slapstick to the more restrained, verbal strategies of the sound film. During the silent-film era Lubitsch directed both epic and comedy films, but I think he will be remembered for efforts such as *Lady Windermere's Fan* and *The Marriage Circle* rather than for the turgid *Madame Dubarry* or the ephemeral hijinks of *Die Puppe*. Even in his comedies, the economy of camera action and plot continuity lack the one quality essential to his adopted dramatic model, the comedy of manners—dialogue.

A Viennese who sought to discover the manners necessary to promote a good, happy life in modern society, Lubitsch, with his co-scriptwriter, Samson Raphaelson, elucidated an old-world ideal. The "Lubitsch Touch" discussed so often is his sympathy for a casual, romantic style so antithetical to the accelerating world of technology brutally exploited in silent-film comedy. While screwball comedy adapted the dynamics and frenzy of silent-film slapstick to the conventions of courtship and marriage, Lubitsch's films are more static and subdued, resolving their conflicts through a veiled gesture or, more frequently, with a decisive verbal retort. Through the presence of dapper, urbane iconoclasts such as Melvyn Douglas and Herbert Marshall, Lubitsch and Raphaelson utilize the ironies of the comedy of manners to reconfirm the old-world pleasures of conviviality, friendship, and, not surprisingly, domesticity. Morally opposed to communism and its blindness to recklessness and love, Melvyn Douglas educates Greta Garbo in the pleasures of high society in *Ninotchka*, while the union of Marshall and Miriam Hopkins in *Trouble in Paradise* is prefigured in their elegance and disdain for their stereotyped opposites. The diplomats, artists, thieves, and people of good will with whom he empathizes illuminate a sweetness and sarcasm unlikely in conventional middle-class society. Notwithstanding the differences between the sophistication of Lubitsch's protagonists and Preston Sturges' deeply felt portraits of small-town America, between the contrived literacy of Sacha Guitry and Marcel Pagnol's rusticism, in each case the propulsive style of silent-film comedy is replaced by an acceptance of the viability of society and the virtues of film comedy's literary and theatrical antecedents. In place of the disruptive mannerisms of the silent-film mime and the chaotic, visually explosive turn of events that he inspires, the major writers and directors of comedy during the first decades of the sound film accept the inevitability of society while reviving a form of satire that emphasizes the protagonist's verbal gracefulness and chicanery.

Whereas comedy developed as a metaphor for America's innocence and brashness in the face of technology and the increasing uniformity of social artifices and amenities, crime films such as Lang's *Dr. Mabuse the Gambler*, with its romantic fatalism and intensely geometric design, and Von Sternberg's *Underworld*, with its atmospheric, psychological gradations, were poetic realizations of a silent-film universe. In *The Testament of Dr. Mabuse* Lang makes a shrewd use of sound, focusing on the power of the invisible voice behind the screen as a vivid parallel to Hitler's use of the radio. *M* offers a similar stylistic condensation by intercutting between the police and underworld, personifying the tension and fear surrounding the German town. But the expressionist motifs of Lang's crime films have little visibility in the work of the most popular crime-suspense film director of the sound film, Alfred Hitchcock.

Hitchcock's craft is emblematic of both the stylistic compromises of the sound film in general and of the crime film in particular. His signature is undeniable—an expert manipulation of the filmgoer through his deliberate exposition of the paradoxes surrounding the psychology of the pursuer and pursued, often resulting in a reversal of their roles and of the audience's sympathies with the major characters. Yet the very nature of his prototypical stylistic and thematic crosscurrents enabled Hitchcock to adapt a variety of treatments of crime during his career. After a generally undistinguished series of silent films and obviously benefiting from his training as a graphic artist, Hitchcock's work in the English cinema allowed him to modify his rigid, at times effectively severe style of thematic development to the dramatic conventions of the theater and the novel of detection. In *Blackmail* and *Murder*, two of his most compressed scripts and film treatments, there is not a shot, camera movement, or sound effect that does not contribute to the physical delineation of the architecture of the crime, the pursuit of the criminal, and the moral ambiguities that confront those drawn into the crime's resolution. They are tight, taut, well-made films, and *Blackmail*, with its horrowing portrayal of the anguish surrounding a female rape victim, is certainly a major statement from its director. But even in these methodical, somewhat mechanical films, and more so in his less congruent though more popular works like *The Lady Vanishes* and *The Thirty-Nine Steps*, the nature of the artifice that Hitchcock perpetrates on the audience becomes increasingly apparent.

The literature of crime has enjoyed a wide, international appeal; unique to English crime fiction is its facility, whether in the nonchalance of Raffles, in Holmes's superiority, or in the transparent social commentary of the country mysteries of the Agatha Christie school. Her crime puzzles, featuring Hercule Poirot or some dandy assuming the role of police inspector, are modestly cerebral parlor games, involving far more social farce than ratiocinative analysis. This then is their appeal: the combination of frivolity and fear, casual social fellowship and sudden self-preservation. In the silent-film era, notably in Germany, the crime film, like the fantasy film, became a record of social and symbolic history because of the rigorous experimentation of visual artists who cultivated styles of art nouveau, primitivism, expressionism, and abstraction, and their underlying recognition that a crime story like a fantasy was a natural metaphor for the political and social ills. In Lang's two probing, early sound films—*The Testament of Dr. Mabuse* and *M*, to which *Blackmail* and *Murder* are closest in style, though less so in content—the social cancer and the personal threads of anguish and alienation are naturally and artistically adapted to a sound film. But Hitchcock's legacy and that of the writers, directors, and designers of crime in the sound film operate within a different social environment, even as the influences of the *Black Mask* or the Poe-like tremors of Cornell Woolrich veer toward the rhetoric of the German films of the twenties without fully embracing it. The trademarks of Hitchcock's style—the sudden juxtaposition of the unusual, the unsettling, and the abnormal to the conventions of everyday life—show an uneasy blending of the more constant motifs of dread and danger in *Blackmail* and *Murder* with the more contrived characters and suspense in *The Lady Vanishes* and *The Thirty-Nine Steps*. The stamp of greatness that Hitchcock's numerous admirers find throughout his career will be consistently achieved only in the fifties, when Hitchcock worked with his most sympathetic and original cameraman, Robert Burks, while adapting a series of scripts that would have been regarded as too perverse and ambiguous in the thirties. The comic banter and romantic interplay in the majority of his English crime films of the thirties, repressed with varying degrees of success in his American films, stand as proof of the continuing appeal of crime, not only as a study in personal or social abnormality, but as one of the most popular and transparent forms of dramatic catharsis.

While the Russian epics of the thirties exemplify the difficulties faced by sound-film directors in translating a country's mores and ideals, several of Jean Renoir's early sound films anticipate the problems facing the development of a humanist ethic in the sound film. Renoir was one of the cinema's most diverse stylists, and one treads on more precarious ground with Renoir than with other filmmakers in selecting a handful of his films. Of the major directors in the first decade of the sound film, no one was more open in testing different styles and themes, no one so interested in using the cinema to instill an aesthetic of pathos and the sublime. *La Grande Illusion* is probably his best film of the thirties and *The Rules of the Game* the most revealing of his limitations as a director, but *Boudu Saved from Drowning* and *Toni* tell us more about the role film will play in the social and intellectual history of the twentieth century. Both films offer an uncompromising example of a primitive humanism, as if Renoir himself were a naïf without the least training in camerawork, cutting, or composition. *Boudu Saved from Drowning* is noteworthy for its treatment of the character of the clown, but as with *Toni*, one's attention should be drawn first to the underlying primitivism of the two films. This primitivism arises out of Renoir's conceiving the world as a reflection of his naive protagonists—Michel Simon's comic anarchist in *Boudu Saved from Downing* and the itinerant, romantic laborers in *Toni*. The films are sloppy, with rough-hewn characters and tentative plot contrivances and climaxes, whether in the rescue of Boudu in which there is a complete absence of any element of suspense or in the scene in which Toni discovers his girl friend making love to the foreman, only to be told by her, "Such is life."

Renoir's intention is to break down the aesthetic distance separating reality and art so that neither *Boudu Saved from Drowning* nor *Toni* will be seen as a contrived fiction, but as a spontaneous, diarylike account of his characters' emotional quandaries. Primitivism in Renoir's films means understanding the natural world through the characters' innocence and placing his faith in the performers' ability to suggest their guilelessness in society. But the arbitrary nature of Renoir's conceptualization and resolution of the sublime severely limit the appeal of the two films. Though he fails to coherently dramatize the comic radicalism of *Boudu Saved from Drowning* or the romantic fatalism of *Toni*, Renoir has begun to fashion an emotionally unvarnished film style. The dialectical treatment of the inertia of the bourgeoisie and the liberating notes of the noble savage that emanate from the movements and speech of Simon's Boudu, the ethnic, communal strains of happiness and the discordant effect of personal emotions in *Toni* reach out to the viewer as moral lessons from nature and society. They have not been cleaned or hardened into the strict, didactic axioms of a scholastic; their meaning is coexpressive with the rambling, disordered nature of the characters' inner feelings. Renoir suggests a way of interpreting people and emotions that will be developed by filmmakers as different as Roberto Rossellini, Luis Buñuel, and Werner Herzog.

1. Ben Hall, *The Best Remaining Seats*, p. 196. Copyright © 1961 by Ben M. Hall. Used by permission of Crown Publishers, Inc.

2. Sergei Eisenstein, *Film Form*, pp. 257, 258, 259. Copyright © 1949 by Harcourt Brace Janovich, Inc.; renewed 1977 by Jay Leyda. Reprinted by permission of the publisher.

# 7

# The Art of the Sound Film (ii)

The preceding survey of key early sound films from Russia, America, England, and France has noted several stylistic permutations from a film reality dominated by silence to one in which sound and the aesthetics of realism were predominant. This review of the apparent technical and thematic properties of the sound film in the "Maxim Trilogy," the comedies of Ernst Lubitsch, the thrillers of Alfred Hitchcock, and Renoir's treatment of the sublime was not meant, however, as a representative study of the Russian, American, English, and French film. The American cinema, with its numerous comedy forms, its topical, highly moralistic crime films, and its westerns and weepies, created a diverse, ultimately unifying style of entertainment for its audience. The English film industry, by drawing on the immense resources of its actors, developed a less individualistic, theatrically oriented form of moviemaking, while the French film encouraged a more experimental yet intuitively classic style of narrative cinema in exemplary productions such as *La Bête humaine, Le Jour se lève*, and *Les Enfants du paradis*. The types of filmmaking that these three countries generated during the thirties and for a good part of the forties gave the medium its textbook identity as a populist, middlebrow art form. From its inception, film enjoyed a relatively resilient identity in twentieth-century social history, but it was decisively affected by World War II and the aftermath of discord, alienation, and rebellion. The development of television and the Supreme Court ruling against the monopolization of theaters by the major American studios would have a major impact on the evolution of the movies. It is the war, however, that first figures in the postwar history of the film medium.

The term "neorealism" has been used to describe the Italian film renaissance of the forties, in a style first defined by Rossellini's *Open City* and *Paisan*. It is meant to define an ambience of poverty and the protagonists' constant moral crises. It is, however, a misnomer because "realism" refers to a stylistic development in which the artist emphasizes the oppressive nature of daily life. Realism is not an incorrect description of the major Italian film plots of this period, but I think the term "humanism" is more representative of their style and meaning. It suggests not only that the overriding stylistic impetus of the Italian cinema lies in its concern with man's moral rebirth, but also that, similar to the role film played in Russia during the twenties and at the beginning of the sound film, the medium becomes a major artistic forum in responding to the physical and social devastation the Italian people have experienced. "Humanism" then is a more precise term than "realism," which implies a manner of representing social history in which the numerous physical qualities of the individual and his environment are enumerated. The term "humanism" forces one to consider these films as a means of establishing an inquiry or dialogue about what it means to be human by examining the social and spiritual hardships facing Italian society in the aftermath of World War II. There is certainly an element of realism in the Italian films, but it is only one aspect and not the crucial one. The humanistic spirit of the postwar Italian film arises out of a common understanding by artists like Roberto Rossellini, Cesare Zavattini, and Vittorio De Sica that the individual, as the focal point of society, must begin anew in defining his humanity. They do not search for the stylistic correlative that Russian filmmakers discovered in montage as the most lucid and expressive means to idealize the victory of the proletariat, but establish a more fundamental historical and aesthetic proposition concerning the viability of man and his society.

This essentially metaphysical approach to the impact of the movies in postwar society is best realized by Rossellini. Our understanding of the Italian films as metaphysical rather than aesthetic, humanistic and not realistic begins with films like *Paisan, Open City*, and *Flowers of St. Francis. Paisan*, like *Open City*, concerns the last years of the war, but it is a more pellucid statement of the ideals of the Italian cinema because its story, performances, and, perhaps most important, the composition of the film reflect the desolation of the Italian countryside. *Open City* is a more conventional narrative, an exemplary study of nationalism in which good and evil, hero and villain are simply and effectively defined. The differences between *Open City* and comparable efforts such as Pabst's sappy tearjerker *Westfront*, Renoir's uncompromisingly didactic *This Land Is Mine*, and *Casablanca*—the American film industry's "classic" statement of the war years—lie in Rossellini's sensitivity to his characters' emotional intensity. There is little that is showy or self-conscious in the performances of the underground fighter and priest, while the vividness with which Anna Magnani's desperation overwhelms the screen cannot be explained by the term "neorealism." Her performance assumes the quality of *verismo*, an accentuated emotionalism which derives from her extreme emotional fragility. It is not simply another distinguished example of the precariousness of women, previously depicted in the American film by actresses such as Margaret Sullavan and Bette Davis; it exposes the vulnerability of an individual to a degree rarely achieved in the movies. One might think of the character of Vera Baranovskaya's mother in Pudovkin's *Mother* or of Beulah Bondi as the aging matriarch in *Make Way for Tomorrow*, but the puissance of Magnani's characterization results from Rossellini's individual, impassioned treatment of the havoc of war. Although *Open City* has the contrived, melodramatic quality of numerous American war films, what distinguishes the film and signals a new era in film history is Rossellini's refusal to dramatically balance the explosive emotional chemistry of the story and characters. This is as true of Magnani's character as it is of the girl befriended and duped by the Nazis.

In *Paisan* Rossellini achieves a similar emotional force by fragmenting the conventional narrative structure in *Open City*. The film is a series of vignettes tied together by the theme of alienation and the total social devastation of Italy. A poignant parallel is established between the protagonists' isolation and the physical desolation of the countryside that was only tentatively fulfilled in *Open City*. A society comprised of the interaction of two or more people, of long-standing mores, and of a cohesive physical reality is nowhere visible in the film. The protagonists are drifters, divorced from any sense of family or friendship; the stories concern their efforts to defeat the enemy and to discover a sign of fellowship and hope. This thematic emphasis leads to the inclusion of *Flowers of St. Francis* as a major statement of the Italian humanist cinema; like the forlorn soldiers in *Paisan*, St. Francis and his followers are faced with a similar social and spiritual challenge. As the devastated Italian terrain in *Paisan* was a metaphor for the collapse of society, the impoverished countryside in which St. Francis and his disciples set up their retreat reflects both their severe asceticism and the hope that their moral and spiritual innocence will serve as the foundation of a social order. It is not, however, the correlation between the physical devastation of nature and the severe moral test facing the characters in *Paisan* and *Flowers of St. Francis* that identifies the two films as emblematic of the Italian humanist ethic. The disheveled nature of society is further evidence of the supervening humanism first manifest in *Open City*; Rossellini, whether out of personal choice or necessity, has renounced any element of contrivance in the two films. Several scenes in *Paisan* make awkward use of a studio backdrop; combined with the insufficient lighting units, the crude camerawork and editing, the amateurish acting, and most notably the extreme sense of poverty conspicuous in every level of the film's style and content, they denote the desperation which must be sounded if society is to be reborn. Rossellini's mission then is not unlike that of St. Francis—to instill the idea of a community and to express the purity of its ideals. A cursory screening of these films may lead one to dismiss them as shoddy narrative experiments, but in terms of film history they mark a turning point in the social and artistic voice of the movies.

Rossellini's primitive film style and his characters' social and spiritual alienation signify his original contribution to the humanism of the Italian cinema. Vittorio De Sica and Cesare Zavattini undertake a more conventional but equally powerful picture of the hardships facing their countrymen in reestablishing society. Although there is an element of physical devastation in their three major works, *The Bicycle Thief*, *Shoeshine*, and *Umberto D*, they do not probe the deracinated nature of society in the extreme manner adopted by Rossellini. In Rossellini's films the impoverished backgrounds and the tentative camerawork and cutting are evidence of the collapse of a social foundation; his characters, like the torn, empty world in which they find themselves, must be remade. In *The Bicycle Thief*, *Shoeshine*, and *Umberto D*, however, a makeshift society has begun to take shape; it is a poverty-ridden world but one in which the major problem is not the reidentification of the individual and society but the reaffirmation of the bonds of family and friendship. The treatment is more straightforward, and in some ways more emotionally explosive. By focusing on the fragility of human relationships De Sica and Zavattini do not encompass the formidable spiritual dimensions in Rossellini's films or in Visconti's *La terra trema*. In their three major films the camera is directly centered on the protagonists—the father and son in *The Bicycle Thief*, the two waifs in *Shoeshine*, and the old man and his dog in *Umberto D*—and their moral integrity in sustaining their humanity through friendships. The humanism of De Sica and Zavattini lies in their commitment to testing the resonance of these relationships as they are threatened by the economic realities of postwar life. There is not, as in the realism of various writers and painters, a predominant desire to comprehensively detail the full measure of poverty at each level of society; the encompassing theme is the exigence of these bonds in sustaining a society.

Of the major works of the Italian humanist cinema, Luchino Visconti's *La terra trema* is the one most interested in interpreting its realistic subject matter in a classic framework. Its intrinsically poetic style derives from the grandiose manner in which Visconti conceives the poverty facing the Sicilian fishermen, as in his epic long shots of the women in black shawls awaiting the return of their husbands along the shore. Although there is a prefatory appreciation for the closed-in quarters of the firshermen and the activity along the waterfront, Visconti's fishermen are not overcome by their squalid existence, but by their hubris in challenging the forces of nature; the film does not present a conflict of man against man as in the films of De Sica and Zavattini, but man against nature.

If humanism then best signifies the visual and dramatic scope of the Italian cinema, it can also be seen as the most formidable social and artistic factor in the development of the movies from the end of World War II through the early sixties; it was not only in Italy where such an extreme form of social regrouping was manifested, but throughout Europe, in Japan, and even in the United States. One can then identify the naturalism of the English cinema, the social anarchism of Kurosawa and the numerous adaptations of the plays of William Inge, Arthur Miller, and Tennessee Williams as elaborating aspects of the humanist perspective of the Italian cinema. This is to overlook momentarily the deification of fin de siècle romanticism in the films of Max Ophüls and the most sustained example of classicism in film history in the films of Yasujiro Ozu. But in our survey of film history numerous styles and filmmakers have been overlooked in order to underline the most prominent developments in film history: it is not a question of favoring one style or director over another but one of discerning the most important social and artistic developments.

Hence the realism of the English cinema with its emphasis on the embittered anti-hero and the grubby materialism of his society, the virulence with which Kurosawa exposes the meretriciousness of various social institutions, and the nascent element of self-doubt and moral ambiguity of the American film of the fifties can all be viewed as tangents of the Italian humanist ethic. The postwar Italian film was imbued with an underlying humanist direction, but there was no such unifying ideal in these other movements. What these different styles commonly signify is a seemingly sweeping change in the sociology of the sound film as it is thrust into the role that the Russian theoreticians had initially forseen in what they termed the "ultimate reality." While there is a deeply felt appreciation of classic and romantic themes in the films of John Ford, Yasujiro Ozu, Jean Renoir, and Max Ophüls, all veteran directors whose training began in the silent film, the Italian humanist cinema of Rossellini, De Sica, and Visconti and parallel styles like Akira Kurosawa's mordant expressionism, and the murky introspection of the American cinema places the movies in the mainstream of postwar social history. It is this identification of film as an ideal medium to express the great ideas of history that Rossellini and the Italian cinema spearheaded.

Yet this humanist ethic enjoyed only a brief period of appeal, in part because of film's changing role in postwar society and the rapid changes in the literature and art of this period. By the late fifties, the pathos and social immediacy of film's postwar stylists had been superseded by a style of alienation and abstraction, first manifest in the Italian and French film and later in the cycle of violent, antiestablishment films in the American cinema and the equally histrionic studies of the individual and society in the Japanese film. This radical change in technique and theme was prefigured in the Italian cinema by films such as Antonioni's *Story of a Love Affair*, Rossellini's *Viaggio in Italia*, and Fellini's *La dolce vita*. The focus changes from the poor to the rich, from a desire to build a spiritual fellowship to documenting its disintegration. Whereas a director like Fellini envisions the world in an increasingly symbolic vein, taking his audience from the commedia dell'arte underpinnings of *La strada* to the tortured autobiographies of *8½* and *Juliet of the Spirits*, Antonioni's love trilogy and his succeeding color films explore the abstracted gloss of modern society and how its dehumanized design leads to self-negation (*Blow-Up*) and fantasy (*Zabriskie Point*). In a period of twenty-five years the Italian cinema completely changed its identity: while originally existing as a profound voice of man's social and spiritual rebirth, it turned to recording his social and spiritual nullification.

The French New Wave, the most formidable group of directors since the founders of the Italian humanist cinema, is a more avant-garde, stylistically eclectic movement. One of the major differences between Italian and French filmmakers concerns the unequivocal commitment to man and society in the Italian film, whereas the French New Wave, led by a group of film critics-turned-directors, is more interested in exploring the continuity of styles in film history. A major principle at work in the films of Jean-Luc Godard, François Truffaut, and Claude Chabrol is an immersion in the entire history of film, from Griffith and Renoir to Hitchcock and Welles. For the first time in film history the director is aware of a well-stocked, self-referential corpus of ideas and images. One scene which intimates the constant interplay of past and present occurs in *Breathless* when Jean-Paul Belmondo stares at Bogey's poster; Belmondo's role is in large part a free-verse interpretation of the tough guy Bogey and other film iconoclasts made famous. To contemporary filmmakers the language of the movies—in terms of its ideas, icons, and images—will become more private and self-conscious.

Godard is in the vanguard of this fight to establish the classic and modern identity of the film medium. In films like *Breathless, A Woman Is a Woman,* and *Alphaville* Godard imbues popular genres with various improvisational and rhetorical techniques; at the end of the sixties he is drawn to a Brechtian-styled collage of film and history, leading in *Le Gai Savoir* to the characterization of his protagonists as visual ideologues in a television studio and in *One Plus One* to questioning his own identity as a director who uses film to express his radical politics.

The politics and poetics of the absurd influenced numerous American and European directors in the sixties, but none rivaled Godard's creativity and integrity in realizing the stylistic cul-de-sac in which the medium found itself at the end of the decade. With the premiere of *Weekend, Le Gai Savoir,* and *One Plus One,* it appeared that film had reached its most extreme form of social and stylistic conceptualization, dramatizing the major social controversies of the sixties while employing the most advanced techniques of the postwar art scene.

By the late sixties the rigorous poetics of Godard and Antonioni had brought the movies to a point of abstraction and spiritual self-negation. In America, where the movies had sustained their most diverse and successful commercial identity, film was experiencing a drastic reversal in its mythmaking potential. The family-oriented, good guy, happy-ending syndrome of the thirties and forties, which had been challenged first in the fifties, was in abeyance. Hollywood was in the midst of a palace revolution; films like *Bonnie and Clyde, The Graduate, Easy Rider,* and *The Wild Bunch* represented a complete departure from the type of film and moral code for which Hollywood had become famous.

But if Hollywood was slow to grasp the change in the social identity of the movies, it signaled the keynote for the cinema in the seventies with films like *American Graffiti* and *The Godfather.* The clean lines and colors of George Lucas's isolated terrain, the rebelliousness of his adolescents, and the romantic fantasies of their pop music idealize the conventions of small-town, middle-class America. The dark tones that envelop Francis Coppola's empathetic study of a family's struggle for survival in the midst of a crime war elevate the clichés and mythology of crime to tragic drama. Their approach prefigures the consistent neoclassic imprint of the American film of the seventies, most often used as a conventional commercial formula—as in the unending cycle of disaster epics, one of the oldest of film genres, and in the proliferation of remakes and sequels. If the term "neoclassicism" can be used then to characterize the styles and themes of the American film, filmmakers such as Lina Wertmuller, Masahiro Shinoda, and Rainer Werner Fassbinder appear to possess a similar interest in reviving conventional if not outmoded characters and stories and infusing them with various modernist touches. In many ways the seventies found the cinema adapting the radical poetics and politics of Antonioni, Godard, Fellini, and

Bergman to classic narrative styles. But it becomes much more difficult to arrive at a generalization of the movies today than in earlier years because film operates in a more dynamic cultural sphere. Whether the radicalism of the sixties or the revisionism of the seventies will have more lasting appeal will not be resolved simply by their artistic validity, but by the role film will play in the technological revolution in the last years of the twentieth century.

# 8
# Film Acting

Why acting? Why devote a chapter to a craft that is often regarded as one of the least craftsmanlike in a medium in which the scriptwriter, designer, cameraman, editor, producer, and director outweigh and clearly shape the manifestations of the actor? Film is applauded as a modern art form—a technological extension of man's cognitive and sensory faculties. The nuances of a film's style are developed through the lighting of the photographer, the dynamics of the editor, the configurations of the designer, the expressiveness of the music, and the intricacies of the plot. The actor, well, he is part of the scenery, a piece of cattle but a nice piece of cattle according to Hitchcock, another film employee who just so happens to be its "star," but whose humanism is carefully modulated by the collective nature of film production. Why, then, not regard the actor as another physical component of the film and dispense with a discussion of acting until the subject of the theater comes up, where a venerable tradition with a rich history awaits us?

The reasons for our suspiciousness toward film acting are many, but the foremost one seems to lie in the desire not to seem too old-fashioned or, even worse, critically naive in thinking that the actor may be a dominant figure in a film's overall design. Yet for all of the investigations into the subtleties of a film through the analysis of camera angles, visual continuity, and the elements of composition, there is a failure to recognize one simple outstanding feature: the actor is the central, unifying presence in the audience's aesthetic consideration of a film. What a film is about—whether in any one of its technical components such as camerawork, cutting, or composition or in its thematic and symbolic imprint—derives from the actor. He is the object that the cameraman shades in varying degrees of light; he is the face and figure around which the editor and art director must center their effects; he is the force that defines the drama, that gives weight and depth to the countless details in a film. He represents its humanization through the ability to transcend film's physical environment and imbue meaning into the two-dimensional world he inhabits. He is the dominant quantity in a film, his quality made known through his humanity.

The actor impersonates; he makes known a character that coheres in the simulated action. By its definition "acting" implies illusion, the ability to ani-

75

mate the inanimate through the performer's physical extensions (the different movements, gestures, expressions, vocal delivery, and speech). A character is created distinct from the performer's, a character who exists only in the dramatic fiction. The reality of a film as opposed to that of the theater further complicates the techniques of film acting. In a theater the audience is continually aware of the nature of the illusion being practiced. One may believe in the autonomy of the vision of the playwright and in the powers of the craftsmen of the theater to transmogrify the playwright's invisible reality onto the stage. But the stage is there, the dimensions of a physically make-believe world inhabiting a common, physical universe through the players' entrances and exits and the various aspects of the stage machinery. A film, however, purports to reproduce reality, to transport the audience to a physical dimension in which the fabrications of a theater's physical space are no longer present. The screen, too, is artificial, but what transpires within its frame is of a nature different from that of the world one inhabits. One knows it is an illusion, but the illusion is practiced with complete freedom and with an acknowledgment of the film's structural and intellectual autonomy.

The criteria that determine an appreciation of acting in the silent film are clearly different from those of the theater, yet closer to the nature of impersonation in a sound film than one might originally believe. The art of pantomime pervades the silent film. Through physical movements and gestures a mime attempts to explain and express an action that in everyday life is supported by the faculty of speech. At the beginning of the silent-film era and most conspicuously in the development of silent-film slapstick, actors function in a world of radical typecasting; their sharply defined makeup, like their nonverbal communications, exists as a transparent symbol in the black-and-white world of the silent film; silent-film performers are not engaged in the realization of a character but in a radicalization of character perpetuated in acute, emphatic signs that function as a type of kinetic hieroglyphics.

The symbolic undercurrents of silent-film slapstick extend into a consideration of the dramatic actor. Because of the absence of sound and the grainy nature of the film stock that encompasses the players in an indeterminate landscape suspended between reality and fantasy, the performer's expressive actions must complement as well as characterize the film's physical reality. The space is not fixed as in the theater so that he must continually redirect and refocus his dramatic impulses in relation to the other actors and to the various permutations in lighting, camera movement, and editing. He cannot "command" one's attention and grasp of reality as in the theater because the frame around him continually changes; he cannot overwhelm the audience in the manner of a stage performer because unlike the stage performer he is not always in the picture where his dramatic presence may be felt even in the presence of other performers. It is his face and figure with which one is concerned; with the exception of the French avant-garde, the performer is involved in a humanistic drama; it is the human form that exists as the most conspicuous, expressive component in a film, the one figure that transcends the physical circumstances of the film medium.

How then does the actor in a silent film transcend the medium's physical reality? How does he make real to his audience the nature of his and our humanity? As he cannot speak, he must channel the techniques of mime acting to the changing physical world around him. Since the silent-film actor is a physical presence who cannot utilize speech as a summation or counterpoint to his physical reality, he must continually redefine his "line" within the changing film universe just as the planets in the solar system use their axes and the gravitational field around them to sustain their orbit around the sun.

Because acting in a silent film is comprised of these different physical extensions and because these extensions are modified within the self-contained, wholly independent world of a film, the aesthetics of silent-film acting must reflect the different art forms that the supporting technicians have utilized. The actor is placed in an imaginary world, his art determined by his ability to adapt his expressiveness to the techniques of visual and dramatic representation borrowed from painting, photography, and theater. The actor's "statements" are then orchestrated into a moving picture by the director and his crew.

The manifold problems that await the critic of silent-film acting arise from the complex process by which film assimilates and redefines these different art forms and techniques. The critic must be able to recognize not only the diverse origins of the visual representation a film intends—such as the combined influences of theatrical melodrama and realism in Griffith's work, the poetic and pictorial symbolism in the German silent film, and the theatrically based identification of the actor as a kinetic, expressionistic force in Russian montage filmmaking—but he must also creatively imagine their resonance as they are reinterpreted through the dynamics of the film medium. Various artistic styles are not simply adapted, but their congruency vibrates within the network of a moving space; the critic must then evaluate the manner in which the elements of film production have affected their validity. Like the cubist painter who alters one's understanding of visual perception, transferring to the eye the dynamics of film while his canvas implodes with the full kinetic force of a moving image, the filmmaker tells his story by imbuing various forms of literary and visual narrative with the dynamic potential of his craft.

The acting manuals of Stanislavski continually instruct the student to think of acting as a gerund. The interpreter of a character does not step in and out of his role but sees his character as a spiritualized presence that is made real in moments of rest and reticent observation as well as in his movements within the dramatic surface of his stage. Stanislavski's characterization of acting through its active voice is a corollary to literary and pictorial styles that treat the nature of thought and the dynamics of literary and plastic form in terms of their organic evolution.

The art of Greta Garbo is emblematic of the controversies surrounding the methods and effectiveness of the silent-film player. Her interpretive powers

illuminate the proximity of photography as well as that of the performing
arts to the silent film. Her appeal originates in her striking physical beauty that
denotes moods of joy and longing, tenderness and aloofness in the many celebrated photographic studies of her face and figure. In the silent film she borrows
from the techniques of the stage actor and dancer through gestures and movements that are inspired by the absence of speech. Like the stage actor her movements have a grandioseness, a concentration of thought that function as a substitute for the unheard declamation. Like a modern dancer, Garbo's physical
gesticulations conceive her face and figure as a cartographic symbol representing the progressions, digressions, and transformations of an inner, emotional
spirit. If, at times, her movements seem too extravagant, it is the result of an
apathetic writer, director, cameraman, or cutter who has not created a symmetrical, supporting physical reality for her heroic, expressionist interpretations. In
her best silent-film roles—*The Story of Gösta Berling, The Joyless Street, A Woman of
Affairs*—even in the two lamentable versions of *Anna Karenina*, a role she improvised on throughout her career, Garbo animates the character in a way that
approximates the plasticity of a photographer, the psychology of a writer, and
the dynamics of a choreographer.

Another problem that undercuts a discussion of acting in the silent film is
that what one terms an actor's mode of symbolic expression is reduced to, or is
in numerous cases, an actor's photogenic expressiveness. How do we differentiate a beautiful face from a beautiful performance when the performance consists
of carefully arranged postures and when its dramatic potential is largely realized through a rearrangement of the actor's physical charms? Clearly the content of the work and the profundity or lack of it are being adjudged, leading to
an appreciation of the performer in a manner not unlike a critique of the formal
arrangement in a Seurat drawing. The utilization of the actor as a physical
component is ubiquitous in the Russian silent film, in both the kinetic, Marxist
action dramas of Eisenstein and Pudovkin, in which the expressive features of
the faces of rich and poor are juxtaposed, and in the plastic dramas of Dovzhenko, in which the Russian visage is interpreted as a type of holy icon in the
new Russian society. This is the most complete form of symbolic expression in
the silent film, adapting the graphic nature of the film image to the dynamic
immediacy of the film medium.

The German silent film provides a similar example of a symbolic physical
extension, but whereas the Russians use the actor as part of an encompassing
Marxist dialectic, the actor in the German cinema dramatizes the film's expressionistic content. Because German films do not attempt the depersonaliza-
tion of history that characterizes the Russian film, the actor, as the most visibly
active element in the symbolic design, retains a dominant humanistic imprint.
In movements and expressions that at times seem too exotic and rarefied, the
silent-film performer in Germany dramatizes the psychological extensions of his
symbolic reality. His gestures, movements, and postures fulfill the role of the
poetic discourse in symbolist drama; his "actions" connote the symbolic motifs
in the drama while personalizing its humanistic undercurrents.

With the addition of sound the film actor's craft is affected by the degree of reality that has been incorporated into the medium. He speaks, but he has not become a theater performer. The dialogue exists as the controlling force in the sound film even as the director may deviate from the continuity of the dialogue. Since the element of sound impregnates the actor's environment, the actor must adapt his movements to the layers of speech that spark his reality. He is no longer a mute presence who enlivens the drama through his elaborate mannerisms; rather, he adapts his actions to the conventions of a physically real world. He remains a presence in his ability to express through nonverbal communication what his words have not said and to reveal the tensions of his character in pregnant physical movements. The director may choose to show his face from an unusual angle or to fragment the expressiveness of his figure and speech by cutting to other players and objects, but the actor exists as the idea inspiring a film's technical embellishments.

A significant portion of the actor's craft, therefore, does not involve verbal interpretation but is an exposition of character through physical extension. Is an actor's presence, then, a matter of his command of various physical extensions, whether a sensual movement across an open space or a virile figure inhabiting a suit or T-shirt? The term "presence" implies an invisible substance, a quality that permeates without being reduced to the performer's physical features. The term "physical extensions" refers to the medium through which the film actor functions and is intended to suggest both the physically real manifestations and culminating idea expressed by the actor. Since film is a medium of physical effects, one cannot avoid discussing the physical aspects of acting; a performance may not be interpreted through the physical dimensions of the actor, yet its meaning and effectiveness derive from the performer's physical expressiveness. In his study of the nude, Kenneth Clark devotes considerable time to measuring the physiognomic proportion of upper and lower body, the space between the breasts, and the volume of the head as opposed to the lower extremities. One cannot deny that, like painting and sculpture, film demands a sense of a physical as well as a spiritual aesthetic, an understanding that the performance exists as our window into the world of the soul. This point is reenforced by the nature of the medium. Similar to the film crew, which builds from the raw material of physical space, the actor must channel his idea of the character through his physical extensions and transformations. Since the rise of method acting, the tendency to shy away from a discussion of the film performer's characterization has been reversed. Instead of minimizing the physical extensions of the performer's characterization, the inner meaning of the characterization is continually manifest in the performer's physical idiosyncrasies and movements.

For all the agonizing over the psychological impetus of method acting, the type or character that the method actor creates is a change only in degree and not in kind from the characterizations in the previous generation of theater and film actors. The different performers who are universally applauded have not created simply profound interpretations, but their physical features and man-

nerisms have incorporated a personality unique to their time. The sum total of
the art of Lillian Gish cannot be divorced from the refined lighting techniques of
Billy Bitzer or the thematic controversies of Griffith and his co-scriptwriters, but
the beauty of her performances lies in her physical apotheosis as the heroine of
Victorian melodrama and Pre-Raphaelite art. Her rich, abundant hair, her
trim, delicate figure, the cherubic face marked by the lightness of the lines of her
mouth and eyebrows, and the crystalline symmetry of her face embody the
vision of contemporary literary and graphic artists. Two of the most popular
and controversial figures in the postwar American film, Marlon Brando and
Marilyn Monroe, personify a mood of anxiety and recklessness, eroticism and
self-destructiveness that writers like Tennessee Williams, Arthur Miller, and
William Inge elaborated in their plays and that directors like Hitchcock and
Lang impressed into their films. But would their magnetism have been possible
without the crude, bulky force of Brando's physique, the element of facial asymmetry created by his nose and mouth, or without Monroe's expression of cupidity, dangling her overripe body in front of her male admirers? John Kobal laments the loss of a classic star appeal in the postwar American film; yet much of
the dramatic focus to the movies over the last three decades lies in the absence
of any period identification among its major stars. The corresponding emphasis
on the denuded topography of the faces and figures of the postwar actor exemplifies our recurrent fascination with the movies as exploratory excavations of
the human soul.

In judging foreign films and actors, the difficulty of discerning the performer's
expressiveness is magnified. An appreciation of the performer's characterization entails an awareness of the social customs and physical mannerisms prevalent in the culture and how the actor's interpretation refines these elements.
There are no universal standards for acting because there are no universal styles
of drama or social behavior. In Chishu Ryu's interpretations of the retiring
patriarch in any one of a number of Ozu's films, his conservative dress, his
sparse physical gestures, and his slight physique and reserved speech play off a
history of social conventions that can be studied in Japanese art and literature
but whose social expressiveness one is sorely ignorant of by not observing them
in everyday society.

Truman Capote gained undue notoriety by characterizing actors as stupid.
No, the actor is not stupid. His intelligence is made known to us through a
physcial medium that reveals, in its most noble manifestations, the intellect in
action. It is our intelligence that is being challenged by a force whose intelligence is well-nigh invisible.

# 9
# Film Criticism

The history of film criticism is a study in the radical changes the medium has undergone in the public eye. In browsing through any one of several collections of criticism that span the history of film, one cannot fail to note the transformation of the critic from a cursory viewer struck by the speed, the topicality, the awesome yet undisciplined physical autonomy of the cinema to a diligent, self-conscious student of the medium who pays homage to the images and styles of the past renewed in the contemporary cinema. The movies were initially viewed with caution if not trepidation by civic leaders and the academic establishment; yet doctorates in film scholarship seem to be awarded today with the facility of a B–movie production. Film has experienced an almost unprecedented catapulting of prestige in the public's consciousness. However, despite all the interest shown by publishers and academia in honoring this modern art form, film criticism and scholarship are adrift in the Ice Age.

Although the silent film inspired several adventurous, speculative accounts of the medium, the appearance of sound seemed to signal to critics that this was to be an art dominated by money and technology. Various actors, cameramen, designers, scriptwriters, editors, and directors had been cited during the silent-film era as bringing to the movies the treasures of theater, photography, even music and architecture, but with the rise of Hollywood as the center of film production, the increasing admiration for the cinema was cut short. As movies became longer and more expensive to finance, as film production assumed the division of labor that is now seen as a paradigm of technological society, the medium settled into its identity as populist and middlebrow. The hegemony of the producer and the American film industry seemed to end the debate over the identity of the movies; the absence of a controlling artistic voice and the wide appeal of the American film apparently terminated any discussion of the artistic independence of the movies. There remained a residue of respect for the aesthetics of film, but it was reserved for European films imported to America.

The most crucial period of film criticism occurred shortly after World War II. It involved a new generation of film critics who responded to the movies as an art form with an undeniable cultural permanence. They were not only aware of the merits of acting, cinematography, scriptwriting, design, editing, and

81

directing but looked to the medium to define the most abstract concepts. The movies were not simply one expression of the sublime, but a profound medium of ideas out of which this new generation of filmgoers would fashion their notions of time and space, truth and beauty. Their predecessors may have traced their youth to the silent film, but they lacked a sense of the direction and validity of the cinema. With a period of fifty years of filmmaking from which to draw, the film critics who began appearing in newly founded film journals in England, Italy, France, and America could establish a historical framework for their own work. They would undertake to write the history of the first two generations of filmmakers, and many of them would go on to constitute the third generation. This postwar phenomenon in criticism, culminating in the *auteur* theory of French critics, has influenced nearly every area of film criticism and scholarship.

Implicit in the proliferation of film journals in postwar Europe and America is the recognition of the medium as an art form worthy of admittance into the pantheon. Film would no longer be viewed as an example of fine acting, writing, or photography but as creating an original stylistic vision. During the first decades of the sound film, film criticism functioned in a sociological context by reviewing movies as an index to social controversies and mores. But postwar criticism would entail a unique proposition: the movies are not shaped by social or commercial interests; they present the most comprehensive, the most advanced, the most "true" picture of reality. This new generation of film critics not only challenged the premises of their predecessors, but also the most basic sentiments of their culture about the integrity of the medium. Film was not a soiled, technological servant of the masses, but its most divine creation; a new aesthetic and, equally important, a new metaphysic would be formulated, exploring both the nature of beauty and the nature of knowledge.

One decisive repercussion of postwar criticism in England and France was that many of the writers were soon to be the major voices in the film revolutions in the two countries. Lindsay Anderson, Tony Richardson, and Karel Reisz played major roles in moving the English cinema away from its stately, bland formulas to naturalism. In France André Bazin set the stage for the more polemic criticism of François Truffaut, Jacques Rivette, Jean-Luc Godard, and Claude Chabrol by championing two different aspects of the movies that were to play a significant part in the *auteur* theory associated with the French critics-turned-directors. Foremost was his appreciation of the inherent superiority of the American sound film to the European cinema. Bazin argued in favor of the multiplicity of the American film, its numerous storytelling forms, themes, and stars. A second feature of his criticism was a cogent defense of the aesthetics of the sound film. Although he erroneously defined patterns of naturalism in the silent and sound film and lacked the incisive theoretical viewpoint of Eisenstein, Bazin's lucid, compassionate essays are among the few examples of film criticism that, like the film classics he discusses, deserve to be passed on.

Bazin then laid the foundations for the *auteur* theory by reversing a long-standing antipathy for the American film, discovering in what had been seen as the most formidable deterrent to the artistic development of the movies and the American film—its underlying breakdown of responsibility and its overriding commercial identity—as the reasons for its success. The intense degree of controversy that surrounds a discussion of the *auteur* theory as formulated by Truffaut and that has affected every level of "movie talk" from cocktail party gatherings to doctoral reviews can be partly assuaged in considering Bazin's role in the evolution of the *politique des auteurs*. Even though the central thesis in Truffaut's essay—and the reason for its general acceptance among critics and academia—lies in his stressing the role of an individual voice in the making of a film, Bazin's more general considerations are implicit in Truffaut's theory. In defending the diversity of the American film, Bazin suggested that its strength did not necessarily lie with the adaptations of literary masterpieces, but in action genres like the crime and western that were usually consigned to the role of B film or supporting work to the major film being distributed. Truffaut's thesis can be seen as a reductio ad absurdum of Bazin's appreciation for the American film: it upgrades the previously downgraded elements of Hollywood commercialism and impersonality, viewing the movies and the American cinema not as a sociological phenomenon but an aesthetic one.

While Bazin and the new group of French critics point to the virtues of the American film and narrative forms held in low esteem like the crime, western, and fantasy film, the "revisionist" thrust of the *auteur* theory is most aggressively expressed in identifying the strengths of a film through one figure, usually the director. It functions as a revisionist development in film history by dismissing a commercial or sociological interpretation of the movies and prescribing a highly romantic reading of the medium. *Auteur* critics discount the eclectic nature of moviemaking and honor one figure as responsible for its success. The romanticism of the *auteur* theory is its most significant feature; Truffaut and his contemporaries call attention to the need for creative superstars who will be seen as more important than the producers and performers previously cited. The reason then for focusing on the postwar *auteur* aesthetic as the most critical phase of film criticism and scholarship is that it disdains a discussion of film in a sociological or anthropological context while choosing to highlight one figure as tantamount to a film's form and meaning.

To admit the romantic drift of the *auteur* theory, whether it concerns the efforts of Truffaut to elevate directors such as Robert Bresson and Jean Cocteau or those of Andrew Sarris to remove William Wyler and John Huston from the pantheon, is to signify its inherent wrongheadedness. The single most consistent truth about moviemaking is its division of responsibilities, ranging from the influence of the producer who finances and often selects the material to the work of the actors and numerous technicians who shape the different images. To look at a film as the "idea" of one man is to overlook the mechanics of making a film. Since the birth of the fiction film, there have been a handful of figures like Méliès, Chaplin, Keaton, and Welles who have figured so prominently in the scripting, acting, and overall design of their films that it would be foolish to deny their signature. But the overwhelming majority of films are made by various craftsmen, who, although conscious of the general theme of the work, contribute nuances of form and feeling that do not emanate from the controlling figure in the production.

If the thesis of the *auteur* theory is so clearly, painstakingly wrong, its continued application can be interpreted as an effort by a new generation of filmgoers to upgrade the "public" and "private" identity of the medium, to underline the notion to both the general filmgoing public and academia that film is an art and not a business. The way they have chosen to undertake the reappraisal of the popular and critical identity of the movies is by idealizing the individual artist with a singular plan and by overlooking the eclectic and hence impersonal nature of moviemaking. Their romanticism lies in the need to identify a film with one voice, similar to the way nineteenth-century romanticism emphasized the independence of the artist and the unique, organic nature of his creation. The popular articulations of *auteur* critics are in direct response to the commercial, eclectic nature of film production, suggesting that the terms by which previous film critics had responded to the medium lacked the one element—that of aesthetic volition—that critics of nineteenth-century literature, painting, music, and dance enjoyed. By refuting the truth of filmmaking, *auteur* critics are gambling on the loss of comprehensiveness, of aesthetic unity, for a name, a style, however minimal, that will give film history a group of superstar figures of similar stature to the "artists" of the past. It has simplified discussion of film by adjudging the numerous elements of a film in terms of the vision of one artist. Certainly one of the major tasks that awaits the next generation of film critics in challenging the validity of the *auteur* theory is to analyze the great films and determine the influence of producer and director, actor and writer, photographer and editor.

The reason that I have associated the *auteur* theory with the manifold changes in film scholarship is that it underscores the acute change in film criticism from a sociological context with its low, populist elements to an aesthetic one in which the style of the director represents the film's form and meaning. The ensuing proliferation of film courses in high schools, colleges, and graduate schools is in recognition of the riches of film history. The seemingly endless number of books about Renoir, Hitchcock, and almost every other director both major and minor implants in the public the idea of the transcendence of style and personality in moviemaking. One indirect consequence of the *auteur* theory is the semiology of avant-garde theoreticians, in which commercial or sociological influences are discounted, and the critic responds instead to the film "image" as a pure form with the same artistic validity as the Madonna or Christ child in a medieval painting. Clearly the problems that have resulted from the popular and academic acceptance of film art are many. This is not, however, to justify every monograph written about the Madonna and the medieval craftsman while lambasting the studies of film directors. These faults in scholarship are not germane to film criticism but to criticism itself.

Perhaps one might argue that there is no need for any ideal or systematic approach to criticism, that rather than advancing any one theory, whether it be

Kracauer's socialist aesthetic with its emphasis on the naturalistic potential of the medium to record the full activity of daily life or the *auteur* theory with its highly specialized concept of style, the critic should rely on common sense, uncommon taste, and a diligent reading of film history in evaluating a movie. Although this viewpoint works in literary, art, and music criticism, where there is a discernible past of greatness, such is not the case in film history. In her preface to Lewis Jacobs's *The Rise of the American Film*, Iris Barry, although disagreeing with Jacobs's estimate of Chaplin, argued that film criticism was at a stage where opinions were still being entertained without definite judgments having been formed about the great, the mediocrities, and the outright failures.

Film scholarship has advanced so rapidly, however, in both the public eye and that of academia, that there should exist a recognizable list of great films and figures and a correct way of evaluating their contributions. This has yet to be achieved, whether in Kracauer's materialist aesthetic, still the most formidable, misconceived theory about film, or in the morass of literature that has resulted from the *auteur* theory. It will be this area of film criticism—the systematic survey of major films and personalities—that I will pursue in the following section in the hope of establishing an underlying framework for a film aesthetic.

Part 2

# The Varieties of the Film Experience

# 10
## The Epic Film

*Enoch Arden – The Four Horsemen of the Apocalypse*

D. W. Griffith's *The Birth of a Nation* has been honored as the first example of the artistic scope of the movies. Several film historians, however, see him as an incomplete artist, a master of visual daring who relied on archaic dramatic devices and a quaint, prissy moralism. Yet among his early, exemplary shorts Griffith's development from an innovative film poet to his mastery of the stylistic gradations of the film image is complemented by a dramatic expansiveness and moral authority. In his shorts Griffith's highly charged romantic temperament experiments with the conflicting passions of human nature and history in tense, melodramatic situations. Unlike his contemporaries in both epic and comedy who innocently exploited the medium's comic treatment of character and action, Griffith's most memorable shorts reveal his sensitivity to the beauty of nature and the individual and their expressiveness on film. He presents his characters as representatives of a dreamlike past and his settings as idealized studies of nature and history. What sometimes appear to be excessive close-ups of steadfast lovers and wives, and lingering, heroic vistas of nature are evidence of a film style that parallels the timelessness of epic poetry. He relies on a sharply edited, scherzo finale and though its application often seems perfunctory, his best work builds toward this fast-paced resolution. In his pioneering shorts Griffith aims for a style of poetic flux, a drama of emotional ebbs and flows that conveys his romantic interpretation of man, nature, and history.

If the qualities that one most vividly remembers from his one- and two-reelers are their symbolic imagery and decisively edited conclusions, they are not so much formulas or equivalents to popular modes of emotionalism in literature, theater, and photography as they are imaginative studies of their dramatic potential through the technical and expressive components of the short. Many of these efforts are tawdry melodramas in which Griffith is in fact an energetic though acquiescent disciple of popular fiction and morality. But the constant experimentation with literary, dramatic, and photographic conventions often results in revelatory studies in which the spatial definition of time and place is animated by the discords and dreams of his protagonists. His most typical early

89

triumphs visualize basic human emotions and conflicts in which the dynamic editing unifies his characters' fate with that of history. This experimentation with combining poetic and pictorial dramatizations through the kinetic under-pinnings of the film medium was the foundation for the more complete histori-cal and narrative authenticity in his feature-length films. In his early treatments of the Civil War—*The Honor of His Family, The Fugitive, Swords and Hearts, The Battle*—Griffith juxtaposes his protagonist's identity as part of an integral family unit to the increasingly refined use of large numbers of soldiers and the dynamics of battle occupying definite areas of space and time. The resonance of time and place is achieved through the resolution of the individual's destiny: by responding to popular dramatic conventions, Griffith transformed theatri-cal and pictorial stereotypes first into episodic and then into transcendent pictures of man and nature.

Among his many early adaptations of classic literature, Griffith's interpreta-tion of "Enoch Arden" is most noteworthy. In his one-reel version Griffith undertakes a simple abstraction of Tennyson's story of nature's tragic intrusion into the lives of a sailor, Enoch Arden, and his bride, Annie, through a handful of images depicting the passage of time and the indomitability of love. A series of parallel cuts between the isolated figures of Enoch and Annie establishes a pertinent corollary between the medium's ability to suggest the permanence of their emotional bond in two separate settings. In his two-reel remake Griffith's increasing control of the medium leads to a more detailed treatment of these themes. Parallel cuts are more extensively used to simultaneously dramatize their fate; the one close-up—a two shot of Enoch receiving a locket of his child's hair from Annie prior to his voyage—represents the idea that will nurture the estranged couple. In transcribing Tennyson's description of Annie's continuing to look through a spyglass as Enoch's ship passes from the horizon, Griffith presents a subjective long shot of Annie's predicament, held until the ship sails slowly out of the frame. During the last moments of Enoch's life, Griffith inter-cuts from Annie, her husband Philip, and their child standing in the left-hand corner of the frame, looking out of their home into the sunlight, to Enoch lying in bed, also placed at the left-hand side of the frame, with a ray of light illumi-nating his figure. The exacting nature of Griffith's camera setups, cutting, and compositions concretely embody the Christian piety and emotional fervor of Tennyson's "Enoch Arden."

The sporadic literary output that several critics have referred to as an exam-ple of Griffith's shallowness and shrillness is of minimal importance in his films. The reason for Griffith's position as the original film poet is his passionate affec-tion for emotional and spatial idealization. In literature he could not convey the power and understanding he developed on film. He discovered the potential of dramatic and pictorial gradation by first isolating the imprint of an individual and his landscape and by then expanding their identity through the dynamic emphasis established by the editing. Griffith's titles were genteel because he could not effectively translate the mood that he had concisely developed in his camera placement, lighting, and cutting. As a romantic he was too attracted to the sublimity of a character or of a setting to repress its expressiveness. This is one of the reasons, as I hope to show, that he was to move from a classic expressiveness to a romantic excrescence.

Griffith's evocative lighting, his sentient, lyrical backgrounds, his sensitivity to the confluent emotions and ideals of his characters that, like Dickens, personify the "hum" of a burgeoning industrial society—all these gain full expression in *The Musketeers of Pig Alley*. He presents old New York as a magical, pictorially compressed stage, marked by the mischievous playfulness among the store owners, families, and ruffians that make up its teeming society. The nubile, seraphic presence of Lillian Gish injects the romantic spark that gives the film its vivid naturalism. Griffith blends together his appreciation of poetry, painting, theater, and the novel into a vibrantly visual narrative that constantly emphasizes the extended photographic realism of the movies. The film's origins lie both in the photographic exposés of working-class districts—poetically abbreviated in the shots of the hobo lying in the background of the alley—and theatrical melodrama—adroitly restructured by subordinating the pursuit of the stolen money to a street rumble brought about by one of the gang leaders' mistreatment of Gish. The integration of different components of narrative art in *The Musketeers of Pig Alley* continues in *Judith of Bethulia*. His earlier triumphs as an effusive film poet taught him how to interrelate more ambitious characters and themes: one no longer experiences moving yet slight images of human pathos but finds an artist discovering new ways to tell a story of man and history. One scene, typical of Griffith's affinity with the film medium, bears comparison to any of his celebrated film passages in the characterization of place and personality. It opens on the city with an iris vignette, as a group of Israelites lies against the houses on both sides of the street, exhausted from the famine imposed on them. Griffith then uses an iris-in to encompass each person, as the character becomes a visual correlative for his or her heroism as recorded in the Bible. The jubilant spirit of the tribal warriors, notably with the characterization of Bobby Harron, is more vaudeville stereotype than biblical archetype, but Griffith's direction of Blanche Sweet's personal moments as the queen and the extended, popular, and profound scene in close-up are magnificently realized; what the film lacks is a more definite, dramatic portrayal of Holofernes's camp. Vachel Lindsay failed to recognize the sweep and sculptural plasticity of Griffith's film while favoring the more formalist, fustian tone of *Quo Vadis?*. But he proposed several attributes for the epic film—"splendor film" and "architecture in motion"—that are ingeniously featured in *Judith of Bethulia*.

In *The Birth of a Nation*, Griffith undertakes his most impressive and controversial study of history as myth and romance. Though the film's odious morality has diffused numerous reviews of the film, Griffith's moral sentiments are an essential part of the film's artistic form. His racist viewpoint is clearly expressed in several titles, but instead of dismissing this issue one must determine to what degree Griffith's racism contributes to his film. Until the ride of the Klansmen, he has emphasized the treachery and demagoguery preceding and following the Civil War. His picture of politics and social unrest is an outer vortex that threatens the stability of his two central families, especially the Camerons, whose pride and honor is embodied by Henry Walthall's Little Colonel. During the ride of the Klansmen Griffith's acute emotionalism conveys both the horror and the heroism of this confrontation. The key to this sequence is in its composition as well as editing; while he cuts from the furor created by the blacks in town to the massing Klansmen, his compositionally distinct characterizations of the whites and blacks give an added dimension to his interpretation.

In dramatizing this confrontation between whites and blacks the Klansmen are conceived as saviors, riding in heroic, awe-inspiring fashion when they converge on the town. Cutting back to the town and dramatically and structurally juxtaposed to his symbol of "white knights," Griffith features the renegade blacks. He is not simply isolating the blacks as an unfocused symbol of evil, but shows them as a swarming, disorderly mob. Therefore in this white-black confrontation, line and order are counterbalanced to a swelling circle; whereas the whites present and represent order and permanency, the blacks present and represent chaos, a symbol of irrational, deadly impulses. Griffith is not documenting the birth of a nation as a historian who is trying to present "all the facts," but as a mythmaker expressing his very personal love of America and how, dramatically, it became a nation. He pictures the South as a fairy-tale world, marked by redolent places like "Love Valley," where a code of chivalry and romance is fulfilled that is more akin to the Crusades than to the Civil War. Griffith sees history as a grandiose surge of social forces and individual passions, for example in the scene in which Walthall departs with the Southern army, his parents' home looming in the background as a symbol of their cause.

Griffith's singular sense of myth and morality plays a critical role throughout his filmography and concerns not only his treatment of blacks. He is as unsympathetic to the revolutionaries in *Orphans of the Storm* as he is to the blacks in *The Birth of a Nation*, but unlike his purblind picture of the French Revolution, the antique morality and mythmaking in *The Birth of a Nation* are manifest in a congruous artistic form. The analogies to medieval epic are not only evident in the extreme characterizations of Walthall's Little Colonel and George Sergman's Silas Lynch and in the light-dark, line-circle juxtaposition during the ride of the Klansmen, but also in his manner of denoting the glory, beauty, and destruction of this conflict. When the Civil War is nearing its end, Griffith divides the action into three planes, predating Gance's Cinerama effects in *Napoleon*. Film becomes our historical, panoramic vantage point: people are shown fleeing in the foreground, complemented by the soldiers marching in the middle space and the burning of Atlanta in the background. When the title reads "War's Peace," Griffith presents its pictorial equivalent, while he often uses an iris-in to depict Walthall's courtship of Gish. Each of these scenes, lighted by Billy Bitzer with an appreciation for either historical facsimile or romantic, heroic portraiture, resolves the dramatic undercurrents of history and the individual through their lyric, mythic iconography. This is not to overlook Griffith's distasteful treatment of blacks; but in his ode to the South and its conservative, aristocratic code, he has adopted a dramatic equation of good and evil that is more prevalent in literary and art history than his critics care to admit. The racist polemics of Dixon's novel, a best-seller and the source of a popular stage adaptation, are abstracted into a less hostile but still problematic romantic epic. Dixon speaks in the voice of the embittered, ignorant Southerner attracted to the Ku Klux Klan as a violent panacea to his social and economic miseries: Griffith elevates these raw passions into a historical passion play.

*The Birth of a Nation*, with *Way Down East* and *Isn't Life Wonderful*—not *Intolerance* and *Broken Blossoms*—are the culmination of Griffith's art. *Intolerance* is not the great epic of the cinema nor is it Griffith's finest work. The major problem with the film is one that figures in Griffith's earliest shorts and that appears more frequently as Griffith's art declines. It concerns his feeling for the sublime and his familiarity with his subject matter as expressed through his visual design. Griffith's sensitivity to the urban setting in the modern-day story extends the social criticism and emotional compassion of his best shorts; but in the three other sections, even in *The Fall of Babylon*, he is not working with derivatives of evil but with the face of evil in the manner of a Gothic artist. Griffith treats the struggles of a young married couple in his modern-day story as a study of corrupt politics and of the harsh economic conditions that threaten the ardor and innocence of Bobby Harron and Mae Marsh: it is as dramatically ennobling as any part of his filmography. But in constructing a film around man's intolerance he presents pictures of villainy, avarice, and evil, instead of exploring their romantic and historic origins as he did in *Judith of Bethulia* and *The Birth of a Nation*. The film seems an outgrowth of late nineteenth-century theatrical melodrama; the majority of scenes and effects show slight dramatic delineation or nuance. Griffith's idea of intolerance through the ages demands a poetic distillation for his study of good and evil. But he is torn between dramatic emphasis and sublime pathos, and the film suffers as a result of his didactic presentation of man's inhumanity.

An artist with similar dramatic failings, Josef von Sternberg came closer to penetrating the sublime in his first film, *The Salvation Hunters*, and in his last, *The Saga of Anatahan*. *The Saga of Anatahan* is the superior work even though the drama is transparent; the jungle island that enshrouds the characters is presented as a mythic setting that mysteriously undercuts and modulates the ensuing action. Von Sternberg's distance from the characters enables him to effectively dramatize the symbolic aspects of man's relationship to nature; Griffith, however, continually identifies with his characters, usually his female leads. In *The Fall of Babylon*, for example, Constance Talmadge's vivacity and Belshazzar's somberness lack the subtlety of Blanche Sweet's Judith or Lillian Gish's disconsolate mother in *Judith of Bethulia*. They are part of an ebullient, kinetic stage, a hotbed of ideas that is closer to the Russian cinema's historical dialectic than to the idealization of myth and romance that Griffith advanced in *The Birth of a Nation*.

To many critics *Broken Blossoms* is Griffith's most exemplary work, evoking the mythlike and the sublime in a more personal fashion than in either *The Birth of a*

*Nation* or *Intolerance*. The plot concerns the tragic love between Richard Barthelmess's Chinese and Lillian Gish's distraught Victorian maiden, culminating
in several of the most effusive close-ups in the history of the cinema. The film is
more like *Intolerance* than *The Birth of a Nation* in its depiction of the sublime and
in its integration of a story for which Griffith had little understanding. In many
of the powerful scenes in *Intolerance*—especially in its apotheosis of the decline of
civilization through an epic, symphonic use of parallel and crosscutting
techniques—Griffith exposed decay and brutality with a puritanlike directness.
In *Broken Blossoms*, a far more simple, humanized fable, Griffith does not manifest a corresponding dramatic purity. His ghetto setting of foreigners, degenerates, and criminals is not imbued with the historical abbreviation and individual exemplification one finds in a classic statement like *The Musketeers of Pig
Alley*.

In his best films Griffith's characters are seen as symbolic expressions of their
environment; for example, Lillian Gish's pubescent charm and New York in
transition in *The Musketeers of Pig Alley* or Blanche Sweet's fragile, heroic innocence and the isolation of her tribe of biblical warriors in *Judith of Bethulia*. But
the three central characters in *Broken Blossoms*—Gish and Barthelmess as the
lovers, Donald Crisp as her savage father—are static, literary derivatives of
good and evil. In attempting a dramatization of the sublime, Griffith proves
that he is the type of film poet who will only evidence the sublime through a
concrete, visually original realization of his material. Unlike Von Sternberg, he
does not have the moral distance from his characters and does not adopt the
allegorical narrative that Von Sternberg used in *The Salvation Hunters* and that
he refined in *The Saga of Anatahan*. Griffith may have discovered a way of personifying the sublime had he decided to shoot the entire film from medium close-
up to extreme close-up range. But instead of dramatically condensing his material, Griffith is reduced to relying on close-ups to express all that he could not
delineate in medium and long shot. Crisp's father is a Victorian fictional and
theatrical stereotype because of Griffith's failure to explain his violent nature in
the context of his environment. Gish is little more than a helpless Victorian
maiden in a hopeless situation; there is one effective scene when Crisp demands
a smile from his daughter and Gish uses her fingers to force her cheeks into one.
The equivalence of the titles and visuals in *Broken Blossoms*, uncharacteristic of
Griffith's visual transfiguration of poetry, is unhappily characteristic of the literal dependency on vapid titles by many silent-film writers and directors.

*Way Down East* represents a triumph over the didactic dramatic platitudes of
*Intolerance* and *Broken Blossoms*. As a film homage to a past social order its emotional and stylistic congruency is matched by few films in the American cinema;
Welles's *The Magnificent Ambersons* is, perhaps, its most formidable successor.
The film's dramatic and plastic vibrancy also reveals the vital differences between Griffith's original standing in the American film and the technician incorporated into the Russian film dialectic of Eisenstein and Pudovkin.

The feeling that this is the film Griffith was destined to make is first intimated
during Lillian Gish's visit to her city cousins. She approaches the door of her

cousins' mansion, then bends backward to appraise the door, which is about three times her size; while in this unflattering position the door opens. Within this short, incisive scene Griffith begins an examination of the two dramatic identities that have played an important part in his filmography and that are conspicuous even in the late, lamentable *The Sorrows of Satan*. It is the juxtaposition of city life—with its social snobbery and materialism—to the country—with its naive manners and innocent idealism. During Gish's stay with her cousins Griffith develops one motif as the major characteristic of city life: its size. Most of the action in Gish's short stay transpires in the living room and ballroom where Griffith isolates Gish and her expressive features from her dramatic opposites.

The dramatic juxtaposition of the prologue is extended by Griffith's direction of what may be Gish's most memorable performance. Though she is dwarfed by the architectural breadth of the mansion, Gish's gaiety and loveliness is contrasted to her snarling, henpecking cousins. Gish's idyllic figure is further underscored when a guest says she looks like an angel, and Griffith shows her as one. During the scene in which she is told of Lowell Sherman's treachery Griffith does not magnify her emotional outpouring as he will in the trial in *Orphans of the Storm*; instead she slightly contorts her facial muscles and expresses her shock by playing with the marriage ring.

After Gish leaves the house where she gave birth to her child, the audience may be unsure of Griffith's dramatic focus. But as Gish returns to the country, Bitzer's lyrical camera eye identifies the splendor of country life in a manner unique to Griffith and Bitzer by visualizing the country as an area suspended in space. The sequence opens with an overhead shot of Gish carrying her child, a lone figure on a country road that is seen as part of an expansive, illuminating field. As she enters the hamlet where Barthelmess lives with his parents, Griffith's empathy with a folk setting and sentimentality is communicated through Bitzer's idealized pictorial framing. When Barthelmess looks up from his work, his parents and several country types are featured in the foreground while Gish stands alone in the background. In effect Griffith shows that the "Love Valley" of *The Birth of a Nation* is a real, permanent part of the American landscape.

The ode that Griffith writes with his camera in *Way Down East* is not cluttered with any historical subplots and possesses and ending much admired by the Russians and identified as an expert montage sequence in textbooks. But unlike the similarly praised rapid cutting applied in *Earth* by Dovzhenko, the most Griffithian of Russian directors, the reason the sequence in which Barthelmess saves Gish from the ice-capped waterfall is only partially dependent on montage concerns the development of archetypes on film. In Dovzhenko's *Earth*, the camera passes over the country and its natural forms as a blossoming tree; Dovzhenko is not concerned with individualized characters inhabiting a realistic narrative but with denoting the land and its people as a cultural archetype. His lovely dissolves interrelate people, animals, and the landscape in a primordial environment that, one day, the proletariat will transform into a nation. The archetype he presents is that of the country as a symbolic wellspring of national unity. During the funeral sequence in *Earth*, Dovzhenko diffuses this enveloping image of his country's natural resources by cutting between the grief-stricken widow and the funeral. The collective idealization of the Russian folk and countryside is undercut through the personalized quality of the widow's grief. Although Griffith, too, regards the land as a transcendent social and pictorial archetype, he distinguishes himself from the Russians—in this instance Dovzhenko—by the progressive association of his characters and plot. Unlike the depersonalized farmers in *Earth*, Griffith's characters possess a distinct meaning because of the expressive nature of their folk origins and their singular roles within the drama. Gish and Barthelmess become individualized figures, representing a larger national ideal; in Dovzhenko's *Earth* the characters are raw, idealized symbols of the good earth. The kinetic features in the last sequence of *Way Down East* resolve the suspense while also personifying the characters' heroic qualities; the conclusion of *Earth*, however, reveals the incongruity between the widow's personalized character and the kinetically impersonal poetics of montage.

After *Way Down East* Griffith's career, with few exceptions, is a classic study of tragic decline. One way to explain this decline is by looking at Griffith's earlier films and trying to discern his failing powers in his earlier triumphs. By the time of *Way Down East* Griffith had worked in the movies some dozen years and was nearing fifty years of age. His shorts not only outdistanced the work of his contemporaries, but also, regardless of whether he saw *Quo Vadis?*, Griffith made the feature film a viable narrative form. Griffith created a grammatical base for the movies through his affinity with the genteel, lyrical side of the American experience. Although one might like to think of this period as one of lucid, uninterrupted growth, it was not. Griffith was repetitious, and at times unbearably crude, as seen in *A Romance of Happy Valley*, which was made at the high point of his career. He often interpreted themes and ideas that were foreign to his temperament. With early masterworks like *The Musketeers of Pig Alley* and *Judith of Bethulia* Griffith became the cinema's first craftsman and artist, laying the foundations for the classic narrative structure of *The Birth of a Nation* and *Way Down East*. During this period, film came of age through the efforts of one man who confronted his personal vision of America's past.

It was necessary for Griffith to master the physical details of his settings, since he could not rely on a preconceived visual style; for example, compare his sappy treatment of rural family life in *A Romance of Happy Valley* with that of *Way Down East*. The many wars he had fought with producers and public and his creative response to a medium in which he was its first classicist and romanticist could have ruined a dozen men. In 1907 he was so ashamed of working in film that he used a pseudonym; by 1920, however, his name was, with that of Chaplin, synonymous with film art.

Perhaps the most complimentary point that can be made about the output of Griffith's last ten years is to characterize it as the work of an uninspired artist. A film like *True Heart Susie* has nothing seriously wrong with it, unlike Griffith's ephemeral evocation of the sublime in *Broken Blossoms*, but one feels the presence of a fatigued artist reviving dated formulas. His picture of corrupt city life, his use of Bobby Harron as the rustic, backwoods innocent and of Gish as the pure one simply lack the passion and dramatic vigor in his earlier work. His first features undertake to transform a folk idiom into a romantically idealized picture of America's past, but in *True Heart Susie* Griffith is wholly absorbed in the quaint, nostalgic virtues of country life.

The depressing, final chapter in Griffith's life, culminating in the interview with the master conducted by Seymour Stern and Ezra Goodman, cannot obscure the fact that Griffith's direction became second-rate. *America* is probably the most ambitious and visually arresting of his later epics; though he characterizes the family as a symbol of national unity, the film is weak in several transitional scenes and does not convey the full dramatic scope demanded by the subject matter. *Orphans of the Storm* contains some of Lillian Gish's finest moments, but Griffith is simply insensitive to the questions and themes germane to the French Revolution; he interprets its historical crisis in a streamlined, melodramatic fashion. The film fails to establish any dialectic or mythic conflict and is wholly attuned to the pathos of the Gish sisters. Dorothy is a moving, energetic presence and Lillian is marvelous, but Griffith is curiously removed from the other characters. Danton is pictured as a kindly old man and Robespierre as a pathetic caricature of the villain. Griffith treats the various anticlimaxes in a tense, theatrical manner as if he realized how little else there was in the film.

When Griffith could not rely on folk charm in the style of *True Heart Susie*, his work became awkward, amateurish. In *Sally of the Sawdust*, a lackluster production, Griffith vainly recalls his old theatrics in Carol Dempster's courtroom defense of her father, played by W. C. Fields. At this early date it is interesting to note how Fields forces a director to conform to his style—as true for Griffith here as for Eddie Sutherland in *It's the Old Army Game*. Fields does not have the bulk nor does he express the torpor and sadism of the older, more renowned cynic he was to become; since Griffith fails to develop any meaningful characters or settings, the most favorable comment one can offer about the film is that it is early Fields. Perhaps recognizing his own decline, Griffith drew on what often stands as a sign of artistic stasis: autobiography. In *The Sorrows of Satan*, a watered-down version of the Faust legend, the devil, played by Adolphe Menjou, manipulates city life. The film's autobiographical element is decisively manifest in its hero: one is made to feel that not only does the hero resemble Griffith in appearance and background but that he is Griffith.

The one notable exception to the shortcomings of his late work, *Isn't Life Wonderful*, shows Griffith's contemporaneousness with the naturalism of the "street film" genre while underscoring his identity as one of its precursors. Its roots are in *The Musketeers of Pig Alley*, with a masterly, atmospheric tonality in its shots of the alleyways and back streets of the city's ghetto. Griffith's use of light to empathize with his struggling, poverty-ridden protagonists shows the twofold nature of its origin: the naturalism that photographers of the late nineteenth century brought to their studies of city life and the idealism of the Dutch school of painting. Its luminism sustains the harmonious simplicity and artifice of *Hearts of the World* and *Way Down East* in a style representative of one of the strongest, most vital tendencies in the American film. Bitzer's panfocus photography isolates the ghetto within the nexus of city life, while his introductory and closing shots of members of the family—absorbed in melancholic loneliness or engaged in household chores—capture a psychological and social truthfulness similar to Ozu's penetration of the family. One may have thought that *Dream Street*, a similar genre study of naturalism and the sublime, with its dramatic stereotypes and its hackneyed presentation of the ghetto, evinced too strong a resemblance to *Broken Blossoms* to hope for a final resurgence from the master. But *Isn't Life Wonderful* remains untarnished by the artistic shortcomings of his work in the twenties.

One can underline Griffith's constant war with his backers and the increasing centralization of film production in Hollywood, but the final chapter of his life presents a grim picture of the fallen artist. The alienated, alcoholic, ruined man, who spent his last years in isolation in the Hollywood Knickerbocker Hotel, had lived out much of the tragedy of the American experience. His battles with producers and public and his depressing decline in the hotel dramatize an aspect of American life that his films never showed. But as he cursed at his interviewers Griffith could still remember the cinema as a magic lamp of the past, present, and future which had lost the poetic sheen of the silent era: "What the modern movie lacks is beauty."

If Griffith stands as the one outstanding figure who gave new meaning to the word "epic" in the American silent film, it is as much because of his appreciation for the medium's imagist, lyrical features as because of his personal genius. Memorable films like *Tol'able David* and *The Last of the Mohicans* seem to mirror Griffith's pathos, his lush pictorial eye, his faith in his characters' heroic immutability. Richard Barthelmess's finely sustained work as the meek, ridiculed young man who discovers his manhood in the encounter with Ernest Torrence's vicious backwoods ruffian, is ably supported by Henry King's rendition of the pastoral splendor of the American countryside. King's repeated, extended close-ups of Barthelmess and the transcendent image of his parents' wooden frame house show the ability of the film medium to blend a style of pictorial naturalism with the idyllic mythology of the American landscape. Maurice Tourneur's *The Last of the Mohicans* is a more ambitious, complex work that depends less on the descriptive passages in Cooper's saga while favoring a more straightforward approach to the grandeur of Hawkeye and Chingachgook amid the turmoil in prerevolutionary America. The first part of the film is too tense and jittery, as if Tourneur were solely concerned with a dynamic transcription of Cooper's story; but his characters' humanism in this grim terrain is gradually, brilliantly realized. His camera does not linger on emotional close-ups but appears to study the profiles and movements of his characters as part of a historical mosaic that, similar to Griffith, uncovers the similarities between the silent film and epic poetry. Tourneur is often remembered as a director of children's fantasies (*The Poor Little Rich Girl*, *The Blue Bird*), but *The Last of the Mohicans* remains an enduring example of American film art.

With the exception of Griffith, King Vidor is probably the most respected of American classicists. His major works of the silent and sound era, *The Big Parade*, *The Crowd*, *Hallelujah*, *The Champ*, *Our Daily Bread*, *The Fountainhead*, *Duel in the Sun*, however, present some of the most high-powered examples of pseudoart in American film history. Whether it is characterized by his long shots of the army platoon marching into battle in *The Big Parade*, his clinical approach to the ethnic drama of *Hallelujah*, or his superficial escalation of sound in the roundup of hundreds of ranch hands in *Duel in the Sun*, Vidor is the classic example of the technician who assimilates every new technique without understanding how his characters and conflicts are affected by his technical, albeit transparent, flourishes. For all of its pious humanism, *The Big Parade* is much closer in tone to the roustabout antics of Laurence Stallings's *What Price Glory* than to the emotional idealism of Griffith's *Intolerance*. There are several moments in *The Big Parade* in which Vidor seems immersed in the tragic experiences that shape John Gilbert's character. Yet in conclusively dramatizing the metamorphosis Gilbert's playboy has undergone, the closing scene attests to Vidor's distance from either melodrama or art. *The Crowd* has several brilliantly executed scenes that underscore the movies' facility to depict man's anonymity in the face of the thousands whose lives intersect in a modern, urban environment. The cutting and camera placement in these scenes are expertly devised, but after one marvels at Vidor's eye-catching pyrotechnics, the pallid nature of his story becomes all too apparent; underlying Vidor's faith in his portentous, technical arrangements is his reliance on stereotypes like the young newlyweds in *The Crowd* and the mush of *Our Daily Bread*. Who else but Vidor could adapt with such literal faithfulness and vigor the pornographic capitalism of Ayn Rand's *The Fountainhead*?

The quasi-artistic nature of Vidor's films reflects the compromise which many producers and directors sought in order to give their movies an aura of respectability and social controversy, if not high art. But it was in their more blatantly melodramatic productions that Hollywood achieved a more resourceful method of allowing the movies to work their magic while showing a profit. One thinks of Douglas Fairbanks, whose athletic aplomb sparked exemplary entertainments such as *Robin Hood* and *The Mark of Zorro*. Fairbanks's star vehicles remain models of the romantic allure and visual exuberance that have made the adventure epic seem at times the best example of what movies are about. Though Fairbanks's *The Thief of Bagdad* is regarded as a less successful, less representative work because of its burlesque treatment of German fantasy films, Fairbanks's prankish spirit is used as a foil to the magical hijinks. In these adventure sagas the emphasis lies in the idiosyncratic interpretation of the heroes and villains of popular fiction and the equally playful resiliency of the movies in illustrating the past.

In the Fairbanks's productions the balance maintained between his interest in perilous quests and in his love of the flighty maiden was the most successful realization of the adventure epic, but it was certainly not the only one. In *The Four Horsemen of the Apocalypse*, scriptwriter June Mathis and director Rex Ingram undertake a more grandiose study of the characters and conventions of romantic fiction and melodrama. The difference between *The Four Horsemen of the Apocalypse* and *Blood and Sand*, in which director Fred Niblo's reverent attitude to Valentino's film presence limits the narrative sweep of the story, is that Valentino's romantic identity is conceived as part of a vast, historical tumult. Ingram's florid, theatrical drama offers some breathtaking moments but, unlike Fairbanks's films, he accentuates the most morbidly mawkish, heavy-handed aspects of melodrama. With the ascension of Cecil B. De Mille, the adventure epic projects a more complacent, middlebrow sensibility, whereby his folk heroes innocently coexist within the decorative artifices of Hollywood technology.

*Destiny–Napoleon*

Griffith's epics, like the comedies of Sennett, Chaplin, and Keaton, play off the brashness and innocence of American folk culture to create a new vision of American society. The German cinema, however, developed along very different, almost antithetical lines. In *Destiny* and *Die Nibelungen*, two of the major epics of the German silent film, the protagonists are situated in a ritualistic society in which they must fulfill the sacred destiny of the past. In the American cinema there is a freedom and independence about the characters' role in history; in the German epics of director Fritz Lang history is seen as an indomitable, iconographic force, manifested in the labyrinthian design and architecture and in the rigid, dehumanized movements of his players. Lang's emphasis on the perverse, gloomy, symbolic underpinnings in a primitively feudal society is paralleled in the moribund nature of the German cinema's contemporary dramas, whether in Pabst's street films or Lang's Mabuse spectacles.

In Griffith's epics the camerawork and cutting are attuned to the gay, inspired gesture that will suddenly alter the mood of his story; *Destiny* and *Die Nibelungen* delineate the repression of the characters' romantic instincts because of their hierarchical society and the oppressively geometric design of their environment. Whether the action occurs in nature or in a town, Lang never wavers in his picture of the encompassing, fatalistic elements of the story. The dreamlike dramatic rhythm in *Destiny* arises from his appreciation that the magic of the movies can illuminate the most unlikely visions in which the allegorical figure of Death appears and disappears, where townspeople walk into the film frame from an unvisualized beyond. If the earliest stages of medieval society suggest a period of darkness and terror, it is a world that Lang and his fellow artisans understand as a natural complement to the chemistry of the silent film.

The slow, piecemeal editing in the two films enhances the austere beauty and permanence of the design, expressing the formal majesty of the period and the psychological subservience of its inhabitants. Unlike Eisenstein's *Ivan the*

*Terrible*, their cutting underscores the absence of free will in the drama: the slightest departure from the foreboding visual schema and the morally rigid treatment of fate and the individual can never be entertained. In *Ivan the Terrible*, Eisenstein's equally grandiloquent, though less ominous design is occasionally fragmented by sharp cuts to augment the political turmoil of Ivan's court. Lang, by refusing to introduce these more personal dramatic motifs, is more faithful to the immeasurable degree of probity and social destiny articulated in the composition.

In the three stories told to the woman by the figure of Death in *Destiny* Lang undertakes a form of cinematic chromaticism that will be more severely and successfully used in *Die Nibelungen*. In the first and second parts of *Destiny*, the mimetic communication, like the language of costume, becomes part of a pictorial vocabulary in which the characters' emotional vibrancy is submerged by the more dominant emblems of culture in their makeup and dress. The third section, however, seems an unnecessary comic intrusion. It shows an unwillingness to develop the characters within the context of their unwieldy environment; it evokes a playful, fanciful spirit at odds with the oppressive imprint of a culture so painstakingly delineated in the first two stories.

In *Destiny* the design is interpreted as the predominant symbol of pagan theocracy and the repression of the individual; in *Die Nibelungen* the enclosed setting of the German court is contrasted to the open air expressiveness and paganism of the Huns' camp. In *Siegfried*, part one of *Die Nibelungen*, the composition assumes the role of Wagnerian leitmotif, in which the formal arrangements and rigid groupings of the actors personify the characters' dependence on the sacrosanct mores of their society. During Siegfried's funeral the mourners surround his figure as the central icon, and the film ends, appropriately, with an iris shot, a world introduced and closed by the camera eye. *Kriemhild's Revenge*, part two of *Die Nibelungen*, shows a more ornate, sculptural design which extends the motifs in *Siegfried* while developing as its dramatic opposite. In the more schematic *Siegfried* the actors are seen as figures in a wall painting or tapestry, but these elements are less conspicuous in *Kriemhild's Revenge*. In the German court a formidable linear pattern is apparent, whereas the Huns' camp is characterized by the sexual motifs in the open terrain and the long, rolling plains of sand. These visual coordinates run throughout the film; when Kriemhild asks Etzel, king of the Huns, to fulfill his marriage pledge and slay Siegfried's murderer, Etzel is photographed against pagan woodcuts as Kriemhild rests against a blank wall. In Griffith's epics the heroes responded to a resplendent countryside, but Kriemhild, like Siegfried, is overpowered by the ominous impersonality of her society. In detailing the perverse anima of a pagan culture Lang shows the Huns appearing out of crevices in the mountains, while in honoring the lovers Lang fulfills the highly schematic design with an image of the mourners surrounding Kriemhild in a manner similar to the idealization of Siegfried as the central unifying icon at the end of part one.

*Die Nibelungen* is one of the prodigious achievements of German studio film art. Its pervasive sense of doom is further reflected in fantasy films in which the demons of the unconscious and fantasy folklore provide telling symbols of social and psychological discord. It is also evident in the films of Friedrich Murnau, but in a different manner. In *The Last Laugh* and *Sunrise*, his two classic studies of the disturbing, dehumanizing elements of twentieth-century life, Murnau discovers modern equivalents for the menacing mood and moral pessimism in Lang's historical epics. In *The Last Laugh* the tragedy surrounding Emil Jannings's doorman is his inability to conform to the mechanical march of modern city life. Jannings is not a romantic, larger-than-life character; his tragedy lies in the personal touches he brings to his job. Murnau's objective portrayal of the people, routines, and structures that permeate our cities does not show modern man dramatically opposed to the mechanical nature of his society. The callous behavior of Jannings's relatives when they learn of his demotion is presented in the same dispassionate manner that the grim evening shadows are shown displacing the afternoon sun. They are part of a formal, utilitarian picture Murnau draws of our anonymity amid a kinetic social order. Jannings's relegation to a lavatory attendant is a personal and symbolic loss, but in watching his bravura performance one wonders whether Murnau and scriptwriter Carl Mayer do not see him as a pathetic figure. The ending forced upon Murnau and Mayer does not obscure the film's fatalism; a happy ending is implausible in a world so thoroughly encompassed by Karl Freund's moving camera.

The Murnau-Mayer allegory of man and technology is dramatically recharged in *Sunrise* as a similar sense of fatalism, of man's smallness in the scheme of things is identified in the country as well as in the city. Margaret Livingston, the city girl who seduces George O'Brien, is no more the dramatic opposite of Janet Gaynor than Jannings's replacement is of him; her cold, ruthless actions, like the new doorman's officious manner, stem from the hardness of city life. This may seem an extreme statement considering that she almost causes the murder of Gaynor, but her erotic identity, like the storm that threatens the country folk, represents the dark underside of our cities and countries. Murnau's ensuing conception of the city, juxtaposed to the equally stylized, light-filled picture of the countryside, culminates in the amusement park. Its glossy design and towering forms represent an exhiliarating yet frightening symbol of the sensuality and power that diminishes the figures of O'Brien and Gaynor who spend an afternoon in its environs rediscovering their love and their separateness from the manic rhythms of the amusement park; it is a technological force, as supreme as that of nature.

The films of G. W. Pabst, particularly *The Joyless Street* and *The Love of Jeanne Ney*, and Josef von Sternberg's work from *The Salvation Hunters* through *The Blue Angel*, combine aspects of realism and melodrama that are repressed in Murnau's vivisection of modern city life. In the films of Erich von Stroheim and Abel Gance the ability of the medium to immerse the viewer in the physical and psychological interplay of social history reaches its most extreme stylization. A sound-film universe seems the next, logical progression, but the special virtues of their films show a potential for development that could have superseded the immediate concerns of a sound film.

Pabst's *The Joyless Street* and *The Love of Jeanne Ney* are acclaimed as the acme of the German "street film," but he seems to underline the more stridently melodramatic features of this genre. The difference between Greta Garbo's characters in *The Story of Gösta Berling* and *The Joyless Street* is in the moral, anti-Victorian fervor of Mauritz Stiller's story and the more precarious emotional relationships in Pabst's film. In the earlier work Garbo's romantic presence suggests the freedom and sensuality repressed by her environment; in Pabst's film she must help her father adjust to the economic hardships in the Germany of the twenties. Stiller's camerawork is marked by a classic, decorous approach to the characters and conflicts; he is most sensitive to sudden bursts of romantic intensity, such as the scene on the ice in which the feelings of Garbo and Lars Hanson transcend his theatrical staging. Pabst, however, moves in closer to the action, as in the scene in which the camera is placed on a trolley and illuminates the faces of the people waiting on line at the butcher shop. Whatever acute strokes he uses to dramatize the scheming and murder, whether sharp cuts or the cluttered, disheveled details of his social reality, Pabst continually accents the oppressive force of his social landscape. His exaggerated cinematographic and compositional descriptiveness depict a disordered social order, an intermixing of personal and social turmoil that places the film medium in the service of dramatic expressionism. His uneven pacing, moving from vivid, harrowing close-ups to detailed tracking shots, interprets expressionism as a study of a declining society and a coexpressive rise in abnormal human behavior.

In his least effective scenes Pabst seems at times little more than a German version of King Vidor, a formalist with no consistent theme or feeling in his direction. His best film, *Pandora's Box*, relies less on the aggressive techniques used in *The Joyless Street* and *The Love of Jeanne Ney* than on the triumphant performances that poignantly declare the loss of humanism and the deadly impulses that are barely controlled in Lulu's presence. Louise Brooks was a perfect choice, with her glistening alabaster complexion, her bow-cut hair, and almond-shaped eyes whose flurried motion seems disembodied from the sculptural symmetry of her face. Her lack of dramatic nuance and her cheery, instinctive nature serve as a dramatic and symbolic counterpart to the deceptive postures of her lovers. Von Sternberg's *The Blue Angel* is the more incisive film because of its intensely personalized study of sexual entrapment while Wedekind's plays achieve their maximum resonance in *Lulu*, Alban Berg's glorious, operatic sex drama.

Von Sternberg's first film, *The Salvation Hunters*, is perhaps, the most allegorical of all silent films that concern the depressing nature of our cities (consider *The Kid*, *Sunrise*, or Cavalcanti's *En Rade*). Von Sternberg draws on his photographic talents in isolating the docks and house inhabited by his three characters: the young man, the girl, and the boy. The action in *The Kid* derives from the tramp's iconoclastic personality and in *Sunrise* from the enveloping camera movements and the voluminous Rembrandt lighting of Charles Rosher and Karl Struss; in *The Salvation Hunters* Von Sternberg adopts a simplified style of poetic naturalism in following his three characters, first as they are engulfed by the shadows of the crane and the wreckage around them. He is not undertaking a documentary presentation of poverty, but he enhances one's appreciation of the ability of the film medium, through only a slight amplification of its photographic antecedents, to transform its realist subject. After they leave the barge, Von Sternberg returns to this area with an overhead shot of the ruffian dwarfed by the shadow of the crane, a terse image that identifies the environment as an inferno-type setting that traps its inhabitants. The boardinghouse to which they drift, like the barge, is also shown as a distinctively isolated stage, with the sunlight failing to penetrate their new home.

Much of the drama develops through Von Sternberg's lighting contrasts. After the young man returns without a job, the girl decides to give herself to another man in the boardinghouse. When she stands by the door inside her room Von Sternberg shades her in darkness. She then leaves the room, hesitates outside, and returns; at this point, as she leans outstretched against the door, a spotlight suddenly illuminates her figure. The film ultimately fails not because of its photographic staginess but because of Von Sternberg's introducing an almost Chaplinesque optimism that is antipodal to the layers of darkness in which he has situated his characters.

Von Strenberg's ability to create dark, symbolic settings that serve as graphic counterpoints to his characters' conflicting desires is impressively advanced in *The Last Command*. The central confrontation Emil Jannings faces is the resolution of his personal honor, first as a military officer in Russia and then as a Hollywood extra. Like Von Stroheim, Von Sternberg focuses on the perverse, psychological paradoxes that result from a collapsed social order and the characters' recognition and control of their sexual impulses; the love of Evelyn Brent's revolutionary for Jannings's tsarist officer is not explored simply for its romantic intensity but as the one moral action within the social upheaval. In *The Blue Angel* he presents a more disjointed society in which Dietrich's Lola innocently signs of its amorality. She is a reborn Aphrodite, who in her fickleness and apathy and in the decline of her five-year marriage to Jannings provides a mirror image to her society. The drama transpires in claustrophobic settings because Jannings has descended into a world cut off from any social outlets and amenities, other than the ephemeral pleasures offered by Dietrich. Her transparency makes the film a study of social negation through Janning's complete self-degradation.

But even in these two fine films in which Von Sternberg was at the height of his powers, his work has critical shortcomings. His understanding of discord as a product of sexual interplay is mawkishly simplified in the way he kills off Jannings in *The Last Command*. He presses for resounding dramatic conclusions that simply are incongruous to his static, exacting studies of characters who are trapped in tense, cloying settings. *The Blue Angel* astutely abstracts Heinrich Mann's muddled novel, but the concluding scene in which Jannings returns to the school and collapses with his hand gripping the desk strikes a falsely affirmative note. Considering the film's immersion into an intensely destructive relationship through the protagonist's social decline and rising sexual awareness, the ending seems an unnecessary concession to theatrical catharsis. While Von Sternberg's eye for composition was flat and formal in *The Salvation Hunters*, more sculpturally alive to his actors' emotions in *The Last Command*, and exquisite in *The Blue Angel*, notably in Lola's dressing room with its mirror, spiral staircase, and hidden trapdoor, his editing is perfunctory in transitional scenes. One speculates that an invisible editing schema or the use of dissolves would more clearly support his cluttered stage.

With the notable exception of *Morocco*, Von Sternberg's career after *The Blue Angel* becomes a wasteful example of self-indulgence. Much of the decline is attributable to producers; one surmises that he exaggerated his flamboyancy in the face of studio executives who wanted him to guide Dietrich through another change of hoisery. *Morocco* is an ironic work in which his distant approach to the romance and comic interplay mocks his characters at the same time that it idealizes them. *Morocco* also shows a dramatic convention first adopted in *Underworld* as Dietrich is torn between two men and continually gives in to the underdog. But analyzing how and why Dietrich chooses Victor McLaglen, Herbert Marshall, and Lionel Atwill over Gustav von Seyffertitz, Cary Grant, and Cesar Romero in *Dishonored*, *Blonde Venus*, and *The Devil Is a Woman* is a question better discussed during the early morning hours of a film convention.

In his silent films the psychologically attuned camera setups, like the languishing low-key lighting, distinguish the characters' discords as well as identify the integral dramatic components of his compositions. *The Saga of Anatahan* is closest to his silent films because of its primordial settings, its use of an invisible narrator, and the modest but effective punctuation created by his tracking movements as an expression of the characters' restrictive living quarters and their common, fatal attraction to the woman living with them. The tentative story line is redeemed by Von Sternberg's adapting simplified dramatic and cinematic motifs to conceive the characters' fate as a study of man and nature. Among his melodramas of the thirities, *Morocco* is the most appealing because of Von Sternberg's emphathetic treatment of both his protagonists' precarious dramatic mask and the conventions of adventure and romance. Jules Furthman is most famous, perhaps, for his scripts for Von Sternberg, but only *Morocco* provided the director with semiorganic embodiments of popular fiction. The dialogue is not as pungent, as seeped in the fast-talking, journalistic froth of Furthman's scripts for *China Seas*, *Bombshell*, and *Only Angels Have Wings*. The characters are melodramatic icons whose appeal rests on their unexpected heroic fatalism; in *Shanghai Express* and *Blonde Venus* this romantic ambiguity is missing, and the characters exist as ornaments: self-caricatures in self-indulgent pictures of erotic entrapment. In *Morocco* the tension between the story fabrications and the protagonists' subtle self-awareness of their romantic virtues—in, for example, Dietrich's sly, self-mocking performance in the nightclub and during Menjou's fete at which he discovers that his acquiescent role in the love triangle has resulted in Dietrich's abandoning him for Gary Cooper—gives the film a buoyancy missing in Von Sternberg's other films. In *Shanghai Express* the more cramped staging makes the photography of Von Sternberg and Lee

Garmes too self-consciously erotic, like romantic filigree. The irony of *Morocco* is missing, and one is left with overly aromatic pictures of feminine pulchritude and romantic adoration.

The viewer may be entranced by the lushness of the masquerade in *Dishonored*, by Dietrich's song and dance as voodoo woman in *Blonde Venus*, and by the gay nonchalance of *The Devil Is a Woman*, but Von Sternberg is playing into and not transcending his melodramas. He is honored for his "personality," while the ludicrous content and antics of these films are overlooked, and his decline from *Morocco* through *The Shanghai Gesture* is obscured. But these films invariably display Von Sternberg's lack of interest in his stories. His choreography of the parties is usually entertaining; the excessive artifice of *The Devil Is a Woman*, however, suggests Von Sternberg's complacency in complementing the costumes of Travis Banton with vacuous theatrical buffoonery. Some of his sound films like *Shanghai Express* are on the level of comic book, while *The Shanghai Gesture*, one of the most autoerotic, degenerate movies in American film history, does not reach that level. Of his post-*Morocco* films *The Scarlet Empress* is the most reminiscent of his earlier more meaningful baroque stylizations in which he centers the drama on Dietrich's richly garbed enchantress and on the subtle gradations of light surrounding her sexual maturity. One commends Von Sternberg for the composition of *The Scarlet Empress*, but I think it advisable to remember those films whose lighting and dramatic treatment defined a period and character. There are several amusing, titillating moments in his sound films, but it is a dangerous game for critics to carelessly exhume the absurdities of his post-*Morocco* sound films in the thirties even as the Russian cinema presented such lukewarm exercises in humanist propaganda as *The Road to Life*.

Erich von Stroheim's *Greed* is referred to as the shining example of the realism of the silent film. Yet even with Herman Weinberg's diligent reconstruction of Von Stroheim's epic, realism does not seem to be Von Stroheim's intention. In his first films, *Blind Husbands* and *Foolish Wives*, Von Stroheim exposes the amorous escapades and decadent manners of the rich. His portraits of the aristocracy are set against a melodramatic backdrop of handsome hotel interiors and lavish parties in which Von Stroheim's dramatic fatalism marks his protagonists' growing recognition of the emptiness of their lives. In *The Merry Widow* and *The Wedding March* he adopts a more formalist approach to fin de siècle Europe. The first part of *The Merry Widow* plays as a study in extravagance: Richard Day's opulent decor overshadows the moral conflicts underlying Von Stroheim's historical reconstruction. Though one is likely to opt for Lubitsch's more straightforward, affable adaptation, Von Stroheim retreats from the excesses of his pageantry by observing its grim, personal repercussions. Mae Murray appears to awaken in a sleepwalker's paradise; she is the one character who is aware that the glimmer and vibrancy of her world have faded. Not unlike the characters in *Fellini Satyricon*, she is conceived as the central figure in a mural that has been animated for a brief time on film.

*The Wedding March* again presents an elaborately drawn costume pageant. Von Stroheim, however, does not languish on the extravagance for its own sake but for its melancholic aura and perverse social underpinnings. His attention to the portentous, prolonged rituals conveys a picture of an etiolated social order in which personal ideals and genuine human emotions are swept aside by the rigorous decorum of the parades and the equally ornate parties that ensue. His protagonists have abjured their humanity, whether it is dramatized in the raw power of the butcher's near rape of Fay Wray or in the exaggerated lyricism of the garden serenade between Von Stroheim and Wray. The brute terror of the butcher's attack and the florid, formal elements of Von Stroheim's courtship underscore the dehumanization of social relationships. The film's aim is not realism but expressionism, the superannuation of personal desires by a rigidly hieratic society. Although he intended to pursue the marriage of his military officer to ZaSu Pitts's wealthy heiress, the film remains one of the best examples of the silent film's absorption in an antiquated social order.

*Greed* differs from *The Wedding March* in many areas. First, *Greed* is set in a primitive environment that allows Von Stroheim's three central characters to develop in a more openly emotional manner; second, unlike *The Merry Widow* and *The Wedding March* in which Von Stroheim has personified social history in elaborate pageants as an epic poet might observe the ruins of a battlefield, *Greed* presents a makeshift society whose inhabitants struggle for survival. Third, whereas the style and meaning of *The Wedding March* was comprised of awesome long shots that impersonally record the languor and the extensive decor and formalism of Vienna, the meaning of *Greed* is rendered in close-up and in the way the characters constantly interact and upset the temporary stability of their world. One such representative scene in *Greed* occurs with Trina's visit to the office of McTeague's dentist as the camera magnifies the emotionally pregnant struggles that will characterize their relationship.

These in-depth, psychological profiles are made all the more intense by the constrictive nature of Von Stroheim's characters' primitive dwellings, a theme that achieves its most devastating, ironic treatment in the final encounter in Death Valley. It shows Von Stroheim as the great Freudian of silent-film directors as he forces his players to move through an unexplored terrain and to uncover a part of the human psyche that has been previously discovered in the baroque exteriors of the German cinema. The acting throughout the film conveys this interest in exploring the desires that his characters must continually repress. This is especially true of McTeague whose rough, brutish nature and contrasting moods of innocence and violence operate within an invisible social matrix. But is *Greed*, in effect, a sound film? When ZaSu Pitts's Trina fondles her coins in bed and bends over them like a newborn infant, running her fingers through the coins as if they evoked a magic drug that heightened her sexual awareness, does one imagine a sound-film continuum? Though Von Stroheim avoids any montage effects that might obscure one's interest in his social environment, his immersion in the vagaries of human corruption connotes an imbalance in the social order that is best characterized as expressionistic, not realistic. The accentuated facial contortions that his characters exhibit are like specimens of protozoa studied under a microscope, whose various transformations negate the premises of three-dimensional portraiture.

Abel Gance's *La Roue* is often placed beside *Greed* in advancing the thesis that the silent film was gradually refined into a realist medium. There are major similarities in the thematic entanglements in the two films—in their grubby, lower-class atmosphere and the sexual tension among the central characters— but Grance's interests are distinct from Von Stroheim's. In Von Stroheim's films the cutting does not fragment the compositions but highlights their most dramatic, psychologically symbolic features. Gance favors a far more furious pace: his camerawork continually upsets the permanence of his settings to expose the dynamic, disparate action and the characters' emotional instability. In *La Roue*, and more so in *Napoleon*, Gance's kinetic camera is distinguished from the fast-paced style of the American comedy film and from Griffith's epics—as well as from the historical dialectic of the Russian cinema—by seeking out the numerous dramatic details of his chaotic reality. Sets like the father's home in *La Roue* or the assembly in *Napoleon* are not presented in rigid, formal terms but as a means of emphasizing the interaction of conflicting social forces and human emotions. The psychological validity of *La Roue* derives from Gance's sudden editing permutations, which seem to explode on the screen with all the forcefulness of the train the father drives; it is a complex and ultimately confusing framework. Gance's experimentation with a variety of camera angles and the different speeds at which various sequences play overwhelm the viewer's hold on reality. He is exploring a theme similar to the one in *Greed*, human obsessions and how they are defined through a myriad of cinematic techniques.

The basic question that Gance appears to have confronted is how to capture the diversity of history: its physical details, its dramatic conflicts, its unique emotional truth. In *La Roue* some tension exists between Gance's interest in his characters' expressiveness and a Balzac-like apprehension of the totality of life. This desire to embrace the interaction of man and society through an outpouring of the characters' passions, set against a richly defined social backdrop, can be seen as a primary characteristic of a realist aesthetic. It is not a realism borrowed from painting or photography but one that connotes the sweep and intensity of social history through a complement of cinematic devices. It is the realism of the silent film, one that will be displaced by the sound film's emphasis on dialogue as the most universal method of understanding man and his world.

The natural affinity between the movies and history—between a kinetic medium and a period of dynamic upheaval—achieves its most grandiloquent stylization in *Napoleon*. In earlier silent-film masterworks such as *The Birth of a Nation* and *Die Nibelungen*, the past was recreated through a style of design and expression unique to the period and characters, but *Napoleon* is a study in primitive filmmaking in which Gance constructs his picture of Napoleon and France's burgeoning republican government through an avalanche of film technology. The snowball and pillow fight during Napoleon's school days underline Gance's preoccupation with the movies as a medium of total involvement. He frees the camera from the tripod, sweeping us into the geography of Napoleon's earliest encounters; his rapid cuts and the masking of the film frame into separate, microscopic images present history as a collective phenomenon. The first part of Gance's epic ends with the battle of Toulon in which he juxtaposes a more humanistic, dramatic viewpoint in vivid close-ups, expressive of the grime, sweat, and destruction the soldiers face to montage effects that denote the encompassing nature of Napoleon's victory.

Gance experiments with various methods of situating the viewer in the heart of the action, using the camera as an acrobatic spectator, whether it is swinging on a chandelier during the ball or experiencing vertigo in the midst of battle; these experiments fulfill one of the essential qualities of the silent film. Griffith had undertaken a scherzo, montage stylization, but only in the final movement to dramatize the protagonist's heroism and his destiny in history; in the Russian cinema, montage would be interpreted as a dialectical force pitting poor against rich. Gance attempts a more radically technical narrative with, however, a less impressive dramatic core. Albert Dieudonné cuts a fine figure as Napoleon, but his growth as a military hero, his relationship with Joséphine, and the role of figures like Marat, Danton, and Robespierre are obscured by the aggregate idea of movies as history in the making. There are no real, living characters in this epic: even Napoleon exists only as the most perceptible shadow cast by history. The intellectual scope of the revolution, the ideas generated by its leading figures, and the voice of the common man are nowhere in sight. Many of the personal episodes involving Napoleon's romance of Joséphine and the principal figures in the reign of terror are tedious: Gance has little interest in explaining characters and ideas or the interaction of the two in history. His picture of the reign of terror is similar to a collection of notes by different journalists whose inconclusive scribblings are pieced together to present an image of humanity in the abyss, a cascading torrent of self-destructiveness. The massing of the armies during Napoleon's Italian campaign, in which Gance uses the triptych to convey the architectonics of warfare, and the final dazzling montage effects in which past and present, the individual and history are triumphantly assembled in a kaleidoscopic reading of history and myth insure Gance's epic a place among the great spectacles in film history. It may be closer to Lang's *Metropolis* than to Griffith's *The Birth of a Nation*: a network of aggressive, ebullient, sensory images in which history as exemplified by movie technology subsumes the viewer's consciousness.

*Strike–Que viva Mexico!*

The Russian silent film is indisputably the cinema of montage. Although there were several filmmakers who did not conceive their stories around a historical dialectic, their work seems to exist as an addendum to the Russian silent film. One recalls Ivan Perestiani's subtle social telescoping in *Three Lives*, certainly one of the most adroit sociosexual studies of the silent era. But it would be the fascination with different methods of editing that characterized the Russian silent film. Their initial study of the scherzo finale popularized by Sennett and Griffith led to the development of a schematic film narrative coexpressive with the dialectic of class warfare. Montage was not simply a form of editing that facilitated the visualization of the dynamics of revolution: montage was a film vision in which each person, object, and dramatic subplot was integrated as a kinetic element in their recreations of the revolution. The editing is the heart and mind of their films, just as the psychological resources of the composition are the connecting thread in the German cinema.

Montage can be defined as a compressed, rhetorical style of cutting, but the meaning of montage in the Russian silent film is that it affects all aspects of a film, from camera placement and the modified use of the moving camera to the composition. The primary import of montage in the Russian cinema, whether in Pudovkin's linear approach or Eisenstein's contrapuntal theory, is that it proposes an equation of animate and inanimate objects; man and nature are characterized by their material extensions, which interact like biochemical properties in the life cycle of man and nature. In Eisenstein's first film, *Strike*, he treats the photographs of police agents in a book as living forms: the title reads "Agent Owl in a Tight Spot," and Agent Owl is then pictured tangled in a rope. Whereas Griffith occasionally presents images that exist as metaphors, Eisenstein continually juxtaposes visual metaphors. As the police slaughter the workers and revolutionaries, several factory owners look over a map of the city, noting the scenes of carnage on the map. One of the owners spills ink on the map; Eisenstein thus establishes an analogy between the assault and the symbolic aspects of the ink-stained map. Both Pudovkin and Eisenstein equate people and objects symmetrical to their identity, for example, the soldiers and statues in *The End of St. Petersburg* and the pig figurine and the butchery of the animals in *Old and New*. Eisenstein's dramatic vitalization of the lion in *The Battleship Potemkin* is one of literally hundreds of examples that illuminates this equivalence of people and objects.

Since their application of montage involves a temporal and spatial framework that can be best defined as an evolutionary continuum, persons, objects, and scenes are wholly defined through their kinetic adaptability. It then becomes impossible to separate a character from his role within the dynamic thrust of revolution; montage as a style and structure expressed in the continuous thread of action and revolt cannot present an individual within a distinct spatial framework. The majority of Russian films advance this use of montage as the unifying aesthetic variable; however, there are several dramatic limitations in using actors as types rather than as expressive individuals. In the epics of Griffith and Lang, even in Murnau's dehumanizing dramas, individual characters are both personalized and abstracted through a repertoire of gestures, emotions, and actions that create their own indissoluble unity and purpose; they attain a dramatic independence that personalizes the drama and its intellectual content. But to Eisenstein and Pudovkin, a Hegelian-Marxist dialectical interpretation of history depersonalizes the individual, assimilating both imperialist and proletarian into a schematic, kinetic picture of the revolution. Nikolai Balatov's impassioned revolutionary in *Mother* and the dancing Cossacks in *October* possess an expressive quality but only to the degree that they denote another link in the war between oppressors and oppressed. This historical linkage is effected through a montage process that displaces a humanistic interpretation with a phenomenological one.

To create distinct, diverse characters, Russian filmmakers would have had to diffuse the mechanistic nature of a Marxist dialectic. As the first historians of a new Russia, they had to picture the past warfare as a collective struggle; thus their films reflect the uniform identity of those who contributed to victory. *The Battleship Potemkin, October, Mother,* and *The End of St. Petersburg* represent the culmination of montage as a means of celebrating the recent struggle; *Earth,* then, marks the beginning of the search for the unifying characters and myths that will inspire this new nation. But the transition from a montage aesthetic to one in which socialist ideals are embodied in the dialogue, composition, and action of a realistically styled narrative will prove a difficult one, perhaps no less complex than the realization of a communist doctrine by its rulers. Part of this aesthetic problem is documented in Eisenstein's films. In *The Battleship Potemkin* he shows various segments of society, such as the sailors on the battleship or the citizens of Odessa as they reach an awareness of the urgency of the uprising; in *October* the Russian people are engaged in the revolution and the film functions as an idealization of their solidarity. In *The Battleship Potemkin* the catalyzing elements of revolution first featured in *Strike* are dramatized in a more interdependent form; in *October* the single, dominant chord is that of nationalism, leading to the storming of the palace and the montage celebration of this historic event on numerous clocks.

Pudovkin, less schematic than Eisenstein, illustrates some of the problems of a sound film in his late silent film, *Storm over Asia.* His treatment of the land and its people evokes comparison to the vibrancy of Dovzhenko's *Earth,* but he eventually rejects the pictorial focus of Dovzhenko's films. His begins with several dissolves on the land that express the affinities the Mongols share with its grandeur. After the protagonist realizes that he has been duped by the tsarist officers, Pudovkin introduces a montage sequence that is incongruous to the mythic qualities he has first uncovered. In Dovzhenko's films the violence of the revolution, poetically recorded in *Zvenigora* and *Arsenal,* results in his appreciation of the primeval splendor of man and nature in *Earth.* But the primacy of the land and its rustic splendor assume a secondary role in *Storm over Asia* because of Pudovkin's gradual emphasis on the mechanistic nature of the revolution through his montage rhetoric.

The central problem faced by Russian filmmakers in a sound-film continuum was twofold: how to adapt sound to their film syntax and how to develop a narrative consistent with the predominant feature of a sound film—that is, the dialogue. Their silent films achieved a consistent artistic form by recognizing the structural affinity between a Hegelian-Marxist dialectic and montage: between an idea of history characterized by repeated socioeconomic conflicts and a style of editing that emphasized the kinetic flux of history and revolution. In a sound film the dialogue and the full complement of the sounds of daily life imbue the characters with an element of empathetic individuality. A static, realistic picture of man and nature replaces the dynamic, abstract thrust of their silent films. The permeability of Marx's collective social philosophy in Russian filmmaking is then identified through its embodiment in a unifying picture of man in history. The composition of a film will now assume the role that editing had previously fulfilled: the fragmentation of physical reality into a dynamic, revolutionary upheaval will be replaced by a search for the most representative, enduring images of the idealism of the Russian folk. *Chapayev*, the "Maxim Trilogy," and Eisenstein's sound films are epics concerning the heroics of individualized protagonists who in their appearance and speech personify the values unique to the new communist society. These films, however, undertake a highly contrived reading of history in which melodrama and mimesis are uneasily intertwined. In their most dogmatic form in *Chapayev* and the "Maxim Trilogy," the heroes of the revolution are reduced to Hollywood clichés. The seduction by a machine gun and the repetitious use of folk songs in *Chapayev*, and Maxim's pursuit of romance and revolution in the trilogy are stilted pictures of the individual as revolutionary archetype.

As the most complex, ambitious artist working in the Russian cinema, Eisenstein attempted to transcend the more literal, psychologically simplistic concerns of the Russian sound film by creating heroes who could be understood only through the symbolic, iconographic makeup of the composition. The advanced degree of visual rhetoric in his sound films interprets the period, the conflict, and the hero as pictorial, textual symbols. The analogies to kabuki drama drawn by Eisenstein and his biographers show his interest in creating a film drama in which the poetic dialogue and music are supported by an equally stylized, symbolic form of acting, costume, and design. His use of Prokofiev's music in *Alexander Nevsky* is particularly instructive. The drama is personalized in the imposing figure and basso profundo of Nikolai Cherkassov's Nevsky and the supporting stentorian force of the two soldier friends who compete for the hand of the maiden warrior. The film begins with a chorus of Russian voices; during the introduction of the German camp, the visual motifs which characterize their menacing presence are complemented by the music. After Nevsky agrees to lead the fight, the chorus summons the people to war, and the visuals delineate their physical awakening and unification on land and sea. The decisive battle on the ice is primarily sustained through the music, with several close-ups of the two friends urging greater effort by their countrymen. The action is not kinetic; although Eisenstein occasionally places us in the middle of the fighting, the isolated close-ups, like the patriotic exclamations of the two friends, are not integrated as part of a physically changing assault. The ending is inspired by Prokofiev's choral hymn, honoring the fallen heroes and then culminating in the people's attack on the captured German leaders.

*Ivan the Terrible* is a more intensive artistic and psychological tour de force. The dialogue is not so much amplified by the music as it directly embodies the dramatic tension. The masterly lighting of Andrei Moskvin defines the characters as evocative psychological types, while the imaginative dress and design work as historical and spatial motifs framing their precise, poignant expressions of idealism and treachery. The staging is triumphantly theatrical through its accentuating instead of underplaying the rigors of court life.

Eisenstein was always skeptical of camera movement, and the few scenes that show some movement—for example, the one in which the camera pans down on the figure of Ivan sitting by his murdered bride and those punctuated by sharp, dynamic cuts, like the exchanges among the populace debating Ivan's war against the Mongols—lend an element of intimacy and dramatic emphasis that he could have used more frequently, especially in his sound films. Though incomplete, Eisenstein's epic is one of the most diligent attempts to interpret the dialogue, music, and sound as a poetic, psychological accompaniment to his awesome mural of the icons of Russian history.

*Que viva Mexico!* seems an even more ambitious experiment in its interpenetration of myth and archetype on film. Although one can only speculate on the possible stylistic relationships among its six sections (owing as much to its incomplete material as to the manner in which Eisenstein would have interrelated the dynamics and symbols in the six sections), few films, silent or sound, convey the movies' unique ability to discover the mythology of a people through its cultural rituals and artifacts. The numerous compilations undertaken in *Mexican Symphony, Thunder over Mexico,* and *Time in the Sun* are approximations of what might have been. The existing footage is a sketch of the outstanding symbols in the culture and physiognomy of the land and people; one questions how Eisenstein would juxtapose the staged bullfighting maneuvers and the exotic posing and physique of the peons to the populist rhetoric implicit in the rape of the peon's wife. Yet for the film student somewhat removed from the politics of moviemaking, there is ample evidence of the unique affinity that Eisenstein, like Griffith and Ozu, possessed with the film medium.

Eisenstein was the greatest theoretician of the movies and one of its genuine artists. Perhaps more than any of the major Russian artists of the first half of the twentieth century, he reshaped the impact of modernism on our intellectual history. His great tragedy was to have been born a Renaissance man, trapped in a society with little sympathy for the Renaissance's artistic and humanistic concerns.

## Nana–Gone with the Wind

In terms of style and subject matter, the films of Jean Renoir are the farthest removed from Eisenstein and his sound-film aesthetic in which abstraction and national symbolism are the dominant effects. To understand the nature of Renoir's work in the thirties, it is important to recall briefly the role of the avant-garde in the French cinema of the twenties.

Although there were several French filmmakers whose films did not project the nihilism and absurdity of the prevailing surrealist and dadaist sensibility, there was a clearly articulated rejection of classic narrative forms in the French silent film. Renoir's avant-garde films display an affection for the bizarre and fantastic, but even in a film like *The Little Match Girl* the surrealistic effects seem mechanical; Renoir evinces a poignant but undeveloped sympathy for the lyrical, mutable expressiveness of his star and wife, Catherine Hessling. *Nana* explores the surreptitious dealings between the aristocratic libertines and the pimps and prostitutes they use, but Renoir is not completely sympathetic to the novel's social realism. The film is most effective in Hessling's fiercely individual moments, when her playfulness or abjection is juxtaposed to the posing and callousness of her admirers. This appreciation for the emotional resources and common humanity of his isolated protagonists proved a major theme throughout his career. It also shows Renoir's growing awareness that, after the excesses and solipsism of the French avant-garde, there is a need for the artist to find some means to express the underlying desires and paradoxes of human nature in a simpler, more direct manner. This is the idea Renoir began to uncover in the thirties, and it is the story of his contribution to film history.

Among his major works of the thirties, *La Grande Illusion*, although the least representative, is his most finished work. His restrained, unaffected camera movements and the gifted ensemble acting interpret this study of war through the friendships sustained between soldiers from opposing sides and different social backgrounds. The detail that Renoir emphasizes in the French barracks and then in the German camp centers on the soldiers' camaraderie, their idiosyncratic behavior, and secret passions. When the French prisoners are moved to another camp, his camera eye never deviates from the framework of their friendships. Renoir is not interested in showing the historical forces that erupt in wartime; he perceives the breakdown of a social order in the relationships of his four major characters: Von Stroheim as the noble, patriotic German officer; Pierre Fresnay as the aristocratic Frenchman who realizes that his duty to his countrymen is greater than his friendship for Von Stroheim; Dalio as the wealthy Jew who tries to win friends through the food his family sends him; and Jean Gabin, the commoner who only hopes to rejoin his friends in the bistros of Paris. The film's anecdotal style may at first seem too removed from the great theme of war. But it is so psychologically true to their regrets and desires that one discerns the double-edged meaning of the grand illusion: the repeated folly of nations and the more profound sentiment that ennobling friendships may not be sustained in a future conflict.

*Toni* is more characteristic of Renoir's commitment to a primitive landscape in which the disarray of his characters' emotions mirrors their barren, destitute environment. Unlike Pagnol in *The Baker's Wife*, Renoir does not rejoice in the everyday pains and pleasures of peasant life; his interests lie in studying nascent human emotions as if he were undertaking an X ray of the human heart. And, unlike Rossellini who was engaged in a similar examination of the moral paradoxes, crises, and triumphs in the human condition, Renoir's sympathy for the unrestrained passions of the migrant workers in *Toni* fulfills a naive idealism distinct from both Rossellini's moral fervor and from Werner Herzog's behavioral exercises. Renoir is not a neorealist who emphasizes the oppressive nature of physical reality; his moralism is directed to the confluent human emotions that give life and meaning to his world. If what critics discover in the

Italian films of the late forties and early fifties is a search for a transcendent humanism, for a moral solidarity that will allow man to grapple with his depressed condition, then Renoir's *Toni* is a definite precursor. The term then that best defines the ideal that Renoir works toward is not "neorealism" but a type of "primitive humanism." Renoir realized that before acknowledging a social order, he must undertake a reexamination of the emotional and spiritual forces that govern the individual through a style with the least amount of narrative and aesthetic subterfuges.

Although there is an undeniable revolutionary impetus to Renoir's dramatic perspective, his denuded, simplified narrative invites numerous problems for him and his successors. The central flaw in *Toni* is Renoir's adopting a fatalistic point of view that does not question the whys and wherefores of his protagonists' actions; Renoir focuses on the emotional interplay without any consistent narrative continuity. One might argue that this is the only method to record the rambling, instinctive habits of his migrant workers, but this admits such a simplistic understanding of the complex, contradictory ways emotions manifest one's true sentiments that the story proves less meaningful than the ballads that the characters sing to themselves. To accept *Toni* as a poetic hymn to the primitive fatalism from which his characters cannot escape is to embrace any instinctive action as an expression of personal humanism. One need only turn to Epstein's *La Belle Nivernaise* to find a more intelligent use of Renoir's close-up, dramatic range, one in which poetry and primitivism are not seen as diametrically opposed values.

*The Rules of the Game* is a much more difficult film to analyze because its classic theatricality and intellectual scope are far more complex than the primitivism of *Toni*. Although it reformulates Renoir's fascination with the conflict between stringent social mores and reckless emotional behavior, Robin Wood's characterization of the work as "the most Mozartean film ever made" is an indication of a general misconception of Renoir's naturalist style. To understand how this film is a radical departure from the exquisite Mozartean excursions in the work of Ophüls and Mizoguchi, one must first acknowledge the basic thrust of Renoir's films: the search for a primeval awakening of human desire. Whether it takes the rustic form of *Toni* or plays against the social backdrop of *The Rules of the Game*, Renoir's intent is distinct from the highly stylized romantic essays of Ophüls or the elaborate paean to Japanese culture in the films of Mizoguchi.

*The Rules of the Game* begins at an airport as a pilot completes a record flight. Similar to earlier films Renoir's camera records the action from up close in order to experience the frenzy surrounding the hero's return. When a radio broadcaster questions the pilot about his feelings, he replies that he has failed because the woman he loves is not at the airport. This opening scene is then cut off most interestingly with Renoir as the pilot's friend taking him away from the crowd so that he will not make a fool of himself and embarrass the woman who is also Renoir's childhood friend. Renoir then shifts the action to the aristocratic woman's mansion, but his cutting maintains the same lackadaisical pace he used in *Boudu Saved from Drowning*, in which it reflected Michel Simon's temperament as an ignoble everyman. But in *The Rules of the Game* the diffusive editing fails to reflect the social tensions embedded in the textures of the city and the country estate. In *La Grande Illusion* Renoir's unaccented rhythms were a natural complement to a drama which unfolded in the displaced world of prisoner-of-war camps and in the ascending emotional fellowship among the characters. But in *The Rules of the Game* Renoir's refusal to penetrate the fabric and manners of upper-class life exposes the characters as children masquerading as adults.

Prior to the party and the final, tragic variation on social conformity and personal desires, Renoir infuses a style of theatrical satire with his own primitivist sentiments. He is most contrived when reworking the conventions of theatrical comedy—for example, during the costume ball. One feels that Renoir would like to violently overturn the rules by which aristocrats play the game of love; however, he is content to comment on their deceitfulness through the characters' blithe self-mocking nature. In the final, dramatic turn of events, a servant girl points to the constant financial crises faced by the artist and dissuades Renoir from running off with his childhood friend. The pilot then attempts to run off with her and is killed when he is mistaken for a poacher. By trying to have the best of both worlds, the aristocratic disdain of a languishing social order and the antipodal currents of his characters' reckless emotional behavior, Renoir has revealed his aesthetic indecisiveness in trying to combine the two.

In reviewing Renoir's work in the thirties one is struck by the variety of literary and aesthetic formulas he uses to transcribe the emotional impulses his characters seem unable to deny. *A Day in the Country* visualizes the tension between society and the vicissitudes of human desire by situating his gay naïfs in his father's impressionist countryside. His empathy with the lyrical puissance of nature is evoked in the saturnalian actions of the family from the city who lose themselves in the splendor of the fields and forests, while the ephemeral sweetness of nature is subtly expressed by the inhabitants of his Edenesque setting. The film's brevity enhances Renoir's pastoral by suggesting that one is only given a short time to revel in this impressionist paradise.

*La Bête humaine* is Renoir's most abrasive study of a society that offers few outlets for natural instincts. In adapting Zola's novel he never diminishes the fatalism surrounding the railroad employees and their inability to express their feelings other than in extreme actions. The foreboding, enveloping shadows that pervade the station become an objective metaphor of the inner torments of the three major characters: Fernand Ledoux as the foreman who is trying to get ahead; Simone Simon as the foreman's sexually destructive wife; and Jean Gabin, the railroad driver torn between the strain of madness in his family and his own precarious emotional desires. The film not only stands as one of the most taut realizations of a novel in the thirties, but also underscores Renoir's search for his literary and stylistic antecedents. This is also apparent in *The Lower Depths* in his use of one setting as a symbolic enclosure for the dregs and outcasts of society, a theme Renoir previously developed in *The Crime of Monsieur Lange*. In its rigid character delineation, in its symbolic use of lighting, exemplified in the Sunday outing in the park, *The Lower Depths* stands as the clearest exposition of Renoir's clarion call to personal expressiveness in the face of scheming villains and tyrannical social forces. Although the film appears to perspire mood rather than evoke it, the characterizations of Gabin and Jouvet possess a classic integrity. The gradual awakening of the outcasts and the murder of the landlord are handled with such conviction and with such a forthright sense of dramatic catharsis that the film can be seen as the archetypal Renoir statement.

John Ford's early years in the cinema were similar to those of Jean Renoir in that he had yet to master an expressive style in the silent film. If Renoir's silent films suffer from his incorporating a style inherently incongruous to his emotional, naive sensibility, Ford's first films lack a dramatic focus in sustaining Griffith's lyrical expansiveness. *Three Bad Men* is an example of Ford's raw folksiness, in which, like *Four Sons*, the film's pathos exists as its lone dramatic device. Even *The Informer*, with its symbolic use of sound and the character of the blind man, seems an uninspired, literal adaptation of theatrical symbolism and lacks the poetic naturalism one finds in Ford's best work of the thirties and forties. Ford's debt to Griffith in films such as *Judge Priest, Young Mr. Lincoln, Drums along the Mohawk, The Grapes of Wrath*, and *How Green Was My Valley* is then inspired by seeing his characters as inheritors of a living past, as true of the garrulous lawyer in *Judge Priest* as of the returning sons in *How Green Was My Valley*. *Judge Priest* shows Ford's fondness for the South as a resplendent world impervious to the changes in the rest of the country, where the native folk wit is illuminated by a seemingly omnipresent midday sun. His maturity as an American folk artist is communicated through his restrained camera movements and in his sympathy with the characters' rustic manners. There is little action or dramatic incident in the film as Ford pulls his camera back to medium shot: a sense of quietude enfolds his characters, some who can never stop talking about the past and others unconscious of their role in history. Like his best westerns, in which he uses one or two locations to emphasize the presence of the land and his characters' dependence on it, Judge Priest's porch becomes Ford's looking glass, encompassing the characters and drama that pass in front of his home, from Stepin Fetchit to the troubled lovers.

Part of the enduring ritual Ford discovers about America is the folk colloquialisms of its people, an important aspect of *Judge Priest* and *Drums along the Mohawk* and an integral part of *Young Mr. Lincoln*. Ford begins *Young Mr. Lincoln* with an address by a politician running for office, cuts to a group of townspeople eloquently framed in front of a store, and moves his camera around to undercut the speaker's pompousness. When Abe Lincoln speaks, the camera remains in medium shot: Lincoln's celebrated words are recognized as a part of America's history upon which Ford's camera will not intrude. His characters tend to slip into a facile folk idiom, for example in Will Rogers's characterization of Judge Priest and in *Drums along the Mohawk* when Arthur Shields's priest outlines the battle plans, but Ford's staging sustains the nascent idealism of both orator and audience. Even as the action reaches its most explosive moments, Ford emphasizes his characters' awareness of their roles in history. When the Indians mount their final attack against the settlers in *Drums along the Mohawk*, the camera is not turned to the full-scale implications of warfare; it shows a saddened Claudette Colbert, who realizes that what she and her husband, Henry Fonda, have worked so hard to obtain is lost, but who also conveys through her firm, resolute manner why they will begin again. It is poignantly rendered in Edna May Oliver's heroic strength in the face of death: she kisses Ward Bond one last time as the house in which the settlers are trapped becomes a stage, symbolic of their strength and solidarity in building a nation.

Like Griffith, Ford sympathizes with characters whose instinctive, often crude behavior disrupts the more solemn moments in his films: the coutroom sequences in *Judge Priest* and *Young Mr. Lincoln* are continually upset, in *Judge Priest* by the festive Negro band outside the courthouse and in *Young Mr. Lincoln* by the lackadaisical manner of one jury member who interrupts the bombastic prosecutor by spitting out tobacco. *Judge Priest* celebrates the American past as an innocent reverie personified by the midafternoon sun that filters through the courtroom. Five years later, in *Young Mr. Lincoln*, Ford centers the historical impact of the drama on Fonda's magnificent characterization of Lincoln, a face no less pure than Dreyer's Joan and no less dominant than Eisenstein's Ivan.

His more well-known films, for example, *The Grapes of Wrath* and *How Green Was My Valley*, are studies in the texture of the land. *The Grapes of Wrath* is a visual symphony in which Gregg Toland's breathtaking photography identifies the countryside and not the suffering Okies as the true subject of the film. Ford is not completely successful in resolving this epic drama because he has never worked with such a large canvas; whereas Griffith would have been more responsive to the film's historical undercurrents, Ford magnifies the pathos generated by the Joads. The dramatic imperviousness in this tone poem of pessimism is similar to the problematic yet sweeping ode of ecstasy he writes to Ireland some twelve years later in *The Quiet Man*.

Though the emotional fervor of his films frequently obscures the characters' dramatic succinctness, a film like *How Green Was My Valley* remains a more convincing work of social turmoil than Carol Reed's *The Stars Look Down*, to which it is often compared. The story originates in the homes of the coal miners and in the surrounding, sloping line of houses that seems to stretch interminably along the valley. This visual motif underlines one major difference between Ford's film and *The Stars Look Down*. In Reed's film the visual line of the homes is much shorter and flater, representative of the town's oppressive squalor; in Ford's film the homes are situated on a hill, expressing the indissoluble unity of the coal-mining families. Reed's film explores the impact of Margaret Lockwood's brazen sexuality and Emlyn Williams's sly Machiavellian on the paling innocence of Michael Redgrave's idealist. In Ford's film the world outside Roddy McDowall's childhood is nurtured by the fabric of family life and the romance between Walter Pidgeon and Maureen O'Hara. Ford intimates that this is a country and story that we can never fully comprehend; Reed's drama is characterized by devious, violent actions, such as the miners' looting of the stores and the cave-in that traps and kills Redgrave's father. To Ford the violence is only part of the story, and for every beating McDowall suffers at the school in the neighboring valley, the village whiskey prophets teach him how to return pride and strength for the scurrilous slap in the face. One does not remember that last cave-in in Ford's film for its destructive, physical impact, but for the image of the sons' holding Donald Crisp's face as they are brought up in the lift. Reed's film interprets history as a remembrance best forgotten; Ford's film sees the past as an indelible memory.

Ford, similar to Griffith, discovers the epic continuity of American history in the innocence and idealism of its people, and in the breadth of the land that reverberates with its pristine splendor. Orson Welles's *Citizen Kane*, one of the great modern epics of the cinema, examines the fate of this idealism through the exploits of Kane's adventurous empire builder. The heroes of Griffith and Ford are impervious to the temptations of modern city life, to the allure of money and power: they are symbols of the moral, inviolable past. Welles's Kane, however, discovers his identity through money and power, and in becoming a great man loses claim to America's mythic innocence; the burning of Rosebud becomes an ironic commentary on Kane's Faustian gambit. Yet from Kane's first day as a newspaper executive, the film adopts a comic viewpoint to Kane's megalomania. This extraordinary film, brought to life by Welles's intertwining the cinematograpic experimentation of Gregg Toland and Herman Mankiewicz's glib reading of the Hearst empire, renders its portrait of America by sardonically probing Kane's mania for transforming his dreams into material forms. In the film's caricature of the decline of a marriage in the famed breakfast sequence, in the camera's traversal of the opera house interiors, and in Kane's last years at Xanadu, the film's cinematic exuberance becomes a stunning metaphor for the deification of extravagance. Welles characterizes America's development as a modern, industrial power through the scope of Kane's projects. He does not, however, isolate Kane as the single example of the fatalistic encounter between history and idealism. During his run for political office the sound of his voice, the magnitude of his poster, and the jolting dynamic cuts create a singularly American realization of "media politics"; when the journalists, communicating with one another in the dark, search through Kane's treasures, the overhead shots show these wisecracking characters, like Kane in his run for political office, as miniatures within our modern world.

Welles's treatment of Xanadu exemplifies the irony with which he approaches both his own cinematic opulence and Kane's empire builder. The monkeys outside the estate suggest a devious analogy to the fairy-tale gloss surrounding Carl Denham and his film crew in *King Kong*. After Susan's departure, Welles presents a near-conclusive image of Kane's identity as an ambivalent idealist. Aging and without a friend to comfort him, Kane walks alone in the deep spaces of Xanadu and passes a mirror; the camera then closes in on the single image of the mirror. With his dreams of transforming America into his own image fading away, Kane is finally faced with the emptiness he has avoided by engaging himself, and thus America, in a swashbuckling climb to the top.

Though the gimmicky Rosebud treats Kane's last word as a joke on romanticism, the final image complicates this caustic effect. The last shot is not of the sled burning in the fire, but of the destitute Xanadu where Kane tried to recapture the lost world of his childhood dream without ever realizing its impermanence and that of his estate. Though several techniques seem arbitrary—such as the isolated examples of long takes in the newpaper sequences—the film's excesses ironically punctuate Kane's dynamic rise to the top. Regarding the similarity between *The Rules of the Game* and *Citizen Kane* it should be remembered that in *The Rules of the Game*, as in his other works of the thirties, Renoir develops the story through his characters' rebellious, effusive actions. The camerawork and editing, whether in *The Lower Depths* or *The Rules of the Game*, are inspired by his characters' obtruding passions. We never understand Dalio's country estate as the dominant social symbol; instead it functions as a backdrop to his characters' need for love and self-expression. The complexity of the composition and editing are not the central issues in Renoir's films of the thirties; these stylistic variants are modulated by his free spirits, whether by Boudu or by Renoir's artist in *The Rules of the Game*. *Citizen Kane*, as much as any film in the history of the movies, defines its conflict and dramatic tone in the context of the settings. The characters' dramatic expressiveness is realized through the baroque interiors of the opera house, the spaciousness of Xanadu, and the sweeping fabric of the party for Kane before his honeymoon abroad. *Citizen Kane* is unequivocally modern in delineating Kane's paradoxical temperament through its use of film technology to celebrate the spiraling currents of money and power.

Welles' *The Magnificent Ambersons*, like the Jacques Prévert–Marcel Carné *Les Enfants du paradis* attempts a different stylistic treatment. Both films idealize the past, Welles by isolating the grandeur of the Amberson estate and Prévert and Carné by telling their story from the manifold stages in which Barrault, Arletty, and Brasseur are pictured as dramatic archetypes. Whereas the Amberson estate becomes the dominant, evanescent symbol of the declining grandeur of American life in the nineteenth century, Prévert and Carné conceive their theatrical setting as a platonic stage brought to life by their three inimitably poetic stars.

Welles as narrator introduces the world of the Ambersons as one immune to any transient social or political controversy. His sparing dialogue establishes their separateness from the townspeople, who function as the chorus in his stylized drama. These introductory motifs serve as a prologue to the return of Joseph Cotten's inventor and the death of George Amberson. The photographic engraving of Stanley Cortez's camera captures the past as a ritualized memory as, for example, in the scene in which the young Amberson sits with his parents and relatives on the lawn, part of a picture-book world made possible by the Ambersons' aristocratic independence. Welles and Cortez enliven the period in short, abbreviated scenes that personify both its beauty and the repressive fastidiousness of their patrician heroes. The sleigh ride, the funeral, and the ball are rich adornments of their world, exquisite in their refinement yet lacking the romantic spark that Cotten's inventor and his daughter, played by Anne Baxter, bring to their love of the Ambersons.

In *Citizen Kane* dramatic outbursts like Kane's applause reverberating through the opera house after Susan's hopeless debut as an opera singer express his power and isolation. In *The Magnificent Ambersons* Welles shows his restraint in transfixing the ambience of the past through the memorable exchanges between Joseph Cotten and Dolores Costello and in Ray Collins's final words to a near invisible Tim Holt in the railway station. A false note, however, is struck in Agnes Moorehead's performance during the Ambersons' decline; her exaggerated emotional breakdown is simply incongruous with the formalist motifs in Welles's tapestry. But even with its dramatically hollow ending, *The Magnificent Ambersons* remains a glowing portrait of the past.

*Les Enfants du paradis* shows none of the tremors of the fading, romantic light of *The Magnificent Ambersons* in its recreation of the past. With the utmost economy in its camerawork and cutting and by introducing its various acts through swelling street scenes, the poetic mask of Barrault, Arletty, and Brasseur becomes a natural, symbolic extension of early nineteenth-century theater. The movie fuses the vivid playacting of the theater, both on and off the stage, with a prosaic sense of scene painting, as if the camera had merely extended the theater's proscenium. It is not so much a stylistic antidote to Renoir's folk dramas as it is a celebration of a period in which Renoir's primitivism achieved its most elaborate fruition in the union of life and art.

The serious, artistic endeavors of Ford and Welles were undertaken at the high point of studio production. Hollywood's "golden age" was a period that best characterized the middlebrow appeal of movies in America. Famous novels and popular historical incidents and personalities were brought to life through the star system; a simplified, invariably romantic reading of history obtained, filtered by the democratic experiences and escapist fantasies of its audience. The popularity of adventure epics in the silent film had established several key elements in engaging audiences—notably a colorful historical backdrop and a fast-paced narrative which centered on the exploits of its attractive, romantic leads. De Mille's epics remain something of an anomaly in the genre; the most famous moments in his films, for example the bacchanalia in *Cleopatra* and the parting of the Red Sea in his remake of *The Ten Commandments*, underscore the medium's inherent propensity for spectacle. Like the most riveting moments in a science-fiction fantasy, they are sensory extravaganzas that display the godlike powers of the filmmaker. De Mille's fame is that of a classic showman, but he was a severely limited director. Though his career spanned some five decades of moviemaking, his most consistent entertainments cover a period of some ten years, from the midthirties until the end of the war. I have not seen *Joan the Woman*, *Old Wives for New*, and *Fool's Paradise*, the three silent films Charles Higham claims are his best work in the silent film. But I have seen *Male and Female*, and S. J. Perelman's riotous send-up of De Mille's folly and foppery as a director of comedy leads one to see the epic as his best genre.

*Cleopatra* and *The Plainsman* show some of the folk humor and melodramatic excesses one associates with popular treatments of romance and adventure in the silent era. They are not as encumbered by the prissy morality and static dramatic tableaux in his silent-film version of *The Ten Commandments* or his early sound film *The Sign of the Cross*. *The Plainsman* is a long, sweeping epic with surprisingly few battles. De Mille is more interested in developing representative scenes of early American life like a series of postage stamps commemorating the frontier. *North West Mounted Police* and *Reap the Wild Wind* are the apex of De Mille's art, more vibrantly kinetic in combining a love story, the protagonists' heroism, and the rival social factions. The game played between the marksmen in *North West Mounted Police* and the raw, muscular physicality of the ship's sinking in *Reap the Wild Wind* draw on the unvarnished folk poetry and visceral power of the adventure epic; these films rise above the simulated naiveté and fulsome technology that De Mille had failed to master in his earlier epics and that would overburden his last works.

His rivals can be broken down into two groups. The first consists of films such as *The Lives of a Bengal Lancer*, *China Seas*, *The Charge of the Light Brigade*, and *Action in the North Atlantic* in which a historical conflict or personality is tailored to the mythic appeal of the star. Cooper's understated idealism, Gable's robust manliness, Flynn's Byronic handsomeness, and Bogart's world-weariness are the focal points of the drama; the simplified story line and supporting stereotypes reinforce the singularly American virtues of heroic innocence, rugged individualism, naive love, and moral fastidiousness. The Warner Bros.' productions, the most successful of these spectacles, sustain an admirable balance between functional character delineation and riveting action sequences which avoid both Ford's more solemn folksiness and De Mille's cumbersome theatricality. They are high-spirited, psychologically obtuse adventures that engage one with their boyish heroes and a picture of history coexpressive with the physical magic of Hollywood's studio craftsmen. The luster of the star system is supported, and at times transcended by the craftsmanship of art directors such as Hans Dreier, Van Nest Polglase, and Richard Day, and by the special effects photography of Farciot Edouart and A. Arnold Gillepsie.

Literary adaptations of the classics also functioned as a means of capturing the past through the Hollywood looking glass. Its writers and directors may have been inadequate in translating the complex literary machinations of Dickens, but George Cukor's direction of *David Copperfield* shows Hollywood's aptitude for illustrating Dickens while abbreviating the novel's most dramatic episodes. Though Cukor was more comfortable with the pieties of Louisa May Alcott's *Little Women*, the strengths of these two films lie in his straightforward theatrical staging and in the performers' emotional viability. Cukor animates Hollywood's theatrical scene painting by highlighting the characters' personal discords rather than emphasizing the novels' literary discursiveness and historical commentary. William Wyler's adaptations of *Wuthering Heights* and *Dodsworth*, like his *Jezebel* and *The Letter*, make for highly effective melodramas which combine the strengths of performers such as Laurence Olivier, Walter Huston, and Bette Davis with the consummate pictorialism of Gregg Toland and Ernest Haller. Hollywood was, perhaps, more attuned to the dramatic clichés in its various remakes of *Beau Geste* and *Back Street,* but the adaptations of Cukor and Wyler make a strong case for the virtues of the star system and of studio art in edited versions of the classics.

Like De Mille, the second group of filmmakers involved in epic cinema during the thirties and forties attempts a more serious, albeit less successful reading of history. One is more conscious of Hollywood's role as a cultural intermediary in *Marie Antoinette, A Tale of Two Cities,* and *Gone with the Wind,* and in biographies starring Paul Muni and Edward G. Robinson. They are studied, static, populist studies of history that bear a strong resemblance to the English quality film pioneered by Alexander Korda, but they lack the theatrical cutting edge of the English productions. *Gone with the Wind* may be the best example of Hollywood experiments to elevate its intrinsically middlebrow scripts to high-art pictorialism. The undeniable erotic chemistry of Gable and Vivien Leigh saves a project that has the heaviness of a De Mille epic with none of his kinky, production-value excesses. The film shows poor continuity, which is sometimes relieved, though not fulfilled, by its more celebrated color photography. The attraction for the three-strip Technicolor process lies in its lush tonal scaling even though it led to a more archaic, self-consciously painterly style of filmmaking. The sensuality and decorativeness of the hues in acclaimed early Technicolor spectaculars such as *Becky Sharp, The Garden of Allah,* and *Gone with the Wind* reproduce painterly gradations that overwhelm the eye with their chromatic brilliance. The style would be most advantageously exploited in musicals, and though they lacked the dramatic vigor that Renoir brought to his celebration of postimpressionism in *French Cancan,* James Agee's review of *Till the Clouds Roll By* noted their unnerving and not unappealing effect. The richness of the colors underscores Hollywood's equation of color film and pictorial dramatization, as if the initial experiments in hand-tinting individual shots by pioneers such as Méliès and Griffith were an attempt to conceive their films as paintings and not as isolated, symbolic effects. The three-strip color method renders its scenes as if they were slides; actors look as though they have been washed in a color solution; an attempt is made to match the radiance of their stars to a period and style of dress in which their beauty can shine. In *Gone with the Wind* Vivien Leigh's opalescent eyes imbue the scene painting with a dramatic sparkle that few Hollywood performers were able to bring to their impersonations of historical and literary figures.

Lee Garmes is credited with photographing the first third of *Gone with the Wind,* and there is ample evidence of his noted atmospheric tonality. His pioneering use of Mazda bulbs to achieve greater tonality resulted in some of the darkest mood pictures in Hollywood, especially in his collaborations with Ben Hecht. In *Zoo in Budapest* he created one of the jewels of thirties photography, where the park setting for the zoo is transformed into an Edenesque haven for the romance of Loretta Young and Gene Raymond through his brilliantly separated, miniscule lighting units. In the opening landscape shots in *Gone with the Wind,* Garmes uses the three-strip color to create a magical foreground landscape; he complained of Selznick's ideas of postcard cinematography, but his short focal range creates an appropriately idealized setting for Scarlett's romance. The benefit ball for the Confederacy develops primarily through the chromatic interplay between the bright colors of the crowd and the black suit and dress of Rhett and Scarlett. The predominantly lighter hues in the first part of the film appear to culminate in the extended crane shot of Scarlett searching for Ashley among the wounded soldiers, in which the blue-gray colors in the foreground are replaced by the darker patches of gray and brown in the background. The return to Tara, highlighted by Robert Edmond Jones's red backdrop, shows a penchant for theatrical decor characteristic of the more cramped staging and the golden, coppery pastels in the second part. The film personifies the historical and emotional undercurrents of history through its layers of colors, a sumptuous array of bonbons wrapped in blue, amber, and red. It is a precursor of both the more tranquil, dramatically harmonious color arrangements in the musicals of the fifties as well as the moody tones and pictorial eclecticism of the seventies with its own *Gone with the Wind, Heaven's Gate.*

### Shoeshine–General Della Rovere

Of the three major directors identified with the birth of the Italian humanist cinema (De Sica, Visconti, and Rossellini), De Sica is the most conventional and straightforward in documenting the central conflicts of postwar Italian society. His major works of this period—*Shoeshine, The Bicycle Thief,* and *Umberto D*—do not attempt any radical treatment of the characters or story line. Their dramatic intensity derives from the strict adherence of De Sica and scriptwriter Zavattini to the protagonists' fight to maintain their personal dignity amid the economic turmoil. The humanism of these films is not of a sophisticated artistic form in which profound philosophic questions are raised; the characters of the young boys, the father and son, and Umberto move us in the way their basic needs are rebuffed by an impervious social environment. The films do not probe their landscapes with the same microscopic eye that characterizes the naturalist movement in nineteenth-century literature: they present a limited number of characters and plot contrivances in order to emphasize the protagonists' fight against a callous, materialist society. Whereas Renoir sees the need for love and personal and emotional expressiveness as the decisive elements of his settings, De Sica stresses his characters' moral persistency. Unlike Renoir's involvement in the characters' emotional discords, their precarious feelings and instinctive reactions, De Sica's films, by documenting the conflict between personal honor and the realities of a postwar environment, are a testament to the characters' humanity. While Renoir's primitivism revolves around the need to assert one's emotional independence in the least propitious surroundings, De Sica's humanism is manifest in the exigence of the relationships between the two boys in *Shoeshine,* the father and son in *The Bicycle Thief,* and Umberto and his dog in *Umberto D.* In Renoir the emphasis is on personalism—remaining faithful to one's emotional needs even as the social order is overturned; in De Sica humanism is conceived as the nexus of society—the spark to the brotherhood of man.

De Sica's films are not imbued with the revolutionary fervor of Renoir's early sound films and seem to exist in a middle ground between Rossellini's metaphysics and Visconti's poetics, but they cannot be dismissed as dogmatic. The major actors in the three films do not betray their awareness of the camera, and it is to the credit of De Sica and Zavattini that the pivotal dramatic confrontations do not seem forced; the viciousness that overtakes one of the boys, the stealing of the father's bicycle, leading him to attempt to steal one, and Umberto's inability to feed his dog appear as a slice of life out of the tragedy of postwar Europe. De Sica has opened a window on one corner apartment in an alienating urban environment; in journeying with his protagonists through their makeshift world, one clearly recognizes the perils of their fight to retain their humanity. In De Sica's films the individual can only hope to retain his personal dignity, because once that is lost one becomes infected by society's callousness; in Renoir's primeval, psychological entanglements, life is not worth living unless one is emotionally liberated. De Sica's films are not as intense, as psychologically exhaustive as the works of Von Stroheim, but their humanism records the pain and frustration of the individual without the cumbersome social rhetoric and transparently virtuous heroes that mar similar Russian films of the thirties.

Luchino Visconti is less interested in the social pitfalls that challenge the individual's humanism and spiritual integrity. Yet of the three architects of the Italian humanist cinema, Visconti remained the most consistent in style and theme. De Sica would reject the moral constancy of *Shoeshine*, *The Bicycle Thief*, and *Umberto D* for the comic absurdities of *Miracle in Milan* while Rossellini would renew his quest for spiritual truth in his historical projects of the late sixties and seventies; but Visconti, from *Ossessione* through *Conversation Piece*, searches for transcendent human emotions as an expression of the mythic core of his drama and characters. *Ossessione* makes for an intriguing comparison with the American version. *The Postman Always Rings Twice* is truer to Cain's gritty mood and his virulent, emotionally descriptive prose; John Garfield and Lana Turner are Depression-era antagonists whose instincts tell them to get what they can; Visconti, however, prefers to expand the characters' romantic vibrancy; his leads appear to have stepped out of the pages of an epic literary romance. The story remains too intrinsically melodramatic for Visconti to distinguish their passions in a more psychologically complex framework. There is one arresting scene that suggests the more objective style of Visconti's later films. Sitting alone in the kitchen, a pile of dishes strewn over the table, the heroine attempts to eat but falls asleep; by then drawing back the camera, Visconti subtly dramatizes the hindrances she faces in renouncing her abject existence. His leads, particularly Massimo Girotti, wearing a T-shirt in which he compares favorably to Gable and Brando, express a pressing, sexual tension that will be fleetingly explored by the movies in the fifties and will become a theme central to the sixties.

*La terra trema* remains a high point in the Italian humanist cinema. Visconti decisively juxtaposes his characters' spiritual integrity as fishermen to the harsh, overpowering force of nature. Though he draws us into their impoverished homes and occasionally uses a hand-held camera to move through the crowds of fishermen at work on the shore, his style is rendered most poignantly in his shots of the women in black shawls looking out at the unfathomable boundaries of the water. It is a film that is most impressive and moving in long shot, presenting a unifying image of the Sicilians in pursuit of their daily livelihood as a symbolic, epic struggle. When the family's fortune declines after they buy a boat, Visconti's characters ramble too long about their mournful condition, but as prolix as these scenes are, one respects Visconti's interest in the romantic discursiveness of these primitives, who by the very nature of their existence become heroic and inevitably tragic figures.

If *La terra trema* leads one to think that Visconti has uncovered new ground in adapting several aspects of epic literature to the Italian humanist cinema, *Senso* reveals Visconti as a man of the theater whose dramatic vision lies in his scenic opulence. This is evident in staging the first scene in the opera house and in representative actions such as Alida Valli's excursion across the battlefield and her walk through the streets after she has denounced her lover. Visconti's visual tapestry is often breathtaking in capturing the romantic breadth of his characters imprisoned within a civil war—whether in his close-ups of the loutish mannerisms of Farley Granger or in the sensually sculptured face of Valli, who reads her tragic fate in the eyes of her lover. But instead of penetrating his resplendent exteriors and showing his characters' social and sexual identity destroyed by the war, he maintains a distant point of view in telling his story. Unlike Mizoguchi, whose calligraphic exteriors presage the conflict between the impassivity of society and nature and individual longing, Visconti's decision to shape the aesthetic of his films along lines similar to the thunderous passions of Italian opera will create more problems for him than is evident in the lovely, supine *Senso*.

Visconti's films are the most removed from the realist or humanist vision of the Italian cinema, but Rossellini's films reassert the validity of these terms. In the humanistic films of De Sica a classic, didactic narrative distinguishes the problems facing man in postwar society as a testing of his personal honor. There is an ambience of distrust and languor; the pernicious nature of society is not seen as resulting from the war but from the dehumanizing, materialist scope of a modern, urban environment. Rossellini adopts a more intense, metaphysical point of view in rejecting the classic protagonists and visual compactness of De Sica's films. In *Open City*, and more so in *Paisan*, he conceives his destitute landscapes as an index of the spiritual hazards facing his characters; although this perspective is most apparent in *Flowers of St. Francis*, it is crucial to an appreciation of these two earlier films and to his position as the original voice of humanism in the Italian cinema.

*Open City* is more exemplary of the nationalist sentiments that inspired films like Pudovkin's *Mother* and Renoir's *This Land Is Mine*. In Rossellini's film Anna Magnani's glowing dramatic presence and that of the underground fighters, particularly the priest, express their intrinsic humanity in a way not unlike De Sica's protagonists. The major difference is that Rossellini's film accentuates the desperate conditions that impinge on their humanism as both individuals and partisans united against the Nazis. Unlike Pudovkin's *Mother*, in which one's empathy for the simple country folk caught up in the fighting is inspired by the devastating images of the massacres, *Open City* explains its conflicts in terms of the characters' emotional commitment. It is less aesthetic, less schematic than Pudovkin's film; Rossellini perceives the violence of the Nazi occupation in the tragedy of the girl seduced by the Nazi officer, in Magnani's hysterical outburst running down the streets as she is gunned down, and in the priest's self-absolution before he is executed.

*Paisan* is a more awkward film than *Open City*. Rossellini's sets, if they can be called that, make the backgrounds in Renoir's *Toni* look like meticulous recreations of the pastoral landscapes of eighteenth-century French painters. His characters so clearly lack any thespian training that De Sica's nonprofessional actors seem models of studied elegance. However, if we are to make any sense of Italy's postwar cinema, *Paisan* should be recognized as the landmark work because of the absence of any dramatic intricacies; it fulfills a visual prose style that delineates the spiritual renaissance man must undergo if he is to survive the war. If Rossellini is indeed the father of the humanist movement, then we must give higher priority to *Paisan* than to *Open City* or to the films of De Sica. The question that Rossellini raises does not concern aesthetics or dramaturgy; it is a matter of how and why man is to live. This change in the social implications of the movies results from Rossellini's realization of the moral crisis facing man in the aftermath of World War II. Like Renoir's first sound films, in which the rustic, primitive settings reflect his characters' emotional upheavals, Rossellini's visually impoverished stage exists as a physical correlative of the spiritual rebirth that faces his characters. Figures like the underground fighters or the black American soldier live in an intermediate world, the former always on the move in order to stay alive, the latter, a twilight figure who seems as misplaced in the ravaged city as he would be on another planet. *Paisan* can be criticized as inarticulate and dramatically oversimplified; but as students of the movies who see the medium operating in the sphere of ideas and intellectual history, we need be more sensitive to the film's spiritual equations. The unsatisfying quality of the vignettes that make up *Paisan* can be readily perceived, but one must first admit the way the film forces its audience to consider the natural world in an entirely new framework. It will be in Rossellini's succeeding films that he will face the challenge of dramatically justifying the spiritually idealistic form of *Paisan*.

Rossellini confronts these questions and raises new ones in his films with Ingrid Bergman. In *Stromboli* Bergman's character of the refugee who marries a poor fisherman in order to escape from a detention center embodies the spiritual conflicts that are sketched out in Rossellini's previous films. By using a narrator Rossellini validates the realism of his backgrounds while asserting the epic quality of Bergman's journey of self-discovery. The story's dramatic simplicity clarifies the psychological turmoils she suffers, from her feeling of isolation as she enters the fishermen's homes to her flirtations with one of the natives and to her moral rebirth when she tries to escape from the village.

There are two major reasons Rossellini succeeds with this strikingly simple parable. First is the brevity and cohesiveness of his story. The most visually refined sequence in the film and one of the most highly stylized he has attempted at this point in his career—the netting of the fish—captures the dynamism and skill required of the fishermen and the brutalizing nature of their work; it also pinpoints Bergman's further alienation from her husband and life in the village. The second reason the film succeeds lies in Bergman's performance. Her forlorn condition is intertwined with her extraordinary erotic presence; her existence among the natives documents her separateness from their folklore while awakening the warm, sensual feelings that have been repressed by the war and by her stay in the detention center. *Intermezzo* introduced a romantic force that even Hollywood's puritan code could not effectively subdue while *Stromboli* studies the cadences, the raw power, and vulnerability of Bergman's incandescent street angel.

In *Viaggio in Italia* Rossellini uses his ever present primitive backgrounds, but instead of the transients in his earlier films, George Sanders and Ingrid Bergman play a rich married couple who are drifting apart. Though several scenes predate Antonioni's interest in the way the furnishings in a home are symptomatic of the characters' insecurity, Rossellini changes his focus to a modernist landscape of estrangement without, however, a complementary change in his dramatic strategies. The folk elements and simplified narrative form of *Stromboli* led Bergman to question her emotional and spiritual feelings. But in his picture of the indolence of the rich Rossellini is too quick to point out their spiritual nullity so that one has no understanding of how they relate to their financially secure world. The sudden reconfirmation of their love during a religious festival seems to inject the very note of contrivance that Rossellini's first films avoided.

Among the changes in the styles of De Sica, Visconti, and Rossellini, De Sica's was the most radical and his last efforts, the least rewarding. But some measure of the cogency of his first films and their influence on Rossellini's later films is seen in *General Della Rovere*. It is a key transitional film for Rossellini; while those who had studied under him and those who had studied him were creating new, more abstract dimensions in filmmaking, he looked to the future by returning to the past. Sergio Amidei's script, like his blueprints for *Open City*, *Paisan*, and *Stromboli*, follows a character's moral fulfillment within a disordered, dehumanized world. Rossellini may have partly adopted this framework because of De Sica's characterization of a roguish anti-hero who knows he is weak and who, until the last scene in the film, allows others to concern themselves with matters such as honor and self-respect. He gives a great performance, but much of the credit must be given to Rossellini, who carefully plays De Sica's cynicism and aristocratic facade against the grim background of the Nazi occupation. He brilliantly extends De Sica's classic point of view by adopting a straightforward narrative that honors personal dignity and not self-expression or self-awareness as the film's central theme. In one of the most spellbinding moments in the postwar Italian cinema, De Sica, awaiting execution, awakens to the sound of the Allied raid. He shivers, he cowers, as fearful as the other prisoners who begin madly knocking on their cell walls. But then he realizes that he has an opportunity to put on the mask of one who is superior to the chaos of war and runs out of his cell and orders the prisoners silenced. It is a moment of extraordinary psychological lucidity in which Rossellini reasserts the rediscovery of man as the basic impetus of the Italian cinema. And then, from General Della Rovere to Socrates, Pascal, Louis XIV ...

## The Reckless Moment–Red Beard

The last films of Max Ophüls and the incomparable stylistic mastery that characterizes the revelation of Japanese culture in the work of Yasujiro Ozu, Kenji Mizoguchi, and Akira Kurosawa underscore the outstanding diversity of moviemaking styles in the postwar cinema. The period from 1945 through the early sixties has acquired a textbook resonance of realism, whether in the Italian derivatives that take us from early Rossellini through Antonioni's middle-period maturation or in the American film with its various shadings of psychological discontent in *film noir* and with the adaptations of the theatrical expressionism of Miller, Williams, and Inge. One can, for the present, interpret the wide-screen epics and the retrogressive classicism exhibited in the cinematography of Harry Stradling, Leon Shamroy, and Robert Surtees—the three tone masters of the epic musicals, love stories, and adventure sagas of the fifties—as a reaction to the small, black-and-white, dramatic intensity of television. The films of Ophüls, Ozu, and Mizoguchi represent the artistic apogee in the departure from critical social and technological developments; they confront the past in a way that achieves further elaboration in the English comedy film, in the kinetic musical collaborations of Gene Kelly, Michael Kidd, and Stanley Donen, and in John Ford's last successful essays in romance and history.

One critic has argued that Ophüls's American films are superior to his work in the French cinema, yet this point of view seems peculiar at best. In America he was unable to imbue the heroines and romantic entanglements in films like *The Reckless Moment* and *Caught* with the effervescent flourishes that mark his best films. The suburban world that Joan Bennett inhabits in *The Reckless Moment* has none of the glitter of Ophüls's French films; her estranged housewife functions as a reverent image for all daydreaming soap-opera fans. *Caught* is a more intelligent film in which Barbara Bel Geddes' shy, unassuming heroine discovers the tragic disparity between the ideal and realistic nature of romance in America. Like Joan Fontaine in *Letter from an Unknown Woman* her fantasies are both encouraged and eventually repressed by society. When Bel Geddes looks at advertisements in a magazine, these elegant images are identified as her fantasy. Ophüls then parodies their everyday embodiment and consequences as Bel Geddes' model is complimented by a woman and is then invited by a man to a party. One of the film's most effective moments shows Ophüls's ability to compress the expansive treatment of love in his European films. It takes place in the doctors' office where Bel Geddes worked after a brief modeling career and a disastrous marriage. As the doctors discuss their feelings for her, the aloof movement of the camera between the desks of the two doctors and the one recently vacated by Bel Geddes offers a poetic, distancing commentary about their unrequited love for her.

*Letter from an Unknown Woman* represents one of the most singular European stylizations of romance in the American film. The film opens on a moving carriage with the camera tracking its movement as the carriage comes into the foreground: this introductory scene will also figure in the film's final fade-out. As Joan Fontaine's letters to Louis Jourdan are read, the past is represented by scenes such as the changing of her parents' residence and the one in which she listens to Jourdan play the piano as she sits on the swing. Ophüls uses his moving camera as a valid metaphor of Fontaine's adolescence, shaping and perceiving her surrounding world through its constant state of motion. Her febrile, romantic memories are further reflected in the way Ophüls isolates Fontaine and Jourdan in a picture-book world. When they sit inside a booth and watch the projection of slides of foreign countries, Ophüls uses this setting to show how Fontaine's love transforms her environment into a romantic fantasy. Spying on Jourdan's amorous adventures, Fontaine crouches in a corner at the top of the staircase and sees him kissing a woman who then enters his apartment. Ophüls uses the same camera setup when Fontaine becomes Jourdan's lover, and thus captures the subjective and objective aspects of Fontaine's love for Jourdan.

In *The Earrings of Madame De* Ophüls enhances the ability of the moving camera to convey the ardor and passion of his heroine. While Danielle Darrieux's wardrobe and jewelry represent the transparent adornments of her aristocratic society, Darrieux's character as an adventurous, reckless woman, magically transfixed by Ophüls's camera permutations, expresses its romantic permanence. Ophüls's emphasis on the comically chaotic aspects of a world in pursuit of romance also characterizes the routines of Darrieux's husband as he runs back and forth to the train station or as he resolves Darrieux's negligent handling of her jewelry. The ultimate expression of this period is the love affair of Darrieux and De Sica wherein Ophüls idealizes their feelings by dissolving on the seemingly endless number of waltzes they dance. Ophüls's translucent image of a fading romanticism, which seems to mirror the prose of Schnitzler, is less successful in his adaptation of Schnitzler's *La Ronde*. Schnitzler's play works as a "snapshot" of the truancy of late nineteenth-century Europe. Ophüls's film, though faithful to the play and highlighted by Anton Walbrook's ringmaster, lacks the astringency of Schnitzler's work. *Le Plaisir* is a better example of Ophüls's unique affinity with an expression of romanticism as one of childlike abandonment and a wholly uncompromised sense of personal fulfillment.

Of his three late masterworks, *Le Plaisir* is the most unbridled in punctuating the energy of its characters and their giddy, make-believe world. Its three vignettes allow Ophüls to create a more densely abstract picture of love and romance as exemplified by his moving camera. The constant flurry of motion in the nightclub and museum and Simone Simon's desperation as the love-struck model are invariably characterized through his sweeping camera movements.

His protagonists are not so much personalized by his moving camera as they are encompassed by its unimpeded force: the moving camera functions as the invisible architect of the emotional labyrinth from which his characters cannot escape. Their frenzied actions are like a dancer's pirouettes with the exception that in Ophüls's film their ebullient playacting and romantic posing unleash a flurry of kinetic convolutions that afford slight opportunity for the more conventional aspects of story theater.

*Lola Montès* is a meditation on his characters' romantic adventures, set against a richly orchestrated social backdrop. The settings convey a greater irony about their identity, from the coach in which Peter Ustinov's circus ringmaster proposes that Lola join his company to the final lineup of men waiting to kiss her. Its dazzling kinetic sweep is not unlike that of *Le Plaisir* in which Ophüls's moving camera seemed to personify his characters' romantic impulses. With the infamous Lola as the transcendent object of his memoir of fin de siècle Europe, Ophüls presents her numerous liaisons in a more pointedly theatrical, operatic style. Lola's recognition of her erotic appeal after her mother's lover has kissed her, like the ringing of the bell at the opera house to signify a further development in her adventures, underscores the contrivances of the theater through the changing parameters of the film medium. The camera elevates the passions generated by Lola into a buoyant study of playacting and reckless love in which the elusive Lola becomes the phantomesque ideal of Ophüls's make-believe world.

Ophüls's films are a classic statement of romanticism as an intensely felt period of one's life and as a highly charged period of history when a belief in the purity of one's emotions and the need for a radical change in the social order ruled out any hope of moderation. In turning to the Japanese cinema and the films of its supreme classicist, Yasujiro Ozu, one not only discovers Ophüls's stylistic opposite, but also the most lucid form of classicism the movies have known. Unlike the first films of Rossellini, there is an unmistakable maturity in the translation of transcendent Japanese themes and emotions in Ozu's work in the thirties and forties; hence, it seems that there is no better place to begin our appreciation of the Japanese cinema than in the work of one of its veteran directors whom one can review with the knowledge that a majority of his work has been seen abroad.

Throughout his distinguished career, Ozu was primarily concerned with the unity and depth of family relationships. In his postwar films, which take one from *Late Spring* through *An Autumn Afternoon* and which coalesce as one family's saga, the tension between parents and children is handled with an austere, majestic subtlety. His first experiments on this subject are more tense and melodramatic, but they are filled with such keen psychological nuances that one cannot fail to admit the authority and steadfast humanism of Ozu's Japanese sensibility. Ozu's silent film, *I Was Born But...*, is a bittersweet study of a young boy's iconoclasm and how it irrevocably alters the family's stability. Ozu's deft editing first draws our attention to the comic tension between father and son, but he then suggests that the child's insouciance cannot be dismissed in the casual manner of Westerners admonishing their rebellious children. In *Good Morning*, his remake of *I Was Born But...*, the boy's aloofness grows out of his desire for a television; the verbal repartee is not as fluid as in the original (although a silent film, the emphasis on the titles and the child's cleverness make it a disguised sound film), yet Ozu's glistening compositions conceive the family squabbles as secondary to the serenity of his Japanese cityscape. In *Passing Fancy* the relationship between the indigent father and the son who is sent away to school is treated in a more tragic manner. The father is a good-natured loafer, but one who is ever aware of the emptiness in his life created by his son's absence. There are several emotionally riveting moments as the father explores his feelings for his absent son, but they lack the cumulative dramatic force in Ozu's later films.

In *The Only Son* and *There Was a Father* there is a greater interest in examining the torment that results from the separation of parent and child; in his postwar films Ozu will repress these emotional currents. The two films develop the simplest of stories in which the poor, widowed parents devote all their strength to the son's well-being; the story seems as universal as that of the ostracized samurai. But Ozu is not concerned with thematic complexities that would exaggerate the parents' hardships or the son's fight for survival in the big city. His interest lies in studying the mood of despair as the overriding feature in the relationship of the parent and child. In *The Only Son* the mother, who has not seen her son for several years, visits him in the city. Before her visit, one realizes that she has happily accepted the additional work that has enabled her to support her son's education and that she has changed her original feeling that it is best to accept one's place in society. The son meets her at the station, and in their walk to his home they pass a lot of poverty-ridden homes that seem to fade away in the light of the bright afternoon sun. The quiet, meek son who was introduced in the first part of the story as a bright, ambitious boy who wanted to make his way in the world tells his mother that he has married. As they continue their walk through the poverty-stricken area, the son's revelation, obsequious in tone, is secondary to the way Ozu films their receding figures amid the myriad clotheslines and desolate houses.

The true wisdom of this film, Ozu's ineffable grasp of things and values uniquely Japanese, is manifest in the moral lesson that awaits the mother. During her brief stay a neighbor is taken ill, and the son gives all of his earnings to the neighbor's wife to pay for her husband's convalescence. The sequence does not emphasize the heroic virtues of the son but his conquering the more difficult problem of becoming a man; he recognizes his duty to care for the family who has suffered with him in their ramshackle environment. Although the mother's reaction is one of the utmost gratification, the last scene reveals Ozu's understanding of the irresoluble schism between social conformity and personal desires. The mother is working at an estate with a friend who asks how she found her son. She replies that he is a great success, but as she returns to her work she breaks out in tears. Ozu's camera then pans from the mother's wailing figure to the gates that surround the estate. What Ozu shows in this last scene is that the son's recognition of his obligation to his fellow man cannot negate the impact of the mother's emotional and financial sacrifices. The mother certainly wished for her son to become a moral man, but far greater was her hope that he become a social success because of the time and effort it demanded of her. In his last shot of the gates Ozu presents a symbol of twofold significance. One is that the anguish the mother has suffered must be repressed; and two, that her enclosed social status, leading to her years of work and ensuing grief, may be an insurmountable barrier.

*There Was a Father* is the father's side of the story, but directed some six years after *The Only Son*; the drama is more complex, the tone more pessimistic. Chishu Ryu, who is to Ozu what Lillian Gish is to Griffith and the tramp is to Chaplin, plays a teacher who leads a group of students on an outing during which one of the boys drowns. Ryu blames himself for the boy's death and decides to forsake teaching. Before placing his son in a boarding school and moving to Tokyo where he will work as a clerk, there is a brief, highly emotional scene in which the father and son go fishing. The image of these two figures with their long rods in the stream is a memory we know will be cherished by father and son because of its freshness, its exhilarating purity, and its isolation. The father tells his son to work hard and become a better teacher than he could have been. The son promises to do well.

The years pass and the son has a reunion with his father. Again they go fishing, and at dinner one evening the son expresses his desire to move to Tokyo and live with his father, explaining that their being together means more to him than anything else. Ryu, however, is adamant; he tells his son to continue his work in the provinces and reiterates the idea that the son must succeed for both of them. What enhances the tragic intensity of the son's pleading is that we have come to realize that Ryu has touched people in a way that the most brilliant teacher could not. Ryu, in effect, is the son of *The Only Son*, some twenty years older. The day after a party given by his former students, Ryu complains of fatigue, and in a scene whose emotional terror is experienced all the more directly because of its brevity and the meaning of the reunion to father and son, Ryu dies. The son then returns to the provinces with his bride, the daugher of his father's friend whom he had promised his father he would marry. But whereas in the last scene of *The Only Son* Ozu interrelates the mother's grief over her son's social failing to the intractability of her social standing, in *There Was a Father* the sorrow is understood through the son's feelings. He is not looking forward to his work as a teacher or living with his young, pretty wife, but turns to her and says, "My father was such a good man," and then stares out the window. His grief is personal, overpowering, suggesting the gulf that will always exist between the newlyweds.

Although *The Only Son* and *There Was a Father* are relatively early films of Ozu and are not imbued with the greater rigors and truths of his postwar films, they evoke sentiment so unsentimentally and interpret the conflict between personal longing and social conformity in such a forceful manner that comparable efforts like *Penny Serenade*, *La Maternelle*, *Make Way for Tomorrow*, and the "Apu Trilogy" are simply not in the same league. One really must talk of Chaplin's *The Kid*, Langdon's *Three's a Crowd*, and maybe De Sica's *The Bicycle Thief*. That, however, is another matter.

But as deftly constructed as his early films are, as sage as he is in his dramatic understatement, Ozu would not deserve recognition as the great Japanese filmmaker, a place Griffith occupies in the American cinema and Eisenstein in the Russian, if the style of his postwar films did not reflect his appreciation of the intransigence of family life and the splendor and significance of the "appearance of things." His introductory or exterior shots, and those he uses in a coda, not only suggest a mood, but meticulously define the spatial configurations in the family living room, the garden, the office where the father works. It is not until *Tokyo Story* that Ozu decides that even the slightest camera movement, which he has used with the utmost restraint since *I Was Born But...*, has no place in his films. For the duration of his career Ozu's camera never once intrudes on his ceremonial compositions; it is as if he thought an incongruous note of familiarity would be introduced into the hieratic nature of Japanese society that he so diligently records. As an extension of his treatment of the family as the most essential, most durable, most representative unit of society, his stationary camera works as a stylistic device, a technical correlative that embodies the artifice, the order, the luminosity, and the symmetry of Japanese society.

Ozu's severe yet poetic compositional style is as keenly felt in his exteriors as it is in interior scenes in which the characters' slight movements and reserved manners sustain his pictorial formalism. The story of these films does not greatly vary; with Ozu as perhaps with no other filmmaker one can say that he was making the same film whether it was about a father trying to marry off his daughter (*Early Spring, Equinox Flower, An Autumn Afternoon*), a mother attempting to find a suitor for her daughter (*Late Autumn, The Flavor of Green Tea over Rice*), or the death of a parent (*Tokyo Story, Early Autumn*). In choosing the family as the single most dominant symbol of the sanctity of the past, Ozu identifies its permanence through his stationary camera and exacting compositions. Whether it is the characters' speech or dress that isolates one aspect of their social identity as they sit around the dinner table or the composition that denotes the encompassing order and gracefulness of their homes, his dramatic and visual motifs reassert the structural uniformity of his society and the family as the most vibrant symbol of the ineradicable continuity of Japanese life.

With the exception of *The Toda Brothers and Sisters*—with its saucy, comical flavor—and *Tokyo Twilight*—whose melodramatic plot includes an abortion—Ozu's postwar work seems to play in one key. At the same time that we are spellbound by the somber beauty of the Japanese home, we realize its repressive features. Though his films present cruel, insensitive characters, he refuses to point to any one individual or social phenomenon as the cause of the tragedy that threatens the family's stability. In *Tokyo Story* when the niece tells Setsuko Hara that she is the lone member of the family who has not acted in a callous manner toward her parents, Hara replies that since she is widowed, she has not been tested in the same manner as the other family members. In *Floating Weeds* the young boy's reaction to being told that the man whom he thought was his uncle is his father may strike us as harsh. But the son's words are softened by the oppressive brown textures, by the unsettling metallic sound of what one thinks is two stones being knocked together but which one later learns is the sound of a clock, and by the casual affairs of the members of the acting company of which the boy's father is the director. There may be a failure to recognize the authority of family life among the younger generation as, for example, in *Early Autumn* with the characters of the daughter who dates various Americans and the young boys who wear sweat shirts and baseball caps instead of kimonos. Ozu, however, does not so much emphasize their insensitivity as he does the parents' increasing isolation as they marry off their children. In *Equinox Flower* the father recognizes the modernization of marriage customs as his daughter chooses her mate; inevitably, his fate is that of Chishu Ryu in *An Autumn Afternoon*, who sits in the kitchen with the lights turned off after seeing his son married. One may be tempted to cite *Tokyo Story*, *Early Summer*, and *Early Autumn* as more profound in their tragic pessimism, but this is not to suggest that his other films are not stamped with his formidable humanism. As a poetic hymn to the uniquely Japanese nuances of everyday life, Ozu's achievement remains unparalleled in film history: the realization of a nation's uniform moral structure through the unifying structural properties of the film medium. No other filmmaker had the same opportunity, but then no other filmmaker, harvesting the fruits of his long-term partnerships in writing, production, and acting, had so clear an understanding of classicism as it is manifest in modern history and art.

The pleasures of Mizoguchi films such as *Ugetsu*, *Sansho the Bailiff*, *New Tales of the Taira Clan*, *Princess Yang Kwei Fei*, and *A Story from Chikamatsu* lie in a different area of film aesthetics. Among Mizoguchi's earlier films one notes his special sympathies for the fate of women and the spiritual quintessence of Japanese culture as reflected in the stately, foreboding design. Both these themes are central to his development as an artist, yet in early works like *Sisters of the Gion*, *Osaka Elegy*, and *The Story of the Last Chrysanthemums* these themes do not receive the masterly irony and compositional depth that characterize his postwar flowering. *Sisters of the Gion* and *Osaka Elegy* show different aspects of Mizoguchi's treatment of women as the doomed heroines of Japanese history. A majority of the camera setups in the most dramatic moments of *Sisters of the Gion* approach the sisters as if looking through a window, suggesting their isolation and their inability to surmount both a temporary and transcendent condition. *Osaka Elegy* is a far more handsome, stylish film. Its concise melodramatic delineation of its characters and milieu lends itself to comparison with similar treatments in the American and French cinema. *The Story of the Last Chrysanthemums* is a more austerely crafted work; the composition shows a more severe treatment of the characters and their fixed identity within the story's theatrical framework. The Mizoguchi motifs that will be crystallized in his postwar films are clearly in evidence, but with its piecemeal dramatic pacing and its strict attention to the gloss of Japanese design—first revealed in its initial glimpses of the stage and culminating in the final procession through the river—the film seems to underscore the ascetic, introspective tendencies of the Japanese cinema one finds in the films of Gosho and Naruse. There is an acute tragic undercurrent about Mizoguchi's fidelity to tradition implied in both the look and actions of his characters, but Mizoguchi has yet to achieve the moral and stylistic control that will enable the filmgoer to experience the tragedy as unfolding within the space of his film drama.

*Ugetsu,* like Kurosawa's *Rashomon,* was one of the celebrated Japanese films that first impressed Western audiences with the original cadence of Japanese filmmaking. Whereas Kurosawa's adaptation of the stories of Ryunosuke Akutagawa illuminates a dreamlike nimbus and a pictorial formalism that are departures from his more familiar tales of revolt and personal redemption, *Ugetsu* distills the paramount themes of Mizoguchi's career. His protagonists are two simple farmers whose families are torn apart by civil war. One of them wishes for success as a military hero, and his unlikely triumphs are ironically juxtaposed to his wife's misfortunes as she is raped, becomes a prostitute, and is later reunited with her husband whom she confronts with their miserably incongruous situations. The other one, more fastidious in the support of his family, is entranced by the spirit of Machiko Kyo. The adventures of the first farmer enable Mizoguchi to expose the folly and tragicomedy of war, while his neighbor's fantasy romance expresses Mizoguchi's understanding of man's smallness in the face of transcendent ritual and his attraction for the grand passions that ultimately remain beyond his understanding. In *Sansho the Bailiff* Mizoguchi's tragic fatalism is again manifest in the way his camera presents the son's arduous search for his mother against the background of the land. Few filmmakers have so strongly emphathized with a protagonist's need for the most basic family attachments while simultaneously evoking the overpowering presence of nature. The primeval countryside against which the feudal warfare is played becomes a metaphor for the unending barriers that stand in the way of the son's reunion with his mother, just as the atmospheric rendition of the forests and lakes in *Ugetsu* diminish the personal losses that the two families suffer.

In *New Tales of the Taira Clan* Mizoguchi undertakes a more heroic, personalized study of the individual confronting a highly schematic society. His use of color serves as a romantic complement to the film's dramatic conflicts without compromising the dynamic interplay between his characters and history. Unlike *Princess Yang Kwei Fei* in which the crystalline color arrangements are seen as the most important feature of medieval court life, the bright colors and extensive rituals in *New Tales of the Taira Clan* distinguish both the elegance of this period of feudal Japan and its accompanying restrictive, autocratic rule. In order to preserve the honor and stateliness of court life, the Taira clan must challenge the warring priest class which has abused its power. Before the final confrontation between Raizo Ichikawa as the reigning member of the Taira clan and the priests, Mizoguchi has only hinted at the deceitfulness and savagery that have enabled the priests to maintain their rule. But in this decisive meeting he brilliantly exploits the terror of feudal Japan as thousands of rampaging priests are met by Ichikawa. One expects them to butcher Ichikawa and begin an unprecedented slaughter, but Ichikawa resists their power and moral inviolability by shooting down their emblem. Mizoguchi not only confers to the Taira clan their moral and political claim to the throne, but exposes the warrior priests' dependency on their religious icons. The rule that they have tyrannically imposed and which they have seen as a divine right is shown to be an archaic symbol. Thus in subtly conveying the conviction of the warrior priests, Ichikawa's destruction of the emblem becomes all the more magnificent and meaningful. Though the film's color proportions are among the most evocative applied on film, Ichikawa's unfocused character denies *New Tales of the Taira Clan* the permanence of a classic. A more decisive social and dramatic tension is needed in the juxtaposition of the priests to the Taira clan and in the identification of Ichikawa's heroic destiny.

In *Princess Yang Kwei Fei* and *A Story from Chikamatsu*, Mizoguchi establishes a tragic three-part equation involving the unwavering formalism of Japanese art, a static social order, and the lack of personal expression among its people. In *Princess Yang Kwei Fei* the natural world is translated in color equations in which the omnipresent warfare is seen as the most formidable aspect of feudal Japan, while the tragic love affair of the king and princess redeems the repressive morality surrounding court life. *Gate of Hell* is honored for its classic portrayal of a Japanese code of honor, but *Princess Yang Kwei Fei* seems more faithful and much more extravagant because of the acquiescent nature of the king and princess, exquisitely rendered by Masayuki Mori and Michiko Kyo (the beleaguered couple in *Rashomon* and the lovers in *Ugetsu*). In *Gate of Hell* the protagonists die because of the oppressive hierarchy of their society; in *Princess Yang Kwei Fei* their death is an idyllic extension of their identity within a labyrinthian world of manners. It is not, however, as complex as *New Tales of the Taira Clan*; the period of history it animates is structured on a moral and ethical system that is not undergoing the self-doubts and conflicts that make *New Tales of the Taira Clan* more appealing and more like the tremors that have been experienced in the West. But the precise, sublime movements of Mori and Kyo as the lovers and the idea of history as an impenetrable, redolent ritual are rendered with the chilling grace that seems to pervade the pages of Japanese history.

If *Princess Yang Kwei Fei* is the least ambivalent of Mizoguchi's major films, *A Story from Chikamatsu* is the most comprehensive in conceptualizing a rigid social structure through his interrelating the constrictive design with the tragic emotional awakening of the lovers. Though it is a black-and-white film, Mizoguchi brilliantly depicts the ominous mood of this key, transitional period of Japanese history in several distinct areas, from the closed-in quarters of the scrollmaking establishment and the virgin forest where the apprentice declares his love for his master's wife to the raft where the lovers, transfixed in a fog, seem to embody the sepulchral stateliness of their time. The film has an identity in Mizoguchi's filmography similar to *Way Down East* in Griffith's and *The Magnificent Ambersons* in Welles's; it presents a more personal, romanticized view of the individual and history than *The Birth of a Nation*, *Citizen Kane*, and *Ugetsu*, but its romanticism offers a far harsher reading of its culture than either the Griffith or Welles films. This is most conspicuous in Mizoguchi's handling of the relationship between sensuality and sexuality among the four major characters; the austere mores and hermetic architecture of the town seem only to encourage the master's lecherous advances to his apprentice's fiancée. Unlike the ennobling features of the son and mother in *Sansho the Bailiff* and of the king and princess in *Princess Yang Kwei Fei*, the apprentice and his master's wife, who by chance are thrown together, are simple figures who spend a good part of the film trying to deny their emotional attraction to each other. The apprentice is a dumpy-looking figure, and while his fiancée has a pert, sexual charm, the wife of his employer, though less attractive, has a more aristocratic demeanor. Since they neither look nor act in the manner of classic heroes and since there is no recognition of an individual rebelling against the social and moral corruption as there is in *Sansho the Bailiff* and *The Life of Oharu*, their ultimate declaration of love may not seem as profound as the unequivocal moral integrity of Mizoguchi's other classic protagonists. But it may be Mizoguchi's greatest film because their idealism is fulfilled in such a stark setting; it is his grimmest film because it is his most psychologically realistic. By rejecting a conventional treatment of the hero at odds with society, *A Story from Chikamatsu* allows one to understand the machinations of the long-standing feudalism of Japanese society on its most personal, tragic level.

Several of Mizoguchi's contemporary films like *Women of the Night* and *Street of Shame* are marked by an absence of the passionate romanticism of his period dramas. *Women of the Night* was made under the control of the American army; Mizoguchi's classical moralism results in a didactic exposé of the plight of prostitutes in postwar Japan. The women continually bemoan their condition, but Mizoguchi is unable to separate his heroines from their grubby, stultifying environment. Representative scenes such as the syphilis test in the hospital and the indoctrination of a new girl are handled in such a crude, bombastic manner that the film's slight documentary value is undercut. *Street of Shame*, like *Women of the Night*, exaggerates the pecuniary difficulties the ostracized women face, while the men are treated as one-dimensional. Mizoguchi's standing in film history is secure: *Ugetsu*, *Sansho the Bailiff*, *New Tales of the Taira Clan*, *Princess Yang Kwei Fei*, and *A Story from Chikamatsu*, along with major portions of *Utamaro and His Five Women* and *The Life of Oharu* are among the most lucid appreciations of the past on film. When one then notes the absence of Mizoguchi's romantic ethos in these contemporary settings, one admits the passing of a uniquely Japanese discernment of the spatial and temporal coordinates of the past and the disturbing relevance of Kurosawa's embittered, westernized studies of isolation and retribution.

Kurosawa's first feature film, *Sanshiro Sugata*, though awkward in tying together the love story with jujitsu confrontations, already suggests a fundamental change in the Japanese cinema. The protagonist is divorced from his surroundings; his development as a master of jujitsu lacks the tension between personal desires and social orthodoxy that has heretofore permeated the Japanese film. The most fluid, engrossing scenes concern the fights, whose aggressive physicality challenges the basic premises of the Japanese film aesthetic in Ozu and Mizoguchi. *The Men Who Tread on the Tiger's Tail* is a Kurosawa anomaly, a charming period piece that adroitly conveys the melodrama and humor of the kabuki play. In *Yojimbo* and *Seven Samurai*, his richest, most exhaustive period dramas, Kurosawa examines the meaning of Japanese history at a time when it was characterized by moods of rebellion and introspection that audiences in the West can readily understand. The sudden, self-referenced bursts of violence in *Yojimbo* and *Sanjuro* and the drawn-out harangues of Mifune in *Seven Samurai*, first against the farmers for their meretriciousness to the samurai and then against the samurai for their insensitivity to their host's destitute condition, connote the uprootedness and the absence of a social matrix that threaten his characters' survival.

Both *Yojimbo* and *Seven Samurai* have spawned numerous imitations, yet their status as classics of the adventure and epic film is undisputed. Kazuo Miyagawa, one of the great cinematographers of the movies, was equally adept in Kurosawa's vividly physical penetrations of the past as he was in Mizoguchi's more ethereal, scroll-painting recreations. In adapting to the wide-screen format, Miyagawa used significant areas of darkness to compensate for the diminutive structure of the Japanese house, and in *Yojimbo* the large expanses of darkness, like the music and editing wipes, augment Kurosawa's black-comic send-up of treachery and violence. The climactic battle in the rain in *Seven Samurai* is, perhaps, the best example of Kurosawa's dramatic and cinematic genius: its tones of idealism, pessimism, and nihilism realized in a sequence of visual grandeur. Again one notes its exacting architectonics, Kurosawa's ability and that of cinematographer Asakazu Nakai to pinpoint the physical interrelationship between the various clashes; the movements of marauders sweeping across the screen and Mifune's raging warrior running laterally to the attack function as decrescendo motifs in the film's final movement of physical devastation and communal harmony. This brilliantly panoramic study of warfare is essential to any epic filmmaker; the final confrontation in the rain is equal to if not superior to any of the clashes in Griffith, Eisenstein, Gance, and Ford because it combines the valor of its samurai warriors with the objective progression of the battle, juxtaposing their personal encounters to the objective constituents of the landscape and rainfall.

The inexorable sense of alienation that characterizes Kurosawa's films and which is poetically simplified in *Rashomon* enables Western filmgoers to feel an unexpected affinity with Japanese literature and art. By closely scrutinizing Kurosawa's filmography, one can see that this conflict involving the estranged individual and a precarious, corrupt society originates in the moral ambiguity he discovers in postwar Japan. In *No Regrets for Our Youth, I Live in Fear, Drunken Angel, Stray Dog*, and *The Bad Sleep Well*, Kurosawa's well-known reverence for Dostoevsky is reflected by his immersing the viewer in tense, emotionally explosive situations. In documenting the traumas of his age, he studies the effects of pacifism in the face of Japan's entry into World War II, the A-bomb scare, the delinquency of postwar youth, the pressures of a police investigation, and the evils of big business. The films recall the humanistic spirit of the postwar Italian cinema, in particular Rossellini, by emphasizing muddy, desolate settings and the characters' rambling monologues of pessimism and optimism. Kurosawa, however, often seems too close to his material to articulate his depression in a cogent, dramatic style; it is only in parts of *Stray Dog* and in the last sequence of *The Bad Sleep Well* that he sees his characters embracing the more profound features of humanist drama. There was some interest in the individual as a tragic moral protagonist in Setsuko Hara's ennobling characterization in *No Regrets for Our Youth*, but even in the ambient *Stray Dog*, Kurosawa seems more concerned with exposing the haunts of Japanese lowlife, from the nightclub to the slum housing projects, than with exploring Mifune's relationship with his police-department superior, played by Takashi Shimura. In *The Bad Sleep Well* it is only after one of the clerks is abducted by Mifune and taken to his own funeral that Mifune's outrage evokes the truly profound cry of pessimism for which Kurosawa became famous. Unlike Rossellini, whose characters' desperation derives from their separation from society, and unlike De Sica, in whose films the economic strain threatens his characters' self-respect, Kurosawa perceives an ineradicable gulf between his protagonists and society. After the mesmerizing scene in *The Bad Sleep Well* in which Kurosawa negates the clerk's identity, Mifune as the avenging son and the pernicious financiers find themselves engaged in a conflict that allows for no social remedy. The retribution that Mifune demands for the murder of his father and the financiers' defensive maneuvers yield a portrait of the darkest, most subterranean shading. The scene in which the Machiavellian father looks at the mirror and then turns away from his reflection only to return to his self-image of villainy and the one in which his crippled daughter tells him that she is leaving forever and he pleads with her to stay only to let her depart when the phone rings are harrowing examples of Kurosawa's rage toward the previously sacrosanct figures and morals of Japanese society.

In *Ikiru*, the culmination of these social allegories, Shimura's dogged, methodical fight to build a playground inspires a comprehensive picture of the layers of apathy and degeneracy in postwar Japan. The stylistic element that makes *Ikiru* such a memorable study of humanism is Kurosawa's holding on a scene until he has exhausted his characters' pretenses, as in the wake for Shimura in which his co-workers, bent over their sake, admit their insensitivity as bureaucrats and promise to reform. This technique is crucial to his two most vivid studies of the fight between humanism and nihilism: *High and Low* and *Red Beard*. He has used this physically static, psychologically introspective approach throughout his career, evident even in the butchered version of *The Idiot*, in which the rigid spacing of his characters recalls the symbolic pictorialism of Eisenstein's sound films, and in *Rashomon* in the scenes before the magistrate in which Mori, Mifune, and Kyo recount their version of the tale. In *High and Low* it is most effectively used when Mifune, his family, and the police await a message from the kidnapper and debate whether Mifune should pay the ransom. It is both a theatrical and pictorial technique, but it gains an added dimension on film because of the filmmaker's ability to simultaneously modify a picture of physical reality and his characters' psychological self-entrapment. It also dramatically clarifies the film's basic theme: how the kidnapper—in his scorched, destitute quarters—renounces his humanity and how Mifune—in his equally isolated setting, with his wife, chauffeur, and the police begging him to pay the kidnapper—discovers his own. The humanism of *High and Low* does not simply consist of its theoretical aplomb in developing this dialectical study of decline and self-redemption; it lies in Kurosawa gradually drawing in all of his participants, from the police to the filmgoer, to a realization of the lower depths of postwar society. It is during the entrapment of the abductor that the searing honesty of the film is fulfilled: first as the police observe the kidnapper who spots Mifune on the street and asks him for a light and then in the journey through the dope den. Mifune's humanity triumphs in the last scene, but Kurosawa does not end the film on a note of moral affirmation with the kidnapper breaking out in a cold sweat but holds on a shot of Mifune's stolid figure as the iron shutter descends, separating him from the kidnapper. He has entered the abyss, but what he has seen and learned will undercut all future statements on the strength of society as the great redeemer.

*Red Beard*, like *The Lower Depths*, is primarily restricted to one set in examining the young doctor's education in the face of disease and social deprivation. One arbitrary scene occurs early in the film when Kurosawa uses a series of jump cuts to show Mifune and the young doctor responding to the cries of an isolated patient. Kurosawa applied jump cuts in *No Regrets for Our Youth* when the students go on an outing in order to suggest its ephemeral mood and in *Ikiru* when Shimura runs after a woman who took his hat at the fairgrounds; it is extraneous in *Red Beard* because the doctor's education derives from his immersion into the abjection and disease at the hospital. The film shows Kurosawa's maturity in the purity of his design, in his filling the screen with the face of the old, dying man and that of the young boy who attempts suicide. The monochromatic backgrounds that surround the numerous dialogues between Mifune—the veteran, sage doctor—and the intern—young and at first pompous—find Kurosawa using an ascetic compositional style and a simple story line to elaborate the crisis of medicine by pinpointing the moral values represented by the doctors and by seeing the degree of pain and the horror of disease in the patients' faces. It is a worthy companion piece to *High and Low*, in which Kurosawa seems to transcend his legacy of anarchy with an inquiry into the nature of suffering. It is part of a legacy that a new generation of Japanese filmmakers will have to confront as the most compelling, pertinent picture of their society and history.

*Samurai—Red Psalm*

The adventure epic enjoyed its greatest success in Hollywood during the twenties and the first decades of the sound era, but some of its formidable postwar entries have come from abroad with the work of Hiroshi Inagaki and David Lean. Inagaki's films in particular show the international stamp of the genre in which De Mille's more ponderous epics with their mixture of theatrical melodrama and gung ho heroics exemplify the genre's dramatic compromises and middlebrow appeal. Inagaki's *Samurai* trilogy reveals its De Mille–like signature in Mifune's tense, overwrought child-hero whose rise to a master swordsman is presented in hackneyed psychological episodes. The audience is not fully absorbed in the pageantry and fighting because Inagaki interprets Mifune's mythic warrior in a solemn historical context. *Samurai Banners* is more faithful to the dynamic, romantic sparkle that has characterized the best work in the genre; Inagaki is not as much concerned with the nationalist imprint of his saga as he is with empathizing with Mifune's celibate swordsman and the valor he displays in what seems to be an interminable number of military campaigns. The singular Japanese virtues of Mifune's hero are honored, but not without losing sight of the spirit of adolescent fantasy that has long been recognized as a trademark of the genre.

David Lean's films expand the virtues of the English film in a style that often seems a near invisible tangent of the American. His first films reassert the strengths of the Korda–Pressburger–Powell tradition with their handsome pictorialism and triumphant theatricality. Films like *Rembrandt, The Thief of Bagdad, The Life and Death of Colonel Blimp*, and *Black Narcissus* are examples of the natural aptitude of British producers and their craftsmen for the pictorial idealization of history and romance that their American counterparts, such as Irving Thalberg and David Selznick, approach with a more contrived flamboyancy. Lean's two adaptations of Dickens—*Great Expectations* and *Oliver Twist*—show a more acute psychological intensity, a surer hand in adapting their narrative complexity to the dynamic proscenium of the film medium. Two of Lean's less successful adventure epics, *The Bridge on the River Kwai* and *Doctor Zhivago*, like several De Mille projects, attempt to elevate their two-dimensional characters into transcendent figures of heroism and romance. The reverence toward Alec Guinness's British officer gives William Holden's wily figure slight opportunity to expose the folly of Guinness's bridge building. Whereas Lean idealizes Guinness through his emphasis on the discipline and painstaking construction of the bridge, a similar, impersonal mood results in *Doctor Zhivago*—his soap-opera prototypes become receding figures in his long shots of the icy depths of the Russian countryside. At his worst De Mille exaggerated the bombast and pseudofolk poetry of the Hollywood entertainment; Lean, as the scion of the English quality film, exposes the increasing dilettante mannerisms of epic filmmakers by magnifying the impersonal grandeur of his stories, an approach toward which his predecessors may have been inclined but were careful to avoid by selecting projects better suited to their threads of historical reverie.

One of the high points of the adventure epic, *Lawrence of Arabia*, expertly blends the vigorous action sequences and dramatic populism of the genre; the film's journalistic idioms are transformed by the cosmic pageantry of wide-screen technology. Peter O'Toole's Lawrence is a much richer, idiosyncratic figure than traditional movie folk heroes, while the supporting cast featuring the elegance of Guinness's Feisal, the coy statesmanship of Claude Rains, and the burliness of Anthony Quinn's Arab chieftain provides stirring tableaux of historical personalities. The story of the incipient unity of the Arab tribes, the long marches through the desert, the attack on Aqaba, and the meeting of the leaders in Damascus seem inspired by the devious emotional makeup of its central character. O'Toole's Lawrence is a poetic, demonic presence, a child of history who embodies historical forces at cross-purposes while fulfilling his singular notion of idealism and tragic self-fulfillment. Robert Bolt's screenplay cleverly avoids the more archaic strategies in Hollywood's final decade of biblical resurrections by conceiving the key transition scenes and battles as resulting from the inner paradoxes of O'Toole's Lawrence.

The continuing surge of nationalism in twentieth-century social history, combined with the mass appeal of the movies, has led to a renaissance of epic filmmaking in Third World countries and in Eastern Europe. In surveying the wreckage of their postcolonial environments, novelists and playwrights like V. S. Naipaul and Athol Fugard adopt a less modernist style by drawing on traditional humanist themes to analyze the conflict between the descendants of colonial rule and the representatives of their newly acquired independence. Their plot contrivances are more realistic and straightforward, their pathos and moral determinism less obscure than that of their contemporaries in America and Europe. They have discovered their voice in the aftermath of violence and social turpitude whereby their estrangement from the more absurdist mannerisms prevalent in modern literature evinces their own burgeoning humanism.

A similar sensibility is to be found in the films of Satyajit Ray. Ray's "Apu Trilogy," consisting of *Pather Panchali*, *Aparajito*, and *The World of Apu*, discerns a Third World macrocosm in the microcosm of family life, beginning with the contrasting hardships and amenities of the family's simple existence, continuing with the death of the father, the mother's growing isolation from Apu's maturing worldliness, and concluding with Apu's spiritual bewilderment following the death of his wife in childbirth and his final reunion with his son. Ray is not as concerned as the Italian humanists in detailing the physical hardships that Apu's parents suffer. *Pather Panchali* is more attuned to the understated gracefulness of the father and mother, fanning each other over a simple meal of curried rice, and to Apu's wonderment at the train that passes through his village. It is the realism of immigrant literature in which Ray chronicles the inestimable family bond as the saving grace of his country's first years of independence. In *Aparajito*, and more so in *The World of Apu*, Ray's treatment becomes less concrete and chronological. The mother's withdrawal from her son following the death of the father and the passing of Apu's wife lead to a mood of disenchantment and alienation. Yet the conflict between the son's increasing worldliness and the mother's retreat into religious passivity in *Aparajito* and Apu's years of soul-searching in *The World of Apu* are not examined with the same detail with which Ray first studied the rubric of family life in *Pather Panchali*. The crises lack a poetic undercurrent in discovering the exigence of family relations. Ray's Eastern temperament interprets Apu's isolation from a wholly emotional vantage point from which he disavows any attempt to externalize or articulate Apu's dilemma.

The *Music Room* and *Devi* show a similar reluctance to probe the singular Indian sensibility of his protagonists. They connote Ray's fatalism in that the music-loving aristocrat refuses to admit his monetary difficulties, while in *Devi* the son and his bride become pawns of his father's neurotic mysticism. The audience can sympathize with the aristocrat's enchantment with the dancers he lavishly entertains, throwing his last coins to them as a token of his regard for their beauty and his disdain for the scurrility of the nouveau riche merchant. But Ray is equally entranced by the persona of the retiring aristocrat. In *Devi* the father's belief that his daughter-in-law is the reincarnation of Devi and the son's inability to challenge his father's power in forcing his bride to become the servant of his father's fantasies demonstrate the overpowering presence of Indian folklore: Ray accepts it as part of a heritage he cannot question or criticize. The idea that his characters are transparent embodiments of their culture also mars his treatment of the indolence of the rich in *Charulata*, *The Chess Players*, and *Distant Thunder*. Ray utilizes the sensual intoxicating design to denote the characters' passivity, their selfish, cocoonlike existence. The most prolonged sequence in *Charulata* concerns the adulterers who lie outside in a garden whose lushness is far too stylized. Ray's camerawork is as listless as his characters; there seems little tension or hope that they will awaken to the duplicity of their westernized condition. *The Chess Players* and *Distant Thunder* find his passive protagonists exhibiting a similar sense of cultural dislocation amid their rich estates. The films lack the discursive, anecdotal ironies of *Days and Nights in the Forest* in which his Chekhovian insights draw off the idiosyncracies of his sensual, college-educated drifters and their emotional suspension between their acquired western dilettantism and an awareness of their dire social environment. Ray is most successful in delineating the foibles and immaturity of his protagonists who assume the mannerisms of their colonial overlords; the tragicomedy in *The Chess Players* results from the husbands' inability to satisfy their wives because of their penchant for chess. Ray remains a humanist in his attention to the social quandary in which his protagonists are placed, but in gravitating to a type of fin de siècle struggle, the materialist sweep of his backgrounds becomes a theoretical contrivance. By failing to personalize the tragic lethargy of his well-to-do characters, the final recognition of their failure as either members of a household or a nation lacks the tension between personal desires and national destiny.

While Ray's films discover the paradoxes of contemporary Indian life in the fragile innocence of his protagonists and their insecurity in a simulated, old-world existence, the films of Andrzej Wajda demonstrate the continuing appeal of the old-fashioned narratives and didactic populism of the Russian epics of the thirties. His war trilogy of *Generation, Kanal,* and *Ashes and Diamonds* relies on an academic symbolism to expose the terrible deprivation wrought by war: its toll on his youthful protagonists in *Generation,* the interminable horror of being trapped in the city's waterworks in *Kanal,* and the inability of love to triumph against the realities of war in *Ashes and Diamonds.* Wajda's dialectic unfolds in a heavy-handed manner in which his humanism fails to invest these conflicts with the essential hubris of heroism. The characters and drama are two-dimensional, set against a social background that expresses its accessible Marxist mythmaking in the characters' simplistic vulnerability and the dramatically reductionist treatment of the horrors of war. Wajda's later films sustain a strict moral imprint, whether the subject remains the war years or more contemporary, romantic themes. In *The Birch-Wood* the two brothers' involvement with the same woman is not suffused with the subjective emotionalism that might have reenforced the cruelty of the older brother to his invalid sibling's more profound attachment; the dilemma is presented as an archaic theater exercise in which the donnish older brother is studied as a curiosity from romantic literature. In *Hunting Flies* the young man's attraction for the fickle girl is treated as a symbolic problem piece in which his cramped living quarters and his inability to fulfill his innocent lusting are seen as psychological parallels to his country's fate as part of the East European bloc. It is a more accomplished work than Wajda's earlier film platitudes, more astute in detailing the nuances of modern life in Eastern Europe. Yet it has all the trademarks of conformist art— the well-made play or popular film—that the West has been taught to regard as the leisurely excesses of its culture. *Man of Iron* shows Wajda's maturation as a director with its uncluttered, incisively drawn portrait of a faceless technocrat whose dormant social consciousness is vitalized by her investigation of a strike leader. The symbolic motifs of Wajda's war trilogy are jettisoned for the journalistic, biographical detail surrounding the strike activist and the self-education of the female documentarian who falls in love with him. The simplicity and honesty of the narrative redeems much of the heavy-handedness in Wajda's previous polemics.

Compared to the other Eastern European and Russian films distributed in America, Wajda's films seek a middlebrow compromise between the crude, naive folk drama of *Ballad of a Soldier* and the bombast of *War and Peace.* Several of the younger members of the Russian film industry evoke a genuine sympathy for a less doctrinaire approach to history and a far richer sensitivity to the artistic legacy of imperial and preindustrial Russia. Sergei Paradjanov's *Shadows of Our Forgotten Ancestors* delves into the arcane rituals and mysticism of Russian history. The film is one of the more overwrought portrayals of a nascent, primitive folk spirit in the contemporary cinema. His portentous camera vistas, his primitivistic regard for sunlight, and the dazzling colors of the countryside suggest a rebirth of the folkloristic cinema of Dovzhenko; he embraces the past with the fervor of an archaeologist who has discovered the lost civilization of his dreams. In *The Color of Pomegranates* Paradjanov's atavistic sensibility results in a more radically pictorial style. The images have a calligraphic delicacy, and although it is not the type of filmmaking that could inspire many successors, Paradjanov's aestheticism offers hope for the return of Russian moviemaking into the mainstream of movie experimentalism.

The films of Miklós Jancsó show a similar strain of avant-garde iconoclasm but with a more determined effort to tie in the stylistic mannerisms of the avant-garde to an orthodox dialectic of myth and history. Jancsó's early films, such as *The Red and the White* and *The Round-Up*, employ a severely sculptural style to distinguish the epic components of men at war: the transcendent coordinates of nature and the ephemeral imprint of the individual and history. He is the least personal of epic filmmakers because of his objective framing of the land and his refusal to disassociate the more fortuitous encounters, for example, the violin serenade in the forest in *The Red and the White*, from his piecemeal study of war. *The Round-Up* is a more personalized drama in which the emphasis changes from the epic breadth of the land and the impassivity of the movement of regiments of soldiers to the fatalism surrounding the soldiers' attempt to spare those incarcerated with the partisans. Jancsó's precise, encompassing camera tracks yield a mechanistic picture of history in which the individual is submerged by the invisible, impersonal thread of his nation's destiny. In *Il Giovane Attila* and *Red Psalm* the restrictive camera movements and schematic use of space interpret history as a series of dramatic tableaux; their craftsmanship is undeniable, yet in his abstraction of the parameters of the medium to a constricted, choreographed folk drama, one never believes in his actors as characters or as dynamic intermediaries between the dehumanized dialectic of war and the humanizing currents of their folk culture. Jancsó's art of plastic puppet theater has none of the irony of Brechtian drama; unlike Ozu's equally stylized studies of space, time, and the individual, he is unable to discover the effects of his rigid staging on the behavior and tensions of his actors. Jancsó's films are the antithesis of Griffith's early shorts and first features. Griffith discovered in the movies a way of perpetuating and expanding classic literature and its modern, melodramatic derivatives; Jancsó turns to the movies as a means of abstracting art and mythology to their most repressively formalist elements.

# 11
# The Comedy Film

*A Skater's Debut–Helpmates*

If any one film genre attests to America's singular role in the social and cultural immediacy of film history, it is the comedy film. The fantasy film reached a high point in the German cinema of the twenties, but its exhaustive, expressionist portrayal of the demons of history and mythology did not allow for the self-renewal that has been a trademark of comedy in America.

One way of understanding why the movies in America so warmly embraced the varieties of comic stylization concerns the original development of silent-film narrative. In the primitive shorts of Porter and Méliès, a critical feature seems to be the precarious appearance of the actors and their chaotic, dispro-portionate actions, whether in Porter's dramatizations or Méliès's fantasies. One may have concluded from their pioneering shorts that the natural inclina-tion of the movies was to distort and caricature: film seemed too idiosyncratic a medium to present a coherent, naturalistic world. A majority of the first successful short films (including the work of Griffith) were comical, oftentimes unintentionally, because there was a striking imbalance between the visual progression of everyday life and its recreation in a film: the medium's comic potential seemed infinite. The fascination with all forms of technology by American artists and inventors, the relative youthfulness of a nation still search-ing for its identity amid the volatile social and political climate at the turn of the century, and the vigorous populism of music-hall comedy in America would give, then, American filmmakers a decisive edge in mastering the dynamics of comedy on film.

Max Linder was an early prototype of the silent-film anti-hero, an elegant, lithe figure much admired by Chaplin. Linder plays a gentleman, without, however, the more paradoxical elements of Chaplin's tramp. The qualities most recognizably Chaplinesque in Linder's work are his incongruity in a mechani-cal, anonymous social reality and his interest in working out a prolonged, dis-ingenuous bit of physical magic. His routines are not as fast-paced as those developed by Sennett. In *A Skater's Debut* Linder's major concern is not an attack on the middle class, but his deft, physical precision in a largely imprecise world, attempting to pick up his hat and falling only after he has appeared to defy the laws of gravity; in another short it is his persistence in attempting to fit all of his groceries into one uncompromising bag.

Unlike Linder's aristocratic manner and aloofness from society, Mack Sennett's pioneering work rejoices in the giddy, anarchic spirit of man and machinery run amok. Sennett was a primitive, an essential ingredient in translating the good-natured violence, the folk innocence, and generally brash mannerisms of American vaudeville theater into a film. The operative term for Sennett's shorts is "speed," manifest in both the fast-paced nature of his stories and in his fascination with all forms of movement and machinery. Sennett's instinctive approach to the dynamic, disorienting nature of the silent film encouraged a repertory of social miscreants, the successors to the vagabond spirits of late nineteenth-century music-hall comedy. Sennett's films explode on the screen like the experiments of a young boy playing with his first chemistry set, aware of the basic ingredients he is mixing, but unsure of the results of his admixture. His shorts do not so much present characters as transparent symbols of light and darkness who find the narrative and moralistic conventions of the vaudeville stage transfigured by the aggressive dynamics of the film medium; they inhabit a world of cosmic indefiniteness, celebrated in a finale of explosive disarray in which the physical force of trains and cars nervously intersecting is juxtaposed to a microcosm of dispossessed husbands and ne'er-do-well types who find their instincts for merriment more than reciprocated by their teetering world. Ben Turpin's cross-eyed figure may well be the representative figure of Sennett's mayhem; his debilitated sleepwalker functions as a mirror image to Sennett's crumbling reality.

Sennett's infectious, primitive folk humor flashes intermittently through *Tillie's Punctured Romance*, one of his early feature-length films. Its weakest segments are in the first part; Marie Dressler's gargantuan figure as the clumsy, unloved maiden who inherits her uncle's estate only to learn that he has survived a fall on a mountain expedition and the young Chaplin as the rake are conventions of the vaudeville stage. Dressler plays her role like an elephant trying to execute a series of figure eights on a tricycle; she is immune to the self-ridicule of her performance, a masochistic figure who uses her bulk to foil Charlie's scurrility and to overcome various physical hurdles which she executes none too dexterously. Chaplin has begun to sketch in the character of the tramp, and his dapper trickster easily lends itself to Sennett's histrionics. Though it runs one hour, the film seems long, not sharp enough in its parodies, and lacks the sustained comic fireworks that explode in the last reel.

The superiority of Chaplin's shorts lies in the character of the tramp. He has borrowed from the mask of Pierrot; although several critics have emphasized his adapting physical features from his contemporaries on the stage and screen, the tramp remains a unique comic outsider, a mixture of hobo and thief, romantic and nihilist, little man and everyman. The history of the tramp is a study in the different masks Chaplin assumes in distinguishing his comic protagonist as the savior of a flawed society. In his early shorts Chaplin perceives each chaotic situation as a stage that will be reconstructed by his sublime sense of fun and benevolence. In *A Dog's Life*, after Charlie knocks out one of the ruffians, his manipulation of the body of the unconscious man pokes fun at the brawling manner of the other toughs and drunkards; in *The Pilgrim* Mack Swain's curious walk is parodied by Charlie in the disguise of a priest. In this role Charlie transforms a church into a vaudeville stage as he mimes the story of David and Goliath; his performance ends with Charlie showing David booting away Goliath's head and with the tramp's returning three times to take a bow.

Chaplin continually undercuts social affectations and morality. His caricature of valor and romance in *Shoulder Arms* reconfirms their validity while uncovering their absurdist potential. The key to these Chaplin shorts is his imbuing standard comic situations with a comic yet compassionate humanism. Even in *The Adventurer*, in which one may first remember Charlie's being chased by the cops and then by the guests, the humor arises from Charlie's upsetting the clichés of social propriety through his use of the cigar and seltzer bottle. In *The Rink* the tramp's actions in the restaurant, at the skating rink, and at the house party poetically transfigure their dull, enervating features. In each of these settings Charlie evokes the poetic signature of the tramp by nonchalantly removing his jacket and walking stick from a stove and by his dazzling performance on the skating rink. Whereas an exemplary comic device such as the revolving door would be transformed by Keaton, as Agee pithily remarked, into a "transcendent juggling act," Chaplin approaches it as an intermediary obstacle in his travels through a benign social setting.

Whether he is trying to catch a fish while the other passengers are overcome by seasickness in *The Immigrant* or innocently patrols the crime-ridden waterfront district in *Easy Street*, the tramp is blissfully removed from the ludicrous uniformity and conformity surrounding him. Instead of leading the characters into a wild free-for-all, a principle Keaton adapted from his training with Sennett, Chaplin elaborates his recurrent film romance with Edna Purviance while sustaining his self-image as a free spirit. The massage routine in *The Cure* is questioned by Charlie, who recognizes its perverse overtones; by challenging its physical suggestiveness he defies our acquiescing to convention. Unlike Keaton who will seemingly penetrate the cosmos to extend the magic and dynamics of the movies, Chaplin subtly subverts the meaning of a kinetic, anarchic world through his idealization of the tramp.

While these shorts are infused with a blithe, romantic spirit, it is in *The Pawnshop* and in the pure poeticism of *One A. M.* that Chaplin distills his vaudeville training into an art inspired by his iconoclastic figure. Unlike *Shoulder Arms* in which the mechanics of war—of good guy against bad guy—are upended and in which society is shown triumphant, the tramp is not nearly so sympathetic in *The Pawnshop*. His outwitting the hobo, like his not so honorable intentions toward the pawnshop owner's daughter, underscores the tramp's aggressively antisocial nature. He is a menace to our world because the tramp is a poet committed only to his free will: it is this independence that causes him to strike out at all forms of social conformity. Charlie's one-shot take with the hobo who tries to sell him a clock is one of many examples of the villainous side of our vaudeville clowns. Charlie's dismantling of the clock by using a variety of instruments, including a stethoscope, is a lucid realization of how the clown builds from an apparently irrational act to destroy the pretenses of conventional behavior. The hobo, who is seen in one reaction shot, can be regarded as Chaplin's audience; he will laugh with him but will not accept the implications of Chaplin's anarchic individualism. One surmises that Purviance as the ubiquitous damsel in distress should be either his mistress or, in a more poetic vein, one of the maidens who sings of his adventures.

*One A. M.* is a remarkable exercise in silent-film comedy; one wonders why more has not been made of the film, at least in evaluating it as quintessential Chaplin in the way that *Cops* is quintessential Keaton. Several of the film's most impressive features derive from its simplified plot: a chamber music exercise played in one key. With the exception of the introductory scene in a cab, the action is restricted to Charlie's home, where he arrives intoxicated. The obstacles Charlie sets in the path of finding his bedroom show the most common objects acquiring new meaning when confronted by a clown. After he realizes that he does not have the key, he climbs through the window only to climb out again and open the door. The bearskin carpet is treated as a live object, and in like manner the pendulum is attacked, not with reason or brute force, but with the balletic movements of the intoxicated tramp. Charlie's inebriation inspires a wholly original plan of attack; his home comes alive with presences that only a drunk would see and that only the tramp could majestically overcome. Chaplin is not concerned with the numerous kinetic variations he can discover in the mechanics of a modern home; instead, the tramp, now in the guise of a well-to-do partygoer, becomes a tightrope walker whose gracefulness in animating the objects in his home is predicated on his dipsomania. By falling asleep in his bathtub Charlie is not simply rejecting another convention of modern life, but shows the tramp's ability to romantically transform the most commonplace objects and settings. *One A. M.* celebrates the magic of the tramp for being wise enough and drunk enough to remake our world.

Keaton's early years in the cinema, first supporting Fatty Arbuckle in several Sennett productions, are as self-expressive but less memorable than Chaplin's novice efforts. His stone-face character and his development of a film syntax that would support his impassive facade seem as much an outgrowth of his earlier vaudeville training with his parents as Chaplin's tramp seems to arise from the pathos and paradoxical humor Chaplin discovered in his impoverished youth. The major differences in their poetic temperaments are clearly conveyed in their work with Sennett; whereas Chaplin's tramp seems to obstruct the dizzying pace, Keaton's presence accentuates the bedlam. While Chaplin suggests an old-world sentimentality, Keaton is both a physical complement to Arbuckle and a type of handy-andy character who propels the chaotic story line. Keaton's agility enables Sennett to extend the encroaching madness, whereas the tramp suggests an otherworldliness.

In Chaplin's films the tramp is situated amid a minimum number of characters and objects. However, in the first shorts Keaton directs, he builds the comedy around numerous conflicting mechanisms between which Keaton—the ideal acted-upon clown—is caught. Shorts such as *The Goat, One Week,* and *The Balloonatic* are examples of an artist who has begun to consider the implications of a Keatonesque landscape, where not only is everything on the move, but where the mechanical and inanimate are treated as living organisms. In comparing *The Haunted House* to *One A. M.,* one immediately recognizes the differences between early Keaton and Chaplin. The Chaplin short plays as a serenade, a sublime tribute to the poet as clown as drunk. Keaton's plot is bare to the point of being invisible; the drama is comprised of his daring choreography within the house in which he is chased by thieves. The cutting is sharply paced, and his understanding of how the traps exist as one unit—an infinitely turning mechanism to baffle the most knowing—exemplifies Keaton's cerebral style: the house is haunted not because the thieves are dressed as ghosts, but because of its mechanical activization. In *One Week, Day Dreams, The Goat,* and *The Boat* Keaton's film sense merits comparison with the best of Chaplin's shorts by more adroitly integrating his technical inventiveness: he creates a technological loony bin in which he is both its most prized inmate and its most constant critic.

The Playhouse and *Cops* are the summation of Keaton's mastery of the short. The two films are inspired by Keaton's awesome athleticism in showing how Keaton, alone among mortals, can cope with the overwhelming power of our new-world technology; also, as Chaplin's dramatic opposite, Keaton's films connote a bleaker view of the clown's romantic potential. One is likely to overlook the moral of Keaton's work and languish in Charlie's pathos because the drama in a Keaton film often seems a minor cog in his dynamic film style, but Keaton's clown is equally distinct. In *The Playhouse,* in which he plays a theater attendant whose fantasies constitute a large part of the film, Keaton's visualization of reality and fantasy reveals their unifying dreamlike components on film. The work could be subtitled "The Dream Life of a Would-Be Actor," as Keaton turns to fantasy as the movies' most viable form of expression. If *The Playhouse* is his most self-referenced, oblique short, *Cops* is his most morbidly humorous look at the frenetic, madcap nature of silent-film comedy. Similar to his other shorts Keaton is chased by a group of people when attempting to romance his girl friend. However, where many of his earlier shorts exaggerated Keaton's interest in accelerating movement, such as the nihilism of *Day Dreams* and the use of his athletic prowess to win the girl in *Neighbors, Cops* interprets winning the girl as the crucial myth that has been obscured in his previous shorts. Keaton also sees that he does not have to draw continually on his Olympian powers; all he need do is sit back and observe the modern world's carnival-type proportions: he has developed comic counterpoint.

In *Cops* Keaton is introduced separated from the girl by a gate that one thinks is part of a jail but that is shown to be the gateway to her mansion. Keaton then attempts to enter a cab but is pushed out by a man who loses his wallet in the tussle; after the cab turns around and the wallet is retrieved, Keaton is shown counting the money. These two scenes characterize Keaton's more subtle comic style; he no longer relies on the exaggerated pacing of silent-film slapstick. His use of an object for a purpose other than its obvious one, first developed in *The Goat*, recalls Chaplin's style of rational insanity as he puts headphones on a horse and telephones directions. He now presents his character as a bemused spectator who will join in the anarchy only at its most extreme stage; through the ironic juxtaposition of his inert persona to the multiple rhythms of modern life, Keaton identifies fantasy as the predominant direction of the silent-film comic. It is evident in his introducing the parade in extreme long shot; simply by cutting to his entering the parade in a horse-drawn carriage and to his mistakenly accepting the cheers of the crowd, Keaton's rueful asymmetry functions as a form of comic counterpoint. He further develops this theme when an anarchist throws a bomb into his carriage, and Keaton then uses it to light a cigarette. The terrified crowd gesticulates at Keaton, who thinks they are applauding him and he bows his head, flicking away the bomb as if it were a match. This sets off the running about in the last ten minutes of the film, which is as cogent a statement of Keaton's film art and personality as is Chaplin's essay on how a poet goes to bed in *One A. M.*

Keaton's flight from the police force, its incarceration, and his final surrender after his girl rejects him comprehensively distinguish Keaton's comic sensibility from Chaplin's. It shows his comic style developing from his mastery of the conflicting dynamics in the action and the editing, unlike Chaplin whose comic vision emanates from his conceiving the tramp as the last romantic in a world gone mad. Whereas Chaplin usually confines himself to one set in idealizing the tramp's tightrope-walking maneuvers, Keaton is constantly on the move; compare, for example, Keaton's cutting of the cops' pursuit of him and its treatment as a football game with the tramp's adaptation of a football-game facade in the café in *Modern Times*. In Chaplin's films social manners and morality are ridiculed in favor of Charlie's liberating spirit. As his opposite, Keaton is always looking for a gimmick or trick that will speed up the film, that bit of imaginative technique that often gives his work the look of surreal trompe l'oeil. In *The Playhouse* Keaton's sweetheart has a twin, and he places a sign on her to distinguish the two; this detail not only works as a variation on the film's theme of the double, but also on the invariably dispossessing nature of silent-film comedy. We are perpetual dreamers in Keaton's films and should remain so, because if we begin to analyze what has happened, as for example in Keaton's surrendering to the police in *Cops*, we are likely to find ourselves trapped in his hallucination.

In his first feature-length films, Chaplin attempts a more full-bodied treatment of the conflict between the tramp and society. *The Kid* is an emblematic Chaplin work in that it personifies the moral fervor and comic humanism of Chaplin's shorts. The film begins with a mother abandoning her child in a garbage can. The tramp appears and sifts through the refuse as if he were sampling lace. Charlie discovers the child and is about to leave the infant when a policeman spots him. The tramp, undeniably, is a warm, effusive soul, but he is not about to go to work for the Salvation Army. In his ensuing education of the boy, Charlie instills a sense of guile and wit that rejects the sophistic rules of middle-class society. But the return of the boy to his mother reminds us that Charlie's poetic integrity can only survive if he is a penniless loner, as the tramp once again takes to the road.

This highly charged romanticism pervades *The Gold Rush* in which his affection for rustic types develops into a most simple, grand metaphor. The dinner sequence with the boot remains one of the great expressions of poetic transfiguration in the cinema in which Charlie's Midas-like transformation of the natural world affects how and what he eats. The difference and conflict between Charlie and the rest of the world is revealed in the way that the tramp can imagine his boot the most delicious repast while his partner, played by Mack Swain, sees the tramp as a chicken, a state of madness and not poetry. But Charlie becomes devious in the final scene. He not only becomes a rich man, but marries the dance-hall girl who has ridiculed him. Why he decides to marry her remains one of the mysteries of film history. One can surmise that Charlie accepts all the evil in the world because he has come into a fortune; in *City Lights* and *Modern Times* he will confront the ambiguity and paradoxes raised by the ending of *The Gold Rush*.

In his best shorts Keaton denotes the uniquely unsettling nature of the film experience; in his feature films his comic nihilism encompasses representative American types and institutions. The less successful of these works—*The Three Ages*, *Go West*, and *Battling Butler*—are examples of a comic personality more enamored of the esoteric magic of the movies than of showing how this magic is camouflaged in everyday life. The sets for ancient Rome in *The Three Ages* suggest that Keaton is more concerned with poking fun at Griffith's *Intolerance* and his interest in historical facsimile than with transposing his comic persona to a different period and setting. A similar comic indolence mars *Our Hospitality*. The humor is not as stilted as in *The Three Ages*, but his treatment of Southern gentility is far too reverent and lacks the sustained comic energy of *The General*. *Go West* is one of many unsuccessful treatments of the West, a genre that will resist the charms of the Marx Brothers, Mae West, W. C. Fields, and Mel Brooks. Keaton dogmatically uses his stone-face identity to set off the anarchic comedy; several examples come to mind, among them his masquerade as Satan in leading the cattle down Main Street in *Go West* and his imperviousness in walking in his shorts and derby in the role of the deadbeat rich boy in *Battling Butler*.

*The Navigator, Steamboat Bill Jr., The General, College,* and *Sherlock Jr.* represent the apex of Keaton's art. In each of these films Keaton is first presented as a fop, without any friends, and attracted to a girl who finds him unattractive. His adversary is the dominant physical structure—the boats in *The Navigator* and *Steamboat Bill Jr.*, the train in *The General*, the athletic field in *College*, and the film medium in *Sherlock Jr.*; it is their technical complexities which inspire Keaton's heroic character transformations. With the exception of *Sherlock Jr.*, Keaton's most extreme realization of how film and dreams are one, each of these confrontations develops its comic point of view from Keaton's methodical approach to its mechanical underpinnings. Keaton then uses his stone-face persona and impassivity in the face of these disconcerting environments to coolly evoke the hazards facing his character; in *The Navigator*, for example, the camera laconically observes the inability of Keaton and his sweetheart to locate each other in the bewildering confines of the boat. His eventual mastery of navigation and the defeat of the natives in a battle on the boat and island result from Keaton's deliberate comic stratagems. He not only scares away the natives in his underwear outfit, but also uses his gear as a rowboat with his arms as oars; his triumph is not one of mind over matter but one in which mind becomes matter.

*College*, with *Sherlock Jr.*, is the shortest of his feature-length films and, like *Sherlock Jr.*, the most dynamic in developing the action through the underlying kinetic adaptability of Keaton's character. Its simple narrative and technical daring lead one to conclude that to Keaton the art of the clown is a science of the most severely intellectual nature. The opening and closing scenes serve as a frame around his college experiences by showing his initial awkwardness and eventual mastery of formidable physical elements. In the opening scene he delivers his high school graduation address at right angles because of his clothes' stiffness following a rainstorm; in the concluding episode he literally becomes the rudder of the school's rowing shell in leading the team to victory. His excursion on the sports field, experimenting with various track and field activities, is a masterly realization of how—touched by God and the love for his girl—the clown as little man is transformed into superman. It is a concise, chilling statement on the art of the music-hall clown as he pole vaults through the cosmos.

*Steamboat Bill Jr.* is a summation of Sennett's cloud-cuckoo country and Keaton's own blending of romance and fatalism. The reason the film seems a more profound work than *The Navigator* concerns Keaton's more personal delineation of the character of the clown. In *The Navigator* his identity is wholly expressed in his Promethean struggles with the boat; but in *Steamboat Bill Jr.* he correlates his personal transformation to the need to win his father's love and respect as well as winning the girl. The first fifteen minutes of the film, one of the expertly cut prologues in silent-film comedy, introduces Ernest Torrence's character of the father, the rivalry he faces on the waterfront, and his image of the returning son as a lusty, broad-shouldered man. Keaton descends from the train sporting a moustache, beret, and ukulele; although they have arranged a signal by which they will recognize each other, Torrence mistakes one person after another until he is faced with the dilettante who happens to be his son. Our laughter is tempered by the shock Torrence has suffered; the physcial tests Keaton's son faces will serve, then, to regain the affection of his father and the love of his sweetheart. Keaton's ensuing confrontation in the jail where his father is imprisoned and the final rescue of his father sustain Keaton's identity as a clown in the context of the father-son relationship. Torrence gained wide acclaim for his performance as the sadist in *Tol'able David*; with his characterization of the father in *Steamboat Bill Jr.* he shows that his emotions match his frame. While the father in *Our Hospitality* was not given any emotional credibility, Keaton displays a keen eye for the pathos and dramatic forcefulness of Torrence's figure.

Were it not for *Sherlock Jr.*, the cyclone sequence in *Steamboat Bill Jr.* would stand as Keaton's finest, funniest, and most frightening picture of the relativity underlying the dynamics of film. He again proves that the man behind the camera, in the cutting room, and working the special effects can devise a phantasm that would shatter Merlin and make for a wary Beelzebub; watching Keaton hanging onto a tree as it is swept along by the hurricane, one begins to understand the reason for Keaton's stone-face impassivity.

If one is likely to experience real fright during the cyclone *Sherlock Jr.* makes each one of us a stone face. While *College* marked the high point of Keaton's identity as the most balloonatic of clowns, *Sherlock Jr.* examines the dream life of a movie projectionist. The self-referential nature of his protagonist enables Keaton to exaggerate the maddening pace and complex trickery in his earlier work; the special effects are not treated as isolated examples of movie madness, but are essential to Keaton's immersion in the elusive, mysterious fragments of the film experience. His film fantasy works on two levels, exploiting the myth of Sherlock Holmes and the dreamlike potential of the movies in projecting his double onto the film he shows at the movie house. His last expression of bewilderment as he imitates the screen lover in the projectionist's booth provides an ironic, paradoxical comment on the magic of his movies. While admitting the terrifying powers of the filmmaker, he appears to question the implication of an art form and artist imbued with godlike powers.

Harold Lloyd's films seem to occupy a middle ground position between Sennett's primitive antics and the spellbinding anarchy in Keaton's films. In exemplary shorts such as *High and Dizzy* and *Lonesome Luke*, Lloyd plays a less helpless character than Sennett stars such as Ben Turpin and Charlie Chase while playing down the violence that is exaggerated by Sennett. The cutting in *Lonesome Luke* centers around the perpetual motion around the bar, with the characters falling into the set by way of the stairs. Buy Lloyd attempts to gain the audience's sympathy without abstracting any one emotion or motif; his makeup and body language is derivative, his slipping on the steps a bit of business rather than poetry. In several shorts he copies many of Chaplin's trademarks; in one, he replays Chaplin's *The Cure*, but Lloyd's staggering dipsomaniac fails as a poor man's Chaplin. When lying by an office window in *High and Dizzy*, Lloyd realizes his boss is standing behind him through the use of his legs; though one may not recall Chaplin's original routine, Lloyd's cleverness diffuses its poetic potential. One continually senses that when Lloyd gets into a jam, it is his perfunctory mask as the boy next door and not as a poetic outsider that enables him to escape. In *Safety Last* there is a piecemeal lifting of the opening sequence from *Cops*; his use of the umbrella to battle the women in a department store suffers in comparison with Chaplin's numerous comic manipulations with his cane.

*The Freshman* may be Lloyd's most personal work, but the major problem with the film remains his screen image. He is presented as a rural curiosity, poor, naive, and wholly out of place in a preppie college environment. There is an effective use of comic irony when he offers himself as a tackling dummy in order to be a member of the football team, but his physical decline is handled in a mechanical manner. He is adept in blending together people and objects, yet the film is not as invigorating as Keaton's *College*. Lloyd created an affable, acquiescent folk hero who steered clear of both Chaplin's humanism and Keaton's kinetic dabblings. A measure of the taste of American audiences can be seen in the fact that while Chaplin would be forced into self-exile and Keaton would assume the wraithlike form in *Sunset Boulevard*, Lloyd's few, unimaginative sound films did little to affect his standing as a classic of the movies and America.

Unlike Lloyd's boy-next-door icon, Harry Langdon's little man inspires a genuine search for a poetic mask; and, surprisingly, what first separates Langdon from other silent-film comics is his limited physical coordination. He relies on an enigmatic gaze, suggesting a little boy who has stumbled into something naughty but is unable to enjoy its naughtiness. In his short films Langdon develops a series of repeated comic gestures; he will look dazzled and then dazed, raise a hand to his face and usually place one or two fingers in his mouth; after maintaining this expression for a few seconds he will run off.

His shorts present an innocent character surrounded by the stereotypes of vaudeville comedy, but without the furious pace in Sennett's work. He is placed in situations, for example, in one short in which he plays a soldier who does not know the war is over, that simplify the comic tension to a most facile level. His work in the sound film was even shorter and more disastrous than Lloyd's, but two of his feature-length silent films, *The Strong Man* and *Three's a Crowd* are sparked by a warm, sensitive film presence that could have developed into a major comic force. *The Strong Man*, an early Frank Capra polemic, concerns Langdon's love of a blind girl and the frail innocence of their relationship; the film's strength lies in the characters' emotional attractiveness, but Capra's undiluted puritanism undercuts the film's cumulative poeticism. *Three's a Crowd* is a superior film and shows why Langdon was at one time regarded as Chaplin's rival. Similar to *The Kid*, the action is restricted to a lower-class setting, but it is a more ascetic film than Chaplin's since a large part of the drama takes place in Langdon's poor abode where he shelters the mother and child. Langdon seems to have realized that he did not have the physical magic of a Chaplin or Keaton, and rather than work around his lack of finesse as the butcher's assistant, he details his tenderness to the mother and child, always looking to provide an added comfort during their stay in his home. The lovely dream sequence in a boxing ring in which Langdon wears an outsize boxing glove is an example of how the truly gratifying moments in Langdon's work arise from his characterization as an effusive, estranged little man lost among grown-ups. His compassionate figure as the butcher's assistant, most luminously expressed in the dream, finds Langdon's undeniably poetic sentiments reflecting the formidable pathos in Chaplin's films.

Langdon's simple, forlorn character is all the more remarkable when one realizes that he was the only product of the Sennett and Roach studios who did not generate a style of comic nihilism. The best films of Laurel and Hardy are more representative of this comic sensibility in that they accentuate the violence in the mainstream of American vaudeville and comedy. Yet they are elusive figures in the history of comedy teams; their silent films have neither Chaplin's comic-tragic idealism nor the brimming ideas and rhythm of Keaton, while their sound films seem minor spoofs when compared to the misanthropy of the Marx Brothers, Mae West, and W. C. Fields. Some of their comedy bits, like the soft-shoe routine outside the saloon in *Way Out West* or Stan's solo in *Sons of the Desert* are among the purest expressions of vaudeville on film. But their more drawn-out comic misadventures, for example, in their attempt to enter a house with a rope and mule in *Way Out West*, are poorly thought-out demonstrations of their lack of coordination. This may explain why the central conflict in two of their best films, *Big Business* and *Helpmates*, concerns their antagonism toward each other. *Big Business*, which was made near the end of the silent era, begins in classic Laurel and Hardy fashion. They first express their tension to each other and to their roles as salesmen and then transfer their irritability to James Finlay, the man who will not buy their Christmas trees being sold in midsummer. The chaos builds slowly; Finlay cuts off branches of their trees, and they retaliate by methodically dismantling his home. Each party answers the other's destructive act as if they were engaged in a chess match; hence the violence of their behavior seems all the more calculating. A point is reached in their destruction of the house when Stan and Ollie relate to the household objects and the crowd that has gathered as the increments of a baseball game. At the end of the film, with Finlay's home destroyed and their car a junk pile, the anarchic implications of silent-film comedy are clearly illustrated: the clown is the ultimate misanthrope.

*Helpmates* is not as encompassing as *Big Business* in exploring the violent thrust of their relationship, but the transparent script perceptively distinguishes their identity in this two-character drama in which Stan comes over to help Ollie clean his house before the arrival of his wife. Stan's awkwardness and Ollie's nervousness are the major obstacles, but somehow they manage to fix up the house. Stan then decides to add a domestic touch by lighting a fire and uses an excessive amount of lighting fluid. The house explodes with only the door frame left standing and Ollie sitting in the one remaining chair. Stan asks if there is anything else he can do as the rain falls. They were beautiful to watch, and it is our loss that there were not better scriptwriters to take advantage of their ironic treatment of a pair of retiring, passive outsiders, befuddled by the complexities of convention.

*Entr'acte–The Great Dictator*

René Clair's early triumphs in the French avant-garde grew out of his understanding of the inherent affinity between slapstick comedy and the absurdist ploys of surrealists and dadaists working in the movies. *Entr'acte*, one of the most appealing films of its genre, begins with a shot of Paris shown upside down, an image brilliantly sustained in the film's zany, elliptical actions. The presence of the camel in the lineup of mourners and scenes like the chase after the coffin show Clair's ability to draw on the surrealist instincts of co-scriptwriter Francis Picabia in reinterpreting the dynamics of silent-film mayhem. Their American counterparts attempt to resolve the friction between lower-class types and a makeshift physical reality; Clair and Picabia give free expression to their darker impulses by mounting one absurd action after another. *The Imaginary Voyage* is a more complex mixture of the unnerving rhythms of silent-film slapstick with the graphic elegance of the French avant-garde. The film is weakest in its character-izations and ensemble humor and most enchanting when its fantasy protago-nists, like Keaton's celestial explorer, appear to fly through their magical set-tings, leading to their harmonious destination in a wax museum whose figures are brought to life. It is one of the more accessible and stylish of surrealist film shorts in which the sudden shifts in its pictorial whimsy convey the dreamer's faith in the lyrical surge of his fantasies.

While *Entr'acte* and *The Imaginary Voyage* liberally blend the rudiments of sur-real design and slapstick farce, *The Italian Straw Hat*, like Lubitsch's *Lady Winder-mere's Fan* and *The Marriage Circle*, is a sound film disguised as a silent one. This is evident in two ways: first by holding to a minimum number of sets and cuts and, more important, by emphasizing the unheard aural components as an integral part of the comedy. The scene that most acutely reveals the exigence of sound occurs in the living room where the unrealized dialogue fails to capture the interaction between the characters and objects in the room. The scene's major comic potential lies in the character of the deaf old man, sitting with his back to the disruptive action. The humor arises from his inability to recognize the confusion around him; as a sound film one would more fully enjoy the comic asymmetry in the old man's inability to recognize the chaos. Clair also shows a Lubitsch-like interest in pointed, drawing-room comedy effects, such as the scene in which the servant opens the door and because of his obscured view, thinks he has entered at an embarrassing moment; it also makes for the film's most humorous episode when the wife motions to her husband to adjust his hat, inspiring the other people in the restaurant to search for the impropriety in their appearance. It is a wonderful bit of theater art, economically expanded on film.

Clair's early sound-film musicals are among the few accomplished examples of a genre that floundered between mediocrity and mindlessness during the late twenties and early thirties. Clair grasped a basic principle of filmed musical comedy that, with the exception of Lubitsch and the combined cinematographic and choreographic extravagance of Busby Berkeley, failed to penetrate Amer-ican producers and directors during this period. *Le Million* is a buoyantly kinetic romp because of the joyous magnification of Clair's giddy characters and elu-sive, ephemeral story through his frenetic camerawork and continuously ex-panding backdrops of Paris. One not only marvels at how Clair, like Lubitsch or Berkeley, has astutely modified his style to the musical rhythms of a sound film, but how a genre inextricably tied to the illusions of the theater has been renewed on film. Whereas Lubitsch modestly extends the parameters of operetta on film, Clair's musicals appear to have captured the poetic sweep of the music through his ambidextrous cutting and staging. In *Le Million* the lyrical sweep of the music does not lead to an abstraction of the characters, but conveys their larger-than-life emotional force; they race through the city back-drops as preliminary stages of their final, romantic self-fulfillment on the theater stage with the confetti falling around them. In *The Love Parade* Lubitsch's fluent mastery of the dynamics of the music continually breaks up the song and dance into rhythmic units of personal expression and lyric sentimentality. One is likely to overlook Lubitsch's musical adaptations because of his success in comedy, but they rechannel the dynamic thrust of silent-film slapstick through the treat-ment of the characters and story as kinetic embellishments of the song and dance. The cosmic potential of the music is most deliriously fulfilled in the major production numbers of Berkeley's *Gold Diggers of 1933, 42nd Street, Footlight Parade*, and *Wonder Bar*, but his attempt to treat the book of the musical as a self-styled uniform fantasy in *Gold Diggers of 1935* lacks the dramatic irony of his more conventional musicals; Berkeley's characters only come alive within the artifices of a theatrical production, whereas those of Clair and Lubitsch embody the glitter of their settings and the humanizing potential of the song and dance.

Slapstick also proved of great interest to Russian filmmakers; though it was creatively elaborated in the films of Pudovkin and Eisenstein, it was used with less success in comedy. Lev Kuleshov's *The Extraordinary Adventures of Mr. West in the Land of the Bolsheviks* and *By the Law* are part of a primitive film culture experimenting with various narrative styles. Kuleshov's simplistic types and his facile use of close-ups are examples of a studied, eclectic film style that borrows from two different forms of comedy: American vaudeville and English theater. There are several adroit character sketches in *By the Law*, but the routines are derivative. Slapstick is limited to its destructive potential, and fragments of the comedy of manners are used in an anticlimactic manner. Abram Room's *Bed and Sofa* is a more interesting work, its literate script probing married life in the first years after the revolution. A man moves in with a married couple, causing a rupture in the marriage; eventually the woman is left alone to face the realities of postrevolutionary society. Room's dialectical look at sexual warfare is not without its penetrating insights; like Lubitsch's silent films, it cries out for sound to more fully express the desires and paradoxes that motivate its three characters.

Two factors played a critical role in Ernst Lubitsch's career: his settling in America and the introduction of the sound film. Lotte Eisner emphasized the influence of Max Reinhardt in Lubitsch's lighting and in his direction of epic confrontations. But her characterization of Lubitsch's historical projects as failed Reinhardt productions misses the mark, and Herman Weinberg has not cleared up this issue. For Lubitsch has only a superficial interest in concep-tualizing the erupting historical forces through the lighting and cutting. The dominant motif in *Madame Dubarry* is the male-female chemistry that is gener-ated by his stars, Emil Jannings and Pola Negri. Jannings was always interesting to watch, but it is Negri's animate, erotic presence and self-conscious play-acting to which Lubitsch is most sympathetic. The problem with the film is Lubitsch's unwillingness to develop the social conflict in terms of their erotic friction; hence, the historical backdrops seem perfunctory, and his picture of the prerevolutionary period wavers between bedroom farce and lurid melodrama.

Though Lubitsch was probably the director most sensitive to the droll, bewitching, and bitching charm of Wilde's plays, *Lady Windermere's Fan* fails to come alive as a silent film because Wilde's elegant humor engages the audience with its crackling epigrams and repartees. Lubitsch shows his theatrical deftness in trapping his players in their homes and at work, and his direction of the garden party is cleverly done, but the film sorely misses the play's scathing verbal taunts. His flair in undercutting the mannerisms of the bourgeoisie is shown to better effect in *The Marriage Circle*; the pacing and his character portraits are less forced than in his historical dramas. One, however, awaits the elixir of language to elaborate their sexual and psychological maneuvers.

With the advent of the sound film the anarchic gracefulness of the silent film is frozen in history. One moves from a world of tightrope walkers, of ethereal romantics, and daydreaming nihilists to a social reality in which one's manners and mores are satirized; the keynote to the comedy films of Lubitsch, Renoir, and Pagnol is the need to morally invigorate a lethargic, stereotyped setting. Classic Lubitsch anti-heroes like Herbert Marshall and Miriam Hopkins in *Trouble in Paradise* and Melvyn Douglas as the wily playboy in *Ninotchka* expose the staid, stolid personality of their dramatic opposites as they pursue their romantic instincts. His characters delight in their cleverness and in exposing their partners' self-conceit, for example, when Marshall and Hopkins read a train timetable in half a dozen languages with a computerlike efficiency and when they reveal what they have stolen from each other. Lubitsch's treatment of their travels through the countryside, in which he incorporates large crowds as a chorus, is brilliantly adapted from his musicals. His natural sympathy for his characters' inspired lunacy intimates the inevitability of their marriage: they must join forces if their wit and sensuality are to survive the dreary, mechanical nature of society. It is as true of Marshall and Hopkins as it is of her reunion with Gary Cooper and Fredric March in *Design for Living* and of Greta Garbo's return to Paris in *Ninotchka*.

*Trouble in Paradise* remains Lubitsch's and Raphaelson's most precise exercise in film comedy; their glib delineation of the characters and intrigue proves as eye-appealing as the work of a card shark. *Design for Living* and *Ninotchka* apply a similar approach to characters whose shrewd plans for self-preservation are most lucidly articulated in their temporary residences: the loft in *Design for Living* and the hotel suite in *Ninotchka*. Lubitsch is not as interested in engaging his characters in numerous subplots and diversions as he is in clarifying the problems they must contend with in sustaining their freedom and humor. The final resolution in *Design for Living*—that mutual respect for another's independence and comic inventiveness can sustain a ménage à trois—and in Garbo's decision to let herself go—"Garbo laughs"—constitute what is called the "Lubitsch touch."

Although Lubitsch's profound regard for his characters' transcendent mischievousness remains paramount in a late film such as *That Uncertain Feeling*, some of his major productions in the thirties and forties like *Angel, Heaven Can Wait*, and *The Shop around the Corner* project a steadfast, moral priority. His more straightforward comedies are generally favored by critics, but in these films, albeit not as clever, as fast-paced, or as much fun as *Trouble in Paradise*, *Ninotchka*, and *Cluny Brown*, his appreciation of his characters' independence develops in a more ambiguous, emotionally unsettled environment. A film like *Trouble in Paradise* shows Lubitsch's consummate professionalism in mastering the rhythms of a sound film, in which his protagonists' aloof mannerisms will, at best, establish a temporary compromise with society. But in *Angel, Heaven Can Wait*, and *The Shop around the Corner*, Lubitsch's heroes are not iconoclasts; their desires arise out of a need to reconfirm the simple harmonies of an ennobling middle-class existence. In *Angel* and *The Shop around the Corner*, Marlene Dietrich and Margaret Sullavan eventually abandon their fantasies in recognizing the ardor and levelheadedness of Herbert Marshall and James Stewart.

*Heaven Can Wait* is the most detailed of these films in expressing Lubitsch's affection for the graces and comforts of a premodern society. The story unfolds through Lubitsch's expert manipulation of Don Ameche's gay sophisticate who is awaiting a verdict on his life as bon vivant and husband from Laird Cregar's divine arbiter. To Lubitsch Cregar's otherworldly offices look no different than one's living room, where the question of whether Ameche is to go to heaven or hell awaits the telling of a good story. Lubitsch's morality is still manifest through a character's sense of style: Ameche meets an old flame in Cregar's waiting room, and when she begins to show some leg, Cregar pushes a button consigning her to hell. Much of the comedy in the film originates in the family gatherings that serve as an effective counterpoint to Ameche's frivolous adventures. Their old-world charm and the ensuing marriage of Ameche and Gene Tierney are among the virtuous emblems of Lubitsch's idealized, premechanized society.

Lubitsch's emphasis on friendship and romance within the framework of the social order was taken to a more extreme point in the films of Jean Renoir and Marcel Pagnol. *The Crime of Monsieur Lange* is a prototypical Renoir work in dramatizing the precarious emotional makeup of his naïfs in a lower-class setting. His characters work on a pulp rag celebrating the glories of American popular culture. Like their own fantasy creations, Renoir's characters are guileless daydreamers whose murder of the ruthless editor functions as an example of the victory of good over evil in the manner of their literary fictions. *Boudu Saved from Drowning* is a more uncompromisingly didactic film in which Renoir turns to the figure of the tramp as society's redeemer. But unlike Chaplin's stylized, paradoxical anti-hero, Michel Simon's Boudu is a clumsy, physically propulsive primitive. During his short stay at the home of the indolent bookseller,

Renoir attacks the platitudes of the bourgeoisie while recklessly honoring Boudu's tramp as its savior. Renoir consistently avoids the poetic, sublime touches that distinguish Chaplin's tramp in order that the primitiveness of Simon's Boudu evokes the anarchy and slovenliness of a child of nature. One applauds Renoir's sentiments, but the film's rambling style and its polemical support of Simon's destructive wild child underline the tenuousness of his Rousseau-like celebration of nature.

In his work with Raimu in the trilogy of *Marius, Fanny,* and *César,* Marcel Pagnol's affection for his working-class heroes and for their emotional quandaries and ever present money problems avoids the dramatic primitivism and emotional fervor that so forcefully resonate in the films of Renoir. The tone of these films is most clearly articulated by Raimu, the pivotal figure in the cafés and camaraderies that permeate French provincial society. Unlike Chaplin's character of a tightrope walker who is defining new laws of gravity and Keaton's characterization of the clown as one continually in orbit, Raimu plays the role of the barroom gadfly, enlivening either a static or a tense situation with his nautral gift of gab. Raimu's prolonged verbal anecdotes and terse playacting allow his audience to sit back and forget their problems; a good story and a glass of wine are the rule of the day. Raimu's character as the father and the predominant folk spirit of the trilogy continually modify its emotional and dramatic continuity. It is Raimu who arranges the wedding, while the reunion with his son is the film's crucial dramatic resolution, underscoring his position as the spiritual godfather of town life and the family as its most essential institution. His love of friends and family makes for the most moving moments in the trilogy. One scene finds him conversing with his friends, lightly mocking their glum facade while proposing new meanings for words when the postman arrives with a letter from his son. His friends realize that as attached as he is to a good yarn, they should quietly leave without expressing their recognition of Raimu's love of his estranged son. In another sequence shortly after his friend's death, Raimu, sitting in a bar and amusing his patrons as the most complacent of tavern owners, suddenly cuts off a long tirade when he spots the empty chair of his recently departed friend.

In *The Baker's Wife* Raimu's character is seen as the source of the story's folk poetry and pathos. In the trilogy Raimu is more often than not commenting on what is happening to others, but in *The Baker's Wife* it is his experiences that embody the problems and virtues of country life. Pagnol's method originates in his adherence to the manners and idiosyncracies of his rustics, just as Lubitsch sustains the wit and wisdom of his adventurers. He adopts the most simple of filmmaking styles, in which the camerawork and editing withdraw from the action so that the voice of Pagnol's commoners becomes the unifying theme and moral of his film. It is his immersion in the poetic truthfulness of his peasants that allows them to transform their primitive settings with their own atavistic impulses. This is most apparent in the scene in which the baker's wife lies with her lover in a quaint picnic area that becomes, for a short time, their Garden of Eden. Compared to Renoir, the rustic spirit of Pagnol's farces lacks complexity.

Their sparkle is wholly dependent on the characters' changing moods; Pagnol refuses to didactically impose the cumulative moral antagonism in Renoir's films. Instead, as in his literal adaptation of Giono's *Harvest*, the moral of the good life is inseparable from his characters' attempts to unify their emotional desires with the regenerative forces of nature.

Chaplin's last silent film, *City Lights*, and his two early sound films, *Modern Times* and *The Great Dictator*, find the tramp in increasingly tenuous situations in which his invigorating romanticism faces a more severe challenge than in his first shorts and feature-length films. *In City Lights* the tramp no longer suspends himself in a world of balletic gracefulness and romantic isolation; he must return to the city where the teeming presocial anarchy in his earlier comedies is replaced by the cold, sobering rules of an established society. It is a key transitional film for Chaplin because the breathtaking antics featured in his shorts are not as dominant. His routine in the boxing ring is as sharply choreographed as any of the liberating performances in his previous films; yet the tramp's support and love of the blind girl do not inspire the triumphant note of freedom and independence in Charlie's relationship to the abandoned child in *The Kid* or to his partner in *The Gold Rush*. *The Circus* is imbued with a similar feeling of loneliness and depression that are closing in on the tramp, but while its setting is the joyous circus world, *City Lights* transpires in an urban background in which a commedia dell'arte story is delineated. Its theatrical texture is most visible in that his love of the girl is not conceived as a secondary theme, but as the single ideal that prompts his exploits. In the final, disconsolate expression that settles on her face when she realizes that her benefactor is not prince charming but a scrawny, weather-beaten little fellow and in his own look of tearful abjection, Chaplin displays his growing uncertainty about the fate of the clown. Perhaps he is fearful of continuing his journey on the road of life alone; his desire to be loved by the girl seems to reflect the ephemeral nature of the clown's existence and a recognition of his incongruity as the savior of humanity. It is a moving, profound variation on the conventions of commedia dell'arte, but if the last scene in *The Gold Rush* has left us wondering as to his future identity, *City Lights* concludes with the moroseness surrounding Chaplin's tramp.

*Modern Times* attempts to extricate the tramp from this perplexing condition through its overt attack on the dehumanizing nature of modern life. The tramp's confrontation with the machine in the factory, his being swept up by the radical mob, and his blithe acquiescence to his short stay in prison present a more uniform story line than does *City Lights*, but his befriending the waif and their eventual return to the road shows Chaplin adopting a more conservative tone. If the moral is more didactic than in his earlier films, a more revealing element is the look of the film. The grainy, primitive texture of his films through *City Lights* reenforces the makeshift, illusory nature of reality. But because of the clearer tonality of the film stock of *Modern Times*, Charlie seems to have stepped out of a time machine and into the streets of our modern cities. Although it enhances the tramp's verisimilitude, the pandemonium he inspires is compromised by the film's more realistic trappings. He has brought the tramp into the modern world, but somehow his antic comedy, like his appearance, seem anachronistic.

In *The Great Dictator* Chaplin challenges the aesthetic incongruity between the tramp and our naturalistic society by directing an ironic attack on Hitler and fascism. He makes a more extensive use of the sound medium, while the tramp, partly visible in his role as the barber, becomes the prototype—with Paulette Goddard—of the good earth. But it is his least successful film because of the stylistic inconsistency between his comic routines and subject matter. The sequence at the train station is contrived, sorely missing the rhythm and energy previously initiated by the tramp. Charlie's characterization of Hitler appears unfocused, lacking in the tension between portraiture and caricature that would have made his confrontation with Jack Oakie's Mussolini in the barber shop a truly inspired study of comic bombast. His pas de deux with the globe is one of his finest moments, but it is such a personal, poetic expression of his earlier film aesthetic that it seems out of place in the film's more naturalistic confines. Chaplin is muddled in the realities of the thirties, unsure of how the elegiac figure of the tramp is to blend into a social environment whose most formidable figure is, as Chaplin noted, a grotesque parody of the tramp.

*Mr. Smith Goes to Washington–The Bank Dick*

Although there seems to be universal admiration for the stylistic diversification of comedy during the thirties and forties in Hollywood, the predominant role of slapstick in disparate productions such as *Mr. Deeds Goes to Town*, *Twentieth Century*, and *The Barber Shop* has gone largely unexplored. Raymond Durgnat, for example, while sympathetic to the energy and frenzy of the major comedies of this period, perceives a confusing mass of sociological impulses that resist any single, stylistic source. Yet there exists an undeniable stylistic thread revealing the irrepressible force of slapstick in American culture.

There appear to be three major comedy forms in the thirties and forties, and each one provides a variation on the slapstick humor of silent-film comedy. The first style embraces many of the characters and themes in the folk poetry of Griffith and John Ford; among its representative works is *Mr. Smith Goes to Washington*, while Preston Sturges' satires make the most artistic use of its admixture of innocence and mayhem. The second comedy style is characterized by the sly, acerbic scripts of Ben Hecht, the nonconformist behavior of stars like Katharine Hepburn and Cary Grant, and films such as *Bringing Up Baby* and *Stage Door*. The third major form, featuring the Marx Brothers, Mae West, and W. C. Fields, presents the most straightforward application of slapstick comedy.

Frank Capra's initial work in the Hal Roach studios seemed to offer a natural outlet for his folk sentimentality. He fully empathized with America's rural origins, its premechanized society, and its puritan political ideology. In three of his major sound films—*Mr. Smith Goes to Washington, Mr. Deeds Goes to Town,* and *Meet John Doe*—Capra fashions a didactic study of the evils of big city life while reconfirming the quaint virtues of the small town. *Mr. Smith Goes to Washington,* less a polemic and more a satire, derives its humor from the characters' idiomatic loquacity and the madcap interplay in settings such as the governor's home, the reporters' club, and the Senate floor. Although the characters of James Stewart, Jean Arthur, and Edward Arnold are imbued with a decisive moral identity, they retain the instincts of their vaudeville forebears. But in *Meet John Doe* and with greater urgency in *Mr. Deeds Goes to Town,* Capra's puritan morality leads to a form of gunslinging populism in which the naive undergoes considerable foreshortening. If the candor and idealism of Stewart's Mr. Smith were extensions of his quirky vocal and physical mannerisms, Gary Cooper's Mr. Deeds is more of a self-caricature, whose first days as a millionaire only expose his inanity, as in his feeding doughnuts to a horse. In *Mr. Smith Goes to Washington* Stewart's comic naïf wins our affection while leading Claude Rains to confess his sins, but the unemployed, hysterical common man who holds a gun on Cooper establishes a far more restrictive sense of both comedy and drama. It is a call to arms all the more contrived when compared to ingenious plot twists such as Stewart's use of the Boy Scouts to combat Arnold's political boss. The most overt expression of Capra's Sodom and Gomorrah dialectic occurs during an unintentionally revealing moment in *It's a Wonderful Life.* One can agree with Capra's admirers that it is his warmest film, his richest penetration of the enduring clichés of the small town. However, when an angel shows Stewart, who is on the verge of suicide, what would happen if he were not born, Capra's apocalyptic vision of Stewart's town is marked by neon lights and strip joints; this underscores the quaintness in Capra's antithetical picture of an American Bethlehem, in which Main Street radiates a *Saturday Evening Post* tranquillity and the local theater shows a Leo McCarey film, *The Bells of St. Mary's.*

Whereas Capra's films shove apple pie into the viewer's mouth, Preston Sturges' work—especially his two films with Eddie Bracken (*The Miracle of Morgan's Creek; Hail the Conquering Hero*)—is more compassionate in its character portraits and moral dilemmas and provides better examples of American folk art. Like *Twentieth Century* and *The Bank Dick,* its theme is the lunacy at the heart of American society. In Capra films the comedy is often used as a platform to express his sentiments on what he thinks unhealthy, un-American, and, in all likelihood, the work of the devil. But in Sturges' films his affection for the comic speech and rhythms of his characters is seen as reason enough for making a film. Unlike Capra who tends to oversimplify each characterization in his fiery polemics against the horrors of the big city, Sturges responds to his characters' absurdist, individualistic behavior. In *The Great McGinty* he does not dismiss Akim Tamiroff and his political cronies as grim symbols of political corruption, but emphasizes the comic interplay involving Tamiroff's Boss Tweed–like characterization and Brian Donlevy's John Doe figure. Instead of exaggerating the devious ways of our political machinery, Sturges sees the inherent humor of villains like Tamiroff, the department store executive in *Christmas in July,* and the mayor in *Hail the Conquering Hero*: they contribute equally to the native folk culture that Sturges shows we can never abandon. In *The Great McGinty* Sturges could have faded out on the great good intended by Donlevy's governor, but he prefers to show Tamiroff and Donlevy brawling in the Mexican town to which they have escaped. He is not calling us all crooks: he conceives his characters' desire to do good and their conflicting meanness as part of the vaudevillelike superstructure that has been made of America.

Sturges' skill as a scriptwriter, combining the idiosyncratic quirks in our language with the reckless behavioral impulses first exploited by Sennett, enabled him to develop the one major comedy style distinct from Lubitsch's genteel, sophisticated humor. Unlike Lubitsch's films, which concern for the most part the well-to-do, and unlike Capra's little-man allegories scripted by Robert Riskin, Sturges distills the posing and awkwardness at both ends of the social spectrum. Sturges' style, like that of screenwriter Sidney Buchman for Capra in *Mr. Smith Goes to Washington*, is intrinsically verbal. Whereas Buchman's most ambitious script, *The Talk of the Town*, infuses the verve of his earlier screwball scripts with a dramatic incisiveness rigorously conveyed through George Stevens's tight cutting and staging, Sturges shows his closer proximity to radio drama than to the theater through his musical integration of rambling fragments of interjection and sudden bursts of commentary from background players. Characters do not simply talk funny in a Sturges film; the dynamics of sound and speech result in the abbreviation of theatrical repartee into musical tropes.

Sturges becomes didactic or sentimental when his protagonists are cut off from their social background. The less satisfying moments in *The Palm Beach Story*—for example, when Joel McCrea and Claudette Colbert debate their marriage woes—lack the energizing social strains of folk behavior and speech supplied by William Demarest and a company of merry twits during the train ride. McCrea's adventures with Veronica Lake in *Sullivan's Travels* fail to inspire any comic banter not only because of Lake's difficulties in enunciation, but also because Sturges unwisely attempts a morality play with only a few, contrived references to the comic vicissitudes of speech and behavior that are found in his best films. Sturges is at his best with groups of people, such as the scenes involving McCrea and his studio executives in *Sullivan's Travels*. However, the soft modeling of the faces of McCrea and Lake by John Seitz's camera and Sturges' reverent treatment of Depression-era America transform the film into a series of Norman Rockwell illustrations. Sturges' work with Victor Milner, the preeminent cinematographer of comedy in the thirties and forties, offers another vantage point in examining his emphasis on the verbal flux of comedy. Milner's high-key gloss in Lubitsch's films functions as a stylistic reflection of the elegance of the characters and dialogue. In *The Palm Beach Story* Milner's equally generous use of light underscores the theatrical staging, but Sturges' dialogue, unlike that of Lubitsch and Raphaelson, is not attuned to the harmonies of theatrical dialogue. He relies on rising, often conflicting currents of sound and speech, the inflection of regional accents and tonalities like those of William

Demarest and Eugene Pallette. In *The Lady Eve* Milner's sparkling photography effectively complements Sturges' most precise theatrical script. The film works in many ways as a contest between the Lubitsch-style spirit of the card sharks, played by Charles Coburn and Barbara Stanwyck, and the receding quirks of folk culture represented by Fonda's gullible fop and the supporting presence of Demarest and Pallette. The gag she pulls on Fonda, which consumes the second half of the film, is a tribute to Lubitsch's comic arsenal, as is her playing on Fonda's credulity when listing her past lovers. The seduction in the cabin is perhaps most typical of Sturges' style; Fonda's stuttering declaration of affection shows the pathos of Sturges' humor making its strongest appeal to Stanwyck's good-natured tease. It is at this moment that one recognizes the inevitability of their union as Stanwyck's affability comforts Fonda's pathetic attempt at courtship. In *Unfaithfully Yours* Sturges interprets the neurotic fantasies of Rex Harrison's jealous husband through Milner's unrepresentative and far-too-dark, low-key photography. The heavy-handed script offers little breathing space for the social and sexual ironies that were previously illuminated by Milner's posh lighting in *The Lady Eve*.

*The Miracle of Morgan's Creek* and *Hail the Conquering Hero* are Sturges' most comprehensive studies of the vaudeville antics and underlying morality of small-town America; in both films he dissects American myths: the character of the sweetheart in the former and that of the war hero in the latter. The characters and chorus that fill his dense canvas are uniquely his own; Sturges emphasizes the fragile nature of the role models they assume as adults and the high-spirited anarchy that surrounds their exploits. It is exemplified in Eddie Bracken's variety of nervous ticks and quirks and in the riotous imbalance during the welcome celebration for Bracken by Franklin Pangborn and a wonderfully inept band. Sturges' spoofing of the manners and customs of rural America balanced against Seitz's prominent, nostalgic front lighting of Bracken surrounded by the Marines shows its social imperviousness, a condition Sturges sees as essential to its moral and comic integrity. Slapstick, to Sturges, is as much a genetic force as a style of verbal and physical comedy.

The second comedy form, blending together elements of the comedy of manners and slapstick and characterized as screwball comedy, was the most successful of the three major comedy styles that flourished in the thirties and forties. The chaotic, physically dynamic elements of slapstick are least conspicuous in this form; yet owing to the stylistic eclecticism of screwball comedy, it has proved the most resilient and to many the most impressive product of American film comedy.

The most recognizable classics of this genre—Ben Hecht's and Charles MacArthur's *Twentieth Century*, with the inspired lunacy of John Barrymore's Oscar Jaffe and Carole Lombard's Mildred Plotka, and the ingenious character transformation of their *The Front Page* into *His Girl Friday*, with the cat-and-mouse fencing of Cary Grant and Rosalind Russell and the complementary staccato editing—prove that there will always be a trace of insanity in the American bloodline. Hecht's resiliency as an adapter of prestigious literary and dramatic works, as well as his coauthorship of *Twentieth Century* and *The Front Page*—two riotous, fast-paced send-ups in which language experiences the same manic rush that their film protagonists bring to their roles as caricatures of the press and theater—stand out as the most vital single force among Hollywood writers. If there is an underlying cynicism to Hecht's comedy scripts, the characters and situations are alive with the immediacy of a journalistic lead-in: the burly voice of America living through Prohibition and the Depression. His scripts invariably reflect the Byzantine nature of Hollywood, both as a social microcosm of ephemeral fame and fortune and as a commercial entertainment.

Among the numerous stars who have contributed to this portrait gallery of the patron saints of nonconformity in our society, none has been quite as distinct as Katharine Hepburn. Lombard was better suited to this style of comedy, and Grant may have been its exemplary performer, but Hepburn's aristocratic charms—her lithe, leonine movements and disdainful retorts—occupy a singular place in this galaxy of shooting stars. Hepburn's fluency as both a comic and dramatic performer is central to the problem several critics have voiced about her screen persona. Bette Davis, her foremost rival, scored a triumph in *Old Acquaintance*, playing straight lady to Miriam Hopkins's scatterbrained scribe, but Davis's screen presence largely derived from her passionate portrayals of destructive heroines in *Jezebel*, *Dark Victory*, and *Mr. Skeffington*. From Hepburn's screen debut in *A Bill of Divorcement*, in which she abandons her lover to tend her ailing father, through her comedies opposite Grant and Spencer Tracy to her interpretations of the tormented matriarch in *Suddenly Last Summer* and *Long Day's Journey into Night*, she has always seemed to resist the attraction either of her comic suitors or of those lending support in her suffering. Her beauty has an aloof, imperious quality, her eyes conveying an intelligence and inner fortitude that make for her early triumphs in *Morning Glory* and *Stage Door* and her self-immolation in *Christopher Strong*, one of her most idiosyncratic screen interpretations and one of the best examples of costume as character in the American cinema.

A characterization of her first stage and screen roles as cold and mechanical is correct but miss the point; her technical control emanates from the self-realization of her perfectibility. She is an artist whose weaknesses of character result from her being wiser and more in control of the emotions she must repress to sustain her identity as the elusive, ideal mate. She may be momentarily nonplussed by the affections of Grant and Stewart in *The Philadelphia Story*, but it is her mask of regal disdain that has inspired their appeals. As the foremost symbol of the modern woman, her verbal and physical powers are clearly more than one man can handle, a theme central to her films opposite Grant and Tracy. Grant's equally mocking delivery and dashing kineticism qualify him as Hepburn's ideal partner in attacking the conventions of high society. When Hepburn plays opposite Tracy's more subdued, paternalistic figure, her superior individuality connotes a touch of madness.

In *Adam's Rib* Hepburn plays a lawyer who defends a client, Judy Holliday, who is accused of shooting her lover; the prosecutor is her lawyer-husband, played by Tracy. During the trial Hepburn's arguments result in a defense of the modern woman; what wins the case for Holliday is not Hepburn's verbal dexterity, but the agile, dynamic use of her athletic skills in transforming the courtroom into a circus. Director George Cukor adroitly utilizes her identity as ringmaster and occasional performer to win over the judge and dazzle both Tracy and the film audience. The strong woman she introduces as an example of a woman's physical strength and Holliday's hapless character present contrasting examples of feminity; Hepburn's role as the promoter becomes a mediating spectrum of male and female virtues. The final moral twist in both *Adam's Rib* and *Woman of the Year* finds Hepburn receiving her comeuppance from Tracy. In confronting Hepburn and a male neighbor with a licorice gun, Tracy reaches into Hepburn's comic arsenal by holding up a mirror to the implications of her defense. She then acquiesces to his more rational point of view, but one speculates that their film marriage will reflect their roles in *Pat and Mike*, in which she plays a professional athlete and he, her agent.

*Woman of the Year* makes perhaps the strongest case for Hepburn as the most awesome female protagonist in American film history—brainy and beautiful, boisterous and beatific. The film is less frantic than *Adam's Rib*, and George Stevens's direction is indifferent, but even in the most commonplace settings the Hepburn-Tracy romance abounds in myth and metaphor. Watching Hepburn's introduction to baseball, one wonders what restrains her from running onto the field, dismissing the players, and rivaling Keaton as a one-player baseball game. *Pat and Mike* presents Hepburn as a modern amazon, but Cukor's direction is weak, and the verbal fencing is less pointed than in *Adam's Rib* or *Woman of the Year*. There are few of the crackling witticisms that charged the dialogue in their earlier confrontations with a social and theatrical resonance; the film offers little more than repeated examples of Hepburn's athletic prowess, as in the scene in which she beats up the two thugs who have come to settle a score with Tracy.

In Hepburn's films with Grant, there is a more consistent slapstick edge. The union of two such gifted, fluent comedians seems inevitable; it is only a question of their mutual recognition that life would be tedious without the other's company. This point is elegantly realized in *Holiday*: Grant's temporary myopia to Hepburn's wit and beauty is overcome at the same time he realizes he is not fated to a tranquil, domesticated marriage. But in *Bringing Up Baby* the lunacy that inspired so many silent-film comics is radically appropriated by Hepburn, who makes the strongest case for the female sex not as the equal of the male but, indisputably, as his superior. There have been several comediennes whose zaniness rivaled their male counterparts'. Mabel Normand's tomboyish personality, her scrappiness and her energy made her an ideal protagonist in Sennett's raucous farces. Marion Davies, in two well-made satires by King Vidor, showed surprising flair as a comedienne whose physical resiliency expressed her cleverness and determination. Davies' attractiveness and athleticism prefigure Hepburn's magic, playing the slumming sophisticate who has become enamored of the raciness and vitality of the jazz age. On the evidence of Davies' devastating parody of the reigning Hollywood queens in *Show People*, one only wishes there had been more of her.

Yet Hepburn's inventiveness gives one second thoughts. The numerous tricks she plays on Grant's priggish pedant is one of the more unbridled examples of castration in the movies: it is not just that Grant is reduced to wearing a dress and whimpering for the safety and security of his research as an archaeologist, but also that Hepburn's idealization of the modern woman with a vengeance denotes a sense of Wildean misanthropy that seems to reject all social conventions. Unlike *The Awful Truth*, in which Grant and Irene Dunne complement each other through their solo turns as the avenging iconoclast, in *Bringing Up Baby* Hepburn combines the disdain of a stripper with the soaring artistry of a trapeze artist in ridiculing Grant's character. Imagine, for example, Hepburn playing Rosalind Russell's role opposite Grant in *His Girl Friday* or her being cast as Grant's wife in *The Awful Truth*. One can see Russell or Dunne having an affair with—even marrying—Ralph Bellamy's twit, but Hepburn would leave him a teetering wreck. Russell, like Dunne, injects just the right sense of irony for a Grant retort to maintain the comic equilibrium. Hepburn's elegance and anarchy, her sexuality and transcendent irony turn the rivalry into a romp; it is no contest. Perhaps more than the Marx Brothers or Mae West, she was the true disciple of silent-film slapstick, adapting its anarchic instincts to the glum propriety of high society. *Bringing Up Baby* is not so much an expert screwball comedy as it is a dazzling exhibition of the revolt of the repressed.

*His Girl Friday* and *Twentieth Century* are among the best screwball comedies because their contrasting gaiety and cynicism seem peculiar to the thirties and to archetypal national institutions such as the press and Broadway theater. *The Front Page* is one of the fun classics of the American theater; the comic repartee escalates with the fury and froth of a pie-throwing jamboree in a silent-film farce. When Hildy is played by a male, even by an intelligent actor like Jack Lemmon in Billy Wilder's adaptation, one is never convinced his romance is for real; by casting Rosalind Russell as Hildy in *His Girl Friday*, the villainy of this classic script is augmented because the rivalry between two reporters is seen as a mask to their identity as sexual protagonists scurrying for the more advantageous, dominant position.

*Twentieth Century* is a delirious satire on stardom. It is brilliantly incarnated by Lombard, one of Hollywood's more instinctive interpreters of the attractive, sassy female whose frenetic personality can never completely hide her love for the leading man. She is not as daring as Hepburn or as frivolous as Harlow in *Red Dust*; she is not as cool and debonair as Russell in *Take a Letter, Darling* or Irene Dunne in both comedy and melodrama, but she has distilled their style of play, cunning, and grace in delineating the male-female antagonism while revealing herself as the ideal female protagonist of screwball comedy. But in *Twentieth Century* it is John Barrymore's explosive self-caricature that makes the film one of the classics of the thirties. Grant would have played the role with his customary aplomb, but it is the self-ridicule in Barrymore's performance that gives the film its parodistic resonance (it also proves why Barrymore with his flair for the grotesque and not Grant should have been cast in *Arsenic and Old Lace*). Hecht's satire concerns the flamboyant nature of show-business entrepreneurs which, through Barrymore's histrionic characterization of Oscar Jaffe, cuts at their pretences while celebrating the vitality and mischievousness their personalities brought to our culture. The film presents a monstrous yet innocent gallery of American con men and would-be artists. The satire becomes decidedly double-edged because of Barrymore's performance and because of the intrinsic puerilities involved in the transformation of Mildred Plotka into Lily Garland. With its vaudeville background and plot twists in the theater and train, the film shows how the comparable exhibitions of lunacy of Barrymore and Lombard enable them, like other screwball partners, to find happiness in their mutual outrageousness.

Howard Hawks, director of *Bringing Up Baby*, *His Girl Friday*, and *Twentieth Century*, deserves much of the credit for their accomplished black humor, but, like George Cukor, his contributions have been misinterpreted by numerous revisionists in contemporary film criticism. While *auteur* proselytes have unearthed several Hawks projects that were best forgotten (*The Dawn Patrol*, *The Road to Glory*), in which his tendency to vaudeville approaches the comic book rather than the comical, Richard Griffith's earlier description of Hawks as "a good all-arounder" seems a fair description of much of the work of one of Hollywood's more competent directors.

The diversity of stars and films that constitute this second major comedy form exemplifies the acuity and accessibility of comedy in particular and of the movies in general. Whether because of the Depression and the resulting need for escapist entertainments or owing to the moral shifts that had evolved in American society during Prohibition and the Depression, Hollywood, especially in its comedy films, reflected many of the changes peculiar to this era through the individualistic escapades engendered by the male-female interplay. These undomesticated renegades enabled audiences to laugh at the conceit of social probity while honoring an unattainable aristocratic independence.

In screwball comedy there is an unerring feeling of the incongruity between the hero's true nature and the mask he must assume in society. In the films of the Marx Brothers, Mae West, and W. C. Fields, the asymmetry between personal instincts and social conformity is energetically exploited. Few of their films were as good as they should have been; it is as if their singular presence as members of a bankrupt vaudeville troupe could not survive in a methodical, rational satire. They were family skeletons who reminded their audience of its proximity to the mean-spirited wit of vaudeville humor: the lower passions and the more Gothic aspects of American morality were served up like a Sunday cartoon supplement.

An example of their emphasis on the solipsistic nature of film slapstick can be found in *My Little Chickadee*. From the moment West and Fields first appear, the absurdity of the setting is underlined, then compounded by an inane, supporting love story. Because of their incongruity in this satire of the West, their gags and mischievousness play as the last laugh from a sinking ship. If there is a predominant reductionist theme to the humor of the Marx Brothers that defeats the purposes of their co-stars and scriptwriters, the comedy of West and Fields develops as a series of nightclub skits—two iconoclasts vying for our attention in their use of body English and other forms of comic disdain. The scenes opposite their earthbound antagonists—when West, for example, is taken for a ride in the carriage with the virtuous journalist—are similar to a surrealist sketch that introduces one disproportionate element in an otherwise conventional setting.

The best of the Marx Brothers—which means *Duck Soup*, most of *The Cocoanuts*, and *Monkey Business*, and celebrated scenes like the selling of encyclopedias in *A Day at the Races* and the stateroom overload in *A Night at the Opera*—plays off their roles as far-too-inventive children who have gained control of the adult world. Their comic choreography on the boat in *Monkey Business* derives from their assuming the role of directors of fun and games, while their ownership of the hotel in *The Cocoanuts* sets the stage for their numerous insane variations on a resort run by escapees from an asylum. One of the more incisive aspects of their onslaughts involves the verbal exchanges between Groucho and Chico; Chico's thick accent and broad punning are a worthy challenge to Groucho in amplifying the verbal and comic repartee. Groucho caricatures the fast-talking, manipulative American salesman while Chico's foreigner lampoons an immigrant's befuddlement, upsetting and at times hoodwinking Groucho. The land auction in *The Cocoanuts* and the encyclopedia sequence in *A Day at the Races* exemplify this point and are among their most inspired moments as Groucho's straight man is continually baffled by Chico's nutty variations. Among their other signature pieces are Groucho's constant ribbing of Margaret Dumont's well-meaning society matron, a serenade gone crazy, while the food, animals, and tools Harpo keeps in his coat suggest a master plan for survival. *Duck Soup* remains their most cogent satire, in which their comic pyrotechnics have a boomerang effect. From Groucho's self-mocking megalomania to Chico's italianate double agent and Harpo's prankster, their spoofing encompasses both the targets of the film's political satire and their own anarchistic nature. It may seem academic to criticize the rest of their work for lacking the unifying hysteria of *Duck Soup*, but to applaud isolated sequences from their films is to overlook their distinctly Rabelaisian potential. As tough and callous as they are to their dramatic opposites, their most riotous moments revolve around their devious, unnerving strategies toward one another.

Mae West's films are less nihilistic than those of the Marx Brothers because her proportions as a type of fertility goddess developed as a slap at Hollywood's priggishness. Her most enjoyable films, *I'm No Angel* and *She Done Him Wrong*, are not as violent as *Duck Soup* or *The Bank Dick*, but they prove most effective in honoring West as a "sexual temple," a mother Buddha who has come to torment man. A striking example of West's use of vaudeville tactics can be seen by comparing her courtroom spoofing in *I'm No Angel* to Katherine Hepburn's equally satiric treatment in *Adam's Rib*. Hepburn upstages the judicial machinery through her febrile movements, engaging the audience with her tomfoolery and inspired athleticism. She makes a case for the superiority of women, one whose logic rests on her own dazzling flights of ingenuity. In *I'm No Angel* the courtroom setting and characters seem lifted from some dated vaudeville skit; when West becomes her own lawyer, challenging the prosecution with her formidable movements, she wins the case by assuming the role of a walking skin flick.

Her two films with Cary Grant are her most appealing because Grant's charm and boyish self-confidence are not overshadowed by West's personality; similar to the Tracy-Hepburn screen rivalry, Grant conveys his admiration for West's daring and lasciviousness while preparing for his revenge. Her other suitors fall into the trap of her former lover in *She Done Him Wrong*; alone with West he can barely speak his lines and appears on the verge of a paroxysm of impotence. Her films differ from those of the Marx Brothers in that their humor derives from transferring their distrust and violence for one another to the surrounding environment; in West's films the various disguises she assumes—like that of the Salvation Army missionary in *Klondike Annie*—transform each of her settings into a nightclub. Considering her unique appearance—a combination of Titian's sprawling maiden and a runaway from a Wagnerian troupe—she could not easily blend into a film satire. She was a presence, better suited to the design of vaudeville comedy or graphic mischief.

Unlike Mae West and her devious impersonations of an American buttercup, the misanthropy of W. C. Fields is not coexpressive with his physical rotundity. His comedy gains as much from his verbal blasts as it does from his ever increasing waistline and bilious nose. Fields's early silent film, *It's the Old Army Game*, finds him turning a nice profit, but one misses the corpulence in his later films, in which he becomes a vaudeville version of the Grand Inquisitor. In combating some of the more freakish aspects of American society, from Baby LeRoy and Deanna Durbin to the mother-in-law, Fields's reliance on the violent strategies of vaudeville humor brutally answers tit for tat, at times without indulging in the physical anarchy for which slapstick comedy is famous. In *The Pharmacist* a customer buys a three-cent stamp from Fields; after pointing to the one in the middle, which Fields then places in a bag, he asks for change of a thousand-dollar bill. Before his departure, after having upset any mortal enough to inspire homicide, he is presented with a gift prize. The subtle, anarchic humor in this sequence rests in Fields's reserve, expressing his rancor in several tall stories and lewd gestures.

Fields's physical dexterity is not limited to clever bits with his hat or cane. In a brief appearance in *Six of a Kind*, Fields talks to a friend as he prepares to shoot a game of pool. While relating several anecdotes, Fields continues to reset the ball, going through a few strokes as if he were in preparation for an exhibition of unrivaled pool aplomb. His friend, who never says a word, is a perfect comedy foil, enabling Fields to dominate the scene and parody the mannerisms of a pool shark. His less rewarding films are similar to those of the Marx Brothers in that his dramatic opposites are abstracted; his sneering in *Never Give a Sucker an Even*

*Break* seems to be directed to all of humanity, while the most favorable comment one can make about *You Can't Cheat an Honest Man* is that it shows off Fields's redoubtable talent at Ping-Pong.

*The Barber Shop* and *The Bank Dick* present some of the funniest moments in sound-film comedy because Fields's misanthropic humor is directed toward more lucidly defined characters. *The Barber Shop* develops as a lampoon on rural America through Fields's malicious innuendos and gestures on the town's main street. Similar to *International House* in which Fields places his hand under a woman's derriere as he reaches for a cat who then gives birth to half-dozen kittens, it is only in a Fields film that one of the characters, upon retrieving his bass from Fields's shop, finds that it has given birth to several cellos. Along with *Big Business* and *Helpmates*, among other concise, pithy essays on mayhem, Fields's *The Barber Shop* offers a doomsday vision of rural America personified in Fields's character.

*The Bank Dick*, a parody on the little man in the environs of a small town, finds Fields barely repressing his villainy, most humorously in his dealings with Franklin Pangborn's bank auditor. Though he appears to fail in his attempts at moviemaking, stock investments, and job remuneration, Fields's eventual triumph is a cunning satire on the daydreams of the common man who feels life has passed him by. Although he has the good fortune to thwart the bank robbers and have his film script accepted, his one comfort remains the bottle. It is the only way to forget a frightening world comprised of characters like the little boy in the cowboy outfit and conventions like the hearty handshake; if vaudeville created a Fields, it also entailed an America as perverse as his iconoclastic figure.

### Kind Hearts and Coronets–How I Won the War

The flowering of the English comedy film, from early Alec Guinness to middle-period Peter Sellers, succeeded because the time seemed ripe to expose modern English society as preeminently Pickwickian. Unlike the classic slapstick signature of the American comedy film with its emphasis on the liberating explosions of unruly behavior and speech, the English comedy vision is inspired by the understated out-of-dateness of its protagonists and institutions; they document the failure awaiting those who attempt to escape its confines, a theme delineated throughout the Ealing comedy films which reaches its seriocomic climax in *I'm All Right, Jack*. Their more classic figures of social debility suggest the following features: Alex Guinness, a wistful schoolteacher who has missed out on a century of progress; Margaret Rutherford, a talented young comic impersonating an elderly woman; Terry-Thomas, a perverted lord; Alastair Sim, Terry-Thomas's perverted father. Though these stars play a number of different roles, the history of this period can be explained in the relationship of two characterizations: that of Guinness and Dennis Price. Guinness is clearly the major comic force in these films; his shy, withdrawn presence represents the entombed

Englishman. In recognizing the stillborn features of his life, he renounces his identity as the prim, correct Englishman in roles such as the bank employee in *The Lavender Hill Mob* and in his Dr. Jekyll married life in *The Captain's Paradise*. In his metamorphosis from a staid, conventional character to one delighting in epicurean riches, he, in effect, becomes the wily debonair character of Dennis Price.

To better understand this character transformation and its role in such seemingly different films as *Kind Hearts and Coronets* and *Your Past Is Showing*, one must first characterize Guinness's timidity as an English form of Walter Mitty-ism. The innocent, daydreaming nature of Guinness's identity is central to both *The Man in the White Suit* and *The Lavender Hill Mob*. The former operates as a parody of England's business world; Guinness's character is not so much that of a mad scientist but that of a reserved, inventive adolescent who is unconscious of his comical mannerisms, as in the helmet he wears during his experiments or in the sound of his machine, which, in a typically English style of under-statement, is the funniest aspect of the film. *The Lavender Hill Mob* is expressly concerned with Guinness's character and the dreams of his anonymous Eng-lishman. And like Walter Mitty's dream life, in which Danny Kaye becomes a comic-book adventurer, Guinness's fantasy leads him to South America, where he pursues a playboy's existence. One can then identify his "Mr. Hyde charac-ter" as being interchangeable with that of Dennis Price because Price is the one major character in the English comedy film who is not, like Guinness, a self-caricature. He will only be seen as part of a P. G. Wodehouse-like menagerie in *I'm All Right, Jack*, perhaps the final and most exhaustive chapter in this decade-long exercise in self-mockery.

It is not only Price's romantic self-assuredness that leads one to offer this equation between Guinness's Hyde-like character and Price's identity. The symbolic nature of Guinness's genteel, timid Englishman is the literal subject of *Kind Hearts and Coronets*, in which his ethereal, Pickwickian style encompasses seven different English figures. It is left to Price to destroy this Guinness-ridden lineage and enjoy a sensual, guiltless existence, just as Guinness himself dis-cards his identity as a decent, ordinary chap in *The Lavender Hill Mob* and in *The Captain's Paradise* in order to pursue his Price-like adventures with Yvonne De Carlo, among other pleasures of the night.

Price's singular identity in the English comedy film is used one last time in *Your Past Is Showing*. In the film several English personalities are confronted with past indiscretions that suggest Hyde-like peccadilloes; in order to maintain their respectable, Jekyll-like facade, they scheme to rid themselves of their blackmailer, played by Price. This casting gem emphasizes Price's unique posi-tion, as if he alone could appear in these films without expressing any Guinness-like idiosyncrasy. Their less-than-professional skill in adapting an Agatha Christie–type plot to do away with Price and his final escape reveal that this classic Jekyll-Hyde split, which for more than ten years was a central theme in the English cinema, remains as relevant today as it was in Dickens's archetype of a Pickwickian society.

The diverse characterizations of these English satires make for numerous effective comedies. *The Lavender Hill Mob*, *The Man in the White Suit*, and *Kind Hearts and Coronets* are probably the best of these films, but the boisterous humor in films such as *Passport to Pimlico* and the series of St. Trinian schoolgirl romps reflect the abundance of comic material in English types and institutions. *I'm All Right, Jack*, however, conveys a different comic emphasis, and this is most apparent in Price's joining the ranks of the self-caricatures and in the original comic identity of Peter Sellers. In his earliest films Sellers's deft, technical interpretations pinpoint the mechanical nature of his comic characterizations. Unlike Guinness's comic persona, which is marked by a spirited sense of irony, Sellers's technical virtuosity reduces each of his characters to a series of gross, awkward tics. Guinness is more poetic and personal; Sellers, perhaps because of his training in radio, undertakes more consistently parodic characterizations. His finest work under Stanley Kubrick's direction in *Lolita* and *Dr. Strangelove* is executed in a comic-tragic vein, in which his facility to assume different masks and voices uncovers a far bleaker and more psychologically penetrating view of his multiple impersonations. In *I'm All Right, Jack*, Sellers's devastating parody of a union leader underscores the passing of the nostalgic tone that sparked the English comedy film through the fifties. Ian Carmichael's happy-go-lucky innocent has little chance of survival in the absurdist social reality of *I'm All Right, Jack*. It is a brilliant, propulsive work whose anarchic point of view suggests that the antiquated nature of English society can no longer be treated in an affable, flippant manner. The revolution has come, but without the redeeming presence of Guinness's daydreamer, only a new generation of funnymen like Peter Cook, Dudley Moore, and the Monty Python troupe who survey the wreckage of English culture.

With the exception of *Lolita* and *Dr. Strangelove*, Sellers's career in America failed to utilize his exceptional vocal and physical technique. In *The Pink Panther* Sellers's comic mask is one of the impressionist specializing in foreign accents whose powers of physical coordination continually fail him. The backgrounds and supporting cast establish a suitable framework for Sellers's misadventures and mishaps, but in *A Shot in the Dark* his awkwardness dominates each scene. *The Party* finds director Blake Edwards and Sellers breaking one of the cardinal rules of comedy: Sellers's characterization fails to establish any comic tension between the rational and the irrational, between normal and abnormal behavior. His Hollywood extra is an indolent Indian who does not seem out of place at the Hollywood party to which he is mistakenly invited; the ensuing anarchy becomes a case study in how slapstick should not work. While *A Shot in the Dark* offered at least a few pleasures in setting the stage for Sellers's slapstick pratfalls, *The Party* recalls Kuleshov's primitive use of caricatures in *The Extraordinary Adventures of Mr. West in the Land of the Bolsheviks*. An equally pathetic attempt at slapstick comedy, *After the Fox*, is wholly dependent on its inert caricatures who would disappear in a cartoon for their lack of ink. Director Vittorio De Sica goes one better than Edwards in having Sellers's character play as a series of caricatures, most glumly in his role as an existentialist director. A definite low point in film comedy occurs when Sellers tells his aide, "I'm thinking, thinking about nothing," and then proceeds to film nothing. The self-conscious has been combined with the senseless.

Richard Lester has resurrected many of Sennett's comic ploys while expressing a genuine attachment to the zaniness of silent-film comedy. *The Running Jumping and Standing Still Film*, however, reveals the differences between an era in which slapstick exploited the energy of a new medium and one that turns slapstick humor into a psychologically reductionist style. Though Lester's timing is far better than Malle's *Zazie*, he oversimplifies the manic rhythms of slapstick by passing from one ludicrous action to the next, from one smirking type to another. Like numerous underground films from the early Richter shorts to Robert Nelson's *Oh, Dem Watermelons*, the anarchy is conceived as a ubiquitous condition and not as a reflection of the characters' revolt against society.

Lester's first Beatles film, *A Hard Day's Night*, is a more effective tribute to the glories of silent-film comedy because he is not passively integrating its self-caricatures and seemingly endless variations on violence. The absurd happenings that arise out of the presence of the Beatles are marked by a sense of the unexpected combined with an appreciation for the inevitability of chaos. The Beatles prove to be charming, guileless pranksters; whether they confront Victor Spinetti's recording manager or the mobs that follow them, they counterbalance one another and the irrationality of their world with their own whimsical merriment. The comic friction of *A Hard Day's Night* arises from the innocent presence of the Beatles and the numerous chases they inspire; rock 'n' roll becomes the self-propelling stage containing all the elements peculiar to vaudeville comedy. *Help!* attempts to superimpose a transparent story in which the Beatles are reduced to comic-book figures; it predates the surreal whimsy of *Yellow Submarine* but lacks the freedom preempted by the animator.

*The Knack* is a less personal work than either of Lester's Beatles films and seems the most objective, the most textbook-oriented of his slapstick reminiscences. His editing extrapolations are often brilliant, but the film's protagonists lack the ingenuity that the Beatles brought to their association with Lester. *How I Won the War* sustains the experiments of *The Knack* by juxtaposing his music-hall idiom and characters to the dialectics of Brechtian theater. But as his characters recede into his nightmarish backgrounds, their mission to build a golf course becomes a gratuitous essay on the horrors of war. The voice of the music hall is poetically realized by Jack McGowran, but the other players lack any identity other than as dim-witted sops who have been appropriated by the anonymous armies of the night. Lester is an accomplished student of silent-film slapstick, but he is unable or unwilling to make the crucial transition to the Brechtian-style collages of Godard's films in which there is a continual interplay of image and idea.

*Born Yesterday–The Family Jewels*

The American comedy film of the fifties and sixties appears to be dominated by the sly, cynical humor of Billy Wilder; some of the reasons for Wilder's ascendant voice can be explained through the characterizations of Judy Holliday. Holliday's roles in *Born Yesterday*, *The Solid Gold Cadillac*, and *It Should Happen to You* differ from earlier comic characterizations in that she does not win us over through the aristocratic aloofness of a Claudette Colbert, the dazzling inventiveness and grace of a Katharine Hepburn, or the hot-blooded, sexually aggressive nature of a Carole Lombard. She could never appear as other than a girl from the wrong side of town, a Runyonesque heroine who has little time for courting and for the romantic superfluities adopted by the female crusaders of screwball comedy. She is most famous for her portrayal of Broderick Crawford's giddy girl friend in *Born Yesterday*, but her most representative role may be in *The Solid Gold Cadillac*, in which her co-star, Paul Douglas, appears as a similarly gruff figure. Her determination as the secretary in *The Solid Gold Cadillac*, her diligence in poring over the books William Holden lends her in *Born Yesterday*, and her refusal to give up the advertising space in *It Should Happen to You* identify Holliday as a lower-class heroine who does not try to hide her lack of refinement and who is unwavering in fulfilling her dreams of success. One of the few Depression-era comediennes with a similar antagonistic nature was Ginger Rogers. Her gutsy, tough-girl retorts in *Stage Door* led to Katharine Hepburn's dramatic awakening, while her simple dedication to working-class ideals in *Kitty Foyle* resulted in her final romantic triumph. Though Holliday's engaging nasal inflection and the cocking of her head show her singular flair for comedy, it is her rugged individualism that makes her seem more real than other screen comediennes. It also explains why her work with Aldo Ray in *The Marrying Kind* affects us in a way Cary Grant and Irene Dunne in *Penny Serenade* cannot. To Holliday and Ray, the loss of a child is tantamount to one's own death; as effective as Grant and Dunne are, their reunion and domestic retrenchment seem inevitable.

Billy Wilder never seems more relevant than in his films of the fifties. *Sunset Boulevard* is probably his best work; the film's cynicism is adroitly reflected through its photography in which the estate and interiors function as a Gothic backdrop to Norma Desmond's acidulous monologues and seduction of William Holden. *The Seven Year Itch* and *Some Like It Hot* are further proof of the relevance of Wilder's cynicism in a period in which Hollywood attempted to remove some of its self-imposed censorial reins. Wilder was one of Marilyn Monroe's more astute directors, and the repressive genuflections of Tom Ewell and Jack Lemmon proved hard-boiled characterizations of America's sexual innocence. If *The Seven Year Itch* suffers from its contrived formularization of prolonged foreplay and eventual retreat, *Some Like It Hot* bristles in its erotic mischief through the self-caricatures of Lemmon and Tony Curtis.

Wilder's alliance with Lemmon would prove a vital link in American film comedy. In his earlier roles Lemmon played the fun-loving prankster opposite

James Cagney's martinet in *Mister Roberts* and Ernie Kovacs's killjoy in *Operation Mad Ball*; in *The Apartment* Wilder attempts a sentimental study of two losers lacking the amorality of their corporate superiors, while in *The Fortune Cookie* the depth of Wilder's cynicism finds Lemmon the target of his attack as Walter Matthau's scheming shyster sets the traps. Lemmon began as a kind of first cousin to Cary Grant's dapper nonconformist, but by the late sixties his comic ingenuity has been exhausted. Wilder retreats to a more nostalgic, neoclassic style in *The Front Page* and *The Private Life of Sherlock Holmes*, perhaps because of both the predominant note of despair in his own work and the increasing vilification of American stereotypes in Hollywood. Both films strongly emphasize period details; there are moments in his remembrance of the Sherlock Holmes myth that appear to transfix the romantic mystique of this withdrawn sleuth, but Wilder is too cautions, too self-consciously the lyricist in confronting his subject. It is also true of his adaptation of the Hecht-MacArthur classic; it is definitely superior to the rickety style of the Pat O'Brien–Adolphe Menjou version, but his mocking players lack the spontaneity of the performers in the Hawks-Lederer *His Girl Friday*. Lemmon is about as sharp, as coolly conceited and naturally vituperative as any actor in the title role could be, but Matthau comes on too strong and nasty as his boss.

Jerry Lewis's films with Dean Martin are significant examples of the nuances of behavior among contemporary comedy teams. George Burns and Bud Abbott, among other comedy straight men, always took a pragmatic approach to their neurotic partner; but with Martin and Lewis, the roles of straight man and idiot child are treated as self-caricatures. The straight man usually draws on the reserve of a psychoanalyst, the steadfastness of a midwife, and the despairing view of a warden in dealing with his partner's lunacy; Martin, however, is a distant, self-indulgent figure who has neither the diligence nor the intelligence to control Lewis's delirium tantrums. One comedy star whose identity is similar to that of Lewis's epileptic is Danny Kaye, but whereas Kaye has a pleasant appearance and voice, the Lewis mask is that of a retarded child.

One of the problems in reviewing Lewis's work in the sixties is that he frequently stars in films that he does not direct. *The Disorderly Orderly*, directed by Frank Tashlin and without Martin or a Martin-like character, is an improvement over his earlier efforts, but there is little evidence that Lewis has taken a more preceptive look at his comic personality. In his directorial debut, *The Errand Boy*, Lewis remains committed to his disruptive presence. Lewis's incongruity in the Hollywood dream factory is sharply drawn in the rehearsal for the musical in which his childish manner upsets the retakes of the actors. Yet the film seems too ambitious; several scenes—in the candy store and in his serving as messenger boy—are hackneyed comedy bits that one feels Lewis added as time fillers. The film's weakest element is Lewis's affected character; his facial contortions and physical ineptitude mindlessly extend the chaos. In *The Bellboy* Lewis's character is that of a poetic, abused little man whose naiveté and reserve recall Langdon's baby-faced figure. Lewis discards his persona of a mechanical wreck and successfully represents two characters—the taciturn bellboy who is ridiculed by the other hotel employees and the film director who is seen as a fantasy figure with his cadre of supporters and sycophants. Scenes like the one in which Lewis's bellboy is ordered to set up several hundred chairs in the auditorium and after a subtle fade to black is shown having completed the job, effectively counterbalance the surreal activities of Lewis's movie director.

The Nutty Professor and The Family Jewels are his most ambitious and controversial films. *The Nutty Professor* won Lewis a major award in France, but it is much too broad in its caricatures. Once again, Lewis expresses his interest in a dual personality, playing the goofy professor and a pop singer. But his role as the professor is a poor substitute for the bellboy because he can only underline the awkward, uncoordinated aspects of his professor, whereas his taciturn bellboy represents the solitary face in the crowd. His day in the gym is funny in spots, but because of Lewis's brash exclamation points around his lack of coordination, his routine is all technique and no meaning. The gym sequence is similar to the various feats he performs as rodeo star and karate expert in *The Ladies' Man*, some of which are quite funny, yet they are not held together by anything other than Lewis's self-evident narcissism. In *The Nutty Professor* Lewis's first transformation from professor to nightclub singer works as a clever parody of the transformation scenes in horror films with, perhaps, specific reference to Mamoulian's heavy-handed manner in *Dr. Jekyll and Mr. Hyde*. Lewis exaggerates Mamoulian's high-angle shots, and his facial changes are concise and funny. Lewis sustains the comedy as his camera passes over the faces of the people in the street, prolonging our anxiety in discovering what he has been turned into. What his Hyde-like figure does look like is the suave, eponymous Las Vegas performer who, in his resemblance to Lewis's show-biz appearance, expresses the self-perpetuating nature of his humor. The film dawdles when Lewis as the singer plays opposite Stella Stevens; he is unable to discover any irony in the bobby-soxers who melt before his self-directed love songs. Lewis often falls back on the hysteria of his preceding films, especially in the scenes in which he plays the singer and in the professor's remembrances of his childhood. It is an inherently weak film because in supposedly dissecting an element of pop culture, the film becomes an outgrowth of it.

Lewis's problematic persona undergoes its richest delineation in *The Family Jewels*. His primary role in the film is as chauffeur and temporary guardian to the waif who must choose a guardian from among her eight relatives, all played by Lewis. In his role as chauffeur Lewis has only to project his simplicity, and this is achieved with little self-consciousness. Lewis's familiar clumsiness is used in his other characterizations, most meaningfully in his role as the photographer. When he sets up the models under the lights, the photographer's camera becomes the film camera so that the one constant image of the models sweating under the lights and the off-camera monologue of Lewis's photographer who has forgotten them as he rummages through his equipment juxtaposes a photographic framework to its cinematically realized humor. Lewis's singular identity is explored most decisively through the chauffeur's relationship to the one relative the girl does not meet, the clown. When he takes her to meet the clown, he overhears the clown saying that he is fed up with his audience and is leaving for Switzerland. Lewis's disgraceful commentary on Chaplin's departure from America is compounded as the chauffeur, in the guise of the clown, becomes the little girl's guardian. Lewis's simple, unassuming character, first evoked as the bellboy and then as the chauffeur, reveals himself as the new Chaplin. It is a most questionable assumption.


## *Limelight–Blood Feud*

The fifties comedies of Chaplin, Renoir, Tati, and Bergman show a far more introspective style than had previously been featured in the movies. They possess a decidedly neoclassic point of view in their stylistic proximity to the theater and in their renewing several of the more celebrated themes and ideas of comic literature.

*Limelight* and *Monsieur Verdoux* seem as removed in tone and dramatic substance from Chaplin's early sound films as from his work in the silent film. *Limelight* introduces the tramp as an aging, ailing figure, whose relationship with the ballerina, played with uncommon gracefulness by Claire Bloom, recalls his love of the girl in *City Lights*. At first Chaplin's dim backgrounds seem distinct from both his first shorts with their makeshift settings and the more naturalistic environs of *The Great Dictator* and *Modern Times*. It then becomes apparent that Chaplin has restricted the movements of his character in order to isolate his dressing room and the theater stage where he performs as the most meaningful backdrops. The film becomes a soliloquy on the fate of the clown; in these two settings, his existence is wholly understood in the context of his identity as a clown. In his earlier films Chaplin has expressed his faith in the transcendent role of comedy through the way in which his depressed environments have been animated by the magical pathos of the tramp; *Limelight,* however, offers no such salvation. The sublime exchange between Chaplin and Keaton in the dressing room, like Chaplin's performance on the stage during which he does not use a single reaction shot, achieves its dramatic intensity from Chaplin's restraint in denoting the emptiness of their world. During their exchange the focus is on the tragic specters of these two great clowns, reduced to playing in a second-rate music hall; Chaplin's one-shot performance moves us because of its sense of failed communication, as if his film audience—like the stage audience we do not see—were unalterably separated from the tramp. The loneliness and despair surrounding Chaplin's performer are crystallized in the final scene in which his death goes unnoticed during a performance. While conveying his estrangement from his audience, Chaplin has confirmed his commitment to the theater and the transcendence of art.

If *Limelight* expresses the bleakness of an aging artist through the opaque, solitary nature of the artist's craft, *Monsieur Verdoux* depicts Chaplin's misanthropy in a world he previously attempted to invigorate through his numerous comic ploys and masks. The opening scene may seem at first a lighthearted burlesque of his characters' slapstick mannerisms, but Chaplin is more interested in exposing their petty, corrupt nature. If *Limelight* explored the failure of the theater and the comedian's mask to inspire the joy and emotional cadences that pervade his previous films, *Monsieur Verdoux* refuses to question the humanity of his victims or the rationality of his murderous endeavors: Chaplin has come to see mankind irrevocably set on a path of apathy, avariciousness, and self-destruction. The romantic, the prankster, the revolutionary of the silent film is unwilling to infuse his settings with the comedic harmonizing that reconfirmed the innocence of humanity. *Monsieur Verdoux*, as both a reaction to his personal troubles in America and as a reflection on postwar society, finds the tramp forced into the role of the grim reaper. Chaplin's first films turned to comedy as an antidote to the grim uniformity of everyday society; he now uses it for our nullification.

*The Golden Coach, Eléna et les hommes*, and *Le Déjeuner sur l'herbe* are, as one expects of Renoir, full of unexpected pleasures and dangers. *The Golden Coach* is one of the most intelligent examples of how the filmmaker can suggest nuances of form and feeling peculiar to film while still adhering to the conventions of a theatrical, literary, or pictorial style. He appears to personify the lighthearted, transparent theatrical satires of Goldoni through the highly visible network of conflicting emotions among his troupe of traveling actors, particularly in Anna Magnani's primitive romantic heroine. It is one of many performances that overflows with the extraordinary force of her folk spirit; however, unlike other celebrated Magnani characterizations that draw on her volatile temper and the fragility of her emotions, in *The Golden Coach* Magnani assumes an almost Dietrich-like deviousness in subverting the ardor of her two admirers. In earlier films Renoir's camerawork and settings were imbued with the precarious nature of his protagonists; in *The Golden Coach* he celebrates a theatrical tradition that is exemplified in its illusory conventions. His direct, fluent cutting; the paucity of establishing shots; the idealization of the actors through the isolated, exterior image of the coach; the stylish dialogue; and methodical character displacements—these create the necessary elegance and distance in accenting the basic virtues of this theatrical form and its unique luminosity on film.

*Eléna et les hommes* may not be as evocative as *The Golden Coach*, yet Renoir's sympathetic, joyous rendition of the artifices of the theater sustains its neoclassical gloss. The film shows a similar pictorial unity in its few exterior shots; like *The Golden Coach*, the film's concise staging of the characters' coy mannerisms and constant playacting creates vivid slapstick tableaux that use the spatial latitude of the film stage to enhance the transcendent effects of both theatrical and film comedy. Ingrid Bergman's performance offers delights similar to those of Magnani's characterization; the sweetness of her smile and the way she seems born into the role of the mysterious, flirtatious princess provide a magical transformation of the intricate, psychological tensions in her work with Rossellini.

Renoir is more devious in his treatment of classical themes in *Le Déjeuner sur l'herbe*. Unlike *The Golden Coach* or *Eléna et les hommes*, in which his camerawork and cutting respect the static, pictorial dimension of his backdrops, in *Le*

*Déjeuner sur l'herbe* he fragments his pastoral setting with sharp, asymmetrical cuts—most aggressively in the scene in which he symbolizes the lovemaking of the scientist and peasant girl by highlighting different aspects of nature. It is one of Renoir's most didactic films as he incorporates the virulent, primitive ethic of his thirties projects into an impressionist canvas. Thus unlike the thematic-pictorial parallels in *Toni* and *Boudu Saved from Drowing*, in which the nascent emotional conflicts transpire in a hazy, primitive setting, in *Le Déjeuner sur l'herbe* Renoir proposes an unbalanced equation between his characters and back-grounds. He undercuts the meaning of his impressionist landscape by present-ing a dialectic of science and emotions that culminates in his characters' incon-gruously radical behavior. Renoir seems to identify himself as the romantic catalyst through the presence of the shepherd whose flute playing inspires the bacchanalia, but his characters' frivolous actions seem as disjointed in their impressionist surroundings as do his pointed cuts and camera movements.

Jacques Tati's films represent one of the more methodical, piecemeal adapta-tions of silent-film slapstick. His style is not so much an example of the influence of slapstick in the sound film as it is a discourse on the art of the mime. He is a lineal descendent of Sennett, Chaplin, and Keaton, but, unlike his forebears, his comedy is inspired by the scientific variations undertaken in the laboratory rather than the pathos and humor of the street. Tati's analytic approach is evident in his comic persona: a reticent figure wearing a mackintosh, carrying a pipe, and walking with a pronounced stoop, as if his cerebral research were responsible for his eccentric appearance. His major comic sequences derive their understated, buoyant charm from Tati's careful orchestration of the dis-proportion initiated by his character, leading to the irregular pattern in the fabric of *Mon Oncle* and the fireworks in *Mr. Hulot's Holiday*. Whether it is his awkward but effective tennis serve or the confusion at the funeral when the tire is mistaken for a wreath and Tati for a friend of the family, the tension that results from Tati's reserved, laconic manner plays as a kind of in-joke in which only the audience is aware of the comic asymmetry. Tati's ratiocinative humor works best when he does not aim for the epic confusion that is characteristic of the silent-film clowns, but when he undertakes a precise interplay between the problems that baffle the characters and their diligent, unemotive approach to their resolution. This is why the last sequence in *Mr. Hulot's Holiday* does not work; there are too many elements that contribute to the chaos; the confusion at the resort develops as a prolonged exercise in silent-film mayhem. The party in *Mon Oncle* during which the waterworks system goes awry is a more succinct expression of Tati's art; he ironically studies the disproportion between the mechanical malfunction and the systematic approach used by Tati and the other guests.

Since his protagonist is an eccentric and does not recall the more frenetic, violent humor of his predecessors, his films refrain from the more comprehen-sive attacks of a Chaplin or Keaton. To further satirize the conventions at the party in *Mon Oncle*, Tati's character would have to be more animated, more clearly out of place in this conformist environment. But this is not what Tati attempts; his major objective is to uncover some of the potentially absurd elements in modern society and to invent a game or routine, like the whistle he uses in *Mon Oncle*, that will offset the torpor and anonymity of his backgrounds. His routines have a tendency to run a little long because, other than Tati, there are no sharply focused characters. This is the problem with *Traffic*, which in its fascination with cars and noise never rises above the level of the cacophony it attempts to satirize. *Playtime* is a superior film because Tati's distance from the other characters is more sharply drawn, while the opening of the restaurant that consumes the last third of the film is his most controlled experiment in collective anarchy.

The strengths and weaknesses of three of Ingmar Bergman's ventures in comedy—*Smiles of a Summer Night*, *The Devil's Eye*, and *All These Women*—are indicative of the artistic choices he has made throughout his career. *Smiles of a Summer Light*, the one most committed to its loving theatrical rhetoric and its delight in the characters' unscrupulousness is one of the high points of early Bergman. It avoids the literalism common to similar film adaptations by gracefully evoking the charms and weaknesses of its married couples in the manner of a tribute to restoration comedy. Bergman never loses sight of his characters' paradoxical expressions of innocence and cynicism; the film comes most alive in his close-ups of Gunnar Björnstrand's cool charm as the husband who perceives the inevitability of his reunion with Eva Dahlbeck's Aphrodite-like stage goddess. *The Devil's Eye* is a less satisfying work because it is a more self-conscious piece of theater, which might even have proved constricted on the stage. One can easily sympathize with Don Juan's fatal attraction for Bibi Andersson as the pastor's daughter, but the dialogue and action lack any dramatic or moral focus, as if Bergman's affection for the legend of Don Juan was too personal and abstract to resonate on film.

Bergman's cinematic inventiveness has made for many fine, disturbing works, but in *All These Women* he blatantly simplifies various silent-film techniques in characterizing the women who have played leading roles in his films. Bergman's overly ripe colors and his supine comedy stereotypes attest to his indifference in dramatizing his feelings as an artist and filmmaker. It is intended as a breezy self-confession, but it emerges as a dreary exercise in autobiographical filmmaking.

Among the various attempts to renew classic comic styles in the sixties, from Lester's epigrammatic satires and the screwball romps in the Italian manner of De Sica and Germi to the brittle romantic escapades in the films of Philippe de Broca, the Czech comedies of the late sixties undertake a more personal, emotional study of classic comedy types and situations. The best of these films, Jiří Menzel's *Closely Watched Trains*, offers a terse, nostalgic analogy between a boy's coming to manhood and his country's precarious position in the last years of the war. Menzel displays an acute eye in juxtaposing the boy's naiveté to the joyous abandon exhibited by his superiors at the railway station. He never seems to overstate his case in observing the young man's attempt to adopt the carefree manner of the other employees and in his protagonist's immersion in the promiscuous activities at the station. Menzel is less successful in *Capricious Summer*, a Chekhov-like study of a resort town, a flirtatious circus performer, and the men who fail to consummate their attraction for her. Its humor is too wistful, as if the film's warm, lyrical pictorialism were unsympathetic to a satire or send-up of the wry townspeople and their bourgeois morals. Ivan Passer's *Intimate Lighting* is a more personal study of provincial life. Although he does not possess Menzel's elegance in uncovering his characters' idiosyncratic mannerisms, there appears to be a more shrewd Pagnol at play. *Law and Disorder*, his first American exercise in seriocomic behavior, concerns a group of city residents that decides to form an auxiliary police force. It is a moody, ambiguous film that lacks an incisiveness in exposing the characters' incongruity as policemen. Passer clearly empathizes with the foibles of working people, but it may be that America is just too large a territory.

Miloš Forman is the most popular of the Czechoslovakian directors because of the controversial nature of his Czech films and his one great American success, *One Flew over the Cuckoo's Nest*. But compared to either Menzel or Passer in whose work there is a genuine folk sensibility, Forman's Czech films—*Black Peter*, *Loves of a Blond*, and *The Firemen's Ball*—look as though they were made by one of his rustic characters. *Black Peter* details the passive, desolate atmosphere of city life in Eastern Europe in a way that seems to unite filmmakers as different as Forman, Wajda, and Skolimowski. There is a poignant sense of wishing to taste those things denied youth in Peter's absorbing study of a photograph of a Titian nude, but the shabbiness of Peter's surroundings, his dreary friends, and the lackluster dialogue give the city the look of a movie set overlooked by a wrecking crew. *Loves of a Blond* is a more professional work, depicting his characters' provincial manners as they shrug off members of the opposite sex at the dance. But it is a less moving film than *Black Peter* because of the smugness of Forman's caricatures, typified by the cruel manner in which the young man treats the blond. Forman's stylistic indecisiveness reaches a point of diminishing returns in *The Firemen's Ball*; his firemen are a group of Sennett clodhoppers who fail to generate any humor by running about and upsetting the festivities. Forman's idea of folk comedy is to close in on a physically gross detail, as if the film's skeletal plot elevated it to the sublime. *The Firemen's Ball*—like Jan Němec's *A Report on the Party and the Guests*, another criticially well-received Czech film that is purportedly a metaphor for the bleak social order—conveys neither the urgency nor the astringent aesthetic vision to dramatize the tragedy played out in Czechoslovakia. What is most unnerving in Forman's direction and Bo Goldman's script for *One Flew over the Cuckoo's Nest* is their inverting the brash radicalism of Ken Kesey's novel. The distressingly innocuous Muzak and the seductively tranquil blue light that surrounds the inmates' routines present a disturbing picture of institutionalization, one made all the more chilling by identifying Nicholson's familiar figure of iconoclasm as symptomatic of dangerous antisocial behavior.

The Italian comedy films of De Sica, Germi, and Wertmuller revitalize the repertory of social caricatures and the send-ups of conventional morality that were first launched in the screwball comedy sound films of the thirties. De Sica is the most straightforward of these parodists in his treatment of the theatrical, romantic fencing between Sophia Loren and Marcello Mastroianni in *Yesterday Today and Tomorrow* and *Marriage Italian Style*. Loren's striking sexuality is distinct from the charms of previous comediennes; in some of her roles her sexual exuberance overwhelms her admirers. However, opposite Mastroianni—a dapper, intuitive performer who is strikingly similar to Cary Grant—Loren's expansive genuflections find their match in Mastroianni's mischievous admirer. The comedy in the two films is only tangentially a study of Italian morality in that it is wholly attuned to the high spirits and sexual compatibility of the stars. The stories in *Yesterday Today and Tomorrow* are prolonged, one-joke comedies, and the second segment lacks the slightest dramatic edge. Yet Loren and Mastroianni are such effervescently complementary performers that Mastroianni's expressing his inability to procreate in the first section and howling like a wolf in the last one when aroused by Loren's striptease remain indelible imprints of sexual devastation.

Pietro Germi is a more fluent director who uses various slapstick maneuvers to uncover the torpor and self-deceit of life in the provinces in *Divorce Italian Style*, *Seduced and Abandoned*, and *The Birds the Bees and the Italians*. *Divorce Italian Style* is the slightest of the three films, but Germi's penetrating look at Italian mores is precisely detailed in the genesis and execution of Mastroianni's murderous scheme. In *Seduced and Abandoned*, however, his sly epilogue in *Divorce Italian Style* becomes his central premise. Germi is not laughing simply at his characters' provincial features—their toothlessness or highly active libidos—but abandons this satiric treatment for a savage indictment of their mores. The deceptiveness underlying Germi's gravitating from the comical to the cynical is vigorously displayed when he attempts to regain the audience's sympathy by hiding behind the fragile mask of Stefanià Sandrelli. Her father has died from public ridicule of Sandrelli's premature pregnancy, while her suitor, having already obtained dentures from her father as part of a marriage agreement, abandons her. During Sandrelli's dream, Germi shows her being pursued by the townspeople, who are pictured not as the progeny of Sennett's merry nitwits but of the lynch mob in *The Ox-Bow Incident*. The suddenness with which he has changed his viewpoint from a celebration of the characters' farcical instincts to their condemnation is not convincing. If he seems to believe in anything, it is Sandrelli's declaration of love in the earlier *Divorce Italian Style*, but it too has been exposed.

*The Birds the Bees and the Italians* is a less violent film than *Seduced and Abandoned*, but it is further evidence that the Wilder touch is not peculiar to the American film. Germi's cynicism is underscored only at the end of a sequence and most effectively in the second story. The subject of his contempt is now the bourgeoisie who entertain a peasant girl who then attempts to prosecute them. One of the wives then offers a bribe to the girl's father; he looks at the money, then at the woman, and jumps on her, telling her to keep the money. She says she will donate it to the church, and in the next scene the girl is brought to trial for slander. Although this story cruelly manipulates its characters, the third segment concerning the shy man's affair with the innocent girl shows the facile nature of Germi's art; he is a director more comfortable with ridiculing his characters and their two-faced morality than with studying the comic-tragic tension of personal desire and social conformity.

Two of Lina Wertmuller's comedies, *The Seduction of Mimi* and *Love and Anarchy*, extend Germi's lampoon of Italian society by adopting a more ironic, personal viewpoint. The lead roles in the two films, played by Giancarlo Giannini and Mariangela Melato, are far more deliberate social travesties than the characters portrayed by Mastroianni and Loren. The two films are concerned with the conflict between social mobility and personal instincts, the antithetical impulses of the mind and heart among lower-class protagonists. Wertmuller's camera seems to be in perpetual motion: she continually closes in on the characters' wild, dramatic postures and affectations, shifting from a frantic editing rhythm to a sympathetic study of the extensive, operalike duets involving the two stars. Her affection for physically overripe gestures culminates in the uproarious seduction scene in *The Seduction of Mimi*; in *Love and Anarchy* she celebrates Giannini's loss of innocence by highlighting the characters' gaiety and physically lush features during a feast at the bordello. But in *All Screwed Up* Wertmuller's faith in her characters' ability to rise above their grim social condition is undercut by their violent emotional upheavals. Her style is more cryptic, as exemplified in her treatment of the Giannini look-alike who, after fathering twins and then quintuplets, takes a night job as a street painter; with one brilliant overhead shot we realize he is too tired to paint a straight line. The other major characters are also treated as foredoomed victims of their instincts or of their materialist society; thus, the likable Sicilian's descent into the kitchen as Mozart's *Requiem* plays on the sound track does not strike one as a definitive metaphor of self-degradation.

*Swept Away* is a more radical departure from the ebullient, parodic effects of *The Seduction of Mimi* and *Love and Anarchy*; Melato plays the classic rich bitch who talks up a most deadly storm of clichés. Though much pleasure is to be derived from her deliberate, delicious performanace—from the juxtaposition of her voluptuous figure and marvelously full-bodied, sonorous voice to Giannini's diminutive appearance with his frizzled hair and rasping nasal tone—the film retains the glibness of its original model, Barrie's *The Admirable Crichton*. The first part consists of Melato's petulantly dull harangues and Giannini's hound-dog mournfulness; during their stay on the island, Wertmuller substitutes Barrie's class metaphor for a Darwinian interpretation of self and, inevitably, social preservation. Her smug handling of the story is most conspicuous in their successive lovemaking, with her stars unnecessarily attired and Melato's running commentary functioning as operatic declamation. It is a dramatic conceit which, although similar to the violent outpouring of the love of Giannini and Melato in *The Seduction of Mimi*, results in a less emotional, more platitudinous style.

*Seven Beauties* avoids the contrivedness of *Swept Away* by conceiving Giannini's little man as the central figure in her cinema buffa study of one man's survival in the Mafia-controlled underworld of Naples and in the Nazi death camps. Her dramatic strategies—equating the feudal nihilism of the Mafia with that of the Nazis and Giannini's admiration for Mussolini as symptomatic of his popularity as a macho, nationalistic hero—are brought to life through her burlesque treatment of Giannini's misadventures. The film largely unfolds through the interplay of Wertmuller's melodramatically styled settings and Giannini's equally flamboyant persona—from the baroque presentation of the various arenas he enters, such as in the confrontation with his sister's seducer in which the elements of a western shoot-out are comically pinpointed, to hyperbolic close-ups of Giannini. The film's theatrical daring underscores its black humor: Giannini's Pasqualino, a verminous vision of humanity, is a trapped rat whose ridiculous airs, elegiacally caricatured in his promenade, lead to his picturesque flight across the rooftops only to be surrounded by the police. Nothing new is discovered in the psychology of Giannini's rascalian survivor, yet Wertmuller's comic tableaux reenforce the nihilism of this period through the increasing blankness of Giannini's face. His courtroom sentence reveals the fatalism encroaching on his character through a series of mute close-ups encompassing Giannini's Mafia mentor, the lawyers, his family, and sweetheart. One may have hoped for a more original moral antagonist than Fernando Rey's anarchist, whose sentiments are retained by Giannini, but the film remains a much needed addition to the banal sociological and fictional interpretations of this most unbanal period.

*Blood Feud* shows Wertmuller's stylistic academicism in her reliance on redolent close-ups and ritualized movements of slapstick romance and revenge. Her film nostalgia is stillborn, but compared to bland, apathetic resurrections such as *Fun with Dick and Jane* and its transatlantic duplicate, *The Wonderful Crook*, Wertmuller's visual energies and the original qualities of Giannini's little man prove that the inherent virtues of classic styles of comedy, while suffering through a decade of excessive formulas and regressive characterizations, can be as pertinent today as they were to those first dabblers in silent-film mayhem.

# 12
## The Crime Film

*Dr. Mabuse the Gambler–Blackmail*

The crime story—whether its hero is the private eye or the secret agent, whether its origin is in those natural encrustations of urban dwellings called the underworld or in the guarded sanctums of international intrigue, whether its subject is the irreducible elements of passion or the grandiose schemes of world domination—is an integral part of the popular culture of the last one hundred and fifty years. It has equally served philosophers and psychologists, either as a tale of redemption or as a cry from the dark, inner forces of the human spirit. Its effects are often ephemeral; its writers discern a microcosm of presocial anarchy that is fated to self-destruction by exposing a conflict or condition that is a sudden departure from highly mechanized forms of behavior and communication. The problematic nature of the crime novel can be dismissed if, like Auden, we admit our interest to be nothing more than a product of our bourgeois moods. But the natural union of the quick read and quicker movies, of a modern pastime and a modern technology, offers fresh insights into the relationship of art and society.

The crime film enjoys a most auspicious beginning in the frenzy and turmoil of Germany in the twenties. Fritz Lang's *Dr. Mabuse the Gambler* rigorously adapts the chromatic, light-dark symbolism of his two major historical films, *Destiny* and *Die Nibelungen*, in his spellbinding study of a criminal underworld; the somber nature of his medieval epics, with their predominant, iconographic severity and the languorous movement of the characters also permeate his modern parable. Like Siegfried and Kriemhild, the detective who pursues Dr. Mabuse is seen as a receding figure of light and moral strength in an increasingly dark world. The expressionist backdrops of the nightclub, the surreptitious meetings covered in smoke, and the paranoia that seems to engulf the characters exemplify Mabuse's systematic reign of terror. Though several murders are shown, along with a final chase and shoot-out that take up the last two reels of the film, Lang does not imbue these clashes with the dynamism and thrilling fireworks for which the action film is famous. It is as if the characters realized that little would be resolved by the capture or death of the criminals; their actions bespeak their lack of volition, their passivity and intoxication courtesy of Dr. Mabuse. The film plays as a chamber symphony whose methodical, exacting pacing denotes the devastation of a people and nation. Though it may strike some viewers as lacking in emotion and depth, the film is no less fatalistic than *Die Nibelungen*; one descends into a world where the nihilistic presence of the underworld is perceived in the design of the rooms, in the murkiness of the environment, and, most decisively, in the characters' moral apathy.

*Spies* is not as comprehensive in examining the power of the underworld in modern society. In *Dr. Mabuse the Gambler* there is a perverse, poignant sense of understatement; in *Spies* the emphasis is on Haighi, a Mabuse-like figure, and the traps he sets for his unsuspecting victims. The action is sustained at a more frenetic pace, as if the characters had awakened from their drug-induced passivity and recognized the grim features of their environment. Haighi is a schemer, a more clearly stereotyped villain than Rudolf Klein-Rogge's expertly drawn Dr. Mabuse, who in his guise as mesmerizer ironically discloses his identity. As a cloak-and-dagger exercise, Lang's attention to the severity of his Bauhaus backdrops and his expert use of the conventions of the crime story make *Spies* a valid addition to the contemporary bestiary created by German filmmakers.

In *The Testament of Dr. Mabuse*, the confusion surrounding both police and criminals results from their inability to uncover the identity of the mastermind. Since Mabuse is in an asylum, the police are at a loss as to the identity of the man behind the screen who orchestrates the various murderous operations, while the criminals are fearful of discovering it. Lang elaborates the theme that there are numerous Mabuses in Germany, that the radio used to instigate the crimes could be appropriated by any malevolent figure who grasps the moral torpor of German society. It is Lang's taut, uncompromising approach to this constant state of fear and suspiciousness that results in an original study on the rise of gangsterism in society and politics.

In *M* Lang presents a more schematic viewpoint, showing Germany as an enclosed studio environment whose tensions are personified by Peter Lorre's child murderer. When he moves to an overhead shot as Lorre is pursued by the criminals, Lang identifies the ambiguous nature of the roles of hunter and hunted: no one can escape from the mazelike horrors of modern Germany. By interrelating the police and criminals as they plan for the capture of the child murderer, by limiting the action to a handful of sets like the police station and the deserted warehouse where Lorre is brought to trial, Lang, like Von Sternberg in *The Blue Angel*, uses his compressed stage as a metaphor for the characters' psychological stigma. Though their most overt symbols are the child abductions and murders of Lorre and the promiscuity of Lola, Lorre's police and criminal avengers and the patrons of the nightclub where Lola performs are judged as coconspirators in creating a precarious, symbolized stage of no exits.

Von Sternberg's *Underworld* makes many of these same points, isolating its characters in a tense, explosive environment in which their emotional entanglements are defined through Von Sternberg's expressive lighting patterns. When the three major characters of his criminal triangle—George Bancroft, Evelyn

Brent, and Clive Brook—leave a nightclub, Brent standing in the center is suffused in light as Bancroft and Brook recede into the impending darkness. The romantic triangle is established, but what distinguishes *Underworld* from *Shanghai Express* or from the Von Sternberg prism of *The Shanghai Gesture* is the way he imbues Bancroft's underworld boss with a heroic identity. Like Lang, Von Sternberg sees the characters as representative of the unrest in society, but he is more interested in the resolution of their emotional and moral integrity. Bancroft's antagonist embodies the dramatic and mythic potential of the criminal anti-hero; his savage nature makes him king of the underworld, but it precludes his escaping with Brent and Brook. His oafish, primitive actions not only set him against the police, but also determine his conflict with other criminals, notably the character who continually harasses Brent and whom he finally kills. Like Jannings's high school professor, Bancroft is trapped within the private world of his emotions and fulfills his tragic identity by giving expression to his violent moods. It is most vividly realized during the party sequence: as Bancroft awakens in the early morning hours, wrapped in confetti, he stumbles across the apartment for the triumphant, murderous quashing of his rival. Ben Hecht, author of *Underworld*, replays this morning-after, confetti-strewn atmosphere in the opening scene of *Scarface*, but there it is used to establish the inexorability of death and not to ascribe any heroic feelings to Paul Muni's scar-faced killer.

Lang's crime films present a conceptual, formalist approach to the turmoil in Germany during the twenties. To Lang the characters and conflicts in a crime story offer a modern counterpart to the symbolic motifs he discovered in the medieval allegories of *Destiny* and *Die Nibelungen*. Von Sternberg's theatrical expressionism leads to a more personal study of the inner paradoxes of his criminal anti-hero, but in many of his sound films one finds his subtle, photographic displacements losing much of their psychological effectiveness because of the cumbersome dialogue. If the problem with Von Sternberg's work in the thirties is a stylistic incongruity between the symbolic potential of the silent film and the more realistic components of a sound film, these aesthetic considerations were absorbed by the traditional dramatic and moral contrivances that were used in the crime film of the thirties. The poetically styled silent films of Lang and Von Sternberg were superseded by a more didactic, clearly defined confrontation between good and evil, and nowhere is this change of perspective more evident than in the films of Alfred Hitchcock.

One way of beginning our "Portrait of Hitch" is by quoting him. In numerous interviews Hitchcock expressed his preference for the chase; but from Sennett through Eisenstein the resolution of a story through its kinetic elements is apt to result in a neutralization of the characters and settings. Hitchcock's emphasis on the chase functions as a parallel to a mystery writer's final plot scheming. It is a mechanical contrivance that is used to resolve the thematic and psychological tensions through the sprightly, kinetic charm of the movies. Hitchcock remains a prime example of the rationale of the *auteur* theory, a craftsman whose popularity combines the two basic elements of the *auteur* theory: honing his techniques while serving the interests of the industry and his audience. But it is only when Hitchcock works with more literate scripts and when his satiric treatment of the characters is not so broadly played that his films provide the necessary texture for the characterizations and the devious turn of events. In *Shadow of a Doubt* he shrewdly reworks the formulas that have been integrated with little irony in his earlier films; from *Notorious* and *Strangers on a Train* through its culmination in *Psycho*, there is an increasingly refined, misanthropic approach to the relationship of the mother and son and the dual personality of his villain.

In *The Lady Vanishes*, *The Girl Was Young*, and *The Thirty-Nine Steps*, Hitchcock juxtaposes the comic banter of his male-female protagonists to the enveloping mystery, but the prevalence of the comic exchanges tempts one to look at Hitchcock as a failed comedy director. Often the tension that he creates is very real, but the indolent nature of these films is exemplified in his treatment of the most unusual spy tandem in film history, that of John Gielgud and Peter Lorre in an adaptation of two of Maugham's Ashenden stories in *The Secret Agent*. Instead of underplaying the differences between Gielgud's reticent, withdrawn secret agent and Lorre's characterization of a Turkish satyr posing as a spy, Hitchcock allows Lorre's outrageous mannerisms to dominate the story line. While Lorre's comic antics prove as ludicrous as the frivolous exchanges between the young ladies in *The Lady Vanishes*, the characters of neither Gielgud nor Madeleine Carroll, a fellow spy playing his wife, seem real; the incongruity of the three agents is exaggerated in order to brutally drive home the hideousness of the ensuing murder of the German. During the murder scene it is not so much Hitchcock's renowned cutting that draws our attention as it is the gripping anxiety of the people involved in the killing. Gielgud and Lorre are invited on a mountain-climbing trip by the German whom they believe is the spy they have been sent to eliminate. Gielgud, who has tried to dissuade Lorre from killing the German, stays behind in a lodge and watches the murder through a telescope while Carroll remains with the German's wife. She serves tea, and her dog, sensing danger, furiously scratches at the door. As Lorre advances on the German, Hitchcock cuts to Gielgud raising his head from the telescope and sighing, and then to the apartment as the dog whines and Carroll breaks down and cries.

The murder scene, the one graphically edited segment in the film, is made real by the helplessness of Gielgud and Carroll and the pathetic nature of the dog's presence. Even if one senses, as the agents learn in the next sequence, that they are killing the wrong man, Hitchcock's deftness in exposing the ugliness of the crime cannot be dismissed. The preceding comic ploys have been excessive if not superfluous, but, for a moment, one is swept into the murderous abyss of international intrigue. In *The Thirty-Nine Steps* and *The Lady Vanishes*, however, Hitchcock is too dependent on the comic friction between his stars, who eventually are drawn together in their attempt to point out the real villain to innocent bystanders. There is no real suspense in the two films because one can never believe in the characters' helplessness; Hitchcock's sangfroid English temperament innocently intermixes comedy and terror. Several scenes play as slightly grotesque exercises in terror and others as ragged attempts at comedy.

Their few redeeming moments result from the graceful mannerisms of Robert Donat and Michael Redgrave, extricating themselves from Hitchcock's incredulous dramatic ploys and tiresome comic setups.

*The Girl Was Young* is such a poor film that it is difficult to understand how Hitchcock developed a reputation as a first-class craftsman. It shows no more feeling for its setting than for its characters. There is an expert scene of sustained terror in which Hitchcock's camera floats through the hotel lounge before unmasking the villain; but he has been honored for these moments far too often. *Sabotage* is a more serious work in which Hitchcock focuses on the desperate, hysterical nature of Sylvia Sidney as she responds to the treachery and violence around her. Though the film has little to do with Conrad's *The Secret Agent*, which it purports to adapt, Hitchcock's treatment of Sidney's husband, played by Oscar Homolka, shows a poignancy missing in his other early sound films. His shrewd depiction of the police and their failure to provide Sidney with a clear alternative establishes a more ambiguous framework for the audience's moral sympathies.

*The Man Who Knew Too Much* employs many of the simplistic plot contrivances used in *The Lady Vanishes*, but the way in which the characters become enmeshed in the deceptive facade of politics recalls the more sustained mood of helplessness in *Sabotage*. At first Hitchcock adopts a distant attitude toward the political intrigue, but this version proves superior to the remake in distinguishing the grim mechanics of violence and its effect on the characters' resourcefulness. Though the Hollywood remake is a more polished entertainment, the English version is more provocative. The wife who experiences the chaos is a more believable heroine than Doris Day, while the suspense surrounding Jimmy Stewart's search for the assassins is compounded by Stewart's persona of the ingenious American who has triumphed in similar adventures. When the wife searches for the assassins in the English version, Hitchcock uses a subjective point of view as her tears fill the camera lens. Her emotional hysteria and not the chase after the assassins is the key motif used by Hitchcock to pinpoint the horror and ambivalence of her situation.

This one scene, with its intertwining a personal and thematic fatalism, figures in the engrossing conclusion. In the last twenty minutes, during the gun battle between the anarchists and police, the bleak mood enfolds not only the central characters, as in *Sabotage*, but also the anarchists and police. It is not just a shoot-out, well executed or not; by restricting the anarchists and police to one setting during their drawn-out stalemate, Hitchcock conveys the scene's irrevocable darkness. The mood in this long, last sequence, whose length is accentuated by the police's inability to overpower the handful of anarchists, is subtlety reflected in the underlighting, whether intentional or unintentional, and by the lack of dynamism in the cross fire. Hitchcock manipulates the audience's response to the encroaching darkness through the gunfire, which is heard but not seen; one does not relate to the fighting through the technical components of a shoot-out, but through the tensions surrounding the repulsed strategies of the police and the confusion that plagues the terrorists.

What is most perplexing about Hitchcock's work in the thirties is that his best film, *Blackmail*, was his first sound film. Although there is an element of academicism in its montage fluency—in first passing through the streets of London in depicting the capturing of the criminal—it is one of Hitchcock's most complex, congruent works because of its ironic treatment of several motifs he disdainfully treats in his succeeding work.

Since the film begins with the arraignment of a criminal, one is wary of the conventional formulas Hitchcock introduces when a rendezvous is then arranged by a policeman's girl friend and an admirer. One's anxiety is cruelly confirmed when the woman is brought to the man's apartment and what appears to be a friendly, amorous tussle, turns into an attempted rape and the killing of the rapist. Leaving the apartment, the woman is conscious of two images: the man's hand hanging out of the bed and a painting of a smirking clown. As the girl walks the streets in a state of shock, Hitchcock uses a series of dissolves to denote her hysteria, which leads her to see various hands as those of her attacker.

With the reappearance of the criminal who was booked in the opening scene, a chilling confrontation unfolds. It runs approximately fifteen minutes as Hitchcock deviates from his conventionally calculating shot-reaction-shot formula, in which Donat and Carroll in *The Thirty-Nine Steps*, Redgrave and Lockwood in *The Lady Vanishes*, and the romantic leads of *The Girl Was Young* tediously draw out his drawing-room formulas. The only similar segments in his films of the thirties can be found in the murder of the German and the paradoxical feeling of the agents in *The Secret Agent* and in the last sequence in *The Man Who Knew Too Much*, which works as a study of a failed action film. The criminal arrives at the heroine's home, where she lives with her parents; her boyfriend, the police officer, is also present. The heroine must gather all her strength while her boyfriend must repress his violent feelings toward the criminal. Hitchcock uses a moving camera to connote the unsettling presence of the criminal who attempts to blackmail them. He brilliantly depicts the scene's repressive, murderous tone through the deliberate movements of the camera in defining their physical and emotional entrapment.

The blackmailer is then pursued in the British Museum, in which he frantically searches for an escape only to be trapped by its enveloping forms. The action then shifts to the police station, where the heroine, about to confess, learns of the blackmailer's death. But her sudden relief is upset as an officer walks by with the painting of the clown, smirking at the woman. Hitchcock, behind the mask of the clown, has the last laugh at his characters' vain attempt to escape the oblique moral twists of justice.

*Little Caesar–Le Jour se lève*

In the metaphysical crime thrillers of Lang, in Von Sternberg's grandiose *Underworld*, and in the best moments of Hitchcock's films, the tensions and ambiguities of crime, whether personal or social in nature, are unmasked. But in the gangster classics of Edward G. Robinson, James Cagney, and Humphrey Bogart, a more conventional approach is taken to the conflict between criminal and society during Prohibition and the Depression. Two of their classic films, *Little Caesar* and *The Public Enemy*, present a straightforward, behavioral study of the inexorability of violence. Robinson's staccato delivery and ruthless behavior and Cagney's febrile, energetic actions and his sudden eruptions of violence set them apart from their contemporaries and also determine their short-lived stay at the top. Unlike the films of Bogart and Gabin, there is an immediacy to the social forces in *Little Caesar* and *The Public Enemy*, leaving Robinson and Cagney with little time to reach the top of the underworld. Mervyn LeRoy's direction is brutally direct in both *Little Caesar* and *I Am a Fugitive from a Chain Gang*, suggesting that the harsh economic conditions that face Robinson and Paul Muni can only result in swift, emotionless decisions.

Whereas Robinson's tough guy was caricatured by W. R. Burnett, author of *Little Caesar*, and by Robinson himself in *The Whole Town's Talking*, Cagney's edginess remains unabated throughout his career. Along with Jimmy Stewart and Henry Fonda, Cagney is one of the original folk heroes of the American sound film; his abrasive feistiness was successfully featured in comedies (*Torrid Zone*; *One Two Three*) and biographies (*Yankee Doodle Dandy*; *Man of a Thousand Faces*). If Stewart's ingenious American innocent is characterized through the quirks of his speech and mannerisms and Fonda suggests the idealism and physical solemnity of his folk heroes, Cagney gives his characters a hyperbolic kinetic authenticity. He was the most dynamic of our stars, the most striking opposite to the morose, painstaking movements of Brando and his generation of methodlike indecisiveness. Cagney borrowed from the hand feinting and dancing feet of Gene Tunney and Willie Pep in his fight sequences in *Winner Take All*, while the emotional and physical nakedness of his portrayal of the framed journalist in *Each Dawn I Die* dramatizes the grim reality of prison to a degree rarely fulfilled. In *The Public Enemy* Cagney's taut, razorlike edge dominates the film in a way that Robinson's criminal does not in *Little Caesar*. Though William Wellman's direction is not as psychologically acute as LeRoy's, Wellman's realist-school perspective gives the film a similar fatalism in its Darwinian study of tough guys who suddenly rise and fade out against the backdrop of an urban jungle. The grisliness of Cagney's demise, like Rico's death against the billboard, underscores the cyclical nature of their violent world and its condemnation by Hollywood's guardians.

The posthumous iconization of Bogart's tough guy is a study of how America has adopted a more cynical, self-mocking attitude to its film stars and Production Code morality. In his early screen appearances opposite Cagney in *The Roaring Twenties* and in *Angels with Dirty Faces*, Bogey plays a sneaky crime partner who acts as a foil to Cagney's more heroic, independent outsider. Cagney dominates these films through his gracefulness and his extravagant ebullience; he is too good for the ingenue in *The Roaring Twenties* and too much of the loner to be copied by the Dead End Kids in *Angels with Dirty Faces*; his death then becomes a fitting tribute to a character who personifies the volatile jazz age.

Bogart, however, in classic performances (Sam Spade in *The Maltese Falcon*, Rick Blaine in *Casablanca*, Philip Marlowe in *The Big Sleep*, and Fred C. Dobbs in *The Treasure of the Sierra Madre*), is a more devious anti-hero than Cagney's tough guy. Although he assumes the pose of a decent, hard-working character, it is his perception of the double-dealing and savagery in his environment that exposes his paradoxical nature; he exists on a precarious border between law and lawlessness. In *The Maltese Falcon* it is Bogart's ability to outwit his adversaries that enlivens the story's fancifulness on the screen. Hammett's glib, tongue-in-cheek sadism is cunningly delineated by its four stars. Hammett plays a con game on readers of mystery novels, and it is this quality of self-caricature in Lorre's Joel Cairo, Greenstreet's Kasper Gutman, and Mary Astor's brilliant characterization of a failed femme fatale that simultaneously deflates and idealizes the pursuit of the prized falcon; Spade is our great debunker. Like that unique fantasy-film classic, *King Kong*, the roguish, cartoon-like characters and spirited sense of adventure and romance of *The Maltese Falcon* seem tailor-made for the movies; surprisingly, few critics have pointed out the difference in the endings of the book and film and the movie's more satisfying realization of Hammett's comic thriller. It may be worth noting that of the two earlier adaptations of Hammett's novel, Warren William's spoofing, donnish impersonation of Spade suggests the diversity of comic and dramatic elements to be found in the masterworks of the *Black Mask* school.

There is much less tomfoolery in *The Big Sleep*, and though it misses the sharp, cutting edge of Chandler's prose, it is one of the most satisfying adaptations of a modern novel, crime or otherwise. The film will never have the public appeal of Bogart favorites like *The Maltese Falcon*, *Casablanca*, and *The Treasure of the Sierra Madre* because it is too tightly structured and levelheaded about the corruption to allow Bogey's ambivalent attitude toward law and order to surface. There is something to Chandler's perference for Dick Powell's irascible, pipe-smoking shamus in *Murder, My Sweet*, and the garish atmosphere of Edward Dmytryk's interpretation of *Farewell, My Lovely* makes for an interesting comparison to other Chandler adaptations. The superiority of *The Big Sleep* lies in the uncluttered abridgment of Chandler's novel by William Faulkner and Jules Furthman, in the suave, martinilike equilibrium in the speech and movement of Bogey and Bacall, and in director Howard Hawks's straightforward direction. Like Ben Hecht, Furthman brought a journalistic spiciness to his scripts while creating satisfying, creditable adaptations of *Mutiny on the Bounty*, *The Big Sleep*, and *Nightmare Alley*. His most representative script may be *To Have and Have Not* in which Hemingway's maudlin, existential adventure story becomes a blatant melodrama of intrigue and romance—largely redeemed, however, by the chemistry of Bogart and Bacall. Their exploratory erotic foreplay, as in *The Big Sleep*, is characterized by a self-conscious irony that evokes a more languorous, ironic picture of the hand-boiled hero and his dame.

*High Sierra* and *White Heat*, both directed by Raoul Walsh, are studies in the psychology of the criminal anti-hero. Bogey's characterization of "Mad Dog"

Earle, a two-time loser who has felt the blows and lies of his partners in crime as well as those of the police, is one of his best pieces of acting. His befriending the girl and her rejection of him is a poignant example of the alienation that is fated for those who have walked down our mean streets, but Walsh betrays his mawkishness with the presence of the dog. Like *Colorado Territory*, which transposes Burnett's *High Sierra* to the West, its sentimentality is part of the mystique of the genre. *White Heat* is one of the more clipped crime films; the cumulative effect of the fast-paced editing plays like a photomontage of the dynamics of a gangster's downfall. The spartan natural exteriors for its major confrontations give the film a documentary terseness as well as a stylistic minimalism. This was hardly unique to Warner Bros., much less to Walsh. Unlike the violence of *High Sierra*, which tragically fulfilled the fatalism of Bogey's character, Cagney's darting, illuminating eyes and his intimidation of his adversaries recall the self-destructive individualism of George Bancroft in *Underworld*. At times Walsh lacks any point of view in treating Cagney's explosiveness, as in the attack Cagney suffers in prison in which he barrels across the dining area. Yet the film is sparked by the nastiness and virulence of Cagney's extreme triumphs of macho, from the primitive emotions that bind Cagney to his mother and to his moll, played by Virginia Mayo, who murders the mother. There is some of the turbulence of Cagney's character in *Kiss Tomorrow Goodbye*, but the Dionysian ending of *White Heat* celebrates the barbarous paganism of the criminal with a purity and ferocity rarely seen in the movies.

*Port of Shadows* and *Le Jour se lève* are among the most heralded examples of French poesy and existentialism on film, but prove terribly cumbersome in expressing the selfsame fear and loneliness of Bogey's "Mad Dog" Earle. As philosophical, moody studies of the drifter—the man who is indelibly marked as unable to join society—they offer slight plot and less action. By restricting the action to the seaport town in *Port of Shadows* and to Gabin's one-room apartment in *Le Jour se lève*, and by their poetic emphasis on Gabin and Michèle Morgan as they lie in her bed and on Gabin as he nestles against Arletty in a hammock, the films attempt to abstract the dread and fatalism surrounding the lovers. The characters are caught in an indeterminate space between the surreal symbolism of French literature and the moody, dirgelike compositions of Davis and Parker; they are not quite parables, nor are they thrillers in the American fashion. It will be left to directors like Lang and Hitchcock, with an appreciation of the special ironies of crime, to create the truly poetic statements on the ennui and chaos of the war years.

*Rebecca–Scarlet Street*

A major theme in the evolution of the crime film of the forties is a growing sense of moral ambiguity; it ranges from *Rebecca*, Hitchcock's most serious attempt at Gothic literary splendor in the grand Hollywood tradition, and Lang's two films with Edward G. Robinson, Joan Bennett, and Dan Duryea

(*The Woman in the Window* and *Scarlet Street*) to the gruesome plot machinations of Cornell Woolrich, the source of several interesting *film noirs*. Hitchcock's unevenness, however, is still apparent in his work in the forties. *Saboteur* shows his broad, at times pedestrian humor, while the escape attempt by Robert Cummings and Priscilla Lane from Otto Kruger's spy ring duplicates an unimaginative flight by Donat and Carroll in *The Thirty-Nine Steps*. Hitchcock's guile makes for most of the best moments, especially the chase through Radio City Music Hall, which ironically challenges the expectations of its dual audience. A subtler scene concerns a conversation between Cummings and Kruger in which Cummings tells Kruger what a terrible person he is and how the little people will get him; when Hitchcock cuts to Kruger's disdainful response, the medium-shot setup reflects Kruger's corrupt character. *Foreign Correspondent* is another in a long line of Hitchcock's studies of the intricacies and malevolence of political intrigue. Several sequences are marred by his awkward comic ploys, when, for example, Laraine Day delivers a speech on behalf of world peace and is unable to continue because of Joel McCrea's flirting; it is an unnecessary diversion from the pernicious plot twists that move even such a callow actor as George Sanders when he sees the torturing of the prime minister.

*Suspicion* and *Rebecca* are more ambivalent studies of psychological suspense than his political thrillers. *Suspicion*, however, fails to rework its theatrically styled premise. The entire film seems an extended prologue awaiting the resolution of Grant's innocence or guilt; its enforced happy ending is no more of a surprise than an unhappy one would be. *Rebecca* is a more rewarding film because the desperation of Fontaine's tremulous wife, unable to penetrate Olivier's reserve or to counter the deviousness of Judith Anderson's housekeeper, is far more urgent than her suspicions about Grant's husband in *Suspicion*. Fontaine is trapped by what Olivier does not tell her and by what Anderson forces upon her, while Hitchcock's sympathy for the convivial splendor of country life further isolates Fontaine's increasing hysteria.

Hitchcock continues to rework his fascination with romantic affairs that result in either one or both of his leads suffering severe emotional hardships. *Notorious* fails because he is an incurable romantic in close-up, as the first half hour proves, and a hardened misanthrope in long shot, most visible in his high-angle shots from the staircase that underscore Ingrid Bergman's predicament. One of the film's more blatant effects occurs when Bergman awakes intoxicated and the camera simulates her inebriated condition. Another problematic scene finds Bergman informing the American agents of Rains's marriage proposal. The camera is on her face as she enters the offices. As one hears the questions and comments of the other agents, Hitchcock cuts to Grant's face in order to explore their emotional bond. There is a cut to Louis Calhern that shows his knowledge of their affection, which proves critical later in the film when Grant comes to Calhern's apartment and talks about visiting Bergman; one is aware that Calhern knows the true reason for the visit while Grant remains ignorant of Calhern's knowledge. But as Bergman leaves the agents, Hitchcock's camera encompasses the entire room; instead of holding on Bergman and Grant, he obscures the impact of this sequence by moving back to an anonymous medium shot. In retrospect the film's significance may be in the way the relationship between the villainous son and mother prefigures the major conflicts in *Strangers on a Train* and *Psycho*.

*Shadow of a Doubt*, Hitchcock's best film of the forties, sustains a mood of psychological terror that avoids the clinical Freudian contrivances of *Spellbound* and the convoluted soap-opera formulas of *Under Capricorn*. Both *Spellbound*— with its pressing psychological traumas—and *Under Capricorn*—with the extreme isolation suffered by Bergman's heroine—show Hitchcock's unease with the more aggressively distraught elements of *film noir*. The superiority of *Shadow of a Doubt* lies in its cold-blooded treatment of the more conventional elements of middle-class morality and romance. The film stylishly assimilates three different points of view: Teresa Wright's niece, Joseph Cotten's uncle, and Hitchcock's distinct attitude to their relationship. The first two sequences concisely identify the characters and the moral values they represent. The film opens with several shots of the city and introduces Cotten, first resting on a bed and then being chased by two men. When Hitchcock moves to extreme long shot he seems to fall back on his cynically simplistic manner of objectifying the story. But it is Cotten's disdain for the two hoods lost in their pursuit of him that is objectified in this distant camera setup. The elliptically styled suspense in this opening sequence, expressive of Cotten's character, is enhanced as Hitchcock moves to the countryside, to its quiet, open, deserted spaces; the camera finally settles on Wright lying on her bed, as bored by her environment as Cotten is challenged by his. One begins to understand Wright's affection for her uncle as the romance of a young girl for a dashing older man which is then complicated by the brother-sister relationship of Cotten and Wright's mother. The mother's love for Cotten as a man of the world who always returns with presents may preclude any physical intimacy, but her love for him, juxtaposed to Wright's more forthright feelings, creates a family drama that gives Cotten's character a devious credibility.

While probing Wright's feelings for Cotten, Hitchcock also clarifies his own feelings for her character. It is apparent in two scenes, first at dinner and later in Cotten's death trap for Wright in the garage. During the dinner sequence the conversation turns to the merry widow murderer, and Wright expresses her antipathy for the man. When Cotten replies that the women deserved to be killed, Hitchcock moves to extreme close-up, reenforcing the severity of Cotten's statement. During the scene in the garage, Hitchcock does not sustain the suspense—will she or won't she get out?—but emphasizes the shadow play that encompasses Wright as a minor figure in a bleak, American Gothic setting. Hitchcock's cool, perverse tone is directly conveyed in the scene in the bar, in which he holds in medium shot, obscuring Wright's figure while magnifying Cotten's aplomb in his manipulation of the waitress. One area that perhaps best expresses Hitchcock's increasing dramatic conciseness is the relationship between Wright and the FBI agent, played by MacDonald Carey. In most of his films Hitchcock manifests little real humor or understanding of romance, but the quaint sentimentality of Wright and Carey is continually superseded by his moral ambiguity. Hitchcock's paradoxical feelings toward his characters culminate in a most cruel, ironic ending. Cotten has died in a train accident and, while attending a service for him, Wright and Carey discuss his character. The priest's reverential speech about Cotten's kindness is barely audible as Hitchcock stays in medium close-up. Wright discusses her impression of Cotten's diseased mind, but then the last words of the priest, honoring Cotten as a religious man, are clearly heard; Cotten's duplicity thus overshadows the pieties expressed by Wright.

Several of Lang's less interesting crime films fail to balance his interest in expressionism with the more popular mythology of the movies in America. *Man Hunt* functions as an exercise in anti-Nazi melodrama; Walter Pidgeon's awakening to the horrors of Nazi Germany is symptomatic of both his overacting and the catastrophic procrastination of democratic countries. Two of Lang's more acclaimed American films, *Fury* and *You Only Live Once*, derive their harrowing mood from the conceptualization of social unrest. *Fury*, however, is a more astringent work than *Man Hunt*; the town's mob violence and Spencer Tracy's retribution are textbook symbols of an unmediated catharsis whose eventual censure exemplifies the pervasiveness of Hollywood's Production Code, whether in the drafting of a script or the final reediting of a film. *You Only Live Once* is a more effective work because of its departure from the prevailing treatment of the gangster as a larger-than-life anti-hero. Lang's protagonists, Henry Fonda and Sylvia Sidney, are unmistakable innocents, much closer in their feelings to Farley Granger and Cathy O'Donnell in *They Live by Night* and the gangster-as-angel syndrome inspired by *Bonnie and Clyde*. There are several taut sequences like the bank robbery, but the film's aesthetic force lies in its evocation of the heroic naiveté of Fonda and Sidney in a manner that combines the social predeterminism of Lang's German films with the more personalized tensions of *They Live by Night* and *Bonnie and Clyde*. *You Only Live Once* is one of the few crime films of the thirties and forties that condemns both the depressed social environment and the machinations of crime itself; a clear reading of the film makes the epilogue superfluous: we have known all along who the good guys and bad guys were.

In *The Woman in the Window* and *Scarlet Street*, Lang interprets the criminal element, not as an alien social sphere comprised of people who feel cheated of the better things in life, but as the "other," unlocked side of one's own personality. These two films stand apart from *film noir* favorites such as *Stranger on the Third Floor* and *The Spiral Staircase* because of the tragic ironies in the characterizations and in the presentation of reality. The distraught characters and constricted design in *Stranger on the Third Floor* or *The Spiral Staircase*, while effective variations on the psychological trademarks of a thriller, do not question the nature of their dreamlike reality. The questions that do arise are of a dramatically mechanical nature. Will the real villain be unmasked? Will the heroine escape? A cat-and-mouse game is played with the protagonists and audience, and it is played very well in reinterpreting the conventions of a Gothic melodrama. In Lang's films, however, Edward G. Robinson's split personality leads to an examination of its physical and moral origins; it is not a question of transcending genre, but of utilizing the basic elements of this genre in a more intriguing intellectual fashion.

Several critics have argued that by identifying *The Woman in the Window* as a dream, Lang reduces the impact of the traumatic events that culminate in Robinson's suicide. But the film's elliptical narrative becomes an expression of the dangers that await Robinson once he deviates from his orderly life as a professor. The deadly, fatalistic turn of events, inspired by the inversion of Robinson's Walter Mitty–like dream of romance, reveals its oblique resonance through the traps it lays for Robinson, from the scissors that are in just the right spot for him to kill Joan Bennett's sugar daddy to the cut he suffers. The film's dreamlike undercurrent is subtly expressed in the way Dan Duryea discovers evidence of the crime, as if someone has told him the exact location of each of the clues. Whether that someone is defined as Robinson's superego or Lang's omniscient director is secondary; the critical point is the absence of free will in Robinson's character or in those of the other actors. They are caught up in a menacing environment that determines their every move and final destiny. Even if the dream label is regarded as a joke, Lang conclusively depicts the tragic conclusiveness of romantic fantasies.

He uses the same trio in *Scarlet Street*, a less tidy but more emotionally charged picture of the repressed nature of middle-class morality. Robinson plays a social innocent who meets Bennett's femme fatale and paints her portrait; it becomes a key motif in the film in explaining Robinson's character and his relationship with Bennett. The portrait personifies her alluring, devious mask and, though one then might conclude that Robinson should not fall prey to her tricks, Lang exposes Robinson's dual personality through its erotic suggestiveness. In *The Woman in the Window*, Robinson's professor could only dream of the tragic series of events, but his dire social status in *Scarlet Street* leads him into a pernicious otherworld. One experiences more fully the sordidness of Robinson's affair with Bennett, leading to his failed suicide attempt. Unlike *The Woman in the Window*, the stark psychosexual drama of *Scarlet Street* offers no moral alternative in its study of Robinson's and America's dark, unexplored other side.

*Odd Man Out–Touch of Evil*

In the late forties and through much of the fifties, the major crime films reflect many of the psychologically ambiguous elements in Lang's *The Woman in the Window* and *Scarlet Street*. The crime and chaos, however, no longer emanate from a single, disturbed figure, but are discovered in the suddenly precarious social order. The more serious, adult scripts, central to the maturation of Hitchcock's art, and the erotic entanglements in Lang's *Human Desire*, *The Big Heat*, and *While the City Sleeps*, identify the crime as originating in a feeling of alienation toward the rigid social mores and intense strains of everyday life. This *noir* style is personified in the expressionistic fireworks of Orson Welles's *The Lady from Shanghai* and *Touch of Evil*, while its more extreme characterizations range from the savage bigotry of Robert Ryan (*Crossfire, Odds against Tomorrow, Bad Day at Black Rock*) to the party-girl persona of Ava Gardner (*The Killers*), Gloria Grahame (*Human Desire, The Big Heat*), and Rita Hayworth (*Gilda, The Lady from Shanghai*), who, while reminiscent of the kittenish appeal of Jean Harlow, lack Harlow's self-humor.

Three English films directed by Carol Reed—*Odd Man Out, The Third Man, The Man Between*—incorporate many of these themes. *Odd Man Out* is the most ambitious of these works as it creates an expressionistic veneer around James Mason's flight from the police; we have returned to the nightmare reality of the German cinema of the twenties, in which man is trapped in the baroque corridors of hallucination and madness. Reed's fluid appropriation of the dramatic rhythms and psychological pictorialism of expressionism is characteristic of many English films of suspense and terror, from the Fruedian motifs in the lighting and backdrops of *The Seventh Veil* through the more decisive Grand Guignol ploys of *Dead of Night*. Their application is adroitly executed, but one often senses a curious incongruity between the characters and settings. It mars *Odd Man Out* in Mason's confrontation with Robert Newton's painter in which Mason is seen as an allegorical figure of suffering prior to his final reconciliation with his girl friend and her shooting of him. The transition from the murky city backgrounds to allegory is awkward, problematic. To superimpose a religious identity on Mason can only be justified by a consistent idealization of Mason's abject condition and by a visual approach that anticipates the visionary shots in the last part of the film. Reed, however, has undertaken a gritty picture of the desperation surrounding Mason in his losing battle against the rain and his increasing physical decline. To then gradually identify the religious leitmotifs as the dominant ones requires that the secondary characters and the political machinations of the revolutionaries and police be more sharply focused in relation to Mason's character. The film loses sight of its dramatic origins, but it remains highly expressive in signifying the pertinence of expressionism in the political and social history of the postwar cinema.

In *The Third Man* and *The Man Between*, Reed juxtaposes the unsettling, nightmarish features of postwar European cities to the paradoxical relationships that threaten the innocents in the two films, Joseph Cotten in *The Third Man* and Claire Bloom in *The Man Between*. Their unique moral twist lies in the devious nature of the law-enforcement officers who force Cotten and Bloom to renounce their love for the villains, played by Orson Welles and James Mason. If *The Third Man* proves more interesting, it is because of the unusual interplay of Cotton's characterization of a writer of Zane Grey–type westerns, who ironically embodies the virtues of his literary protagonists, and Welles's deadpan characterization of Harry Lime. The film's original appeal derives from its casual, tongue-in-cheek presentation of Vienna's sordid nightlife and its conflicting impact on Alida Valli's mistress and Cotten's writer. Valli becomes the victim and Cotten the unlikely hero of the deadly games played by Welles's associates and the equally sordid implications of the passport exchange between the Russians and the English. Cotten's interpretation of the innocent abroad is his fourth brilliant characterization in the forties. (Jedediah as an older man in *Citizen Kane* is unconvincing, but there is little to find fault with in Cotten's performances in *The Magnificent Ambersons* and *Shadow of a Doubt*.)

In *The Man Between* James Mason's character is not as engrossing as that of Welles, and unlike Welles's affection for Cotten in *The Third Man*, Mason's love of Claire Bloom enables her to understand Berlin as a city of illusion, from the hypnotic appeal of the bicycle ride and the numerous deceptions played by the characters—each one warning Bloom to be wary of the others—to the masks in the nightclub. The treatment is not as caustic as *The Third Man*; the characterizations lack the emotional incisiveness that gives the players in *The Third Man* a life independent of the city's contrasting glamour and grime.

In Fritz Lang's *The Big Heat, Human Desire,* and *While the City Sleeps,* the torturous personal relationships become a sign of the malevolence in the political and social machinery. *The Big Heat* adopts a conventional story line; Glenn Ford's tough-minded cop hunts down the killers of his wife and, in the process, destroys the crime organization that controls the city. With its violent actions and rich cast of supporting characters, from the virulent love-hate relationship of Lee Marvin and Gloria Grahame to the ignominious figure of the politician's widow who collects blackmail money from the syndicate, Ford's pursuit of justice is characterized by a puritan determinism. Although it is a foregone conclusion that crime reigns supreme, Ford's cop does not question its origin, but acts as a moral agent who makes his presence felt before the curtain can be drawn on him.

Since crime is not limited to one sector of society, the more moving crime films expose the omnipresence of evil and its impact on the individual's behavior and friendships. *Human Desire* is not as consistent in its grim behavioral analysis as Renoir's *La Bête humaine,* but it has a cumulative psychological truthfulness in showing how Broderick Crawford and Glenn Ford, because of their jobs on the railroad, are unable to resolve their attraction for Gloria Grahame's fickle, sultry housewife. In Renoir's version Gabin's passionate, murderous nature is partially explained by his fear of hereditary insanity; in *Human Desire* it is the oppressive nature of their work that inspires the wayward behavior of Crawford and Ford. *While the City Sleeps* extends many of the probing, psychological nuances of *Human Desire* in what is one of Lang's most underrated American films. It is an important addition to Lang's filmography because the protagonists are not members of a police force who combat the crime in society, but are employees of a communications empire in which the desire for achievement is more subtly developed than in *Human Desire*. From Rhonda Fleming's adulterous wife to Thomas Mitchell's scheming editor, Lang features a devious group of supporting characters whose desires and ambitions are personified in the psychopath who terrorizes the city. The killer's dialogue with his mother is puerile Krafft-Ebing, and Dana Andrews's reporter, who literally challenges the killer on television, is too clean-cut, but Lang's sensitivity to the way the employees of Vincent Price's communications empire respond to the killer uncovers a social cancer whose existence had not been admitted in the thirties or forties.

Whereas Lang's work in the fifties concerns the multifaceted nature of crime, its widespread social origins and its appearance in the least suspect individuals and institutions, Hitchcock's art studies the moral crisis that arises when his naive protagonists are drawn into a physical and psychological underworld. In *Strangers on a Train, Stage Fright, I Confess,* and *Vertigo*—the most cohesive and gripping work of his career—Hitchcock examines the previously unexplored affinity between criminal behavior and his innocent protagonists.

*Strangers on a Train,* Hitchcock's best film since *Shadow of a Doubt,* is a masterly example of the artful manipulation of the suspense film into a sardonic psychological thriller. Robert Walker's Bruno, the most interesting male character in Hitchcock's films since Joseph Cotten's misogynic murderer in *Shadow of a Doubt,* is a key transitional figure in Hitchcock's treatment of homosexuality and mother love. In *Notorious* the son-mother relationship of Claude Rains and Madame Konstantin was used as an unsettling counterpoint to the romantic passions of Cary Grant and Ingrid Bergman; in *Psycho,* Anthony Perkins's Norman Bates will function as the most perverse counterpart to Hitchcock's romantic leads. Though Walker does not make any overt advances to Farley Granger's athletic, virile Guy, their relationship implies their identity as a split personality, a theme developed as Walker kills Granger's sultry wife and then asks Granger to kill his father. This character fragmentation gives the film its devious charm in conventional settings such as the party that is upset by Walker's menacing presence and oddball behavior. It is sustained throughout the film by Robert Burks's theatrical light-dark lighting effects surrounding Guy and Bruno and by the acute editing permutations that elaborate the suspicions of the supporting players and Guy's increasing isolation from his friends and the law. It is much less explicit than the novel in the interpenetration of its two characters, and, for once, Hitchcock's paradoxical point of view is enriched by Walker's performance. Because Hitchcock sees the conflict as a deadly cat-and-mouse game rather than as an agonizing psychological profile, the audience understands the subconscious implications as a parallel to the basic black-comic tensions that spark the film. Its cleverness and gripping suspense are made real by Walker's Bruno, a character whose blatant abnormality would have been unlikely in earlier times in Hollywood.

There are occasional lapses of frighteningly inane dialogue in *Stage Fright,* such as in the scene involving Michael Wilding and Jane Wyman in the taxi, that ruin an altogether creditable work. Hitchcock's interrelationship of two points of view, that of Richard Todd and Jane Wyman, provides a cogent parallel to the film's theatrical backgrounds. But one must turn to *I Confess* to more clearly understand what Hitchcock is attempting in these films. A major area of improvement is in the dialogue between Montgomery Clift and Anne Baxter: they are real, fragile characters whose emotional ambivalence never seems mannered or false. Clift's characterization is further enhanced by his sense of being trapped in the city's enveloping shadows. Hitchcock's brilliant collaboration with cinematographer Robert Burks results in a graphic realization of the city as a visual correlative for Clift's tortured conscience. Their subjective cross section of an isolated protagonist and the grim specter of a dark urban background are effectively recalled in *The Fifth Horseman Is Fear*, Zbyněk Brynych's World War II horror story concerning Nazi-occupied Czechoslovakia; in *I Confess* it results in a probing study of the ambiguities that are dormant in the most rigidly ordered lives.

*Rear Window*, like *Dial M for Murder*, however, exposes Hitchcock's continuing commitment to a theatrically conceived mystery drama. The film inevitably cheats its audience owing to Hitchcock's blasé interiors, or what I earlier characterized as his being a romantic in close-up. Hitchcock again plays the clown through his use of the newlyweds and the lonely widow who live opposite Stewart. They are meant to exist as dramatic counterpoints to Stewart's temporary Peeping Tomism, but when one considers the film's psychological premise, they are as banal as the countless drawing-room stereotypes in Hitchcock's earlier films.

Throughout his career Hitchcock has usually focused on one character as he confronts an unusual and dangerous situation. In *Rear Window* he is faced with the more difficult problem of drawing out Stewart's relationship to the apartment of the murderer, even when he is not looking at it through his binoculars. He achieves this by using the fade to black. Like other film techniques, the fade to black can be used as other than a simple editing device. The most notable use of the fade to black is in Bresson's films, in which it compresses the action and isolates the setting as another fixed point in his static universe. In *Rear Window* it is brilliantly adapted as both Stewart's state of mind—falling asleep and awakening three times in his first night watch of Raymond Burr's apartment—and as an objective abbreviation of the actual passage of time—in the fourth and final return to the apartment complex, during which Burr leaves with his girl friend, ending with a pan showing Stewart asleep. But Hitchcock pads his story with tepid dialogue; only once does Hitchcock show his characters seriously responding to Stewart as a Peeping Tom, when Grace Kelly, at her wit's end, confronts Stewart. This is the one moment in the film that shows Kelly as other than a mannequin; for a brief moment she is a living part of this gruesome drama. Hitchcock's delineation of the murderer, played by Raymond Burr, however, works as a subtle variation on the audience's perception of good and evil. When Stewart's investigation becomes apparent to Burr, his exchanges on the phone with Stewart reveal a man with whom one could almost sympathize, a man whom one realizes is telling the truth when he says he has no money and who has probably suffered through a miserable marriage. If only Hitchcock could have integrated this ambivalence in other parts of the story— but then, as Hitchcock cultists would argue, that would not be Hitchcock.

*Vertigo* is a more radical departure for Hitchcock, first evident in his shrewd manipulation of Jimmy Stewart's innocent. During the scene in which Stewart goes to a restaurant and is entranced by Kim Novak as she walks by, Burks's camera separates the two without fully closing in on Novak, immediately defining her as a mysterious, idealized object. By then associating Novak's identity with the painting she returns to stare at in the musuem, Stewart's fascination with Novak during the first hour of the film is treated as a neurotic attraction, her everyday habits an anomalous routine that Burks records in an objective, distant fashion. The few weak moments in the first part concern Stewart's relationship to Barbara Bel Geddes, a slight concession to conventional behavior that Hitchcock will not make in *Psycho*, even with Vera Miles's character. Bel Geddes's Midge is an amorphous figure who appears in too many of Hitchcock's films, and in *Vertigo* she looks and acts like a displaced Hitchcock heroine. A second unsatisfying feature is Stewart's dream in the sanitarium; like Bergman's fade-out in the garden in *Notorious* or Gregory Peck's nightmare in *Spellbound*, it is a glib execution of a hallucination. But after Stewart is released from the sanitarium and finds Novak, Hitchcock returns to the icy style of psychological fixation he had sustained through Stewart's rescue of her. Stewart then forces Novak to fulfill the dreamlike identity she assumed at the beginning of the film, but the audience is now removed enough from Stewart to understand his neurosis and why he forces Novak to play out the drama into which she first drew him. With her death Hitchcock dramatizes the bleak, irrevocable nature of love, and the ever tightening moral authority that he exercises over his characters.

The major postwar crime films of Lang and Hitchcock undertake a more tenuous approach to the origins of crime. Walker's Bruno in *Strangers on a Train*, the psychopathic killer in *While the City Sleeps*, and the images of the femme fatale of Gloria Grahame and Kim Novak represent only the most overt signs of social and psychological unrest. In the crime films of the thirties and forties, a clear dividing line between law and lawlessness was established; Lang and Hitchcock, however, resolutely avoid equating crime with the manic gangsters who reject all social and moral standards. Their postwar work is distinct from the premises of *Dr. Mabuse the Gambler*, in which the criminal is seen as a distortion of Machiavelli's *The Prince*. Their psychological style identifies Lang's *M* as the less obvious but equally compelling archetype; the criminal is seen as the sum total of the perversities that are repressed by society. In *The Asphalt Jungle* and *The Killing* there is a similar stylistic principle that diminishes, if not dismisses, the question of good and evil.

With their emphasis on the planning, execution and post-caper aftermath, the mechanistic elements of *The Asphalt Jungle* and *The Killing* present a departure from traditional presentations of the criminal. In the films of Robinson, Cagney, and Bogart, a major failing of their characters is their sudden, explosive irrationality that separates them from their partners in crime as well as from society. In *High Sierra*, for example, one responds to Bogey's jittery, distrustful "Mad Dog" Earle as characteristic of his fatalistic character and to the heist as a culminating expression of the characters' emotional insecurity. But in *The Asphalt Jungle* and *The Killing* the participants in crime are commonplace losers who wish to escape from their dreary, blue-collar jobs. They are not moral renegades whose exploits have been covered in the tabloids; compare, for example, the differences between Barton MacLane's scheming cop in *High Sierra* and Ted De Corsia's debt-ridden policeman in *The Killing*.

The characters in *The Asphalt Jungle* and *The Killing* connote an unmistakable weariness—whether as a result of past misdeeds or, more prominently, of having suffered too many insults and wisecracks, as in the case of James Whitmore in *The Asphalt Jungle* and Elisha Cook, Jr. in *The Killing*. As the leader of the heists in the two films, Sterling Hayden projects a nervous, restless energy that embodies the desperation of his gang members. Director Stanley Kubrick's previous film, *Killer's Kiss*, was a neurotically eclectic film with a final showdown right out of *Rashomon*; in *The Killing* he documents the mechanics of a caper, but relies on one of the most archaic motifs in criminal or classic mythology: man falling prey to woman. *The Asphalt Jungle* is less stringent in juxtaposing the idiosyncracies and failings of its criminals to the stolidity and precision needed to execute the heist. There is a more acute romantic fatalism about the personal dreams of the criminals in *The Asphalt Jungle*; both films, however, identify the allure of crime as a means, if only for a short period of time, to redeem the characters' flawed past by their impersonal execution of a theoretically perfect crime.

The ominous mood that hovers over each of the characters in *The Asphalt Jungle* and *The Killing* is abrasively exploited in Welles's *Touch of Evil*. While the films of Reed, Lang, and Hitchcock present the representatives of law and decency as being as corrupt as the villains they pursue, Welles offers the most exhaustive evidence for this moral ambiguity. In *The Lady from Shanghai* Welles identifies Rita Hayworth's seductive sexual presence as the source of bewilderment and chaos; in *Touch of Evil* his suspense-filled editing and his fascination with intensively baroque angles becomes a metaphor for the omnipresence of crime in the border town. The essential stylistic equation in *Citizen Kane* is Welles's ability to delineate the movies' evocation of space as an expression of Kane's larger-than-life desires and dreams; in *The Magnificent Ambersons* it is his ability to isolate the Amberson estate as a static, somnolent social ideal; in *Touch of Evil*, it is the explosive action that fills the film frame and which is exaggerated in his disengaging camera angles. Welles's tour-de-force characterization of Hank Quinlan, the local sheriff, forces a showdown not with a gangland boss, but with Charlton Heston's Mexican police officer. By dwelling on the passionate trust of Welles's aide and through the final, ironic epilogue in which it is revealed that Hank's hunch about the murderer was right, the film suggests that a police official like Hank Quinlan is needed to instill order in the troubled environment of postwar America. Though one is made to feel the hideousness of Hank's methods in cross-examining the murder suspect and in brutalizing Janet Leigh, one never believes that Heston's simple devotion to the law can prove successful. Welles appears to have reintroduced a conception of crime more suited to the twenties and to Lang's *Dr. Mabuse the Gambler*. *Touch of Evil* lacks the fatalism of Lang's crime epic, but it is a stunning, paradoxical study of the social maxims that support law and order.

*Psycho–Bonnie and Clyde*

*Psycho* is the fourth of Hitchcock's masterly studies in misanthropy. But its truths are more shocking than those in *Blackmail, Shadow of a Doubt,* or *Strangers on a Train* because the subjects of his attack are the very characters he has sympathized with throughout his career. When the camera begins to move in on the deserted apartment complex and finds Janet Leigh and John Gavin having just consummated a brief midday union, Hitchcock is exposing his characters, both literally and metaphorically, to a degree never undertaken in his previous films. The one lawless act that Leigh commits and her decision to return the stolen money increase the moral ambiguity of her situation. Like the distraught heroine in *Blackmail,* she flees to a world that proves hostile and alienating, from the eerie presence of the policeman with his dark sunglasses to the blank stretches of space and ominous rainfall that lead her to the Bates motel.

In *Notorious* and *Strangers on a Train,* Hitchcock plays with the queer mannerisms of the characters of Claude Rains and Robert Walker as displaced symbols that envelop his principal performers and action. In *Strangers on a Train,* his most dangerous and successful blending of the comical and surreal, Walker's psychopath is both a foil to and an extension of Farley Granger's Guy. But in *Psycho* Hitchcock is far more direct in linking the homosexuality of Anthony Perkins's Norman Bates with his attack on one of the cherished maxims of American folklore: love of mother. Bates's sheltered existence, as a counterpoint to Leigh's harried, precarious circumstances, does not offer the viewer a very attractive set of alternatives. Unlike Hitchcock's earlier films in which a certain moral choice rests with the viewer's character preferences, the nightmarish configurations in *Psycho* do not yield any redeeming figure or moral perspective. Neither John Gavin, Vera Miles, Martin Balsam, nor John McIntire inspires the necessary strength or authority to deny the immeasurable impact of the killings at the Bates motel. As a study of American Gothic it manifests the bleak vision of the magistrates of New England; by exposing the characters' weaknesses and the inexorability of a preconditioned moral code, Hitchcock presents one of the most overpowering examples of the crime film as, inescapably, a matter of conscience.

*Topaz* is one of his most effective spy thrillers, the erotic entanglements more decisively juxtaposed than in his coy, prefabricated thrillers of the thirties and forties. Hitchcock has reaped the benefit of the increasingly cynical, erotic scripts of the sixties, whether manifest in his showing the wife of the French undercover agent having an affair with the KGB agent or in such secondary figures as Roscoe Lee Browne's wily spy and the defecting Russian who only becomes conciliatory when he is rewarded by his CIA protectors. It underscores Hitchcock's camerawork in tracking across the room as the head of Cuban security kills the double agent and expresses both his attraction to her and his greater commitment to the state. The film displays an intelligent balance between the perils of the spy game and the romantic sheen of its characters and backgrounds; one only wishes that Hitchcock cultists would be more careful in warning the public about his hits and misses. This is more important than ever with films such as *Torn Curtain* and *Frenzy*.

*Torn Curtain* applies many of the vapid touches in his first spy thrillers, notably in the cartoonlike characterization of the German scientist and in Paul Newman's overly dramatic disclosure to Julie Andrews about the true nature of his mission. It contains little of the dramatic aplomb that makes *North by Northwest* such a refined exercise in suspense, a film whose commercial seriocomic congruity complements the grimmer tension in his other films of the fifties. *Frenzy*, however, makes one pine for the tedious escapades of *The Thirty-Nine Steps* and *The Lady Vanishes*. It may be the worst film Hitchcock ever made; it is so psychologically fraudulent and so casually photographed, as in the camera setup during the rape and strangulation of Jon Finch's ex-wife, that one might label it Exhibit A in the demise of a filmmaker. There is a representative scene of subtle, spellbinding terror, when the camera withdraws from the apartment of the murderer as he escorts his next unsuspecting victim, but Hitchcock shows such a callous attitude to the sexual tensions that it is as if Norman Bates had taken over as director.

Many of the stylistic components of the caper films of the fifties undergo a more rigid stylization in the sixties. The criminal and crime buster as technician is the subject of Peter Yates's *Robbery* and *Bullitt*, two films almost wholly attuned to the mechanics of crime and the technical dynamics involved in the execution of a crime and in the apprehension of the criminals. It is as if the Marxist economists had assumed control of the crime film; the call is out for specialists, while the Renaissance man of crime becomes an outmoded symbol of social protest. By documenting the increasing dehumanization of the genre, *Robbery* presents a group of technicians who are no more animated than the technology they confront; it is the single emotional response by one of the gang members who calls his wife that proves their undoing. *Bullitt* is a more personal film, yet how much of one's interest in the car chase involving Steve McQueen and the hit men derives from one's identification with McQueen as a reticent, war-games specialist—whether in the old or new frontier—and how much stems from his role as a troubled police officer? There is an exciting, burly approach to San Francisco and the rigors of police life, but it is compressed in a two-dimensional world of gunplay and chases.

A similar ephemeral mood mars Yates's direction of *The Deep*. Yates shows little interest in drawing out the characters' feelings in their foreboding tropical paradise. The underwater sequences and the titanic physical struggle of the white-black adversaries are decisively executed, but the star appeal of Nick Nolte, Jacqueline Bisset, Robert Shaw, and Louis Gossett, Jr. functions as bland ornaments of romance and danger. Yates's immersion in the cold-blooded mentality and dynamics of crime finds an ideal subject in George Higgins's *The Friends of Eddie Coyle*. The idiosyncratic jargon and ruthless cycle of revenge are the central motifs in a refreshingly real exposé of the underworld. Articulated with a genuine poetic harshness by Robert Mitchum, Peter Boyle, and Richard Jordan, Yates's austere direction underlines the genre's classic fatalism. How ironic then for Yates to have enjoyed his greatest commercial success with the pithy, Capraesque cartoon types in Steve Tesich's *Breaking Away*, in which his jolting, two-fisted montage rhythms are subordinated to the wistful charms of small-town life.

The dehumanization of crime may be one of the reasons for the proliferation of special effects in the spy serial, especially in the Bond films. Unlike the spellbinding serials of Louis Feuillade, with their languorous mood of understated terror, the Bond films adopt a more straightforward action story line while venerating the supersleuth for his solipsistic nature. It was imperative in Feuillade's serials that an antiquated tone of innocence and danger be maintained, in the Bond films, only that his tuxedo not be stained by the blood of his victims.

In the gangster profiles of the thirties and forties, the conflict between a depressed social setting and a flawed anti-hero defined these efforts as largely sociomythic in design. In *The Rise and Fall of Legs Diamond* Ray Danton's characterization of Diamond ironically integrates the popular mythology of the gangster. Diamond is not presented as a heroic antagonist to society; he plays at being a gangster, one whose machismo consists of his dancing grace, his ability to fool Karen Steele's dumb broad, and to set their dancing opponents' clothes on fire. After he is gunned down while working as a minor aide-de-camp to Arnold Rothstein, Danton painstakingly learns all about toughness and guns in order to become a full-fledged gangster. When he announces himself before killing his assassins, and during his following victory over Leo Bremer's mob, Danton's scalding, supercool portrayal characterizes Diamond as a thinking man's gangster who wittily and brutally applies the classic formulas of the rise of the gangster with none of his tragic, explosive shortcomings. Diamond's most devastating triumph not only is a testament to the gangster's murderous blending of cynicism and administrative know-how, but it also works as a lucid picture of the devastating nihilism of gunplay in America. Danton speaks over the phone with his rivals, and after they agree on a battle site, where they have already arrived, the camera pans to the next window where Diamond is shown one step ahead of them.

The murder of Diamond is the final variation of director Budd Boetticher's parallel study of machismo and murder. Two assassins burst into Diamond's bedroom, and he is able to scare one of them away by shouting, "You can't kill me; I'm Legs Diamond," as if the myth and the man were one. As in the earlier assassination attempt on Diamond, the gun of the remaining killer is turned on both Diamond and on the audience; even Legs Diamond is not immune to the murderous rationale of crime. It is a skillful, frightening film because by pitting Diamond against the other criminals rather than against the police, one can applaud Diamond's victories for their style and cunning and for his idealization of machismo as the supreme virtue of the criminal anti-hero.

*Murder Inc.* presents a similar rise-and-fall treatment of a most sordid chapter in American crime. Its handful of characters and sets gives the film a journalistic thoroughness that is augmented by the teledramatic immediacy surrounding the intimidation of Stuart Whitman by Peter Falk. Falk's performance is one of the grittiest portrayals of the primitivism of an underworld henchman on film; the supporting relationships of Whitman's cowardly, acquiescent innocent and May Britt's beleaguered wife perversely juxtaposed to the unusual pathos generated by the crime boss and his aide delineate the glumness of the crime world with few concessions to moral righteousness.

Joseph Losey's *The Concrete Jungle* and John Boorman's *Point Blank* show a more representative severity in their treatment of the underworld and its mercenaries. Losey's taut camerawork and relentless pacing characterize Stanley Baker's internment and his relationship with Patrick Magee's screw. The psychologically expressive nature of Losey's high-angle shots during Baker's incarceration and the grating buzz-saw rhythms of his prison routines work as a detailed prologue to Baker's fated rendezvous with death during his brief time on the outside. Losey makes a terse statement on the chaotic, short-lived life of the gangster by compressing the biographical and social allegories of *Little Caesar* and *The Public Enemy* within the limited time frame of *The Concrete Jungle*. *Point Blank* is similar to *The Concrete Jungle* in its emphasis on the frenetic nature of a gangster and his environment. But, unlike *The Concrete Jungle* which was set mainly in a prison, *Point Blank* transpires in the beautifully blank exteriors of California. In Losey's film the forceful editing was generated by the harsh dialogue and manic exchanges between Baker and Magee; in *Point Blank* the dizzying high-rise structures and cold, harsh colors create a mazelike effect in which Lee Marvin's violent actions seem the only way to obtain a response. He is engaged in a ceaseless fight against the encroaching anonymity of his world, not only of Alcatraz and the faceless, business orientation of modern crime, but also in the Disneyland of modern urban planning. The lone, desperate acts of Marvin, his razorlike edge, and his persistency in seeing justice served show the gangster as our last romantic.

In *They Live by Night* director Nicholas Ray features the clash between the lack of worldliness of his outcasts and the unbridled antisocial identity of their partners in crime. The emotional vulnerability of Farley Granger and Cathy O'Donnell sustains an unequivocal aura of sympathy in depicting their alienation as adults and as criminals. In *The Rise and Fall of Legs Diamond*, Ray Danton's braggadocio in outmaneuvering his enemies and his belief in his own immortality create an unmistakable romantic aura about the criminal; in *Bonnie and Clyde*, these themes achieve a richer poetic and psychological treatment. The protagonists—Bonnie Parker, Clyde Barrow, C. W. Moss, and Clyde's brother and sister-in-law—continually show off for one another, interacting like children who play at being criminals. One of the major motifs in the film pictures the robberies with their sudden, brutal violence as an extension of their childlike playacting. Whether it is Michael Pollard's moronic bashfulness, Faye Dunaway's simulating the pose of a tough guy's moll, Estelle Parsons's frantic tantrums, Gene Hackman's good-natured, acquiescent sibling, or Warren Beatty's pathetic attempts at male dominance, each character, as the victim of his or her fragile, innocent, emotionally flawed makeup, reclaims a role as adult and as hero to their partners in crime through their bravado as members of the gang. The tragic, sublime beauty of the deaths of Bonnie and Clyde, as their bodies seem to float as if suspended in a dream, is a poignant fulfillment of their play-acting; the innocence of their intentions and the violence of their actions cannot be separated in life or death. Their criminal exploits and misadventures conceive Depression-era America as a self-styled escapade in which scriptwriters David Newman and Robert Benton, cinematographer Burnett Guffey, and director Arthur Penn rediscover America's past as a make-believe fantasy by interpreting the Barrow gang as fabled innocents.

### *Bob le flambeur–The Godfather Part II*

Two films by Jean-Pierre Melville, *Second Breath* and *The Samurai*, recharge the symbolic, existential motifs discovered earlier in *Le Jour se lève* and *Port of Shadows* with greater elegance if less commitment. They are not as fanciful as the crime-film inversions of Godard and Truffaut; yet Melville's mechanistic reading of crime has proven unusually pertinent as a unique precursor of the neo-classical design of the crime film of the seventies. *Second Breath* is an exhaustive study of the fatalism that marks those who have spent time behind bars. Unlike their gritty, brash American counterparts, Lino Ventura and his cohorts do not challenge society once they escape from prison but are involved in a cat-and-mouse game that forces them to suspect every person they meet and to take the least visible position they can. Melville foreshortens the vigorous, descriptive components of the crime film; the opening prison breakout, with its abbreviated movement and silhouetted figures, is one example of his stylistic abstraction. Ventura's relationship with his sister and the policeman's attraction for her are simultaneously repressed and redefined through the film's laconic delineation of the criminal, the woman under suspicion, and the law. *The Samurai* is a more self-conscious departure from the vivid emotional interplay and highly charged suspense of the crime film. Alain Delon's performance, like the minimal exterior shots, is so cryptic that it makes Hammett's *The Continental Op* stories seem Dreiserian. The question *The Samurai* raises is to what degree can the abstracted characters and routines of a crime film be interpreted as symbols? One is unable, however, to answer this question because there is no intrinsic meaning to Delon's autistic characterization of the killer in a role that recalls the equally withdrawn mannerisms of George Raft in *Scarface* and *Quick Millions*. Like Melville's initial exercise in underworld iconography, *Bob le flambeur*—with its montage of the characters' entrances and exits through bars and nightclubs and with the romantic punctation of the criminal through the classic apparel of its protagonist—*The Samurai* reduces its protagonists and their passions to pictorial emblems without the dramatic and social folklore that have made these emblems both poetic and personal.

The popularity of *Z* and *The Battle of Algiers* finds the crime film adopting an entirely different set of priorities. In *Z* Costa-Gavras prefaces the story by telling us that the drama is a true historical incident. However, instead of presenting his characters in a simple, documentary fashion, Gavras conceives the military junta as dramatically and visually simplified symbols of villainy. The characters of Yves Montand and Jean-Louis Trintignant inspire similar emotional responses, as if they were involved in a gang war during Prohibilition-era Chicago. The political and moral currents are resolved in a facile manner; Gavras's picture of social malaise in a true-to-life situation dramatizes the same conflicts and gut emotions long appropriated by Hollywood. *The Confession* is a more honest film, but again it is Montand's resourcefulness as a conventional hero who foils the brainwashing of his invisible persecutors that gives the film its emotional impact. *State of Siege* is the most interesting of these Gavras films; but nowhere in *State of Siege*—any more than in *Z* or *The Confession*—does he deviate from the moral and dramatic clichés featured in American crime sagas. Unwilling or unable to transform his politics into a more didactic or distilled dramatic fable, he relies, and quite effectively in *Stage of Siege*, on the suspense elements essential to a political thriller.

*The Battle of Algiers* operates from an antithetical point of view. No documentary footage was used, but in its slow, methodical approach to the hero's rising political awareness and the activities of the revolutionaries, the film plays as a compilation of newsreel footage. The crime film has made a simple, transcendent jump in perspective, from crime as the province of those wishing to satisfy their instinctive, violent impulses, to crime as a means of political salvation. Television docudrama replaces the romantic mythology surrounding the criminal outsider in the literature and movies about crime.

While Melville abstracts the crime film into an elusive shadow play and Gavras reclaims the genre as a vehicle of social criticism, American crime films, from the nonstop action sequences of Clint Eastwood's Harry Callahan series to the operatic strains of *The Godfather* saga, undertake a comprehensive reexamination of their mythology. Clint Eastwood's Harry Callahan, like Gene Hackman's Popeye Doyle in *The French Connection*, is a sullied protector of society who must adopt the illegal actions of his adversaries. Eastwood's figure evokes the innocence of the West, directly featured in the earlier *Coogan's Bluff*; it identifies him both as an outsider and as the savior of society. Hackman's Popeye Doyle is a more contemporary figure representing the look and language of the streets, who understands that the face of the criminal has only undergone slight cosmetic surgery. In *Dirty Harry* the film's brutality illustrates its vigilante polemic through the use of its San Francisco backgrounds as an extended arena for Eastwood's tracking of the killer. *The French Connection* comically exploits the documentary features in postwar crime films such as *The Naked City* and *13 Rue Madeleine* through the blustering mannerisms of Hackman's police officer as he races through the city's environs; veteran action director Don Siegel gives the chases in *Dirty Harry* a more manipulative, kinetic authenticity punctuated by the impact of Eastwood's gun. In *Magnum Force*, however, Eastwood's folk hero becomes a fetishistic symbol of revenge who, with his black sunglasses, combats the anonymous, dark-clad vigilante police force. The numerous clashes and explosions—in the airplane, at the supermarket, on the highway—present a far more destructive, pagan celebration of gunplay than *Dirty Harry*. Its fascination with guns and the dynamics of death is one of countless examples of the technological pop-art pandering of filmmakers in the seventies.

The popular and critical success of Coppola's crime-world epic lies in the script's shrewd treatment of archaic literary and dramatic formulas; De Mille's pioneering innocents are replaced by an immigrant family that has risen to the top of the underworld. A second decisive element is the chromatic pictorials that give the family's personal conflicts as well as their gangland confrontations a classic atmospheric and iconographic density. While the family's struggle for survival achieves a social, archteypal expressiveness, the underlying dark brown tone of *The Godfather* elevates family life and criminal warfare into moody genre studies that treat the protagonists with a solemnity and grandeur that painters have usually reserved for portraits of kings and republican statesmen.

In *The Godfather Part II* the dramatic continuity and pictorial mythology surrounding the family saga is strained. Coppola, cameraman Gordon Willis, and production designer Dean Tavoularis continue their family epic through a series of genre paintings, from the icy exteriors of Nevada to the naturalism of the streets of New York and the pastoral rubric of Sicily. It is more self-consciously a spectacle, yet there is an ensuing appreciation for the moral paradoxes and stylistic expressionism surrounding the rise of the Corleones; the American folk idiom of success, slyly delineated in *The Godfather*, has led to the Freudian excesses of *The Godfather Part II*. One, however, cannot overlook the mesmerizing effect of Al Pacino looking melancholic for a little over three hours and the finely textured supporting performances of, among others, John Cazale's distraught underling. The lush romanticism of American social and movie mythology in *The Godfather*, which showed the Corleones as immune to the violence of the crime world by their faith in the family, now finds them reenacting the passions of the House of Atreus.

# 13
# The Fantasy Film

*The Cabinet of Dr. Caligari–Vampyr*

The fantasy film offers the film student a unique philosophical and stylistic vantage point. Since its inception the film experience has worked as a type of voyage into the unknown; whether it was the Lumières' arrival of a train at a station or Méliès's delightful, daydreaming excursions, the magic of the movies was an irrepressible aspect of the silent film. The Lumières and Méliès were equally handicapped by the primitive state of film production and the tentative effects used in documentaries and dramatic shorts. But Méliès surmounted these technical limitations through his performers' playacting and the innocently surreal nature of his studio imaginations. Fantasy, in the early silent film, seemed a natural component of a movie: Méliès, as the first film poet and parodist, underlined a central preoccupation of fantasy filmmakers by exploiting the medium's potential for extravagant illustrations and disconcerting special effects.

The one period of film history in which the fantasy film blossomed into an effective dramatic genre was in the German cinema of the twenties. In this explosive era, German writers, directors, and designers approached the demons of the past and future with the same intensity and introspection that mark films like *Die Nibelungen* and *The Last Laugh*. Some of the major fantasy films of this period—*The Cabinet of Dr. Caligari, Waxworks, Metropolis*—miss an essential ingredient in conceiving the horror as a resonant nightmare, yet they manifest a fascination with grotesque symbols and tales of evil as an index to the traumas of classic mythology and modern history.

While much of the praise for *The Cabinet of Dr. Caligari* concerns the stark, painted sets (more abstract than expressionistic), the conventional ending forced upon the filmmakers, in which the audience finds that the distorted backgrounds represent the imagination of a psychotic instead of Caligari's devious social presence, reduces much of the film's stylistic daring. The slow, fatalistic opening and closing of the camera shutter and the mesmerizing performances of Werner Krauss and Conrad Veidt pinpoint the vertiginous, mazelike features of their fantasy entrapment. But the cutting and continuity are poorly developed, even when one considers the impoverished nature of German film production at the end of World War I. It is not, as often cited, one of the great German films of the twenties. Its place in film history is, perhaps, most attributable to Kracauer's story regarding its origin and the controversies surrounding its filming. It does, however, strikingly suggest that a new filmmaking style is about to challenge the romantic thrust of Griffith's work and the kinetic farces of American film comedy.

*Waxworks* also attempts to dismiss its thinly veiled parallels to modern history by defining the story as a dream; like *Destiny*, it too suffers from an acute stylistic incongruity with the comedy sequence in the second story. The first part of *Waxworks*, starring the most poetic of all German faces, Conrad Veidt as Ivan the Terrible, is a brilliant example of an actor's personifying the mood and design in a setting. While the low-arched tunnels and winding staircases become an extension of Ivan's paranoid character, director Paul Leni's dramatic interests are centered in Veidt's facial contortions and emotional frenzy. After the astrologer tells Veidt that he will die when the hourglass runs out, he turns it back and forth in trying to escape his fate; Veidt's spellbinding performance leads the spectator to realize that there is no object that can rival the beauty or terror of the actor. Leni's facile staging in the second story is at the mercy of what Lotte Eisner calls Emil Jannings's "doughy personality." In the last sequence—the shortest, the most brutal and overpowering of the three—the camera passes through the carnival as a foreboding, enveloping surface, an enlarged Venus's-flytrap that awaits the entrance of its next victim. Two motifs are presented to the viewer in this last segment; first, that Jack the Ripper is the lone surviving figure in both *Waxworks* and *Pandora's Box* and, second, considering the nihilism of the German cinema of the twenties, that this final sequence may be the most representative, riveting metaphor of the social disorder and violence in modern Germany.

Fritz Lang's *Metropolis* reflects many of the strengths and weaknesses in later science-fiction fantasies such as William Cameron Menzies' *Things to Come* and Stanley Kubrick's *2001: A Space Odyssey*: their intrinsic technological texture and their often invisible dramatic credibility. Like Menzies and Kubrick, Lang diligently creates a future world by drawing on the most visionary contemporary design, but the love story is simplistic, and the villainous rulers of his technocracy are treated as stereotyped symbols of social control. Lang sees that the true strength of a futuristic fascist order would lie in its ability to imbue inanimate forms with human features, such as in the sexual identity of the false Maria who diverts the revolt of the workers. But he is unwilling to impose a similarly rigorous interpretation of his narrative; the love affair and eventual overthrow of the tyrannical ruler rely on the outmoded storytelling formulas that have permeated science-fiction literature and moviemaking from *Flash Gordon* to *Star Wars*. This reluctance to question the nature of human intellect and behavior within a radically technological society reveals a heterodoxy in creating future worlds; while the social order is scientifically, physically transformed, the individual is seen as retaining his personal dignity and a capacity for emotional involvement. This Rousseau-like reverence and mysticism is more acutely manifested in Lang's *The Woman on the Moon*. There is a stunning recreation of the planning and launching of a rocket ship, but once the characters are featured, the drama is reduced to the level of "baby talk." Whether it is epitomized by the youthful protagonists of *The Woman on the Moon* or by Luke Skywalker, the inarticulate child-hero of *Star Wars*, the innocence and babbling of children function as a symbol of the redemption of humanity in a futuristic, scientific metastructure.

The two most complete realizations of fantasy during this period, the second version of *The Golem* directed by Paul Wegener and Murnau's *Nosferatu*, experiment with the cinema's propensity for disturbing, chaotic images as an expression of social and personal disorder. *The Golem*, like Dreyer's *Vampyr*, develops as a study of persecution and repression in which the extreme theatrical expressiveness of the actors and the imposing spatial fragmentation of the sets denote a mood of anguish and torpor. Only *The Cabinet of Dr. Caligari* and *Warning Shadows* attempt a similar painstaking definition of the theatrical texture of the actors and environment as symbolic of a tortured, nightmarish world. In *The Cabinet of Dr. Caligari* it is delineated through the jagged, asymmetrical lines in the paintings; in *Warning Shadows* the characters' shadows are used as the pervasive psychological motif in conveying the imbalance of their world. But *The Golem* executes these themes with greater force; it embodies a mood of persecution and fear through the thickness of the doors, the oblique shape of the windows, and the unyielding configurations of the buildings. The characters' anguish is reflected through the physical density and spatial imbalance in each part of the town and through their painfully slow movements as they pass from one room to the next. The few exteriors in the film, such as the gate that encloses the ghetto and the bridge crossed by the rabbi and the golem, are further examples of the film's spatial expressionism, in which each object looms as a symbol of the religious oppression the Jews suffer. Within this psychologically stylized setting, the golem's slow, mechanical movements become the most profound example of a world in which not the slightest natural movement is allowed to obtrude. And this, perhaps, is the tragic irony of the golem's death as he naturally responds to the little girl who unknowingly removes the key that brought him to life. The film may seem too theatrical in its stylistic objectives, but so much of the glory of film history lies in its filtering the genius of other art forms. The golem is a resonant figure of Jewish mythology and drama which has been artfully expanded on film.

Murnau approaches the nature of terror from an altogether different point of view in *Nosferatu*. The action is tense, continuous, as if Dracula alone were capable of surviving amid the menacing shadows and the aggressive, dynamic thrust of the editing. Unlike Dreyer, who looks at the diseased, haunting world of vampires from the viewpoint of an estranged Jonathan Harker, Murnau unleashes a case study of madness. The demonic characterizations of Alexander Granach as Renfield and Max Schreck as Dracula are the most gruesome products of the psychological terror, which is punctuated by Murnau's febrile camerawork. He does not allow for moments of emotional relief and contrast, such as the dinner scene in *The Last Laugh* and the walk in the city by George O'Brien and Janet Gaynor in *Sunrise*. His unrelenting baroque compositions present images of such a morbid, melancholic nature—for example, in the scene in which Mina awaits Jonathan's return in a sand dune or the one in which Dracula is seen attacking Harker in shadow play, followed by a cut to Mina screaming—that he appears to underscore Dracula's reign of terror. Whether the story transpires in Transylvania or London, the ghoulish otherworldliness with which one associates the image of Dracula remains paramount. It is Murnau's most pessimistic film and one of the most bruising studies of terror because it is not presented from a distant point of view. The terror is in the film, in its imagery and in the dramatic interconnectedness of its motifs of terror, as if Dracula himself had appropriated the kaleidoscopic magic and power of the movies.

While Murnau's *Nosferatu* subjects the viewer to a constant barrage of disturbing figures and settings, Dreyer's *Vampyr* impresses one by its subdued emotions. Rudolph Maté's camera frames the characters in a manner similar to *The Passion of Joan of Arc*; Harker replaces Joan as the trapped, tremulous victim, and the vampires become his persecutors. It also reminds one of the agonizing, spiritual drama of *The Golem*, but whereas Wegener's film emphasized a mood of repressed emotional intensity, Dreyer sees Harker as an outsider to the phantomesque world of vampires. In Dreyer's deliberate approach to the presence of supernatural beings—from the silhouetted figures of the vampires to the sepulchral tones of the castle—the film's cadence becomes the most lucid expression of its horror. An exemplary scene is the priest's killing of the old woman. After a stake is driven through her heart, Dreyer cuts to a shot of the clouds, then to the priest's hammering, and finally to her face as she turns into a skeleton. Like his use of organ music, these effects find the atmosphere providing all the essential dramatic components that are needed to tell the story. Although Harker proves a most elusive figure, this is no imagist film; it is as dramatically compressed as *The Passion of Joan of Arc*.

### The Cat and the Canary–King Kong

In the German studio film, legendary demons such as the Golem and Dracula exist as the most vivid symbols of a living nightmare. Thus, for any mythological figure to engage one's interest, the "creature" must function as a correlative. Carlos Clarens, in his history of the horror film, was completely wrong in his judgment of *The Cat and the Canary*, a critical work prefiguring the interpretation of fantasy in the American film. The characters assembled at the haunted house are dramatic stereotypes, while the house is no more real in its otherworldliness than the murderer's glass eye. The conventions of a haunted house story are used as a transparent backdrop to support the ludicrous comic melodrama. A more interesting aspect of this film, which Clarens fails to note, is how the suspense is dependent on the copious titles; in effect, it is a sound film.

One of the few American writers-directors with a genuine fascination for fantasy was Tod Browning. The original nature of his work derives from the empathy he generates toward abnormal figures and abnormal behavior and from his sensitivity to the problems his outsiders face as they try to lead normal, emotionally fulfilling lives. Film historian William Everson, however, believes that Lon Chaney's work in *The Phantom of the Opera*, *The Hunchback of Notre Dame*, and *The Penalty* is more satisfying than his performances in Browning's films; Everson considers Browning's films morbid and static while citing these films as examples of first-rate melodrama. But as melodrama these three films fail to stir the emotions because Chaney is the only vivid, living presence while the other players are treated as stereotypes lifted from trashy magazines and second-rate Gothic theater. In the flogging of the hunchback there is no period or dramatic authenticity; Chaney's tortured face is the one image to which the camera returns. *The Phantom of the Opera* is the most rewarding of the three, especially in its exciting final chase; but it is Chaney alone who dazzles us with his extreme makeup, his tremendous animal passion, and his convoluted expressiveness as the doomed outsider.

Browning's work with Chaney in *Where East Is East* and *The Unknown* and his more well-known films like *Dracula* and *Freaks* are characterized by his affinity with a unique gallery of undesirables. *Where East Is East* is the least memorable of these films, but one still finds evidence of Browning's fascination with languorous, morbid settings and his reluctance to use any dynamic camerawork or cutting. Chaney plays a professional game hunter who, while preparing to marry off his daughter, is upset by the return of his wife after an absence of seven years. Prior to the appearance of the wife, Browning mawkishly develops the daughter's courtship but remains sensitive to Chaney's remarkable physical authenticity even in a role in which he is not playing a physically grotesque figure. During the journey on a steamship, Browning uncovers the conflict between the estranged couple; one not only feels Chaney's unease in her presence but also the fear Chaney's manly game hunter has for his wife's strident sexuality. This emotional tension, resulting in the wife's seduction of her future son-in-law, is physically complemented by the oppressiveness created by the hundreds of Chinese laborers on the ship. To ensure that the marriage takes place, Chaney releases a gorilla from its cage, leading to his wife's death and his own eventual eventual demise. What is most interesting about *Where East Is East* is how Browning implies much of the ugliness of his characters' passions in sudden, vivid close-ups and actions, such as his introduction of the wife and in the release of the gorilla. The film is not as successful in interrelating its backgrounds and characters, but as an early Browning film and as a primitive example of the American fantasy film, its morbidity is to be savored as a flawed though genuine expression of melodramatic upheaval.

*The Unholy Three* is his most admired silent film, but *The Unknown* is a more perverse, personal work. Browning's isolated setting is the circus in which Chaney, working his act with Joan Crawford, performs as an armless rifle expert who shoots with his feet and toes. The first unsettling feature concerns Chaney's physique; while hiding his arms to escape capture by the police, he still possesses a sign of abnormality with a webbed thumb. A second devious factor involves Crawford who declares she is unable to love any man except Chaney, whom she thinks armless. When Browning opens one scene with a man holding a cigarette, it is likely that the viewer will take a moment to realize that the cigarette is being held in Chaney's toes. This is not a clever or eerie shot; Browning studies the displacement of a normal, balanced world by an abnormal, unbalanced one. After Chaney kills one of the circus employees and Crawford recognizes the murderer by his webbed thumb, Chaney is faced with a problem. He thinks he has the solution when Crawford tells him that because she has witnessed the murder she cannot be embraced by any man; Chaney then decides to have his arms amputated. When Chaney returns from the hospital Crawford tells him that she has recovered from her neurosis; with the camera holding on Chaney, Browning absorbs the audience in his hysterical collapse, one of the most truly terrifying moments in the history of the fantasy film.

Browning does not attempt to balance the grotesque nature of his story by showing Crawford attracted to a dashing, romantic figure. She falls in love with the circus strong man, and in the brutal last sequence Chaney tries to bring about the loss of the strong man's arms. But the true hideousness, the real "Browning touch" is not in Chaney's demonic actions, but in those of a lady in the audience who raises her binoculars and stares at the strong man, her voyeurism accentuated by Browning's slow camera movement toward his figure. Browning was not a complete artist, but his immersion in the feelings of his social and physical deviants, and his special sympathy for Chaney's tense, supercharged presence prove far more real than the pseudodemons in conventional Hollywood fantasy films.

*Dracula* and *Freaks* are more familar examples of Browning's unique blending of emotion and violence. Though *Dracula* lacks the apocalyptic terror of *Nosferatu*, it is a far more intelligent, craftsmanlike work than has been acknowledged by film historians. Browning's collaboration with Karl Freund brought together two distinct sensibilities. One again notes Browning's methodical, ominous pacing; supported by Charles Hall's intelligent design—with the magnified spider webs set against the enormous deep space of Dracula's castle—and by Lugosi's mournful, demonic presence, the film avoids the dramatic incredulity that characterized the major Hollywood adaptations of otherworldliness in the thirties.

Freund's cinematography is a noteworthy addition to his legacy in the German cinema; his camera angles maintain a distant point of view, augmenting the sense of fatalistic entrapment, as in the camera setup for Lugosi's indoctrination of Dwight Frye's Renfield. His close-ups of Lugosi, one eye in shadow and the other illuminating his ghoulish condition, faithfully convey the story's mordancy. Lugosi's Dracula, like Frye's Renfield, lacks the devastating, definitive mask of madness in the portrayals of Schreck and Granach, but they remain distinct from the numerous campy derivations they inspired.

A more personal effort, *Freaks*, has a singular place in the American horror film by fully empathizing with its outcasts. Browning does not portray them as symbols, but humanizes their condition in a way that is similar to his treatment of Dracula as a foredoomed, melancholic lover. Again, I feel that Clarens is in error in stating that, as the freaks corner Olga, one's sympathy turns away from them. The contrary is true. Since Olga and her lover have grossly abused the feelings of the freaks, their revenge is emotionally and dramatically justified as a necessary action. The party that precedes the assualt is among the few rapturous moments in his films, made memorable by Browning's lyrical camera movement that shows them as children at a wedding feast. It is a gross spectacle only to those eyes unwilling to see the freaks as human beings; the film becomes a testament to Browning's private, passionate regard for physically marred figures who attempt to resolve their very human, pressing emotions.

*The Old Dark House*, more representative of the Hollywood fantasy cycle, recycles the formulas of *The Cat and the Canary* in which a group of comic stereotypes is trapped in a haunted house. Boris Karloff, who brought a level of intelligence to the most soporific productions, is sorely tested in his role as the malodorous manservant; director James Whale uses the Gothic backdrops as theatrical props, as fake as the skin pigmentation of the old man locked up in the mansion. *Frankenstein* is not as silly as *The Old Dark House*; the self-humor and folly exhibited by the characters, culminating in the search for the monster in a miniscule studio forest, is redeemed by Karloff's original animation and entanglements with Dwight Frye's assistant. In *The Bride of Frankenstein*, probably the most successful of all horror-film sequels, Whale employs a less heavy-handed approach, treating each of the major characters—from Karloff's monster and Ernest Thesiger's Dr. Praetorius to Elsa Lanchester's bride that never was—as sympathetic caricatures of a child's fantasy. Praetorius's artificial people, like Frankenstein's quest for a mate, are part of an entertaining hoax perpetrated on science and fantasy; from the monster's smoking of a cigar to Thesiger's facial contortions as he awaits the outcome of his joint venture with Dr. Frankenstein, the film evokes the gay, irreducible nature of our most fanciful dreams.

Whale's adaptation of *The Invisible Man* is an uncommonly literate fantasy film. Claude Rains's speaking voice and delivery, with its commanding raspiness, its cadenzalike trills of megalomania and despair, are endemic to the appeal of the film, much in the way Lugosi's sickly pallor and moroseness embody the spirit of Dracula and Karloff's slow, moronic expressions and movements bring home the horror of medical skulduggery. John Fulton's special effects in these fantasy films, like the makeup of Jack Pierce for most of the gruesome faces of Hollywood horror folklore, innocently fulfill the sparkling sham of Gothic melodrama. Arthur Edeson, cinematographer for *Frankenstein* and *The Invisible Man* and co-photographer with John Mescall for *The Bride of Frankenstein*, shows his customary expertise, surrounding this gallery of gargoyles with colorful, contrasting shadow effects that recreate the gloss of Victorian illustration in the glitter of Hollywood back light. Several town scenes in

*Frankenstein* and *The Bride of Frankenstein* use a deep focus composition to show the townspeople clamoring for revenge, while the voluminous space in the laboratory and mansion adds to the sense of horror emanating from an indeterminate point in the mind of the filmgoer and in the characters' physical surroundings. Not to be overlooked, the art direction of Charles Hall intelligently translates the melodramatic detail of Victorian illustrators. Craftsmen like Fulton, Pierce, Edeson, and Hall—like cinematographers Günther Krampf, Fritz Arno Wagner, and designers Robert Herlth, Walter Röhrig, and Hermann Warm in the German fantasy film—were essential to the meaning of these fantasies. If the artists of the German cinema possessed a greater dramatic uniformity about the implications of their work, there was no lack of commitment by those entrusted to animate our nightmares in the American cinema of the thirties.

An interesting example of how the different styles of Browning and Whale were integrated by one director is seen in two films by Karl Freund: *The Mummy* and *Mad Love*. *The Mummy* qualifies as a Browning-type project through its deliberate editing and Freund's penetration of his claustrophobic sets. The ritual that shows Karloff in ancient times has sufficient spectral mystery, and one believes in his power to mesmerize the girl who resembles the queen. But its serenely understated pacing and Karloff's ennobling performance as the solemn, priestly mummy fail to inspire a transfiguration of the popular culture of Victorian Egyptologists. *Mad Love* is a much weaker film, its melodramatic bombast characteristic of nearly every return-and-revenge sequel to the stories of Frankenstein, Dracula, and the Wolf Man. Peter Lorre has a few sensitive moments as the doctor, but invariably he plays his role for laughs. In *The Mummy* Freund centers the drama on Karloff's mythological presence; in *Mad Love* he is the servant of the banal dialogue.

The first sound-film adaptation of Stevenson's *Strange Case of Dr. Jekyll and Mr. Hyde* proves even more ponderous than the interpretations of the Frankenstein monster. The Paramount version, directed by Rouben Mamoulian, unintentionally shows how much easier it is for its star, Fredric March, to conform to the manners of a beast than to those of a scientist and scholar. Mamoulian may have been Lubitsch's most serious rival in musicals, but his succeeding productions present an outmoded example of showmanship, whether in Stevenson's London or Blasco-Ibáñez's Spain. Unlike Karl Struss's high-contrast lighting in the glossy Paramount version, there is a more discretely handsome stylization of Victorian England in Joseph Ruttenberg's cinematography in the MGM version, culminating in the final chase of Spencer Tracy through a series of elegant, miniature backdrops. There is also a prolonged, psychological treatment of Ingrid Bergman's gamine suffering from the brutality of Spencer Tracy's man-beast. It is her contradictory feelings of shame and fear in those moments preceding Tracy's attacks that give this version a credibility lacking in other ones. A minor footnote to this period is the unusually uninventive treatment of the Wolf Man, but the transformation scene in *The Werewolf of London* is pure film fantasy. Henry Hull's metamorphosis as he slithers around the pillars in a nocturnal fog briefly illuminates the magic of the movies and the myth of the demon.

*The Raven, Murders in the Rue Morgue,* and *Island of Lost Souls* undertake more graphically sordid penetrations of the unknown than generally favored in the adaptations of the Frankenstein, Dracula, and Wolf Man myths. Like the Bauhaus backdrops of *Son of Frankenstein* and the cavernous setting of *Svengali,* the high-ceilinged torture chamber of *The Raven* shows the influence of European art directors on American filmmakers and is equally sensitive to the respective masks of alienation of Lugosi and Karloff. *Murders in the Rue Morgue* is a fast-paced exercise in Grand Guignol, highlighted by Freund's savory lighting, by the effectively cluttered design, and by the forcefully abrupt editing. *Island of Lost Souls* may be the best of these ghoulish entertainments. Laughton's performance as the villainous scientist and Lugosi's spokesman for the man-beasts bring to life one's childhood fears with an expressive blending of hysteria and hokum. Karl Struss won more acclaim for his use of the moving camera and the dark shadows in Mamoulian's *Dr. Jekyll and Mr. Hyde,* but his work in *Island of Lost Souls* seems superior. Although one is conscious of the small, physical space meant to represent Dr. Moreau's island retreat, the moving camera assumes a darker note of mystery. Whereas the lighting poetically defines Laughton's diabolical character by continually shading his face against the outsized vegetation, the camera dollies reveal the manifold layers of evil created by Laughton's experiments.

The psychological currents of horror and fantasy are explored in a more low-key vein by Val Lewton and in several films by John Brahm and Edgar Ulmer. Though they lack the stylistic acuity of such a landmark work as Lang's *M,* they are intelligent, often gripping studies that treat the characters' madness as a meaningful statement on commonly experienced fantasies and depression. In both *Cat People* and *The Curse of the Cat People,* the hallucinatory visions of the two female protagonists arise out of their forlorn, disconsolate existence. In *Cat People* Simone Simon's tremulous victim is encompassed by cinematographer Nicholas Musuraca's familiar florid lighting, where every object casts its shadow on the characters' faces. In *The Curse of the Cat People* director Robert Wise is more interested in studying the young girl's independence from her parents, and for the first half of the film he sustains a touching psychological profile. *The Body Snatcher* is a well made, tightly organized exercise in terror that shows Lewton's ability to juice his settings for every ounce of creepiness. In *Murders in the Rue Morgue* the abrasive editing and pungent design seem to trap its victims; in *The Body Snatcher* the juxtaposition of Karloff's malevolent figure as the body snatcher to the scientist's experimentation and the mother's devotion leads to an unusual dramatic mosaic.

The films of John Brahm are similar to Lewton's in depicting the tortured imaginations of psychopaths while revealing them as examples of a doomed romantic spirit. Brahm's two Victorian melodramas—*The Lodger* and *Hangover Square*—are dominated by Laird Cregar's massive frame and lugubrious demeanor, the unique combination of fear and delicacy that his presence inspires.

Watching his almost religious sense of pain as he sits through a cancan revue or his dedication as he plays Bernard Herrmann's Ravel-Rachmaninoff pastiche in kitsch major, the viewer has ample evidence of his dementia. *Guest in the House* is Brahm's richest, most detailed work, his physical and psychological effects proof of Anne Baxter's scheming, neurotic character. Her guile in convincing her prospective in-laws of her innocence and her gradual manipulation of them are deftly elaborated through their increasing isolation on the estate. Brahm shows considerable restraint in his sensitivity to Baxter's finely textured performance and to the genuine literacy of the script.

In *The Black Cat* Edgar Ulmer's skillful art direction results in what is literally one of the darkest of all horror films. But even with its poignant confrontation between Lugosi and Karloff, Ulmer's talents seem those of a specialist and not those of a storyteller. In *Bluebeard*, however, Ulmer displays a sure-handed poetic style in presenting Paris as a series of enclosed, painted backdrops that surround John Carradine's puppet theater. Carradine's performance as Bluebeard complements Ulmer's understated approach to the murders in which Bluebeard becomes the victim of his stage fantasies.

*Things to Come* is the second major study of a future world. It is less involved with symbolic conflict and dramatic catharsis than Lang's *Metropolis*; its underlying theme is the resonance of cleanliness in a futuristic society. The first third of the film concerning a modern-day holocaust plays as a newspaper montage compilation and is well-done, though without the graphic artistry one imagines a Russian director bringing to this project. The second part consists of the lull after the fighting as mankind awaits the next savior; it is the dullest, most didactic section. In this segment, Raymond Massey acts not so much as a dramatically redeeming agent, but as a type of scientific Mr. Clean who comes to clear away the debris and filth. The film's anonymous portrait of Armageddon and man's rebirth extends into the third part, in which the future world appears to be run by the Department of Sanitation. Science is engaged in its idealistic course, but it is the sparkling, architectural arrangement of massive groups of people filmed against a spiraling, voluminous backdrop that impresses the viewer. While the story is negligible in *Metropolis*, the invisibility of the drama is more apparent in *Things to Come*. Director William Cameron Menzies, one of the prominent art directors in the English and American cinema, creates several startling designs, but the narrative shows little of the imagination he has brought to the settings. One only hopes that our hygenic, mechanically supreme city of the future will create a human being slightly more complex than a model for a toothpaste commercial.

Although fantasy was treated with little insight by Hollywood filmmakers, the prevalence of dramatic self-caricatures and production-value excesses contributed to the making of the one classic American film fantasy. *King Kong* has won lasting fame through its ingeniously intertwining a romantic adventure with the spectacular model animation of Willis O'Brien. The combined splendor of its artful matte painting—featuring the Doré-like island setting—and the meticulous, magnificently coordinated movement of Kong, are far superior not only to the earlier *The Lost World* of Cooper, Schoedsack, and O'Brien, but also to half-baked derivatives like *Mighty Joe Young*, *Gorgo*, and the Mattel-toy machinations of the postwar Japanese monster film. The beauty of *King Kong* lies in O'Brien's artistry elaborating the elements of heroism and fantasy originally personified in the treatment of Robert Armstrong's Carl Denham as the archetypal documentarian filmmaker. Its innocent, spellbinding romance, from the first sighting of the island through the crew's fight for survival to Kong's final act of hubris, works as a monument to an unabashed love of mystery and intrigue and to the movies' ability to fulfill this quest. The magic of the movies in general and of Hollywood in particular has been redeemed.

## The Little Shop of Horrors–Kill Baby Kill

Fantasy filmmakers have adhered to the conventions of the thirties and forties to a much greater degree than recent crime films have to earlier models. Whether set in the past, present, or future, fantasy remains the most innocently archaic of film genres. There has been a change in tone from the more blithe, inane dynamics of science and religion in the thirites to the incipient camp sensibility in the nickle-and-dime oeuvre of Roger Corman, but in both cases, mediocrity reigns triumphant.

The two major institutions that have sustained the public's penchant for gargoyles and gaga are Corman and the Hammer studios. Corman has become one of the most major of minor cult curiosities, mainly because of his administrative known-how in churning out B-movie schlock on a shoestring budget. Some of the younger generation of film critics have applauded, for example, Corman's *The Little Shop of Horrors* as a perverse exercise in black humor; its cult status, however, bespeaks the more dangerous perversity of its fans. Corman's pre-Poe style, equally influenced by financial consideration as by his debased aesthetics, discards the resplendent Gothic trimmings of earlier fantasy films and thus creates a more self-consciously absurdist setting. There is no question that Corman is a modernist, but one whose minimalist settings and off-key performances prove most meaningful to the devotees of drive-in movie theaters. Corman fanciers are free to choose their favorite moment of movie madness; one that scared me occurred at the end of *"X"—The Man With the X-Ray Eyes*. For the most part it is a standard tale of the scientist gone wrong, with a few diversions resulting from the doctor's increased vision. At the end of the film, after Ray Milland's eyes have been transformed into black dots, he stumbles into a revival meeting. The zealots tell him to remove them, and as Milland plucks out his eyes, the ghastliness of his experiments and the movies' ability to revel in excesses of all sorts are made strikingly clear.

Corman's Poe filmography is more directly modeled on Hollywood prototypes of horror while expressing a parodistic approach toward its characters and moods. In Hollywood's age of innocence a slight moral nudging tempered the audience's interest in the scientific brouhaha and the infamous alchemists of the soul; Corman's films visualize the specter of the unknown with greater romantic intensity. Corman's appreciation of the stylistic dimensions of fantasy, however, is marred by his allegiance to this very age of innocence. An exemplary Corman scene in *Premature Burial* shows a character lost in an atmospheric forest, its coarse reds and grays replete with sexual overtones. Corman prolongs the scene in which the protagonist runs about and finally bumps into the groundkeeper. The formula is sententious and is repeated in many of his Poe adaptations. Starring Vincent Price, the most doleful of all male leads, Corman's films waver between a tone of disquietude and disdain; the exception is *The Raven*, which is played strictly for laughs, with Peter Lorre's foul-mouthed leprechaun striking a merry balance between the hocus-pocus of Karloff and Price.

In Corman's more deliberate films the talents of cinematographer Floyd Crosby and set designer Daniel Haller create an attractive series of illustrations to a child's abridged copy of the horror classics. In *The House of Usher* the hyperbolic color tones overshadow the wooden dialogue and stilted characterizations. *The Masque of the Red Death* is a more coherent yet supine work. The film's pictorialism results in a series of color slides of debauchery in a tentatively realized morality play. Its simplistic dramatic-pictorial equation underlines the uniformity of Corman's films and his unquestionable roots in Hollywood's earthly cosmology.

The Hammer productions are more conventional. Their faithfulness to the innocuous trimmings of the Hollywood fantasy prototypes lacks the occasional luster of Corman's work, but their sensitivity to the intrinsic power of the classics in the genre has made for several satisfying efforts. *Horror of Dracula*, begins with the demon's residence in London, and is characterized by an unblinking dramatic tension in the relationship between Dracula and Van Helsing. The composition offers no new insights into the psychologically gripping prose of Stoker's novel, but in developing the Dracula–Van Helsing clash as a series of chase sequences, the film does not circumvent the audience's expectations. A more invigorating approach to the classics, *The Revenge of Frankenstein*, finds the venerable doctor settling in a German town. One notes the original quality of the laboratory design and that of the monster, who looks like he is suffering from a drug overdose. The monster's indoctrination, his growing affection for the nurse, and his escape and recognition of the doctor at a town gathering are treated in a low-key manner. The beating of the doctor by the inmates, while reminiscent of the uprising in *Island of Lost Souls*, strikes its own terror because these are real people with no reason for attacking him except their own scurrility. Most memorable is the ending, with Frankenstein's assistant restoring the doctor to life. How refreshing to find the man of science win in the end, especially in a film in which his pioneering experiments have made for a creepy two hours.

*The Curse of the Werewolf* avoids Hollywood's maudlin moralistic juxtaposition of science and religion and shows instead the horror originating in the diseased world of the aristocracy. It begins with the appearance of a minstrel at a wedding ceremony; the emphasis is on the decadence of the rulers, the feigned gaiety, and the minstrel's pathetic attempts to bring laughter. After the lecherous prince locks up the minstrel, a narrator informs us that many years have passed and that the princess has died. The prince is a wasted, syphilitic figure whose desiccated skin color is more striking than the minstrel's decrepit condition. The jailkeeper's daughter has looked after the minstrel, but after she rejects the advances of the prince, she is thrown into the minstrel's call. She is raped and escapes.

Prior to her escape it is one of the few fantasy films undertaken by either Corman or the Hammer company that is imbued with an acute feeling for physical decay and gross passions. This is no small achievement in the fantasy genre, but the middle and last sections of the film fail to fulfil these motifs. Its most symptomatic feature may be the appearance of Oliver Reed as the werewolf in one of his first starring roles. It is a tense, loud performance that works better here than in the less animalistic confines of human society.

This interest in period atmosphere is more consistently developed in *The Kiss of the Vampire* in which the cult of the vampire leads to a sympathetic, stylized picture of their murderous, aristocratic bond. Our interest in the newlyweds who arrive in the vampires' domain centers on the wife, awestruck by the magnificence of the vampire estate; one realizes that her attraction for the scion of the vampires is not simply induced by a drugged cocktail. This theme reaches its most lyrical treatment during a masked ball. When the wife is eventually indoctrinated into their cult, her assault by the father evokes the spiritual as well as the sexual aspects of this act. The final sequence is the most unnerving one in the film. The vampires gather in white robes, fearful that their persecutor may soon destroy them. Throughout the film the physical beauty of the vampires is seen as one of the outstanding traits of their diseased dynasty. Thus, their dressing in white robes makes an ironic point about their deviant behavior. Their persecutor calls upon evil to destroy itself, and as the bats mass in the castle, the film bears comparison in composition and dramatic emphasis to any of the birds' attacks on the townspeople in *The Birds*; one is led to consider a world without vampires, in which their elegance and stylish manners will have faded away like an outdated feudal ceremony.

One director who seems to have been singled out by fantasy film cultists is Freddie Francis. A brilliant cinematographer, equally adept in the muggy, gray naturalism of *Saturday Night and Sunday Morning* and the lustrous, formalist compositions of *Sons and Lovers*, Francis has specialized in fantasy films. The decorative color tones of *Asylum* and *The Creeping Flesh*, however, show Francis, like his predecessors in the Hollywood fantasy films of the thirties, more interested in mood than in drama or characterization. In *Tales That Witness Madness*, only the last sequence, in which the blind inmates trap the corrupt administrator, fulfills its grisly potential. *The Skull* is probably his most accomplished film. Like the best work of Mario Bava, his probing camera not only traces the murderous scent of evil surrounding the characters' pursuit of the skull, but also appears as a manifestation of the skull's chthonic force.

Mario Bava is a more instinctive primitive than either Corman or the Hammer studios' Terence Fisher. The exaggerated backdrops for *Black Sunday*, like his use of the subjective camera, have the quality of an unsettling camp fire tale but with a nastiness missing in the Corman and Hammer variations. At the same time that one is conscious of the fabrications, the storyteller's intensity gives free rein to our most dreaded fears.

Bava's *Black Sabbath* is another in a long line of anthology fantasy films that rarely work. The second part of *Waxworks* is a heavy-handed parody, whereas only the segment with Michael Redgrave's psychotic ventriloquist in *Dead of Night* conveys the full impact of a madman's reality. The first story in *Black Sabbath* is an extended exercise in fast cutting, as if Bava were experimenting with this one technique in building a mood of fear surrounding the woman's stealing of the ring. The second one is of more interest if only for its creepy combination of the dreaded phone calls and the voyeuristic entrapment of the heroine. The third story is far more engrossing, beginning with one family member's flight from a vampire. The succeeding piecemeal entombment of the family into the vampire cult is then seen as an inevitable consequence both of their isolation and of the incestuous feelings that have arisen from their alienated existence.

*Blood and Black Lace* is a trashy work similar to Michael Powell's *Peeping Tom* in that the glittering backgrounds are used as a parallel to the characters' emotional traumas. Like Powell, Bava impersonally denotes the characters' perversity through the overly stylized settings. *Kill Baby Kill* is the odious title of Bava's most serious film. During the first half hour Bava engages the viewer in a somber, introspective study of a landscape of terror. His camera passes through a terrain of scorching reds, illuminating the hellish nature of the protagonists' backgrounds. Though the two central characters are unconvincing, Bava's conception of evil—a little girl with a ball—is a more frightening, otherworldly image than Fellini's deadly nymphet, who premiered in the same year in *Toby Dammit*. There are several scenes whose shock potential lies in their suggesting the spiritual conflict at the heart of the terror, especially the one in which the protagonist runs through what appears to be an endless number of rooms— which in reality is only the same room—to confront his phantom self. If Bava doesn't quite fulfill this unsettling period tale, his interest in spooky fantasies is far superior to their reckless treatment in Corman's films.

### Village of the Damned–The Empire Strikes Back

Fantasy films set in the present utilize a variety of ideas as the source of the terror. Some point to the bomb as the cause of the gruesome horror that follows (*Village of the Damned*, *The Damned*); several show nature or a supernatural force attempting to destroy mankind or assuming control of one's life (*The Birds, Rosemary's Baby, The Exorcist, Invasion of the Body Snatchers, Omicron*); and others consider the psychological ambiguity that arises when a person undergoes a physical transformation (*Seconds, The Horror Chamber of Dr. Faustus, The Face of Another, Le Testament du Docteur Cordelier*).

The difference between *Village of the Damned* and *The Damned* is one of emphasis. In *Village of the Damned* the social and psychological implications of the children's stigma are secondary to the actual mechanics of terror, as in the motorist's death or in the children's final confrontation with their teacher: their luminous eyes become a striking metaphor for their identity as outcasts and for their unique power resulting from experiments with the bomb. But in *The Damned* director Joseph Losey is not interested in such hocus-pocus. He attempts a statement about the fascistic nature of scientific experimentation by establishing a cause-and-effect chain, from the military's control of the children to the violence of the teenage gang and the mannered sculpture of Viveca Lindfors. In developing the characters' precarious emotional relationships, Losey simplifies their meaning as individuals. He is not interested in what they are, only in what they represent. Without the few conventional chills that made *Village of the Damned* a straightforward exercise in terror, Losey's inability to communicate through his actors becomes the true origin of the violence he has tried to symbolize.

*The Birds* presents an interesting premise, but Hitchcock's unwillingness to deviate from the conventions surrounding the romance of Rod Taylor and Tippi Hedren limits the meaning of the sudden, inexplicable onslaught of the birds. His formula-ridden study of male-female discord turning into love makes for a tendentious beginning. Until the birthday party for Taylor's sister, Hitchcock presents a picture-book world of sunshine and romance, but his leads prove stubbornly two-dimensional. During the party Hitchcock isolates Taylor and Hedren on a sand dune and, as in many of his films, uses a strict shot-reaction-shot perspective. Robin Wood sees this as a decisive sequence, discovering in the sand dune and in the shot-reaction-shot dynamic an effective symbol of the plight of modern man and a personification of the Taylor-Hedren relationship. But Hitchcock's use of the sand dune, like his depiction of the characters of Taylor and Hedren, is characteristic of his indolent dramatic staging. The repeated close-ups treat Taylor and Hedren as stereotypes: their identity is that of two soap-opera figures languishing outdoors. In this sequence, in which Hitchcock's performers must resonate as characters, his naive romantic style fails to distinguish a vivid, dramatic stage. Wood states that he has seen the film seven times and suggests that one might have to screen the work this many times to appreciate Hitchcock's rhythm and meaning. I have seen the film twice, and after the second screening I found it more suspect. After the first viewing, I though its ability to shock one—for example, in the mother's discovery of the neighbor, the massing of birds as Hedren sits on the bench, and the attack by the birds on the children, the gas station, and Taylor's home—was representative of the film's virtues and Hitchcock's study of nature as an opaque, destructive force. During the second screening I found the film less rewarding because the nihilism seemed divorced from what Hitchcock tries to express through his characters, especially in the relationship of Taylor and Hedren and that of Jessica Tandy and Hedren. One is impressed by the horror while depressed by its surface glitter.

In *Rosemary's Baby* and *The Exorcist* the otherworldy force is the devil; in *Rosemary's Baby* he is portrayed as a classic demon, while in *The Exorcist* he is transformed into a ludicrous composite of our repressed thoughts, of our foul-mouthed speech, and of the things we eat. Polanski's earlier exercise in film terror, *Repulsion*, was a savage study of madness; although it was marked by a surfeit of bloodcurdling images, the visceral impact of its gross actions engaged the viewer; it disdained the emotional sympathies in Val Lewton's productions for a more cynical joyride into the unknown. But *Rosemary's Baby* is so cool in its treatment that only one indoctrinated in demonology could accept its bland, supercilious devil worshipers. *The Exorcist* was deservedly a greater financial success because it had the good sense to treat demonology with all the restraint of a group-encounter session coordinated by a zealot on speed. It is the type of fantasy film that one feels Hollywood has wanted to make for some time, spoofing the very techniques and symbols that have made the genre such a durable form. It may seem cavalier to see the film as a parody when so much debate and instant paralysis was generated during its premiere. Its numerous blatant effects, however, mark the beginning of a cycle of anarchistic shock films—*The Omen* series perhaps the most reprehensible—that displaces both the solemn horror projects of the thirties and Corman's more wry treatments.

The transformation of human beings into mechanically destructive automatons offers filmmakers and science-fiction advocates the opportunity to explore many of the bleak horrors in the novel of alienation. The replication of human behavior and speech presents a direct, disturbing statement about the effects of technology on modern man. Since, to borrow from the title of a celebrated study on the subject, mechanization took command, society has appropriated to the machine various functions performed by man or ones that man thought best left to God. Although we are apparently working toward a more leisure-oriented society, there appears to be a greater social uniformity because of man's dependence on technology in enjoying the fruits of this social mechanization. In *Invasion of the Body Snatchers* the metamorphosis of man into pod becomes a metaphor for the dynamics of conformity; in *Omicron* this idea is comically interpreted as the ultimate level of productivity to be reached in a technological society. The original *Invasion of the Body Snatchers* has proved a chilling tonic since its release a quarter of a century ago because its unaccented depiction of the townspeople's transformation into pods exists as a looking glass to the many ways man has given his blanket endorsement to the antiseptic anonymity of technology. *Omicron* is a furious, anti-Marxist parable in which the bosses and workers vie for control of Renato Salvatori's superhumanoid. Similar to *I'm All Right, Jack*, both sides are petty and self-centered, while the boss's eventual triumph results in a paradoxical last image as they finish their cigarettes in one puff. From the English anarchist satire to the Italian science-fiction parody, there is a transition from a declining society to one in which both the leaders and laborers accept the crazy-quilt world of superhuman efficiency.

In *Seconds*, *The Horror Chamber of Dr. Faustus*, *The Face of Another*, and *Le Testament du Docteur Cordelier* the physical transformations express man's unblinking approval of the discoveries of the scientific community. *Seconds* is the weakest of the four films because director John Frankenheimer is overpowered by James Wong Howe's wide-angle lens distortions, penetrating John Randolph's suburban existence as a reticent dreamworld dominated by Caligaresque phantoms. The film sees Randolph as a representative American who signs over his soul in the form of his life's savings to Will Geer's rustic incarnation of the devil. His transformation, while reflecting society's acceptance of transplants and cosmetic surgery, is too contrived in exploring its dangerous psychological repercussions; his tragedy, inevitably, is linked to his inability to forget the sweet conformities of suburbia.

Georges Franju's *The Horror Chamber of Dr. Faustus* is imbued with the hushed, somnolent tones in his other black-and-white films. Franju's style originates in the poetic sweep and mystery of a variety of film and literary archetypes, identifying him as the most severe neoclassicist in the French cinema. In *The Horror Chamber of Dr. Faustus* he avoids the moral dichotomy that characterizes most treatments of scientific pioneers; Pierre Brasseur as the doctor, Alida Valli as his mistress, and his disfigured daughter are trapped in a maze of repressed emotions. Franju's empathy with their devious, subterranean world is reflected by his unwillingness to delineate the spiritual crisis in similar film adaptations. By capturing the daughter's excitement as she stares at the kidnapped girl's face that will soon be hers, by the pervasive look of chagrin that marks Valli, and by the estrangement of Brasseur's doctor—neither saint nor sinner—Franju distills the truly dispossessing qualities of this romantic genre.

Teshigahara's *The Face of Another* attempts a more classic, introspective study of the moral ambiguities that are all too smoothly effaced by the medical profession. Kobo Abe's novel is written in a tense, philosophically overwrought style, but Teshigahara's film analyzes the patient's problem in a sensitive, aloof manner characteristic of the doctor-patient relationship. One is first aware of his stylistic emphasis in the distortion of the scientific apparatus and plastic appendages in the doctor's office. It is a surreal dungeon in which the doctor appears as just another displaced figure of our imagination. The central confrontation concerns Tatsuya Nakadai's victim and the doctor; during their first night out together, Nakadai's vocal and physical awkwardness are visually isolated by the camera and analyzed by the doctor. With his new face, Nakadai seduces his wife only to learn that she saw through his attempted deception; he expresses his anguish to the doctor and then kills him. In the final scene he walks out to the street and sees a crowd scarred like himself.

There are some confusing elements at the end of the film. Is Nakadai's victim distraught because his masquerade was not successful, or does he realize the horrible implications of a world in which anyone can assume another's identity? But it remains one of the more original variations on the psychological crisis underlying physical transformations. It is always a pleasure to watch Machiko Kyo, though it is slightly disconcerting to see her in the role of the wife since she is best remembered for the exquisite softness of a face that invoked the passions of medieval Japan. With his performance as the victim, Tatsuya Nakadai reconfirms his position as one of the most intelligent of film actors. He does not possess the manic force of Toshiro Mifune, but has more cunning in his physical resiliency; he is a little like Jack Lemmon in his gracefulness while possessing the charm of Mastroianni and the essential presence of all fine actors.

Jean Renoir's *Le Testament du Docteur Cordelier* is the only fantasy film classic that concerns the impact of science on society and the individual. Renoir's Jekyll-Hyde protagonist is not played as a persevering scientist who exceeds the boundaries of his profession; in Jean-Louis Barrault's stunning portrayal he is seen as a poet manqué, the sweetest and simplest of souls who unleashes his latent, sadistic other self. Renoir's treatment of this classic tale is only subliminally concerned with the spiritual nihilism of modern science. Barrault's Jekyll-Hyde character is pictured as a refined, retiring scholar who in his first appearance as the Hyde demon—with his swagger, disheveled hair and dilated pupils—does not so much suggest the netherworld of man and beast as that of beatniks and drugs. His first attack is not the act of a monster, but a murderous extension of the ramblings of a midnight prowler whose diseased appearance reveals a world that no legislation can resolve. Hence, what is implicit in this classic study of repression gains an added dimension because of Renoir's modern-day setting in which Barrault's shy elegant figure seems even more out of place than Dr. Jekyll does in Victorian England. The moral antipathy of his Hyde identity also unfolds in a more paradoxical manner; unlike Stevenson's Dr. Jekyll, who admits his unwillingness to refrain from his experiments in bestiality only when nearing death, Barrault is continually aware of the danger and of his desire to discover an aspect of his nature that he has refused to acknowledge. It is more severe than Stevenson's tonic because it delineates the tale's psychological symbolism in a more personal, romantically misanthropic style.

During the thirties and forties Hollywood approached classic fantasy myths with a childlike abandon that one imagines readers of Victorian melodrama brought to their excursions into terror and fear. The ascending element of self-parody in the Corman and Hammer productions, however, projects a distant, disdainful attitude to fantasy folklore, as if our technological society were somehow inherently superior. Movie monsters become transparent creations, as mechanical in their movements as the camera that has brought them to life. But a more respectful attitude is adopted toward the future: the awe and mystery that once characterized our response to mythological demons is transferred to future worlds.

*Destination Moon* gives further evidence to the archetypal nature of Lang's *The Woman on the Moon*. The preparation and launching of the spaceship fulfills one's initial interest in this Herculean technological venture. But once the voyage is underway, the characters prove no more complex than Lang's comic-book stereotypes; the astronauts seem more concerned in polishing the grease on their hair than in realizing the humanistic dimensions of their expedition.

Of the two controversial French entries in the futuristic sweepstakes—Truffaut's *Fahrenheit 451* and Godard's *Alphaville*—the latter proves more appealing because of its less reverent approach to the classic formulas of science-fiction literature and film. By faithfully adapting Bradbury's moral tale, Truffaut's film exposes the amorphousness and pretensions in the literature of science-fiction. Unlike Frank Herbert's *Dune*, which diligently constructs a mythical cosmology, avant-garde science-fiction writers like Ray Bradbury and Samuel R. Delany adopt tentative, often fragmented literary styles to mirror the spatial vicissitudes of their post-Einstein universe. In *Fahrenheit 451* one never believes in Truffaut's future world because it functions only as a lukewarm symbol of radical politics. His transcription of Bradbury's wall-to-wall television, pill popping, and book burning offers no new insights into an imperious socialist technology; the only moments of artistry in the film are those created by Oskar Werner, as he cradles a novel by Dickens and suggests how much he has missed.

Godard's *Alphaville* is an ingenious, ephemeral film whose irony derives from its combining various popular genres and motifs. The difference between Godard's seriocomic parable and other Lemmy Caution thrillers is that Godard takes a caustic approach to Eddie Constantine's cartoonlike pungency and humor. In his long shots of Constantine driving on the highway or in Constantine's interrogation by the computer, Godard spices the audience's pleasure in the adventures of this unabashedly hard-boiled detective. Unlike Bond, Flint, Helm, and countless other superspies who are, in essence, futuristic secret agents because of their familiarity with the gadgets they must use to foil the equally devious technology of their enemies, Constantine's cavernous face and blank expression recalls the serials of Louis Feuillade, the thrillers of Edgar Wallace, and the tough, mean streets that Bogey patrolled. While setting his futuristic film in an obliquely framed Paris, Godard juxtaposes clever, kinky symbols of contemporary paranoia to Constantine's indefatigable, sleepy-eyed avenger. The real measure of the film's appeal is Godard's ability to remain within the conventions of a Constantine film and not to abstract the already elliptical world of the private eye.

Two major American future-world productions of the sixties and seventies, Stanley Kubrick's *2001: A Space Odyssey* and George Lucas's *Star Wars*, exemplify many of the shortcomings of science-fiction films that were first manifest in Lang's *Metropolis* and William Cameron Menzies' *Things to Come*. Kubrick's *2001: A Space Odyssey* is not as obtuse as *Things to Come* and seems closer to the architectural imprint of Lang's epic. Kubrick's approach is linear and archetypal, two decidedly romantic elements that have long permeated futuristic fables. The opening sequence with the apes presents a symbolic reading of man's first days. The next segment with the space station in orbit is a concise intermixing of the old and new; the Strauss waltz denotes its romantic splendor, while the space station embodies the combined religious and scientific luminosity of space technology. But the reappearance of the monolith on the moon and the cryptic political tension in the space station do not sustain Kubrick's initial symbolic schema. The confrontation between Hal and the astronauts is well-done, but it seems as if Kubrick changes styles in midair; after the allegorical episode involving the apes and the monolith, he undertakes a grim study of the politics and anxiety of space technology. His work with special-effects-coordinator extraordinaire, Douglas Trumbull, is striking, often breathtaking; the ship's interior is both placid and unnerving, while Keir Dullea's entry into the outer galactic horizons of space and time, using Trumbull's stroboscopic, slit-scan photography is a believable compendium of fluid, sensual colors, with its initial projectile force evaporating into a lyrical, synergistic light show. Dullea's transformation into a De Chirico embryo is a pithy, poetic hallucination, yet neither Dullea nor the monolith have become sufficiently meaningful to exist as transcendent symbols. *2001: A Space Odyssey* is certainly the major science-fiction film since Lang's *Metropolis*, but its technological insights, like those in Lang's film, have not been matched by a similar dramatic profundity.

One of the most gifted filmmakers of his generation, Kubrick has recently experienced a decade of filmmaking in which his interest in boldly conceptual scripts has resulted in several cumbersome productions. *The Shining* contains shortcomings in its script and performances similar to those in *A Clockwork Orange* and in *Barry Lyndon*. Yet even as Kubrick makes a fatal misjudgment in having Jack Nicholson play his role as a caricature—revealing his inherent disdain for the more dramatic, albeit Gothic conventions of Stephen King's novel—Kubrick's staging offers hope for the resurgence of this once formidable talent. The introductory aerial sequence featuring the curvilinear composition of the mountain range, valley, and highway is a prologue to the curved space in his pop-art mosaic of the Timberline Lodge interiors. Kubrick's collaboration with cinematographer John Alcott results in an imaginative rearrangement of fantasy clichés of entrapment and isolation. While the interview between Barry Nelson's hotel representative and Nicholson's alcoholic writer recalls the tension in the space station in *2001: A Space Odyssey*, the residence of Nicholson, Shelley Duvall, and their son at the lodge is rendered in a series of wide-angle foreground compositions with various brightly colored household items surrounding the victimized figures of Duvall and her son. There is also one shot and camera movement set in the hotel lobby—a burning cigarette in an ashtray, a pack of Marlboros, and a typewriter completing the foreground composition while Nicholson throws a ball against the wall in the background— that magically personifies Nicholson's writer's block. Kubrick partially compensates for Nicholson's disastrously off-key performance with Duvall's riveting characterization. Yet whatever the odds may be against his fulfilling the promise in his earlier films, Kubrick will have to be considered one of the distinct film painters of the contemporary cinema, his vision of a curved space in *The Shining* worthy of consideration alongside *2001: A Space Odyssey* and the film canvases of the great Antonioni.

*Star Wars* looks more to the past than Kubrick's *2001: A Space Odyssey* in envisioning its future world. Like Godard, director George Lucas has turned to the serials and pulps as source material for his adventure hero and his fight against an intergalactic hegemony. But, unlike Godard, who abstracts the kinetic features of the crime novel and science-fiction serial without losing sight of their inherent charm and chemistry, Lucas painstakingly replays the grade-school mythology of the *Flash Gordon* serials. It results in blissfully inane dialogue and in the picture of a superhighway of the skies in which his moronic protagonists show the same attachment to their wheels as did the teenagers in *American Graffiti*. It is difficult to understand why the director of *THX-1138* and *American Graffiti* would make the artistic choices that glorify the most childish fantasies about future space. The unique quality about *THX-1138* and *American Graffiti* is Lucas's craftsmanlike settings and his objective camera eye, which characterizes the teenagers in the American Southwest as being as trapped in their environment as the protagonist in *THX-1138*. Though *THX-1138* is not as gripping as his short on the same subject, Lucas's methodical interpretation of the conventions of science fiction is fresh and uncompromisingly direct in its visualization of an individual fighting against the antiseptic rigors of his future world. *American Graffiti* shows an advance in Lucas's understanding of the way a landscape encompasses the dreams and fantasies of his characters: he made a film both for and about teenagers in postwar America. In *Star Wars*, however, he respectfully incorporates science-fiction juvenilia in what becomes a lily white paean to the daydreams of a schoolboy. In adapting the latest film hardware for the four hundred and fifteen composite shots in *The Empire Strikes Back*, Lucas has not only revived the drama and dialogue of the old serials, but also their innocently prefabricated staging. The bright colors and fanciful designs of comic-book illustrators have resurfaced, yet Darth Vader is one of the few creations that shows the acuity that fantasy illustrators such as Stan Lee and Marvel Comics pioneered in the sixties, while the whimsy surrounding the character of Yoda lacks the sensuality of Ray Harryhausen signature pieces like the dancing skeletons or his nubile, mesmerizing Medusas. With the exception of the bar sequence in *Star Wars*—a raunchy send-up of a western shoot-out—Lucas celebrates the underlying tediousness of science fiction. The references to pinball and video technology are refreshingly contemporary; but where is their dynamism—the electric blasts of a pinball reverberating through a flashing, macabre landscape of hits and misses? If only Lucas would fulfill the erotic, machismo fantasies of pinball and video wizards.

One is tempted to search for a more devious explanation for the unrivaled box-office success of *Star Wars* and *The Empire Strikes Back*. But this would be looking at the films as philosophy, or worse, as sociology. The fact is they play as the revenge of the straight-shooting, popular folk heroes who have taken a back seat to the modernists and technocrats who have tried to make something of popular culture that it is not.

# 14
## The Religious Film

*Leaves from Satan's Book–Une Femme douce*

Carl Dreyer's studies of spiritual ideas and figures encompass the diverse stylizations of religion on film. His first major religious film epic, *Leaves from Satan's Book*, impresses one by its understated mood and by his ability to create a small-scale, believable stage in an era in which the movies were admired for their technical and melodramatic excesses. Like *Intolerance*, it is divided into four parts, but whereas Griffith as film's first poet-mythologist romantically embellishes his allegory, Dreyer adopts a more distant, introspective style in discovering the presence of God. Unlike Griffith, who uses numerous editing techniques to express the power of this infant medium to define and unify archetypal forms and situations that bind man's past and present, Dreyer's subdued settings isolate the spiritual struggle in each of his stories.

In his dramatization of Christ's betrayal, the majority of the introductory shots are in medium-shot range. His deceptively simple camera angles conceive the story as a somber, spiritual conflict involving one person's recognition of God and another's ignorance as to His ways. Dreyer's reserved treatment represses the grand passions one associates with the great artistic interpretations of this drama. During the Last Supper he uses an iris vignette not as an exotic pictorial effect, but to better understand the pregnant religious imagery in the faces of Jesus and his disciples. Dreyer's Judas is not the physically coarse, sensual figure portrayed in numerous Hollywood productions; he is a bald, nondescript character, a role as adroitly underplayed as Dreyer's interpretation of the betrayal. In Seville the priest's anguish in responding to the woman's advances results in a more radical, sensual conflict, but Dreyer does not accentuate its personal, psychological tremors. When the priest sees the woman's figure in a religious artifact, the image is not exaggerated, but seems proportionate to the other symbolic features in Dreyer's distilled setting. A similar spiritual equation is made in the third section: a flock of birds, one of the few "liberating" shots of nature in the film, passes over the jail in which a woman awaits execution. The birds' freedom becomes a clairvoyant symbol of the eventual release of the woman's soul.

In *The Passion of Joan of Arc,* one of the three definitive portraits of a religious theme on film, Dreyer interprets the persecution and immolation of Joan through the unique dimensions of the medium. The major stylistic effect he uses is the juxtaposition of the judges—shot from a low angle, usually in full-figure shots in the center of the frame—to Falconetti's Joan—presented in eye-level or slightly high-angle compositions which show her from the shoulders or neck up, often to the side of the frame. Dreyer's sharp editing underscores the frenzied nature of Joan's persecution. Contrary to its reputation as a static film, it is a vividly dynamic work wherein Dreyer's visual dialectic identifies the inviolability of Joan's face in relation to the oppressive features of her persecutors. This visual-spiritual dialectic is reenforced by his rigid staging of the people at her trial and by his claustrophobic use of space in the courtroom, torture chamber, and cell in which she is further questioned and to which she is returned after fainting in the torture chamber. In each of these stark, skeletal settings the pressing, penetrating force of the close-up augments the physical as well as spiritual entrapment Joan suffers. Though several scenes show Joan's full figure in the frame with a priest, barber, or her guards, Dreyer uses his first full-figure shots of Joan alone in the frame only as she is carried and placed on the stake in anticipation of her salvation.

*Day of Wrath* transpires in a foreboding medieval setting that is similar to one of the stories in *Leaves from Satan's Book,* but Dreyer's appreciation of the luminous beauty of the pastor's wife leads to a more complex, paradoxical treatment. In *The Passion of Joan of Arc* and *Vampyr,* he isolates one person within an obliquely styled environment; but in *Day of Wrath* there is a more naturalist approach to the conflicting icons and images underlying the struggle between freedom and repression. In the first part of the drama he introduces the character of the pastor through his involvement with a former prisoner whom he freed. Although knowing she was a witch, the pastor released her because of his attraction for her daughter, whom he has married. Since these facts are disclosed by a woman who is being tortured, her old, decayed body exists not only as a condemnation of witchcraft, but also as a prefatory explanation of the husband's attraction for his young, shapely wife. The major section of the film, the union of the pastor's wife and her stepson, is presented in an elliptical fashion, as if to denote their predestination as lovers. But Dreyer is not an unabashed lyricist; in showing them out-of-doors, their passion is treated as a natural consequence of the pristine clarity of nature. He sees the lovers not as lustful sinners, but as two people who wish to experience life in a manner antithetical to their stern social and moral code.

But Dreyer adds certain ambiguous elements in what originally appeared as a straightforward presentation of a spiritual-worldly agon. After the wife says that she wishes her husband were dead, Dreyer cuts to a shot of the husband returning home and suddenly faltering. The wife has truly inherited supernatural powers; her otherworldliness seems a natural extension of the predominant theism in her society. If the audience sympathizes with her, it too is damned, and if the wife is condemned, the audience must support the mournful, proscriptive ideology of her persecutors. Dreyer further delineates the wife's character through the prohibitive mask of her mother-in-law who has prophesied the love affair and who also accuses her daughter-in-law of being a witch. Dreyer astutely realizes an element of ambiguity in the viewer's feelings about the mother-in-law's suspicions and the wife's adulterous behavior. In exploring the existence of witchcraft, Dreyer appears to acknowledge the presence of God and the Devil, while revealing his own paradoxical stance toward the sweet, sensual nature of the pastor's wife.

The only major American filmmaker associated with religious themes during the silent or early sound era was Cecil B. De Mille. His *The King of Kings* shows little of the furious action and rich array of adventure heroes and profligates that characterize his best work; its demure, quiescent tone is highly expressive of the lack of sympathy American moviemakers have experienced with religious subjects. H. B. Warner's portrayal is the sweetest, if not the softest Christ on film, while the vaudeville antics of the two Schildkrauts lead one to believe that De Mille can barely restrain his natural inclination to fill the screen with all the mayhem and comic excess that figure in his later films. *The Sign of the Cross* is a more frivolous work than *The King of Kings*; De Mille's Christians are treated as dreary party crashers, and the satyrs of ancient Rome are reduced to Fredric March brandishing his whip and Charles Laughton imitating Oscar Wilde. His remake of *The Ten Commandments*, like *Samson and Delilah*, is marked by theatrical bombast and lacks the helter-skelter gaiety which made several of his epics such admirable examples of popular folk art.

Roberto Rossellini's two early ventures in religious drama, *Flowers of St. Francis* and *The Miracle*, are a striking departure from the enveloping religious and historical ambience in Dreyer's films. These two films present stylistic and moral equations which parallel his two celebrated studies of the upheavals in Italy during the last years of the war. Like *Paisan*, *Flowers of St. Francis* is the more purely Rosselliniesque in featuring a stark, destitute environment in which the very crudeness of his storytelling manner, the awkward camera angles, and the stuttering expressions of his nonprofessional actors are offered as the purest expression of their spiritual conflicts. There is an undeniable absence of stylistic and thematic clarity and counterpoint in *Flowers of St. Francis* because, as in *Paisan*, he is reducing the nature of the art and film experience to a series of transparent visual impressions that signify the spiritual omnipresence of St. Francis's world. To Rossellini, Italy in the thirteenth century looks no different from the ravaged, depressed countryside in the waning months of the war; his characters move through a moral and physical vacuum in which their steadfastness and their belief in the communicability of the word of God are their lone comforts.

With the exception of the confrontation between St. Francis and the pagan chieftain, the action is passive, almost stilted; the drama unfolds with all the pain, misery, and simplicity that surrounded St. Francis and his followers. Each action in the film becomes a testament to their ardor, their sincerity, and their faith in exemplifying an ascetic, religious life. Some scenes are directed in too primitive a manner; for example, a beggar who has joined them tells one of the mendicants that he is hungry. The brother then attempts to trap a pig who rushes into the bushes; he calls to the pig, "Brother pig," and returns with part of the pig's foot. Other scenes—such as the one in which St. Francis follows a leper, walks up and kisses him, and then raises his eyes to the sky—divine a sense of the sublime. Rossellini accepts the quaint lives of these "poor souls" as visual proof of the indomitability of God.

*The Miracle* attempts a more philosophical treatment of the permanence of religious figures and values. Based on a story by Federico Fellini, Rossellini shows a far greater skepticism in exploring the viability of belief through the character of Anna Magnani's village dullard. The film begins with Magnani encountering a man whom she thinks is St. Peter; after a fade to black, Rossellini returns to the hill site to find Magnani awakening. She returns to the village and tells two priests that she has talked to St. Peter. One passes it off as the daydream of a retarded woman, while the other priest says he sees the Madonna every day. Rossellini underlines the dichotomy in the rational and spiritual apprehension of the Divine, and through Magnani's character implies that belief is the primary way to recognize the spiritual. This viewpoint is personified in the last sequence in which the village and surrounding hills are incorporated as part of a symbolic stage, from the shelter from which Magnani is ejected to the cave in which she gives birth. Since she is not shown sleeping with anyone with the possible exception of the man she first meets, her persecution by the villagers transforms her simple faith into a supreme justification of belief. After Magnani's head is covered with a washing bowl, Rossellini uses a still shot of Magnani to suggest her transfiguring the bowl into Christ's thorns through her self-imposed religious identity. This terse script, as the second major religious film archetype, boldly extends the scope of neorealism by dramatizing an essential dichotomy that has been debated throughout intellectual history.

In considering Rossellini's early films, the student must question to what degree an impoverished world signifies an underlying religious presence or idea. The films of Robert Bresson present a more difficult problem in that his abstracted narrative style is unsympathetic to the more overt portrayals of a spiritual epiphany that have characterized so much of religious art. With the exception of *Les Anges du péché*, all of Bresson's films through *Une Femme douce* utilize his static, denuded filmmaking style. In his films it is not a question of making God's existence known, but of using the simplest, most unaccented techniques to identify the religious conflicts that confront his characters. In *Les Anges du péché*, the protagonist's anxiety inspires an emotional tableau that is as intensely experienced as the acute lighting effects surrounding the movements of the nuns at the convent.

But the emotionally gripping relationships and staging in *Les Anges du péché* are nowhere visible in *Les Dames du bois de Boulogne* or *Diary of a Country Priest*. These two early prototypical Bresson projects do not result in a manifestation of the Divine, but play as elliptical religious configurations. Bresson adopts a straightforward narrative that does not allow for permutations in the delineation of character or dramatic motif that would uncover the spiritual crisis unique to his characters. He chooses to establish an equation between the elliptical and the religious, between an austere presentation of reality and the omnipresence of the spiritual challenge that overwhelms his protagonists. Unlike *Mouchette*, *Pickpocket*, and *The Trial of Joan of Arc*, in which there is a more acute stylization of his drama and characters, in *Les Dames du bois de Boulogne* and *Diary of a Country Priest* the viewer's recognition of the religious anguish is dependent on one's willingness to admit the equivalence of character and symbol. It is unclear, however, whether the fallen girl in the former is a cherub or is simply angelic and whether Maria Casares is evil incarnate or simply a very cruel woman. In *Diary of a Country Priest* these questions are not as relevant because the drama unfolds from the priest's point of view; he becomes a symbol of goodness because his passivity in various meretricious relationships documents his distance from the devious politics of a secular life.

The aesthetic choice that Bresson asks the audience to make—one that André Bazin was among the first to accept and elaborate—is that whatever is seen or heard be understood as part of a spiritual design from which none of the characters can escape. Bresson does impose an emotionally constricted tension in the two films; for the film student to accept the literal and religious as one, the characters and ensuing conflicts must then evoke the religious as the only possible issue in their lives. But to see the drama in *Les Dames du bois de Boulogne* and *Diary of a Country Priest* as unequivocally centered on the spiritual makeup of his characters is to offer a poor estimate of the artistic and intellectual factors that contribute to the rationale of religious art.

The problems implicit in Bresson's style gain greater dramatic complexity in *Balthazar* and *Mouchette*. *Balthazar* is intended as a series of symbolic actions in which each person is "led" into a situation in which he or she becomes the personification of good or evil; but Bresson's story is too opaque for one to understand the religious significance of his characters and their actions. An exemplary scene involves the donkey, Balthazar. Separated from his owner, Balthazar enters a circus where Bresson cuts between the donkey's face and the caged animals. One first questions the reason underlying Balthazar's entry into the circus grounds. Is Bresson suggesting that the distance between Balthazar and the animals is symmetrical to the distance between Balthazar and the central characters? Is one then to conclude that Balthazar—without identity in the animal kingdom or as a beast of burden in the human—exists as a spiritually indeterminate figure who enables the audience to determine the inherent goodness or evil of the people around him? In the scene in which the Christlike character is seated on Balthazar, the analogy to Christian drama is left unfocused because, like the country priest, Bresson prefers to record acts of desperation and violence instead of distilling a vision of religious catharsis for the viewer.

*Mouchette* is one Bresson film that enlivens its spiritual configurations in decisive dramatic terms. From the grimy abode in which Mouchette lives with her parents—illuminated by passing car lights that penetrate this hovel like an underworld terrain—to the ditch from which she throws mud at her classmates, the symbolic nature of Mouchette's forlorn existence is clearly defined. Unlike the girl in *Balthazar*, whose tragic identity was obscured by her affair with the gang leader, Mouchette's acceptance of her torn clothes, her dirty face, and the general squalor of her surroundings reveals her distance from the other characters and the original manner in which she will resolve her spiritual identity.

Whereas the depressed setting in which the priest found himself did not sufficiently explain the inherent goodness of the priest, the gruesome events that shape Mouchette's existence—for example, in the scene where she loses her virginity to the demented actor—enhance her identity as a fallen girl. Bresson's succinctness in detailing the tragic and religious nature of her life as an outcast is sustained in a final scene which underscores the differences between the opacity of *Balthazar* and the luminosity of *Mouchette*. In the last scene in *Balthazar*, during which the donkey dies among the sheep, Bresson uses a series of fades to black to further distinguish Balthazar's inexorably tragic condition; it reenforces the feeling that one can make little sense of the disparate, complex turnings in the life of the donkey or in the lives of the characters he has briefly crossed. In *Mouchette*, however, her death further elaborates the consequences of her isolation while existing as her deliverance. Wrapped in a white shawl, Mouchette rolls herself into the river three times; though the shawl may seem a contrivance, like the cross to which the priest is related at the end of *Diary of a Country Priest*, Mouchette has appropriated this sign of purity into her own fantasy world.

*Pickpocket* and *The Trial of Joan of Arc* may be Bresson's most abstracted films; his two central characters are literally locked in their skeletal surroundings. Again one notes Bresson's scrupulousness in suppressing any motif that would dramatically enrich either Joan's existence or that of the pickpocket. Like a faithful scribe, Bresson evokes the spiritual grandeur of these figures in terms of the symbolic starkness of their environment and in their refusal to question the somber course of their lives. The predominant settings are the pickpocket's oneroom closet abode, the room in which Joan's trial is held, and her cell. But as grim and dark as the pickpocket's home is, with its affinity to the flat, whiteblack, good-evil surfaces in Joan's incarcerated existence, Bresson effects a transfiguration of people and their surrounding world on a minimal level. The only way one can relate to Joan as a symbol of purity or the pickpocket's one-room apartment as a sign of decay and evil is by accepting Bresson's underlying spiritual-stylistic equation between the characters' stasis, his rigid camera setups and compositions, and the idea of spiritual omnipresence.

Some scenes are more extreme than others in characterizing the spiritual dimensions of his characters and environment. After the pickpocket steals a man's wallet, they both leave the train at the next station. The man approaches the pickpocket, asks for his wallet, and tells him that he will not call the police. There is silence for a few seconds; the pickpocket then returns the wallet, and Bresson terminates the action with a fade to black. During the scene one is aware of the players' precise movements, a sense of the predetermined nature of their clipped words and movements; the fade to black then separates this incident as one symbolic stage in the pickpocket's spiritual decline and eventual reawakening. The transcendent spiritual implications of the fade to black are present throughout the film, yet the relationships of the pickpocket to the prostitute, the pickpocket to the policeman, and the pickpocket to his devious friend are not as dramatically compressed as the scene in the train. Having to rely on his characters to mean something as human beings within a severe, albeit naturalistic setting, Bresson's impersonal, acquiescent style prefigures a metaphysical equation, the world of ideas rather than the evolving dramatic transfigurations that a religious style must express.

Though the conflict is emotionally resolved in the two films through the union of the pickpocket with the prostitute and through the final release of Joan's soul from her body, neither film dramatically justifies its religious idealism because such distinctions as good and evil or body and spirit have no meaning in Bresson's films. A comparison between Bresson and Ozu may be helpful in clarifying this point. Ozu elaborates a story, delineating his characters through their identity as part of a family and in terms of the cultural uniformity in their homes and environment; the drama unfolds through a remarkably disciplined style that selects concise, expressive angles to define a character and his role in the hierarchy of Japanese society. Discord and symbol are discernible in Ozu because he discovers the essential signs of order and tradition and their heterodoxical meaning to his family members. Though there is an acute difference between the format of the religious film and Ozu's studies of family life in Japan, can one regard the pickpocket or Joan as characters "involved in" or "experiencing" a spiritual conflict? Does the pickpocket's telling the police officer that certain people are exempt from the law or the simple reaction shots during Joan's trial express anything other than Bresson's oversimplification of classic dramatic themes? If either the actors or the settings were developed in greater depth, Bresson would be emphasizing a religious passion that, while still leading to an acknowledgement of God, would imbue the individual protagonist with more choice and dramatic forcefulness in shaping his life and in recognizing or rejecting his soul. Though one readily admits that Bresson is not working toward a Dreyer-type study of Joan—unlike Dreyer's Joan who is involved in a passion, Bresson's film records a trial that exists as a prelude to the eventual release of her soul—allegory must yield some slight, aesthetic permanence. Since the characters and sets in the two films are not abstracted to the point of their purest, quintessential meaning, one can reject these films on Bresson's terms.

*Une Femme douce* is similar to *Mouchette* in its idealization of a fallen girl, but Dominique Sanda's aristocratic appearance and wayward existence do not engender any unique spiritual conflict or identity in the manner of Mouchette's isolation and transfiguration. The problems with the film result from the stasis that marks most of Bresson's work: Bresson asks the viewer to accept an idea of spiritual omnipresence without an understanding of how Bresson's religious schema transforms physical properties into spiritual ones. Though he distinguishes various aspects of Sanda's character such as her tremulous reaction to a performance of *Hamlet*, her moodiness is handled abruptly, didactically. There is an almost existential purity to Sanda's actions—for example, in her questioning her husband about why they sleep together—but her bold, intemperate behavior fails to elucidate any one moral paradox. Her final, most desperate act, that of suicide, does not, like the death of the priest or Mouchette's suicide, explain or epitomize her tragedy. Whereas the priest's death from tuberculosis exemplified his destitute existence and his final test before meeting his Redeemer, Sanda's suicide is only the most extreme example of her instinctive response to the moral imbalance of her life.

## The Virgin Spring–Gertrud

Bresson's films are perhaps more important as religious experiences than as artistic expressions of God's impenetrable mask. Bresson "knows" of the ubiquitousness of God, but he prefers to show his constancy instead of dramatizing the complex manner in which the spiritual is manifest in one's daily existence. Compared to Bresson's films, Ingmar Bergman's *The Virgin Spring* and *The Seventh Seal* adopt a completely different tone, one in which his symbolic landscapes are charged by characters whose emotional upheavals denote the spiritual anguish of their times. The strengths of both these films do not lie in apocalyptic images like Max von Sydow playing chess with Death or the eruption of the spring, but in Bergman's belief in Von Sydow's ability to convince the audience that his pain and suffering are tantamount to spiritual unrest. Whereas Bresson rejects the idea that a religious drama is similar to other styles of dramatic, symbolic expression, Bergman's two films present the religious symbols as a natural feature of the settings, from the ritual of the penitents whipping themselves to Von Sydow's ablution before he kills the rapists. Bergman directs simple parables in which the straightforward character portrayals provide an acute rendering of the spiritual traps that have plagued man in the past; their didacticism is more important than their art, but at least Bergman is willing to share this religious passion with us and does not, like Bresson, dismiss the emotional and formal motifs that can interpret a religious experience as, simultaneously, an aesthetic one.

In his trilogy, *Through a Glass Darkly*, *Winter Light*, and *The Silence*, Bergman attempts a more psychological study of religious anguish, in which he avoids the overt religious symbols in *The Virgin Spring* and *The Seventh Seal*. The spiritual dread that overwhelms the characters in the trilogy is more sharply defined than in Bresson's films, but their malaise is too abstracted for one to understand how and why they become symbols of the emptiness of modern life. In *Through a Glass Darkly*, Von Sydow's impotent husband and Gunnar Björnstrand's selfish, noncommunicative father are treated as objects rather than as characters, while the gray, overcast sky and the dark shadows in their house are part of an inconclusively drawn setting, stylistically antithetical to the densely symbolic staging of *The Seventh Seal* or *The Virgin Spring*. The voices and spirits that trouble Harriet Andersson's wife do not arise from any particular turmoil that affects their family life: they represent the unease that plagues modern man. The play that prefigures the incest between Andersson and her brother is a facile, contrived way of showing their helplessness; Björnstrand's eventual commitment to his family is expressive only of Bergman's moral weakness in confronting the darkness his characters cannot evade. If Bresson gives too little evidence for his characters' spiritual transcendence, Bergman first overindulges the cynic's point of view that all is nothing and then, inexplicably, suggests that communication is possible.

*Winter Light* is the least cluttered of Bergman films; it simply depicts the moral and spiritual demands that are made on Gunnar Björnstrand's priest. Bergman does not emphasize Björnstrand's crisis in grotesque, Gothic visions, but records his pain and frustration as entries a priest might make in his diary. Von Sydow's dulled, immobilized laborer who questions Björnstrand about the Chinese and the bomb and the intensely beautiful scene, in which Ingrid Thulin's face overwhelms the film frame while her accusatory love letter to Björnstrand is read, are as evocative and symbolic of the spiritual emptiness of their lives as are the allegorical figures in *The Seventh Seal* and *The Virgin Spring*. Bergman seems to suggest that even if man cannot penetrate the meaning of God by examining his life, he will come to a more satisfying understanding of his own place in the universe. *Winter Light* is not a profound film, and though it fails to convey the loneliness of an ecclesiastic in the somber, pitying manner of Bresson's *Diary of a Country Priest*, Bergman's immersion in the formidable truth and beauty of his actors attests to his underlying faith in art and humanity.

In *The Silence*, however, Bergman's actors, the most meaningful aspect of his films, exist as unfocused symbols of man's suppressing the need to communicate. Bergman presents pictures of decadence and dissipation that do not adequately illuminate the allegorical nature of his story. Bergman perceives a penumbra of spiritual ennui and nihilism in his shots of the tank maneuvers, but he prefers to encourage the characters' fears instead of exploring their roots. For example, if the foreign city to which the two sisters travel is representative of the desolation of modern society, why does he refuse to sketch in any details about its people? Instead he features extreme actions that prove unoriginal examples of moral turpitude. Gunnel Lindblom's pickup at the café and Ingrid Thulin's masturbation are rhetorical statements on the irrevocable separateness of the two sisters: one's heterosexual nature leads to her sexual desperation; the other's intelligent, bookish nature becomes synonymous with her physical decline.

Bergman's interest in symbolic drama and behavior results in his unwillingness to discover any rational instincts about his characters. Thulin's relationship to the hotel servant is marked by their inability to speak the same language; although the young boy does innocently play with some people, they are dwarfs. Why, then, when his characters are so close to disgusting and ravaging one another, when modern city life is identified in terms of its sexual deviancy, does Bergman refrain from a final, definitive resolution? If a pervasive silence exists, why doesn't he express his faith or scepticism in a more direct manner by admitting or dismissing God? Is it because, as suggested by the ending of *Through a Glass Darkly* and by the last words of Thulin to her nephew in *The Silence*, he wants to make another film about the possible nonexistence of God?

The films of Luis Buñuel elucidate a well-known paradox. As filmdom's most celebrated atheist, Buñuel's films forcefully evoke the evil that foils the virtuous; he attacks the world with the ardor and virulence of a cynic who cannot fail to admit an ongoing spiritual struggle. But a long-standing philosophical question about art and religion remains. Is it possible to conceive a world of symbolic identities in the religious film without realizing the presence of the spiritual? Do not the metaphysics of a visual medium suggest an essential link between the abstract—the world of ideas—and the religious?

In *Nazarin* the priest's persistence in hoping to change the ways of the syphilitic beggars, the robbers, the whores and the neurotics on whom his shutter opens exists as a vigorous assertion that belief is the ballast of Christian theology. Unlike Bresson's country priest, who accepts the characters' lies, the destitute terrain, and his humble abode as symbols of a transient, materialist fate, Buñuel's cleric attempts to awaken a sense of spiritual compassion in the townspeople. But it is a weak film because the brutalizing characters and events that resist the priest's benevolence are tautological—not in the manner of Bresson's films in which the physical world's transparency and the indomitable presence of the Divine are continually manifest, but tautological in that Buñuel's cockroach vision of the world remains unchanged by the priest's efforts. A later work, *The Milky Way*, is a sardonic treatment of religious belief, but Buñuel is too abstruse in delineating the symbolic journey undertaken by his tramps. Instead of personalizing his scatological interpretation of a morality play, Buñuel glibly dismisses the visions experienced by his tramps; by the time they reach their destination, they are neither wiser nor wearier. *Simon of the Desert* is the beguiling anecdotal inversion that *The Milky Way* was not. Buñuel avoids the bland, heuristic style of *The Milky Way* for a more caustic point of view. Simon is a sly figure, more self-conscious of his role as saint than other spiritual characters in Buñuel's films. The misfits who come to ridicule him are the dregs of society, like those the priest encounters in *Nazarin*. They regard Simon, like God, as a joke; if Simon can cure their diseases, they won't attempt to discover the way the trick is played. Like a tale from Boccaccio, *Simon of the Desert* lambasts people's abuse of religious beliefs without dismissing the mystery of their genesis.

*Viridiana*, Buñuel's richest, most compelling work and the third major film study of religion, is similar to the Dreyer and Rossellini classics in that it concerns the persecution of a woman. However, unlike Falconetti's Joan and Magnani's retarded peasant who know the identity of their oppressors, Silvia Pinal's Viridiana never realizes who has forced her to renounce her life as a nun. She probably thinks that it is her virile, pragmatic cousin who has destroyed her faith in the Divine, but it is her uncle, Don Jaime, played by Fernando Rey who, after being rejected by Viridiana, displays a mischievous smile before committing suicide and leaving the estate to her.

Viridiana learns two things during her ensuing education: deprivation is boundless, for example, in the scene with the dog tied to the cart and the miserable beggars she tries to comfort are so far gone in vice that they are best left alone. Their physical and moral decline, culminating in a primordial celebration of their incongruousness in the splendor of Viridiana's estate, is reminiscent of the feast in *Freaks*. Browning's outcasts gain our sympathy because their physically anomalous condition does not preclude their joyful innocence in fulfilling the marriage ritual. Buñuel's outcasts, however, exult in their gross, outrageous behaviour, thus confirming the cousin's advice that Viridiana give them a few coins and try not to be a martyr. The rape of Viridiana may seem excessive, yet it is a viable expression of the tragic consequence of her naiveté and the insurmountable odds against her altruism. Since he is unwilling to accept Bresson's spiritual passivity or to sympathize with the French film-maker's understanding of evil as mere physical obtrusion, Buñuel dramatizes his anguish in the chaotic pillaging of the estate and in the rape. In the last scene Buñuel subtly underscores Viridiana's loss of faith as she joins her cousin and his present mistress, the maid, in a game of cards. Viridiana has given up her fight to purify the world; Don Jaime has won, not because he was the Devil incarnate but, perhaps, because God asks too much of his servants.

One of the few directors in the contemporary cinema with a genuine interest in religious themes was Pier Paolo Pasolini. In *Accattone!* he combines Rossellini's moral compassion with De Sica's gritty character studies to show the aimlessness of his delinquents. But Pasolini's empathy with his characters' anti-social behavior results in a straightforward Marxist dialectic of the torpor and aridity of the countryside and his characters' amorality. His condemnation of physical reality is dogmatic and sorely misses the psychological acuity and stylistic experiments of other Italian modernists.

In *The Hawks and the Sparrows* and *The Gospel According to St. Matthew* Pasolini experiments with aggressively avant-garde themes and techniques. The two films, however, awkwardly blend their aesthetics and metaphysics. *The Hawks and the Sparrows* jumps from satire to allegory wherein his use of slapstick effects diffuses the raffish pilgrims' spiritual journey through his full-scale assault on narrative clarity. The film functions as a polemic in which Pasolini's disdain for dramatic logic shows a director attempting to discover God through his own godlessness. *The Gospel According to St. Matthew* is a more rewarding effort, partly because it makes one more conscious of the bombast that has characterized numerous film interpretations of Christ. From the documentary-style recreation of the birth of Christ to the dance of the pubescent Salome—a poignant foil to such exercises in buffoonery as Rita Hayworth's show girl on the make—the film's unvarnished style, whether characterized by its poverty-ridden ambience or by the veritable anger of Christ, reexamines the spiritual anguish and moral puissance of Christ's life as a folkloristic drama.

Pasolini's tentativeness in adopting a variety of classical myths and infusing them with the absurdity of the avant-garde reached its most inglorious fulfillment in *Teorema*. It is among the few truly allegorical films ever made, but it makes little effort to explain the spiritual in analogous cinematic terms. One might be reminded of *La strada, Ordet,* and several films by Cocteau, Bresson, and Godard, but none of their films expresses the disinterestedness in dialogue and in psychological and dramatic clarification of Pasolini's *Teorema*. He is not concerned with distinguishing good and evil through the spiritual depth of the family members who cohabit with the archangel played by Terence Stamp. Rather, like Bergman but in a far more radical style, Pasolini attempts to symbolize the vacuity of modern life by dispensing with the artifices of drama and art. This creates more problems than it solves, because when he first introduces the upper-class family which has just bequeathed their plant to the workers, there is no sense of their Christian compassion or lack of it in running their business. When they each engage in intercourse with Stamp, one is unsure of their understanding about their relationship with Stamp's spiritual figure. Even in Bresson's elliptical films one perceives the reason and nature of the spiritual transfiguration; in *Teorema* Pasolini assumes a more anarchistic viewpoint by showing the characters' transfiguration without any qualifying scenes.

The maid makes advances to Stamp, who shakes his head; disgusted with herself, she returns home and fasts. When Pasolini returns to her later in the film, he shows her hanging in midair. The wife undresses before Stamp, then picks up two men, reaches a level of self-revulsion similar to that of the maid, and is last seen entering a church. The son, also attracted to Stamp, lives in a studio where he urinates on a painting, while the father, after cohabiting with Stamp, strips at a train depot and runs on a sandy plain that Pasolini first featured during the titles. In each of these encounters Pasolini's refractory material does not lend itself to a literal or symbolic meaning; he illuminates the characters' personal quiescence as if he were a seer who had experienced the truth but refuses to share his secret vision. To accept *Teorema* as art is to overlook not only the complex emotions and ideas necessary to any statement on the human condition, but also to simplify religion to its most simple, repressive denominator: belief as ignorance.

The paradox that certain filmmakers feel exists in visualizing and, hence, vulgarizing the invisible, ineffable properties of the spiritual is central to Dreyer's *Ordet* and *Gertrud*. In such original films as *The Passion of Joan of Arc* and *Vampyr,* Dreyer experimented with the phenomenological and psychological presence of evil. In *Ordet* Dreyer attempts to affirm the corporeal presence of God as an expression of faith through the purity of the family's life and its apotheosis in the wife's resurrection. The film's ascetic, subdued story line becomes for Dreyer a measure of his belief in a spiritual universe. The film fulfills its exemplification of cinematic pietism, but it fails to produce the intellectual or artistic stimulus that all but pietists require.

*Gertrud* proposes a more radical denial of the sensual and dissonant experiences that affect one's life. As Gertrud tells her story in her living room, the outside world and her former experiences undergo a thorough abstraction. Dreyer's austere, ethereal compositions underscore the acute differences between the spiritual expressiveness of *Day of Wrath* and the spiritual minimalism of *Gertrud*. In *Day of Wrath* the characters—like nature itself—are alive, tremulous, passionate. In *Gertrud* the outside world is seen as a stilled, sepulchral illusion, formerly animated by one's ephemeral emotions. Like other testaments to man's faith, *Gertrud* is a religious statement that transcends the literal, the symbolic, for the spiritual quintessence—the substance that Dreyer knows is in each person and in every part of the physical universe. Inevitably, one responds to *Ordet* and *Gertrud* as a religious experience rather than an aesthetic one. Though some may think the two inseparable, they are not; in the former, belief dominates; in the latter, understanding is the paramount value.

# 15
# The Documentary Film

*Grass–Berlin–Symphony of a Big City*

The ideological concerns of the documentary film have been largely defined by the realist axioms of Grierson, Kracauer, and Rotha. Their populist advocacy of realism originates in the verisimilitude of the first movie shorts: it was a real train that the audience saw arriving at a station. But the event was recorded in such a strikingly individual manner that a further scruinty of the Grierson–Kracauer–Rotha aesthetic is requied. The idea of reportage which each of these historians advanced in his documentary proselytizing denies the nonfiction filmmaker the dramatic alternatives available to other artists. In the major documentary films before the advent of television and *cinéma vérité*, one is impressed by the efforts of Flaherty and Lorentz, among others, to discover the underlying mythological permanence in what Kracauer called the "continuum of natural existence." To imply that the documentarian uses his camera simply to record daily activities is to belittle the task he faces, which is to give shape and meaning to the life of his subject. Since the introduction of television, the social realism of Grierson, Kracauer, and Rotha has gained greater validity; but here, too, one finds that the search for truth by advocates of *cinéma vérité* like Jean Rouch and Richard Leacock results in ambiguous stylizations that suggest the natural continuum is not as straightforward and self-evident as some historians would have us believe.

One of the first works of poetry in the documentary film, the Schoedsack-Cooper *Grass*, is an example of how the ethnographic, anthropological interests of the documentary film parallel the classic narrative virtues of the epic film. Like Flaherty, they painstakingly depict the epic struggle of the tribe that must abandon its village and then journey to a new home across a treacherous mountain range. It is a story of heroic endurance rather than an exposition of sociological behavior; the theme is one of survival. Our interest in *Grass* is inspired by emotional antagonisms common to classic drama and literature. The natural, surface expressiveness of people, nature, and history is captured by depicting their dynamic, unifying, cultural and romantic validity.

In *Nanook of the North* Flaherty had yet to master the distant, objective style

249

with which he would securely define the relationship of man and nature in *Man of Aran* and *Louisiana Story*. His camera is less turned to the stunning long shots of man and nature that characterize his later films; he is more interested in expressing Nanook's constancy through his unwillingness to surrender to the elements. The film's roots are in both primitive epic cinema and the more random naturalism envisaged by Kracauer as ideal for documentarians. Flaherty's style ranges from the objective to the subjective, from waiting with Nanook and recording his encounter with the seal to Nanook and his family in friendly recognition of the camera.

*Tabu* is a more tentative film not because it is a joint effort on the part of Flaherty and Murnau, but because the film fails to fulfill its dramatic fatalism. During the opening scenes the physical beauty and unique freedom the Polynesians enjoy in their fishing and dancing show Flaherty and Murnau searching for the transcendent features of their native folk drama. Their aim, like that of Eisenstein in his Mexican epic, is to discover the mythic-poetic origins of their subject—to show naturalism and the sublime as mirror forces in the lives of the Polynesians. The film's incompleteness is most conspicuous in the marriage during the couple's stay on the island and in their final separation which seems to take them by surprise. Characters like the merchant and the village chieftain are unfocused symbols, but the final scene is certainly a great moment of silent-film poetic fantasy: the hero fights against the elements and almost enters the boat, only to have the rope cut while his bride remains unaware of his proximity.

*Man of Aran* is Flaherty's most sweeping study of nature's power over man. As the natives of Aran follow a more predetermined course than Nanook or the young explorer in *Louisiana Story*, Flaherty sees them as symbols of a primordial endurance whether they walk along the mountainous terrain or as they navigate through the rough waters. They become the single humanizing metaphor in the film; the more dominant, complementary image of nature is underscored by the overwhelming impact of the water on the land and the receding nature of the father's words to his son about mooring the boat and those of the mother which express her concern that they get some sleep. The film's contrived, epic style may seem less involved and moving than that of his other films, but Flaherty uncovers a truth about man's relationship to nature that bears favorable comparison to similar treatments in the fiction film. For example, in Rossellini's *Stromboli* the savage fish hunt reveals the islanders' primitive mores while expressing the alienation of Ingrid Bergman's refugee. In *Man of Aran* the encounter with the fish illuminates both the intransigence of nature and the heroic determination of the Aran islanders.

*Louisiana Story*, the least acclaimed of Flaherty's major efforts, is in many ways his most personal, vibrant film. He subtly blends fictive and documentary elements in searching for the underlying myth of two distinct worlds: a virgin, expansive wilderness and the haunting, unsettling power of the geyser. In *Nanook of the North* and *Man of Aran*, Flaherty imbues his subjects' struggles with the absolute force of nature; in *Louisiana Story* he decentralizes the drama by characterizing the young boy as a mythic explorer, first traveling through the luminous, foreboding backwoods and rivers, and then discovering the men at work on the geyser. Flaherty's lyrical yet still distant camera eye celebrates the formidable breadth in both nature and man-made structures.

The evocation of the dramatic, mythic permanence of nature is also central to the films of Jean Epstein and Arne Sucksdorff. Epstein's films continually experiment with a variety of film techniques; his nature films parallel many of the themes in Flaherty's films, notably *Man of Aran*, as well as those in Visconti's study of Sicilian fishermen and their battle against nature. In *Finis Terrae*, however, the fast cutting undercuts his initial interest in the precarious bond of man and nature. This incongruity between technique and subject matter is even more sharply mainfested in his use of the hand-held camera, which obscures his mosaic of the hands and faces of the women as they watch the sea hitting the land. Like Flaherty, Epstein is fascinated by the paradoxical quality of nature, its cruelty and immense beauty. But his immersion in the conflicting aspects of this unending struggle diffuses the mythic unity that binds the sea and those whose existence is dependent on it.

*Mor'Vran* does not feature the dissolves and acute editing that mar *Finis Terrae*, but Epstein is still unable to construct a cohesive story line. There are signs of a poetic understanding of the raw power of his material, for example in his long shots of the sea that he juxtaposes to close-ups of the people awaiting the sailors' return. This theme is extended in *L'Or des mers*, in which the postsynchronized dialogue is used as an operatic coda. But the treatment remains too contrived for his material—a shot of the intoxicated old man stumbling across a rock is followed by a shot of a cross set against the image of the man lying on the ground.

*Le Tempestaire* is one Epstein documentary that sympathetically humanizes the power of nature in the lives of a married couple. He is not simply interested in the grandeur of his abstracted images of nature, but in the way they permeate the relationship of the husband and wife, nonprofessional actors whose contrary understanding of the awesome world they inhabit dramatizes an essential truth about marriage in such primitive surroundings. It is exemplified in the scene in which the wife, after seeking shelter at a neighbor's house while her husband is at sea, is confronted by the sudden appearance of her husband, who asks why she was not at their home. The film reflects the control nature exerts over their destiny; the husband seems immune to the power of nature, whereas the wife, sensitive to its beauty, is more conscious of its terrifying force.

The major problem in Epstein's films is his indecisiveness in resolving two apparently antagonistic viewpoints: his appreciation of the objective, timeless features of the land and his development of a microcosmic social or personal drama. In the films of Arne Sucksdorff a different problem arises; because of his reverence for nature, man's presence is barely visible; hence, his lyrical studies of nature lack the epic stature of Flaherty's films. In *Shadows on the Snow, Trut!*, and *A Summer Tale* Sucksdorff's identity is that of a naturalist mesmerized by the wonders of nature. In the opening scene of *Shadows on the Snow* his camera passes over snowcapped mountains at night, a private paradise where birds search for insects, which is then marked by the appearance of a bear. In the following daytime scene the sounds and sights of birds chirping fill the screen as a young boy skies into the valley but leaves when the bear is spotted. A man and dog then come to track the bear, but they also are scared away. The last, epigrammatic shot reenforces the idea that man has no place in this setting; the final image of the bear on a rock shows that the bear, too, is a lone, miniscule part of nature.

Like *Shadows on the Snow, Trut!* and *A Summer Tale* do not contain any dramatic subplots; Sucksdorff is content to revel in vast kingdoms in which animals fight among themselves. The killings by the eagle in *Trut!* and by the foxes in *A Summer Tale* belong to a splendrous world whose one variable is the Darwinian balance that nature imposes. In *A Summer Tale*, the most exemplary of these three short films, he does not introduce the animals in their natural habitat until he has shown the insects and plants. To Sucksdorff, there are no oblique lessons or paradoxes to be learned; the audience is asked simply to immerse itself in the multifaceted levels of existence in nature—watching a fox eating insects off the plants or the sunlight filling the forest. Man's role is to record this daily spectacle, to marvel at the freedom and symmetry of an untrammeled paradise.

Sucksdorff's reluctance to derive a dramatic framework from his unfledging celebration of the sundry pleasures and mysteries of nature receives a problematic treatment in *The Great Adventure*. The first part of the film is an ode to the wonders of nature that looks as if it were lifted from any one of his shorter films. There is a semblance of a story with the child-heroes who cope with the problems of raising an otter at home. But the brothers in no way express the heroic aspects of Flaherty's young adventurer in *Louisiana Story*; they are two figures from a Disney dreamworld who finally learn that the otter's place is not as a pet, but in nature; the viewer can be thankful that Sucksdorff is absorbed in attractive but somewhat repetitive sights of nature. Unlike Flaherty who can only understand and give meaning to nature as it prefigures man's heroic destiny, Sucksdorff purposely removes man from nature, delighting instead in the glories of his Edensque landscape. Sucksdorff's pantheism is an undeniable antecedent of the numerous *National Geographic* specials on American television.

A second major attribute of the documentary film concerns the social and political crises and personalities that have shaped twentieth-century history. The social immediacy of documentarians from Leni Riefenstahl and Joris Ivens to Chris Marker and Alan Pennebaker has been largely superseded by television, yet each of these filmmakers stylizes his material to a degree that documentary television, at least in America, has shied away from. The controversy surrounding Leni Riefenstahl's *Triumph of the Will* and *Olympia* originates in her emphasis on the mechanization of modern politics and the architectonic grandeur of the human figure; her impersonal film style captures the madness in the former and the abstract beauty of the latter. It is not Riefenstahl's intention in *Triumph of the Will* to examine the political rhetoric of the

Nazis; her theme is the rigorous, dehumanizing behavioral ethos that was generated during the Nazi party convention. Riefenstahl's camera eye is unyielding in capturing the ebb and flow of this expression of party unity and strength; the horror of her historical document is not in the articulation of any one Nazi doctrine, but in its orchestration of national hysteria. The fascistic nature of her film lies in her exposing its structural underpinnings and not in supporting any one racist element. She shows us, somewhat naively one suspects, how the camera can serve as the most expressive vehicle in celebrating national unity through its manipulation of the actions of hundreds of thousands of people. It is one of the most cold-blooded documents of twentieth-century social and political history; it inspires one's anger and disbelief in the way each segment of German society unhesitatingly functions as a mechanical cog in Riefenstahl's sweeping fabrication of Nazi social technology.

In *Olympia* Riefenstahl finds a perfect subject for her religious passion for mechanical power and splendor: the Olympian figure. The various techniques of the film medium, from epic camera angles to diverse editing patterns, are perfectly matched to the titanic achievements of the athletes. But her fluid camera angles and editing rhythms miss the sense of competition—of personal pain and triumph—that makes the games both human and abstract. Her objective treatment was better suited to *Triumph of the Will* because she stylized the party convention as a three-ring circus honoring the mechanized march of modern Germany. In *Olympia* she probes the athletic contests like an anatomist explaining the muscles and tissues that are used in each event. Her cold, detached camera eye denotes the architectural, ritualistic sweep of the convention, but it dehumanizes the unique elegance and strength that the athlete possesses. After the activities have ended for the day, Riefenstahl shows the stadium lights illuminating not the stadium, but the sky; Riefenstahl dissolves to the torches and then to the lights shining in the sky. The absence of a human figure in this scene reveals how Riefenstahl's fascination with the mechanical underpinnings of her subjects in both *Triumph of the Will* and *Olympia* documents her lack of interest in people and personal emotions.

The natural attraction of the documentary film to the mechanical components of modern life was not the sole province of Leni Riefenstahl. Three of Joris Ivens's films—*The Bridge, Rain,* and *New Earth*—delineate the camera's intrinsic ability to pinpoint the abstract dimensions in various social forms and activities. The opening shot of *The Bridge*—an architectural drawing of the bridge—identifies the film's subject. Ivens then cuts to the bridge and tracks horizontally, vertically, and diagonally; he then visualizes the different dynamic relationships between the bridge and the train that passes over it. The film's message, similar to that of Riefenstahl's films, lies in the abstraction of a natural event.

Though *Rain* explores the effects of wind and rain on people and objects, it shows a similar mechanical dynamic in dissecting this interplay. There is some lyrical coloring in the film, suggesting that the raw material documentarians rely on is as resilient as any fictive character or event. *New Earth* is a Flaherty-type study of nature in which the construction of the dam is characterized by the workers' ongoing struggle with the sea. Ivens chooses to distinguish a symphonic study of this confrontation; the dam's completion inspires a sense of exhilaration that is not unlike the epic heroism of *Grass* or parts of *Olympia*. Ivens's *The Spanish Earth* is far different in style and scope; its rambling narrative and camera angles are used as a poetic metaphor for the Spanish Civil War. Unlike the dramatic commentary provided by newspaper collages in Frédéric Rossif's *To Die in Madrid*, Ivens's film assumes the form of an essay without any vantage point to the pain and pathos of this tragic period. It is closer in style to Resnais' *Night and Fog*; the war is relived through fragmented episodes that are meant to suggest the devastated nature of the land, but it lacks the cogency of Resnais' terse study.

Alberto Cavalcanti's *Rien que les heures* is an experiment in documentary filmmaking in which his celebrated wipes show the life cycle of food in Paris. It is an imagist film, from its pictures of onions and potatoes being marketed and sold to a shot of a woman lying in a garbage heap. Cavalcanti's Paris is a ruined city, characterized by the gastronomic interests of its inhabitants. His unsettling camera movements propose a sly but ultimately unconvincing equation between the raw material of life and the more symbolic concerns of the French avant-garde.

Walter Ruttmann's *Berlin—Symphony of a Big City* offers several interesting parallels to Vertov's *Man with a Movie Camera*. In Vertov's film city life is characterized by the constant state of motion that is sustained by his editing and tracking shots and that is most stunningly realized in the numerous double exposures—cubistic collages of the cameraman and editor intersecting with the people and streetcars on the major thoroughfares. Ruttmann and cinematographer Karl Freund, however, attempt to uncover the distinct qualities of the city's multifaceted activities. The slow movement of the newspapers sliding down the chute is juxtaposed to their naturally fast distribution; the shots of the river are not isolated lyric images, but are part of a larger formalist picture as they move to an overhead shot of the bridge and river. Their use of dissolves, unlike a more parodic application in Vertov's film, identifies the city as a complete, autonomous structural unit. While Vertov's *Man with a Movie Camera* implicates the entire city as a cog in the wheel and the wheel as an image invented by the camera, *Berlin—Symphony of a Big City* offers no moral judgment. When Ruttmann cuts from people eating to the feeding of animals at the zoo, man is not being ridiculed; both actions are examples of the film's mechanistic interpretation of modern city life. The magic of our modern cities, in *Berlin—Symphony of a Big City* as in many other silent films, finds the movies an ideal medium to capture its sensuality, its energy, and, perhaps most disturbingly, its anonymity.

*Land without Bread–The Sorrow and the Pity*

The mastery of television, with its unique ability to transmit the immediacy of news happenings, has lead to an increased specialization of the documentary film's social realism. One film which shows the variety of stylizations potential to the naturalism advocated by the English triumvirate of Grierson–Cavalcanti–Rotha is Luis Buñuel's *Land without Bread*. He rejects any overt naturalistic ploys through two distinct techniques. First, instead of featuring the townspeople, Buñuel's invisible narrator establishes the irrevocable distance between audience and subject. The second and more incisive technique is Buñuel's reliance on distant camera setups on the land which dramatize the pervasive bleakness of daily life in this region. For example, when Buñuel shows a donkey, heavily packed, walking on a steep hill and falling to his death, his impersonal long-shot range interprets the tragedy as part of the impassive cycle of nature. Because of the distance—both physical and social—that separates the audience from the film's subject, any hope of empathy is negated. The absence of sociological editorializing is one example of how the documentary film is in many ways more, not less, poetic than other film genres.

Several American film documentarians like Willard Van Dyke and Pare Lorentz try to achieve a classic parity between poetry and fact, but Van Dyke's films in particular point to the ascendancy of the more rigorous, didactic naturalism of the English cinema. This parity is often indistinguishable from paradox in Van Dyke's *Valley Town*. The film begins with a poetic use of dissolves to establish the mythic unification of the land and its people. Aaron Copland's score—at this stage of his career most imitative of Prokofiev—attempts to evoke the depression that paralyzes the town. There are several benign close-ups on the workers' faces complemented by a voice on the sound track: "Gotta get out of this place. When is the mill gonna open again?" The treatment becomes increasingly problematic when a woman sings her troubles at the dinner table and reaches a point of ludicrousness as the men walk through the town while their voices are heard on the sound track: "But why? We're all good men here." *Valley Town*, as an experiment in poetic naturalism, invariably undercuts the agony of the townspeople through its crude, proletarian folk devices.

A similar stylistic incongruity mars Van Dyke's *The City*. In visualizing various areas of city life, he uses sharp cuts, ludicrously imitative of Murnau's stylization of the city in *Sunrise*. The jittery, mechanical movements of the city dwellers become part of a puritan polemic; Van Dyke then turns to the countryside as the last refuge of innocence and goodness. In making his case for country life, Van Dyke unwittingly shows it to be a city in the making—its highways and supermarkets cry out of expansion. But Van Dyke refuses to admit the conclusiveness of his findings and dogmatically urges a return to a preindustrial Eden which his camera has shown no longer exists.

The essential shortcoming of *Valley Town* and *The City* lies in Van Dyke's lack of faith in his visuals, as if the urgency of his social commentary could not be discovered in the expressive features of the countryside and its inhabitants. Pare

Lorentz, whose films also concern man's dependence on nature, sees the American landscape as a wilderness whose grandeur remains constant, impervious to the crises that are inspired by its mighty waterways, plains, and mountain ranges. In *The Plow That Broke the Plains*, the poetic spacing of the animals grazing in the countryside recalls Dovzhenko's epic compositions. The only sequence that does not celebrate the pastoral qualities of the land concerns the Depression; Lorentz introduces a montage stylization of newsreel footage to present a cause-and-effect chain, from the stock market reports to an arid landscape. Inevitably Lorentz renews his sweeping, lyrical style to emphasize the transcendent beauty of the American countryside, epitomized in an evocative image of a dog sleeping next to parts of a discarded machine.

*The River* shows a similar mythlike design. Like Van Dyke's *Valley Town*, Lorentz introduces the Mississippi as an integral part of the American economy, but unlike Van Dyke neither his visuals nor his narrator conceives the river as a forum for social discourse or proletarian piety. In visualizing the immeasurable beauty of the river and its use for transporting cattle and cotten, Lorentz presents a modest picture of its profound impact on daily life. When the water rises and destroys several towns, neither the narrator nor Lorentz's camera interprets the disaster as a tragedy in a sociological context. Like the narrator's objective report, the camera passes over the devastation as part of a recurrent and much larger drama that man cannot challenge.

The English documentary filmmakers approached their social history without the poetic sentimentality that mars Van Dyke's sociological essays and which Lorentz sees as basic to penetrating the American environment. In the films of Alberto Cavalcanti, Harry Watt, and Basil Wright the various problems they confront—from coal distribution to the rescue of sailors caught in a storm—are presented in a straightforward, journalistic manner. Cavalcanti was probably the most dramatic of the three, showing a greater integration of movement and pulsating emotions, and an effective use of nonsynchronous sound in his dramatizations. Though he gained some notoriety in the underground film, his contrived, heavy-handed study of a married couple in *Pett and Pott* suggests that his eventual contributions to the English documentary film best expressed his artistic potential.

Humphrey Jennings's *Listen to Britain* is an emblematic English documentary; it functions as a call to arms in the face of World War II, in which his fresh, uncluttered visuals celebrate the mainstays of English culture, from Myra Hess performing Mozart to Gielgud playing *Hamlet*. Few documentary films give one such a feeling of national unity; unlike Riefenstahl who idealized the mechanical ardor and mechanical unity of Germany, Jennings stresses his country's emotional permanence. *The Silent Village* is another example of English documentarians using the film medium for its journalistic immediacy. It is a staged drama depicting the destruction of a Welsh village; the film's earnestness alerts its audience to the terrible fate that may await them. Wright attempts a more stylistic treatment of his material in *Night Mail*; however, the fact that the post office is regarded as a subject for film art underscores the sociological bias of the

English documentary film. It is similar to Ivens's study of the construction of the dam, symphonically joining the employees' chatter with the train en route during its night run. At best, it makes the job of mail clerk seem less dreary.

In the Harry Watt–Basil Wright production of *Song of Ceylon* the emphasis on dissolves—used in *Night Mail* to integrate and animate various parts of the English countryside—tends to depersonalize the unique emotional and spiritual qualities of the Ceylonese as they pray before the statue of the Buddha. The film's epic, objective approach is first characterized by the dynamic editing, but compared to Flaherty and Lorentz who sought out the singular features of their landscapes, the first section of *Song of Ceylon* exposes the neutralizing effects of this film technique. Their rhythmically styled cuts work much better in the second and third parts because in following the Ceylonese as they build a home or work in the fields, the constant human activity is aptly expressed through their fast-paced editing. The fourth segment is the most impressive; the editing is less intense, as it dutifully observes the Ceylonese at worship. Had Watt and Wright shown a little more sensitivity to their material in the opening section, the symphonic form that works so well in *New Earth* could have achieved an even greater resonance in *Song of Ceylon*.

Paul Rotha's *World of Plenty* is a striking example of the prevalence of a factual interpretation instead of a fictive one among English documentarians. Its style seems to embody the benevolence, the good will, and the international forums of sociological dialogue of the United Nations. The narrator speaks to a person who remains off camera and who represents the uninformed public's perception of the problems of nutrition. The dialogue between the two develops on the level of a children's primer. In one representative scene the narrator introduces himself to a farmer—"Hello Mr. Farmer. I'm glad to meet you,"—while the invisible spectator frequently interrupts the narrator by interjecting, "Hey, Mister." Through his reliance on charts and statistics Rotha transforms the documentary film into an extended arena for classroom instruction. A weak, at times pathetic work, *World of Plenty* typifies the conventions surrounding the application of film and television in the postwar age as an instrument of polemic controversy.

Although the documentary film was a natural vehicle for generating national unity in prototypes such as the "Why We Fight" series—in which the crude chauvinism of Hollywood films such as *The Purple Heart* is only slightly modified into an acerbic polemic against the rise of Imperial Japan and of Nazi Germany—John Huston's *The Battle of San Pietro* eschews Hollywood's blatant nationalism and moral righteousness for an unremitting study of the deadly tension of men in battle. Huston's journalistic involvement is not geared to the heroics or integrity of the Allied camp, but is intended to convey an insider's feel for the nerve-shattering effects of war. Like Huston's *The Battle of San Pietro*, Tomotaka Tasaka's *Mud and Soldiers* confirms the dramatic concerns of documentarians by simply recording the hazards and duress under which the soldiers live. By refusing to personalize the grueling, solitary nature of the soldiers' existence, Tasaka searches for some basic truth about man's courage, and he invariably identifies Flaherty's epic, timeless style as the classic source for the documentary film. In *Five Scouts* he develops a more personal study of soldiers removed from the main field of action. Tasaka uses a hand-held camera to follow the scouts as they track through the swamps, leading to a scene of Fordian sweep and clarity in which the soldiers sing together while awaiting the return of the two soldiers separated from their platoon. Tasaka's films are imbued with the passions of a naked human drama, exploring man's inner resources with both the discipline of a social scientist and the more romantic instincts of a poet.

There are several factors that contributed to the rise of *cinéma vérité*. In the war films of Rossellini there was a rejection of the stylistic flourishes in previous depictions of national and international conflict; Rossellini confronted a landscape whose physical scars mirrored an equally severe spiritual crisis. While television seemed to usher in a new age of more direct involvement in and examination of social and cultural controversies, the original architects of *cinéma vérité* in Europe and America dissociate themselves from the more contrived formulas of television documentarians by experimenting with a more personal, rough-hewn portrait of their subjects. In the Rouch-Morin *Chronicle of a Summer* the camera remains close to the faces of its subjects. But the questions asked are no more probing than those on a television talk show; Rouch and Morin seem to believe that they can symbolize the vacuity of modern life through tedious dialogue. To enliven their dreary subjects, they resort to silly, heavy-handed questions. For example, they ask a man who has told them that his life consists of nothing but eating and getting a good night's sleep whether he has seen *Last Year at Marienbad*. In the case of *Chronicle of a Summer*, *cinéma vérité* becomes pop sociology.

A more honest, penetrating examination of the role of *cinéma vérité* is provided in the prologue to Chris Marker's *Le Joli Mai*. His aerial shots of Paris illuminate its renowned, mythlike luster. Marker sees the ornate, romantic veneer of Paris as a barrier to one's understanding of its inhabitants. In the ensuing one hundred and forty minutes, Marker mirrors the diffuse, unsettled qualities he sees as representative of modern life through awkward camera angles, seemingly interminable interviews, and his refusal to infuse an underlying moral viewpoint around the people being interviewed. In *The Koumiko Mystery* Marker's kinetic editing is used to personify the commercial gloss and unnerving rhythms that surround the Olympic games in Tokyo. This whirlwind movement treats Koumiko, however, as only another example of the elusiveness of Japanese culture. Marker avoids the neutrality of television commentators for the more personal, prolix prose of *cinéma vérité* but without any secure sociological or aesthetic bias.

In the films of Richard Leacock and Don Alan Pennebaker *cinéma vérité* explores the idiosyncracies of various American personalities. In focusing on the preparations and advance work and on the aides and supporters of political and pop figures such as John F. Kennedy, Hubert Humphrey, Bob Dylan, and Joan Baez in *Primary* and *Don't Look Back*, Leacock and Pennebaker do not so much demythicize these public performers as they seek out the magic presence their coteries and professions force upon them. *Primary* is the more interesting film because there seems to be a greater complexity of people and moods that contribute to the stumping and political infighting of primaries than in a concert tour. Leacock's camera and editing shift back and forth from close-up views of the candidates' forced expressions of anger, joy, and honesty to the voters' puzzlement and fascination. Though they fail to seek out any larger national myth about primaries and politics in America, it is an effective antidote to the glib, pseudoobjective commentary of television newscasters. Pennebaker's and Leacock's subjects in *Don't Look Back* seem curiously indolent; the camera fails to sketch in the details that give the pop-music industry its wide appeal. There are moments when they appear to isolate Dylan and Baez and to trace in the icon of the performer at bay. But the mood is quickly upset by a rotating interest in their legions of publicists and fans.

Frederick Wiseman takes a more studied, ethnographic approach to his material than either Leacock or Pennebaker in his Darwinian-styled exposés of American institutions. *The Titicut Follies*, his most abrasive, doctrinaire work, does not underline the dramatic conflicts and the grim, ironic moments of doubt and self-parody that appear in his succeeding films. His aggressive camera angles and close-ups function as a brutal indictment of the asylum. The suffering and anguish is never studied from a sociological point of view—what caused the neuroses, what can be done?—but immerses the viewer in the horror of the inmates' routines through his primitive, journalistic style. In *Hospital* and *High School* Wiseman uses fewer exclamation marks. His camera remains in medium close-up range and records what seems to be an infinite number of examples of the characters' pathetic behavior, from the reading of the poem in class in *High School* to the scene in *Hospital*, in which the hippie, while telling the doctor of his dislike for the city, continues to vomit. Though one admires Wiseman's ability to discover the comic-tragic elements in these institutions, the lack of any moral or social viewpoint in his impersonal camera angles allows him to poke fun at these miserable figures instead of exploring the origin of their bleak condition.

From the dry, diffuse, humorless study of the Parisians in Marker's *Le Joli Mai* to the smug, patronizing vignettes of Wiseman's *Hospital* and *High School*, the documentarians' search for the truth through an extrapolation of the anonymous news items that pervade our television screens is limited by their refusal to offer some point of view on the frictions surrounding man and his society. But this penchant for rambling psychological profiles, though it has proven to be the most popular of modern documentary methods, is not the only manner in which filmmakers have responded to the raw material of modern history.

In Alain Resnais' *Night and Fog*, a cogent, chilling statement about the Holocaust, the horror of the camps is rendered in a series of black-and-white stills, while color film is used to show the railroad tracks and forest that remain from this tragic period. Resnais has taken an unusual point of view in discussing and denoting this historical crisis; instead of overwhelming his audience with the immensity of the mechanics of destruction of the death camps or citing examples of the Nazi's gruesome social rhetoric, this dire period of history is characterized by a narrator whose memory is encompassed by devastating images of death.

A more direct treatment of modern history is realized in such films as *Africa Addio* by Gualtiero Jacopetti, Frédéric Rossif's *To Die in Madrid*, and Marcel Ophüls's *The Sorrow and the Pity*. *Africa Addio* is one of the most aggressive documentaries ever made, highlighted by muscular camera movements and a use of the zoom that seems to be repeated to the point of madness; it effectively mirrors the cultural and personal crosscurrents in Africa's transformation from a colonial empire to an independent one. The film works on a graphic, sensationalist level; there is no intellectual discourse on or distance from the tumult that is brutally reenforced in each sequence. The intensity Jacopetti instills in the numerous clashes between whites and Africans, brutally underscored by the rape of the land, serves as a vivid reminder of the ability of the documentary film to mirror the dramatic vigor in conventional dramatizations.

Rossif's *To Die in Madrid* is the dramatic opposite of *Africa Addio*. In its use of newsreels and judicious selections from the writings of Unamuno, it is a model compilation film. Marcel Ophüls's *The Sorrow and the Pity* finds the superficial ethnographies first undertaken by *cinéma vérité* blending in historical footage in the style of *To Die in Madrid*. Ophüls confirms the basic humanistic virtues of *cinéma vérité* through his extensive interviews with those who lived through the occupation of Clermont-Ferrand and with wartime leaders of England and France; they are infinitely more complex and emotionally engrossing than the common-man profiles of *Chronicle of a Summer* and *Le Joli Mai*. The historical footage he uses—clips from Nazi propaganda shorts and shots of the entertainers who performed during the Nazi occupation—works as a social and dramatic backdrop to his overriding interest: the memories and personalities of those interviewed. A moving recollection, the film proves that the raw material of history, whether past or present, has no fixed identity; it only awaits the documentarian with the courage and insight to penetrate the luminaries and landscapes that constitute our identity.

# 16
# The Avant-Garde Film

*Ghosts before Breakfast–Beauty and the Beast*

The underground or avant-garde film, by definition, proposes a more inherently radical point of view and style than is pursued in conventional genres. Because of their reputation as experimental artists in painting, photography, and literature, original members of the French film avant-garde of the twenties such as Hans Richter, Man Ray, and Jean Cocteau won far greater attention from cultural mandarins than writers and directors working in the commerical cinema. In the case of the postwar American underground the emphasis shifts from the aesthetic to the metaphysical, with numerous "hunger artists" using the medium as a diary to liberate themselves from what are considered the archaic demands of self, society, and story cinema. But their old-fashioned contemporaries who labor in the narrative cinema achieve more complex, resonant styles by integrating classic myths and narrative forms. And, as I hope to show, the most adventurous works of the avant-garde, like Kirsanov's *Ménilmontant* and the films of Jean Vigo, succeed because of their use of the very themes and devices that the underground, theoretically, has looked upon with disdain.

In a prototypical French underground short, *Ghosts before Breakfast*, hats and ties jump across the screen like astronauts floating in a vacuum. It is a clever film, though perhaps it accents the filmmaker's flippant disregard for realism in too facile a manner. The variations that Richter and other avant-garde filmmakers propose between animate and inanimate objects was a theme central to numerous American comedy films and only one aspect of the high art of Chaplin and Keaton. In *Ghosts before Breakfast*, once its freeze-frame machinations are acknowledged, a trick that has undergone countless variations since Georges Méliès and R. W. Paul, there is little else to engage its audience.

Several Man Ray films draw on this film chicanery to a more extreme degree, while his most memorable short, *The Mystery of the Chateau of the Dice*, evokes a menacingly real drama, unlike the majority of French experimental shorts. *Return to Reason*, like *Emak Bakia*, is a study in the dynamics of twisting, oblique patterns; it is a more appealing work than *Emak Bakia* because Ray is not simply isolating deceptive geometrical patterns, but uses the cinema's animating force

261

to discover the comedic elements surrounding their abstract form. In *The Mystery of the Chateau of the Dice*, Ray expands the dramatic potential of the visual sleight of hand he uses in his other avant-garde films. Though we never fully understand the role of his masked pranksters, the fantasy images do not seem exaggerated. During their activities at the estate—from playing with the beach ball to swimming in the pool and walking around the inert body, an action repeated with numbing permutations—Ray's phantomesque figures and their bizarre actions intrigue us because of the tension between his protagonists' imaginary improvisations and those of the filmmaker. But few French filmmakers show Ray's interest in exploring the medium's affinity with dreams and fantasy; a more representative work, *Anemic Cinema*, uses its spiraling forms to spell out a phrase.

Léger's *Ballet mécanique* is a cerebral work that seems inspired by the elusiveness of man and nature on film. Unlike numerous fantasy filmmakers who recklessly exploit the medium's facility to fragment various subjective and spatial relationships, the different speeds Léger applies to the circle and triangle or to the repeated advance of the woman on the stairs reveal the unique way the medium negates and then reconstructs visual patterns and relationships. By characterizing each individual and object only as it is defined by the medium's dizzying kinetic properties and editing equations, Léger's short exemplifies a major objective of the French avant-garde. A basic premise was that film should distort man's perception of the world; few, however, were able to effect a coherent substitute.

The Buñuel-Dali *An Andalusian Dog* is the most renowned example of the chaotic, dreamlike potential of the silent film. Like other surrealist works, its graphic, exhortative symbolism resists a piecemeal analysis, but one speculates that the initial slitting of the eye exists as a metaphor that brutally announces the filmmakers' intentions to cut into the audience's vision. But the succeeding images and symbols—the ants, the donkey in the piano, the hand—are inconclusive remnants of the natural world that are more important as examples of the surrealists' commitment to the destructive, irrational force of the unconscious. The film then depends on the immediacy of its images to suggest, without fulfilling, analogies to less explosive, everyday routines. A title like "Eight Years Later" works only as a shallow attack on the spectator's sequential expectations, but compared to the more mechanical efforts of the French avant-garde, there is an undeniable propulsion and savagery to *An Andalusian Dog*.

Although less manic in its pacing, their following collaboration, *L'Age d'Or*, has been interpreted as an ambitious assault on religious and erotic themes. Yet its intrinsically symbolist conception of a universe inspired by man's lascivious, nihilistic impulses results in a more prosaic, didactic film experience. The extensive episodes on the beach and at the aristocrat's party rely on tautological symbols of sexual and social conformity; the antagonist's peculiar fixations lack the artistic innocence and imagination that would make him seem other than a malcontent at a Marx Brothers reunion.

*Ménilmontant*, a more impressive example of the hallucinatory potential of the silent film, finds Dimitri Kirsanov creating a palpable landscape of terror through his radical extension of several themes and techniques made famous in the narrative cinema. The most prominent of these revolves around the presence of Nadia Sibirskaia, who not only resembles Lillian Gish, but also poignantly accents Gish's manner of expressing joy and fear through her use of the objects around her. Kirsanov's film moves one because he decisively, dramatically juxtaposes Sibirskaia's innocence to the grim horrors, first realized in the sharp cutting which accentuates the horrible butchery of her parents, and then in his use of dissolves and double exposures to express the fantasy and fright of Sibirskaia and her sister upon their arrival in the city. There are a few weak moments, notably in Kirsanov's treatment of Sibirskaia's pregnancy. But his sensitivity to the sisters' jarring emotional adventures and to the symmetry between the city's frightening specter and the cinema's fluency in illuminating its eerie features are evidence of his unique talent.

Jean Vigo strikes a lyrical balance between the avant-garde's penchant for raucous, nihilistic symbols and the more dramatically realistic concerns of narrative cinema. Several of the images in *A propos de Nice* seem tenuous, but Vigo's film cadence sustains a joyous, felicitous profile on the playfulness underlying much of the theoretical daring of his contemporaries. His grainy, dreamlike haze captures Nice as a self-enclosed world caught in the gravitational pull of one's waking and dreaming self. *Zero for Conduct* is a more lustrous example of Vigo's affection for reverie. His unwavering faith in the poetry of a child's world establishes an irrevocable bond between the Chaplinesque instructor and his pupils. It shows Vigo's ability to imbue such scenes as the disorderly classroom, the pillow fight, and the jaunt through the town with the discernible motifs of freedom and emotional inventiveness. He was a true poet of the cinema, and like Kirsanov, should be appreciated in the context of artists like Chaplin and Renoir.

Perhaps it can be argued that it is the mysterious affinity between the real and the imaginary and between the human and the mechanical that gives the French avant-garde and films like *The Mystery of the Chateau of the Dice*, *Ballet mécanique*, and *An Andalusian Dog* their special identity. This point of view is basic to the films of Watson and Webber and Jean Epstein. In their five-minute short, *The Fall of the House of Usher*, Watson and Webber evoke Poe's tale as a state of mind in which they do not make the slightest concession to the real world. Their cutting immerses the spectator in the Usher estate as a labyrinth that nullifies any hope of escape. In *Lot in Sodom* they display a fine eye for the muscular, sculptural sweep of the human body, but their reliance on an accelerated editing rhythm to depict the destruction is typical of the narrative resolutions of the avant-garde.

Epstein's *The Fall of the House of Usher* is a flawed but genuinely poetic adaptation of Poe. Although the final fireworks scene, in which the Usher estate is shown as a plastic miniature, is a self-conscious effect, a good part of the film works as a probing study of the stilled and distilled emotions which pervade Poe's tales. Epstein visualizes Roderick's anguish and his sister's death mask as the predominant signs of Poe's imaginary dreamworld. Epstein's use of the subjective camera when Roderick carries his sister, of slow motion when Roderick gazes at her coffin, and of the shots from inside the coffin that show the swaying of the leaves embodies Poe's morbidity.

Epstein's *La Glace à trois faces* may well be his best film. It shows Epstein's dramatic flair in reflecting the mannerisms of his donnish protagonist while creating a harrowing picture of the deadlier passions of the jazz age. His camera studies the corrupt features of his modern satyrs without parodying their gross habits. One example of his ironic subjective-objective viewpoint is the scene in which he cuts between the man studying himself in the mirror as he buttons his vest and the woman's voyeuristic fascination.

If any one filmmaker can be said to represent the avant-garde aesthetic in its most crystalline form it is Jean Cocteau. Parker Tyler, among other avant-garde film historians, argues that Cocteau's films present the most comprehensive example of the purist-symbolist aims of the French avant-garde. *The Blood of a Poet*, Cocteau's most individual work, offers a critical equation between the cinema's unlimited visual resources and the world of ideas. But the lyre, like the tower that crumbles and the rooms through which the poet passes, is identified as a symbol because of its classical iconography. In visualizing the world of the subconscious, Cocteau does not undertake a transformation from the literal to the symbolic and spiritual. He unintentionally shows his lack of interest in how the movies, like other art forms, create unique structural and figurative equivalents to these symbols. To approach the film medium as synonymous with symbolic drama—in the images of the artist's hand or the card game—involves a refutation of the inherent transfiguration underlying the aesthetic experience. What is most surprising is that film historians remain in awe of the pseudoart of *The Blood of a Poet* and an artist whose beguiling strategies in poetry and the novel more faithfully express his true muse.

*Orpheus* elucidates this symbolism with greater specificity because its myths are not the products of Cocteau's intuitive fantasies as they were in *The Blood of a Poet*. The most formidable question that is raised concerns the manner in which Cocteau visualizes the "real world." While he sees his impoverished exteriors as a natural stage for his philosophically styled drama, Jean Marais's poet is equally transparent; neither his speech nor manner denotes the poetic. In his final treatment of the legend of Orpheus in *The Testament of Orpheus*, Cocteau's style becomes increasingly autistic as Cocteau himself will travel through space like a spirit from *Miracle in Milan*. Some may argue that symbolist drama demands a wholly different set of critical priorities and that the audience must accept symbols like Maria Casares's Death and her band of motorcyclists without questioning their dramatic origin. But Cocteau fails to illuminate how these symbols and spirits haunt one's everyday world. Why, for example, is Death's council as unstylized as the natural world? One can argue that Cocteau interprets both the real and spiritual world as undifferentiated by time and space and that he is only concerned with the questions Marais's Orpheus asks himself; for example, what type of poet is he and what does he represent to himself, to his wife, and to his audience? But Orpheus's love of Death is never explained as being purely physical, purely spiritual, or purely aesthetic; like Maria Casares's characterization of Death, it wavers between the literal and symbolic.

Cocteau's significant contributions to modern art—his undeniable talent in discerning the genius of modern painting, literature, and dance and his irrevocable commitment to the parodic fictions of the surrealists and dadaists—preceded his involvement with the film medium. His *Beauty and the Beast*, among film's most elegiac and elegant literary adaptations, finds him rejecting the philosophical design of the avant-garde. It is one of the few films that successfully recreates the innocence of fables on film and suggests that Cocteau's best work in poetry, literature, and film conveys the mystery with which a precocious child sees the world. Though he is an epochal figure as critic, advance man, and historian of the avant-garde, his own efforts in fashioning a film aesthetic negate the irony and conceit that made him such a witty observer of the twentieth century.

### The Great Blondino–Why Not

The renaissance of the underground film in America underscores the acute differences in the French cultural ambience between the two world wars and an American scene marked by beats, hippies, and other antiestablishment figures who review their personal and social history on film. The most prominent feature of the French avant-garde was its conception of film as the prototypical modern art, in which the symbolic figures of one's dreams appear with the same facility that one records people crossing the street. To the surrealists and dadaists who saw the medium as heaven-sent, their films became a way of exorcising the linear, narrative, and rationalist conventions that they felt repressed the demons and fears and the poetry of the unconscious. It was their instinctive marriage of aesthetics and metaphysics that imbued their films with a curious form of ambiguity and didacticism, of stylistic abandon and geometric precision.

It is more difficult to generalize about the American underground because it has proven to be less uniform in its theories and films than the French avant-garde. Though there remains a strong commitment to both the comical aspects of the dadaists in films like Robert Nelson's *The Great Blondino* and to the more explosive, nihilistic energy of surrealists in the opium-dream films of Kenneth Anger, one must look to other sources to discover the unique features of the American film underground. Its special viewpoint, which has gained expression in the polemics of Jonas Mekas, Amos Vogel, P. Adams Sitney, and Annette Michelson, finds the filmmaker using his personal experiences or his rambling studies of the world around him to personify the absence of any moral or physical center. On one level it takes the form of Stanton Kaye's *Georg* or *David Holtzman's Diary*; in the more abstract work of Stan Brakhage in which the camera records the director and his wife making love, the medium becomes the modernist's equivalent to a diary or journal.

But these filmmakers' moral absolutism is not the only manner in which the American underground approaches the medium. In Brakhage's *Anticipation of the Night* and S. Arakawa's *Why Not* the camera dissects the physical makeup of their settings without attempting a synthesis of their meaning and form. The parallels that are drawn between the car travelers, the sights to which they return, and the children at home in Brakhage's film, and the relationships between the girl and the table and between the girl and the bicycle in Arakawa's work find the filmmaker celebrating a universe of abstract indefiniteness. Like much of contemporary science fiction, in which disjointed styles and transparent otherworlds purport to mirror a smorgasbord of the latest cosmic theories of the scientific community, the underground film in America projects a sensual, solipsistic sensibility.

The early films of Andy Warhol reject the acutely discursive camera designs of his contemporaries in favor of prolonged, static monodramas. Warhol attempts a wedding of two seemingly antithetical forms—that of the documentary and the underground film—in attempting to understand how the movies can be most expressively used in modern American society. Like Flaherty, he holds on the faces and monologues of his deviants in the belief that whatever they say will uncover a basic sociological truth, yet, like Cocteau, he realizes that their inherently autistic nature results in a substratum of fantasy intrinsic to the underground film. Listening to Taylor Mead's extravagant monologue in *Nude Restaurant* or watching the young man play with his beautiful blond hair in *The Chelsea Girls*, one senses Warhol's interest in replacing pictorially motivated abstractions with the similarly abstracted consciousness of the descendents of French dadaists. Like a bemused social scientist, Warhol fills his films with social renegades that intrepid television journalists would never dare to show; he prefigured the solecisms of cable television and the experimental video psychodramas that the newest personalities in the American avant-garde are currently exploring.

Whether the "spiritual" vantage point of Warhol's films or the more expressive, imagist exercises of Brakhage will predominate is an unnecessary rhetorical exercise; what both directors have shown is the American underground's lack of interest in the art of our museums, literature, and langauge. Rather, they use the camera as an anthropological tool of self- and social discovery or as a building block to reorder the appearance of the outside world.

# Part 3

# The Contemporary Cinema

# 17

# The American Film in the Fifties

*Scarlet Street–Sunset Boulevard*

Somewhere in the forties the fifties began. Women were no longer exclusively portrayed as innocents, whether as the mirthful creature of screwball comedy or the forlorn heroine in a back-street romance. The seductive, innocent pallor of Gene Tierney's Laura, the voluptuousness of Ava Gardner's temptress in *The Killers*, and the sexual swagger of Rita Hayworth's Gilda share a mask of allure, danger, and perdition. In *The Woman in the Window* and *Scarlet Street*—both directed by the great German expressionist Fritz Lang and photographed in classic, enveloping shades of darkness by Milton Krasner—Edward G. Robinson plays a middle-class everyman who journeys on the road of erotic gratification and self-debasement with his siren, Joan Bennett. At the end of *The Woman in the Window*, Robinson's grim adventure is dismissed as a perverse fantasy that he has dreamed. In *Scarlet Street*, however, Robinson roams the streets of our cities, indelibly marked by his fatalistic attraction for Bennett. He has painted a portrait of her that becomes an expression of his own desires and a symbol of the qualities of romantic discord so many of the protagonists of the forties discovered in their love object. Executed in primitive symbolist style, she is pictured as a phantom—a bewitching, doll-like specter whose disembodied eyes await the appearance of her next victim.

The history of the vamp dates back to the halcyon days of the silent era where she was fabricated out of the Freudian depths of puritan morality and Victorian melodrama. In her original incarnation by Theda Bara in *A Fool There Was*, she exists as a demonic symbol of carnality; exposing little more than her pudgy ankles, Bara's deadly, hypnotic spell was personified by hedonistic outbursts of laughter over the efforts of her victim's family to bring him to his senses and by the ubiquitous darkness surrounding her mansion. The vamp was associated with the deadly menace of city life, its gangsters and nightclubs, or with foreign, exotic settings. With her languorous, distant manner and impervious eroticism, Greta Garbo's characterization of the "other woman" in several MGM romances of the twenties underscored the identity of the vamp as a dark, damned, irresistible force. But in Robinson's portrait of Bennett or with the faces and figures of Tierney, Gardner, and Hayworth, a more acute element of self-destructiveness, a more brazen sexual ripeness becomes apparent. The forties are often characterized by the cheerful, rosy-cheeked attractiveness of Betty Grable and the mature, matronly presence of Greer Garson. But the nocturnal, sensual shadows of Bennett, Tierney, Gardner, and Hayworth present a far greater challenge to the sanctity of the family and flesh than previously encountered in American movies.

The more prevalent, popular image of women in the American film had been one of indomitable innocence. An integral feature of America's first master of the movies, D. W. Griffith, was his profound commitment to the idealization of woman. He envisioned his heroine as a rustic innocent (*Hearts of the World, Way Down East, True Heart Susie*), as a virgin warrior (*Judith of Bethulia*), or as the transcendent sign of purity that inspired a national reawakening (*The Birth of a Nation*). Other variations found Mabel Normand playing the tomboy, and although Anita Loos's scripts for Mary Pickford and Constance Talmadge drew some rough edges around our little darlings, they remained pure, playful, asexual spirits. The Depression did little to change the wholesomeness of film heroines. If Katharine Hepburn and Myrna Loy were models of aristocratic chic, Ginger Rogers came to embody many of the virtues that Americans were taught to pride themselves in—hardworking, tough-talking, yet inescapably a romantic, whether as the object of Fred Astaire's song-and-dance courtship or as the strong-willed heroine of *Roxie Hart*. The film industry had become an axiom of American life; owing to its happy endings and saccharine treatment of the family, the vamp remained a contrivance—a transparent symbol of desire who represented the abyss from which the hero extricated himself.

The persona of Tierney, Gardner, and Hayworth, however, connotes a considerable change in our romantic fantasies. Studio executives had long recognized that an essential fabric of the film experience, especially in the Hollywood star system, was the crafting of a film around the publicity photography distributed to fan magazines. One recalls the distinct photoportraiture that preceded and often personified Hollywood productions and the background in still portraiture of the industry's most noteworthy cinematographers and their long-term association with Hollywood's movie queens: Charles Rosher and Mary Pickford, Arthur C. Miller and Shirley Temple, George Barnes and Marion Davies, William Daniels and Garbo, Oliver Marsh and Joan Crawford, and the most famous of all Pygmalion-and-Galatea relationships, that of Von Sternberg and Dietrich. In the publicity photos of, among others, Tierney, Gardner, and Hayworth, there is a not-so-subtle departure from the smoky, seductive, often abstracted eroticism in the stills of Hollywood's most legendary women of danger in the twenties and thirties. The treatment of Tierney, Gardner, and Hayworth is far more provocative, more palpably physical and pornographic. The soft, cool radiance of Tierney's face presents an image of the seductive debutante who will assume her role as a lady of society with an adroitness that will repel any expressions of endearment. Gardner is a more classic incarnation of the temptress—dark-featured, with perfectly symmetrical lines of eyes, nose, and mouth, the exquisite cylindricality of her face complemented by a figure that would need no padding and invite no shadow play. Hayworth does not possess Gardner's classic beauty and proportions; her nose is too prominent, her lips too full. Yet her magic is perfectly captured in a publicity shot for *Gilda*. Set against a dark backdrop, Hayworth stands slightly off-center in a strapless, shimmering dress, casually holding a mink coat which falls by her side and a cigarette held high in her other hand, its smoky residue billowing atop her thick, wavy, exotically styled hair. Her aloofness is conveyed both through the artifices of the coat and cigarette and through a smile that is equally manifested in her eyes and closed lips. The figure is not as curvaceous as Gardner's, yet the shadow forming in a V-pattern from her thighs to her ankles, and her slightly tilted posture create an original study of her identity as the high priestess of seduction. Whereas Gardner presents herself as an object for our satisfaction, Hayworth suggests the intentions are mutual. She was Gilda, and in her performance she embodied the nuances of destruction, both inner- and outer-directed, of the femme fatale in the romances of the forties.

The suddenly numerous pictures of dangerous, destructive women in the forties were not isolated examples of the moral turpitude in the American film. Although the characterizations of Joan Bennett, Gene Tierney, Ava Gardner, and Rita Hayworth denote a major feature of the style labeled "*film noir*," they represent only one piece, perhaps the centerpiece, in the oblique treatment of romance and mystery in the forties. Bette Davis, the foremost romantic heroine of the first decades of the sound film, enjoyed two of her greatest successes in two of Hollywood's most accomplished romances with *Mr. Skeffington* and *Now Voyager*. She imbued the romantic adventuress with a regal individuality, whether in her role as the lubricious, reckless partygoer finally confronted with the sins of her amorality in the spellbinding, Dorian Gray image of physical decay in *Mr. Skeffington* or as the ugly duckling transformed into a polished, handsome, celibate socialite in *Now Voyager*. Yet the fate of Barbara Stanwyck, an equally representative thirties dame, reveals the perversity of the heroines and temptresses of the forties. Stanwyck had enlivened several of Frank Capra's Depression-era comedies and melodramas, but with her inviting, cross-legged figure in *Double Indemnity*, she joined such film icons of seduction as Lana Turner's silky, turbaned heroine in *The Postman Always Rings Twice* and the not-so-obscure object of Louis Calhern's desire in *The Asphalt Jungle*. Among these numerous images of sensuality is a prophetic spotlight that encompasses the embracing figures of Stanwyck and Burt Lancaster in *Sorry, Wrong Number*. Only her left eye is kept in darkness, signifying her tragic fate as the paralytic who will suffer the anguish and death inspired by her salacious behavior.

But it was not only women who embodied this fatalism. If *Citizen Kane* remains a harbinger of the romantic and stylistic ironies of the forties, Chaplin's *Monsieur Verdoux*, released in 1947, provides an equally compelling cumulative archetype of its social frictions and personal nihilism. Chaplin's impassive persona and the distinctly archaic look of his settings and staging do not project the motifs of psychological unrest that Welles instilled into a film whose paradoxical rhythms can be discovered in a number of genres, *film noir* perhaps its most commercialized form. But Chaplin's difficulties with the American press and the increasing realist themes he chose for his sound films make an inclusion of his pancultural figure seem more justifiable. If Welles is the voice of a new age, Chaplin's is that of the past, expressing his complete, irrevocable divorce from society through a reversal of his traditional features and comic empathy. Assuming the mask of an elegant, fastidious gentlemen, he disposes of his female victims with none of the exuberance he brought to his earlier escapades. He is a man at peace with himself, fulfilling a final, devastating social contract in which his apprehension and execution become an epilogue to his wasteland killings; Welles's Kane, the dreamer and Chaplin's Verdoux, the nihilist, the former prefacing his age's tensions, the latter writing its last chapter of mordancy through his misanthropic dramatic voice.

There then appears a dualistic image of carnality and evil, attributable to the chaos of the war years and its natural expression in the unnatural visions of the literature and art of expressionism. Many of these films of social and personal strife are adaptations of a deleterious pulp romance (*Out of the Past, Thelma Jordan*); the hard-boiled literature of Raymond Chandler (*The Big Sleep, Lady in the Lake, Murder, My Sweet*) and James Cain (*The Postman Always Rings Twice, Double Indemnity, Mildred Pierce*); or the eerie, twilight zone of human aberration explored in the writings of Cornell Woolrich. Woolrich's stories and novels were the basis of a dozen crime-suspense films, and his numerous credits lead one to see him as the archetypal poet of *film noir*. He was a fantasist who, like Poe, suggested the hallucinatory nature of imagination by erasing the boundaries separating reality and illusion. His fiction reads like a diary: painfully subjective records of drifters whose psychotic, paranoid depression is filtered through their repeated excursions into the lower depths of romance and intrigue. His narratives are set in classic social spheres of romantic turbulence—high-class parties, low-class ghettos, international danger zones—but they all unequivocally originate within the mind of his protagonists. Like James Hadley Chase, another popular writer of sordid affairs and subconscious upheavals, Woolrich was a primitive—primitive in his use of language to convey his characters' psychological pressures, primitive in his development and resolution of plot, yet a resourceful and not unappealing primitive in his understanding of expressionism as the representative voice of the individual in the twentieth century. The marriage of Woolrich and the movies was one of the most felicitous in the American film, the union of a writer absorbed in his tormented, recurrent nightmares becoming his everyday reality and a medium naturally sympathetic to the subjective tremors of expressionism.

Expressionism is the ultimate, interlocking network of ideas and imagery for the more ambivalent films of the forties and fifties. If Orson Welles's work from *Citizen Kane* through *Touch of Evil* represents the single most conclusive, cohesive repertoire of expressionist techniques—the extensive, foreboding deep space, the use of the wide-angle lens to create an element of distortion in the juxtaposition of foreground and background, the aggressive, staccato editing rhythms, and the oblique camera angles, whether in tilted close-ups or the preference for floor shots—its origin lies in the German film expressionism of the twenties and in the artistic unification of classic literary and pictorial studies of isolation with the unique psychological dynamics of the silent film. Not surprisingly, many of the foremost craftsmen and directors of American film expressionism were German refugees who had received their training in the German film studios of the twenties and who had come to America to escape Nazi Germany. Franz Planer was a masterly proponent of the moving camera as a personalizing instrument of fear and obsession. One of his most eloquent tracking shots in *The Chase*, an adaptation of a Woolrich novel, begins in complete darkness across the exterior of a ship, slowly descending for the dreamlike iris effect of a muted Michèle Morgan seen through the porthole. The deft sensuousness of Planer's movement is a testament to the devious ironies of Woolrich's plot and to the camera's unique affinity with his intricacies. Planer was behind the camera for Ophüls's elegiac *Letter from an Unknown Woman*; in *The Chase*, *Champion*, and *Criss Cross*, his magnified shadow play is ubiquitous; no attempt is made to key the shadows to a light source, as in the less ominous lighting of Joseph LaShelle (*Laura*, *Hangover Square*, *Fallen Angel*). By using a Garutso lens for greater contrast and depth in his lighting, Planer's encompassing shadow play comes to represent the specter of fate; in LaShelle it suggests the latent, destructive potential of the characters' erotic instincts. Planer's densely expressionist lighting, however, was one of the major reasons for the failure of the film version of *Death of a Salesman*, neutralizing Miller's poetic realism; Planer's symbolic, light-dark tones in *Not as a Stranger*, a medical soap opera directed by Stanley Kramer, and in *The Nun's Story*, a religious soap opera directed by Fred Zinnemann, failed to compensate for the films' lightweight dramatic urgency. In the work of Nicholas Musuraca, the preeminent photographer at RKO (which Alain Silver characterizes as the quintessential studio of forties melodramas), there is a similar florid eroticism to the shadow play, a pregnant mark of the protagonists' psychological stigma. Darkness is a pervasive factor throughout the forties, and in two of its idiosyncratic, postwar stylizations by Stanley Cortez in *The Night of the Hunter* and *Shock Corridor*, the lighting abstractions are supported by Gothic distortions in the staging, from the apselike configurations of the bedroom where Robert Mitchum murders Shelley Winters to the symbolized deep space of the corridor in the insane asylum.

One of the isolated expressions of critical condemnation in the back issues of *American Cinematographer*, an original source of the technical and stylistic priorities of Hollywood filmmakers, is manifested in their reviews of several major German films during the late twenties. Hollywood technicians found the effects of a moving camera mannered, disconcerting; but the art of camera movement, associated with Karl Freund's cinematography of *Variety* and *The Last Laugh*, and that of Karl Struss and Charles Rosher in *Sunrise*, was a significant achievement in the last years of the silent film. Its revived use in the film expressionism of the forties reaffirms the implications of a moving camera in characterizing the protagonists' inner turmoil and the precariousness of their social reality. If the nuances in the shadow play of Krasner, Planer, LaShelle, Musuraca, and Cortez are an essential motif in these film stylizations, then the prevalence and geometry of their camera tracks further delineate the tensions of these perverse romances. In the climax of *Hangover Square*, Laird Cregar's composer premieres his piano concerto. As Cregar begins his performance, LaShelle's camera undertakes a long, spiraling tracking shot across the faces of the audience, leading upward for its eerie accompaniment to Laird's discordant melodies. His camera floats above the gathering, accentuating the increasing shrill effects of the concerto and ends with a zoom on its creator. In the last scene, this alienating movement is repeated as Cregar, who has set the house on fire, sits at the piano engulfed in the carnage and flames as the camera continues to withdraw from this infernal image. The symbolic fire and expressive music are parallel motifs of romantic dread that are personified in the figure of Cregar, absorbed in his piano playing and the flames of his obsession.

Robert Siodmak and John Brahm achieved their greatest success in the moody, romantic fatalism of the forties, utilizing their extreme low-key lighting as effective counterpoints to the desperation of their heroines (*The Spiral Staircase, Phantom Lady, The Dark Mirror*) or to the hysteria of their antagonists (*Hangover Square, The Lodger, Guest in the House*). Edgar Ulmer, a noted designer in the German studios, enjoyed one certifiable success in *Bluebeard* with the wholly fabricated backdrops of Paris complementing the puppet theater of John Carradine's melancholic murderer. Equally attractive for the designers and directors of expressionism was the use of latensification, a method of predarkening the negative that allowed cinematographers to employ a much lower lighting level while functioning as a major cost-reducing device during the budget-conscious war years. Hollywood executives had imposed a self-restriction of $5,000 for the construction of new sets during the war, and latensification was incorporated in numerous crime films throughout the forties and into the fifties.

The psychologically pregnant shadow play, the unsettling camera setups, the fatalistic camera movements, and the cloying, claustrophobic sets are among the most commonly used aesthetic motifs that interpenetrate a world of fugitives from the law, of unsuspected murderers, and of characters trapped in their own private hells. Claims have been made, most exhaustively by Alain Silver and Elizabeth Ward in *Film Noir*, for an impressive number of films and filmmaking teams as original stylists of the era. I have seen less than half of the three hundred films they discuss, but their approach seems to be characteristic of the dangers of "sign reading" among numerous structuralists, and not only in film criticism. A film like *Suspense* can be acclaimed as an exemplary *film noir* owing to the fateful symmetry between Philip Yordan's script, Karl Struss's camera, and Paul Sylos's art direction. But I am not sure how many of the films in the genre do not utilize their symbolized landscapes to become the audience's cognitive stereotypes.

These grim stylizations of sexuality and hallucination invert basic thematic, moral, and technical axioms of Hollywood moviemaking: our fundamental assumptions about Americans and their institutions are continually under attack. It is against this background of love turning into eroticism, reality into nightmare, that the postwar American film must secure its identity. And perhaps no better point of origin can be found than *Sunset Boulevard*, a self-referential film about Hollywood. The film sharply differs from earlier studies of the movie colony and moviemakers in its acidulous treatment of Gloria Swanson's movie personage. Previous film portraits had characterized the industry as a primitive social environment that was redeemed either by the fun-loving craziness of film production (*Show People, Boy Meets Girl*) or by the self-fulfillment of the characters' fantasies of becoming stars (*What Price Hollywood, A Star Is Born*). The movies are America's Shangri-la, a dreamworld marked by its illusory grandeur but one that invariably reveals the ideal of romance and fantasy in a way unique to the movies. In the Billy Wilder–Charles Brackett–D. M. Marshman, Jr. script for *Sunset Boulevard*, the meaning of the movies is delineated in Swanson's Norma Desmond, an aging, bitchy, vituperative whore who reminisces about the good old days with her own "whore" played by William Holden. One of the film's most evocative scenes, a soiree attended by movie luminaries of the past, works as a gruesome analogue to a zombie horror film. No longer active in the movies, they appear, only to one another, as the stars they once were, while the audience, with William Holden, sees them as the specters they have become.

Wilder's association with cinematographer John Seitz is particularly instructive. Seitz's fascination with intricately lit, extravagantly romantic compositions, magnified Valentino's appeal and made *The Four Horsemen of the Apocalypse* one of Hollywood's most impressive studies of romance and history. But after his mutually advantageous collaborations with Rex Ingram, Seitz's career floundered until his work with Wilder (*Double Indemnity, The Lost Weekend*) and in other noteworthy productions of the forties (*Sullivan's Travels, This Gun for Hire, The Miracle of Morgan's Creek, Hail the Conquering Hero, The Unseen, Night Has a Thousand Eyes, The Big Clock*). Seitz's voluminous shadows were, with James Wong Howe's cinematography (*Kings Row, Hangmen Also Die, Body and Soul*), among the best examples of low-key photography and its dramatic resourcefulness in the psychological melodramas of the period. He favored greater front-lighting than Howe, but there is no mistaking the relevance of his shadow play in Wilder's productions. The Wilder-Seitz etching also uses latensification to enhance its dark, enshrouding tones. Hollywood, to William Holden's aspiring scribe, is Norma Desmond, and what a compelling yet mordant figure she is.

*Ace in the Hole–Marty*

If *Sunset Boulevard* conveys a striking change in the movie iconography of Hollywood into an isolated, Gothic fiefdom in which its past servant has become its aging mistress, Billy Wilder's abrasive style seems to find its ideal film projects in the fifties. Kirk Douglas's brash movie presence was rarely better used than in *Ace in the Hole*. Wilder's flair for sharp, biting dialogue and dramatic characterizations made *Stalag 17* and *Witness for the Prosecution* sartorial star vehicles for Holden and Charles Laughton. His best comedy, *Some Like It Hot*, is a frenzied, brittle screwball romp that lacks the fluidity of earlier classics, but its romantic trio-turned-quartet featuring Tony Curtis, Jack Lemmon, Marilyn Monroe, and Joe E. Brown makes for one of the more happily cynical films in Hollywood annals. The fifties was a critical transition period for Hollywood in its treatment of adult, controversial topics; by adapting or writing some of its most expressive dialogue, coupled with a brilliant handling of actors, Wilder merits consideration as the most effective director of the decade.

The scathing literary quality of Wilder's films and his interest in exposing strong-willed characters are closely paralleled in the films of Joseph Mankiewicz. Like Wilder's *Some Like It Hot*, Mankiewicz's *All about Eve* is an acidic satire that reclaims the conventions of its theatrical drama to suggest its underlying element of self-caricature. Mankiewicz is not as misanthropic as Wilder, and, thus, there is less strain about the successful reunion of the married couples in *A Letter to Three Wives* or in that of his Ibsenian outsider and society in *People Will Talk*. Like Wilder's *Sunset Boulevard*, Mankiewicz's *The Barefoot Contessa* is another in a long line of fifties movies attacking Hollywood, among other communication industries (*A Face in the Crowd*, *Sweet Smell of Success*, *The Great Man*, *A Star Is Born*). One of the film's more intriguing features concerns Bogey's characterization as the compassionate, wizened press agent. As the least virtuous hero of the star system, Bogey's posthumous iconization rests mainly on his work in the forties. *Casablanca* is an archetype of the period through its adroit intertwining of social concern and individual heroism. The film's charm lies in the redoubtable romantic luster of its stars and the luminous, estranged tone in the decor and lighting of the nightclub. Ingrid Bergman, Claude Rains, Paul Henreid, Peter Lorre, and Sydney Greenstreet enliven a didactic drama in which Bogey's Rick is the most memorable of characters because his involvement in the film's anti-Nazi rhetoric does not undercut his resonance as an outsider, as cool in his dealings with the Nazis as he is with Ingrid Bergman. But after *The Big Sleep*, *The Treasure of the Sierra Madre*, and *Key Largo*, Bogey's impenetrable tough guy is transformed into a defender of our laws, an aging, incorruptible moral agent who was really one of us all along. In *The African Queen*, *The Enforcer*, *The Harder They Fall*, *Beat the Devil*, and *The Barefoot Contessa*, Bogey's previous distance from the moral righteousness of the good guys and the pernicious behavior of the bad guys is diminished: his craggy appearance, the more cautious movements, and less frenetic speech suggest that there is little room for Bogey's outsider in the fifties. It is time to choose sides; while his wiseacre riverboat captain in *The African Queen* acquiesces to the spinsterish gloss of Katharine Hepburn in one of the more contrived screen romances, his weatherbeaten con man in *Beat the Devil* is won over by the energy and beauty of Jennifer Jones.

If Bogey's romantic outsider remains the most appealing of Hollywood's film rebels of the forties, Marlon Brando's heroic anti-hero exists as a vivid expression of the thread of alienation, of reticence and unhappiness, of nonconformity and a profound distrust of social conventions that began appearing in the late forties and that would prove a major force in the next three decades of the American film. While Brando's Stanley Kowalski, a wild, raging bull, unleashes a primitivism in the depiction of male sexuality, the recent characterizations of Richard Gere (*Looking for Mr. Goodbar, Bloodbrothers, Yanks*), with his garbled speech and highly charged physical mannerisms or the fragile romantic identity and relationship of Robert De Niro and Christopher Walken in *The Deer Hunter* underscore the contemporaneousness of Brando's destructive male animal. His illiterate yet sensitive Terry Malloy and his characterization of Emiliano Zapata as a brooding, failed Marxist revolutionary are further examples of the poignancy and pertinency of his anxious primitive. Brando's face became the paradigmatic symbol of individual unrest that a generation of film, theater, and television actors would use as its model. The slow, reflective tilts of his head, the ripples of movement along his eyebrows or lips that express his lingering self-doubts and preface his explosions of violence use the geography of his face, not merely as an accompaniment to his speech, but because of the thinness of his voice, his reedy tone, and his grappling with the simplest expression of confusion and pain as a centralizing motif to the psychological exposition of the mentality and behavior of a primitive. His influence would range from such an ephemeral yet mesmeric figure as Elvis Presley's angelic androgyny in *Love Me Tender* and *Jailhouse Rock* to the more poetic presence of De Niro, Nicholson, and Pacino, three actors in the seventies and eighties vying for recognition as heirs to Brando's mask of discontent.

With its emphasis on flawed characters, *film noir* prefigured many of the changes in the role models and moral resolutions in both action films and dramatic adaptations. The raw, physical persona of Burt Lancaster, Robert Mitchum, and Kirk Douglas attest to this new appreciation of the male anti-hero. Whereas Lancaster's characterizations vary from the tragic *film noir* protagonists of *The Killers, Criss Cross,* and *I Walk Alone* and his lively involvement in roles made famous by Douglas Fairbanks in *The Crimson Pirate* and *The Flame and the Arrow* to his more wooden dramatic interpretations in *From Here to Eternity, Come Back Little Sheba, All My Sons,* and *The Rose Tattoo,* the murkier film presence of Robert Mitchum (*The Night of the Hunter, Cape Fear*) and Kirk Douglas (*Champion, I Walk Alone, Ace in the Hole*) repudiates the manly appeal of Gable with elements of violence, sexual domination, and a general sense of social perfidy. These qualities undergo a poetic transfiguration in the films of Brando, Montgomery Clift, and James Dean owing to more expressive roles and their more acute interpretation of social nonconformity. Clift's face, like Brando's, suggests a sexual vulnerability and his tentativeness in fulfilling his social identity. His role as the priest in *I Confess* is noteworthy for the use of Clift's highly expressive, troubled gaze in defining the tentativeness of his spiritual faith in his relationship with Anne Baxter. Playing opposite Elizabeth Taylor's melodramatic heroine in *Raintree County, A Place in the Sun,* and *Suddenly Last Summer,* he fulfills her erotic wanderlust while expressing his own social ambivalence in his wandering eye and pale, anxious appearance. He is both an idealist and a misfit, leaving unresolved the question of which sprang first.

Dean's sense of the cool, remembered in numerous posters that fill the college dorms in the movies of the sixties, makes him a more transparent, tenuous figure than either Brando or Clift. His tragic death limited his film characterizations to that of the youth at bay, adrift from his parents (*Rebel without a Cause*), or rebelling against his lack of social identity (*Giant, East of Eden*). His good looks invite a more straightforward response and create a more concrete, romantic allure than Brando's misshapen hulk or Clift's more poetic, distraught figure. Owing to the paucity of his film work, he has become a definite icon of postwar delinquency, less self-pitying than Brando and more independent than Clift. His films show him in search of the right girl or mother figure; in the one film image of Dean as an older man—the dissipated oil baron of *Giant*—the tragedy of an alienated youth has marked him for life. Each of his characterizations are distinct in thought and technique, and although Paul Newman's mythic figure of the sixties reminded audiences of Dean's romantic, self-destructive antagonist, we are fortunate that Hollywood's dream merchants selected Dean over Newman for the lead role in *Rebel without a Cause*.

The estranged anti-heroes of Marlon Brando, Montgomery Clift, and James Dean underline the often overlooked role of contemporary adult literature in Hollywood. If Hollywood was incapable of absorbing the novels of Saul Bellow—perhaps the most distinct voice in the literature of the fifties of a mood of existential despair blending with the more traditional regional realism and comic pathos of American novelists—it showed no reluctance in adapting the poetic voice of alienation and dramatic expressionism distinguished in the postwar American theater by playwrights like Tennessee Williams, Carson McCullers, William Inge, Arthur Miller, and Robert Anderson. Dramatic and literary adaptations have long been one of Hollywood's chief sources, but the reasons for this interplay change continually. For example, Hollywood's fixation on the American musical theater during the first half-dozen years of the sound film exemplified the lack of ingenuity of Hollywood producers in meeting the challenge of the sound film; it was hardly the expression of a prevailing cultural sensibility. At best, a musical like *Rio Rita* or the annual compilation of music-hall bits in the *Paramount on Parade* series are valuable documents of once-famous productions or routines. Since Sarah Bernhardt's performance in *Queen Elizabeth*, the medium has functioned as an archive not only of fresh, imaginative works and the more obvious social-science interests of documentarians, but also of stars and productions that may gain little added resonance on film. At least they survive.

In the case of the postwar American theater and its relationship to contemporary moviemaking trends, a striking affinity is manifested between the two in their flawed, ambivalent protagonists and their derisive attitude to traditional morality and institutions. While the *film noir* of the forties exposed and exploited the ambiguous psychological tensions of self and society, the postwar American theater fulfilled a similar expressionist discontent with the social malaise of Miller and Inge and the desperate cries of loneliness and frustration in Williams,

Anderson, and McCullers. Clearly, the film work of Brando, Clift, and Dean is not coexpressive with these dramatic voices. Some of their best films animate the dreams and anxieties of a different period. Though many if not the majority of these original dramas become static, lugubrious films, they give expression not only to a new voice in the American literary scene, but also prefigure the style of teledrama, the dominant, popular dramatic voice of the fifties on the stage, television, and film.

Teledrama refers to plays written for television, made famous by such programs as "Studio One" and "Philco Playhouse," and the work of Paddy Chayefsky. Though this genre encompasses many of the realist trappings of the American theater of the thirties, the focus is not so much on the deleteriousness of the social environment. Chayefsky's characters evoke a more personal, emotional despair in attempting to ameliorate their miserable social condition through a close personal attachment. A teledrama like *Marty* appears as a cross between the desperate anguish of the contemporary American theater and the more romantic trimmings of soap opera. The introspection of both the postwar theater and teledrama and the concern with everyday figures and the serial-like development in both soap opera and teledrama underscore their stylistic and thematic proximity. The relevance of teledrama, however, is more apparent in a sociological context than an aesthetic one. With television implanted in the American home as the most accessible form of entertainment and information, teledrama—with its roots in the American realist theater of the thirties and its equally strong affinity with soap opera and its serial format, its paucity of settings, its close-up camera angles, and its middle-class protagonists—looms as the most significant sociological-cultural hybrid in television programming of the fifties. If such terms as "escapism" and "entertainment" are characteristic of the American film during the Depression, one can then point to television as the most evocative popular medium of the fifties and to teledrama, with its ties to both our theatrical heritage and film expressionism, as the most paradigmatic, popular dramatic genre of the decade. This is not to posit the hegemony of television over the movies or that of the writer over the director, but to expand our understanding of how popular art forms in America respond to the most widely held values and to the paramount crises in society.

But instead of attempting to pigeonhole postwar American society with such terms as "McCarthyism" or the "White Negro," the "organization man" or "teledrama," the telltale clue to the nature of American popular culture lies in its structural and intellectual democratic uniformity. Because television, like the film industry, is inextricably committed to public support of its form and content and because both media invite a communal response—although television adds significant extensions on this public bond through its placement in the home—both television and film assume similar identities within our democratic matrix. There was a stronger imprint of realism and of older dramatic devices in the teledrama of the fifties. Yet the undeniable social thrust of the postwar American film, combined with the long-standing popular identity of the film medium, leads one to correlate the underlying sociological design of film and television drama. This proposition is not offered as a simplification of the wide-ranging economic, moral, and technical considerations that influenced the industry and art of Hollywood or of television. There are several impressive films and styles in the American cinema of the fifties—the flowering of John Ford's work in the western; the rigorous epics of George Stevens; and the vibrant, kinetic musical collaborations of Stanley Donen, Michael Kidd, and Gene Kelly—that are far removed from the psychotherapy worked on the American character in postwar theater and television. But if popular culture is a primary component of the film experience, teledrama signifies a decisive development in popular culture through the social, thematic, and stylistic proximity of film and television.

## Boomerang–Touch of Evil

In the crime film of the late forties, two trends appear to dominate. One is the genre's increasing realism, evidenced either by location shooting or the use of documentary footage. *The Naked City*, *Kiss of Death*, and *The House on 92nd Street* are among the first examples of a style sustained in the fifties in such films as *On the Waterfront*, *The Phenix City Story*, and *Riot in Cell Block 11*. The second trend is characterized by an ambience of violence, elaborated in the primitivism of Robert Aldrich (*Kiss Me Deadly*, *Attack!*, *The Big Knife*); the paranoia of Samuel Fuller (*Pickup on South Street*, *The Steel Helmet*, *Shock Corridor*); and the grim fatalism of *The Asphalt Jungle*, *The Killing*, and Orson Welles's *Touch of Evil*, the high point of fifties nihilism.

The realism of Elia Kazan's first crime-film entry, *Boomerang*, a facile, behind-the-scenes look at a police investigation, derives from its character study of Dana Andrews's idealistic district attorney. The film's linear treatment of the apprehension of a suspect plays like a journalist's recreation of police work, substituting the nuts and bolts of a criminal investigation for a more romantic study of the criminal outsider. *On the Waterfront* utilizes a far richer framework, juxtaposing the redemption of Brando's strong-arm lackey against the congressional investigation of racketeering in the waterfront union. Boris Kaufman's exteriors combine a muscular realism with a poetic look at the dreary waterfront locations. The film's dynamic intensity, which centers on Brando's resolution of his feelings toward Rod Steiger's tentative brother, Lee J. Cobb's tyrannical union boss, and Eva Marie Saint's crusading heroine, imbues the commonplace outlines of the first postwar documentary-type crime films with a classic, dramatic humanism.

*The Phenix City Story*, like *On the Waterfront*, is concerned with the menace of criminal control of city hall. The film astutely intertwines elements of newsreel reporting and dramatic urgency in delineating Richard Kiley's transformation from a reserved, apolitical teacher who, following the murder of his father who had worked as editor of the local paper, runs successfully for district attorney. The film conveys a journalistic immediacy in showing the mob's murderous hold on the town; the brilliantly underplayed suggestion of terror in the meeting between Edward Andrews's mob chieftain and John McIntire's editor reveals that director Phil Karlson's strength as an action director builds from static, ominous, dramatic confrontations, as in the hotel-room scene between Larry Gates and Richard Conte in *The Brothers Rico* and in the erotic underpinnings involving Brian Keith and Ginger Rogers in *Tight Spot*. Karlson's recent immersion into the dramatic populism of *Walking Tall* results in the extravagant, Diego Rivera–like mosaic of an avenging body politic; *The Phenix City Story*, however, fulfills its realistic fervor through the social awakening of Kiley's avenger.

In *Kiss Me Deadly, Attack!*, and *The Big Knife* the tightly drawn social settings do not allow for the personal or social catharsis of *On the Waterfront* or *The Phenix City Story*. The claustrophobic environs of *Attack!*, in which a small group of soldiers are trapped in a town caught between the fire of retreating Germans and the advancing Americans, and *The Big Knife*, which transpires in the living room of a Hollywood actor who confronts his studio head with his desire to leave the business, are as anxiety-ridden as any theater or television drama of the fifties. Unlike Karlson's films, whose virulence is expressed in the repression of the characters' feelings, Aldrich's films present characters at the end of their tether who cannot hide their fear or anger. Whereas *Kiss Me Deadly* extends the violence of Mickey Spillane by treating Ralph Meeker's private eye as just another sordid inhabitant of Spillane's gutter world, piling up expressions of violence the way a marine biologist might record the activity of sharks, *Attack!* and *The Big Knife* document each painful step in the characters' descent into madness until the final, inexorable explosion of death. There are no heroes or redeeming social statements: Aldrich has identified both the bunker and the movie colony as areas marked by the time bombs of his characters' psyches. They are proximate movie analogues to the guilt-ridden dramas featured in postwar theater and television, demolishing their protagonists as the most diseased figures in a world past redemption.

Fuller has become one of the key cult heroes of contemporary film criticism, yet his least effective and most original works are representative of traditional stylizations of psychological unrest in postwar film, theater, and television. *The Steel Helmet* is a moody teledrama involving a group of American soldiers who have captured a North Korean agent; its single setting dramatizes their tension with the same hackneyed, psychological formulas one finds in television and theatrical productions. With the exception of the opening scene in *The Naked Kiss*, Fuller's small-town psychodrama interprets its sexual malaise in the clumsy, overwrought fashion of *The Steel Helmet. The Crimson Kimono, Pickup on South Street*, and *Underworld U.S.A.* are far more successful because of their empathetic delineation of the characters' precarious emotional stability as a reflection of their sordid backgrounds. The most riveting encounter in *The Crimson Kimono* concerns a Japanese-American police lieutenant and the girl friend of his partner, alone in his apartment. An emblematic Fuller scene, employing a minimum of cuts, their attraction to each other is communicated through their defensive emotional postures; one is drawn into the scene and inside their feelings through what at first seems a prolonged, superfluous preface to the final shoot-out in Little Tokyo. In *Underworld U.S.A.* and *Pickup on South Street* extensive, intensely close-up encounters are effectively applied to depict the growing bond between Cliff Robertson and Dolores Dorn as they rest in bed and that of Richard Widmark and Jean Peters as they lie in his waterfront hammock. Other equally moving dramatic statements explode with the characters' violent instincts, like Widmark's discovery that the gang with which he bargains over the stolen microfilm is a group of Communist agents. Fuller's settings and protagonists differ from the middle-class terrain of American theater and television, but his techniques, like those of Aldrich and Karlson, underline their common psychological origin and exposition.

The *Asphalt Jungle*, *The Killing*, and *Touch of Evil* document a similar note of fatalism in more conventional settings. The cast of *The Asphalt Jungle* is treated as nostalgic, warmed-over clichés, each one made dramatically credible in the performances of Sterling Hayden, Jean Hagen, Louis Calhern, Sam Jaffe, James Whitmore, Anthony Caruso, and Marilyn Monroe. It is not the caper that engages the audience, but how each character's personal flaws lead to its failure. Orson Welles's stated preference for *The Killing* may lie in director Stanley Kubrick's removing these melodramatic conventions through the mechanization of each person's role. Yet the clichés remain, whether in the character of Marie Windsor's femme fatale or in the more questionable use of the dog as a symbol of fate. Its pinpoint dramatic clarity and documentary trimmings make it a more contemporary work than *The Asphalt Jungle*. One is not forced, however, to decide which is superior; each shows the influence of a different period and style: *The Asphalt Jungle*, with its roots in the romantic pessimism of hard-boiled literature and *film noir*, and the caper dynamics of *The Killing*, a precursor of the abstraction in the action films of the late sixties and seventies.

*Touch of Evil* can be seen as the culmination of *film noir* in the fifties for two reasons. One is that it is the most accomplished example of the techniques of violence in the genre. The second reason concerns the film's treatment of the loss of innocence, a motif central to both Welles's career and *film noir*. Kane's empire builder, Joseph Cotten's inventor in *The Magnificent Ambersons*, and Welles's Hank Quinlan are idealists who lose sight of their original dreams by pursuing them in society. If *Citizen Kane* can be considered the progenitor of *film noir* with its baroque camerawork, expressionist settings, and its essentially romantic viewpoint of an idealist whose dreams are corrupted by his own paradoxical nature, then the two idealized relationships in *Touch of Evil* involving newlyweds Charlton Heston and Janet Leigh and that of Quinlan and his aide (played by Joseph Calleia) ironically expose the tragic repercussions of love and justice.

In the films or Brando, Clift, and Dean, it is their expressiveness as actors that denotes society's tragic flaws; the films of Fuller and Aldrich present similar anxiety-ridden characters whose loss of innocence predates the film. Only Hitchcock can approximate the reality of terror in Welles's *Touch of Evil*, but Hitchcock's protagonists are too withdrawn and too locked in their own netherworlds for one to infer a social parable. In *Touch of Evil* a defense of Quinlan's attitude to the law is reflected in the nature of physical reality, a Grand Guignol landscape that erupts with the fury of a smoldering volcano. One sequence alone indicates the film's transcendent perversity—Quinlan's trapping and murder of Akim Tamiroff's local crime boss in the hotel room. Their gritty fight is an original bit of sordid melodrama involving two aging, decrepit figures: the torturous, staccato cutting with its barrage of close-ups and shock cuts jolts the viewer like a succession of lightning quick jabs. Quinlan leaves, only to be trapped by his failure to take his cane, the conclusive proof that he has had to manufacture in his defense of the law.

### The Big Heat–Psycho

Fritz Lang's best work in the fifties (*The Big Heat, Human Desire, While the City Sleeps*) combined with the most expressive of Alfred Hitchcock films of the decade (*Strangers on a Train, I Confess, Vertigo, Psycho*) offers a comprehensive picture of the psychological ambivalence of *film noir*. Lang's earlier excursions into the grim underworld of erotic fantasy in *The Woman in the Window* and *Scarlet Street* were among the forties' most nihilistic statements about wayward behavior. Whereas the majority of *film noir* classics involve the conventional romantic anti-heroes of crime literature, Edward G. Robinson plays a dreary, middle-class innocent who is unable to cope with his subconscious impulses outside his home and job. In *The Big Heat* Lang returns to the classic crime formula of police and criminals. Gloria Grahame replaces Joan Bennett as the femme fatale, but Glenn Ford's protagonist does not replay Robinson's role of the naive everyman. As the police officer and returning army veteran in *The Big Heat* and *Human Desire*, he is better able to confront the violence around him. Ford's plan of revenge in *The Big Heat* centers on the characters of Grahame and Lee Marvin (the latter correctly identified by Hunter Thompson as the true embodiment of a motorcycle gang member in *The Wild One*), two wild swingers whose fatalistic relationship leads to the demise of the underworld's control of the city. *Human Desire* is also charged with this deadly combination of eroticism and violence; the setting changes from a corrupt city government to the environs of a small town characterized by the hellish sounds and visual arabesques created by the railroad on which Ford works. The social cancer is not identified in the figure of a criminal, but in Ford's adulterous affair with Grahame's housewife and the character of Broderick Crawford's husband, unable to satisfy his wife erotically or with more conventional means of social ascension. It is a pulp-literature triangle, but Lang's uncompromising treatment of their romantic dreams and tragic shortcomings gives the film a social expressiveness it might otherwise lack. *While the City Sleeps* combines elements of *The Big Heat* and *Human Desire*, using an urban communications empire and its Machiavellian manipulators as the social backdrop surrounding the pursuit of a sex maniac. The duplicity exhibited by the characters offered a top job in the conglomerate if they break the story of the criminal's arrest presents a picture of society as sordid as that of *M*. Whereas the earlier film established a parallel between the psychology and methods of the police and criminal underworld through a deliberate crosscutting technique, *While the City Sleeps* defines its social cancer in the glib, amoral behavior of the power elite.

The psychological proximity of hero and villain is one of the central themes in Alfred Hitchcock's films of the fifties. Unlike his most famous English suspense films like *The Thirty-Nine Steps* and *The Lady Vanishes* which innocuously flirt with elements of comedy and terror, his work from *Strangers on a Train* through *Psycho* is far more dramatically compressed. *Strangers on a Train* transforms Patricia Highsmith's mordant, introspective study of a doppelgänger into a black-comedy portrait of an innocent protagonist, who, locked in a subterranean world by his adulterous wife and a psychotic traveling companion, escapes not only unharmed, but with the girl of his dreams. Hitchcock's adroit use of Robert Burks's light-dark lighting motifs surrounding the characters of Guy and Bruno introduces elements of mischief and humor that undercut Guy's attempt to clear himself. While the lavish decor of *Dial M for Murder* and the conventional character and plot delineation of *Rear Window* reveal Hitchcock's enduring affinity with the theatrical and literary transparencies of the crime film, the delicate balance of comic understatement in Ernest Lehman's script and the proximity of danger communicated in Hitchcock's direction of *North by Northwest* undergo a far more penetrating treatment than in his work in the English cinema. There is no apparent reluctance, however, to enmesh the viewer in a web of terror in *I Confess*, *Vertigo*, and *Psycho*. Both *I Confess* and *Vertigo* present unusually fragile protagonists in Montgomery Clift's cleric, who must reexamine his own feelings toward a former lover while being a chief suspect in a murder, and in Jimmy Stewart's duped, love-struck innocent. Although Hitchcock admits that the basic premise of *I Confess*, in which a priest hears a murderer's confession but refuses to act on it, is dramatically erroneous, the film subtly externalizes Clift's anxiety in its psychological cross section of city life. *Vertigo* is a more poetic work in which Hitchcock conveys Stewart's fascination with Kim Novak through a series of intermediate shots that identify her as an illusory, dreamlike figure. The film's repressed, methodical, highly expressive pacing becomes a reflection of Stewart's neurosis, as he forces Novak to play out the consequences of her deceit and his love.

*Psycho* marks the culmination of Hitchcock's study of terror and madness. The film's relentless entrapment of Janet Leigh's confused heroine, sustaining a style of paranoia as vivid as any of the great German expressionist films of the twenties, makes it the ideal Hitchcock film to be applauded by both film specialist and general moviegoer. The strength of the film does not lie in arcane visual motifs, but in Hitchcock's refusal to diffuse the film's nihilistic treatment of loneliness in the character of Leigh's embezzler and Perkins's psychotic. If the fifties remain fundamentally a movie decade about estrangement, then the maturation of Hitchcock's art from *Strangers on a Train* through *Psycho* leads us to consider this group of films not only as Hitchcock's most artistically expressive, but also as the most profound of the decade.

## The Gunfighter–The Incredible Shrinking Man

The western, like the crime film, is infused with a similar moral ambiguity resulting in such didactic works as *The Gunfighter, High Noon*, the series of Budd Boetticher–Randolph Scott films, and the more ambivalent, violent psychodramas of *The Furies* and *Johnny Guitar*. *The Gunfighter* and *High Noon* are not so much isolated examples of the anti-western as they signify a change in the treatment of the West as a pastoral to a period marked by the self-introspection of postwar literature and art. They exhume the romantic iconography of western mythology with equally straightforward examples of virtue and villainy, the major departure being that the heroic gunslingers of Gregory Peck and Gary Cooper secure the honor of the West without the communal support that inspired earlier defenders of the law and masculine virtue. They initiate a reappraisal of western mythology, presenting the first examples in a long line of glum antiheroes who will survive until the infamous spaghetti westerns and their artistic transfiguration by the shaggy-dog archetypes of Sergio Leone's *The Good The Bad and the Ugly*.

*The Furies* and *Johnny Guitar* displace the moralism of *The Gunfighter* and *High Noon* with a primeval sense of Freudian politics. *The Furies* is the less artistic, with its overly compressed camera angles exaggerating the erotic tension between Walter Huston's imperious patriarch and Barbara Stanwyck's delinquent daughter. *Johnny Guitar* juxtaposes the erotic rivalry between Joan Crawford and Mercedes McCambridge to a richer dramatic mosaic of the social miscreants of western folklore. The characters are not the egregious symbols of good and evil that have long permeated the western, but evoke a mood of nonconformity similar to Nicholas Ray's romanticized study of social misfits in *Rebel without a Cause*. Compared to earlier, traditional Hollywood portraits of outsiders, the tenuous dramatic identity of the characters in *Johnny Guitar* is refreshing and real, but Ray was not enough of an artist to refine the conventions under attack. The film offers several exciting pictorial groupings—the lone figure of Crawford cornered in her saloon, the elliptical coach ride with Hayden and Crawford, and the lynching scene with Ward Bond's darkly clad vigilantes and Crawford in her white dress. One is not certain, however, if more credit is due Ray or cinematographer Harry Stradling. *Johnny Guitar* is sufficiently nasty, but there remains a lack of subtlety in the character of Hayden's guitar-toting loner and in the degree of sordid behavior Ray discovers in his collection of western drifters. If the trend in contemporary film criticism is to upgrade esoteric stylizations, then I would cite *Terror in a Texas Town* as a more radical example of the neurotic western, in which Hayden's avenger carries a harpoon into the final gunfight.

One can agree with numerous admirers of Ray's work who see him as a quintessential director of postwar anxiety. *In a Lonely Place* meets all the requirements of a classic *film noir*: the symbolic Hollywood backdrop and the conflicting expressions of love and hate, control and madness exhibited by Humphrey Bogart and augmented by Ray's lighting and camera angles. But, like his *Rebel without a Cause*—a studied, teledramatic treatment of adolescent chagrin in CinemaScope—Ray treats his characters' ambivalence in an extremely convoluted, melodramatically streamlined fashion. His relevance among the writers and directors of teledrama can be acknowledged without accepting the inflated conclusions articulated by his biographers.

A more conventional but far more coherent picture of the savagery of frontier life permeates Anthony Mann's westerns. They are dramatically simplified allegories that pinpoint the recurrent dramatic stages and tensions of the classic western. With the exception of the shoot-out in the hotel, each of the major clashes in *Bend of the River* is set in an isolated, exposed river encampment, a primitive arena for the defense of the western settlers by Jimmy Stewart and Arthur Kennedy, concluding in their gunfight against each other. The transcendent beauty and dangers of his virgin backgrounds and the supporting cast of scarred losers and anti-heroes give his films the scope of a prehistoric epic; by simply changing the dress and artifacts of his films, they could be set in ancient Greece or the Middle Ages. Some of his Technicolor films show an incongruity between their settings and the drama—the soft, warm, azurelike exteriors of New Mexico and the psychologically exposed frictions involving Stewart, Kennedy, and Alex Nicol in *The Man from Laramie*. *Winchester '73* may be his most cogent work owing to the stronger Gothic undercurrents of its interior compositions and to the unifying metaphor of the gun and its fate in the hands of those striving for its possession. It is the story of the classic West—continuous chases and gun battles surrounding the pursuit of the gun—that is told through the classical symbolism of patricide and revenge.

*Invasion of the Body Snatchers, The Day the Earth Stood Still, It Came from Outer Space,* and *The Incredible Shrinking Man* can be read as social parables concerning the most pertinent crises of the fifties: the pervasiveness of conformity in *Invasion of the Body Snatchers,* the McCarthy-like hostility toward outsiders in *It Came from Outer Space* and *The Day the Earth Stood Still,* and man's recognition of his insignificance in *The Incredible Shrinking Man,* one of the most allegorical of fantasies. Unlike the German fantasy classics which used their distorted backgrounds to symbolize the victimization of man by a social or supernatural force, these films depict society's Babel-like helplessness at a time when vast strides in space research are being made. *The Day the Earth Stood Still* and *It Came from Outer Space* most closely resemble the style of teledrama; the alien being inspires the social friction between a sympathetic scientist and the most menacing social forces. *Invasion of the Body Snatchers* and *The Incredible Shrinking Man* are more stylistic treatments of the paranoia in postwar art; both films center around the protagonist's increasing isolation and helplessness. They play as more straightforward examples of terror, and if one is inclined to relate them to other socially expressive films, future generations may be less wont to take our moralizing for granted.

## Dead End–The Best Years of Our Lives

The references to *Citizen Kane* as the archetype of the expressionism of the forties and the anxiety of the fifties exemplify the dangers in simplfying the tendencies in an industry and art like the American film. The romantic fatalism surrounding Kane's exploits is, in fact, a remarkable precursor of the paradoxes that would characterize many idealists and anti-heroes of the postwar film. The style of the film, drawing on the talents of Herman Mankiewicz's sardonic reading of the press, the jarring editing maneuvers of Robert Wise, the plastic lighting configurations and panfocus range of Gregg Toland's camera, creates a baroque commentary on the film's American themes of fame and fortune. The energy, the florid expanses and textures of the baroque, achieves a harmonious cinematic manifestation through the pervasive mood of unrest inspired by Kane's megalomania and sustained through the cinematic subterfuges of Welles and Toland, the art direction of Perry Ferguson, and the optical reprinting of Linwood Dunn and Vernon Walker. In *Dead End*, one of Toland's first experiments with the faster lens and film stock made available in the thirties, his selective focus distorts the characters in the background, sometimes at a distance of ten to fifteen feet, never more than fifty feet from the foreground action, in a style that presages the more abstracted compositions in *Citizen Kane*. Unlike one of his mentors, George Barnes, who used a panfocus range as a symbol of the encroaching darkness of city life in the film adaptation of Elmer Rice's *Street Scene* six years earlier, the psychologically charged compositions of *Dead End* remain an anomaly in the American film. While Toland characterized his style as one of realism, one notes that the play's juxtaposition of its ghetto setting to the skyscrapers is translated by a matted background in the film adaptation. In the case of *Citizen Kane*, Toland's realist claims must be considered in relation to the fact that over 50 percent of the footage in *Citizen Kane* results from the lab work of Linwood Dunn and Vernon Walker.

Toland's use of the faster lens and emulsions was not restricted to the theatrical realism of *Dead End* or the baroque expressionism of *Citizen Kane*. In *The Long Voyage Home* and *Wuthering Heights* it is not the extended depth of field that is emphasized, but the plastic, classical iconography of his effusive compositions. The "luminism" which Edgar Richardson saw as the predominant influence of Dutch painters on American landscape, portraiture, and genre painting is reflected in the traditional, dramatic integrity of Toland's lighting. O'Neill's weary, meditative sailors lying on the deck or in their bunks and Olivier's Heathcliff peering through the windows and discovering the dense social configurations of the ball are characterized by a classic pictorial and dramatic harmony. Toland's last effort as a cinematographer for Robert Sherwood's postwar tearjerker *The Best Years of Our Lives* can be seen as a testament to the pictorial realism of Hollywood film studios. Several scenes, drawing on the talents of both Toland and production designer George Jenkins—the opening terminal scene, the exterior airport sequence involving Dana Andrews walking amid the discarded airplanes, several shots of the department store where Andrews returns for a job—make use of the depth of field to dramatize Andrews's symbolic anonymity. One scene provides an adroit psychological commentary through its foreground and background images as Fredric March, after confronting Andrews with his advances to his daughter, stands in the right-hand corner by the piano in Hoagy Carmichael's bar while in the background, some twenty feet away, Andrews, in the left-hand corner, telephones Teresa Wright, March's daughter. The diminutive background figure of Andrews and March's reflective foreground presence present a physical and psychological insight through the distancing effects of the shot's composition. The film then seems more noteworthy for its stationary dramatic setups and Toland's genre-study punctuations. In the final scene, the wedding of Harold Russell's paraplegic and Cathy O'Donnell, Toland makes a surprising, symbolic use of a northern-light aureole atop the two figures of the reconciled Andrews and Wright. The luminism one associates with Dutch and American genre studies and portraiture is now incorporated into postwar movie realism.

Succeeding technological advances, however, found Hollywood returning to a more archaic form of drama and filmmaking. In his study of the old masters at The Metropolitan Museum of Art undertaken for Magnifilm, Lorenzo del Riccio discovered an aspect ratio of 1.85:1. The proximity of the aspect ratio Riccio found in the old masters and that of the wide screen underscores the classical ideals common to both. The major change in the rectangular wide-screen productions of the fifties from the previous 1.33:1 aspect ratio lies in its ability to duplicate the 160-degree lateral vision of the naked eye. The objective properties of the wide screen at first diminished the supporting definition of extended camera tracks, close-ups, and camera setups. Original studies of camera movement in a wide-screen format recommended a two-thirds decrease in their application because of the accompanying fuzziness in the background images. While there would be a significant curtailment of close-ups because of the truncated appearance of the characters in a two-shot or a one-shot, camera setups were also radically reduced; in several major productions of the thirties, such as *Anthony Adverse* and *Les Misérables*, there were more than a thousand camera setups; in *The Robe*, the first CinemaScope production, there were some two hundred. One's absorption in a film as a pictorial narrative is featured rather than a realistic treatment of the story line. However, there were exceptions to this static, overly pictorial style of filmmaking. One of the magical sequences of film art occurs in the last twelve minutes of *Some Came Running* when the artifices of the wide-screen compositions come alive with the dramatic denouement; the continuous movement of the figures of Frank Sinatra, Dean Martin, and Shirley MacLaine is enhanced by a beautifully executed, poetically expressive, moving camera. The painting has been brought to life without reducing the symbolic effects of the colors and configurations.

But this was an exception. The numerous wide-screen musicals, romances, and historical sagas exaggerate the importance of the composition through their theatrically pictorial construction. The lavish, lush, and more than slightly ludicrous scene painting of Leon Shamroy at 20th Century-Fox and Robert Surtees at MGM became Hollywood's alternative to television's small screen and the contemporaneousness of postwar theatrical and television drama. It is the single most conspicuous example in the history of Hollywood of the promotion of its technical resources and its disdain for contemporary dramatic realities; one is tempted to search for an encompassing term like *film noir* or "expressionism" to characterize the stylistic currents in postwar filmmaking, but there is no such congruency about its technological developments. While the fifties is recognized as a period of discord and depression, it also generated such triumphant filmmaking styles as the musical flowering at MGM; the epic nationalism of George Stevens's *Giant*, *A Place in the Sun*, and *Shane*; and the vibrant romanticism of John Ford's *Wagonmaster*, *She Wore a Yellow Ribbon*, *The Searchers*, *The Wings of Eagles*, *The Horse Soldiers*, and *The Quiet Man*.

*An American in Paris–The Quiet Man*

During the initial mastery of the sound film in the late twenties, Hollywood producers turned to the Broadway stage as a natural source for the newly increased potential of the film medium. It was, at best, a compromise between the neutralized power of the camera and the all-singing, all-dancing resources of the musical; at worst, it was one of the most soporific chapters of filmmaking in the American film. Because of the necessity of blimping the camera in sound-free booths, there could be little movement or dynamic involvement in the stage drama; it would be several years before Busby Berkeley or the Astaire-Rogers musicals would work their magic on the genre. As an interested spectator at the opening of Miles Kreuger's retrospective of the early movie musicals at The Museum of Modern Art, I had hoped to discover the artistry of performers and production numbers that might have transcended the cumbersome nature of their direction on film. Yet I must admit my failure as a film student to endure this festival after two weeks of the most painful, tedious, retrogressive examples of filmmaking that I have encountered. If there is an inherent disproportion between the conventions of musical theater and the dynamics of film, these primitive film musicals passively record the contrivances of the book and the excesses of the performers and design. In a theater, one's eye can delight in the absurdity—ironic or not—of the musical drama by selecting details in the action or background that magnify the fate of the protagonists through the expansiveness of the action or the largess of the design. Once the camera locks us into a set point of view, the self-generated extravagance of the musical drama is lost, and one is forced to respond to the musical as drama with music. One begins to feel like Malcolm McDowell in *A Clockwork Orange*, strapped to a seat, his eyelids forced open, and overwhelmed by repeated examples of violence. There is violence too in these musicals, and if I can offer any movie analogy, it is to the equally painful pornographic films that cauterize their performers' sexuality through the mechanical punctuation of thrust-counterthrust. Although I lost out on discovering some of the interpreters of song and dance of the twenties, after a dozen or so examples of movie anality, I was fearful that I would avail myself of some critical absurdity and, like McDowell, begin to enjoy the pain.

The nature of the success of the Berkeley musicals and those of Astaire-Rogers reveals the profound enervation of their predecessors. The delirious camera movements and grandiose stage configurations in Berkeley's musicals are not a repudiation of the conventions of the musical theater, but a celebration of their inspired, cosmic silliness. They contain some of the finest moments of filmed musical theater; their fragmentation of the theater stage is the first step in their apotheosis of musical theater as a cultural alternative to the equally precarious fantasies of surrealist literature and art. The Astaire-Rogers musicals incorporate several elements of Berkeley's phantasmagoria with the airplane sequence in *Flying down to Rio* or the Continental number in *The Gay Divorcee*. Even in an imperfect production like *Follow the Fleet*, one is continually swept up in the razzle-dazzle of the production numbers and by the ability, through involved camera setups and artful editing, to expand the pleasures of these production numbers on film. In their most accomplished efforts, like *Top Hat* and *Swing Time*, the fabrications of musical theater are mastered, not to the degree of their transfiguration as in Berkeley's musicals but, in the opposite direction, to support the fabrications of the book through a modestly extended proscenium in the staging of dance numbers specifically set in a theater or the stagelike setting of a nightclub.

The MGM musicals of the late forties and fifties, under the aegis of lyricist-turned-producer Arthur Freed, brought together the talents of performers like Astaire, Judy Garland, and Gene Kelly; writers like Betty Comden and Adolph Green; and choreographic talents like Kelly, Michael Kidd, and Gower Champion. But they often duplicated many of the problems in the movie musicals of the thirties. Vincente Minnelli's work as stage director at Radio City Music Hall made him naturally sympathetic to the dramatic realities of the stage story, and his films underscore both the inherent virtues and limitations of a film style transposed from the theater. In *An American in Paris*, there is the Berkeleyan tendency to physical transcendence in the final ballet number, where the gorgeous physical textures are brought to life by the sweeping camera movements; it is only during this stage fantasy that Minnelli attempts to fulfill the cosmic expansiveness of the music, dance, and design. Major sections of *An American in Paris*, like *Kismet* and *Brigadoon*, his two outright failures of the fifties, are suffocated by the straightforward conventions of musical theater. Minnelli was the most literal of the major directors of movie musicals; his cinematic resiliency was analogous to the irony or lack of it in the musicals. *Gigi*, an original screenplay, crystallizes the musical nostalgia through the natural union of the shimmering color tonalities to the picture-book artificies of the story and the theatrical expressiveness of the Lerner-Loewe score. Minnelli, however, was unable to match the magic of *Singin' in the Rain* with *The Band Wagon* because of his fidelity to the story; the sequences that are most happily frenetic, that spill over with the cynicism and artistry of its performers, are those written and choreographed with an eye, ear, and mind for their dynamic exploitation on film: Astaire's opening song-and-dance meditation on 42nd Street, Jack Buchanan's riotous selling of the musical to the financial backers, the brilliant use of dissolves on the paintings to convey the show's original failure, and the montage of the musical production numbers. But several of the interior scenes, especially in the middle section, in which Astaire, Nanette Fabray, and Oscar Levant suffer through Buchanan's domination, replay the clichés of musical theater. There is continuous evidence of Minnelli's decorous scene painting, the short focus sustaining colorful pictures of chagrin among the performers, but they lack the more elaborate self-parody in the major production numbers.

It would be Gene Kelly (usually in collaboration with Stanley Donen and Michael Kidd) and not Minnelli and his revival of nineteenth-century operetta that would prove the true glory of the movie musical of the forties and fifties. *Singin' in the Rain* is probably the most universally acclaimed American film classic of the fifties, and the reason for its wide appeal is that the apotheosis that Berkeley sought in the major production numbers is generated by the screenplay of Comden and Green; the cynicism, the chicanery, and the spoofing of the performers are happily juxtaposed to the absurdity of film production. Kelly is the pivotal figure, a Broadway ham who spices the conventions surrounding O'Connor's gullible partner and Debbie Reynolds's struggling show girl. The tart dialogue is complemented by the musical numbers; they become natural expressions of the giddiness of their stage and movie backdrops. The characters live as song-and-dance performers in the film as well as in our imaginations, magically envisaged in the number that the producer remarks he has trouble visualizing after we have been entertained by ten minutes of production and choreographic whimsy.

Kelly's rake is basic to the story and choreography of these films. Sometimes the action is too frenetic in conveying their more sardonic tone. *On the Town* begins with a fluid collage of New York exteriors. Its most evocative setting, however, is the glittering neon recreation of New York seen atop the Empire State Building at night, a sublime moment of musical theater elevated by the increased splendors of trick photography. But the playacting among the performers soon degenerates into college foppery, nonstop explosions of epileptic convulsions. The choreography of the Kelly–Donen–Kidd musicals, like the less constricted story line, is not as formal in its style and dramatic placement as are the dance numbers in the Astaire-Rogers musicals. Astaire's solos are discourses on the style and elegance of his dapper leading man; together with Rogers, they become images of the grace and vitality of high society. In the Kelly–Donen–Kidd musicals the more dramatically integrated dances result in elastic, gymnastic explosions of character through movement; one example is the opening number of *It's Always Fair Weather* in which Kelly, Kidd, and Dan Dailey race through the streets like a steeplechase. It is a film style that complements the original presence in Broadway theater of Jerome Robbins. Robbins's signature is common to both the vigorous athleticism of Michael Kidd's *Seven Brides for Seven Brothers* and the more disjointed clusters of jerks in Twyla Tharp's interpretations of rock 'n' roll. While George Balanchine used American music and folklore to expand the abstract repertoire of classic ballet, Robbins's *Fancy Free*, like his succeeding works in Broadway theater and classical ballet, experiments with more personal, emotionally fluid lines and movements for his dancers: visions of men and women as living, reflective characters whose vicissitudes of motion suggest those of their emotions. His sailors in *Fancy Free* are not simply instruments of kinetic arabesques, but three guys whose fanciful, self-mocking gymnastic solos are used to impress the girls in the bar. In the Kelly–Donen–Kidd musicals it is the seemingly spontaneous outbursts of a jet-propelled force suddenly inhabiting their spirit that convey the essential freedom in this new style of movement. They have borrowed from the cynicism of postwar literature and art, but there is little doubt about their assumption that the road to salvation lies in their happy feet.

George Stevens's three major works of the fifties—*A Place in the Sun, Shane, Giant*—are among the most formidable examples of epic filmmaking in the American cinema. *A Place in the Sun* is the least distinct of the three, and the ending is putrefied Production Code. Stevens's fidelity to Dreiser is best expressed in the omnipresence of the dark, Germanic lighting, in Montgomery Clift's unease toward Shelley Winters's Zolaesque misfit, and in his understated wonderment in capturing Elizabeth Taylor's delicious debutante. Though none of the major confrontations matches the prologue for its depiction of a drifter caught up in a vast, industrial landscape, Stevens's clipped pacing provides an effective streamlining of Dreiser's Darwinian tome. One of the pure examples of movie allegory, *Shane* sanctifies the most redundant clichés and stereotypes of western folkore: its symbolism is consistent with its rigorous character delineation and piecemeal story line. The film's straightforward didacticism conceives the western landscape as an ideal setting for American ritual in which its simplified plot removes the period charm and social history of traditional movie westerns. Its imperial visual style personifies Hollywood's reserved, republican attitude toward the art and morality of the West; it is both an anodyne to the embittered western fables of the fifties and a celebration of the archetypes of western literature, painting, and moviemaking.

In *Giant* the sensual, majestic dissolves during the train journey, the long shots of the Texas plain suggesting both its menace and beauty, the elaborate interiors marked by the handsome varnish of the antiques and the heroic imprint of family life, the prosaic picture of alienation surrounding the isolated figure of James Dean at the banquet—are textbook examples of film art. *Giant* loses as much in dramatic expressiveness as it gains in pictorial splendor from Rock Hudson, while the anguish-turned-malevolence of James Dean more than compensates for Elizabeth Taylor's melodramatics. The shortcomings in narrative and dramatic characterization and the richness of camerawork and composition in Stevens's films underline an inherent dichotomy in Hollywood moviemaking that only Griffith successfully resolved through the discovery of classic literary and pictorial motifs in the kinetic, psychological impetus of the silent film.

While the majority of postwar westerns effuse the violence and psychological alienation of contemporary theatrical and television drama, John Ford continues to distinguish its heroism, camaraderie, and stately pictorialism. Ben Johnson's initial meeting with Ward Bond in *Wagonmaster*, as he leans against a fence while cutting a piece of wood, is a masterly rendering of two men sizing each other up; the sparse dialogue enables them to measure each other's honesty and toughness as they prepare for the long wagon trek. John Wayne's work in Ford's westerns remains an integral part of our understanding of the West; playing opposite Henry Fonda's Lear in *Fort Apache*, Wayne's strong, silent, enduring hero leads to a reaffirmation of America's expansionism; his avenger in *The Searchers* is a noble, solitary wanderer who reenforces the more orthodox ideals of family and social justice. The films are often marred by Ford's affection for corn, yet as difficult as it is to accept the historical platitudes of *Rio Grande* or the prolonged exercise in macho self-determination in *The Horse Soldiers*, the glories of these films derive from Ford's sense of epic cinema—with Ben Johnson's spectacular horseback riding in *Rio Grande* or the march of the child drummers and the ballads of the cavalry in *The Horse Soldiers*. *She Wore a Yellow Ribbon* is part folk reverie in its tribute to Wayne and part folk caricature with the comic clichés surrounding Victor McLaglen's oafish innocent. Its virtues are not tantamount to the autonomous majesty of the long shots of Wayne riding in Monument Valley; they are equally manifested in Wayne's memorable close-up reminiscences by the grave of his wife. In *The Wings of Eagles*, Ford appears to respond to the more theatrical and pictorial demands of the wide screen, but the film retains the same buoyant, dramatic interaction that infuses the moody genre paintings in the saloon of *My Darling Clementine*. Wayne's towering portrayal shows Ford's dramatic pinpointedness in using his radiant compositions to probe Wayne's fulfillment of his historical destiny.

Among the masters of the American sound film, Ford is the most serious contender to the mantle of D. W. Griffith. He was not, however, like Griffith, an original interpreter of American history. He drew from the resources of his writers, cinematographers, and production staff to suggest the essence of human dignity in his period settings. In *The Prisoner of Shark Island*, one of his most Griffithian projects of the thirties, Ford immediately brings out the pathos of the story. Warner Baxter's protagonist lacks the innate dramatic strength that his role demands, but Bert Glennon's tableaux—from the impassive yet formidable figures of the soldiers at the trial to those of the blacks suffocating in the dungeon on the island—are historical archetypes that express both Ford's lack of interest in dramatic complexity and his faith in the idealism of his scene paintings. Even in *The Informer* where one would imagine that Ford's feeling for the subject would result in a more personal statement, the static, transparent stage lighting and direction show his acquiescent dramatic style. Working in the wide screen, Ford's association with Technicolor specialist Winton Hoch resulted in a flowering of these emotive, pictorial motifs, but they also showed his nostalgic and at times antiquated voice. The claims made for *The Searchers* as the classic western underscore a belief in the simplified methodology and mythology of western literature and art. The film is centered on the brilliantly abstracted metaphor of the isolated house, with the major protagonists identified from the point of view of those indoors. But the dialogue and drama remain quintessentially Fordian in replaying the comic platitudes with the character of the immigrant and in the supporting romance involving Jeffrey Hunter and Vera Miles. An archetype must suggest a distillation, a poetic purification or expansiveness. The dramatic solemnity of Wayne's quest repeats the clichés and ennobles them, but it does not transmogrify their content or style.

Ford's sentimentality, as problematic in *The Long Gray Line* as it is in *The Iron Horse*, is transcended in *The Quiet Man* by his lyrical treatment of the Irish countryside, the unabashed romanticism of Wayne's courtship of Maureen O'Hara, and the undiluted folk excesses culminating in Wayne's clash with McLaglen. It is one of his most personal and profound films, asking us to see his characters and settings as the embodiments of a rustic romance. Its artistic virtues are not to be denied, even as Ford's most fervent admirers equate it to such lamentable exercises in folk poetry as *Two Rode Together* or *Seven Women*. Ford's triumphs in the fifties circumvent its anxiety and alienation; the reason for their success may also explain the failure of his final work in the sixties.

# 18

# The American Film in the Sixties

*The Misfits–The Sand Pebbles*

Whether it is the sociologist or mythologist who speculates about Hollywood and the American film experience, the movies remain an elusive, enigmatic part of American society. Contrary to the pure Hollywood mosaic of its interpreters and their emphasis on the medium's influence on the country's mores or its fulfillment of the audience's most personal fantasies, Hollywood refuses to be oversimplified. When the Hollywood studios functioned most effectively in the thirties and through most of the forties, the American film was a nexus of society: moviegoing became a unifying experience for its disparate audience. Although the medium adapted many features from popular art forms of the nineteenth century, it inspired original variations on popular art for two major reasons. One was the dynamic makeup of America's social and political institutions—the movies became an extension of the democratic experience. The second reason derived from the film experience—a dreamlike nimbus of magnified figures who literally engulfed the audience on a journey of myth, romance, and adventure.

Prior to the breakdown of the studio system and the rise of television, the American film experience was not only our single most popular pastime, but also a means of creating and sharing American values and fantasies. The movies were entertainment, but because of the democratic nature of American society, the movies invariably revealed the most commonly shared symbols and myths at the heart of the American experience. The moral, idealistic core of American society was interpreted by movie stars who became visual icons of the innocence and individuality of American history or what the film audience perceived to be its heritage. Underlying and unifying their characterizations were the energy and dynamism of American life, which the movies so uniquely reflected. The popular cultural identity of the movies during the thirties and forties exemplified both the centripetal and centrifugal nature of the American film: because film was our most powerful and popular art, the movies were forced to satisfy the dreams of their audiences.

During the fifties, the American film undertook a comprehensive reexamination of long-standing platitudes about the inviolability of the American individual and society. It began in the crime film of the forties, but the effects of *film noir* then spread to more conventional settings and to characters who would have been thought immune to the psychological rumblings of expressionism. With the rise of teledrama, a central proposition of postwar culture was underlined: the introspective analysis of daily life and prototypically American characters, resulting in the dissipation of traditional American myths and values. The sixties found this crisis reaching a cul-de-sac; the psychological ambivalence at the heart of the fifties film experience led to more violent expressions of antisocial behavior. A fundamental schism was occurring in Hollywood— the very identity of the American movie experience as an inherently conservative and positive force was severely challenged. Hollywood's elders vainly attempted to rework outdated formulas, while younger filmmakers had either received their training in the anxiety-ridden environment of teledrama or were more symphathetic to the contemporary aesthetic of contempt and cynicism. No film better underlines these social and artistic tensions in the early sixties than *The Misfits*.

John Huston, one of Hollywood's veteran filmmakers, directed *The Misfits* from a script by Arthur Miller, featuring Clark Gable and Marilyn Monroe, two stars representative of two different periods of moviemaking in America. Whereas the heroic presence of Gary Cooper suffered through an indifferent farewell in *The Naked Edge*, Gable's role played off his identity as the tough, romantic individualist who scorns the conventional thinking of his contemporaries. In his best films, opposite Spencer Tracy in *San Francisco, Boom Town, Test Pilot*; in comedies like *It Happened One Night* and *Red Dust*; and, of course, as Rhett Butler in *Gone with the Wind*, Gable's manly figure, his hard-driving business sense, and no-nonsense approach to the ladies proved one of the most simple yet appealing of Hollywood stars. In *The Misfits*, however, his characterization of the cowboy develops into a commentary on the decline of American myths. And nowhere is there better evidence of his fading individualism than in the contemporaneous identity of his co-star.

Throughout her film career, Monroe personified both the tragic (*The Asphalt Jungle, Niagara*) and comic (*Gentlemen Prefer Blondes, Some Like It Hot, The Seven Year Itch*) tensions of the sexual waif. By the time of *The Misfits*, when her increasingly turbulent personal life had become page-one news, there was a more acute sense of unease in her characterizations. Thus, with a supporting cast that featured the Kafkaesque Montgomery Clift, the hard-boiled Thelma Ritter, and the hard-edged Eli Wallach, rarely did the title of a film so aptly denote its story and characters. Arthur Miller, like William Inge and Tennessee Williams, had exposed the deterioration in the social veneer so essential to Depression-era playwrights like Clifford Odets and Elmer Rice. In *The Misfits*, he juxtaposes rural America, the West, and the cowboy as embodied in Gable's character to the neurotic frictions of city life that Monroe represents. Each character and subplot, from Wallach's coarse behavior to the pursuit of the stallions, are conceived in broad, symbolic terms, but Miller's script proves as schematic, as psychologically shrill as his studies of witch burning, guilt, and cowardice (*The Crucible, All My Sons, Incident at Vichy*). There is a lack of humanity in his characters; the innocence and idealism of the thirties is displaced by a postwar aimlessness and apathy. Though Miller tried to inject a spark of valor and romance in the ending, one realizes how little chance there is to sustain a film marriage of Gable and Monroe, as their symbolic identity was cruelly emphasized shortly afterwards: Gable, the most virile of movie adventurers, succumbed to a heart attack, and Monroe, the emblematic, albeit commercialized other woman of movie melodrama, committed suicide.

Huston's postwar filmography details many of the changes that the film experience has undergone in America. His best films—*The Maltese Falcon, The Treasure of the Sierra Madre, Key Largo, The Asphalt Jungle*—derive their brisk nihilism from Huston's adult, ironic treatment of the conventions of popular literature. After filming *The Treasure of the Sierra Madre*, in which he exposed the cruel, sadistic side of Bogey's tough guy, Huston fails to instill the necessary tragic dimensions in productions like *Moby Dick, Moulin Rouge, Freud, Reflections in a Golden Eye*, and *Fat City*. His experiments in symbolic color tones are reminiscent of the grandiose literary adaptations of the thirties, while prophetic of the penchant for pictorial abstraction in the numerous cases of "flashing" among filmmakers in the seventies. His interest in exotically perverse themes reflects the changes in the literary and dramatic sources of Hollywood writers and directors from the journalistic raciness of the thirties through the alienation of its postwar period.

Two films directed by Robert Aldrich, *Whatever Happened to Baby Jane?* and *The Flight of the Phoenix*, are further evidence of this modern soul-searching in Hollywood. *Whatever Happened to Baby Jane?* is a study in Hollywood Gothic that cruelly documents the decline of the pristine masks and myths of the thirties. The film is almost all Bette Davis, but Aldrich shrewdly delineates Joan Crawford's character as a damsel in distress. Since the stars are identified with the strong-willed heroines of the thirties, their mummified appearance provides a double-edged acuity in this gruesome melodrama about the backside of stardom. This may be more true of Crawford considering the ill-advised attempts in her film romances of the forties and fifties to renew her appeal at a time when she was undergoing some midlife physical crisis, usually through disconcerting close-ups of her lightly garbed figure or her bare legs. Davis's tour-de-force victimization of Crawford, her lewd impersonation of Crawford on the phone, and most vividly the image that Davis projects as the seducing virago of the thirties transformed into a cancerous carbuncle isolate the tragic grandeur of the primal myth of stardom. Ernest Haller was instrumental in the romantic iconography of both Davis (*Jezebel, Mr. Skeffington*) and Crawford (*Mildred Pierce, Humoresque*); his evocative pictures of their physical decline suggest an inherent uniformity and inevitability about the studio system and its stars. *Whatever Happened to Baby Jane?* led to other films in which Davis and Crawford were situated center stage in a Grand Guignol entertainment, but none of their future projects have the cynicism that makes Davis's bravura as the antique Baby Jane so compelling. What is most intriguing about *The Flight of the Phoenix* is its manner of subverting the melodramatic conventions of the action-disaster genre. In such modern disaster epics as *The Poseidon Adventure*, *The Towering Inferno*, or the *Airport* cycle the oftentimes breathtaking special effects and the complexity of the escape are secondary to the films' romantic entanglements. In *The Flight of the Phoenix*, Aldrich's all male cast led by James Stewart and Ernest Borgnine are featured in a long-winded self-examinaton of machismo. As they struggle to rebuild the plane, our interest is drawn to agonizing, dramatically incongruous monologues. Though the plane is reborn, the film's inordinate spirit of self-revulsion leads one to conclude that it will take more than the spark of a Greek myth to renew the audience's sympathy for the heroic figures of the adventure saga.

This radical, modern iconography not only encompasses Hollywood's older performers, but also affects its newest starts. While the initial anti-hero appeal of Marlon Brando, Montgomery Clift, and James Dean looms as the pervasive postwar screen persona, the films of Paul Newman and Steve McQueen soften their mask of discontent. Newman's original characterizations in *Somebody Up There Likes Me* and *The Helen Morgan Story* show a street-wise toughness and romantic invincibility more akin to Cagney than Brando. In *The Left-Handed Gun*, one finds the Newman trademarks that will be utilized until his transformation into a mellow, middle-aged hipster opposite Robert Redford in *Butch Cassidy and the Sundance Kid* and *The Sting*. He is a pretty boy, more self-conscious and confident about his appeal to women than Dean; like Brando, he possesses an insecure vocal range that makes him more human and vulnerable. His acting nuances—a tightening of the upper torso, the depressed, sullen shoulders, and the recurrent image of Newman as the precarious romantic idol bent over on his knees in his big dramatic scenes—recall both Brando and Dean. Of his major films of the sixties, only *The Hustler* works as a dramatically incisive portrait, while *Hud*, *Hombre*, and *Cool Hand Luke* are similar to such Steve McQueen projects as *The Cincinnati Kid* and *Nevada Smith*: they combine equal strains of antisocial behavior with a viable romantic presence—a classic Hollywood compromise of the flawed hero.

The decline in John Ford's work is emblematic of a traditional imperviousness in Hollywood mythology. Whereas a pallid sentimentality overruns such cornball films as *Seven Women* and *Donovan's Reef*, *Two Rode Together* and *Cheyenne Autumn* pay homage to the clichés of western literature that had barely survived into the forties. The quaint, rarefied, folk poetry of his earlier work, the simple yet believable studies of valor and camaraderie are reduced in *Two Rode Together* to the stilted heroics of James Stewart and Richard Widmark and a pathetic self-parody of Indian folklore in Woody Strode's war dance; *Cheyenne Autumn* is a less problematic work only because the narrative is replete with the conventional, half-baked archetypes of the West that directors less original than Ford perpetuated in Hollywood's golden age. It is the time for westerns like *One-Eyed Jacks*, *Welcome to Hard Times*, *The Professionals*—films that have yet to achieve a coherent blending of romance and revenge, but that point to Sam Peckinpah's lyrical treatment of gunplay as the essential link between the Fordian rigor of the fifties and the solipsism of Clint Eastwood's lone rider of the seventies.

Other directors who significantly contributed to Hollywood folklore but whose style appears dated in the sixties include William Wyler, George Stevens, George Cukor, and Robert Wise. Wyler's direction of *Ben-Hur* is a technological summation of the wide-screen epics of the fifties. Its cinematographer, Robert Surtees, was behind the camera on many of the spectacles of the fifties (*Quo Vadis, King Solomon's Mines, The Bad and the Beautiful, Oklahoma!*). The beneficiary of the latest improvements in the Panavision lens and Eastman film stock, his work shows a tonal clarity originally articulated by De Mille and fulfilled in his associations with Victor Milner. Along with the cinematography of Leon Shamroy in similar historical and musical epics, Surtees' glittering illustrations represent a last effort by Hollywood producers to celebrate the splendor of the wide screen in the face of small-screen television dramas. The silent-film version of *Ben-Hur* was the most ambitious technical undertaking of its time, highlighted by the fireworks surrounding the sinking of the slave ship and the chariot race and by the wizardry of Karl Struss sliding a graduated filter across the lens to simulate the healing of the lepers. The remake projects a more rigorous solemnity, a more consistent undercurrent of religious epiphany in its reverential treatment of one of the best-sellers of nineteenth-century American literature. Its fustian tone would characterize Hollywood remakes of *Mutiny on the Bounty, Cleopatra, Cimarron,* and *The Greatest Story Ever Told*, where the increasing pictorial and production artifices result in a disastrous diminution of the essential star chemistry in the originals. The most top-heavy of these production caravans may be *The Greatest Story Ever Told*. A strong blue light suffuses the actors standing in profile, transforming the drama into picture-book configurations in the style of Florentine art. A dramatic failure and commercial flop, its director George Stevens, an exemplary Hollywood craftsman, disappeared from the Hollywood scene. Wyler tried to adapt but was doomed to failure. In *How to Steal a Million*, his hip comic mannerisms fail to imbue the art world with the same curiosity with which Peter O'Toole and Audrey Hepburn regard each other; in *The Liberation of L. B. Jones*, he makes another in a long line of distasteful, Freudian studies of racism that ludicrously dramatize Hollywood's turnabout from the quaint pictures of history it had effortlessly produced in the thirties.

George Cukor, whose film triumphs range from the Hollywood fantasy of *What Price Hollywood* through his brilliant handling of Judy Holliday in *It Should Happen to You* and *The Marrying Kind*, experienced a similar decline in the sixties. While the casting and nonsinging of Audrey Hepburn received most of the bad press concerning the film version of *My Fair Lady*, her performance makes for the few redeeming moments in the film; Rex Harrison's Henry Higgins, showing the effects of too many nights on Broadway, is a waxen, senile figure. Cukor, spellbound by its celebrated stage tableaux, compresses the Lerner-Loewe operetta into a badly staged television production, while the Academy Award bestowed on Stradling seems a belated recognition of the romantic textures that he more richly explored in musicals of the late forties. The theatrical flavor of Cukor's films is much admired, but when the material is based on a theatrical source his direction is constrained. *A Bill of Divorcement, Dinner at Eight,* and *The Women* make no attempt to hide their theatrical origins. For such negligible dramatic fare as *A Bill of Divorcement* and *Dinner at Eight,* and considering their early adaptation to film, it hardly matters; *The Women,* however, immobilizes Luce's stinging rhetoric and offers only modest concessions with the handsome, portrait photography inserts of Norma Shearer and Joan Crawford. Cukor's direction of *Gaslight* is more outdated than its Victorian melodrama; both the scenic changes and emotional climaxes lack any sense of cinematic time— perfunctory transpositions of a theatrically conceived story. Cukor's most well-received film of the seventies, *Travels with My Aunt,* is so empathetic with Maggie Smith's affected persona that his romantic recreation of the past seems modeled on her overbearing, lachrymose character. But Cukor is still to be applauded for his restraint and suavity in directing the first joint appearance of Katharine Hepburn and Laurence Olivier in *Love among the Ruins.* The telefilm is unusually sensitive to the genius of its two stars, and though old-fashioned, it is a remarkably fresh, invigorating film, whether reviewed in the context of regular television or movie fare.

Robert Wise first gained prominence as the editor of *Citizen Kane* and *The Magnificent Ambersons*; his piercing montage rhythms were most successfully incorporated in the brutal ring drama of *The Set-Up* and the fateful criminal caper of *Odds against Tomorrow.* Wise's dramatic resiliency has made him a respected survivor. He has directed several of Hollywood's more anonymous though often intriguing technical productions, from the computer story dynamics of *The Andromeda Strain* to the technological protagonists of *Star Trek—The Motion Picture.* In two of his big films of the sixties—*The Sound of Music, The Sand Pebbles*— he welds together Hollywood technology with the platitudes at the heart of the major productions of the thirties. *The Sound of Music* is probably the fastest paced operetta Hollywood has ever undertaken. The major difference between the filmed operettas of the thirties and Wise's production is the dehumanization that steadily creeps into Wise's film. In the MacDonald-Eddy operettas, the conventions of the theater were upheld in the stage-bound settings and contrived story and characterizations; in *The Sound of Music,* however, the faces of Julie Andrews and Christopher Plummer are treated as saintly icons, while the adventures of the singing family become an exercise in mindless exuberance. *The Sand Pebbles* is as constricted as *The Sound of Music* is excessive. Unlike his schematic approach to musicals, Wise adopts a solemn, ponderous tone that is most reminiscent of De Mille's last epics. He attempts a more cynical viewpoint, but owing to the substitution of John Wayne's popular adventurer with the distant, reticent figure of Steve McQueen, the film becomes a lethargic dirge on American heroism.

*Exodus–Inside Daisy Clover*

Otto Preminger, Fred Zinnemann, Robert Rossen, and Elia Kazan began directing at the height of *film noir* and are associated with celebrated literary and dramatic adaptations; Stanley Kramer, Sidney Lumet, Richard Brooks, Martin Ritt, and Robert Mulligan show a similar interest in controversial topics whose treatment is derived from the more intimate, scaled-down television screen.

Preminger has shown an equal flair in classic *film noir* adaptations and epic moviemaking. The noteworthy quality of his melodramas is in his creating a romantic prism out of the most sordid material. If *Laura* is just a bit too emotionally unruffled for a forties melodrama, Joseph LaShelle's light, low-key photography illuminates the contrasting glamour and mystery of his high-society backgrounds. In Preminger's two most interesting *film noir* studies, *Fallen Angel* and *Anatomy of a Murder*, the conflict centers around the erotic identity of Linda Darnell and Lee Remick and the precarious moral stance of those mesmerized by their destructive sensuality. *Fallen Angel* is a more convincing work because the tightness in the staging and camerawork around the diner where Darnell works mirrors the passions of her admirers. Dana Andrews is not a very expressive actor, but his anxiousness in pressing his lips against Darnell when they dance exhumes the clichés of romantic fatalism with a psychological immediacy that undergoes a more detailed, journalistic interpretation in *Anatomy of a Murder*.

Like Clifton Webb's stance as that man in the tub in *Laura*, Preminger often assumes a glib attitude toward his devious stories, whether it is manifest in Keir Dullea's shrill performance as the psychotic brother in *Bunny Lake Is Missing* or in the psychologically facile use of color and black-and-white photography in *Bonjour tristesse*. Preminger's epics of the sixties—*Exodus, Advise and Consent, The Cardinal, In Harm's Way*—are more phlegmatic and not as fraught with the heavy-handed symbolism in the social statements of Zinnemann and Kramer. The perverse politics of *Advise and Consent*, the most sophisticated of the four, stays so within its energizing, potboiler conventions that Preminger's lack of depth begins to look moral. Because of his faithfulness to their best-seller trimmings, the films have a punch and narrative directness that is more proximate to the bathos of the thirties than to the more serious and complex scheming of high art. Preminger's breezy treatment of the religious and social controversies in *The Cardinal* gives Leon Shamroy ample opportunity for his colorful scene painting, and the exterior crowd scene of demonstrators against the Nazis in Vienna is one of his most brilliant compositions. But in *Advise and Consent*, Sam Leavitt achieves a more subtle effect with the steely demeanor of the senators at the hearing, their silent, background figures the arbiters of the political infighting. *In Harm's Way* is one of the few war epics of the sixties that provides an intelligent, admirable study of John Wayne's screen presence, delineating with little dissimulation the ardor and pride of men at war.

Fred Zinnemann's shortcomings lie in his failure to animate his hoary projects. In *The Nun's Story, Behold a Pale Horse*, and *A Man for All Seasons*, his lackluster

staging conceives the words and actions of Audrey Hepburn's missionary and
Gregory Peck's revolutionary with the same reverent, close-up view he uses
toward the pious witticisms of Robert Bolt's Sir Thomas More; their confrontations are leaden, without the slightest suggestion of the spiritual darkness Peck
and Hepburn suffer. *A Man for All Seasons* is among the more polished pseudohistorical tragedies which, like Eliot's *Murder in the Cathedral*, tries to reconfirm
the sanctity of the theater. If Eliot's play fails because of his ascetic view of the
theater, Bolt's play and Zinnemann's film adaptation are too neat and balanced, without the hard, piercing edges and poetic density that would lift the
characters out of their prim self-esteem. Zinnemann's recent direction of Lillian
Hellman's *Julia* underlines an inherent affinity between Hollywood highbrow-
ism and the more ponderous soul-searching of social realists. Hellman's major
efforts as a playwright, like Hollywood's more inert productions, suffer from a
similar simplemindedness—the lack of a sensuous artistic texture that would
elevate the characterizations and moral imprint from a dull two-dimensionality.

Robert Rossen achieved several brilliant credits as a scriptwriter and producer prior to directing *Body and Soul*, an archetypal study of romance, guilt, and
heroic redemption sparked by one of James Wong Howe's most effectively inventive efforts as the camera poet of psychological realism. Rossen's adaptation
of Robert Penn Warren's *All the King's Men* is more satisfying than Zinnemann's
version of James Jones's *From Here to Eternity*, but in focusing on the demagogue
instead of the journalist, the film becomes an abrasive yet negligible political
profile. He was less successful with *Alexander the Great* and *They Came to Cordura*,
two of the most catatonic films of the sixties which by shearing the physical
richness of their backgrounds identify the protagonists as existential figures who
could as easily be situated in a teledramatic enclosure as in ancient Greece or
the West. This motif reaches the proportion of self-parody in *They Came to Cordura* where the three major characters, Gary Cooper, Rita Hayworth, and Van
Heflin, relate to their surroundings on a subliminal level: they act out their roles
as the righteous one, the fallen woman, and the bad man as if they were locked
in a morality play in which their slow, painful movements and mournful
speeches are superimposed on more redolent movie memories of the West.
Though Rossen's last film, *Lilith*, is typical of Hollywood's trivialization of
psychological traumas, *The Hustler* remains one of the most engrossing studies of
the winners and losers in America's underworld. Rossen's sensitivity to the enclosed, private world of pool hustlers provides a telling picture of the Hemingway maxim of grace under pressure. One could easily imagine the film as a live,
television play, but the smokiness of Eugen Schüfftan's lighting and Harry Hor-
ner's pool halls and the hermetic nature of the hustler's life and love affair offer
striking movie variations on the open spaces and rousing romances in the movie
adventures of the thirties.

Elia Kazan's first films instill his naturalistic stage with a liberalism that
Hollywood had perforce rejected. His prosaic appreciation for his characters'
passions and flaws was instrumental in the recognition and relevance of the
mumbling, fumbling, psychologically charged style of Marlon Brando. Some of

his early films, for example, *Boomerang* and *A Face in the Crowd*, are dogmatic yet effective exercises in teledrama; in *Panic in the Streets* and *On the Waterfront*, his exposés of a criminal conspiracy make more expressive use of the medium. In *East of Eden* he combines his interest in gripping, psychological portraits with a more epic study of the American Southwest. Though less self-consciously theatrical than *A Streetcar Named Desire*, its backgrounds are still treated as backdrops for the characters' confessions, for example, in the climactic garden scene involving James Dean and Julie Harris.

While the contrived theatricality of *A Streetcar Named Desire* was saved by the magnificent performances of Brando and Vivien Leigh, *Splendor in the Grass* is overwhelmed by the method-ridden characterizations and the soured romanticism of William Inge's script. In *Wild River* and *America America*, Kazan strives for a more folkloristic, Fordian point of view. Ford needed the dialogue film to establish a one-to-one relationship between what his characters say and what they do, but Kazan wavers between an idiomatic and artificial dramatic structure. *Wild River* is most effective in conveying the underlying tensions of Montgomery Clift and Lee Remick, their sense of isolation from the other characters and the depressed social environment. In the family memoir of *America America*, Kazan's sensitivity to his characters' soul-searching is given little room for expression. There is an undeniable classic texture in Haskell Wexler's picture of the Greek countryside and in the interiors of the home of the protagonist's fiancée, but Kazan fails to evoke a similar magnitude about his protagonist's heroic idealism and suffering.

Stanley Kramer is the most severely teledramatic of the postwar generation of Hollywood directors. His major productions—*Inherit the Wind, Judgment at Nuremberg, Ship of Fools*—are textbook examples of the message film, characterized by Ernest Laszlo's straightforward, psychological portraiture. Though Kramer has been the victim of the more liberal-minded critics of the sixties and seventies, his strained, earnest films are an essential link between the sappy, naive message productions of the thirties and the cynical, antiestablishment films of the late sixties and seventies. Obviously their primary value is as sociology, but we often forget that sociology, certainly of a more savory nature, was central to Hollywood's golden age. By lambasting Kramer's pious, middle-class emotionalism, we admit our preference for the inviolable optimism and playfulness of the past.

Kramer's contemporaneousness is further underlined in the proximity of his films to those of Norman Jewison. *In the Heat of the Night* is, in effect, a remake of *The Defiant Ones*, while *The Russians Are Coming the Russians Are Coming* shows the same muddled handling of its epic slapstick material as *It's a Mad Mad Mad Mad World*. At least to Kramer's benefit, his commitment to preachy filmmaking was sustained into the seventies, whereas Jewison's producer mentality transformed *Fiddler on the Roof*, a magical, dramatically kinetic folk revelation of the American musical theater, into one of the more glib, lifeless movie musicals of the seventies.

The films of Sidney Lumet are examples of the effects of television, both technically and thematically, on Hollywood's changing identity. Lumet's approach is to remain on top of his characters, as if the psychologically shrill scripts of the fifties created an encounter group on film. A model teledrama, *Twelve Angry Men* is the most cogent of his early films; its datedness exemplifies a style of sociological screenwriting and direction that modestly affirms the liberal ethic of its time. Lumet seems a studied, diligent director who puts himself in the service of his scripts; if his direction of *Long Day's Journey into Night* exaggerates the play's intensely constricted form, there is also evidence of his respect for the text. Katharine Hepburn's performance could have used some toning down, but Ralph Richardson's intelligence as an actor has never seemed more incandescent. *The Pawnbroker*, one of Lumet's most acclaimed films, suffers from the contrivedness of its analogous tensions—between Rod Steiger's concentration-camp memories of his wife and his present liaison and between his camp experiences and the problems he faces as a pawnbroker in Harlem. Yet Lumet's feverish recreation of the Holocaust as a painful cancer embedded in Steiger's consciousness and Steiger's heroic evocation of anguish provide an uncompromising embodiment of a Holocaust survivor. In *Dog Day Afternoon* Lumet's taut, probing style finds its most sympathetic material. Al Pacino's unsettling presence as the homosexual bank robber inspires an engrossing emotional mosaic involving the bank employees, the crowds, and the police. Lumet takes a journalistic account of the holdup and adds an element missing in journalism— infiltrating the bank employees' roles as hostages, exploring their changing feelings to Pacino and his gang and to the media that have made them instant social celebrities. But Lumet's immersion in his material finds him transforming Agatha Christie's *Murder on the Orient Express* into a beautiful, yet blank dramatic facade. He accentuates the self-irony characteristic of English adaptations of her work; it is especially true of Albert Finney's Hercule Poirot, which plays as a caricature of Peter Sellers's Clouseau caricature. *Network* shows a further inflation of Lumet's style, and that of Paddy Chayefsky's as well. Chayefsky's bombast at first makes for a coarse satire of television, but he then interprets his characters and setting as modern-day counterparts of a morality play. Lumet's fidelity to Chayefsky's pretensions, like his stylized valentine to Christie devotees, exposes the inherent limitations of these popular sentimentalists.

A more clear-cut example of Hollywood's failure to adapt to the growing alienation of the sixties can be found in shabby film treatments of classic literary and dramatic statements of discontent. In the course of Tennessee Williams's transformation from Southern tragedian to Southern parodist, Burl Ives's Big Daddy in *Cat on a Hot Tin Roof* becomes a representative symbol of Hollywood abnormality. In his film adaptation of *The Brothers Karamazov*, director Richard Brooks casually changes the ending as if it were an oversight by Dostoevsky, while his versions of *Lord Jim* and *Elmer Gantry* treat the novels as cumbersome studies of cowardice and the con man in desperate need of Hollywood editing. Brooks's most riveting film adaptation, *In Cold Blood*, is brought to life by Conrad Hall's atmospheric treatment of the windswept flatlands of Kansas and the striking disjointedness in the performances of Scott Wilson and Robert Blake.

But soon into the film, Wilson's generalizations about our corruptibility become as offensive as the Clutter's pathetic wholesomeness. Brooks's contrived editing reduces the irrationality of their crime to a textbook prissiness; it is as if the engrossing photography and characterizations were in need of a tonic, as if the straightforward recreation of this gruesome event were not shattering in its own right. There is a similar sociological and dramatic artificiality about his interpretation of *Looking for Mr. Goodbar* and the surfeit Gothic flavors of William Fraker's compositions, but the searing expressiveness of Diane Keaton personalizes the tensions of being single to a degree that even Brooks cannot efface.

Martin Ritt, who reduces the Hemingway and Faulkner material in *Hemingway's Adventures of a Young Man, The Sound and the Fury*, and *The Long Hot Summer* to second-rate teledrama, proves more effective with the chilled dialogue of *The Spy Who Came in from the Cold* and the brusque characterizations of *Hud*. Paul Newman and Patricia Neal bring a congruent, melodramatic spark to their roles, but the presence of Brandon De Wilde as the virginal younger brother, a role he first played in *Shane*, and the overbearing somberness of Melvyn Douglas, similar to his performance in *Billy Budd*, diminish their inherent chemistry. The cliché-ridden dialogue is treated as poetry, but the acute facial frontlighting that James Wong Howe uses to illuminate the characters in their most intimate moments gives the film a poignancy missing in its oppressively drawn symbolism.

Robert Mulligan is one of the few directors who tries to suggest a modernist thread of nonconformity while resurrecting the myths of Hollywood's golden age. *Love with the Proper Stranger, The Rat Race*, and *Up the Down Staircase*, however, prove the most unequivocal expressions of the lowbrow seriousness and antique-style romance originally explored in the work of Leo McCarey. Mulligan's films function as love stories that integrate a contemporary psychological motif, but he invariably simplifies the tragic flaw or urban horror that engulfs his characters. Perhaps the high point of Mulligan's career is *Inside Daisy Clover*, in which the stillborn acting of Natalie Wood and the always difficult-to-digest Ruth Gordon become, like Norma Desmond, part of a Hollywood dreamscape.

## All Fall Down–The Graduate

At the same time that directors and stars from the silent and early sound era found long-standing moviemaking axioms and dramatic clichés largely rejected, several of Hollywood's most promising directors—graduates of television drama like John Frankenheimer and Arthur Penn, a maverick like Stanley Kubrick, and those with roots in the American film avant-garde like Shirley Clarke and John Cassavetes—undertook to infuse traditional genre material with a more modern sensibility. When an exemplary fifties cold warrior like Samuel Fuller was given the opportunity to direct an offbeat, French-styled existential caper like *Dead Pigeon on Beethoven Street*, he was unable to utilize the congruent emotional discords that made *The Crimson Kimono, Run of the Arrow,* and *Pickup on South Street* such intensive studies of characters at the edge of society. Even his more conventional action films like *Merrill's Marauders* and *China Gate,* with their ever present, explosive battle sequences, have little relevance in the thematic and stylistic ambiguities of the sixties. John Frankenheimer's films present another side of the problems facing action directors. *All Fall Down* begins with a gritty picture of Warren Beatty slumming around the country, but the film falls prey to the attenuated Freudian poetic in American literature. In *The Manchurian Candidate* Frankenheimer's sharp, abrasive cutting creates a volatile dramatic facade that places the characters in the service of the suspense: the film is so bruising to its audience that one feels trapped in its murderous juggernaut. His tendency to depersonalize the characters, as in his introductory shot from the back of Burt Lancaster in *Seven Days in May,* while magnifying the mechanics of the plot, retains some dramatic interest; in *The Train* the mechanics are heightened and the drama nonexistent. In Frankenheimer's least satisfying films, he works toward a more humanistic study of his outsiders but mawkishly treats their emotional conflicts. It occurs in *The Fixer* when Alan Bates's Jew questions whether to go to bed with the gentile played by Elizabeth Hartman and in the all-too-quick romance of Gregory Peck and Tuesday Weld in *I Walk the Line.* It mars *French Connection II* in his reluctance to use Gene Hackman's character as the film's dramatic focus; his reverie about trying out for the Yankees while being brought out of his drug overdose is emotionally effective, but it is removed from Frankenheimer's perfunctory handling of the French underworld.

Arthur Penn has enjoyed one great success with *Bonnie and Clyde,* but his other films remain largely unsatisfying. *The Miracle Worker* is an earnest, somewhat overwrought adaptation, while with *Mickey One,* Penn earned the dubious distinction of having directed one of the best and worst American films of the sixties. Penn has experimented with different narrative styles, from the social expressiveness of *The Chase* to the surreal *Mickey One,* from the folksy *Alice's Restaurant* and the epic comedy of *Little Big Man* to the oblique literalism of *Night Moves.* In each case he only shows a marginal understanding of his material. *Mickey One* is an exercise in abstraction handled with more intuitive flair by the avant-garde; *The Chase* is a more representative example of the stylistic indecisiveness in the American film of the sixties whose few incisive moments surprisingly arise from its excessive treatment of Southern depravity, first with the Wagnerian fireworks in the deserted car lot sequence and then in the pummeling of Marlon Brando's sheriff. In *Alice's Restaurant* Penn fully embraces the whimsy of his hippie outcasts and seems simultaneously to make a film for and by them. He crudely uses the hand-held camera during the motorcycle race, while his distant, poetic shots at the funeral are as much a sign of his own failure to question their actions as it is of their own indolence. *Little Big Man* is not as heavy-handed as *The Chase,* but his social polemic undercuts Thomas Berger's richly textured, old-fashioned yarn. *Night Moves* is only further evidence of his dependence on scripts, in this case a contrived, pseudothriller that mixes elements of the modern novel and the whodunit.

*Bonnie and Clyde* remains a recognizable high-art achievement of the sixties owing to its acute reversal of the low-art clichés of the genre. The astute screenplay of David Newman and Robert Benton imbues the criminals with the radical, wild-child poetics of the counterculture of the sixties. Bonnie and Clyde become innocent misfits of the Depression, transforming the crime tale into a folk ballad characterized by the recklessness and daring of modern anti-heroes. Warren Beatty gives what is probably his best performance, in large part poking fun at the image of macho that he has nurtured in his earlier work. Faye Dunaway is a revelation as a newcomer, who, with her curly locks and sprightly, casual sexual energy, plays Bonnie as a child's embodiment of the tough moll. Gene Hackman, Estelle Parsons, Michael Pollard, and Gene Wilder head a supporting cast that joyously fills out this remembrance of the thirties as a time of independence and romance, of cartoonlike energy and irreverence. The past has been redeemed, but the fatalism of *Bonnie and Clyde* suggests that its reinvigoration of the thirties is too harsh and pointed to exist as a wellspring into the seventies.

From *The Killing* through *2001: A Space Odyssey*, Stanley Kubrick made the most ambitious attempt of any postwar American filmmaker to achieve greatness through a cogent, methodical reinterpretation of conventional narrative ploys. *The Killing* may be just a bit too clean, too much of a textbook study of the failure of a caper, but it is executed with telling psychological detail. *Spartacus* is one of the more intelligent epics produced in Hollywood, and if more care had been taken in the development of Kirk Douglas's rebel hero, it could have merited attention as the type of entertainment Hollywood in the thirties is too often credited with achieving. *Lolita* is the most devious of major novels adapted in Hollywood, and though without the cunning and romantic misanthropy of the novel, it offers many fine characterizations and a moving, adult picture of Humbert's predicament. In *Dr. Strangelove*, the most successful American black comedy of the sixties, Kubrick's deadpan approach underscores the lunacy of political and military doublespeak. *2001: A Space Odyssey* is undoubtedly his great achievement, an apotheosis of advances in space technology that were first adapted by Fritz Lang in his early science-fiction melodramas and that the American film has drawn on from the time of *Destination Moon*. It may not be wholly convincing in its symbolism, but there is an appreciation for the aesthetics of space technology that earns the film a singular place in movie history. But even if one applauds the idea behind *A Clockwork Orange* and *Barry Lyndon*, Kubrick, who first seemed to be striving for greatness through the literacy of his scripts, overshoots the mark with painfully excessive stylizations. With its puerile admixture of classical music and silent-film slapstick, *A Clockwork Orange* distorts the roguish ear of Anthony Burgess. *Barry Lyndon* is, perhaps, most representative of Kubrick's overly conceptualized scripts—a pictorial feast, yet an intellectually static rendition of Thackeray's study of man-

ners and morals. Kubrick's future efforts await the verdict of an umpire looking at a batter with two strikes against him, the bases loaded, and his team
trailing by three runs.

The disenchantment with American myths and institutions—the self-
abasement and apathy that replace the self-confidence and determination of an
earlier time—are incorporated into the avant-garde gristmill in the films of
Shirley Clarke and John Cassavetes. Two of Clarke's films, *The Connection* and
*The Cool World*, are experiments that attempt to prove that the more naturalistic
the sets, the greater the opportunity for the actors to uncover a humanistic and
perhaps aesthetic truth. But what the two films reveal is Clarke's misappropria-
tion of naturalism. The pose of the dope peddler in *The Connection*, for example,
is much closer to Robert Strauss's persona in Preminger's *The Man with the
Golden Arm* than he is to the grubby figures who lurk in ghettos. When Duke, the
young war lord of *The Cool World*, is given lines like "I see death everywhere,"
the pseudopoetic dialogue conflicts with Clarke's upclose, jittery camerawork.
The more moving, expressive characterizations in the two films—Warren Fin-
nerty as a junkie who seems to be the only character not playing for the camera
and Yolanda Rodriguez as Duke's girl who keeps asking him to take her to the
beach—transcend Clarke's claustrophobic settings through their more stylized
sense of pain and yearning.

In John Cassavetes' *Shadows*, a modest, breezy film essay of the fifties, there is
a scene in which the female lead walks in front of a movie house. She is accosted
by a man, and Cassavetes then enters the scene and pushes the man away.
Cassavetes the filmmaker becomes Cassavetes the actor, documenting the ups
and downs of his career as a moviemaker. Unlike Clarke whose camera often
holds on a scene or monologue that is begging for a cut, Cassavetes captures the
disquieting tone of his characters' edginess. In following the adventures of a
group of beats, Cassavetes connotes the ephemeral nature of their high, whether
in picking up girls and in the beating they receive from the girls' boyfriends, or
by capturing the atmosphere of a place and its effect on the characters, as in the
brief nightclub scene in Philadelphia. Unlike Clarke, who is convinced that the
logic of a so-called improvisational form lies in her passive absorption of her
stultifying characters and tensions, Cassavetes adapts to the changing moods of
his characters who realize that they must move on even though they feel depressed or hung over from a bad night out.

But in parts of *Too Late Blues* and throughout *Faces*, the upbeat, laconic style
of *Shadows* becomes solemn sociology. In *Too Late Blues* Cassavetes' itinerant
jazz players are older, more weary than their careless counterparts in *Shadows*.
In a poolroom or during a softball game, they seem more studied and self-
conscious of the depression that surrounds them. In *Faces* Cassavetes extends
this introspective inquiry into suburbia but falls into a Clarkesian trap. His
middle-aged couples convey their hostilities and hang-ups in a prolix manner
that only sporadically displays humor or insight. Other than those few moments
of self-revelation shared by John Marley and Lynn Carlin, laughing uncontrollably over a bitchy, erotic anecdote about a neighbor, seemingly drawing off

each other's presence only to find themselves more removed from each other, the one genuine performance is by Seymour Cassel. He is a character out of *Shadows*, whose irony and playfulness force the characters to momentarily forget their abject condition. Twelve years later, Cassavetes would attempt to apply his stylistic primitivism to the clichés of *Gloria*; yet the tediousness with which he executes its fanciful dramatic and photographic motifs finds Cassavetes as equally confused by the artifices of storytelling as he was by the poetics of alienation in *Faces*.

Hollywood has always seemed to pride itself on its resiliency, a native shrewdness in pandering to the changing fads in our culture. It could rival the lowbrowism of competing American hucksters and, if necessary, imitate the more serious experiments of high art. Yet in attempting to adapt to the style of alienation and contempt in the sixties, Hollywood was forced to invert the very formulas that had made it a melting pot of self-assured middlebrowism. This stylistic paradox can be discovered in numerous films of the decade, but if one searched for an example of Hollywood's tentativeness in drawing on the anxiety of contemporary writers and prevailing social discords, the films of Mike Nichols, particularly *The Graduate*, serve as a representative example of a decade-long crisis that would carry over into the seventies.

Nichols gained a considerable reputation as a deft comedy performer opposite Elaine May and then as Broadway's most consistently creditable director. His first film, an adaptation of *Who's Afraid of Virginia Woolf?* showed some amateurishness in its blatant close-ups and undercut the play's congruency by moving the party outside the home. Although George Segal and Sandy Dennis act more like students than as a member of the faculty and his wife, Nichols deserves credits for generating more out of Elizabeth Taylor's bitchery than one might have expected, while Richard Burton's George remains one of his most demonstrative screen portrayals. *The Graduate* provides Nichols with a literate, comic script that is strongly reminiscent of Preston Sturges' verbally kinetic studies of Americana. In the first part of the film—until the unmasking of Ben's seduction—Nichols artfully blends Sturges' self-humor with a touch of the torpor and mordancy that rained so unevenly on the American film of the sixties. He still shows a tendency for the blatant effect, but because of Dustin Hoffman's wry delineation of a virginal twit, one is engaged. Nichols then gravitates to a more grim analysis of his protagonist, as if the tightly drawn ensemble humor did not provide a secure enough footing. The dramatization of Hoffman's lassitude through a subjective camera and then through the blue note of discomfort suggested by Robert Surtees' inappropriate prefogging—a technique similar to that of latensification in darkening black-and-white film to heighten the tonal expressiveness of the color photography—invariably reveals a lack of faith in the characters. Sturges' faith did not waver; whether it was because of a more secure technique or the self-conviction of America and Hollywood during the thirties and forties, comedy at the end of the sixties is no longer experienced as a self-perpetuating force.

Nichols's later projects show the extent of the abyss in the second part of

*The Graduate.* Joseph Heller's *Catch-22* is simply too exhaustive, too comically extravagant for Nichols's farcical instincts, and the film is reduced to an awkward, disjointed exercise in black humor. In *The Fortune* Nichols tries his hand at period comedy, juxtaposing the elegant settings to the failed comedy antics and con game of Warren Beatty and Jack Nicholson; its single, amusing element is in observing Nicholson's ratty, devious charm expose the self-conceit of an actor who had considerably undercut his macho in *Bonnie and Clyde. Carnal Knowledge* seems better suited to Nichols's comic counterpoint, but after obtaining some laughs at the expense of America's sexual innocence in the forties, his characters are engulfed by the same mood of meaninglessness and despair that await Hoffman and Katharine Ross in *The Graduate.* The marketing of this despair would confront Hollywood producers and moviemakers as the decisive challenge of the seventies.

# 19

# The American Film in the Seventies

While the thread of dissension and revolt that characterized American society in the sixties continued into the seventies in the controversies surrounding the Vietnam War and the Nixon presidency, the American film industry returned to more conventional themes by adapting several commercially viable elements from the more controversial films of the previous decade. A style of neoclassicism entered the American cinema; the appeal of the star system and genre filmmaking, two mainstays of Hollywood's golden age, were reinvigorated with the cynicism and stylistic eclecticism from the late sixties. While rebuilding the star system and reembracing the more popular storytelling formulas, the American film industry recognized a change in the makeup of its audience: younger groups of people had replaced the family as the most representative, powerful faction, and their interest in violent, erotic themes was reflected throughout the films of the seventies.

Neoclassicism, however, does not simply imply a return to the past, a dull imitation of previous themes and techniques, but a rediscovery of the past in the fusion of a modernist viewpoint with those hoary archetypes. It is often equivalent to the transparent commercialization of a once popular classic (*King Kong, A Star Is Born, Hurricane, The Big Sleep*) or to the revival of an enduring though recently overlooked story or genre (*Star Wars, Superman*). It is also represented in the proliferation of movie sequels and in the ubiquitousness of murderous car chases, nudity, and four-letter words. These, too, are ingredients of American film neoclassicism, lest we forget that the period and style of filmmaking that is being revived were also characterized by their dramatic uniformity. Just as the "happy ending" and virtuous heroes were at the center of the film experience of the thirties, the violent, electric chase sequence, the dangling bosom, and the undeleted expletive remind audiences that the specter of the late sixties, however crudely it is employed, has entered into the mainstream of movie imagery and vocabulary.

If the term "neoclassicism" suggests a style and period of artistic gracefulness, a return to and reappreciation of older, wiser, more profound themes and

311

myths, the neoclassicism of American moviemaking in the seventies contains a more paradoxical, less securely classical identity. It is not simply explained by the fact that the style and period that are being renewed lack the aristocratic munificence and stylistic independence that characterized previous examples of neoclassicism in literature and art. The film experience in America identifies its roots in the social myths and controversies that bind its audience as a nation and culture; since the catalyst for this period of social and cultural reassimilation is one of despair, alienation, and stylistic experimentalism, there remains an underlying incongruity in matching a period and style of conservative populism with one of radical revolt. Furthermore, the role of the movies in American life has changed considerably from the time of Prohibition, the Depression, and New Deal politics to the Vietnam War and Watergate. Film production no longer exists as a self-perpetuating dream factory, but it has been affected by changing social attitudes to the movies, first manifested in the postwar society by Congressional investigations into Hollywood's purportedly Communist affiliations, and the final, effective Supreme Court ruling against the monopolization of movie production and distribution by the film studios.

The role of television is exemplary in showing how in a relatively free-enterprise, democratic-society popular art forms undergo permutations both social and stylistic in a sudden, shocking manner. I have already discussed the interrelationship of television programming and the Hollywood film of the fifties and sixties. By the early seventies, the American public was engaged not only in a "living-room war," but also, in the case of the Watergate hearings, with a criminal docudrama that further revolutionized the country's conception of the power of television as an educational, social, political, and cultural instrument. If television's crucial role in the public's involvement and interpretation of Vietnam and Watergate underscored the medium's formidable immediacy, the dramatic stereotypes and glib dynamics of television sitcoms, action shows, and telefilms had as great if not a greater impact on film scripts and productions than that of live television drama. In the fifties Hollywood was still adhering to the older moviemaking formulas of the forties while incorporating themes and styles prevalent in teledrama. But by the early seventies television was no longer seen as an inconclusive, mixed bag of education and entertainment; its stereotypes of entertainment were now acknowledged as the archetypes of American enlightenment.

While television productions have largely duplicated the poverty-row cheapie, the influence of various European styles of the sixties, from the constricted existential dramas of Bergman to Leone's baroque, expansive pop-art caricatures, has infiltrated the more esteemed and expensive Hollywood productions. There is a less definable American core to these movies, unless one regards these cultural implants as a sign of American resiliency and pragmatism. The marketing of a conservative populism from the midtwenties through the midforties enabled Hollywood producers and artisans to cultivate their own formulas of social idealism: in a period shaped by the misanthropy and eclecticism of the late sixties, there results an inherent asymmetry between a motive of dissension and its stylistic duplication. Hence there are elements of tired academicism and blank pessimism—an underlying thread of emptiness, pretension, and deceitfulness about Hollywood's efforts in the seventies to build on this mood of revolt in reconstructing the Hollywood galaxy of the thirties. The American film in the seventies clearly distinguishes American film neoclassicism from its resonance in earlier periods; a residue of cynicism and contempt, rather than a style of cynicism and contempt, has obtained.

*The Getaway, The Last Picture Show,* and *American Graffiti* are three examples of the inherent virtues and limitations of the neoclassicism of the American film of the seventies. *The Getaway* is particularly expressive in unwittingly exposing the ephemeral quality of the violent, misanthropic style of the late sixties. Directed by Sam Peckinpah (*Ride the High Country, Major Dundee, The Wild Bunch*) and starring Steve McQueen, Ali MacGraw, and Ben Johnson, the film concerns an ex-convict who is reunited with his girl friend, who had originally planned to double-cross him; they execute one last haul and escape from both the police and criminals into Mexico. McQueen, one of the familiar adventure heroes of postwar American cinema, is a cool, taciturn anti-hero who has the appearance of a burned-out case, similar to Bogart in *High Sierra* and Cagney in *Kiss Tomorrow Goodbye.* He no longer suggests the innocence and self-confidence of his earlier roles in *The Magnificent Seven, The Great Escape,* and *The Cincinnati Kid.* He is looking for a way out, and MacGraw's sudden, inexplicable murder of Johnson and their successful escape from numerous criminals and police offer significantly modern variations on the crime film and its heroes. The "bad guy" wins out and gets the girl; even as one may argue that McQueen is morally superior to any other character in the film, his escape into Mexico in a pickup with the cash and the girl is an unequivocal reversal of traditional characterizations and morality. With *The Hunter* McQueen seemed consigned to a more shabby farewell than Gary Cooper in *The Naked Edge,* but the stolid drama and imperial landscapes of *Tom Horn* place him in a suitably austere, romantic setting for our last images of his silent marksman.

Another revealing aspect of *The Getaway* is Peckinpah's use of contrasting techniques of slow motion and sharply edited punctuations of violence, which had originally appeared as a timely development in the western. Though only *Ride the High Country* successfully integrated Lucien Ballard's penetration of the red Sierra mountains and forests with Peckinpah's empathetic treatment of the genre's primitivism, both *Major Dundee* and *The Wild Bunch* make valid statements about the prevalence of nihilism in the history of the West. But in *The Getaway,* as in future Peckinpah projects of the seventies, he is unable to fashion a new statement about the pervasiveness of violence among different social groups: the CIA in *The Killer Elite,* a Nazi regiment in *Cross of Iron,* truckers in *Convoy.* These shortcomings are prefigured in *The Getaway* by the repetitiveness of slow-motion close-ups and shock cuts in the various encounters McQueen faces on his way to the border. Since Peckinpah refuses to treat his characters other than as pawns in his apocalyptic battle scenes, his films play as contrived, perfunctory statements about violence. Although the elegiac tone of *Pat Garrett and Billy the Kid* would find Peckinpah returning to a classic reappreciation of the West, the richness in the film's hues—from the golden light of a midafternoon sun to the coppery tones of sunset—was only partly successful in matching the autonomy of its romanticized Mexican backgrounds to the contrivances of Bob Dylan's folk ballads and the Christian symbolism of Rudolph Wurlitzer's script. In *Bring Me the Head of Alfredo Garcia*, Peckinpah's most idiosyncratic film, the colors, at first, look as faded as Warren Oates's autobiographically styled hero. Yet its perverse references to primitive mythology and Peckinpah's own primitive westerns ironically fulfill the fatalism that would be increasingly depersonalized in his films of the seventies.

*The Last Picture Show* is one of the earliest and most striking examples of the ambience of the past in the films of the seventies. The use of black-and-white film highlights its nostalgic tone: the film has the look of a burnished photo album of rural America. The story line further connotes a mood of reverie with its innocent protagonists experiencing first love and their passage into adulthood. Larry McMurtry's screenplay is hardly an original memoir of life in the Southwest, yet it is the very simplicity of his dramatic confrontations involving the three major characters—Timothy Bottoms, Cybill Shepherd, and Jeff Bridges—that gives the film its wide appeal. Released at a time when varied sordid characterizations were inundating the American film, the softness of its characterizations, juxtaposing its troubled adolescents to their equally confused parents, absorbs audiences in a less agonizing period in American history while treating more adult themes than one finds in past Hollywood films about the loss of innocence. Director Peter Bogdanovich projects a distant, somber mood in which Ben Johnson's quiet, manly figure and Cloris Leachman's sorrowful, alienated housewife fill out an ensemble of heroic yet flawed figures.

Bogdanovich's career is emblematic of the changes in the background and interests of writers and directors in the seventies. A former film critic, Bogdanovich is one of a large group of filmmakers who, as a result of their training as film critics or students, infuses his work with pointed references to previous films. Bogdanovich's first project, *Targets*, was a pretentious, hackneyed study of violence with enough self-referential icons to satisfy a convention of movie buffs; his later films showed how much he depended on McMurtry's quaint, dramatic devices in making *The Last Picture Show* a commercial success. In *Daisy Miller* the wooden characterizations of Barry Brown and Cybill Shepherd and the picture-book interpretation of James's novella fail to duplicate the charms in previous Hollywood adaptations. *Nickelodeon*, even more than *What's Up Doc?*, suffers from Bogdanovich's inability to create an original variation on the adopted genre of screwball comedy. *What's Up Doc?* at least evinced Bogdanovich's careful reading of classic comic formulas; the escape by Barbra Streisand and Ryan O'Neal on a bicycle cart is an original tribute to the expertly timed physical mayhem of silent- and sound-film slapstick. Bogdanovich undercuts the extended chase through the sloping contours of San Francisco by the efforts of two men perilously balancing a large piece of glass, caught between the bicycle cart's losing fight against gravity and the improvised pursuit of the black sedan—a witty variation on a pinball racing through its obstacles. But *Nickelodeon*, like *Paper Moon*, is far too dramatically timid about its pictorial recreations. *Saint Jack* marks a more perilous decline. The overly kinetic editing of the opening seems the work of a director unsure of how to adapt the cuts to the fast-paced dialogue; the later sections are equally problematic, reducing the comic excesses of Paul Theroux's derivative novel to pictures of diminishing carnality.

George Lucas's *American Graffiti*, like Bogdanovich's *The Last Picture Show*, celebrates the past, but by taking more risks in selecting hot rods and pop music as major motifs in its recreation, he shows the more enriching attributes of neoclassicism. Though one can fault Lucas for selecting musical hits that were not made in the fifties, the dominant role of canned music as both an expression of the characters and the period marks an original development in the movies of the seventies. Numerous black-exploitation works and films like *The Wanderers* and *American Hot Wax* incorporate pop music as an objective mirror image to the characters' adventures and state of mind; several, however, for example, *Saturday Night Fever*, have only their music to compensate for their tenuous story line. The style is one of artifice, but it works in Lucas's films because the pop tunes comically support his deliberate camera movements on the hot rodders as they drag through the town's main streets. His pop-art mosaic of the fifties is as sentimental as Bogdanovich's, but he artfully blends his protagonists' sentimentality with their roles as fantasy figures within his rose-colored landscape. Lucas's triumph in *American Graffiti* is to have made a personal, introspective statement about a period bursting with energy and extrospection. These qualities are nearly invisible in *Star Wars*, a project whose immense box-office success defeats any facile sociological or aesthetic explanation. Unlike its sequel which follows the more standard science-fiction serial plot devices of *Flash Gordon*, *Star Wars* is a haphazard collection of literary and movie science-fiction symbolism that attempts to satisfy science-fiction junkies of both the pre- and postwar period. It invites the audience to rummage through its storehouse of space gadgetry while creating a seemingly mystical high as it recreates the most glorious moments of inanity in science-fiction folklore. It exists, its mesmerizing effect to be accepted on faith alone.

## Super Fly–The Electric Horseman

The intertwining of the styles, themes, and mythologies of two different periods of moviemaking—the basic feature of the neoclassicism of the seventies—is most vividly and coarsely displayed at the beginning of the decade in the black-exploitation movie cycle. The term "black exploitation" is a derisive approximation of film fantasies such as *Super Fly* and *Black Caesar*. For if we first try to deduce some general characteristics about the *Super Fly-Shaft-Blacula* series; the films of Jim Brown, Pam Grier, Fred Williamson, and Jim Kelly; the two film adaptations of Chester Himes's novels (*Cotton Comes to Harlem* and *Come*

*Back Charleston Blue*); and the two plantation sagas (*Mandingo* and *Drum*) one is struck by their emotional resoucefulness, and how, like the movies of the thirties, they offer rich escapist fare for their audience.

These similarities are blithely underscored in *Super Fly*, one of the first and most popular of these films. In the viewer's first introduction to Priest, lying on his plush bed with his white mistress and an ample supply of cocaine hanging around his neck like a religious medallion, the extraordinary changes that have been worked on the image of the American black from the time of the actors in blackface in *The Birth of a Nation* through the soft shuffle of Stepin Fetchit and the "invisibility" of Sidney Poitier are readily apparent. He is no longer the servant of his masters, but the master of America's free enterprise, who has casually taken to dealing in drugs as if it were the one avenue of capitalism in which he could successfully compete. The film is poorly made, redeemed only by Curtis Mayfield's riveting score; yet a feeling of exquisite, deadpan nonconformity has been captured for black America, announcing to its audience that Hollywood's halfhearted efforts on behalf of brotherhood no longer serve as the barometer of assimilation by blacks in white society.

While performers like Jim Brown, Fred Williamson, and Jim Kelly often portray the role of the avenger of some grevious wrong perpetrated on the black community, most vividly in *Three the Hard Way*, a more important aspect of their screen image is the way their good looks, financial success, no-nonsense approach, and incredible good fortune represent the Horatio Alger syndrome finally working to the benefit of the black. The one major difference in the moviemaking ethic of the white-exploitation films of the thirties and the black-exploitation films of the seventies is that whereas in the thirties there was a conservative ideology that Hollywood believed was shared by its diverse audience, the grim sociological backdrop and irreverent solipsism of the black-exploitation film are geared to only one segment of society. No black-exploitation film that I have seen is quite as surly as *Super Fly*, but in the films of Richard Roundtree, Jim Brown, and Fred Williamson, there is an unequivocal sense of individuality and of paying heed to no man that enlivens many of the repressed dreams of a new generation of black moviegoers. In the thirties middle- and lower-middle-class audiences accepted Hollywood's quiescent, pious picture of American life because the movies proved a unifying form of entertainment and social realignment. Although numerous black artists have voiced their disapproval of these films, there is a simplicity and oftentimes a rank oversimplification similar to the films of the thirties. As typified in *Super Fly* it pits the heroic nonconformity and "badness" of Priest against malicious, two-faced, white police officials.

But there is more to these films than a carefree repudiation of the pie-in-the-sky syndrome. *Across 110th Street, Sparkle, Book of Numbers*, and *Come Back Charleston Blue* show some flair in penetrating the rough edges of black exploitation; even a campy improvisation like *Mandingo* invites such a playful, mocking approach to the most bleak period of Afro-American history that one cannot simply applaud the genre for its commercial successes and be done with it. *Book of Numbers* is perhaps the most literary and thoughtful of these films in which the hero's coming of age avoids the maudlin pitfalls of a more conventional work like *Cooley High*; there is a sage humor and a zest for life in Raymond St. Jacques's picture of life in the South during the thirties that is neither affected nor artificial. In *Across 110th Street* there is one scene in which Antonio Fargas primps in front of a mirror, enjoying the high from a heist that he and his partners have brought off. Fargas's self-mockery is so real one can literally feel the audience sharing his brief moment of sardonic self-conceit. Director Barry Shear must also be given credit for his gritty look at white-black relations in the environs of a police precinct and for obtaining one of the few workmanlike performances from Anthony Quinn in recent memory. The ending is a cop-out, but the tension between the black and white mobs is as real as the disquieting helplessness of the police, caught between the duplicity of their political superiors and the violence of the crimes.

While *Cotton Comes to Harlem* shows a lilting insouciance, *Come Back Charleston Blue* more richly integrates Himes's surrealization of Harlem. When the bad dope is used, and the camera raucously illuminates the ghetto as if it were celebrating July fourth, when the gangster, in imitation of James Cagney, squeezes a grapefruit in his girl friend's face, or, with more self-humor, when he offers his white rival a watermelon, the film, like the most uncompromising lyrics of soul, makes the black experience shout and cry and, equally important, laugh and howl. *Mandingo* is a more problematic work. Unlike the majority of black-exploitation films which are set in a modern urban environment, *Mandingo* recreates plantation life as if it were a costume drama in which the tragedy of slavery is reduced to the oversexed nature of the slave owners. Whereas other films might use their simplistic formulas to drive home a bitter truth, *Mandingo* ironically exploits Boris Leven's poetically decorous setting with its sexual impulses: a joke is played on an audience that must be willing to make fun of any subject.

A more exemplary feature of neoclassicism concerns those movie stars whose screen iconography proves to be the most important ingredient of their films. The popularity of Hollywood stars like Douglas Fairbanks, Mary Pickford, and Harold Lloyd during the silent era; that of Tracy and Hepburn, Gable, and Ginger Rogers during the thirties and forties; and more recently that of Brando, Monroe, Elizabeth Taylor, and Steve McQueen was not dependent on the number of good films they made, but on presenting a character whom audiences could see as unique to their time or as representing an enduring American trait. Among the film stars of the seventies, male performers most uniquely fulfilled this function. Perhaps no male star of the seventies etched out the dramatic iconography of Jane Fonda. Yet few female stars amassed the formidable public following of Charles Bronson, Burt Reynolds, or Sylvester Stallone. Although they have worked in many films of dubious artistry, these actors' unvarnished appeal stands out as the dominant factor in the popularity of their films. Clint Eastwood and Robert Redford better fulfill the traditional role models movie stars have pursued, but the success of Bronson, Reynolds, and

Stallone sharply details the sociological genesis of stardom in the seventies.

The quality of Bronson's work, not surprisingly, is similar to that of black-exploitation films. His most striking feature is his reticence; in an early, quasi-Bronson vehicle, *Chato's Land*, he does not speak a word. His most succinct role is in Leone's *Once upon a Time in the West*, in which his craggy face suggests countless nights on the prairies and mountains and memories that one is not likely to pass on to children. Throughout his films in the seventies, Bronson plays the loner whose lack of wit or polish precludes any romantic interest to a degree rarely, if ever, sustained in Hollywood. One speculates that his earlier box-office successes in Europe and South America, like those of Clint Eastwood's Leone films, rest on his individuality, his lack of uncertainty in destroying the evil around him; in comparison, Cooper is garrulous and Wayne pedantic. His breakthrough film, *Death Wish*, then serves to acquaint American audiences with his primordial appeal by situating him in an urban environment and by its drawing on the gut psychology of movie westerns. *Hard Times* uses Bronson's weather-beaten, Depression-era persona to make a poetic statement about the period. The central fight in the cage is among the most exciting action sequences in the movies of the seventies, but the script, most noticeably in Bronson's relationship with James Coburn and compounded by Coburn's complacent acting manner, fails to extend its pictorial assumptions about the Depression. Yet the visually astute style and the detailed friendship of Bronson and Alain Delon in *Farewell Friend*, Bronson's recognition of the wayward mood in *Rider on the Rain*, and the uncluttered narrative of *Breakheart Pass* and *The Mechanic* are examples of an oeuvre not without interest. They not only show the icon at work but as his better films document becoming an almost cherishable defender of innocence and manhood.

Burt Reynolds earliest films are noteworthy for his physical resemblance to Brando, while his later appeal derives from the crass commercial interplay of film and other mass media. Like several silent- and early sound-film stars whose films were predicated on their popularity in a medium other than the movies and on a logic based on accounting, Reynolds is a creation of our media, notably television, where he has promoted himself as a good-natured, virile personality. The reason his initial success leaves a sour taste is that Reynolds suggests nothing so much as being in love with his breezy, fortuitous manner. His style is similar to that of nightclub entertainers who, from Al Jolson to Dean Martin, seem to be crooning to themselves; he presents a lovable, transparent image of the simple country boy who made good and cannot believe the women and fame that are his. In the role of the quarterback who sells out his team in *The Longest Yard*, Reynolds seems to be playing the character in his sleep, as if by merely cracking a smile at his cell mates, looking chagrined at the screws, or beaming his sexuality to Bernadette Peters's starry-eyed self-caricature he, like Barrymore, expresses his superiority to the material. What is most depressing about *The Longest Yard* is veteran, hard-boiled director Robert Aldrich's lackadaisical direction, mechanically appropriating the split-screen dynamics of sporting telecasts; it is a deceptive concession to video electronics which will undergo further dramatic inflation in *Twilight's Last Gleaming*. John Avildsen, director of *W. W. and the Dixie Dancekings*, makes a better case for Reynolds's acting by poking fun at his wily operator.

With his ascension into the ranks of superstardom, Reynold's projects seem to aspire to a modest self-humor. *Gator* begins with some exciting chase sequences that humorously treat both the law-enforcement officials and Reynolds's guile. The film suffers from a maudlin ending, a failure to be as tough as the presence of Reynolds originally intimates. This moral, invariably stylistic flabbiness also mars *The End* in Reynolds's meeting with his daughter, but his work in the first suicide attempt shows signs of wit and intelligence that one would have thought was all but negated in his rise to the top. But if one is willing to applaud Reynolds's image as the savvy innocent and overlook the more crass elements of his commercialization, a film like *Hooper* exposes the fatalistic nature of media miscegenation. At this point in Reynolds's career, he relies on a self-conscious laugh that, like Goldie Hawn's, sounds like someone tickling his rib cage, but without the truly liberating silliness in her giggles; it reduces the dialogue and drama to the level of the sexual self-satisfaction in *The Longest Yard*. Another example of the film's dishonest presentation of machismo occurs in the stunt sequences, especially in those that attempt to show Reynolds as a legendary stunt performer. They are clearly fake, leading one to surmise that if the nature of Reynolds's appeal, as one comic has suggested, rests in his two and only, then they are no more real than the daredevilry he supposedly performs in *Hooper*. The problematic nature of stardom has always seemed to originate in the star's attitude to his appeal; *Hooper* once again shows Reynolds as the good-ole-boy, laughing his way to the bank.

Sylvester Stallone's Rocky Balboa is a more direct flashback to the past, a Frank Capra naïf who makes the classic protagonists of Gary Cooper and James Stewart seem overbearing aesthetes. *Rocky* offers two striking variations on Capra's cornball populism. One is that Stallone, unlike Cooper or Stewart, does not suffer the profound moment of embarrassment and self-doubt that in Capra's films led to the massive public outcry and eventual victory of the small-town innocent. The second feature concerns the role of the girl, who in Capra's films first ridicules the protagonist; in *Rocky* she is presented as a veritable dolt who, through Rocky's love, becomes an intelligent, attractive woman: Rocky is the redeemer of the lumpen proletariat. His refusal to strike out at those who make fun of his awkward speech, his benevolence to his manager, and his Herculean effort in the ring, transform the Joe Palooka caricature into a figure of Olympian proportions. Stallone's script and John Avildsen's direction carefully avoid making his adversaries, particularly Apollo Creed, appear as evil figures; Creed's braggadocio serves to oil the money machinery of the fight game, whereas Rocky's workouts become the embodiment of his dedication. But it is the absence of any irony in Rocky's fantasy figure that makes his character a loathsome one. A fantasy involves an idealization and not a simplification or untruthful characterization; in a film that purportedly concerns a primitive anti-hero, the falsification of primitive behavior is all the more despicable because the expression of a primitive sensibility is one which the American public is most likely to mistakenly perceive as real and truthful. Or, perhaps, more ominously, although recognizing the duplicitly in the film's characterizations, the public still applauds Rocky as one of its own.

A small measure of relief is won in the dismissal of Stallone's *Paradise Alley*, a less distilled example of lumpen moviemaking aesthetics. In *F.I.S.T.* Stallone's Rocky persona is transposed in a quasi-historical project about the life and times of Jimmy Hoffa. Joe Eszterhas's script and Norman Jewison's direction lack the incisiveness of Stallone's and Avildsen's work in *Rocky*. The period locations and piecemeal, biographical style are hand-me-down Coppola; there is no fineness of eye or dramatic focus to the growth of the union. Stallone impersonates Hoffa through the roughhouse tactics of a gang leader taking control of a neighborhood. It may be that audiences simply could not accept Stallone's brutish figure in a broad sociopolitical setting; yet the blending of stupidity and strength in Stallone's character make him a figure to be reckoned with. If pornography involves the exploitation of the human figure, then Stallone can be considered one of America's most successful pornographers.

*The Sting, The Way We Were, Klute*, and *All the President's Men* situate their star players in more traditionally congruent roles. Yet in attempting to update the star appeal and story conventions of the thirties, directors George Roy Hill, Sydney Pollack, and Alan Pakula invariably reflect the more acute self-consciousness in contemporary American filmmaking. George Roy Hill's stylistically eclectic *Butch Cassidy and the Sundance Kid*, borrowing themes and techniques from *Jules and Jim* and *Bonnie and Clyde*, makes the work a less fluid entertainment than *The Sting*. The film's recourse to various modernist effects is one of the earliest expressions of the impact of mannerism on the American film of the seventies. Hill's panoramic camera eye and use of dissolves are reminiscent of George Stevens, one of the Hollywood's more efficient yet cold-blooded directors; whereas these techniques enhanced the symbolic mythology of *Giant* and *Shane*, they undercut the bittersweet romance of William Goldman's script for *Butch Cassidy and the Sundance Kid*. Equally noteworthy is the relationship and screen iconography of Newman and Redford. One of Hollywood's more engaging images of manliness and individuality through the sixties, Newman, sporting some gray in the seventies, assumes a passive role, no longer given to outbursts of self-revulsion. It is Redford who plays the anxious, young honcho, and although he has yet to relax in front of the camera, his tenseness is more bearable playing opposite Newman's coy, retiring figure. The picture-book gloss of *The Sting* superimposes a more amenable framework for the chemistry of its two stars. Newman replays the role of the sage, self-mocking prankster, hoodwinking Robert Shaw's malevolent swindler in the amusing poker game on the train. Redford's dapper figure is also put to better use, a young hustler whose phony come-on to Shaw sets up the sting. With a fine supporting cast and its recycling of Scott Joplin's music, *The Sting* enfolds its skeletal story line in a compact production.

Sydney Pollack's direction of Streisand and Redford in *The Way We Were*, of

Redford in *Jeremiah Johnson,* and of Redford and Jane Fonda in *The Electric Horseman* makes fewer concessions to modernism. *The Way We Were* reclaims the prefabrications of its period romance through Streisand's near mystical adoration of Redford's incarnation of a Jack Armstrong doll. Harry Stradling, Jr. continues the family tradition, coloring and moving through the period settings as a visual approximation of Streisand's swooning lyrics. In *The Electric Horseman* Pollack again attempts a thirties love story, this time involving the city sophisticate and the country rube. The film is a project for its two stars, yet Redford was more appealing as the innocent in *Jeremiah Johnson,* while Fonda essayed a more expressive role in the same year as the plastic newscaster-turned-committed-reporter in *The China Syndrome.* The supporting cast offers few diversions, and the escape is painstakingly straightforward; only the most un-suspecting filmgoer would not forsee the outcome in the confrontation between Redford's cowboy and Fonda's reporter. We have seen this done many times before and one concludes the only reason to do it again is that the names of the stars have changed.

One of Alan Pakula's first films, *The Sterile Cuckoo,* showed little promise for him other than as a director of *Saturday Evening Post* pastiche. Liza Minnelli as the film's chatterbox protagonist engulfs the screen in a Bergmanesque torrent of self-pity; Pakula fails to create any distance between his secondary players and Minnelli's pathetic heroine. He fares no better with the conspiracy para-noia of *The Parallax View;* at best, the film shows the commitment of its star Warren Beatty. Pakula's reliance on his supporting technicians, particularly Gordon Willis and his genre-study pictorialization of the West makes *Comes a Horseman* one of the more ill-fated western canvases since Lee Garmes's *Hannah Lee.* But in *Klute* and *All the President's Men* Pakula combines dramatic contem-poraneousness with star appeal in a style that reaps further dividends in the Michael Douglas production of *The China Syndrome.* With the adult treatment of a call girl's impassivity and the contrasting intentions of a psychopath and would-be lover in *Klute,* with the disingenuous intertwining of historical realism and dramatic license in *All the President's Men,* and with the shrewd packaging of the nuclear power controversy as an ideal feminist project for Jane Fonda in *The China Syndrome,* these films closely parallel the style of William Wyler.

Wyler's intelligent direction of such imported dramatic and literary works as *Counsellor-at-Law, Dodsworth, The Letter, The Little Foxes, The Heiress,* and *Detective Story* confirmed an essential attribute of Hollywood. While making fine use of the camerawork and art direction in distilling their period flavor, his direction of John Barrymore (*Counsellor-at-Law*); Walter Huston and Mary Astor (*Dods-worth*); Bette Davis and Herbert Marshall (*The Letter, The Little Foxes*); Ralph Richardson, Olivia De Havilland, and Montgomery Clift (*The Heiress*); and Kirk Douglas and Eleanor Parker (*Detective Story*) fulfilled the films' underlying dramatic authenticity. He is faithful to the original virtues of the star system, and though these qualities may be used in the service of middlebrow art, how many directors achieved the consistency and professionalism one rediscovers in these projects?

In *Klute* Gordon Willis's devious camera eye establishes an aura of conflicting beauty and tension about Fonda's call girl. The viewer senses both the objective allure of the city and Fonda's subjective entrapment; her relationship with Donald Sutherland's country investigator adds to the ambiguity in this suspense film turned love story. In *All the President's Men*, however, Willis's distant, atmospheric camerawork undercuts the historical repercussions of Woodward's and Bernstein's investigations. The central office unit created by George Jenkins is a stunning piece of technology, but Pakula makes the Washington backgrounds—from the initial burglary through Woodward's meetings in the garage with Deep Throat—assume an ominousness more germane to a Hitchcock thriller. William Goldman's episodic, seriocomic look at their investigative efforts is equally problematic, diffusing the film's intensity in recreating one of the most fascinating periods of postwar history; the comic, melodramatic adventures of Bernstein and Woodward transform Watergate into a study of two newspapermen making good. The characters of Bernstein and Woodward also suffer from this point of view; Hoffman's Bernstein is sloppy in appearance, obnoxious in character but tenacious in his job, while Redford's Woodward is portrayed as a smart, cool operator. Jason Robards, Jr.'s Ben Bradlee, however, not only ennobles the man, but may be his most precise film characterization to date. This symmetry between its star performers and dramatic history continually sought after by Hollywood receives one of its most successful interpretations with Jane Fonda's newsreporter in *The China Syndrome*, blending her symptomatic transformation with a tough-minded look at the doublespeak of the nuclear power company and the news agency. The film's cunning delineation of Fonda's reporter shows how neoclassicism need not be characterized by such flabby exercises in star gazing as *The Electric Horseman*.

*Five Easy Pieces – Popeye*

A measure of the commercial and artistic realignment of American movies in the seventies is the way audiences are willing to experience films whose style or subject matter would have been considered too offbeat in earlier periods. During Hollywood's golden age there was little opportunity for dramatic experimentalism; but owing to the changes in the makeup of movie audiences and the rival identity of television as America's predominant medium of entertainment, the movies have assumed a more controversial identity. Another, more subtle factor is that the redefinition of the American film in the seventies entails not only a receptivity to classic narratives, but also a greater sensitivity to the social and artistic diversity of the American film experience. Such films as *Five Easy Pieces*, *Badlands*, *Blue Collar*, *Mean Streets*, and the work of Robert Altman are not in the mainstream of the American film, but their proximity to prevalent social issues and more experimental filmmaking styles is much greater than that of previous maverick films and filmmakers.

Among directors involved in attacking our most cherished values and institutions in the late sixties, Bob Rafelson appeared to be the safest bet to enter the Hollywood fraternity. The virtues of *Five Easy Pieces* and *The King of Marvin Gardens* largely originate in an intimate, psychological study of a group of outsiders. The approach is not unlike the teledramas of the fifties that examined the anxieties and miseries of lower- and middle-class figures. The characters in Rafelson's two films tend to more perverse, violent emotions, but the dramatic intensity of Jack Nicholson's drifter in *Five Easy Pieces* and the ambivalent relationship of the two brothers played by Nicholson and Bruce Dern in *The King of Marvin Gardens* recharge the emotional fireworks and introspection in the teledramas of the fifties. Nicholson's characterizations as the feisty, forlorn anti-hero adrift from his family and society and as the shy, sensitive sibling unable to stop his brother's self-destructiveness are among the handful of original, heartfelt film creations that avoid the specter of Brando's hubris. Laszlo Kovacs's camerawork in the two films remains some of his best work. The script for *The King of Marvin Garden* calls for a poetic, pictorial rendition of the characters' estrangement, set against the fading splendor of Atlantic City; Kovacs's telephoto lens extends these dramatic entanglements, defining the characters' isolation amid the ashcan pomp of this once popular resort. Rafelson's direction, illuminating a Salinger-like mood of alienation, effectively integrates the feeling of moroseness and helplessness in Antonioni's triumphant style of the sixties.

Yet like many of his contemporaries who returned to the classics and conventions of Hollywood moviemaking, Rafelson's sensitivity to the psychological antinomies of the individual and society could find no point of contact in his remake of *The Postman Always Rings Twice*. George Jenkins's production details are far superior to the shanty cafeteria in which the original transpired, but neither Jack Nicholson nor Jessica Lange are able to instill any feelings into the simple, emotional dialectic of Cain's prose. The Tay Garnett original was a rather shabby work, but at least John Garfield and Lana Turner existed as true embodiments of two street angels trapped in the purgatory of their desires. The remake is submerged by its formalism; Jenkins's set pieces, from the musty decor of the café to the art deco of the bus depot and the airbrush languorousness of the courthouse lack any resonance other than as museum fabrications. Sven Nykvist's photography is equally craftsmanlike, yet the characters seem divorced from their surroundings: the passions of Nicholson and Lange are those of two sexual iconoclasts of the eighties whose lack of involvement in their roles reflects Rafelson's cursory attitude to the novel. Perhaps the chief culprit is David Mamet's screenplay, a sullen study of behavioral abstraction that gives no indication of the wonderfully lyric ear of his plays. The film's thorough alienaton from its characters, their problems, and their period is one striking example of mannerism as the single most ominous, retrogressive development during a period of revival.

A stronger aesthetic impulse but a less satisfying dramatic viewpoint punctuates Terence Malick's two films, *Badlands* and *Days of Heaven*. Malick's direction is more conceptual—his films present the protagonists as receding figures in his pictorially imitative recreations of America in the fifties and at the turn of the century. *Badlands* attempts to evoke and explain the love affair and ensuing killings through its impersonal configurations, visualizing small-town America as a dry pastoral typified by clean, iridescent streets. The film's formal beauty invests the town with a Hopper-like quietude; the violence displayed by Martin Sheen seems to challenge its ethical as well as structural formalism. Sissy Spacek's diary and voice-over narration, while characteristic of the film's distant tone, fail to personalize her character or relationship with Sheen. Her diary is a dumb, ethnographic rehash of the trash magazines she reads, and while it makes her a more genuine creation, it limits her dramatic viability.

The contrived, disjointed quality of Linda Manz's diary also mars *Days of Heaven*. A young, backwoods innocent again serves as narrator of a love triangle involving two migrant workers and their underage, sickly employer; like Spacek, her awkward, plaintive memoir further distances the story line and its impersonal encapsulation by Nestor Almendros's lyrical photography. Malick's unduly formal pictorial style and the girl's receding voice allows him to emphasize the visual dynamics of sharecropping. But since there is no inherent interplay between her narrative and the luminous still work, one questions the effectiveness of Malick's treatment. If he had wanted to explore the idyllic sweep of this period of American history, he could have concentrated on establishing a fluid editing format in the way Dovzhenko used dissolves in *Earth* to create a unified visual archetype involving the farmers, the land, and their animals. At best the film is an arty, self-conscious folk drama.

The films of Martin Scorsese offer a more varied yet strained example of modernism. Scorsese's novice effort, *Who's That Knocking at My Door?* makes an effective use of a jazzy, improvisational style. Like Cassavetes' *Shadows*, Scorsese conveys his characters' fluctuating moods without the prolixity in similar film journals. In *Mean Streets* Scorsese again features a group of rambling social misfits; his camera angles and cuts, however, are too enamored of their erratic behavior, and the tensions surrounding Harvey Keitel's relationships with his epileptic girl friend and moronic companion, played with an authentic lumpen swagger by Robert De Niro, are not resolved. Yet their torpor and then sudden bursts of violence are captured with an immediacy that fulfills Scorsese's improvisational style and the actors' methodlike, psychological permutations. In *Taxi Driver* the spontaneous violence and grim lassitude in *Mean Streets* are placed in the service of Paul Schrader's allegory of love and revenge. Both De Niro and Cybill Shepherd are treated as devious symbols of a once tainted innocence: De Niro because of his tour of Vietnam and Shepherd because of her association with the glib, populist presidential candidate. The numerous stultifying episodes, from De Niro's inviting Shepherd to a porno movie to Scorsese's backseat monologue as the abused husband are rhetorical examples of a defrocked priest trying to explain his loss of faith. Unlike Keitel's precarious innocent, who was constantly tested and invariably overwhelmed by the reckless actions of his friends, De Niro's antagonist is a primitive warrior whose increasingly psychotic behavior leads to his self-destruction in the garish sounds and colors of a New York cesspool. Similar to *Who'll Stop the Rain?*, where the nerve-shattering effects of California's drug culture transform Nick Nolte's drifter into the last marshal of the frontier, the violence of *Taxi Driver* becomes an abstraction of social and personal ills. At least Nolte's heroic defense was more honest in acknowledging his fated identity in a cast featuring the scarred veterans of Vietnam and the sixties; De Niro, however, is a self-styled dragon slayer whose attraction for the darker corners of urban life neutralizes Scorsese's and Schrader's tragic metaphor of national atrophy during the war years.

Scorsese fares worse with the nostalgia of *Alice Doesn't Live Here Anymore*. The coy juxtaposition of Keitel's neurotic cowboy to a representative movie cliché like Ellen Burstyn's precocious child removes the fluff of traditional portraits of the romantic heroine and results in a brittle project. *New York New York* is a more extreme example of Scorsese's flawed reinterpretations of classic movie projects. He is unable to follow through with his characterizations and opts for splintered, pictorial reminiscences concerning the half-baked musical archetypes of the forties. He tries to uncover the hard edges of his musical performers usually softened in musicals and musical biographies, but his digressions only extend the bathos and banality in what was originally a sugarcoated version of the musical world. De Niro, one of our most daring performers, seems to be laughing at his lines; Minnelli belts out two high-powered numbers, but it is simply the wrong film for Scorsese. I have not seen the full-length version, but *New York New York* seems to me one truncated work whose fragmentations lie in the imagination of its director.

*Raging Bull* combines the Group Theatre acting dynamics of *Mean Streets* and *Taxi Driver* with the pictorial nostalgia of *Alice Doesn't Live Here Anymore* and *New York New York*. In *Raging Bull* Scorsese's fascination with the violence in American culture is communicated by interrelating the guttural speech and emotional conflagrations of the family gatherings to the redolent clichés of boxing films. Its homage to the boxing-film genre is most directly and artistically fulfilled during the fight sequences; the dynamics of the introduction by the ring announcer, the choreography of the fighters' movements, and the crescendo montage of the bloodspilling knockout and the ringside reaction of flashing cameras isolate the ritualistic motifs surrounding this most brutal of sporting encounters. The exacting use of both slow motion and dispossessing jump cuts to show De Niro's jealousy and his animosity toward one of the Mafia lieutenants reveals a character whose most vivid self-expressions are manifested in his outbursts of violence. Yet the narrative is choppy; De Niro's towering inferno and the supporting characterizations, especially Joe Pesci's elusive sibling, often seem divorced from the period and fight-film stylizations. Its craft seems best exemplified by Michael Chapman's cinematography. Chapman worked as camera operator for Gordon Willis on *The Godfather*, and his extreme aperture opening and short focal range for the fight arenas and nightclubs with their pervasive clouds of smoke and darkness offers a black-and-white rotogravure counterpart to his mentor's work in color. Scorsese's involvement in the intimacy of De Niro and Pesci, and Chapman's piercing light backdrops for their encounters at home as well as his dark halos for the fight and nightclub settings present an experimental though valid compromise between the orthodoxies of fight films and the subjective intensity of Scorsese's psychological primitivism.

Schrader, who began his film career with a dogmatic study of spirituality in the films of Bresson, Dreyer, and Ozu, and whose scripts for *The Yakuza*, *Taxi Driver*, and *Rolling Thunder* are among the most existentially overwrought in the contemporary cinema, has directed three curiosities in the films of the seventies. His direction of *Blue Collar* is surprisingly literate, almost old-fashioned. The film concerns three factory workers, one white (Harvey Keitel) and two blacks (Richard Pryor and Yaphet Kotto), their stealing an unofficial company ledger listing illegal funds, and the dire events that ensue. Keitel provides another of his gripping, tormented characterizations, but the film's most dramatic moments involve the two black performers. The murder of Kotto, underscored by the hellish sounds of the factory and his gradual acquiescence to the poisonous gases, is one of the most stinging deaths in recent film memory. Pryor's performance begins with his customary raucous humor, but in meeting with his union boss, Pryor's paradoxical predicament, unable to further protest Kotto's murder without putting his own life in jeopardy, seems both pathetic and real. His confrontation with Keitel over Kotto's death further underlines the fate of his black worker; angered by the loss of his friend he expresses his resentment toward his superiors by telling Keitel how much more difficult it is for him as a black to protest the killing. We are back in the social realist environment of the fifties; even if *Blue Collar* does not extend the dramatic and social consciousness in a film like *Edge of the City*, one welcomes the author's interest in its straightforward behavioral exposition.

*Hardcore* is a more contrived project involving George C. Scott's tormented village elder and a prostitute who aids him in search of his runaway daughter. Unlike *Blue Collar*, which gives full expression to the tensions of its three major characters, *Hardcore* is a didactic narrative in which Scott's supreme indifference to the prostitute after she has helped him rescue his daughter proves dramatically implausible. Schrader indicts the callousness of Scott's religion and its dogma concerning those predestined for grace, but the film's conclusion makes the preceding drama superfluous. *American Gigolo* is a more deceptive work, combining thin scholasticism with a swank reading of sexual politics. Schrader's reverence for Bresson's *Pickpocket* shows not the slightest irony in transplanting Bresson's Catholic study of the lower depths to the California flesh-and-sex hustle. One simply notes the borrowings as a footnote that may be recorded in some future study of the French filmmaker. Schrader's absorbtion in the airy, sensual surfaces of California's high society barely sustains the decadent beat of Blondie and her bass-amplified drones; at this point in his career, Schrader receives low marks for his derivative symbolism.

Robert Altman, like Stanley Kubrick, is a maverick filmmaker whose stylistic independence has often led to flat, emotionless, overly conceptual interpretations. His least effective films, *Images* and *Buffalo Bill and the Indians*, are marred by his experimenting with a theme or style (fantasy in the former, Brechtian theater in the latter) that he treats with little insight. In *Images*, the fantasy becomes hopelessly muddled; Susannah York's precarious state of mind fails to resolve the nature of the interplay between real life characters and her inner demons. *Buffalo Bill and the Indians* never warms up to its material; the underlying epic theater motif of Buffalo Bill and Sitting Bull performing in a circus arena is explored only in the penultimate scene. In parts of the film Altman highlights the rhythmic activity and the overlapping dialogue of circus life; while this was a natural expression of his repertory of country-music bohemians in *Nashville*, it is incongruous to the stately, inhibitive drama of *Buffalo Bill and the Indians*.

*M\*A\*S\*H* shows Altman's flair for the disengaged comedy of the sixties, but after a decade of black humor, its flippancy seems better suited to television. In *McCabe and Mrs. Miller*, Altman turns his eye to the folk heroes of the West and their role in the transformation of a primitive country into an industrial empire. His characters, however, seem removed from the conflicting beauty and violence of their microcosmic social setting. The film presents a polemic of their innocence set against the gradual socialization of the West, but Vilmos Zsigmond's compositions with their heavily diffused light are too self-consciously pictorial for the characters' improvisational behavior. *Thieves like Us* and *The Long Goodbye* are similarly contrived neoclassical experiments that undercut the distinct appeal of the two works. Altman's adaptation of the Edward Anderson novel places greater emphasis on the formal pictorialism of the period than on the idiosyncratic speech and volatile emotional relationships that were featured in Nicholas Ray's *They Live by Night*. In *The Long Goodbye* he plays much looser with the original, substituting Elliott Gould's fumbling shamus for Marlowe's tough-mindedness—kinky eroticism for tragic corruptibility. Though intended as a fresh interpretation, the film is suspended in the social ennui and artistic eclecticism of the sixties.

*Nashville* remains Altman's most impressive work because of his choice of the effervescent drama around the Grand Ole Opry as the film's emotional and stylistic thread. The political campaign is adroitly used as a mocking, mysterious motif that is eventually incorporated into Altman's extravagant mosaic. The film's sage humor is generated by a confluence of personalities whose lives briefly intersect. The assassination of Barbara Jean is the one false moment in the film; it is as if Altman felt the need to politicize the carefree, joyous, and perhaps soulless spirit of his characters. A more honest, revelatory scene is that moment of illumination for Keith Carradine's lovers when his song explains the guiltless pleasures of his lovemaking. In capturing the characters' involvement in the giddy, make-believe world of fame and fortune, Altman refuses to compromise the sincerity of their emotional gambits even as one recognizes the duplicity it demands of them.

If the engaging amorality of *Nashville* lacks the decisiveness to render it a film classic of the seventies, *Three Women* reveals Altman's strengths in the very areas *Nashville* seemed weakest. Whereas *Nashville* is most alive to the frivolous, seemingly disjointed quality of the conversation and mood through a fluid, rhythmic editing flux, *Three Women* explores an intimate psychological bond with rare sensitivity. The acting rapport between Shelley Duvall and Sissy Spacek builds on their respective inadequacies in adjusting to their bare environment. The complete reversal in roles after Spacek's suicide attempt is baffling, but one believes in Duvall's recognition of her selfishness and Spacek's desire to hurt her for her previous insensitivity. Such touches as Duvall's dress caught in the car door, her babbling to her co-workers who regard her as an alien, Spacek's washing of her underwear after coming home, and her wonderment upon first seeing Duvall's mail-order decor apartment are examples of Altman's shrewd psychology in detecting the idiosyncracies of time and place in his characters' behavior. But similar to *Nashville*, *Three Women* ends inconclusively. This is not only true of the perverse ending, but also of Janice Rule's elusive, Cassandra-like patroness of the Dodge City Saloon. Her murals in the bar, shooting gallery, and swimming pool are suggestive of the deadly erotic undercurrents that bind the three women. But as explicit as Altman is in detailing the reverberating emotions in the relationship of Duvall and Spacek, we never discover the proximity of Rule and her murals. One could only wait and learn if Altman would combine the singular ironies and subtleties of *Nashville* and *Three Women* to make one great film or if he would fragment his talent in varied experimental efforts.

The answer, unhappily came much faster than one would have expected. *A Wedding* is a rank work. The techniques are similar to those encountered throughout his films of the seventies, but the story, the characterizations, and the texture of the drama have been jettisoned in Altman's send-up of American sham. *Popeye* is an unusual project for Altman but a similar disappointment. It stars Robin Williams, one of the few reasons kids had for watching television, and Shelley Duvall, who, with her recent work as Wendy in *The Shining*, continues to enrich our feelings toward her characterizations of plain, awkward females. The supporting cast does not measure up to this pair's talents, but I approached the film hopeful that the energy of comic books and the association with famed European cinematographer Giuseppe Rotunno would enable Altman to strike a new direction for his art. However, the arrow points south and not north. The treatment is nonverbal—when it is not inaudible or incomprehensible; the luminous designs, employing some of the softest colors Rotunno has used since *Amarcord*, create scenic backdrops that are substitutes for the graphic and action dynamics of cartoons. However, there is no continuity, none of the whiplash kinetics and violence of the Popeye caricature or the Max Fleischer cartoons. In my count Altman has single-handedly negated the mimetic appeal of Williams and Duvall, the visual magic of cartoons, the innocence of fables, and the idea of movies in the seventies and eighties as a blending of myth and art. Its lone competitor is *Superman*, an incompetent megabuck production whose earth-shattering, head-splitting process effects fail to compensate for the innocent heroics of the comic book or television series.

*The Driver—The Outlaw Josie Wales*

The cycle of black-exploitation films and the appeal of stars like Charles Bronson, Burt Reynolds, and Sylvester Stallone are isolated expressions of the film neoclassicism of the seventies. The impact of neoclassicism on the American movie experience of the seventies must then be explained through its effect on the most popular, representative movies and filmmaking styles of the decade.

Two of the more stylized approaches to the conventions of action filmmaking appear in the films of Walter Hill and Steven Spielberg. Hill was responsible for the script of *The Getaway*, and his own films accentuate its streamlined mythology and methodology. If the weaknesses in the script for *Hard Times* were overshadowed by its classic delineation of Bronson's persona, Hill's scripts and direction of *The Driver*, *The Warriors*, and *The Long Riders* are among the most acute examples of the mannerist tendencies in the neoclassicism of the seventies. *The Driver* is one of the more cool evocations of a hot genre. The machismo of Peckinpah's anti-heroes, which triggered his kinetic explosions, is transformed into a mask of indifference for Ryan O'Neal's racing technocrat. The chases are not treated as supporting episodes, but become the subject of Hill's and cinematographer Philip Lathrop's distillation of this classic movie convention, breaking down O'Neal's pursuits into concise, Mondrianesque boxes, the horizontals of the car interiors juxtaposed to the verticality of the cars encompassed in the larger rectangles and squares of the city streets. It is a minimalist, mechanically autonomous interpretation of the genre.

The superannuation of character and conflict becomes more problematic in *The Warriors*. The movements of his fugitive gang through the streets and subway stations sustain an attractive elasticity, but without one's empathy with the characters. The film's assumption of urban nihilism and high-art decor makes the work seem a pastiche of New York City Ballet modernism subsumed by American Ballet Theatre story gristmill. In *The Long Riders* Hill finds his most sympathetic material. Because the elements of myth and romantic metaphor have long characterized interpretations of the West, one is less wary of Hill's decision to pictorially abstract contemporary journalistic accounts of the James-Younger gang through the sepia-toned compositions featuring three families of brothers. The chases and gunfights, however, are rendered with the architectural iciness of *The Driver*; the film lacks the linking motifs that Peckinpah brought out in his treatment of Bob Dylan's folk ballads and the adobe fortress of the gang in *Pat Garrett and Billy the Kid*. Hill's distant, depersonalized style is well suited to discovering the physical attributes of his settings and characters, but not to the dynamic cross section of the gang's fate during the numerous chases and gunfights. These are the least interesting parts of the film, without the paradoxical currents of savage self-fulfillment and surreal horror in Peckinpah's editing of *The Wild Bunch*. The most rewarding moments absorb one in the West as a series of photoengravings of pioneer towns and their marauders.

One of several college-trained directors now working in Hollywood, Steven Spielberg first attempted to refine action filmmaking to its most elementary components. In *Duel* Spielberg's crosscutting between an invisible, crazed truck driver and Dennis Weaver's innocent traveler achieves a Porteresque simplicity in the repeated assults on Weaver. Like George Lucas's award-winning college short, *THX-1138, Duel* derives its intensity from the crisp, repetitive use of editing techniques that have usually functioned as the denouement in action films. *The Sugarland Express* combines *versimo* drama and action filmmaking. The characters of William Atherton's fugitive from the law, Goldie Hawn's tremulous wife, and the policeman with whose car they abscond perpetuate their psychological portrayals in an automobile extravaganza that encompasses small towns, mobile home parks, and the open countryside. Both Atherton and Hawn give remarkably controlled portraits of emotionally distraught outsiders, mainly within the confines of a police car. Spielberg has fashioned a tight essay on the colorful yet dehumanized nature of their backgrounds, and although much of the film is too schematic, his immersion in Hawn's live-wire heroine manages to hold one's attention.

Spielberg's next two projects, *Jaws* and *Close Encounters of the Third Kind*, utilize dramatic and cinematic clichés in a more commercial manner. *Jaws* again shows Spielberg's highly constricted mise-en-scène, his arrangement of the island resort into distinct physical units, the most menacing area being the beach to which his camera returns in the manner of a Peeping Tom whose gaze shifts from one window to the next. His trio of struggling macho types provides some amusing moments, especially in the self-mockery of Robert Shaw, who appears to be cutting at the heavy he first played with aplomb opposite Sean Connery in *From Russia with Love*. *Close Encounters of the Third Kind*, with its high-voltage, symbolic sound effects and its glorification of middle-America fantasies about alien beings, projects a *National Enquirer*–type mentality. The mysteries or perhaps the banalities of outer space are experienced through Richard Dreyfuss's kid in man's clothing. He is an apocryphal lowbrow whose childlike behavior fails to engage one in his inevitable meeting with the aliens. The arrival of the spaceship is indeed one of the magical sequences in science-fiction film history, but one wonders why these supremely intelligent aliens want to meet and mate with such an ephemeral species as Dreyfuss's clodhopper.

With *1941* and *Raiders of the Lost Ark*, Spielberg's elevation to the direction of the most prestigious pop productions results in more anonymous stylizations. The commercial failure of *1941* may have resulted from its impersonal dramatic voice; no one character leads its chaotic assault on movie mayhem and social frenzy in the manner that Dreyfuss personified UFO fantasies. There is an overriding element of mechanical contrivance in its slapstick configurations, but Spielberg shows far better timing than did John Landis in *The Blues Brothers*. Whereas Landis's production excesses undercut the spoofing of John Belushi and Dan Aykroyd, Spielberg imbues *1941* with a randiness one associates with silent-film comedy. This is hardly a leitmotif of Wagnerian proportions, but it gives the film a socially kinetic stimulus lacking in the repetitious, disconnected exercises in chaos in *The Blues Brothers*. Other than the scene involving Ray Charles and Aretha Franklin, where the iconographic posing of Belushi and

Aykroyd is unexpectedly invigorated by the naturally funky predisposition of Charles and Franklin, the self-consciousness of *The Blues Brothers* finds the mannerist features of seventies moviemaking equating its slapstick tone to its surfeit of physical explosions. Landis's *National Lampoon's Animal House* is not as polished as *The Blues Brothers*, but its bellicose, ebullient undergraduates at least were given ample time to express their nonconformity. Spielberg's production has too many climactic send-ups of physical comedy, and there could have been a sharper juxtaposition of its sexual innocents to their make-believe backgrounds. But the performers never seem to affect their merriment, and the state-of-the-art miniature photography coordinated by William Fraker, A. D. Flowers, and Gregory Jein creates a hallucinating metaphor of its characters submerged within a wartime playland.

*Raiders of the Lost Ark* shows the influence of producer George Lucas in its more straightforward magnification of the fabrications of the serial film. The film's pinpoint storyboard editing, however, abbreviates the dramatic self-irony in its execution. The problem with the film is that the action precedes the characters' involvement: the audience is propelled into successive episodes of danger without any comic, romantic, or thematic buildup. Its most acute film homage is not to any serial, but to *The Ten Commandments*, and particularly the process work of John Fulton. It underscores Lucas's and now Spielberg's commitment to filmmaking in terms of the mechanization of character and plot. Mannerism, the most dangerous by-product of neoclassicism, here receives its most professionally glib exploitation.

Among the major crime films of the seventies, *The French Connection* and the continuing saga of Harry Callahan (*Dirty Harry, Magnum Force, The Enforcer*) offer modern variations on Hollywood crime films. There are two reasons for the dramatic incisiveness of *The French Connection*. First is Gene Hackman's Popeye Doyle, a ludicrous, pop-art figure of a policeman, who with his soiled shirt, unshaven face, and blustering manner, could be mistaken for a criminal. Yet it is Hackman's uncouthness and mercilessness as a police officer that give his character a genuine street-wise contemporaneousness. There have been tough, scary policemen in movies, but few who won our sympathy. From *Little Caesar* through *Bonnie and Clyde* the police remain supporting social symbols: it is the criminal who holds the viewer's interest and who best captures the social unrest. But it is Hackman's tenacity as a policeman and the quirks of his behavior that inspire the most intriguing, dramatically unifying parts of the film. The second distinct feature of *The French Connection* is the urban background and chase sequences. Owen Roizman's pungent colors and Dean Tavoularis's art direction incorporate the city as a dynamic, organic component. The chase sequences, particularly Doyle's pursuit of the hit man, derive their impact from both a personal and technological quality. Not only are two different modes of transportation juxtaposed, but the circumvention of the law by policeman and criminal augments its nihilism. The chases in *Bullitt* and *The Driver* are technically more beautiful, but it is the nature of our empathy with Doyle that makes the chases in *The French Connection* more riveting.

In his role as a police officer, Clint Eastwood remains a loner owing to his suspiciousness of social legislation and sociological maxims that profess a belief in rehabilitating antisocial types. His adversaries, particularly Andy Robinson's psychopath in *Dirty Harry*, are shown as metaphors of destruction whose absence of any redeeming human features simplifies our attraction to Eastwood's tough-minded cop. The chase ending in Keezar Stadium in *Dirty Harry* graphically fulfills a quality of Eastwood's tracking of criminals established at the very beginning of his first contemporary crime drama, *Coogan's Bluff*, in which he confronts his adversary in the desert. In Eastwood's films good and evil are not analyzed, but involve a confrontation of wits and macho between two uncaged animals. With the exception of Charles Bronson, no other major folk adventurer so uniquely assumes the role of a hero who, because of his realization that he is a professional gunslinger, can only hurt himself and society by observing its rules.

Essaying the role of the criminal in *Escape from Alcatraz*, Eastwood, cinematographer Bruce Surtees, and director Don Siegel have fashioned a study of blue-on-blue to warm the heart of William Gass. The work has strong overtones of the formalism and constrained dramatic sequentiality one associates with Jean-Pierre Melville. Eastwood's lithe, hard, gaunt figure heads a group of outcasts who wear their blue denim shirts and navy pea jackets as an emblem of their spiritual passivity. The interiors of the cells and dining area as well as the exteriors of the Pacific yield nuances of blue that imbue the planning and escape with a style of supercool. This is in sharp contrast to the more "hot" dynamics of the heist that have been featured over the last decade. *Escape from Alcatraz* was released the same year Eastwood began his travels with a simian soul mate in *Every Which Way but Loose*, a one-two, artistic-commercial success that one surmises makes Burt green with envy. *Bronco Billy* showed, however, that even this most enterprising of superstars was not immune to the pseudofolk poetry of the seventies.

The last films of John Wayne, when combined with Eastwood's characterizations of the western gunslinger, provide telling examples of how this genre has adapted a mood of violence and cynicism without suffering any significant changes in its narrative simplicity and primitive morality. The basic difference among the figures of innocence portrayed by James Stewart, Gary Cooper, Henry Fonda, and John Wayne is that Wayne sustained his popularity while rarely attempting the more controversial roles they undertook. Wayne's towering figure made him ideally suited to personify the archetypal hero of the West pioneered by Tom Mix and Hoot Gibson. He is a presence whose physical dimensions and limited dramatic repertoire embody the virtues of western manliness and frontier justice.

With its elements of farce and self-humor, *True Grit* applies some frizzles to the classic Wayne portraiture. Wayne is surprisingly resilient, playing his role with what one is tempted to call "gay abandon." In *Cahill—United States Marshal*, a more typical Wayne project of the seventies, he is given little opportunity for the truculent independence that characterized his work with Ford. He is an aging, tired defender of the law who must cope with the delinquent behavior of his sons who have drifted apart as a result of his selfless devotion to the law. There is one expressive moment when Wayne, tending one of his ailing sons, wonders what went wrong and remembers the last words of his wife: "Go get 'em, J. D." He has been "gettin' 'em" for over forty years, but in such a hack work as *Cahill—United States Marshal* he seems an anachronism. *The Shootist*, however, admirably serves as an epilogue to Wayne's career, and to the first fifty years of the western in the sound film. It is a reverie on the legend of the West that is John Wayne. In it Wayne confronts the numerous stereotypes of western folklore who reveal to him the painful truth that his identity has been as the fastest draw. Both his old acquaintances, such as Sheree North's bad girl, and his new companions, such as Ron Howard's admiring, troubled youth, see him only as a myth, which leads to Wayne's recognition that he must fight one last battle to satisfy his enemies and admirers. The references to his terminal cancer are unusually evocative, not simply for combining the real and mythic, but also in denoting the modest contemporaneousness of the western. Had director Don Siegel decided to reject the conventions of western narrative and allowed Wayne to survive the pell-mell shot in the back after he has killed his three adversaries, the film might have become a truly Bergmanesque dirge in dealing with the death of a legend. By remaining faithful to western clichés, Wayne's death serves as a romantic coda, even if some of us might have preferred a more modern, fatalistic intertwining of realism and mythology.

Wayne's imposing figure and general taciturnity are filtered through Eastwood's character in three westerns that significantly altered the genre. In *A Fistful of Dollars*, *For a Few Dollars More*, and *The Good the Bad and the Ugly*, Eastwood plays a loner who transforms Wayne's ideal western protagonist from a figure of indomitable morality to one of amorality. He remains the good guy, but one whose goodness is defined by his asocial stance and shrewdness, his uncanny instinct for survival, and a willingness to settle all disputes in a shootout. He is an outsider who sees that his ability to stay alive is dependent on his cynical attitude to society; unlike Wayne or Cooper he does not conceive fistfighting or gentleness to the ladies as essential virtues. The West of Sergio Leone is more brutal than that of John Ford and Louis L'Amour, and Eastwood's nameless loner is its champion because he stands apart and remains the fastest draw.

Eastwood's original effort behind the camera, *Play Misty for Me*, proves an effective compendium of scare techniques while dissecting his own nasty appeal. His direction of *High Plains Drifter*, however, dilutes the spice of his first two Leone films. Like most directors of the post-Leone western, he relies on baroque camera angles and excessive use of close-ups and shock cuts, but without the humor or hyperbolic violence in Leone's best work. The popularity of Eastwood's westerns from *Two Mules for Sister Sara* through *The Outlaw Josie Wales* is consistent with Leone's aura of violence but without a restructuring of the sparse dramatic conventions of the genre. The lack of dramatic expansiveness has long been a trademark of the western, and the clichéd treatment of violence and currently acceptable perversity of Eastwood's rakish figure loom as replacements for the pristine charm of John Ford's West and the incontrovertibility of John Wayne's crusading hero.


## The Exorcist–Alien

If the techniques of violence have transformed the western from a quaint, rarefied tale to a mechanical, manipulative landscape of destruction, the fantasy film has reverted to the most basic dynamics of the genre: the special effects. Such films as *The Exorcist*, *The Omen*, *Carrie*, and *The Fury* overwhelm the audience with brutal, hedonistic displays of carnage and production whimsy.

*The Exorcist* brilliantly updates the contrivances of horror through its use of the child as the unknowing medium of the horror. While this generates the audience's sympathy for Linda Blair's possession, one responds to the spectacle of terror as a hallucination that is not meant to be explained. Each trip to the child's room is like entering a sideshow at a carnival: the audience knows it is being tricked, but the very bestiality of the effects works as a narcotic, the increasing ugliness of the child's appearance revealing the power of the supernatural force. Director William Friedkin is to be given credit for a sympathetic cast of supporting players, particularly Jason Miller's doubting acolyte. His anxiety, like that of Ellen Burstyn's mother, is based on a common emotion—devotion and love of family; the realism of their torment makes their helplessness before Linda Blair's possession all the more gripping.

Brian De Palma's companion telekinesis films, *Carrie* and *The Fury*, pursue a slightly different viewpoint. The power of the three telekinetic children in the two films is not treated as a contemporary sign of the struggle of good and evil, but as an uncontrollable force of nature. In *Carrie* the vestiges of classic Gothic remain through the association of Piper Laurie's psychotic, evangelical mother and Carrie's telekinetic powers. By refusing then to incorporate any parallel elements of abnormality into the parents of the telekinetic children in *The Fury*, De Palma seems to have opted for a more facile drama; one is entranced by the various explosions of anger as independent, surreal forces that permeate his films the way a rainbow marks the horizon. For this reason, I find *The Fury* a more exciting film, a better example of pure terror, even as one acknowledges the depth of the cult worship of Sissy Spacek's pubescent monster. The opening raid on the Israeli resort, the car chase under the subway which seems to transpire in a subterranean world of no exists, the devastating attack on the Arabs at the shopping center–amusement park, the son's destruction of his mistress, and the girl's evisceration of John Cassavetes function as creative organizations of the raw technology of the medium—extravagant attacks on the unsuspecting filmgoer. John Williams's score is a brooding counterpart to De Palma's juicy visuals, one of his few film compositions that avoids the repetitive crescendoes in his brass-orchestrated space sound tracks.

A "cult" favorite of the seventies, *Night of the Living Dead*, is one of countless examples of the decreasing credibility and increasing self-consciousness of the genre. One of the reasons that fantasy films, more than other genres, attain cult status, a phenomenon that seems to have proliferated with Roger Corman's entry into the field in the fifties, is because of the freedom given the spectator to infer some symbolic meaning from the transparent narratives. The absence of character, plot development, or visual elegance in Corman's initial science-fiction efforts overturns the moral didacticism of the genre with the solipsism and chicanery of a pop-art scavenger. Not as solemn as television's "The Twilight Zone" or as scientifically precocious as "Star Trek", Corman's films are pointlessly absurd parodies of both the Gothic formulas of the thirties and the anxiety-ridden space fantasies of the fifties. George Romero's *Night of the Living Dead*, with its home-movie gloss, its amateurish acting, and overall miserable production values, continues the Corman tradition—another example of the mystical power of camp.

*Halloween* is a more straightforward tale, a minimalist exercise in terror that strips the genre to its most fundamental properties and emotional associations. John Carpenter's use of the subjective camera does not exploit our common fears about the dark as do numerous horror films dealing with a group of isolated wanderers. His simplified camera strategies, like the house in which Jamie Lee Curtis is trapped as she is pursued by the bogeyman, effectively reduce the fantasy film to a fearful realization of a child's nightmare. Yet if one had thought that the visual control exhibited in *Halloween* and in the preceding *Dark Star*, like that of Lucas's *THX-1138*, would reap further dividends in Hollywood, Carpenter's succeeding projects exposed him as an odious opportunist. His association with Kurt Russell in *Escape from New York* and *The Thing* were characterized by Carpenter's unsuccessful rip-offs of original sources—underground comic books in *Escape from New York* and the special effects of *Alien* in *The Thing*.

A writer-director more sympathetic to the moral crisis engendered by science is David Cronenberg. His interests lie in balancing the mechanics of horror with an attack on its social origins—mind control in *The Brood* and the use of drugs as a genetic and environmental panacea in *Scanners*. In *The Brood* his sharp cross-cutting between Samantha Eggar's self-immolated mother and her family of disfigured offspring works as a simple dialectic of inner withdrawal and physical and emotional autonomy. In *Scanners* his story of two brothers who resolve the effects of the drug their mother took while pregnant with them creates a more consistently hallucinatory experience. His sound track, beginning with the nerve-shattering crowd scenes, conveys the sensory impact of sound on his protagonist's altered consciousness. With the exception of the final drawn-out psychic blow-out between the two brothers and its conclusive imagery of eyeballs spinning around like symbols on wheels in a slot machine, Cronenberg suggests the threat of terror through his elliptical editing of the good brother's search for his other brother. The subjective undercurrents of fantasy achieve one of its more poetic treatments through the penetration of the mordant sounds and colors on the hero's exposed psyche.

Two films stand out in a period that has seen the exploration of the unknown characterized by faceless symbols of evil whose multiple murders necessitate the use of a computer. One, *The Texas Chainsaw Massacre*, uses the clichés of the genre—innocent, college-aged kids on an outing, rural backgrounds, horrific acts of violence—to make a classic statement in American Gothic. The second, *Alien*, juxtaposes the unnerving demands of space travel to its hip crew in a manner that redeems Corman's fulsome metaphors of anxiety and social caricature. *The Texas Chainsaw Massacre*, written and directed by Tobe Hooper, immediately declares its antecedents in the evil of Welles's *Touch of Evil* and Hitchcock's *Psycho*. Its opening image of the mutilated graveyard figures makes the first of several analogies to celebrated pictorial abstractions of horror, in this instance to the tortured baroque creations of Aleijadinho. After a perverse, prefatory scene involving the paraplegic relieving himself, the action inside the van briefly introduces the victims and modestly delineates our feelings toward them. The key figure is the paraplegic, and his oafish, obnoxious manner alerts one to the fact that he will suffer the cruelest fate. One problem with the van sequence is that it is too manipulative; once they pick up one of the crazed members of the family, Hooper refuses to show any sunlight penetrating the van. It has the look of the studio, and though one is engrossed by the foredoomed nature of the innocents' questioning of the psychotic, it is the only scene in the movie in which one is conscious of its contrivedness.

The ensuing killings are terrifyingly real. It is not until some twenty minutes into the film that the slaughter commences, with a pig squeal from the kitchen that is dramatically accompanied by three jump cuts. After the savage directness of the first attack, the victim's girl friend enters, and in a scene that typifies Hooper's emotional gambit, she falls into a room filled with the bones of animals, the camera panning with her this excremental vision. Her girl friend experiences the most devastating image of her attackers' cannibalism, when upon first escaping, she encounters a gas station attendant, and while he runs off, apparently looking for help, she turns her head to find an interior barbecue pit filled with human and animal flesh. It seems meaningless to dwell on the protracted chase, capture, and final escape of the heroine, its revved-up editing matching the power of the masked villain's chainsaw and the heroine's continuous, hysterical cries of fear. We have entered the world of the death camps, of the apocalyptic murders devised by Charles Manson, and of those culminating images of shock and horror of Akim Tamiroff's death mask placed above Janet Leigh's drugged, abused heroine in *Touch of Evil* and of Anthony Perkins's skeleton in *Psycho*.

Whereas *The Texas Chainsaw Massacre* interprets its backgrounds and characters as representative models of American Gothic, *Alien* studies the effect of the gloss and abstraction of its spacecraft interior on its cast of genuine, quirky characters. The production, costing some $10 million dollars, makes a far more intelligent use of effects gadgetry than several more famous megabuck productions. Director Ridley Scott and his crew have done a beautiful job with their spacecraft set, tracking through its long, silent corridors to give the viewer a feel for its layout and logistics while emphasizing the unsettling spell of its futuristic architecture. The opening incubation scene and the numerous encounters with the central computer called "mother" capture the rhythms of technology in a way that is beyond the imagination of the creators of "Star Trek." The alien and crew members show an equally savvy blending of film and social folklores. The metamorphosis of the alien becomes a cross section of movie monsters, culminating in its final transformation into a mechanically recharged creature from the black lagoon of outer space. The crew is a comic vitalization of the allegorical protagonists in Corman's miniscule productions; their emotional rapport strikes a welcome note of kinship with the audience. The production design, whether of the spacecraft or of the interior dwelling of the alien, establishes a poignant affinity with the grim visions of modern artists. The journey through the alien's shrine seems to pay homage to Henry Moore's famous cave drawings of post-Holocaust survivors. *2001: A Space Odyssey* became the space-age classic for imbuing the hardware sheen of its subject with a mystical, religious aura; *Alien*, however, with its mesmerizing design and spooked characters rediscovers the basic paradoxical emotions of expectation and dread surrounding our space fantasies.

### The Producers–Next Stop Greenwich Village

Of the numerous genres that have contributed to the hegemony of the American film, the comedy film has usually functioned as the best example of its charm, energy, and artistry. The revival of slapstick in Mel Brooks's films, in those of Woody Allen prior to *Annie Hall*, in Peter Sellers's Inspector Clouseau series, and the popularity of farceurs such as Gene Wilder, Dom De Luise, and Richard Pryor attest to the strength of slapstick as a living part of our cultural heritage. Slapstick, however, has never achieved the preeminence it possessed during the silent era. As often as one returns to the films of the Marx Brothers, Mae West, or W. C. Fields, they rarely work as coherent parodies of our manners. Their outlandish appearance and prankish behavior invite the audience on a fantasy adventure in which, similar to Samuel Butler's *Erewhon*, there is a complete reversal of the role models and values upheld in everyday society.

The films of Mel Brooks show the most comprehensive application of slapstick in the contemporary cinema. *The Producers*, his first, most simple, and still perhaps his best film, derives its humor from the disparate comic masks of Zero Mostel and Gene Wilder. The deliberate pacing in Mostel's office as he hoodwinks Wilder into believing that millions are theirs for the asking is a brilliant tour de force. His glib speech and corpulent figure entice Wilder like a mother convincing her child to drink a glass of milk. The intelligence of Wilder's performance lies in conveying his understanding of Mostel's ingenious plan through a gradual animation of his facial features. Mostel, an overpowering theatrical performer, finds an ideal comic opposite in Wilder's catatonic bookkeeper, yet the emotional and stylistic chemistry in this updated vaudeville skit is not developed in Brooks's later films. His work as a writer for "Your Show of

Shows" is acutely exploited in *Blazing Saddles* and *High Anxiety*, wherein he satirizes the conventions of the western and suspense films. *Blazing Saddles* lacks a focus other than its roughshod treatement of western clichés. Brooks attempts a surrealization of the West, but the elaborate chase sequences and other forms of split-second mayhem in the silent films of Chaplin and Keaton are sadly missing. Brooks's most successful genre inversion, *Young Frankenstein*, juxtaposes Gerald Hirschfeld's tribute to the backlighting in the Hollywood fantasy films of the thirties to the blissful idiocy of its caricatures, most winningly evidenced in Peter Boyle's pragmatic transplant monster. *High Anxiety* is a more subdued work, but Brooks's comic protagonist is neither cleverly destructive nor effectively ineffective, and the burlesque characterizations of Harvey Korman and Cloris Leachman seem too extravagant in this film satire. A more amusing treatment of Hitchcockian motifs permeates *Silver Streak*. Jill Clayburgh's performance shows a diligent reading of her screwball mentors, and the hysterical comic persona of Gene Wilder, effectively restrained, sustains the comic ironies through their incongruity in a suspense film.

Other names to consider in the revitalization of slapstick are Andrew Bergman and David Walsh. Bergman has one of the more cultivated ears among writers fascinated with the catalyzing properties of comic hyperbole. His script for *The In-Laws*, like his mystery parodies (*The Big Kiss-Off of 1944, Hollywood and LeVine*), display a cunning absorption of popular movie and literary conventions. Peter Falk gives one of his more affable characterizations, but Bergman is not as successful with the frenetic tantrums of Alan Arkin. Ryan O'Neal replays the frozen innocent of *What's Up Doc?* in Bergman's *So Fine*; Bergman's script, however, misses the voice of Falk's bravura parody, and his direction is too quick to jump the gun on its numerous chase sequences. Walsh appears to be the favorite cameraman of comic writers and directors (*Sleeper, Murder by Death, Silver Streak, Foul Play, The In-Laws*). Although often at the mercy of his scripts, his bright colors have reconfirmed the wisdom of high-key photography in the genre. *Murder by Death* is one of Neil Simon's more effective satires as much for its stylish repertoire of acting talents as for Walsh's parodic configurations. If there is an interchangeability about his lighting for Woody Allen and Neil Simon, the lighthearted, melodramatic hijinks of *Silver Streak* result from the interplay of Clayburgh and Wilder in its flavorsome compositions.

Woody Allen's schlemiel, the most popular of contemporary comic protagonists, updates the misadventures of the funny man. His first four films are poorly made, yet the appeal of Allen's pathetic underdog is undeniable. His slight, awkward figure is reminiscent of both Langdon's fumbling man-child and Lloyd's boy next door. Although Allen's schlemiel is hardly a representative type, and his one attribute, his wit, would seem to inspire comparison with a comedian of the sound era, the contemporaneousness of the anti-hero is not unlike that of the silent-film clown in the first stages of mechanization. The similarity between Allen's schlemiel and Lloyd's persona rests on the absence of a strong athletic or balletlike quality in either of their characters. Lloyd's routines were derivative; although his repeated adventures hanging onto a skyscraper were performed without a safety device, he succeeded not because of an inherent skill, but because of the conventions of the genre. Chaplin and Keaton distinguish themselves from their dramatic opposites through their ethereal, death-defying grace; Allen, like Lloyd, depends on luck in escaping unharmed from his perilous misadventures.

The best of Allen's screen portrayals, and the only one in which his mastery of physical comedy does not, as in *Bananas* and *Love and Death*, lead to innocuous though often amusing time fillers of spastic paralysis, is as the nebbish film buff in *Play It Again Sam*. The film makes good use of Owen Roizman's stylish, nostalgic tones for Allen's fantasy entrapment and heroic character transformation. In *Annie Hall*, a similar metamorphosis occurs, not in Allen's character but in that of his inamorata, Diane Keaton. Allen still plays the schlemiel, but in the surprising conclusion in a movie repertory house showing *The Sorrow and the Pity*, Keaton's hapless character is transformed into a secure, independent woman largely because of her recognition of the wisdom of Allen's flippant expressions of shame when they previously watched *The Sorrow and the Pity*. The schlemiel may still end up alone, but his comic insights have contributed to the self-education of another human being. This was an essential feature of Chaplin's art. In his succeeding films, however, Allen disassociates himself from the comic ethos of slapstick. After a disastrous imitation of "Playhouse 90" in a hand-me-down Ingmar Bergman style in *Interiors*, Allen turns to safer, more familiar ground with the simple, unencumbered nostalgia of *Manhattan*. Allen does not try to reinterpret a period or style; Gordon Willis's classical homage to the textures of black-and-white photography treats the characters and their emotional vicissitudes as a reflection of their romantically civilized decor. It is certainly easier to watch than *Interiors*, but why, when Allen seemed so close to fulfilling a personal comic style and persona in *Annie Hall* has he retreated to the lazy, self-indulgent, piano-bar lyric drama of *Manhattan*? If the answer is in *Stardust Memories*, then those who applauded the mellow-yellow of *Manhattan* are confronted with the hung over, mirror image of a comic trying to be both funny and wise and who at a relatively early age is faced with his own dissipated image.

One comedy genre the American film has experienced the greatest difficulty in renewing is screwball comedy. During Hollywood's golden age film studios were blessed with a number of performers who sparkled in stories about courtship and those moments of crisis in marriage which lead to the recognition that their partner was indeed the best of all possible choices. But among the more popular performers and writers involved in reinterpreting the battle of the sexes, there is a quality of sour, strained humor left over from the sixties that undercuts the irrepressible social misanthropy that this genre exhibited in the thirties and forties.

Two films starring Warren Beatty, *Shampoo* and *Heaven Can Wait*, characterize both the modern and archaic approaches to screwball comedy in the seventies. In *Shampoo* Beatty's role as a hairdresser and his affairs with Julie Christie's call girl, Goldie Hawn's hippie, and Lee Grant's housewife underscore the amorality in contemporary comedy. In the screwball classics marriage was conceived as a dangerous, but not impossible arrangement, and while one initially empathized with the idiosyncratic resistance of performers like Cary Grant, Katharine Hepburn, Carole Lombard, and Spencer Tracy, there was an underlying recognition of the wisdom in the inevitable union or reunion of the male and female leads. But in *Shampoo* Beatty's love god distrusts marriage; he also senses an inherent perniciousness in trying to live out the love ethic of the sixties. The film has several amusing, offbeat encounters—the initial romp with Lee Grant, the bathroom sequence with Julie Christie, the brief encounter with Carrie Fisher, and those in which Goldie Hawn's jerky leg movements intimate her impatience in renewing their sexual dalliances. These portraits of the late sixties are sharply sketched, but as the film begins with a radical thematic and moral premise in the coupling of Beatty and Grant, the characters' lackadaisical erotic adventures cancel out the option for a return to conventional morality and the numerous comedic turns that secured this transition. What is most surprising about *Heaven Can Wait* is Beatty's choice of *Here Comes Mr. Jordan*, a minor, dated vehicle when it was first made. The film offers few conventional delights other than Dyan Cannon's scatterbrained adulteress. The most intriguing aspect of the film is how Beatty, whose comic persona proved the most wooden feature of *Shampoo* and was further ridiculed in *The Fortune*, uses the film as an autobiographical statement about the inviolability of Julie Christie as his love object. What ideal, contemporary roles he has found for himself as a football player and Christie as an outspoken activist; it may be the most benign characterizations among our screwball adventurers since the final pairing of Tracy and Hepburn in *Guess Who's Coming to Dinner*.

Another example of the failure of screwball comedy to sustain its good-natured assaults on American morality concerns the comic persona of Jack Lemmon. Lemmon's original roles in the genre—as Judy Holliday's equally obtuse romantic foil in *It Should Happen to You*, as the bongo playing warlock in *Bell Book and Candle*, and as the fun-loving prankster in *Mister Roberts*—were followed by his development as a major comic actor in four Billy Wilder films—the deliciously dumb brunet in *Some Like It Hot*; the ill-equipped hustler in *The Apartment*; the confused, miserable protagonist caught between the duplicity of his wife and brother-in-law in *The Fortune Cookie*; and his virtuoso characterization of Hildy Johnson in *The Front Page*. Although there is an undeniable souring in Wilder's treatment of Lemmon's hyperkinetic figure, these films are among the most literate comedies attempted in Hollywood in a period which also used Lemmon as the good-natured sexual panhandler in such impotent exhibitions of male menopause as *Under the Yum Yum Tree*, *Good Neighbor Sam*, and *How to Murder Your Wife*. In the seventies Lemmon completes his transformation into a grouchy, middle-aged malcontent. His roles as the beleaguered tourist in *The Out-of-Towners* and as the fired executive in *The Prisoner of Second Avenue* evidence a change in comedy from a spirited attack on American values to a feeble stab at the American dream.

This transformation is largely exemplified by Neil Simon whose sententious formulas characterize the influence of television's situation comedies on film comedy stylizations. There is hardly a moment in Simon's films that does not expose the contrived nature of his work; the dialogue is reduced to a constant banter of sophomoric repartee, as if his protagonists were auditioning for the *National Lampoon*. He has created a large body of literature that interprets such issues as marriage separation, joblessness, and the specter of loneliness and old age as an invitation to borscht belt Jewish humor overladen with Noël Coward insouciance. *The Sunshine Boys* is one of his less offensive works because the bickering between Walter Matthau and George Burns originates in their work as vaudeville performers. The vast majority of his films, however, show the canned effects of television comedy in which the clever rejoinders obscure the characters' problems while infusing various segments of American life with the simulated, sly rebuttal. His style of cocktail-party ripostes permeates television with the wiseacre banter and demographic conviviality in the Norman Lear and Grant Tinker productions.

One of the few departures from the Simonizing of American comedy comes from another veteran of the television medium, Paddy Chayefsky. In *The Hospital* he draws out the black humor surrounding the running of a big-city hospital, creating a more believable character cross section than one finds in Simon's work. Chayefsky returns to more familiar material in *Network*, in which he combines elements of a morality play and situation comedy. He is more concerned with the subject of his satire, network conglomerates, than with uncovering the rudiments of film comedy in the paranoia and infighting generated by the industry.

Paul Mazursky blends the venerable formulas of screwball comedy with the more manipulative conventions of situation comedy. In *Bob & Carol & Ted & Alice*, he substitutes the comic entanglements in a film like *Libeled Lady* with the ponderous soul-searching of today's couples; unlike the classic Hollywood pairings whose reunions were intimated in their ability to counter each other's flights of fancy, the couples in *Bob & Carol & Ted & Alice* are no more exciting together than when they drift apart. Marriage was never taken seriously in the comedy films of the thirties; as the subject of a couple of hipsters and their apprentices swinging into "alternate life styles," it is filmed with all the caring vapidity of their cupidity.

Mazursky makes a complete turnabout in *Blume in Love*, still one of the most compassionate of American love stories of the seventies. George Segal's kibitzer is, for once, subdued, the unlikely romantic hero of a film that explores the contradictory desires of its three central characters with a heartfelt richness that is missing in the scripts of Neil Simon. It makes the best use of Kris Kristofferson's scrawny screen presence, while Susan Anspach's romantic viability proves that Antonioni and Bergman have not abstracted the effectiveness of male-female relationships. Mazursky is less successful in *Harry and Tonto*, in which the cuteness of his story prevents him from dissecting Harry's feelings toward his children. In *Next Stop Greenwich Village*, the facile dramatic undercurrents of *Harry and Tonto* are recycled; Mazursky's clinical recreation of life in the Village during the fifties exudes an optimism that is both coy and antiseptic. Mazursky makes sure to include every conceivable stereotype, as Lenny Baker's mannered mimic and Shelley Winters's monstrous mama bring our social history in line with the canned conventions of situation comedy.

### *Patton–Heaven's Gate*

The epic film, whether in the form of a saga involving the destiny of a nation or of a sweeping, adventure-action melodrama first crystallized in Hollywood around the dashing figure of Douglas Fairbanks, seems ideally suited to exploit the riches of film technology. Battle scenes and sundry crowd movements, the shifting of viewpoints from the individual to society, and the passage of long segments of time are aesthetic propositions uniquely fulfilled in the movies. In the American film of the seventies, three aspects of epic cinema appear to dominate: first, the tale of adventure featuring a hero in an exotic setting (*Papillon, Islands in the Stream*); second, the disaster film, which has replaced the biblical epic as the most expressive cinematic metaphor of destruction and the fallibility of mankind; third, the historical biography or literary adaptation which functions as a recreation of a period and which received its most grandiloquent treatment in Coppola's *Godfather* epic.

Franklin Schaffner gained some attention with *Planet of the Apes*, which is worthy of a footnote in the history of the contemporary cinema for transforming Charlton Heston, the most famous film icon of Judeo-Christian culture, into its lone survivor, painlessly removing him from the pseudohigh culture of the fifties into the pseudolow culture of the sixties. In *Patton, Papillon*, and *Islands in the Stream* Schaffner and cinematographer Fred Koenkamp make a serious effort to combine the splendor in the Paramount epics of De Mille with the rousing dynamism one associates with Warner Bros.' productions directed by Raoul Walsh and Michael Curtiz. *Patton* is the most successful of the three, and considering the shortcomings of *Papillon* and *Islands in the Stream*, a good deal of the praise for the paradoxical treatment of General Patton must be given to Coppola's coauthorship. George C. Scott's feisty, individualistic portrayal verbalizes and dramatizes many of the unspoken axioms represented by John Wayne and other legendary heroes. Scott's aggressive interpretation of Patton's hubris and Schaffner's empathetic treatment of his burly manner and raspy-toned speeches achieve an effective compromise between De Mille's gung ho attitude to the glories of America's past and the more critical psychobiographies of modern mythmakers. The continuous dynamics of the battles, architecturally rendered by Koenkamp's long focal lens and complemented by Jerry Goldsmith's fife-and-drum musical motif, cogently articulate the film's nationalism through the epic theatrics of warfare.

But in *Papillon* and to a greater degree in *Islands in the Stream*, Schaffner and Koenkamp seem detached from their story, limiting their focus to the dense verdure in *Papillon* and the tropical vistas in *Islands in the Stream*. At best, the resplendence of their backgrounds shows a faith in the medium's facility for panoramic spectacle. But in *Papillon*, neither Steve McQueen nor Dustin Hoffman seem real in the way characters in *They Died with Their Boots On* or *Passage to Marseille* came to life. Schaffner lacks a kinship with his players, an ability to explain their involvement in the folklore and camaraderie of the adventure film. *Islands in the Stream* is as tenuously structured and romantically prolix as the novel. But how heroically Scott recreates the Hemingway hero, and how interesting to find David Hemmings, the quixotic protagonist of *Blow-Up*, playing the rummy and playing it as well as it has ever been played on film.

The disaster film is among the most contrived of film narratives. The basic formulas of the genre were established in *Grand Hotel*: an imposing superstructure is the lone setting in which numerous dramatic situations involving star performers transpire. Each one of the major stars is marked by some shortcoming so that the ensuing drama becomes a microcosm of society. The critical development in contemporary disaster epics is that the backdrop assumes a dynamic dramatic force. In *Grand Hotel* the interest, invariably, is in the personal interaction—the self-discovery of romantic, heroic qualities by the characters of John Barrymore and Greta Garbo. In the contemporary disaster film, trick effects play a greater role; hence, a stronger emphasis is placed on how the characters respond to the inoperative technology. Failing or fallen airplanes, submerged ships, and burning buildings possess a unique resonance: the spectacle of technological disaster functions as a symbol of man's arrogance, just as the Frankenstein monster represents the hubris of men of science. The contemporary treatment of man's Faustian aspirations combined with the element of fate in striking down some and saving others (Jennifer Jones but not her cat in *The Towering Inferno*) creates an effect similar to the numerous adaptations of biblical tales of fall and redemption. The strong appeal of disaster films in the seventies finds Hollywood juxtaposing a purportedly perfect technology to a cast of flawed characters who, in their heroic awakening, reconfirm Hollywood's continuing commitment to personal interaction in the face of the ever increasing solipsism of composite photography and other forms of special-effects hocus-pocus.

The work of three directors—Hal Ashby, Roman Polanski, Francis Ford Coppola—is concerned with translating and often transfiguring literary narratives. Ashby's films are among the strongest story-oriented films in the American cinema. His background as an editor results in a filmmaking style in the service of his scripts. This would appear to be an admirable goal, but his films rise and fall on his writers' profundity or lack thereof. At its best, *Shampoo* was a sour sitcom of the future, a shape of things that come. *The Last Detail*, a modest, intimate, ethnic slice-of-life drama, was "Playhouse 90" revisited with one of Jack Nicholson's finest portraits in realism. *Harold and Maude* found Ashby accenting its inane black humor with the same facility that he drew one into the rancorous behavior of his Navy flunkies in *The Last Detail*. To have treated Bud Cort's delirium tremens and courtship of Ruth Gordon's nursing home representative with the degree of empathetic sophistication Ashby brought to the project marks him as an emblematic Hollywood pragmatist.

After *Bound for Glory*, a disastrous period epic in which the diffuse delineation of its folk hero was languorously supported by Haskell Wexler's soft blue light, Ashby found more sympathetic material with the war romance of *Coming Home*. The film has little to do with Vietnam in either its plot or its romance of Jane Fonda and Jon Voight. It is the Dana Andrews–Harold Russell vignettes of *The Best Years of Our Lives* expanded around Fonda's heroic reincarnation of the Florence Nightingale persona of Teresa Wright and Cathy O'Donnell. *Being There* removes some of the excrement that engulfed the last decade of Peter Sellers's film work; *The Fiendish Plot of Dr. Fu Man Chu* was only the final rung on the ladder of Sellers's artistic debasement. It is also Jerzy Kosinski's cleanest, most honest, and humane vision since *The Painted Bird* and *Steps*. An entrepreneur of angst, Kosinski joined the growing fraternity of writers in the seventies whose skeletal visions of hell read like rejected film treatments of self-negation. In *Being There* Kosinski's sparse drama of nothingness is elevated by Caleb Deschanel and ennobled by Sellers. Deschanel photographs Sellers's initial isolation by using a hot, harsh backlight, suggestive of Sellers's time warp entrapment. Sellers's convalescence at the home of political boss Melvyn Douglas and his wife, played with a surprisingly sympathetic nonchalance by Shirley MacLaine, is imbued with the solemn, low-key grandeur of their palatial mansion, an entry by Sellers's medieval icon into the secular world of classical, political portraiture. The film plays like a symphony of Hindu rhythms currently favored by musical modernists, centering around the motif of Sellers's receding, repeated, whispering self-acknowledgments. Hal Ashby was the director.

Roman Polanski seems a curious subject for consideration as a director of epic cinema. Yet after a balefully surreal interpretation of *Macbeth*, Polanski's direction of *Chinatown* and *Tess* shows a richness of sensibility that one would never have expected from the director of *Macbeth* much less *Repulsion*. With a shrewd script by Robert Towne, Polanski, cinematographer John Alonzo, and production designer Richard Sylbert stylize *Chinatown* as a moody reverie on romantic myths. The stereotypes of the flawed hero and heroine and the conventional juxtaposition of low- and high-society backgrounds undergo a subtle transfiguration, replacing the archetypal black-and-white photography with dark but not black, settings whose expanded wide-screen prominence brings out the classic harmonies of time and place. If the darkness conveyed through the acute lighting contrasts in the mysteries and romances of the forties functioned as a correlative to the characters' emotional conflicts and desires, Polanski and Towne define their protagonists through the underlying objectivity and comprehensiveness of the wide screen. It is characteristic of the film's genre-study approach, the melancholic tone of its settings reflected through the look of the actors and their final, tragic destiny. Alonzo attempted a similar low-key treatment in *Farewell, My Lovely* with the supporting, voice-over narration of Robert Mitchum's Marlowe and Dean Tavoularis's decisively dark, neon-lit backgrounds; but Towne's script and Polanski's direction underscore the difference between neoclassicism as a rebirth and neoclassicism as rehash.

One shortcoming of *Chinatown* was that, although projecting the seductive glamour of the period, it did not capture the voice of Nicholson's private eye. In *Tess* Polanski achieves an even greater fruition of neoclassicism by conceiving his atmospheric landscapes as an extension of his heroine's feelings. This consanguinity between Nastassia Kinski's fragile heroine and the romantic vibrancy of the backgrounds gives the film a subtlety unmatched in any of David Lean's epics, with the exception of *Lawrence of Arabia*. Scences which may at first seem overly pictorial or passive examples of the medium's ability to immobilize the eye with the majesty of its landscapes provide evocative insights into the plot or the vagaries of Kinski's Tess. Her walk across the countryside after leaving her husband, the pictures of the bucolic Kinski gathering in the wheat, the close-ups of Kinski and her female companions show an isolated romantic spirit finding her dramatic identity in the psyche of romantic landscapists and portrait artists. The last work from the eye and mind of Geoffrey Unsworth, it is a film whose symmetrical toning bespeaks the artistry of Ghislain Cloquet, who finished the work; enriched by the incandescence of its youthful star, the film's artistry can also be acknowledged as the director's "mea culpa." The romance that producers and directors from Goldwyn and Cukor through Korda and Lean sought to idealize becomes a psychological as well as a physical reality through the unimpeded romantic instincts of the neoclassicists of the seventies.

The first films of Francis Ford Coppola show diverse stylistic influences that often become the excesses of his own laboring experiments. His first film, under the aegis of Roger Corman, *Dementia 13*, is an emotionally charged, though trim exercise in Gothic horror. In *The Rain People*, a more ambitious project, there is an uneasy blending of television drama in the tensions surrounding Shirley Knight, James Caan, and Robert Duvall and the pictorialism in its shots of the American countryside. His most cumbersome early project, *You're a Big Boy Now*, lacks an appreciation for the rudiments of film comedy; his boob's-eye gallery of half-wits features the all too appropriately cast Peter Kastner and the excessively loud colors and energy of Andrew Laszlo's camera. In *The Conversation*, made after the first *Godfather* film, Coppola makes a conscientious effort to adapt Antonioni's masterly 1960s *Blow-Up* to America. While, on the surface, the differences in the films of Antonioni and Coppola may seem marginal, they comprise the differences between art and artiness. In *Blow-Up* the photographer's rising self-awareness through his penetration of the oblique murder develops with the naturalism of everyday life and the symbolism of a parable; in *The Conversation* the tension is far more manipulative, its fatalism coexpressive with the technology first used by Gene Hackman for his employers and then used by them on him.

At the heart of the popular and critical success of *The Godfather* and *The Godfather Part II* is their absorption in the classic mythology of the crime film—in the self-consciousness of their heroically styled characterizations and in the underlying belief that the conventions of the genre can be interpreted with the seriousness, even the dignity, usually reserved for traditional symbols of social and cultural reaffirmation. By focusing on a family of Italian immigrants, Coppola and co-scriptwriter Mario Puzo integrate a family saga with the feudal warfare among America's crime organizations; they cunningly direct the audience's sympathies to the Corleones by depicting the treacherousness of the other criminals while elaborating the Corleones' irrevocable family bond. At the same time the two films invest the conventions of the drama—its emotional melodrama, its gangland assassinations, its didactic moralism—with an unlikely grandeur, they uncover the darkness of the American dream through the social success and personal tragedies that characterize the family's assimilation.

Why, then, call the style, of which *The Godfather* and *The Godfather Part II* remain the best examples in the American film of the seventies, one of neoclassicism rather than baroque, abstract, or simply romantic? I have chosen the term "neoclassicism" because of its predominant origins in a past style and because of the variety of sources and techniques utilized in its examination of the past. The classicism of Coppola's epic lies in its using pictorial archetypes for its redefinition of the gangster film. The two films propose an intuitive symmetry between the classicism of art history and movie iconography and are characterized as neoclassic owing to Coppola's delineating his original empathy for the films' unlikely heroes through the expressiveness of their classical pictorial models. The film's textual beauty lies in two major areas: first cinematographer Gordon Willis's low lighting levels and various shades of light and dark brown filters for his classical iconography of an American underworld and second the stunning definition of physical types, highlighted by Brando's physical embodiment of a world-weary immigrant acting around his physical scars and sagelike presence. The eclecticism underlying neoclassicism, however, often results in an overabundance of sources, a tendency more acutely manifested in *The Godfather Part II*. The inclination to the home-movie realism of the wedding festivities juxtaposed to the introspective hues of Brando's inner sanctum is further complicated with Robert Duvall's visit to John Marley's studio boss. Nino Rota's music functions as the editing bridge between the wedding party and California, which is introduced through a dissolve on a painting of an art deco exterior meant to represent Hollywood. A more questionable, lengthier stylistic anomaly concerns Michael's exile in Sicily; its abundance of bright colors plays as a sunlight serenade, an extravagant operatic interlude.

*The Godfather Part II* substitutes the more fluid pictorial narrative of the first film for a murky, expressionistic study of the further perils of the Corleones. Analogies to Aeschylus and Greek drama rather than Verdi and the Italians are pronounced, resulting from Coppola's fateful examination of the tragic undercurrents of America's criminal dynasties. Although the pictorial framing calls attention to itself in the manner of a series of slides of great painting styles, this family saga becomes a modern American tragedy that moves us in a way that few movies do. The narrative cohesiveness is fragmented, but what a tapestry of acting styles is contained in the characterizations of Al Pacino, Lee Strasberg, Talia Shire, John Cazale, Michael Gazzo, and Robert De Niro. The film's operatic veneer seems to challenge the viewer with its dramatic and picturesque excesses, whether in the extravagant behavior of Don Fanucci or the creamy corruptibility of Havana. It does not fulfill its Aeschylean apex, but its intrinsic parallels to Verdi's historical tempests create an attractive romantic niche for movie neoclassicism.

*Apocalypse Now* is a starry-eyed gamble that fuses traditional war-epic moviemaking with the more unnerving strains of modernism. It recalls the highly expressionist, often ecletic viewpoint of *The Godfather Part II* in its stressing of individual, pictorial configurations that fragment the war experiences of Martin Sheen's agent provocateur into personal, fantasylike episodes. The film's inchoate magnitude, like that of *The Deer Hunter*, is a counterpart to the straightforward, personal war memoirs from *The Big Parade* through *The Best Years of Our Lives*. The selection of Vittorio Storaro, Bertolucci's chief cinematographer, fulfills a role similar to that of Willis. In *Apocalypse Now* it is the film's psychological pictorialism that shapes its story line and editing rhythms. With the exception of the assignment of Sheen to the murder of Brando, in which the fluid yet ominous editing explores the unexpressed tensions of Sheen and his superiors, Storaro's camera eye functions as the film's orchestrator. The opening scene introduces the film as Sheen's surreal reverie, its leitmotifs of energy and electricity sustained in its linking shots of helicopters and other forms of electric power or military destruction. It assumes an Odyssean resonance in its journey upriver, leading to its Bosch-like rendezvous with Brando's camp, its Rembrandt shading of Brando's Buddha, and culminating with the final devastating ascent from the water in the ritual killing of Brando, a scene that simultaneously recalls the most sacred mysteries of primitive culture and a memorable shot of Eduardo Ciannelli's crazed demagogue in *Gunga Din*. It is this feverish juxtaposition of art and movie history that typifies Coppola's acid-trip nightmare. The self-generated rhetoric of carnage draws on the contrivances and clichés of Hollywood war films to reveal their tragic destiny in Vietnam, from the excessive palpitations of Robert Duvall's military caricature to the cinematic pyrotechnics of the helicopter raid. Coppola and Storaro appear to have taken the self-indulgence, the solipsism, the despair, the overwhelming eclecticism of contemporary filmmaking to an extreme and, if not completely satisfying conclusion, far more exemplary of Hollywood filmmaking than critics care to admit. One only hopes that the dramatic dissipation and transparent window display of romantic metaphors in *One from the Heart* is not evidence that *Apocalypse Now* is a premature Armageddon for its creator.

*The Deer Hunter* is an interesting companion piece to *Apocalypse Now*, investigating the nature of the American experience at home with an intensity and disquietude similar to that with which *Apocalypse Now* reflects on the American experience adrift in a foreign culture. Like Coppola and Storaro, director Michael Cimino and cinematographer Vilmos Zsigmond examine the raw, surface density of their characters and settings, interpenetrating their environment the way newsmen with their cameras and tape recorders try to record the full activity of our surrounding world. The first section, some ninety minutes in length, is among the best examples in the history of feature-length moviemaking of film as novel, its camera tracking through the volcanic steel furnaces, the neon-lit bars, the icons of the Greek Orthodox church, and the clusters of people and disparate actions during the wedding festivities. It is one of the longest, most detailed first chapters in the novel writing that has been a major preoccupation of American filmmakers. Though it loses whatever cogency' it had maintained with Michael's first return home, it retains our interest in its brutal pinpointing of Vietnam in the game of Russian roulette and in its capturing, if not fulfilling the heroic nature of the love Michael has for his doomed friend played by Christopher Walken.

*Heaven's Gate* is a more difficult work to review. The numerous delays and charges of reckless budgetary abuses have obscured the basic proposition the film confronts: a reexamination and an ensuing reconstruction of the mythology—social, political, and cultural—of the western as an archetype of the American experience, of our art, literature, and movies. If we briefly review the major features of movie westerns, we can better understand the reasons for the conflicting incoherence and artistry of *Heaven's Gate*.

*The Covered Wagon*, one of the first satisfying film epics of the West, interpreted its mythology as a poetic saga, a series of collective actions of honor securing the destiny of its western settlers. One scene emblematic of its poetic clarity concerns a dangerous river crossing. Simply, magically edited by Dorothy Arzner, it has no individual or emotive charge; its unobtrusive naturalism equates this stage in the lives of the pioneers to an objective rendering of their fate in history. The film utilizes a number of iris shots to suggest the symbolic identity of the characters and landscapes. Although there is continuing evidence of the popular mythologizing of the West in its love story and in the characterization of Ernest Torrence's backwoods scout, there is no diffusion of the ideals that sustain its journey. The numerous shots and scenes centered around isolated wagons culminate in a communal prayer of thanks by the side of a line of wagons as the settlers reach their western settlement.

Two of John Ford's most famous silent films, however, are more representative of the sentimentality and unvarnished romanticism of the West. *The Iron Horse* and *Three Bad Men* are marred by the hokey camaraderie and populism that were dramatically foreshortened in shoestring productions starring Tom Mix or Hoot Gibson. A general equation appears to have been made among the writers, directors, and stars of primitive movie westerns between the dime-novel stereotypes of Zane Grey and Louis L'Amour and the dramatic transparencies of silent-film westerns. There have been nine adaptations of *The Virginian*, three of which I have seen, and they all play as dime-novel fabrications. The pancultural strains of loneliness and violence that Owen Wister explored in his classic novel were clearly at odds with the more exuberant fantasies of western filmmakers.

Ford's maturity as a director led to the enrichment of the movie iconography of the West. Though Ford adapted the plays of O'Neill and O'Casey, there is no better evidence of his identity in their dramatic vision than in the poetic naturalism of his westerns. *Stagecoach* is probably the most famous work in the genre. Prior to its surprisingly staged conclusion, Ford's treatment polishes off the clichés of Dudley Nichols's script. Cinematographer Bert Glennon turned to John Singer Sargent's paintings of the West for his inspiration, and the individual framing of the travelers, either as they look out of the stagecoach door or as they sit in their seats, expresses a classic luminosity, whether in the flawed heroic demeanor of John Carradine or the silken softness of Claire Trevor. The stunt work of Yakima Canutt as he jumps on the horses running uncontrollably after the driver has been shot is not only one of the electrifyingly real moments of movie adventure, but it is also a dynamic juxtaposition to the more staid dramatization of the characters inside the stagecoach.

The intermediate resting points are perhaps the best examples of Ford's development as a director, the appropriately used high- and low-angle compositions defining each of the characters' responses to the dangers of their passage. After having reached their destination, there is a climactic gunfight involving John Wayne avenging a previous murder. The entire sequence is coordinated through a moving camera. Lighted with a darkness uncharacteristic of westerns, the participants' hulking shadows make them barely visible, prolonging the audience's anxiety as to the outcome. It is a brooding scene, full of deep-focus compositions, in which the moving camera assumes the role of fate in leading the spectator through dark alleys. It is estranged in tone from the rest of the story; although one questions the scene's dramatic necessity, it abstracts the resolution of the characters' symbolic stagecoach journey through the depersonalized, if not invisible presence of Wayne's heroic avenger.

In succeeding westerns Ford continued to delineate its representative virtues of place, time, and personal honor, like the winding desert plain which Henry Fonda's Wyatt Earp surveys from the porch of the saloon in *My Darling Clementine*, similar in its historical permanence to the hill on which the miners live in *How Green Was My Valley*. Yet one of the key transitional westerns of the postwar period, the Howard Hawks–Russell Harlan–Borden Chase *Red River*, reflects the interest of the period and genre in a style of psychological turmoil further paralleled in the muscular landscapes and classical conflicts in the Anthony Mann wide-screen epics of the fifties. The dramatic modernization that Ford avoids is central to the appeal of *High Noon, The Gunfighter, The Furies*, and *Johnny Guitar*, films that reverberate with the teledramatic tensions and staging familiar to the audiences of the fifties. It is a central theme in the films of Randolph Scott and Budd Boetticher, extended studies of Scott as loner or lawman undergoing the introspection of the so-called anti-westerns. In *Red River*, the formidable backgrounds in the films of Ford and Mann are combined with the psychopathology of the anti-western and the Scott-Boetticher films, rewriting the dime-novel clichés with the contemporary erotic schisms of postwar teledramatists.

Filmmakers, however, were slow to act on the success of *Red River*, its combination of physical formalism and psychological trauma. The most saddening example of this stylistic conservatism is in the last films of Ford and Hawks. Whereas *Seven Women* pictures its women warriors as the embodiments of a woman's romance wedded to a comic book, the enervating pictorialism and perfunctory use of "Old Tucson" in *Rio Lobo* and *Rio Bravo*, the setting for hundreds of westerns for over thirty years, result in the type of winsome melodrama that would have been rejected by the producers of "Wagon Train".

A corollary comes to mind between the imperviousness of movie westerns, especially among their veteran directors, and the critical stance assumed by one of the key figures in American film criticism, Andrew Sarris, characterized by Stuart Byron as the Van Wyck Brooks of film historians. Byron compares Sarris's immersion in the archives to Brooks's pioneering studies of the flowering of American literature, yet this shrewd equation needs further scrutiny. In his autobiography, Brooks recounts that when once discussing a novel by William Dean Howells with Edmund Wilson, he was surprised by Wilson's outright rejection of the work. The reason for the disparity in taste between Brooks and Wilson is not simply explained by Wilson's heightened critical powers, but by noting that Brooks's position as America's foremost literary archaeologist seemed to preclude the more exacting literary analysis that Wilson and his generation brought to their appraisal of American literature. Sarris's cinematic excavations have led to a similar schism. I do not think it possible to routinely dismiss Sarris as an ecstatic cinéaste; yet I equally resist the claims of *auteurs* in charge of publications like *Film Comment* who feel their position is proof that the battle against the pharisees has been won. Sarris's voice signified a revolutionary change in the social and academic resonance of film. New expeditions must be arranged; the maps might be redrawn, but a victory was won, though it has often seemed to be a Pyrrhic one.

The painful anachronism and underlying stylistic vacuity in the last films of Ford and Hawks underscore the radical changes in the mythos of the West. Although there are signs of darker, misanthropic themes and stylizations in such westerns as *One-Eyed Jacks*, *Welcome to Hard Times*, and *The Professionals*, it is only with three of Peckinpah's films—*Ride the High Country*, *Major Dundee*, *The Wild Bunch*—and two films directed by Sergio Leone—*The Good the Bad and the Ugly*, *Once upon a Time in the West*—that the modernist elements suggested in the earlier postwar westerns achieve their richest crystallization. *Ride the High Country*, the most dramatically and visually congruent of Peckinpah's westerns, shows a far more pertinent psychological proximity to Lucien Ballard's immersion in the Sierra wilderness than in Ballard's work in Budd Boetticher's westerns. The apparent lushness, yet underlying notes of danger and violence of the background complements the classic movie persona of Joel McCrea and Randolph Scott and their antithetical resolution of the gunman's destiny. The paradoxical treatment of western scenery and characterization and the supporting motif of a rustic romance that almost results in the groom's family rape of the bride provide a more effective commentary on the changing historical continuity of the West than the Boetticher-Scott series. Its final gunfight neatly prefigures the aesthetics of violence that dominate Peckinpah's future films but that still hit the mark in *The Wild Bunch*.

Leone's westerns proved far more problematic for American audiences. *The Good the Bad and the Ugly* received no push from any major critic, while *Once upon a Time in the West* enjoyed only a few belated acknowledgments. Yet in these two films Leone creates an extravagant shaggy-dog film saga and follows it with a lavish, delirious ritualization of western archetypes. *The Good the Bad and the Ugly* celebrates the funk, the lubricity, the braggadocio of western romance with a rousing, blunt, pop-art energy and wit. Its trio of comic-book adventurers of Clint Eastwood, Lee Van Cleef, and Eli Wallach renew their fabled roles with a welcome edge of self-parody, further exploited by the dazzling music score of Ennio Morricone.

*Once upon a Time in the West* is as hyperbolic as its predecessor, but here Tonino Delli Colli's stunningly sculpted faces and vistas are part of a symbolic meditation in which the clichés of western drama undergo the same idiosyncratic stylization as Charles Bronson's silent avenger, Henry Fonda's vicious bad man, Claudia Cardinale's bride, and Jason Robards, Jr.'s loner. If *The Good the Bad and the Ugly* was a sprawling comic fable that exploited the violence and chicanery surrounding its treasure hunt, *Once upon a Time in the West* projects an epic solemnity about its theme of revenge. In the previous film the dramatic masks of the three central characters drew out the perverse irony in its send-up of the clichés of machismo—from the reversal of roles involving Eastwood and Wallach humiliating each other during their desert treks to the undeniable majesty of the final shoot-out. In *Once upon a Time in the West* there is greater detail to the architecture and climaxes in the treatment of the conventions of western folklore. The opening gunfight at the train station parodies the posing of its three desperadoes while simultaneously delineating the physical sweep of this confrontation. Unlike the dynamic editing that was most rigorously used by Peckinpah in *The Wild Bunch*, Leone's piecemeal, linear editing achieves a literal expansiveness in identifying the emotions and reactions of those involved through his establishing shots, the brief dramatic panning shots, and close-ups.

But it is the overriding bravado in its staging that enriches and transforms the clichés Leone has assimilated. The prolonged buildup to the town as Cardinale walks disconsolately along the train tracks and the town's introduction through a magnificent, epic crane shot give this archetype of history and western movie mythology a subjective and objective grandeur. The more extravagant settings—for example, the halfway station with its amphitheaterlike proportions, its hanging rolls of sausage and bottles of wine, its deep space rendered in sensual textures of red, green, and brown, and the train interior reconstructed into a palatial drawing room for the land scheming of Gabriele Ferzetti—suggest a poetic interplay of historical narrative and mythological reverie. The ingenious, comic-book artifices of *The Good the Bad and the Ugly* remain: accentuated, aural exclamation points surrounding the various physical confrontations from the ringing of the bells to dramatize Fonda's murder of the boy to Robards's arrival at the halfway station, rendered through the grunts and explosions on the sound track. However, it is the profoundly individual triumph of the composition that places the film in the classic mainstream of movie westerns. The heightened colors of the performers' faces—reddish, sunbaked masks— the russet browns of the sagebrush, the rising clouds of dust in its main street settings have a romantic splendor never before achieved in western film scenery. So much of the legend of the West lies in the symbolized virgin terrain of its actors and backgrounds; while some critics are confounded by the artful, pulsating sound track, the truthfulness of Leone's compositions fulfill the classic narrative scope of the West. The beauty of the film is not extraneous to the story—pretty pictures that flavor our popcorn indulgences—but is integral to our understanding of the myth and melodrama of the West. Leone never loses sight of the origins of his dramatic, pictorial and musical archetypes, and it is this dangerous though never false treatment of tragic irony in *Once upon a Time in the West* that complements the comic irony of *The Good the Bad and the Ugly*.

The decisiveness, the completeness of artistic vision with which Leone re-made the West had some effect on Hollywood in the seventies but with con-trived concessions to kinky behavior and redundantly baroque configurations. Wayne survived the seventies, but for every *True Grit* there was *Cahill—United States Marshal*; for every *The Shootist*, a *Rooster Cogburn*. Eastwood modified his anti-hero into our most successful entrepreneur of the clichés of the past. The West had returned to its safe niche of innocuous romanticism, strongly flavored, however, with the stinging rhetoric of violence.

*Heaven's Gate* seems as much inspired by the mythology of the Hollywood western as by the role of the western in the mythology of the settlement of America. It injects a strong socialist-communal dissonance into the nationalist epics of *The Covered Wagon* and *Red River*. It is the story of an aristocracy of cattle barons usurping the rights of proletarian immigrants, concluding with their contract on these settlers. The protagonist, Kris Kristofferson, is a member of the aristocracy who after graduation from Harvard during America's centen-nial assumes the role of frontier marshal to patrol and possibly mediate the rivalry between representatives of America's political and economic leaders and the immigrant settlers. A crucial weakness is in the opening section during grad-uation ceremonies at Harvard. The slightly tilted, ominous camera movement on the tower begins a baroque cross section of university life. The paradoxical elements of architectural power and social decadence of this sequence, how-ever, are not fulfilled with John Hurt's address, with the more congruent yet otiose pontification of Joseph Cotten, or with the festive waltzes that follow. Cimino, like other modern disciples of technology, is far too attuned to the mechanics of his opening scenes; his sound mixing in Dolby of the chorus of chatter and laughter is abstracted, as if influenced by the computer dynamics of Morton Subotnick. Where is our hero, and where is our story?

The voice-over narration and titles that Cimino added in the shortened ver-sion, with Kristofferson relating the allure of the West, clear up a major gap, inexcusably overlooked in the original. Our first introduction to Kristofferson, twenty years later, is a complex shot. Asleep in a train, Kristofferson's adven-turer is illuminated by a ray of light. This visionary shot, with its acute symbolic overtones, introduces a major leitmotif in Cimino's drama. Until the final con-frontation between the hired guns and the immigrants, Cimino will consistently envelop his proletarian folk heroes in light. One remembers the cock fight scene;

the pastoral intimacy of Kristofferson, Huppert, and Walken in Huppert's bordello; and Kristofferson's walk through the living quarters of the immigrants. Each of these scenes is suffused in light, a poetic, imagist motif that is a vital part of the West as fable. In one interior train shot of the arriving gunmen and during their attack on Walken and his friends, Cimino and Zsigmond cover these icons of evil in light as well. Though this might be interpreted as further evidence of the film's amorphousness, it works in these later scenes by underlining their symbolic dimensions: they too have entered into a medieval dramatization of good and evil.

Yet Cimino's decision to delineate the symbolism of the West through its pictorial textures is symptomatic of the problem writers and directors of the West have faced in adapting the glories of western art to the narrative demands of the movies. Painters have long influenced film studies of the West, but few films have successfully used their pictorial models as dramatic narrative. In *Pat Garrett and Billy the Kid*, the last significant film from Sam Peckinpah, the picturesque southwestern exteriors in *The Man from Laramie* assume a primary role in his stately, solemn study of classic western protagonists assuming the poetic mask of their pictorial predecessors. The film's dramatic-pictorial integrity is obscured by the wooden persona of James Coburn and the heavy-handed Christian symbolism in the killing of Billy the Kid, but a majority of scenes sustain the historical and romantic imprint of the West through the juxtaposition of the characters' repressed dramatic instincts to the predominant wide-screen harmonies of time and place. In the first shoot-out involving a group of bounty hunters who have come to the hideout of Kristofferson's Billy the Kid, the prelude to the shoot-out is comprised of a series of deft, campside close-ups that suggest both the menace that is about to explode and the memorable artifacts of this isolated western setting. The shoot-out is handled with Peckinpah's noted flair: the individual movements of the combatants are executed with an eye for the objective dynamics of the confrontation and for the subjective fate of those involved: the painting has been abbreviated into short panels of dramatic punctuation. In an interior, jailhouse setting R. G. Armstrong's sheriff expresses his intense dislike of Billy and his marauders. Peckinpah has repeatedly used Armstrong as a towering figure of puritan idealism (the gun-toting preacher in *Major Dundee* and the zealot pioneer in *Ride the High Country*). After he finishes his tirade, Peckinpah uses a dissolve on his figure, isolated in a corner of the jailhouse, a testament to Armstrong's dignity as a dramatically real icon who personalizes the grandeur of the reddish-brown interiors and the twilight of the skyline that seeps through the window.

In the first sequence involving Isabelle Huppert's whore-mistress in *Heaven's Gate*, there is a ground-level shot of Huppert's shoulders and face set against a florid background that works as a sudden epiphany in its reference to Botticelli's *Birth of Venus*. Yet the Montana backgrounds have no distinct meaning other than as symbols of the primitive sweep of western landscapes. There is one breathtaking execution of cinematic sky painting involving a train conductor awakened from his sleep on a hilltop by one of the desperadoes. He begins to run away as the camera pans across the golden blue expanses of the horizon, suddenly marked by the presence of a dozen hired killers. Though much of the one hundred minutes that were cut out in the second version concerns its epic, exterior scenery, there is no specific visual or nature motif that is lost, only, perhaps, the hypnotic spell of languishing in the wilds of Montana.

The sepia toning added by Cimino and Zsigmond brings out a darkness in their virgin backgrounds, but a more important technical factor is the flashing favored by Zsigmond. Flashing has been described as a corollary to fill light in black-and-white photography; it accentuates the mood of a shot or scene by softening or sharpening the color textures through a preexposure of the film to light. While indicative of the growing attraction for dramatic abstraction among film neoclassicists, the suggestive shading is often used as an inconclusive substitute for a murky narrative, or worse, as an oppressive, symbolic equivalent to the film's theme. The scenes in Huppert's bordello represent Zsigmond's most liberal execution of flashing. Billows of gray wood-burning smoke cut across the trio of Kristofferson, Huppert, and Walken much in the manner that dust is used to decorate exterior scenes. They are the most personal expression of the romance and beauty Cimino and Zsigmond see in the West, but they are also the most dramatically static, self-consciously pictorial scenes in the film.

Cimino and Zsigmond are too much the lyrical folklorists in the scenes with their three central characters, but those involving Sam Waterston are as evocative as any portrayal of the forces of evil in the iconography of the West. The speech Waterston delivers during a luncheon of the cattle barons brilliantly conveys the atmospheric potential of a national folk genre like the West. The composition of the darkly clad businessmen and military officers works as a formal execution of social etiquette while conveying their underlying smug self-confidence. Its references to Rembrandt's burghers are ensconced in a perfectly edited sequence that clarifies our empathy with Kristofferson and antipathy toward Waterston.

The roller-skating sequence and the final shoot-out have been cited as representative of the film's ostentatiousness and its empty, solipsistic style. The roller-skating sequence, like the earlier waltz scene, or the car demolition derby in Cimino's *Thunderbolt and Lightfoot*, is a prolonged exercise in the baroque. During the roller-skating sequence, the majestic rush of the camera, enfolding and punctuating the movements of the skaters, works as a controlled, dynamic reverie on the folk spirit of his proletarians. The music, too, with the simple, brusque rhythms of violin and accordion, has its roots in the recorded folk music from the turn of the century; here, in its most florid movement, it sweeps us into the friendship and innocence of the immigrants as an enduring staple of their culture. The two battles that comprise the final confrontation are dizzying, objective studies of tumult and hysteria. Cimino is not interested in showing us who is winning; the focus lies in the montage of families fleeing in their wagons only to be overturned by a broken wheel, overlapping with circular camera movements that grind our eyes in the dirt, the sweat, the confusion and horror of this historical clash. We, too, like Kristofferson are spent, looking up to see the oncoming army platoon to the rescue of the cattle barons and their mercenaries.

The final sequence—in the original a crude, blatant, and wholly confusing analogue to Keir Dullea's "ages-of-man" scene in *2001: A Space Odyssey*—has been abridged in the reedited version and makes for a stunning epilogue. While remembering the brutal killing of Huppert, Kristofferson walks on the deck of his yacht in Newport. Moving to long shot, Cimino and Zsigmond's stumbling yet prodigious epic achieves a magical, poetic coda with a shot expressing symbolic alienation, not only of its hero, but of a genre, an art, a country.

The seventies brought out some cool, exciting treatments of movie formulas and imagery (*American Graffiti, Come Back Charleston Blue, The China Syndrome, The French Connection, The Exorcist, The Texas Chainsaw Massacre, Alien, Play It Again Sam, Blume in Love*). Its prevailing tone of psychological disengagement inspired Altman's most memorable work in *Nashville* and *Three Woman* and Scorsese's *Raging Bull*. Its inherent self-consciousness—discovering the iconographic resonance of its movie heroes in the stylistic interaction of classic myth and contemporary mythologizing—received its most ambitious and invigorating treatment in *The Good the Bad and the Ugly*; *Once upon a Time in the West*; *The Godfather*; *The Godfather Part II*; *Tess*; *The Deer Hunter*; and *Apocalypse Now*. *Heaven's Gate*— the culmination of the stylistic eclecticism of the period—was inundated with the paradoxes that characterized a decade-long exercise in the revitalization of past genres, of classic art and literary archetypes. A measure of the increasing rupture in the American film of the late seventies is that while Coppola and Cimino were undertaking a more dangerous interpretation of neoclassicism, the commercial instincts of the guardians of Hollywood led to their bestowing awards on a series of domestically oriented social dramas whose most prominent model was not any movie genre, but the teledramas of the fifties.

The style of the movies of the seventies may be characterized as one of neoclassicism, but its triumphs and failures pose a classic issue. The two extremes of Hollywood moviemaking over the last decade—the mannerism of its least original and often most commercially successful productions and the experimentation that ruined the projects of some of the most adventurous filmmakers—underscore the tentativeness surrounding a period attempting a compromise between its postwar legacy of alienation and abstraction and its prewar ideals of conformity and convention. We have always seemed to reach for a median in our society, and by duplicating this goal in the art and industry of Hollywood, the movies continue to exemplify the paradoxes of our populism.

# 20
# The English Film

*The Bridge on the River Kwai–The Stepford Wives*

Jean-Luc Godard's statement that the English cinema does not exist presupposes that the only films worthy of study are those of a uniquely cinematic nature. Although the artist is at liberty to present such an extreme point of view, the critic or student of the movies should be sensitive to those pleasurably middlebrow conventions entailed in the word "entertainment," whether it is the American, English, or Japanese derivative. Critics have often selected English films as illustrious examples of film art, but like Kracauer's discussion of *Pygmalion*, they are making a mountain out of a molehill. The simple pleasures of the English cinema lie in the use of an elegant backdrop to fashion a form of didactic, eclectic entertainment, a style of historical nostalgia illuminating the treasures of the past. Their most consistent virtue is the abundant acting talent, and how rich a resource this has proven to be, not only in Korda productions, but also in such equally telling examples as Ralph Richardson's reserved scientist in *Breaking through the Sound Barrier* or Kay Kendall's delicious solo on the saxophone in *Genevieve*. To remember for example the performances of Michael Redgrave in *The Stars Look Down, Fame Is the Spur, Dead of Night,* and *The Browning Version* is not simply to recall a most distinguished repertoire of dramatic interpretations, but to discover the different emotional and technical gradations of the film actor. Redgrave's characterizations inhabit these films, a continuous presence who effaces the illusion of the screen and camera; we observe the vicissitudes of his life in the manner of our absorption in the countless properties of nature, unable to grasp all the nuances of his behavior yet continually aware that his emotional and moral quandaries are the source of the close-ups and cuts on the supporting players and actions; the verbal and physical sparks of the theatrical performer have been transposed to the verisimilitude of film.

From the earliest efforts of R. W. Paul and Cecil Hepworth, English filmmakers have incorporated the most significant techniques in advancing the art of film. If Paul's trick films and Hepworth's pioneering exercises in crosscutting were overshadowed by Méliès's hyperbolic fantasies and Porter's more dramatic, kinetic variations, the flowering of the English cinema—in the epic, hoary narrative illustrations of Pressburger and Powell; in Olivier's Shakespearean adaptations; in Carol Reed's taut, expressionist thrillers; and most luminously in the acute self-irony of the English cinema's cycle of comedy films—remains one of the richest and most successful translations of a distinct cultural legacy to the eclectic potential of the movies. The talents of producers and directors like Pressburger and Powell, Olivier and Reed immediately come to mind, but their successful application of the film medium was made possible by the art direction of Alfred Junge and Hein Heckroth and such brilliant cinematographers as Jack Cardiff (*Black Narcissus, The Red Shoes*), Robert Krasker (*Henry V, Odd Man Out, The Third Man*), and Douglas Slocombe (*Dead of Night, Kind Hearts and Coronets, The Lavender Hill Mob, The Man in the White Suit*). Adding the names of Jack Hildyard, Geoffrey Unsworth, and Freddie Young, cinematographers whose imaginations were critical to some of the major English and international productions of the last twenty years, one finds an array of talent that bears favorable comparison to any similar renaissance among the major film countries of the world. Their innate craftsmanship, ironically, has been ostentatiously sustained in the single most original series of films in the English cinema of the sixties and seventies—the Bond spy cycle, with its ever increasing giddiness and its celebration of childlike fantasies of power and sex, characterized by the erotic foreplay of Maurice Binder's titles, by the razor sharp cinematography of Ted Moore, and by the delirious production spoofs of Ken Adam.

Yet the uniquely craftsmanlike nature of the English film is not without its drawbacks. If Alexander and Vincent Korda and Georges Périnal are the pivotal figures in the creation of the English quality film, their attention to period detail often resulted in stillborn historical dramas and fantasies, in which little opportunity was given for the cinematic and psychological twists that German and American moviemakers brought to their treatments of history and hallucination. This tendency to static, simplified cinematic embellishments is most evident in the Pressburger-Powell production of *Stairway to Heaven*. The medium is used as an extended proscenium for the essentially theatrical rhetoric of its cosmic courtroom drama; this approach also mars their most handsome production, *Black Narcissus*. The exact, rigorous contours of this religious drama center around Deborah Kerr's lovely, pastel heroine and the melodramatic fireworks inspired by the sisters' secluded existence. One's lone reservation is that the film's cinematographic textures are far too rich for the story's spiritual agon; the exotic colors of Jack Cardiff's compositions, from the plangent reds of his exteriors to the darkness surrounding the nun's suspiciousness and hysteria, fail to reflect the characters' feelings. It is a beautiful, adroit film, but one cannot believe in its ornate, sensual design as a sign of spiritual penetration.

This attention to lavish production detail is characteristic of other than historical and fantasy productions in the English film. It is an essential component of the Bond genre, which encouraged the flippant, comic-book adventures and parodic gloss in the Helm and Flint spy films; it underscores Jack Hildyard's and John Guillermin's treatment of the prosaic platitudes in Agatha Christie's *Death on the Nile*. Hildyard's exaggerated romantic compositions and the film's deftly fluid editing rhythms transform Christie's protracted, mundane mystery into an elaborate, sumptuous period drama. The decorative backgrounds and theatrical mannerisms of its stars infuse Christie's tease with an extravagance her theatrical and literary audience could only dream of; one is not offended by the waste, but by the nature of their dedication.

Perhaps the most noteworthy example of the ambivalence of the English quality film in the postwar era—the appreciation for the treasures of the past yet the tendency to highlight its physical, albeit artificial permanence—is in the career of David Lean. Lean's background as an editor, combined with his sensitivity to the long-established integrity of the actor, make his preepic films among the more impressive portrayals of a literary imagination on film. *Great Expectations*, *The Passionate Friends*, *Madeleine*, *Hobson's Choice*, and *Summertime* achieve a cogent blending of dramatic literacy and romantic vibrancy. The expressive physical detail and emotional ebb and flow of *Great Expectations* have a far more gripping urgency than one finds in the theatrical pastiche of Korda's films. *Madeleine* and *Hobson's Choice* offer more modest pleasures. The psychological tensions of *Madeleine* are effectively magnified through the terse editing in Ann Todd's meetings with her lover and in her courtroom trial; Lean personalizes the theatrical flavor of *Hobson's Choice* by capturing the idiosyncratic behavior surrounding the dramatic tug-of-war between Laughton's father and Brenda de Banzie's daughter over John Mills's suitor. Guy Green's tasteful photography in *The Passionate Friends*, lyrically bridged by Lean's editing, becomes a metaphor for the characters' romantic memories, while the picture postcard backgrounds of Venice in *Summertime* are punctuated by Katharine Hepburn's exuberant, romantic self-fulfillment. Lean showed himself as equal if not superior to renowned American directors assigned to Hollywood's most important adaptations and star vehicles.

With the notable exception of *Lawrence of Arabia*, Lean's collaborations with Jack Hildyard (*The Bridge on the River Kwai*) and Freddie Young (*Doctor Zhivago*) magnify the cumbersome nature of the Korda–Pressburger–Powell productions through the personification of the story's psychological currents in the icy, evanescent exteriors. Owing to its idealization of Alec Guinness's professional soldier, *The Bridge on the River Kwai* emphasizes the epic strategies of the bridge's construction while undercutting the discontent of his fellow officers. Unlike Roger Livesey's Colonel Blimp, Guinness's mask of dedication does not invite the graceful pageantry and sympathetic tribute to English patriotism in the Pressburger-Powell production; Guinness's ideologue becomes a final symbol of Kipling's chauvinistic adventurers. *Doctor Zhivago* is a more mechanical epic. The initial inclination to physical metaphor finds Freddie Young's objectification of the characters' desires in his long shots of the Russian countryside interpreting Boris Pasternak's novel as a historical soap opera: the romantic icons of Omar Sharif, Julie Christie, Rod Steiger, Tom Courtenay, and Geraldine Chaplin become receding figures of personal longing and fear.

Other veterans of the English film like Carol Reed and Anthony Asquith suffered far greater declines. Reed's postwar thrillers—*Odd Man Out*, *The Third*

*Man, The Man Between*—are exemplary works in fashioning an expressionist veneer around their political and social quagmire. But Reed shows no similar facility with the more existential mystery of *The Running Man* or the epic canvas of *The Agony and the Ecstasy*. *Oliver!*, his best film in many years, lapses into several stagy, boxed-in production numbers that detract from the exhilarating, dynamic impetus of the score. Asquith was one of his country's first major filmmakers whose early films give some support to Godard's ringing indictment. *Tell England* applies a montage-school finish to a lachrymose story about the effect of World War I on two schoolboys, while *A Cottage On Dartmoor* is an academic exercise in suspense. Two of his last films, *The V.I.P.s* and *The Yellow Rolls-Royce* are case studies of the probity of the Korda–Pressburger–Powell tradition gravitating to the tense, psychological introspection made famous in teledrama. *The V.I.P.s* is based on a script by Terence Rattigan, who was practicing soap opera long before its evolution on American television. Like other soap-opera-type studies, *The V.I.P.s* builds on many of the themes common to the movies of the thirties, in this case the *Grand Hotel* metaphor, in which various representatives of English society are lumped together in an isolated setting. The dialogue is harsher than in previous Hollywood models; whereas one was absorbed in Garbo's elusive presence or Joan Crawford's beauty in the original, Rattigan's contrived psychotherapy and Asquith's blatant direction treat Maggie Smith's love confession and Louis Jourdan's gigolo with a degree of seriousness more prominent in the teledramas of the fifites than in the romances of the thirties. *The Yellow Rolls-Royce* is a more acute example of strained teledrama. Asquith uses the luxury car as a symbol of the decline of romance, and the characterizations, from George Scott's hammy mafioso to Omar Sharif's saccharine revolutionary and Ingrid Bergman's lovesick patroness, fail to inject any feeling into their shopworn situations. What becomes apparent in the first story, in which Rex Harrison finds his wife in the car with one of his employees, is the turgid nature of Asquith's love elegy—the repression of the emotional excesses that offered some relief to audiences in an earlier time.

A new direction in the English cinema is struck by Harry Saltzman and Albert Broccoli, producers of the James Bond and Harry Palmer spy series. It is a signature which has come to represent the mechanization in the contemporary packaging of entertainment. The first Bond films are sparked by the presence of Sean Connery, whose dilettante mannerisms transfigure Ian Fleming's small-scale, nuclear-age action stories into a heroic disdain for the polemics of the cold war. The second Bond film, *From Russia with Love*, with its cool treatment of the theme of deception and with the pungent characterizations of Robert Shaw, Lotte Lenya, and Pedro Armendariz, brings out the hyperbole of the Bond films with surprising elegance. The next three Bond films—*Goldfinger*, *Thunderball*, *You Only Live Twice*—evidence the increasing undertones of camp and caricature. Film craftsmen enjoyed a field day in conjuring new weapons of death and stunning sequences of cartoonlike mayhem, complemented by and often culminating in wet-dream fantasies. This affinity with kitsch, however, is abbreviated by the accentuated kinetic thrust and the almost nonstop chase sequences in *On Her Majesty's Secret Service*. Directed by Peter Hunt, editor and second unit director of the preceding Bond films, the film seems to attempt to compensate for the loss of Connery through its exaggerated dynamic charge. Pauline Kael's admiration for Hunt's interpretation of the Bond myth seems to acknowledge its now accepted dramatic diminution, owing in part to its new stars. Yet George Lazenby's hulkish impersonation and Roger Moore's phlegmatic Beau Brummell reduce the ironies surrounding their numerous chase routines. Hunt's choreography of the ski chase, while suffering from some pooly executed composite photography, could be adapted into any one of the kiss-and-kill thrill spectacles of the seventies; Moore, who showed some promise in his original incarnation as Simon Templar, displays little involvement as Bond; we never enter into his physical culs-de-sac, whether in the drawn-out self-parody involving Moore's detached observation of Richard Kiel dismantling his van in *The Spy Who Loved Me* or the impersonality of the motorboat chase in *The Man with the Golden Gun*. His more recent transformation and that of the Bond films into the surreal, pinball artifices of *Moonraker* underscore both the technology of the Bond films and their appropriation by a new generation of video fantasists.

Michael Caine achieved far less acclaim in the Harry Palmer series; only the first, *The Ipcress File*, retains some interest for its abject treatment of the cold-blooded mentality of its intelligence administrators and agents. Caine's desultory manner has been used in various prototypically English films of the last two decades. In *Alfie*, his most acclaimed film of the sixties, Caine's glum confession treats Alfie's conquests as glib excursions into low-life lovemaking. Caine has worked in epic clinkers like *Zulu* and pseudoart films like *The Romantic Englishwoman*; his best, most detailed characterizations, however, have been in two films that juxtapose his strong cockney accent and raffish mannerisms to the theatrical airs of his co-stars—*Sleuth* and *The Man Who Would Be King*. For the most part, however, the lazy, apathetic figure Cain cuts in *Alfie* is emblematic of the English anti-hero of the sixties. Whenever he is called on to emote, his face takes on a diseased, Cagneyesque facade, but without the accompanying physical edginess in Cagney's performances. This is why, despite all the excitement Michael Hodges generates with his immersion in the criminal underworld of *Get Carter*, Caine's villainous hit man fails to distinguish any motif other than his empathy with the film's gritty violence. In *Pulp*, a pop-art travesty of the crime film, Caine's performance as the writer lacks any irony in dealing with the film's caricatures; but then Hodges and not Caine is the chief culprit in *Pulp*.

This voice of estrangement also characterizes the inability of English moviemakers to renew longstanding dramatic protagonists and entertainment formulas. The imprimatur of producer Michael Balcon and the Ealing Studios signified to the public the merry assortment of nitwits, half-wits, and Pickwicks who fumbled their way through the comedies of the late forties and fifties, but an attempt to revive their irony and self-humor results in the comic fatalism of *Charlie Bubbles*. In Albert Finney's adaptation of a Shelagh Delaney story, Finney plays a successful writer who becomes increasingly alienated from society.

The film revives the poetic spirit common to both the Ealing comedies and Fellini's first ventures, but Finney's impassivity to the self-ridicule of his family and friends leads him to adopt Keaton's mask of dramatic invisibility. Like Keaton in *The Balloonatic*, he challenges the absurdity of his world through his final flight in a balloon, suggesting that there is little hope of regenerating the comic anarchy of the Ealing comedies. A mutation of the Ealing comedies, Joan Littlewood's *Sparrows Can't Sing* equates its farcical tone to the crude habits and gross physiognomy of its lower-class figures. The film's slobbering, physically grotesque types are stripped of any redeeming features; Littlewood's idea of comedy is to pile one gross action or facial contortion on another: a pitiful example of self-abuse. If Littlewood's film reduces comedy to a form of autistic scribbling, *Time Lost and Time Remembered* finds its working-class heroine, played by Sarah Miles, unable to establish any emotional contact with English society. Unlike Monica Vitti, whose adventures in Antonioni's trilogy detail numerous associations between the individual's dislocation and the haunting features of the Italian countryside and cities, Miles's quest for love superimposes the sappy, antiquated clichés of the thirties on its contemporary facade of alienation. One example finds director Desmond Davis spinning the camera to convey Miles's happiness as she rides her bicycle.

*Privilege* is similar to celebrated Hollywood big-issue films that project such a solemn tone and contrived plot that the singular dramatic expressiveness of the subject is undercut. That rock 'n' roll has affected the younger generation in a far more encompassing and devious manner than that of Paul Jones's caged, immolated rock star seems obvious. The film then plays as a ponderous essay by one of those many social prognosticators whose appearance on television seems a more ominous phenomenon than that of rock 'n' roll. In *The Ruling Class* director Peter Medak uses the self-willed anachronism of the English aristocracy as the most pernicious and potentially the richest comic feature of English society. Although Peter O'Toole's performance as the aging but unruffled madman never confuses energy with inspired gracefulness, the film's full-scale blast on the meretricious behavior of the upper class is too broad and without any focus other than exploiting the deceitfulness of O'Toole's guardians. It is similar to *It's a Mad Mad Mad Mad World* and *The Russians Are Coming the Russians Are Coming* in that the anarchy at the center of the film has no single target other than reconfirming the already admissible fact that the characters live in a loony bin. It is a more intelligent and genuinely wicked work than the two American productions, but the cancer is too immense to be overcome by the disruptiveness of O'Toole's incarcerated man of leisure.

*The Lion in Winter* attempts to inject a healthy dose of bitchery into the inflated dramatic exegesis of *A Man for All Seasons*. If the problem with *A Man for All Seasons* was the bland, antiseptic formulas that Robert Bolt used to revive historical drama, *The Lion in Winter* suffers from a strained sense of parody. The one performance that shakes the foundations of historical drama with an enriching woolliness and self-mockery is Peter O'Toole's King. He responds to the meanderings of his children and the beatific rage of Katharine Hepburn as if they were members of a stock company who were not sure in which style and period they were meant to perform. The film accents the play's theatricality, but it could have worked to the advantage of director Anthony Harvey had he adopted a more resilient tone of self-parody. Harvey, a noted film editor, has even less success with *The Abdication*, in which the star presence of Peter Finch and Liv Ullmann functions as receding icons of saintliness. Harvey's sharp cuts isolate the ascetic nature of court life, but the successive close-ups of Finch and Ullmann become far too melodramatic images for the period and the subject.

Among the directors involved in England's more prestigious film productions, Peter Glenville has shown the least inventiveness. He was the director of *Becket*, a film memorable for the bellicose behavior of O'Toole and Burton and Geoffrey Unsworth's intelligent use of the matted backgrounds to duplicate the cramped staging and pictorial foreshortening of the high Gothic. Glenville's adaptation of *Hotel Paradiso* is one of the very worst undertaken on film, while *Term of Trial* suffers from the incongruity between a middlebrow approach to sexuality and an overtly erotic script. *The Comedians* promises more, but Burton's riveting moments of self-revulsion are overshadowed by a miscast Peter Ustinov, by a distasteful characterization of Lillian Gish, and by Elizabeth Taylor's worst performance, a sure sign of dramatic overstatement if not social malaise.

Guy Green shows no more expertise in handling the ambivalent themes of the modern cinema. *The Mark* is such an unrelievedly glum study of child molestation that Stuart Whitman's hangdog expression becomes the most tangible proof of Freudian unrest. Rod Steiger's accent and analysis often slip into Brooklynese, while Whitman's guarded relationship with Maria Schell is dramatized in a tenderly facile moment as he touches her back. If all neuroses could be so neatly explained, the doors of our institutions could be opened without any reservations. Whereas *The Mark* misses the rough edges, the sudden, inexplicable emotional frictions necessary to explain Whitman's tragic stigma, *The Magus* lacks the necessary distortions to make one believe in Michael Caine's fantasylike sojourn. Instead of experimenting with different stylistic touches in expressing the devious continuity of the past, Green painlessly fragments the theme of alienation like a magazine editor putting the finishing touches on his copy for a vacation in the sun.

Among the major English directors attracted to the narrative models established in America and England during the thirties, Bryan Forbes has made the most serious, sustained effort to revive their modest, melodramatic appeal. His strength lies in his sensitivity to his performer's emotional fragility, for example, in the character of Kim Stanley's alienated medium in *Seance on a Wet Afternoon* and in that of her husband played by Richard Attenborough, who remains faithful to her while subverting his need for affection. It also characterizes Forbes's handsome, soap-opera treatment of the lovers played by Nanette Newman and Malcolm McDowell in *Long Ago Tomorrow*. Forbes's study of the fallen woman in *The L-Shaped Room* is too self-conscious in its ethnographic recreation of the realism of the fifties, but it conveys a higher regard for its characters than a similar Hollywood film such as *Love with the Proper Stranger*. *King Rat*, Forbes's most entertaining work, is highlighted by Burnett Guffey's scorched backgrounds and pale-figured POWs. Forbes avoids the moronic strategies of *The Bridge on the River Kwai* or the leisurely frivolities of *The Great Escape* through a more straightforward exposition of the psychological hardships of camp life, especially in the engrossing relationship of James Fox and George Segal. Forbes has had less success in his more recent projects, beginning with *The Wrong Box*, in which his ethereal vision of an inebriated Victorian England is an idea waiting for its execution. *The Madwoman of Chaillot* takes a second-rate, inflated Giraudoux play and treats it as a most civilized piece of antisocial rhetoric; *The Stepford Wives*, however, does not even have second-rate Giraudoux to fall back on. Although Forbes's career seems estranged from the drift of the contemporary cinema, his earlier work, like that of David Lean, is a striking example of how the English quality film is a sure-handed derivative of Hollywood entertainment.

### Look Back in Anger—Yanks

The abeyance of the English quality film is a telltale sign of the decline in traditional cultural and artistic values. England's language, literature, and actors, the living embodiments of its past, whose savory tones of elegance assured earlier generations of moviegoers that amid the physical embellishments of this new medium the art of verbal discourse would remain inviolable, are inundated by the rumblings of discontent initiated by the English theater's "angry young men." In the postwar American film, the teledramatic vision of Miller, Inge, and Chayefsky influenced the movies with a more static sense of dramaturgy: audiences experienced a taut, cathartic exercise that substituted the high spirits and self-confidence of its Depression-era film fantasists with a mood of introspection and alienation. In the English theater of Osborne, Wesker, and Delaney, greater emphasis is placed on the depressing ambience; hence the characters' speech is more evocative of their slum surroundings than are the poetic mumblings of their American counterparts. The protagonists are not involved in a straightforward pursuit of truth or spiritual redemption evident in American drama, but seek instead to strike back at the representatives of English society who have denied them their personal dreams.

Tony Richardson directed four of the most celebrated works by the angry young men. Although his direction of *Look Back in Anger*, *The Entertainer*, *A Taste of Honey*, and *The Loneliness of the Long Distance Runner* shows little subtlety, his commitment to the authors' restlessness and chagrin heats up an already inflamed polemic. His adaptations are marked by their pervasive dimly lit settings, by their ubiquitous tones of alienation, and by the forcefulness of the characters' self-disgust and unfulfilled erotic desires. The sexual tension underlying and gradually overriding the relationship between Burton and Claire Bloom in *Look Back in Anger* is all too apparent, but their intensity confirms the historical permanence of Osborne's fiery rhetoric. *The Entertainer* is even less valid on film; yet how astutely Olivier makes us appreciate Archie's selfish self-aggrandizement. The painful adolescence of *A Taste of Honey* is diffused by Richardson's absorption in the clatter and clutter of the heroine's materialist society. The script of *The Loneliness of the Long Distance Runner* is a more personal study of social alienation, yet Tom Courtenay's delinquent is fated to reconfirm the apathy of his working class anti-hero.

Richardson's adaptation of Fielding's *Tom Jones* has been criticized for simplifying the novel's portentous comic vision. But even as we admit the absence of genius in his film version, it retains the novel's picaresque humor through the sunny, sensual hues of Walter Lassally's color cinematography, the slapstick arabesques of Osborne's script, and the assortment of self-mocking characterizations, highlighted by the roguish delineation of Albert Finney's Tom Jones. Fielding's exhaustive comic rhetoric is considerably abridged, but there is an undeniable affinity between the film's sumptuous backgrounds and the tendency to playful excess among its performers. Richardson's comic timing seems even better in *Tom Jones* when compared to a future effort like *The Loved One*, in which his sledgehammer effects and Gielgud's Shakespearean mask of unease diminish Waugh's deadly, elliptical prose. In *The Charge of the Light Brigade* he undercuts the epic characterizations and historical facade necessary to penetrate Victorian England. The love affair between David Hemmings and Vanessa Redgrave is extraneous to his parodic treatment; his send-up of the military results in Trevor Howard and Harry Andrews dilating their eyeballs and elbowing each other for position in a Punch-and-Judy pantomime.

Karel Reisz's first feature-length film, *Saturday Night and Sunday Morning*, is one of the more radical examples of the underlying Darwinian impulse in the naturalism of the English cinema. It also proves, with greater matter-of-factness though less emotion than *Look Back in Anger* and *The Loneliness of the Long Distance Runner*, that the protagonist's antipathy is not directed at the upper classes or at any one ideal with which English society has been associated. Finney's swaggering self-assurance must not contend with any upper-class or authoritarian figure, but with Rachel Roberts's husband; he ends the film by stating that the only important thing in life is to have a good time, all the rest is propaganda. Although Burton's Jimmy Porter and Courtenay's long distance runner detect a malodorous stench that pervades every sphere of English society, they are on a self-destructive course that one suspects would have taken its toll had they been raised in more propitious surroundings. Finney's character in Reisz's film, however, connotes the tragic stasis facing the English anti-hero: he refuses to admit that something exists beyond what he eats, drinks, and touches. Whereas Richard Harris will undertake the most aggressive and heroic interpretation of this oppressed anti-hero in *This Sporting Life*, Finney projects a new kind of authenticity about two-dimensional portraiture.

*Morgan!* makes greater use of Reisz's training as an editor by either juxtaposing the movements and mannerisms of humans and animals or by slowing down or speeding up the action to convey Morgan's unbalanced condition. Some of the effects and analogies are amusing—for example, the physical surges of love-making among man and animal or Morgan's illustration of the assassination of Trotsky through his breaking an egg—but David Warner's character is in need of an expanded comic and intellectual irreverence in order to make sense of the mayhem of modern England. Reisz is less successful in *Isadora*. The script is as didactic in its romantic epiphanies as the comic visions of *Morgan!*. What is most revealing about Redgrave's characterizations of Isadora and of Morgan's flighty wife is how acutely she evokes the differences between a theatrical and a film presence. I once saw Redgrave on the stage in *The Prime of Miss Jean Brodie*, and she was breathtaking: regal, elusive, and with an undeniable iconoclastic fervor. In her film roles her dramatic possession of a character is far too extreme. One responds to her tremulous gestures like a doctor recording the effects of a drug on a patient. She realizes the moods and masks of her character, but without allowing for expressive pauses and repressed, reflective dramatic moments. I find her elusive flirt in *Blow-Up* more credible than her ethereal Julia because her constant genuflections seem endemic to her role in Antonioni's metaphysical thriller; in *Julia* she is a spirit, and, while one admires her intelligence, it is like the artistry of a singer or dancer superimposed on the story's dramatic realism. In *Isadora* her interpretation of the legendary dancer as an icon of religious intensity is not only hindered by Reisz's perfunctory staging, but also by her mannered, demonic portrayal of a free spirit. On the stage, she alone can magnify the dramatic and emotional threads of her character; on film, her expressive strategies seem removed from the film's dramatic continuity. We observe her manifestations of sublimity with little understanding of their proximity to or distance from her real life hardships and dramatic transfigurations.

Jack Clayton directed what is often described as the archetypal study of working-class rancor, *Room at the Top*. The problem with the film is similar to the admirable though constrained literacy in Jack Cardiff's direction of *Sons and Lovers* and in Clayton's direction of *The Pumpkin Eater* and *The Innocents*. In *Sons and Lovers*, the most interesting of the three films, Cardiff adopts a distant tone to D. H. Lawrence's tremulous prose; only Trevor Howard seems willing to project a heroic individuality in his performance as the father. One is not asking Cardiff to take the chances Ken Russell recklessly abuses in *Women in Love*, but his stately design fails to animate the sensual trajectory of Lawrence's industrial settings. In *Room at the Top* Laurence Harvey's social ascent and spiritual decline is too cut-and-dried: his attack on the upper class is rooted in dramatic formulas that lack the particularities of time and place in the more representative though often less cogent works of the angry young men. Harvey and Simone Signoret provide several moving images of the lovers who, in fulfilling a passion, realize the inexorability of their separation; it is in their moments of romantic isolation that we experience the tragic impact of Harvey's lower-class upbringing. One of Harvey's lesser known though equally compelling roles, the zestful, scurrilous theatrical agent in *Expresso Bongo*, exposes England's pop-music industry as a sore-ridden yet active prostitute. The film's musical score lacks the fluency of moods in *The Harder They Come*, yet it imbues the clinical naturalism of the English film with a rude feistiness it sorely needs.

Clive Donner's direction of *Nothing but the Best* and *The Caretaker* makes for a revealing comparison to Clayton's work. *Nothing but the Best* is not as mired in Pavlovian theater as *Room at the Top*. Alan Bates's character in *Nothing but the Best* differs from that of Harvey and other English malcontents in that he does not suffer from their antipathy; he is a faceless social climber who goes about his rise to the top as if he were taking a correspondence course. Although there is an effective contrast between Bates and Denholm Elliott's wry, delinquent aristocrat, the most striking aspect of the film is how the dramatic fatalism of *Room at the Top* is here manifested in its distant point of view, its refusal to juxtapose the pettiness of the little man to the disdain of the rich. It is an appealing film, but it does not take the chances to fully circumvent the angry-young-men ethic of the power of negative thinking. Donner is less successful with *The Caretaker*, even though he is not working with the Pinteresque platitudes of *The Pumpkin Eater*. Pinter's three estranged figures seem the voices of a grim, nightmarish fantasy in which Donner's stagy, shadowy backgrounds leave the play unfocused. Bates's characterization is the most problematic: his innate film presence as a tough, wily street kid digresses to that of a method performer ferreting his way through the devious maze of Pinter's prose. The absence of a stylistic viewpoint in Donner's direction is most conspicuous in *What's New Pussycat?*. The disparate acting temperaments of Peter Sellers, Peter O'Toole, Woody Allen, Romy Schneider, and Capucine intersect like chickens during mating season. The cumulative effect of their erotic abandonment may deaden one's critical impulses, but Donner removes himself from consideration as a fledgling interpreter in his adaptation of Murray Schisgal's sickly comedy, *Luv*.

John Schlesinger is one of the few directors who has survived the uses and abuses of naturalism in the contemporary English cinema. His earlier film ventures, *A Kind of Loving* and *Billy Liar*, are among the first signs of the protagonist's romantic longing overcoming his crass behavioral instincts. Similar to other works in the film canon of discontent, they suffer from their stereotypes of dramatic and social repression and, in the case of *Billy Liar*, from banal images of poetic liberation. The fate of the young lovers when they first decide to make love in *A Kind of Loving* is all too familiar, but Thora Hird's portrayal of Alan Bates's mother-in-law imbues her role with a ferocity that explodes across the screen; a similar scintillating presence in *Billy Liar* is that of Julie Christie, who seems so real, so touching that one feels she is bound to happily transcend her grubby confines.

She does transcend them in *Darling*, and, with a cleverly detailed script by Frederic Raphael, Christie's wayward model, like Dirk Bogarde's servant, becomes a clairvoyant symbol of the corrupt materialism at the center of the English cinema of the sixties. Several critics have judged the film a failed work of art, as if Schlesinger were striving for the same abstract form that characterized the major statements on alienation from the European cinema; his intentions, however, are considerably different. He conceives Christie's lovers as ephemeral figures in her unsuspecting rise to the top. He has carefully crafted the film so that each of Christie's romances evokes her lover's guile or lack of it. During her affair with Dirk Bogarde's journalist, one sees them trying to expand their initial attraction into a sobering middle-class existence. During her stay on Capri, with the camera setup in extreme long shot, Christie is picked up by a man on a motorcycle, and in the next scene, still in long shot, they return to the same spot with the only evidence of their previous night out the fact that they are wearing the other's sweater. The film assumes a still more depersonalized tone in her encounter and marriage to the Italian prince; it first plays as a behind-the-scenes look at the making of a commercial and then as a magazine editor's clipped notes on romance among the jet-setters. Schlesinger has fashioned a suave, amoral autobiography; although we never penetrate the surface of his characters, his breezy rhythms reflect the soulless nature of Christie's heroine.

In *Midnight Cowboy* Schlesinger attempts a similar cross section of New York's slimy outsiders, but his glossy visuals are incongruous to the city's pimps, pushers, and prostitutes. Dustin Hoffman's "Ratso" Rizzo is typical of the deceitfulness in Schlesinger's treatment of the Times Square abyss; Hoffman's guttural snap, like his limp, is too acutely dramatic, an acting-class tour de force rather than an expression of his physical and psychological alienation. Jon Voight's performance rises above the material to convince the audience that there is more to growing up in the Southwest than the wide-eyed goons and gang bangs that Schlesinger features. Schlesinger's innocuous journey through his characters' underworld is ironically exposed when the guests at a party are asked why they have come. In *Darling* such a question would never have been raised; in *Midnight Cowboy* it reveals Schlesinger's self-consciousness. The incisive editing of Schlesinger's *Sunday Bloody Sunday* interrelates his characters' repressed emotional tensions with the more visible yet anonymous physical trademarks of their backgrounds. The young artist caught between the affections of Peter Finch and Glenda Jackson is reasonably sympathetic, but it is the film's two stars who articulate how the need to be loved cannot be alleviated by their jobs. Jackson has given nastiness a new sexual edge in *Women in Love*, and how well she plays her role as the older woman. Finch was one of the few credible, mature male presences in the contemporary cinema. Less petulant and not possessing as pronounced a sense of homosexual unease as Jean-Louis Trintignant, he convinces the viewer of the tremors the modern adult male faces.

Schlesinger's expert editing has given him a decided advantage over his contemporaries whose identity has submerged with the decline of the voice of disenchantment of the fifties and sixties. If there was a glibness about *Sunday Bloody Sunday* that was previously incorporated into the dramatic paradoxes of Christie's paramours, *Marathon Man* shows a more accomplished reading of the suspense film than *Black Sunday*, whose director, John Frankenheimer, comes from a similar background in television and the cutting room. There are several awkward transitional scenes in Schlesinger's film, and Hoffman's history student lacks the dramatic animus that Roy Scheider and Olivier bring to their roles. Yet how invigorating it is to find the clichéd notes of terror instilled with a dramatic fatalism that personifies each of the major characters and the thematic crosscurrents in their pursuit of the gems. Frankenheimer disposes of the supporting characters and leads us to the climax in a linear, mechanical fashion; in Schlesinger's film, the characters become an extension of the pervasive note of doom.

Schlesinger fares less well with the period dramas of *The Day of the Locust* and *Yanks*. In his earlier adaptation of Hardy's *Far from the Madding Crowd*, Schlesinger seemed most sympathetic to Hardy's absorption in landscape but was indifferent to Hardy's dramatizing the emotional discords through the upheavals in nature. In *The Day of the Locust* he makes a critical mistake in transforming West's bitter fable into a tragic epiphany; his tendency to depersonalize his characters' emotional tensions through his dynamic editing is exaggerated by Conrad Hall's golden, dreamlike hues. The extravagant production design exposes the characterizations of Burgess Meredith, Karen Black, and Donald Sutherland as caricatures, and the film misses the voice of dramatic fatalism in West's narrator. *Yanks* is a more cogent example of the evocative echoes of time and place. One again notes Schlesinger's preference for character displacement through the emotional counterpoints of his editing; the characters, however, never come alive other than as transparent, though attractive icons of romantic nostalgia. Schlesinger seems to be more fond of Richard Gere's nervous mannerisms than of the genuine romantic pulsations of Lisa Eichhorn's performance, and the ending seems tentative. But the intelligence of craft has survived.

*Petulia–Altered States*

The films and filmmaking styles that grew out of the angry-young-men school, as a result of their faithfulness to the playwrights' language and listlessness, failed with few exceptions to inspire a new cinematic vision. In the films of Richard Lester, Joseph Losey, Lindsay Anderson, Nicolas Roeg, and Ken Russell, there is a greater diversity of literary and cinematic sources, yet the very exuberance of their treatments conveys the absence of an underlying, unifying dramatic or stylistic core.

The stylistic paradox in Richard Lester's comedy films, with the exception of *A Hard Day's Night*, is not so much peculiar to him as it is to a generation of filmmakers who were trained in television, whether in live drama or commercials. Lester's mastery of different editing dynamics—as a form of hyperbolic, communal anarchy (*The Running Jumping and Standing Still Film, A Hard Day's Night*); as a collage of hyphenated cartoon gestures and episodes (*Help!*); as a choreographic reverie that jumps across the screen in increasingly complex patterns and kinetic rhythms (*The Knack*); and as a Brechtian fantasy that denotes various layers of character inversion and social allegory (*How I Won the War*)—results in a highly prefabricated style lacking a consistent comic voice or protagonist.

In *Petulia* he applies his multiple editing tracks to a contemporary marriage drama. The flashbacks and flash-forwards intercut the dialogue with the visual and aural strains of his characters' social setting; Lester uncovers the sensual fabric of San Francisco's high society but fails to capture those elements of regret and longing that inspire his successive streamlined images of social stasis. The miserable attempt at reconciliation involving George Scott and Shirley Knight suggests a dramatic alternative to the mindless marriage of Richard Chamberlain and Julie Christie, but Lester opts for a mood of impersonal, kaleidoscopic dislocation. In *Robin and Marian* and *The Three Musketeers* Lester, surprisingly, turns to classic narrative genres but, not surprisingly, with a dominant note of contrivedness, notably in the tension or lack of it between his period details and the characters' inclination to parody. There are scenes in *Robin and Marian* which portend the elements of a comic-book send-up, but Lester's gradual emphasis on the romance misses the necessary dramatic buildup in its recreation of the legend. *The Three Musketeers* is more characteristic of his association with cinematographer David Watkin. There is a greater emphasis on the decor and on replaying the clichés of comic melodrama; his setups, whether in long shot or close-up, are cued to the period authenticity, with only a few concessions to his distancing, editing experiments. The film strikes a pose of neoclassical serenity, one that has been judiciously disembodied by Lester's foremost successors, the Monty Python troupe.

Joseph Losey's *The Servant* is similar to Schlesinger's *Darling* in that he does not try to transcend the characters' corrupt facades or their decadent surroundings. From our first picture of James Fox looking emaciated and dozing to the last image of his doped stupor, the film traps its characters in their precarious social identity. Harold Pinter's juicy, mean-spirited script continually closes in on Fox's insecure, foppish manner, on Dirk Bogarde's barely controlled smirk, and on Sarah Miles's brazen sexuality. The script's multifaceted layers of verbal and visual exposure are comically exploited in a restaurant sequence: Fox conveys his confused idea of Brazil to his fiancée, and in surrounding booths Pinter engages in a conversation with a woman while a priest, played by Patrick Magee, insults a waiter as his secretary looks on. The snatches of conversation show them as mercilessly exposed by their words as by their gestures; unbeknownst to them, they have engaged in a striptease. It is the most callous scene in the movie, but even with the more distant framing used by Losey and Pinter —for example, in the scene at the fiancée's in-laws in which they question the meaning of a poncho—their indolent speech and postures create a surreal frieze of upper-class conviviality. It may seem that Losey and Pinter are only interested in surfaces, in systematically revealing the characters' perverse behavior in their etiolated social setting. But, like *Darling*, *The Servant* never intimates that there is anything beneath the characters' erotic impulses; the sound of the water hitting the basin as Miles seduces Fox is not simply a crude, obvious effect, but an inexorable variation on the decline of the stiff upper lip.

But what was hot and seductive in *The Servant* is cold and constricted in *Accident*, autoerotic in *Eva* and *Secret Ceremony*, and self-indulgent in *Boom!*. There is no surprise when Bogarde pins Jacqueline Sassard to the floor in *Accident*, but there was when Fox's fiancée momentarily succumbed to Bogarde's advances in *The Servant*. We never understand how the characters fulfill their roles as teachers and students, whereas the manservant metaphor provided an expressive framework for the erotic degradation in *The Servant*. The characters have no identity other than as sexual fantasists whose subconscious desires become the physical terrain of their university setting. *Eva* is the opposite of *Accident*. Douglas Slocombe's constant camera movements are meant to denote the fragmented characters and the oppressively erotic mood. But as a study of sexual obsession, *Eva* presents a conventional picture of decadence: while we never get inside Stanley Baker's tormented figure, the other characters drawn to Jeanne Moreau's temptress lack the depth to make their descent enlightening to any degree. *Secret Ceremony* is a more flagrant example of autoeroticism simply because of the extravagance of the script and casting. The film features Elizabeth Taylor's overly suggestive figure; two senile aunts, who are lesbians; Robert Mitchum, an ideal masturbatory image, who also happens to be the laziest actor on God's earth; and Mia Farrow, who plays a game of substitute gratification with Taylor. The dense, harsh colors, like the art objects that clutter Farrow's home, accent the characters' identities as sexual gnomes. *Boom!* takes this absurdist formula one step further by playing Tennessee Williams's shrill threnody strictly for laughs. Taylor is cast as one of the world's richest women, Burton plays the angel of death, Noël Coward is a transient blithe spirit, and Michael Dunn is Taylor's groundkeeper. The potential for sexual delinquency in Dunn's character lies in his being a dwarf.

Losey's more recent efforts, *The Assassination of Trotsky* and *Mr. Klein*, dangle numerous tenuous motifs involving the individual and his destiny in history. *The Assassination of Trotsky* suggests an analogy between the mosaics that are interspersed throughout the city and the fatalistic encounter between Burton and Alain Delon. But neither the dialogue between Trotsky and his assassin nor the relationship of Delon and his mistress, played by Romy Schneider, explains their characters on either a personal or historical level. Whereas Burton's Trotsky is played as an ecclesiastic who awaits his deliverance, Delon's killer seems a matinee idol who has been struck by the method style of acting. *Mr. Klein* is a more engrossing film, and the two opening scenes—one in which a woman undergoes a physical examination as the doctor searches for Semitic features and the other, an exchange between Delon and a Jew on the run who must sell his paintings—evoke layers of tension and possible victimization. It is interesting to watch Delon, whose career has drifted from playing punks to charming rakes, feel his way through the role of a dilettante mistaken for a Jewish member of the underground during the Nazi occupation of Paris. But Losey and scriptwriter Franco Solinas give one little information about Delon's feelings concerning the identity of the other Mr. Klein. Only those who pay homage to the movies' power to mystify will be satisfied with the film's obscure references to *Moby Dick*, with its failure to pursue Delon's relationship with Jeanne Moreau, and with Delon's final acquiescence to the fate of his double.

Unlike *Darling* and *The Servant*, *This Sporting Life* is the only one of the three definitive studies of discontent and disdain in the Engligh cinema of the sixties that draws on the bile of the angry young men. One of the reasons that Richard Harris's rough-hewn, inarticulate rugby player proves a more original creation than the alienated intellectuals and wistful daydreamers in the works of Osborne, Delaney, Sillitoe, and Naughton is that the target of David Storey's novel is not the rigidly oppressive nature of English society. Unlike the socially inspired rancor of contemporary film anti-heroes, Harris is not concerned with class inequities, but in communicating—through his attention to his physique, through his brutal confrontations on the field, and through his primitive cry for help that overwhelms Rachel Roberts's widowed landlady—the inner paradoxes that impede his successful rise to the top. Lindsay Anderson, like several other English directors, first worked as a film critic, but he avoids the studied, self-conscious effects in the films of Richardson and Reisz. The camerawork and editing never treat Harris as a perfunctory symbol; the film derives its poetic force from Harris's faltering expressions of a primitive using his physical vitality as a means of self-protection as well as a means of establishing an emotional rapport with his society and friends. Roberts's character is a little stale, but the rowdy camaraderie among the team players is infused with the idiosyncracies of Harris's characterization. The novel is good if somewhat cumbersome; because of the heroic dimensions Harris discovers in his rubgy star, the movie is more personal and profound. Harris's performance inspires favorable comparison to Brando's work in the fifties and shows how essential this Brando-like chagrin and animal passion are to the contemporary English cinema. In many ways Harris does things Brando would not and could not do; there is a tragic vulnerability about Brando's persona while Harris is so instinctive in his actions, so happily the innocent as he boozes with his friends that one can cite his performance as an original variation on the humanism first explored in the Italian cinema.

But Anderson's sensitivity to the humor and pathos of *This Sporting Life* is nowhere apparent in his next films. *The White Bus*, an adaptation of a Shelagh Delaney story, is further proof that the dream life of the English working class is no more invigorating than its daily conventions; while Jimmy Porter would have laughed at half the fakes in the film, he would not have admitted the existence of the others. *If . . .* is a more imaginative work, but as much as one admires Anderson's rueful study of English boarding schools, his story line avoids the more pointed treatment his material deserves. The characterizations and vignettes are sharper than in *The White Bus*, and his handful of fantasy images, for example, the two boys and the girl on the motorcycle, are subjectively, poetically liberating. However, the film shows an uneasy blending of classicism and modernism, as if Anderson were not sure whether he wanted to make a parody of *Tom Brown's School Days* or a Godardian blast at the establishment. In *O Lucky Man!* Anderson embraces a more acute, modernist viewpoint in directing one of the most ambitiously Brechtian films of the last decade. It begins most wittily as Malcolm McDowell learns to taste coffee, and Alan Price's title song augurs well. But McDowell's adventures do not isolate any one aspect of the little or lucky men of this world. The initial theme of social satire is enveloped by a mood of wistfulness, yet the transition to fable fails to reveal its origin in the makeup of its protagonist or in the devious charms of his dramatic reality. Inevitably, the film is most reminiscent of a stately, stodgy English production like *Stairway to Heaven*, in which an innocuous, middlebrow approach is taken to film as fantasy. Anderson's film attempts a more disengaging picture of fantasy, but one senses, without believing in the gay antirationalism of contemporary filmmakers.

Nicolas Roeg and Ken Russell offer a more radical, and often painful example of the revived romanticism of the English film. Roeg's *Performance* is one of the more corrupt works of the modern cinema, yet the film's nastiness, its vigorous descent into the polymorphous corridors of rock 'n' roll, remains so peculiarly of its time that it works as one of the more impressive examples of the sensibility of the outsider on film. Roeg's sharp cutting may at first alienate the viewer, but his recreation of the ethnic garble of the British hoods and James Fox's unlikely characterization as the vicious, sadomasochistic gunman create a vivid portrait of the underside of the criminal world. It is not the decadent, pseudoart of *Dead Pigeon on Beethoven Street* or the facile parody of *The American Soldier*. The intense editing rhythms underscore Fox's fascistic satisfaction in brutalizing his victims, making it one of the few pictures of the criminal that looks at this misfit from inside his turbulent world. Fox's escape to Mick Jagger's home finds Roeg exploring the sensual, subterranean quality of Jagger's narcissism and its expression in his loud, abrasive music. Much of the dialogue is inaudible and the change in roles between Fox and Jagger is not convincing; but the film brings a hard, corrosive realism to its treatment of a singularly unrealistic subject.

The photographic sheen in Roeg's succeeding films leads one to conclude that the abstracted drama of *Performance* exemplifies his seductively superficial style. The brother and sister in *Walkabout* are dogmatic characters who are less engrossing than Golding's hierarchical schoolchildren. Roeg's approach is too distant and civilized for his harrowing story, but this works to his advantage in *Don't Look Now*. Similar to *Performance* and its transporting the viewer inside the characters' perverse habits, the pleasures of *Don't Look Now* are those of making sensible those aspects of our memories that are insensible. It may execute this theme in too impersonal a style, with too much of a photographer's aplomb, but few indeed are those directors capable of achieving this tone. *The Man Who Fell to Earth* is a splintered science-fiction tale. Roeg generates some feeling in the relationship of David Bowie and Candy Clark, and the special effects make sense when seen in the context of America's foreboding wilderness. The negligible subplots, however, suggest that the genre of science fiction is too inherently anarchic for such a cool temperament as that of Roeg. It will be interesting to see if he will survive the one-shot-success circumstance of *Performance*.

Ken Russell's films easily qualify him as the most wrongheaded director working in the movies. *Women in Love* is his only film that merits serious analysis; Russell's stylistic equation between D. H. Lawrence's purple prose and his continuous camera movements and tense framing oversimplify Lawrence in a way that is strikingly similar to Jack Cardiff's seemingly antipodal direction of *Sons and Lovers*. Only Glenda Jackson captures the spirit of her character, but with one of Russell's telefilms, *Isadora Duncan, the Biggest Dancer in the World*, they are his most accessible works. The problem with *The Boy Friend* is that for all the care Russell has shown in designing the film, his performers never seem to infiltrate his Berkeleyan backdrops. His straightforward adaptations of the drug visions of *Tommy* and *Altered States* represent his least paradoxical equations between filmmaking and fantasy. *Tommy*, blissfully inane, fulfills its acid-trip symbolism; *Altered States*, with its drug addicts masquerading as drug analysts, revives the spirit of Roger Corman's primitive science and space allegories. Although they are less fraudulent than *The Music Lovers* or *Valentino*, the critic is still inclined to analyze Russell rather than his work. That they are puerile, schlocky, extravagantly bad films is superfluous; what I think they do illuminate, however, is a romantic sensibility that has never been given much credence in the English film. They are the muck and mush that the sensible, stolid curators of the English cinema have successfully repressed and which, through Russell's fervid subjectivity, are reclaimed as the cry of a miscast Hercules who has begun work on the Augean stable.

# 21
# The French Film

## Alain Resnais

With the exception of Jean-Luc Godard, Alain Resnais is the most prominent modern filmmaker to base his films on the dynamic, dialectical editing style most commonly associated with the Russian silent films of Eisenstein and Pudovkin. But unlike the Russians who used montage both as an objective idealization of the dynamically interconnecting nature of their revolution and as a means to intensify the cathartic charge of their social uprisings, Resnais finds no similar unifying thread about montage. He utilizes the highly schematic, acutely rhythmic montage style of the Russians to penetrate the hazards of the past and its varying interconnectedness with his protagonists' present fate. Resnais' early documentary study of the Holocaust, *Night and Fog*, remains a gripping execution of this theme: his invisible narrator and the bleak horror of the concentration camps provide a cogent synthesis of a tortured, fractured memory and the objective truth of the camps as part of a collective social history. But when Resnais deviates from this personal-historical interplay, his introspective editing rhythms seem arbitrary, unconvincing.

Resnais' precarious blending of the subjective and objective remnants of the past in *Hiroshima mon amour* is filtered through Emmanuelle Riva's actress. In her memories of Nazi-occupied France where she had a love affair with a German officer and was ostracized by the community which shaved her head, Riva is seen as a martyr who is unable to identify her persecutors. During her stay in Hiroshima, which is marked by demonstrations against the bomb, Riva's vulnerable figure is confronted by a seemingly endless stream of confusing images. Her alienation is directly featured during her walk at night where she is surrounded by the harsh neon lights and scorched backgrounds. Resnais suggests that wherever she turns there is little chance to understand her past or present circumstances, but some hope is offered in her relationship with Eiji Okada. Whereas Riva plays an actress, someone who simulates the emotions of make-believe figures, Okada is an architect—strong, self-confident, a builder for the future. Riva does not leave Japan any more sure of the intercontinuity between past and present but seems more aware of the inescapable tenuousness that characterizes one's grasp of the two.

Resnais sustains our interest in Riva's confused character through the explorative nature of her relationship to Okada, but there is no similar point of contact in the French town in which *Muriel* is set. Neither Delphine Seyrig's character of the mother who hesitates in renewing a love affair with a man who visits her with a mistress masquerading as his niece nor her son who goes about filming what seems to be a minidocumentary on guilt provides a discernible viewpoint on the disheveled town and chaotic series of events. While the Algerian War serves as the historical backdrop, with fleeting references made to the torture of a girl and the betrayal of several underground fighters by Seyrig's former lover, the son's involvement in the Algerian campaign is no more clearly defined than the nature of Seyrig's feelings toward her ex-lover. Her son is played as a divinely inspired mystic who becomes the prototypical *cinéma vérité* documentarian, searching for fragments of man's inhumanity as he walks the streets of his town. Resnais has purposely situated the characters in a colorless, desolate environment, but this deprives them of a dramatic focus for their pursuit of self-knowledge. Without either a meaningful visual design or an arbitrary understanding of the characters' present condition, the viewer can only agree with Resnais' premise of the fragile nature of our memories while criticizing its exemplification.

A major problem in *Muriel* distinct from both *Night and Fog* and *Hiroshima mon amour* is that Resnais' modernist approach undercuts the film's romantic and historical tensions. In *Last Year at Marienbad* his adherence to Robbe-Grillet's manipulative formulas creates a similar impersonalizing tone, while the more conventional theme of *La Guerre est finie* results in his most satisfying work. Had Robbe-Grillet or Resnais the honesty to identify with the trickster, *Last Year at Marienbad* might have expressed a more satiric, devious point of view. But without a centralizing conflict between the author's objective ambiguities and the characters' subjective, defensive maneuvers—a point of view that distinguishes such absorbing Robbe-Grillet novels as *La Jalousie* and *Le Voyeur*—the sundry camera and editing permutations reinforce what one knows at the film's inception: the characters and their memories are complete fabrications of an author who never gives them a chance to escape from his endless reconstruction and restaging of the past. This is not to dismiss Robbe-Grillet's literary or film aesthetic, but it is a problem unique to modern art, wherein the contours in the subjective and objective shadings of truth are permanently obscured. The characters seem to be pawns in a chess match between two malicious grand masters; whatever spark *Last Year at Marienbad* possesses as a literary abstraction is lost as a film.

In *La Guerre est finie* there is a similar element of polemic simplification in Yves Montand's revolutionary—caught between the ineffective ploys of his contemporaries and the more violent measures advocated by the young radicals. But because of Montand's engrossing characterization of the weary gunrunner, the probing quality of Resnais' discontinuous time scheme works as a morally affirmative tract on the revolutionary. The abstracted treatment of

Montand's lovemaking with Geneviève Bujold may seem at first incongruous, but it effectively draws out the more personal, emotionally erotic undercurrents between Montand and Ingrid Thulin. The characters are not treated as symbols of the revolutionary as existentialist, but as compassionate individuals whose entire lives are absorbed by their involvement in the fight against fascism. If Montand occasionally rattles one too many metaphysical axioms, Resnais is invariably moved by the very real, piercing feelings that fill the screen and that negate any excursion into the past that would refute his protagonists' identity as revolutionaries.

Since *La Guerre est finie* Resnais has become one of the least visible of major directors in the contemporary cinema. In *Je t'aime je t'aime*, his most simple, but in this case his most lamentable film, Resnais is unable to invest the memories of his characters with any social or dramatic substance. The man's tragic love affair shows little passion, and the scientific backgrounds seem perfunctory. *Stavisky* is his least dramatic, most romantically felicitous excursion into the past. Sacha Vierny's cinematography, with its pastel hues, conceives the past as a lovely summer idyll, but one whose sensual fragrance subordinates the characters' personal desires and fears to a receding, decorative imprint. *Providence* does not even possess these slight, ephemeral overtones of time and place. The pleasures to be derived from the honeydew cadence of Gielgud's voice—the continuous manifestations of an intellect in action through his pregnant, poetic physical postures—have a diminishing effect in this painfully sophomoric treatment of one man's fantasies becoming his family's reality. The film becomes a parody of the ambiguities of self and society which Resnais attempted to methodically reconstruct in his first films. Considering the ambitiously abstract undertakings in the French New Wave and Resnais' initial commitment to classic formulations of man's humanist identity in twentieth-century social history, his inability to extend this inquiry into the seventies hits home just a little bit harder because of the declining sense of historic continuity among Resnais' contemporaries.

## François Truffaut

In the final scene of *Stolen Kisses* Jean-Pierre Léaud sits on a park bench with his wife. A stranger who has been following her approaches and declares his love for her. He asks that she go away with him as true love can only be experienced once in a lifetime. She refuses, and as they walk away, she remarks to Léaud that he must be crazy. Léaud mutters his disagreement.

This most pellucid moment in Truffaut's film autobiography seems to question not only the carefree romanticism of *Stolen Kisses*, but the direction of Truffaut's succeeding films. There are several poignant, humorous episodes in the film, from Léaud's misadventures as a detective who follows a woman who then calls a policeman, to his masquerade as a shoe salesman trying to discover why the owner is unpopular with his employees. This leads to the exquisite preamble to the film's last scene in which Delphine Seyrig, the wife of the shop owner who has overheard Léaud's declaration of love for her, decides to spend the afternoon with him. Although these scenes possess a delightful irony, one senses that Truffaut refrains from scrutinizing the consequences of Léaud's reckless behavior. Truffaut's indecisiveness will lead to the bland, mechanical marriage infidelities of *Bed and Board*, the soured fatalism of *Such a Gorgeous Kid like Me*, and the precious, perfumed romanticism of *The Story of Adele H.*. One must then turn to the very first expressions of his poetic sensibility to see why his romanticism suffered such a quick, precipitous decline.

Perhaps the single most arresting moment in *Les Mistons* occurs when the young boy kisses the seat of the girl's bicycle. Truffaut accentuates this perversely passionate sentiment by shooting it in slow motion, but it is not until *Jules and Jim* that Truffaut further embellishes his already considerable romanticism. *The 400 Blows*, Truffaut's first feature film, is composed in a more naturalistic style. It continues to impress one because of the surprisingly mature humanism in its story of a young boy becoming a hardened adolescent. The film avoids the cynicism that mars similar projects by intertwining moods of flippancy and realism; it draws us into the young man's ramshackle existence without pointing the finger at any one member of his family or society. In contending with his disconcerting life at home and school, the young Léaud engages one's interest through his mischievousness, his desire to win the affection of his abused father, and his playful excursions around Paris. Whereas Truffaut's later films, beginning with *Stolen Kisses*, have a more episodic quality, Léaud's anti-hero is so vibrantly alive in each scene, whether he plays around with his father or upsets the classroom, that one is aware at every moment of his aging—of his energy and cleverness being reproved by his elders. Although the last sequence involving his incarceration is too abrupt, as if Truffaut felt the audience didn't get the point, the film imbues Léaud's frighteningly fast maturation with a compassion rarely seen in first films.

*Shoot the Piano Player* and *The Soft Skin* appear to renege on the promise of *The 400 Blows*. *Shoot the Piano Player* lacks the irony and innovation of Godard's *Breathless* and the more full-bodied whimsy of *The Bride Wore Black*. Aznavour's diminutive form works well in intimating the inexplicability of the criminal world, but unlike Moreau's sleepwalker in *The Bride Wore Black*, whose ethereal figure draws out the idiosyncrasies of her husband's assassins, Aznavour functions as a transparent icon of helplessness. *The Soft Skin*, with *Such a Gorgeous Kid like Me*, bears strong consideration as Truffaut's worst film, and only takes second place because of his commitment to the fashion-magazine poetics of his tale of adultery. One awaits some evidence of Truffaut's deviousness in adapting this straightforward story of an amoral man who wants the best of both worlds, but Truffaut matter-of-factly transposes the rules of modern lovemaking. At least he does not completely empathize with the husband in the way he celebrates Bernadette Lafont's lack of chagrin in *Such a Gorgeous Kid like Me*.

In *Jules and Jim* Truffaut undertakes an extravagant summation of romanticism on film. Raoul Coutard's buoyant, feverish camerawork and Truffaut's sympathetic, impressionistic pacing, whether personified in the magnified image of Moreau's face or those sudden bursts of editing jumps, crystallize an era of history while punctuating his characters' tremulous moods. Henri Serre's Jim is a colorless intermediary, but the performances of Moreau and Oskar Werner are so richly drawn that the movie seems to overflow with the immediacy of their pain and pleasure. If Moreau's classic beauty and wild, intemperate actions appear to inspire the film's dramatic vicissitudes and cinematic exuberance, Werner's prematurely wizened, soulful presence impresses one with the foredoomed nature of man's attraction to Moreau's free spirit. In *Two English Girls*, his second adaptation of a Henri-Pierre Roché novel, Truffaut attempts a less paradoxical interpretation of romantic fatalism. Similar to the unruffled dramatic tensions of *The Soft Skin*, Truffaut represses the subjective tones of *Jules and Jim* for an objective, literary recreation of his characters and period. The quintessential Truffaut touches remain—lyrical tracking shots of his characters enjoying a picnic on a lake, the double exposure of the mother's face as her letter is read—and the amber, autumnal colors of Nestor Almendros typify both a time and a state of mind. Yet the voice-over narration suggests a note of predestination that is paralleled in Léaud's insentient hero, an absence of the living, dangerous presences that inhabit *Jules and Jim*.

Unlike the classic, storytelling textures of *Jules and Jim*, *The Wild Child* is an intuitively styled meditation on a celebrated moment of social history. By using black-and-white film, Truffaut seems to establish a parallel between the inherent lyricism of black-and-white photography among the masters of the silent film and the historical and metaphysical leitmotifs of innocence that intersect in this study of a dual education: the child's discovery of society and the doctor confronting the boy. The film refrains from the straightforward dramatic and psychological delineations of Arthur Penn's *The Miracle Worker* and René Allio's *Moi, Pierre Rivière*. But it is far more interesting than Penn's stagy, didactic interpretation or Allio's static, historical recreation because of its emphasis on selective personal details as emblematic of this highly charged encounter. Truffaut's characterization as the doctor, however, is an unfocused symbol of libertarian virtues; but the frenetic exchanges between the doctor, his servant, and the boy whose feelings are translated in tentative, high-pitched shrieks, sensitively evoke their emotional gambit. Perhaps the subject matter is too intrinsically intellectual for Truffaut's impressionistic style, but it is a valid, courageous attempt to use the movies to illuminate a unique conflict in our realization of a good society.

One often looks at a certain film as a director's quintessential project, as the one film he was destined to make, but rarely is this more joyously true than of *Day for Night*. From the very first scene, in which we watch a movie set in action, one is swept along in the effervescent story; the numerous parallels between the movie being made and the personal lives of the actors and technicians coalesce as a valid expression of the dreams of a moviemaker and his audience. Since his first shorts, Truffaut has been honored for the fluidity and emotionalism of his films, but nowhere is this as evident as in *Day for Night*. It is lovingly manifested in the flirtatiousness among the director's assistants and in his reverence for those magicians behind the camera and in the editing room who fulfill our illusory moviegoing. Truffaut's sympathetic idealization of the movies shows how the ephemeral, romantic impersonations of the actor are naturally duplicated by the actor's offscreen identity, whether in the self-assuredness of Jean-Pierre Aumont's matinee idol or in the theatrical mannerisms of Valentina Cortese. Perhaps it is most remarkably illustrated in Truffaut's handling of Jean-Pierre Léaud and Jacqueline Bisset: while he exposes Léaud for his callous treatment of Bisset's fragile character, he creates an intelligent picture of her vulnerability as a soap-opera heroine. If Keaton's *Sherlock Jr.* asks us to consider the frightening implications of a movie-made universe, *Day for Night* embraces its fancifulness.

The fact that *Day for Night* is the ultimate Truffaut film seems cruelly borne out by *Bed and Board, Such a Gorgeous Kid like Me*, and *The Story of Adele H.*. The critical difference between *Bed and Board* and his previous film autobiographies is that Léaud's protagonist is no longer the inventive drifter of the earlier films, but a married man whose misadventures are all too familiar. *Such a Gorgeous Kid like Me* is evidence of a more dangerous decline; the Léaud-type protagonist is played as a sap, the victim of Bernadette Lafont's raffish, soulless love object. If *Bed and Board* finds Truffaut growing weary of Léaud's character, *Such a Gorgeous Kid like Me* is the low point in the career of a director honored for his compassionate gallery of heroes and heroines. In *The Story of Adele H.*, Truffaut attempts to redeem the loutishness of Lafont's vixen with Isabelle Adjani's frail heroine. But Nestor Almendros's exaggerated lyrical compositions, with their suffocating tones of darkness, and Truffaut's empathetic treatment of Adjani's morbid fixation embrace the clichés of romantic literature with little irony. After apparently experiencing an emotional glut in his autobiographical reveries, the contrived, stylistic decor of *The Story of Adele H.* seem a dramatic compromise for a director whose romantic temperament was expressed through his characters' emotional resourcefulness. Adjani's Adele is certainly a paragon of romantic passion and isolation, but Truffaut and Almendros are content to idealize her pathos with the derivative motifs of romantic painting and fiction. Similar to *Two English Girls*, Truffaut attempts to discover his romantic precursors through his fidelity to their style.

*The Man Who Loved Women* marks a return to the personal, spontaneous moods of Truffaut's first films. It is always a pleasure to watch Charles Denner, an intelligent dramatic actor who plays his character of the woman watcher with a sense of poetry and introspection that are not, however, apparent in Truffaut's overall conception. Several scenes, such as Denner's confrontation with the baby-sitter or his doctor inject new life into anecdotal comedy, and one only wishes there were more of Brigitte Fossey. But as a reverie on the fate of love in the modern world, *The Man Who Loved Woman*, at best, resurrects some lovely sentiments about the fair sex. The film plays more like a series of vignettes than as an extended study of Denner's incandescent skirt chaser; for a director of Truffaut's emotional depth, the film is a meager compromise in reviving the romantic daring of his work before *Bed and Board*.

## Claude Chabrol

Claude Chabrol's films present one of the more uneven showcases of talent in a period when consistency has not been the filmmaker's most visible trademark. Although his subject matter remains uniquely of a piece, most cryptically in the treatment of his wife, Stéphane Audran, Chabrol's films often enmesh the viewer in perverse happenings without demystifying the erotic dilemma facing the characters. In an emblematic Chabrol work, a short film called *La Muette*, Audran plays a harried housewife who falls down a flight of stairs, while her son, wearing earplugs to drown out the noise in their home, is unable to come to her aid. The action leading up to Audran's fall is abrupt, vulgar, messy, epitomized by Chabrol in the role of the husband who eats his food as if he were testing its symphonic potential.

But as autoerotic as his films become, they provide an interesting study of a stylist who has refrained from the more overtly abstract ploys of his contemporaries. His first efforts in black-and-white clearly distinguish his position among New Wave directors. In *Le Beau Serge* and *Les Cousins*, there is an interesting reversal of roles by Jean-Claude Brialy and Gérard Blain; in the former Brialy plays a convalescent who returns to the country and attempts to instill hope in Blain's disordered, debilitated marriage, while in the latter Blain plays the country innocent who is confused by the corrupt manners of Brialy's dilettante. *Le Beau Serge* immerses the viewer in the psychological tensions surrounding the precarious friendship of Brialy and Blain. Bernadette Lafont plays Blain's sister-in-law, and her identity as the cruel, Zolaesque misfit of the modern cinema is already in evidence as she comforts both Blain and her stepfather. Unlike *Les Cousins*, which ridicules Blain's dull, priggish character, in *Le Beau Serge* Chabrol empathizes with Brialy's devoted friend, who in the harrowing final sequence runs around the village looking for Blain to bring him to the side of his wife who is delivering their child. The bleakness of the setting, as Brialy finds Lafont with her stepfather, while Blain, inebriated, has passed out in a cave, is dramatized by Brialy's determination to unite Blain with his wife, even if it only proves a temporary reunion.

*Les Cousins* shows both Chabrol's fluidity and flippancy in exploring the decadent ambience surrounding Brialy and his friends. When Blain's letter to his mother is read on the sound track, in which he expresses his steadfastness and desire to succeed at school, Chabrol's camera tracks from Blain writing the letter to the erotic artifacts in the room and then to the living room, where Brialy receives a visit from a girl demanding money for an abortion. It is a clever, cruel, yet invariably ephemeral variation on the fatalistic relationship of the cousins. One admires Chabrol's aplomb in leading the viewer into Brialy's, carefree, sensual existence, but one also senses Chabrol's unwillingness to probe beneath the glitter of Brialy's seven-day weekend. Chabrol is not a ponderous or academic director, but we never experience Brialy's sensuality as other than a sign of his financial security.

*L'Oeil du malin* is one of Chabrol's lesser known works; it is among his most cogent films and one of the most satisfying to come from the French New Wave. It concerns a Peeping Tom who shatters the secluded love nest of Audran and her husband, a famous German writer, played by Walther Reyer. Using his camera as an analytic instrument, Chabrol photographs their home through the underbrush and trees to establish a prevailing note of mystery and unrest. Although the narrator is an unpleasant figure, Chabrol exposes the husband and wife as silly, foolish characters who live in a make-believe world. After the narrator decides to gather material to destroy their illustions, he follows Audran when she goes to the city, spots her with a man and photographs their encounter. Prior to showing the pictures to Reyer, the narrator inspects them: the first picture in long shot is not very incriminating evidence; the next in medium shot is more damaging; the last is an extreme close-up of Audran kissing the man. When Reyer opens the folder, Jean Rabier's camera begins in medium shot, and as the camera slowly moves in on him, Chabrol uses a jump cut to make a parallel between the final, most devastating photograph of Audran and her lover and the extreme close-up of Reyer. Reyer looks up and says, "Happiness is fragile," runs after Audran, and kills her. The film ends with Chabrol using his first overhead shot as Reyer is taken away by the police while the narrator says that he has related this episode to various people, but they do not believe him. *L'Oeil du malin* may not have the sweep of Chabrol's later films, but it suggests that his study of the state of love in the modern world is best served when he does not engulf the viewer in the characters' erotic mischievousness.

*Les Bonnes Femmes* is Chabrol's most ambitious early film yet one that also reveals his imperviousness in depicting his heroines' fatalistic charms. Chabrol exposes their reckless desire for adventure and pleasure, but he fails to move us through their inexorable decline. When Bernadette Lafont is brought to an apartment by two male friends, neither their grisly demeanor nor her lack of hesitation in entertaining them both is shocking or sorrowful. The scene in the nightclub when the men don the masks establishes their self-debasement, but it is so glumly portrayed that it is as if one of the characters were filming the scene. The one truly perverse relationship involving the virago and the man on the motorcycle, whom she thinks is the prince of her dreams but whom we realize is a dark knight on a dark horse, exemplifies Chabrol's manipulative dramatic formulas as she is raped and possibly killed during an outing in the park. After the man hurries away, Chabrol begins one of his ubiquitous swirling camera movements while a group of children is led for a walk through the park, accenting his distant, icy tone. The final scene is even more detached, focusing on the face of a girl in a dance hall who suggests both the angelic and destructive side of women. The camera then languishes on the movement of the mirrored spheroid overhanging the dance floor, an inconclusive symbol of the opaque, circuitous nature of those searching for love and adventure.

*Landru* is a brilliant experiment in historical reconstruction. Unlike the predominantly personal motifs Chaplin brings to his interpretation in *Monsieur Verdoux*, Charles Denner's Blueheard is a dandy whose murderous romantic liaisons illustrate the decline of romance during World War I. Denner's disdain hides behind a mask of fastidiousness. When, for example, one of his conquests is so overcome by Denner's charm that she eats berries from his hand, Denner, disapproving of her childish behavior, hands her his handkerchief. Françoise Sagan's script characterizes Denner's Bluebeard as a morose bibliophile, but Chabrol spices her treatment with Jacques Saulnier's exquisite design. He isolates several locations, particularly the opera house, bank, and police station as emblems of Landru's theatrically transparent society. Chabrol sees the impassivity of his anti-hero and the artifices of the design as imaginative parallels to the war years. The beauty of this film is that underneath its pictorial formalism and the donnish stance of Denner's Landru lies Chabrol's realization that Landru is both product and victim of the romantic ethos of the late nineteenth century.

In the late sixties one figure, that of Stéphane Audran, becomes central to his films. Preceding her screen iconography as one of the cinema's most erotic and mysterious of sexual luminaries, Audran had played several different roles—the easygoing, blond-haired sensualist in *Les Cousins*, the most comical of Chabrol's four good women, the dark-haired, hysterical wife in *La Ligne de démarcation* and Bluebeard's red-haired mistress. Beginning with *Les Biches*, in which she plays a bisexual vamp who delights in wearing different-colored wigs through her roles as the unfaithful wife in *La Femme infidèle*, the evanescent schoolteacher in *Le Boucher*, the oppressed heroine in *La Rupture*, and the country decadent in *Wedding in Blood*, Chabrol undertakes one of the most riveting examinations of sexuality on film.

One of the problems with Chabrol's study of the darker expressions of love and eroticism is his penchant for exhibiting its destructiveness instead of exploring his characters' sexual drives as part of a larger social and intellectual drama. This is not to advocate that sexuality should be regarded as an example or substitute for social history, but Chabrol unfairly handicaps those characters caught in his erotic webs. The characterization of Jacqueline Sassard in *Les Biches* is one example. Sassard is first shown drawing doves on the street where she meets Audran, who befriends her. When Audran takes her to her country estate, Chabrol does not pursue the possible differences between Audran's life in the city and country or how her relationship with Sassard affects her nonconjugal activities. When Jean-Louis Trintignant appears at her home and begins courting Sassard, Audran seduces him. Their lovemaking is breathtakingly erotic; while Sassard expresses her anguish on the door that separates her from the lovers, Audran suggests that her enjoyment of Trintignant is not exclusive of her adoration of Sassard. Sassard eventually kills Audran and then puts on Audran's wig and makeup. One wonders, however, whether Trintignant will notice the difference or even care that a change has taken place.

In *La Femme infidèle* and *Le Boucher* Chabrol uses Audran's persona as the central motif, whether she rests on her bed waiting for her husband, played by Michel Bouquet, to join her or most dramatically in the last scene of *La Femme infidèle* in which Bouquet pauses to look back at her and their son as he is led away by the police and Rabier's inquiring camera eye remains in long shot, studying her distilled erotic facade. Identified within the context of their pastoral home and the presence of the child, Audran exists as the most beautiful and mystifying of objects. Chabrol thus uses her enigmatic erotic mask as a metaphor for the perversion of woman's fate in the modern world. This theme is brilliantly exploited when Bouquet visits the home of Audran's lover, played by Maurice Ronet. He tells Ronet that they are a liberated couple and that he is simply curious about Ronet's apartment. Ronet is somewhat piqued but takes Bouquet on a tour. Yet upon entering the apartment, Bouquet turns deathly white; in suddenly killing Ronet, he expresses his shock at the corruption of love. His exactness, then, in wiping off his fingerprints and disposing of the body is further proof of his need for and love of Audran and his family.

*Le Boucher* is a more paradoxical study of Audran's romantic presence; her role as the white-haired schoolteacher becomes the purest sign of the pristine beauty of the village where the story transpires. Chabrol prefaces several scenes with long shots of the tranquil countryside, where the movement of the police car in the background threatens his quaint setting. This ominous motif is elaborated through the butcher's unfulfilled attraction for Audran. Jean Yanne's butcher is presented as a shy, retiring figure sympathetic to the bucolic pleasures of the country, as in the scene in which Audran's students rehearse a play in costume; they are led by Yanne who, in costume and smoking a cigarette, partners Audran. Chabrol suggests that the idyllic fragrance of his settings contains some repressed element of savage nonconformity, but the most concrete proof of its origin is a cross section of angles on Audran's face when she drives Yanne, who has wounded himself, to the hospital. After Yanne is taken away by the hospital attendants, Audran stares at the elevator signal as Chabrol cuts from its flashing light to Audran's face, a possible metaphor for Audran's role in inspiring Yanne's killings. The film ends with a series of five jump cuts, perhaps to emphasize the alienating nature of Yanne's actions or the isolation that Audran now feels. The final scene seems arbitrary, but Chabrol has fashioned an original variation on the imperfectibility of love in a near perfect world.

Chabrol's exploration of wayward behavior still shows signs of cynicism toward its resolution. In *This Man Must Die* the father, who has searched out and discovered the identity of the man who ran over his son, has arrived at the man's house and is introduced to the man's wife, to the man's partner and his wife, and to the mother of Jean Yanne's killer. Yanne's wife asks for the father's opinion of French literature; the asexual business partner talks of zoology; the mother laughs like a hyena; the partner's wife looks sexually troubled; and the father's mistress (the sister-in-law and former lover of Yanne) looks sexually declined. Rabier's camera punctuates their dialogue like a sadist torturing his victims while the father, lacking a viable dramatic and moral authority, becomes a receding figure in Chabrol's collage of narcissistic sexual delinquents. *La Rupture* may be Chabrol's most radical study of sexual deviation and social abstraction. He features a disproportion of psychotic characters while Audran, in the role of a mother whose husband has been committed to an asylum after attacking their child, attempts to hold onto her son and her sanity. She moves to a boardinghouse, where her neighbors include a greedy landlady and her alcoholic husband, their retarded daughter, an actor who sees the boardinghouse as his stage, and three pixilated women boarders. In the background lurks Audran's villainous father-in-law, played by Michel Bouquet, and Jean-Pierre Cassel as the man Bouquet hires to discredit Audran in order to gain possession of his grandson. The odds are not in her favor, and inevitably she goes insane.

Chabrol diffuses the dramatic tensions surrounding Audran's precarious grip on reality with dispossessing camera movements. His use of the zoom lens through the corridors of the boardinghouse suggest both the fragmentary nature of Audran's struggle for survival, as well as denoting her reflective isolation as she lies in bed as if in a coma. It is an absurdist setting, marked by coarse symbols of sexual promiscuity, for example, in the telephone scene in which Bouquet outlines his plans for Cassel to trick Audran while Cassel's girl friend strikes from below. There is also one of the longest takes in Chabrol's filmography in which Audran relates her troubles to her lawyer while Rabier photographs different sides of her face and her reflection in the window. Similar to the car scene involving Audran and Yanne in *Le Boucher*, Chabrol seems to see her identity as an elusive symbol of modern romance and tragedy. Cassel eventually kills Audran's husband after his release from the sanitarium, while Audran tours the park with the three women boarders and responds to its colors and figures as abstract, visual patterns. Audran's decline, however, lacks the impact it should have.

*La Rupture* appears to have been a key transitional film; in Chabrol's more recent work, the fragmentation of the social order or of the individual is admitted from the start. In *Wedding in Blood* neither Audran as the adulteress nor Michel Piccoli as the indolent clerk challenges any aspect of their drab country life. Their amorous escapades are a self-fulfilling revolt against their emotionless society; Audran and Piccoli artfully convey the liberating quality of their lovemaking, but their erotic exuberance is foredoomed. *A Piece of Pleasure*, starring Paul Gegauff, Chabrol's longtime script collaborator, is Chabrol's most overt expression of sordid behavior. Yet Gegauff's transformation into a psychopath and his wife's pitifully acquiescent nature develop in such a barren environment that their alienation seems further proof of Chabrol's unquestioning acceptance of the banality of evil. There has never been a consistent dramatic resolution of eroticism in Chabrol's films, and with the proliferation of pornography, one hopes that Chabrol will rediscover the link between our social history and its erotic undercurrents.

# Jean-Luc Godard

Jean-Luc Godard's filmography has inspired mixed reaction among critics, some hailing him as the most brilliant of modern artists, others considering his work half-baked or pointlessly absurd. In first reviewing a career that takes us from the disengaging black humor of *Breathless* to the eclectic symbolism of *Pierrot le fou* and the anarchic Brechtian design of *One Plus One*, one is struck by Godard's adventurous experimentalism—his desire to test the imprint of modern cinesthetics and political radicalism through a diversity of narrative reconstructions. The pleasures of such films as *Breathless* and *Alphaville* are as apparent as the excesses of *Pierrot le fou* and *Weekend*. But by first identifying Godard as an exemplary modernist, we can better understand his spirited experimentalism as an attempt to resolve the pervasive abstractions of postwar literature and art by using the techniques and technologies of filmmaking as a regenerative form of communication. Even in his best work, however, there is a frenetic, stylistic elusiveness; but one must return to Rossellini or perhaps even to Eisenstein to find a filmmaker who so vitally responds to the movies' humanistic and aesthetic scope. However inconclusive his absorption in the radical poetics and politics of the sixties, he underscores the role of the movies as the most pertinent and profound art form of our time.

Since one of the characteristics of Godard's career as the modernist par excellence is the diversity and, one must add, the inconsistency of his subject matter and stylistic treatment, it may be helpful to separate his films into two major groups. The first one consists of *Breathless*, *Alphaville*, and *A Woman Is a Woman*, in which he playfully expands the disruptive potential of such genres as crime, science fiction, and the musical. In *Le Petit Soldat* and *Les Carabiniers* he experiments with a more intrinsically symbolic narrative that functions as a stylistic bridge between his initial genre rearrangements and the acute eclecticism in his succeeding films. In the second group—*My Life to Live*, *Contempt*, *Pierrot le fou*, *La Chinoise*, *Two or Three Things I Know about Her*, *Weekend*, *Vladimir and Rosa*, and *One Plus One*—Godard adopts a prolix, Brechtian point of view in which his characters assume a more self-conscious, fatalistic affinity with the protagonists and ideas of art and literary history.

*Breathless* remains the most arresting of his first films because of his ironic integration of themes and techniques that are not readily associated with the crime film. Belmondo's flippant anti-hero and Seberg's phlegmatic femme fatale are peripheral figures, either as social outcasts or as variations on the role models of crime fiction: they are equidistant from the juvenile delinquents of the fifties and the more conventional bravado of their predecessors in crime. The film works as a nervous, edgy statement about nonconformity through the adventures of a free-spirited drifter and a mixed-up kid, unsure of where their posing will lead them. Godard's stylistic irreverence—with Belmondo addressing the viewer or through the jump cuts—reflects Belmondo's disengaging personality and Godard's iconoclastic fragmentation of the moral inevitability of crime. But the penultimate sequence, in which the lassitude of Belmondo and

Seberg is expressed through their improvisations in method nonconformity, shows Godard's tentativeness in blending in elements of parody with a style of existential despair. *Breathless* is a dizzying, dazzling work, caught between the understated poetry of its cinematic precursors and the encompassing fatalism of postwar art.

*Alphaville* is a less intricate work. Eddie Constantine's Lemmy Caution treats the futuristic horrors with the same no-nonsense approach he has used in disposing of gangsters in his more familiar action roles. The film's flippant humor lies in the displacement of Constantine's conventional adversaries through its cool abstraction of the more rowdy tone in the underground comic books and spy films of the sixties. *A Woman Is a Woman*, however, is the most rhetorical of Godard's early films. He reduces the extravagance of Hollywood musicals to a series of fanciful commentaries on the genre, from Jean-Claude Brialy cycling around his apartment to the image of two lovers outside the apartment. Among his earlier works, it is the one in which his background as a film critic overshadows his interest in the mechanics of the genre, substituting self-conscious rhetoric for plain old Hollywood pep and emotional chemistry.

*Le Petit Soldat* and *Les Carabiniers* are key transitional films for Godard. *Le Petit Soldat* is his most economical film narrative. In the film's most expressive moments—when the revolutionary trails his victim with a gun while the streetwalkers passively move on, when the protagonist makes the celebrated statement that film is truth twenty-four times a second—Godard's minimalist narrative combines the poetry of a fable with the contemporaneousness of *cinéma vérité*. The unusual juxtaposition of the distancing effects of irony and the empathetic notes of commitment gives the film a sense of being suspended between two worlds: that of its creator's imagination and that of television docudrama. *Les Carabiniers* works as a similar cinematic paradox, its caricature of the absurdity of war paralleling Godard's references to the fabrications of the filmmaker. The film's allegorical vignettes center on the exploits of two mischievous, moronic brothers. This might appear to make it easy for Godard to baffle us, and to fragment whatever analogies we might draw between his protagonists and other unblinking followers of society. However, the film shows a sustained level of intellectual ellipsis, from the ingenious use of gunfire on the sound track to his visualization of the brothers' fighting in what appears to be a Tin Pan Alley war. The film's quixotic appeal is best expressed in that magnificent parable of moviegoing, in which one of the brothers searches for the best angle on the woman taking a bath and finally walks up to the screen and tears it down. Few films have so shrewdly challenged our acceptance of the inherently illusory nature of the film experience.

*Masculin-Féminin* does not have the jazzy brilliance of *Breathless* or the ironic literacy of *Le Petit Soldat* and *Les Carabiniers*, but a strong case can be made for it as the best of Godard's films. Godard uses the basic format of a television news program—its eclectic, impersonal point of view—and transforms it into a Brechtian collage of the personal and eponymous. Several episodes, such as the interview with the winner of a beauty contest entitled "Interview with a Consumer Product," parody the more innocuous features of television news. The segments involving the man who confronts Jean-Pierre Léaud with a knife only to strike himself and the woman who pulls a machine gun on the blacks in the subway are offered as representative, symbolic stagings of the chaotic sweep of history. Like brief descriptions of senseless riots or murders buried in a corner of a newspaper, Godard uses them as oblique, poetic indexes to the anonymity of our journalists. Underlying these pungent, pregnant parallels to television news, Godard features the adventures of Léaud's rambling, inquisitive teenager and his infatuation with a pop singer as a personalizing metaphor of Parisian life during the summer of 1965. Léaud's paradoxical instincts, drawn equally to the rhetoric of revolution and to the charms of his consumer society, free Godard from the cant of his *cinéma vérité* contemporaries in filtering social and political controversies through the vicissitudes of Léaud's teenager. Léaud's death, however, seems a betrayal of his subject, an apocryphal, symbolic punctuation that reveals his greater allegiance to Brecht's concept of distancing than to his characters' laconic moods.

Among the second group of Godard's films, *My Life to Live* is the most uncompromisingly didactic. Godard conceives the Parisian underworld through the symbolism surrounding the life and death of a prostitute, played by Anna Karina. The major problem with the film is that his severely opaque framing fails to crystallize any single religious idea of Karina's understanding of her fall and possible redemption. Unlike Bresson's ascetic characters, who are irrevocably locked within and defined by a spiritual transfiguration, Karina's heroine is a more tentative figure. When she cries while watching Falconetti's persecution as Joan of Arc, the parallels between the two films seem arbitrarily drawn. In one scene, which is similar to Bresson's depersonalized study of a pickpocket's routine, money is transferred from prostitute to pimp; we are not sure, however, whether Godard is paying homage to Bresson's film or whether he is underlining the sordid inexorability of Karina's life. Another apparently revealing episode begins with Karina's pimp telling her that women are three-faced; Godard provides a visual parallel by shooting the reticent Karina from three angles. But he then introduces different camera angles that obscure his experiment in symbolist drama and Karina's role as its fated heroine.

Godard has stated that he thought the color in Antonioni's *Red Desert* was in the landscape and not in the camera; whereas he finds Antonioni's camera tracking along a red desert, the color in *Contempt*, he believes, is in the camera. Within Raoul Coutard's colored camera obscura, Godard shapes a statement concerning the condition of love in the modern world through the relationship of Michel Piccoli as a screenwriter, Brigitte Bardot as his wife, and Jack Palance as the film producer of *The Odyssey*, undertaken by Fritz Lang. Although Godard shows little interest in the formal grandeur of Homer's epic, continually alienating his audience through his contemplative digressions, he achieves an original formulation about the relationship of classicism and modernism in the cinema.

The film begins with a shot of Piccoli and Bardot in bed as he strokes her derrière. Although one anticipates Godard's emphasis on Bardot's role as an object of love, this scene, similar to his intercutting on statues of the Greek gods from Lang's epic, only hints at the possible analogies to and deviations from classical motifs. The one sequence that most successfully explores the interrelationship of the classical and modern involves Piccoli and Bardot in their apartment; they are dressed in white sheets, having just moved in. As they walk through the rooms or as Bardot lies in the bath or on a couch and Piccoli criticizes her behavior, the contrived, schematic treatment of their estrangement is complemented by the formalized design and the rigorous choreography of their movements and the positions in which they are photographed. They walk around the apartment as if trapped in a maze; when, for example, they sit at the dining table, Godard undercuts the dialogue by showing them as objects caught within Coutard's austere, abstracted landscape. The final sequence, however, may be most characteristic of the film's aloof, reflective tone and Godard's unevenness in blending poetic and cinematic metaphors. Palance, wearing a red sweater and driving a red sports car, is killed with Bardot in a collision; after her farewell note to Piccoli is flashed on the screen, there is a short, powerful image of their smashed bodies. The action then shifts to the movie set, where Godard, playing Lang's assistant, asks him if he is ready and gives instructions to the crew. The camera moves in on a long shot of the ocean, absorbed in the suffused colors of an afternoon sky. This final image is entrancing yet indecisive, leading one to speculate that the film's fragmentary allusions may result from Godard's feeling that the modern filmmaker is unsympathetic to the objectivities of narrative that would make *Contempt* not only a great idea, but also a great film.

If *Contempt* is the most opaque of modern movies, *Pierrot le fou* is certainly the most oblique. It is the one Godard film that most forcefully asserts his feverish experimentalism, juxtaposing the harmonious resonance of the past to the chaotic undercurrents of political modernism. The opening scene—in which he intercuts between a tennis game and Belmondo reading from Faure in a bathtub—presents a thesis similar to that of *Contempt*. Though Belmondo carries along Faure's history of art and Anna Karina has her copy of the *Rover Boys*, Godard's references to countless other books and protagonists, from their being characters in a commedia dell'arte troupe to the romantic rebels of crime fiction, negates any singular identity for either Belmondo or Karina. If the film can be said to be inspired by any one theme, it is Godard's paramount belief in the movies as a volcanic treasure trove, where ideas and myths from our literature and art history are nervously funneled through his protagonists. But just as we are about to make some sense of the disjointed imagery, Godard reconfirms his attraction for the alienating signature of the modernist.

For example, when Belmondo walks through the rooms at a party, Coutard's saturated colors and Godard's rigid staging function as a pictorial and dramatic abstraction of Belmondo's middle-class existence. Belmondo then encounters Samuel Fuller, who caustically informs him that the movies are emotion—the one element purposely missing in this scene. Godard's singular sympathies for improvisation and the ironies of Brechtian theater are symptomatic of the edginess in Godard's stylizations—the uneasy alliance between the polished objectivity of his predecessors and the disruptive nature of his experimentalism, between the overriding objectivity of art and the underlying subjectivity of his political consciousness. The one conclusive motif that he appears to draw through Fuller's presence is the oppressiveness of Belmondo's middle-class existence and his need to escape. Another example of Godard's proclivity to fascinate and infuriate occurs in the following drawn-out sequence involving Belmondo and Karina in a car. The intriguing quality of this segment is that Godard never conveys any movement of the car; they talk, and talk, and talk, even as we are led to believe they are on a highway. Is he playing on the power of the movies to fool us? Is he negating a sense of motion to emphasize the transcendent nature of the dialogue, as in similar didactic episodes in his other films? Is he simply bypassing the illusory methods used to convey movement in so many films? Some of these elements are suggested, and there are probably a dozen or so other ones as well, but one's interest is sustained through an awareness that Godard inverts dramatic and cinematic conventions in order to discover the voice of Belmondo's existential adventurer, buried beneath his numerous dramatic and cinematic identities.

One of the more straightforward scenes looks to the social and artistic formulas that he will probe in *La Chinoise* and *Weekend*. Belmondo is in a movie house showing newsclips from Vietman while Jean-Pierre Léaud sits in front of him. As Belmondo continues to turn from Faure to the film, Godard seems to confront one of the major issues facing modern artists: the possibly irresolvable conflict between an aesthetic and political consciousness. Léaud's presence may be extraneous, but one believes in the poignancy of this visually rhetorical scene. Godard's almost spiritual belief in experimentalism as a way to attack the objective congruity of art also characterizes the last scene, in which Belmondo and Karina commit suicide. The camera, similar to the ending in *Contempt*, passes over a bright afternoon sky while we hear the voices of Belmondo and Karina saying that this is not eternity only the sea. Godard violates the role of catharsis or death as the final action of their lives: he cheats the audience of any feeling of release or empathy by confounding an already perplexing situation. It may be Godard's way of accentuating their bizarre adventures, taking obliquity to its most impenetrable end.

*La Chinoise, Two or Three Things I Know about Her*, and *Weekend* find Godard as polemicist, presenting his movies as instructive fables for the politicization of his audience. *La Chinoise* plays as a series of Maoist placards in which his "actors" not only read from the Chairman, but are dressed in revolutionary garb to underline their identity as tautological images. From the living room in which the film is shot and where we watch Godard making the film, he exemplifies filmmaking as rhetoric in motion with special reference to the films and writings of Dziga Vertov. Several images, such as the one in which Léaud is framed by a bikini-clad teenager and a corpulent, middle-aged woman, work as examples of visual ideology; the film becomes a demonstration of a television station commandeered by a disciplined group of Marxist revolutionaries.

*Two or Three Things I Know about Her* is a less radical example of moviemaking as social protest. Whether it is the invisible narrator speaking in soft, hushed tones, discussing the political controversies affecting Paris as the camera tracks along new construction sites or Marina Vlady's revolutionary who masquerades as a prostitute, assuming the role of both narrator and protagonist, Godard's experimental filmmaking is surprisingly simplified. Godard resolutely avoids his characteristic stylistic subterfuges; he is not interested in attacking the complacency of the filmgoer or in inundating the film with the abstract propositions that previously fragmented his narratives. Its light, breezy tone and its piecemeal, simplified collage style utilize the commercial Parisian backgrounds as an extended arena for Vlady's instructive attack on bourgeois society.

*Weekend*, however, finds Godard reembracing the polemics of his outstanding predecessors, particularly Eisenstein and Brecht. Like Eisenstein, he is drawn to the sensory immediacy of montage; whereas Eisenstein used his fast-paced, contrapuntal editing to personify the revolt and eventual triumph of the masses, Godard uses montage as the primary comunicative style of our television age. And, like Brecht, he often subverts his story for a more incisive, tautological attack on his own artistic formulas and the expectations of his audience. In *Weekend* Godard begins by showing the wife sitting in her bra and panties as she relates an incident that she is not sure really happened. But this prefatory scene is all wrong for the film: Godard is not interested in a film fantasy, but in a brutal bloodletting in which the generation of Marx and Coca-Cola experiences the middle-aged blues with a vengeance. Unlike *Masculin-Féminin*, in which his youthful protagonists are treated with a shrewdly paradoxical understanding of freedom and love, and unlike *La Chinoise*, in which his social rhetoric is translated into video propaganda, *Weekend* presents a series of capricious attacks on representative symbols of society, such as the seemingly endless line of cars jammed on the highway and the married couple who kill and eat the husband's mother, after which the wife devours her husband and then joins the guerrillas. The film's polemicism—intercutting the long-winded narrative of revolutionary politics with abbreviated, arcane episodes of social collapse—seems an indecisive compromise between the sly, black humor of his earlier film projects and the rigorous styles used by Eisenstein and Brecht to illuminate the revolution as both a social and artistic experience.

That Godard should then situate Jean-Pierre Léaud and Juliette Berto in a television studio in *Le Gai Savior* seems the most logically conclusive dramatic stage for an artist who has so closely scrutinized the relationship of the film and television image. *Le Gai Savior* presents a less problematic style than *Weekend*; Godard's word-image dialectic directly unfolds through the juxtaposition of Léaud and Berto to sensuous photographic images of consumerism and revolution. One admires Godard's exacting style of polemical filmmaking by trapping his protagonists in a television studio and by using them as the predominant symbols in his collectivization of word and image. Although not as accessible as the poster art of *La Chinoise*, it is an intelligent formulation of the role of television as a medium of ideas, equally conducive to a capitalist or a communist ideology.

*Le Gai Savior* can be seen as one of the last films of the sixties and as Godard's least cluttered statement on television as the most effective weapon in a revolutionary's arsenal. *Vladimir and Rosa* seems to confirm its culminating viewpoint; as in Brecht's lesser plays, his restaging of the trial of the Chicago Eight is so straightforward, so narratively streamlined as to suggest that Godard has wiped out the memory of his work in the sixties and has decided on an equation of revolution and art that could be used as a learning primer in a utopian society. But in *One Plus One* Godard shows that there is no logical termination for a filmmaker committed to exploring the explosive interaction between the artist and society.

The title of *One Plus One* refers to modern art, which to Godard means the linking of two strips of celluloid; as a dialectically oriented director, it represents the cross sectioning of words and images, which is duplicated in the actions of the revolutionaries who interrelate various words and images on the placards they carry. Godard's dialectic focuses on two distinct symbols of the counterculture: the self-indulgent, autistic expressiveness of the Rolling Stones and the polemics of the black revolutionaries. He presents the Rolling Stones's studio as a modern-day labyrinth; members of the group, technicians, and groupies move about the studio as if they were lost in a subterranean world. Juxtaposed to the enclosed space of the recording studio, Godard introduces supporting examples of the indolent nature of the counterculture. There is a narrator who reads from comic books, and Anne Wiazemsky in the role of Eve reborn as a hippie; but the most prominent symbol that is counterpoised to the recording studio is a junk heap where a black power advocate lectures his audience. Godard is not simply interrelating the degenerate passivity of the recording studio to the regenerative activism around the junk heap. He photographs them in a way that most concisely illustrates their singular features: whereas his camera tracks through the maze of the recording studio, his short, horizontal panning shots in the junk heap underscore the didacticism of his revolutionaries.

Had Godard chosen either the recording studio or the junk heap as his final setting, his ironic treatment of the innocence and self-consciousness, the self-humor and violence of the counterculture would have been impressively realized. But he selects a more subtle motif than in *Contempt* in which he played Lang's assistant. In *One Plus One* we see Godard directing a scene on the beach as a black revolutionary leads along a white girl dressed in a white sheet. When Godard begins running, we hear machine-gun fire, and the girl falls dead in the seat of the camera. Godard then sends the camera crane in motion. Not only does Godard question his role as a revolutionary and artist in filming this paradox, but in the last image of a camera moving through space, he identifies his artistic dilemma as a politically oriented filmmaker as the film's central, unifying theme.

It is difficult to try to project where Godard will focus his energy in the social and artistic history of the eighties. There is a severe element of theoretical bias in his work, and few of his films seem the product of a meticulous craftsman. We might like our art neat, and the styles and themes of the filmmaker to be consistent. Godard is certainly the least neat and least consistent of our major artists, but how many other modernists have renewed the history of film art and aesthetics with such fervor and with such a keen sense of intellectual commitment?

## The French Cinema

Since the premiere of the first works of the New Wave, there appear to be two interesting trends among the more well-known directors in commercial French filmmaking. In the films of Vadim, Demy, Varda, Lelouch, Sautet, and Robert, the romantic esprit in such past models as *Pépé le Moko* and *Casque d'or* is vibrantly renewed with a surprising diminution of the poetic fatalism in their precursors. Whether expressed in the romantic sensibility of *Lola* and *Live for Life* or in the comic buoyancy of *Happy New Year* and *Salut l'artiste*, there is little evidence of the painful, teledramatic traumas that pervade the pursuit of romance in the postwar American film. One can further argue that the uninhibited lyricism exhibited in their films is simply one aspect of the predominant faith in classic narrative formulas in the films of Georges Franju, Eric Rohmer, and Louis Malle.

One of the more controversial though less successful of this group of directors is Roger Vadim, a Svengali of less-than-mystical repute. His adaptation of Laclos's *Les Liaisons dangereuses* plays as a slick portrait of the peccadilloes of the rich. Vadim shows some flair in exposing the nuances of lethargic self-waste, and the lack of chagrin of Gérard Philipe and Jeanne Moreau is absorbing. But one wonders why Truffaut should have lambasted Vadim for any possible decline when such a sure-handed sense of the effete is displayed in *Les Liaisons dangereuses*. He later directed Jane Fonda, who was then his wife, in several films in which her eroticism is diluted by his mannered style. *Circle of Love* is trendy pornography, while *Barbarella* lacks the visual flair to work as a pop-art parody. *Spirits of the Dead* is more acutely self-indulgent: the actors' mask of sexual indolence seems more germane to a documentary on the jet-setters. Vadim will be remembered as a woman's director who cheated us of the glittering sensuality of his stars and gave us instead a glum picture of decadence.

In the romantic melodramas of Jacques Demy, Angès Varda, and Claude Lelouch, there is a more elaborate expression of the romantic spirit that is celebrated in French culture. Demy's early films, *Lola* and *Bay of Angels*, are among the most uniquely two-dimensional portraits of the female on film. Unlike Lelouch's *A Man and a Woman* or *And Now My Love* which faithfully adapt the saccharine prose of women's romances to fashion an ornate pictorial drama, Demy's single motif is the sexual mystique of Anouk Aimée in *Lola* and the erotic mask of Jeanne Moreau in *Bay of Angels*. His camera enfolds their faces and forms like an adoring curator at home with his prize paintings; narrative detail is equivalent to Aimée fixing her face in front of a mirror or Moreau crossing her legs. *Lola* is too mannered in its evocation of the musicals of the fifties, but it is difficult to find fault with Aimée's exquisite posing as a waterfront Cyd Charisse. *Bay of Angels* avoids the self-caricatures of *Lola*; Demy's operatic treatment diminishes the dramatic components of the genre while magnifying its emotional currents. Unlike the more famous brief encounter of Celia Johnson and Trevor Howard which gains its intensity from the straightforward reaction-shot dialogue and their recognition of each other as forlorn, vulnerable characters, *Bay of Angels* lyrically extends the precarious rules by which Demy's lovers meet, substituting dangerous excitement for the compassion and tenderness of the English romance. Demy's *The Umbrellas of Cherbourg* and *Donkey Skin* are less appealing because he depersonalizes the characters' vibrancy while heightening the story's supporting textures. *The Umbrellas of Cherbourg* is too literal in its operatic execution; he tries to give birth to an idea that was treated with greater insight in the equally operatic *Bay of Angels*. *Donkey Skin* is a tongue-in-cheek satire of Cocteau's fantasies that evokes little of Cocteau's reverence for fairly tales in Jean Marais's incestuous love of his daugher, played by Catherine Deneuve.

Agnès Varda's films explore a more intuitive, modernist point of view than the romances of Demy. Her first film, *Cleo from 5 to 7*, is marred by the characters' self-conscious interplay in the apartment and by its suffocating mist of existential despair replacing the luminous backdrops in the film romances of the thirties and forties. *Les Créatures* is a more intelligent film, in which the elliptical story line enhances the very real tremors that surround Michel Piccoli's pursuit of Catherine Deneuve. Unlike the explicit social allegories in the majority of fantasy films, the elusive features of Varda's haunting fable personalize her characters. In *Lions Love*, a variation on *Cleo from 5 to 7*, Varda's maturity is evident in the way she captures the reckless, fickle nature of her counterculture protagonists. They are not as affected as the characters in the earlier film because their offbeat mannerisms have a boomerang effect that is missing in the rambling picture of alienation in her first film. Varda's meandering tone of estrangement probes their facade of irreverence with the insight of a sympathetic journalist. *One Sings the Other Does Not* sustains her sweetly sympathetic study of outsiders, in this case modern-day feminists who experience the pitfalls of unhappy romances and marriages. Her approach is less didactic than one might expect, showing their innate romantic susceptibility and surprising resiliency. They become not so much anarchic free spirits as survivors who have learned to accept the freedom implicit in modern romances, achieving an independence usually reserved for more traditional romantic heroines.

With the premiere of *A Man and a Woman* Claude Lelouch seemed destined to become the French Leo McCarey. Employing a glossier style than McCarey, Lelouch glorifies the pieties of romance and love with the same unquestioning faith of McCarey and other disciples of a rarefied, *Saturday Evening Post* humility. Although he has shown occasional lapses, such as *And Now My Love*, a sugar-coated family album that skips over three generations of French life, Lelouch has become one of the surprises of commercial filmmaking. In *Live for Life* he still favors a prolix cinematic sentimentality, but one's admiration grows for Lelouch's empathy with Yves Montand's adventures in Africa. The characters are subordinated to his florid picture of Paris and the tropics in a manner similar to *A Man and a Woman*; yet there appears to be a greater sensitivity to the fact that their emotional vicissitudes are often at odds with his extravagant exteriors. In *Love Is a Funny Thing* he no longer tries to translate the emotional drama through an opulent, dehumanizing tour of the backgrounds, but gives us a more personal, adult look at his characters' adulterous affairs. His camera eye is still turned to romantic vistas, but he does not equate the characters' feelings to an elaborate visual showcase. There is less self-consciousness about the gay or alienating features of their backgrounds—from the raucous, carefree atmosphere of the Las Vegas hotel and the drive through the desert where the leads imagine themselves caught up in a cowboy-and-Indian film to the pathos of the final scene in which Lelouch holds on Annie Girardot's face as she waits for Jean-Paul Belmondo to step off the plane. Belmondo has decided not to leave his wife, and with the camera absorbed in Girardot's eventual realization that she will not see him again, Lelouch personalizes her pain in a most moving way.

The pleasures of *Love Is a Funny Thing* achieve a greater emotional and stylistic depth in *Happy New Year*. From the opening scene in which Lelouch has some fun at the expense of *A Man and a Woman* by showing the final scene being screened at a prison where it is booed by the inmates to those cunning colloquies between Lino Ventura and Françoise Fabian in which his static camera seems to ask the audience to simply look at and listen to these engaging performers camouflaging their mutual attraction through their verbal fencing, one senses a tribute to the enriching sexual warfare in American comedies. Lelouch's fondness for the genre invests the film with the conviviality of Hollywood's screwball romances, whether in the winning characterizations of Ventura's partner and the manager of the jewelry store or in the scene in which Ventura, who has enticed Fabian with his sly manner, fails to consummate the seudction because of his poor choice of words when inviting her to his room. Fabian, as always, seems a gift from the gods, but it is Ventura's performance that shows Lelouch's maturity as a film director. Ventura's craggy face and heavyset appearance seem eminently suited to the crime films for which he is best known. In his courting of Fabian, however, he combines Spencer Tracy's crafty entrapments of Katharine Hepburn and the gracefulness that Cary Grant perfected as the exemplary male star of the genre.

Philippe de Broca is probably the most well-known interpreter of the rustic, Gallic spirit of French comedy films. His first films starring Jean-Pierre Cassel and Jean-Paul Belmondo seem more accomplished in their sensitivity to the characters' whimsical behavior than his recent comedies. In *The Joker* his lyrical camera movements become a substitute for the self-conscious loquacity of Sacha Guitry's protagonists. However, unlike Guitry, whose films are clearly rooted in theatrical plotting, De Broca attempts to transcend the family's repetitious expressions of iconoclasm through Cassel's exaggerated choreographic solos as a free spirit in his dealings with the family and in his affair with

Anouk Aimée. *Cartouche* is a more conventional comic melodrama that shows Belmondo's natural affinity with Fairbanks's atheletic daring; yet the film misses a greater irony by not imbuing its backgrounds and supporting players with a complementary slapstick irreverence. *That Man From Rio* may be his best film because of its felicitous casting of Belmondo's frenetic adventurer opposite the scatterbrained charm of Françoise Dorléac. Their comic ingenuity and romantic communicability sustain an artful interplay between De Broca's melodramatic spoofing and the kinetic hijinks inspired by his stars' masks as unlikely adventurers. *King of Hearts* became a modest cult phenomenon, and though one is tempted to dismiss its whimsy, the film's light, mocking tone gives full expression to the dramatic rapport among its cast members.

Claude Sautet is a more conventional satirist than De Broca. In *Cesar and Rosalie* he undertakes a detailed picture of the pleasures and pitfalls of Yves Montand's marriage and business; Montand's romantic escapade and marriage reunion reconfirm the underlying merriment surrounding the pursuit of romance in middle-class French society. In *Vincent François Paul and the Others*, a buddy film times two, the hardships of middle age and marriage fail to erode the characters' joyful camaraderie. Though Sautet tends to dwell on pastoral close-ups as they enjoy one another's witty repartee and to force one comic routine after another without studying the effects of his amiable, sensual gatherings, the film radiates a good will, a lust for life among its middle-aged malcontents that one hopes Sautet will examine more discerningly in future films. *Salut l'artiste* is a probing, lilting study of the underlying sympathy between the poetic instincts of the middle class and the singular romantic splendor of their surroundings. Any one of the dinner sequences involving Marcello Mastroianni as an actor, Françoise Fabian as his mistress, and their friends or those with Mastroianni and his family find the director, Yves Robert, blending their emotional quirks with a larger statement about his characters and settings. In one scene Mastroianni plays a Chaplinesque figure in a commerical who suffers through several retakes in which he is thrown into the water by a couple in a boat. Robert does not choose to accent the quaint features of the commercial but subtly evokes Mastroianni's pathetic predicament as he waits to speak to his son who has unexpectedly returned after running away. Although one might think there are few things in this world to rival Fabian's Apollonian sensuality, her attraction to Mastroianni is perceptively balanced with the independent nature of his wife and children; that it is Mastroianni's richest performance in years seems almost a bonus in Robert's rediscovery of the pulse of romantic screen comedy.

In the films of, among others, Demy, Lelouch, and Robert, one senses an appreciation for the lush presence of their stars—an immersion in the social environment through the fulfillment of the characters' romantic or comic persona. This simplified style of dramatic empathy was a central feature of the American cinema of the thirties and forties; it should not surprise us then to find that the neoclassicism that gradually predominated in the American film of the seventies gains expression, with a more acute commitment to its classical origins, in the films of Georges Franju, Eric Rohmer, and Louis Malle.

Of the three directors, Franju best embodies the idea of neoclassicism; it is difficult to see how films like *Judex* and *The Horror Chamber of Dr. Faustus* could be reviewed otherwise. *Judex* shows his sensitivity to the atmospheric tension of Feuillade's serials while discovering an element of dramatic irony missing in the originals. Whereas Feuillade's serials seem to accentuate the murkiness of his lurid plots and his characters' romantic mystique, *Judex* balances its eerie tone with a more extravagant delineation of the characters' valor. The hero's walk through the ball with the dove is faithful to the original while isolating its most overtly romantic elements. Unlike Feuillade, who magnifies the fear and fatalism that surround his players, Franju reveals the vulnerability and resiliency of his heroes and villains. The slow, solemn pacing in Feuillade is an extension of the numerous plot complications; in Franju there is a methodical inquiry into both the charm and deviousness of the genre. *The Horror Chamber of Dr. Faustus* is a cerebral film in which Franju approaches the story as a poetic reverie. He first evokes the irrevocability facing each of the characters—from Alida Valli's repressed love and the daughter's anxiousness over her new face to Pierre Brasseur's alienation as the doctor—but Franju is not as successful in fulfilling the conflict between their fragile human needs and the terrors they face. In *Judex* he has transfigured a period; in *The Horror Chamber of Dr. Faustus* he underlines the inexplicable mysteries of the genre.

Franju has had mixed success in his adaptations of novels. *La Faute de l'abbé Mouret* is mired in his pedantic treatment of the novel's dichotomies. The major section of the film—the priest's convalescence and romance of the country spirit—is awash in their tender feelings, with no attempt at a dramatic distancing of their emotional fervor. The chilling fantasy of Cocteau's *Thomas l'imposteur* is clearly more congenial to Franju's contrived style. The clouds and mist that mark the protagonist's journey provide an effective backdrop, and the characterizations are possessed of a Cocteau-like blending of wistfulness and tragic self-awareness. But the film limits the charm of Cocteau's literary fable instead of enriching it in the way Franju injected new life into the serial film. The viewer keeps waiting for those moments in which his introspective camerawork will illuminate the reality of the tale on film through a romantic punctation of Cocteau's original treatment of love and patriotism. *Thérèse* is a more ambitious narrative; its subject possesses a physical substantiveness lacking in the fragrances and the silhouettes of *Thomas l'imposteur*. The lassitude that overcomes Emmanuelle Riva like a playful spirit is lucidly mirrored in Franju's editing cadence. Yet Franju hesitates in clarifying the effect of the characters' taciturnity, their sense of dread in what seems the least dreadful of settings. Franju's restrained, thoughtful treatment of cinematic and literary archetypes makes one eager for his neoclassicism to ripen into its most fertile expression.

The neoclassicism of Eric Rohmer's moral tales lies in their unwavering moral resolution. In *My Night at Maud's* the visual clarity of Nestor Almendros's cinematography denotes the asceticism with which Jean-Louis Trintignant looks at his world, from his brief promenades through the town where he spots the woman he knows he will marry to his admirable strategies during his encounter with Françoise Fabian. The film is not so much a philosophic inquiry into the question of free will as it is a reflection of Trintignant's delicate, guarded movements through a bourgeois environment that one senses he finds all too appealing. The film's merits, then, are those of its stars: Trintignant's intelligence cuts a fine line between self-doubt and self-assurredness; Fabian's sensual radiance suggests a softer yet more dangerous romantic presence than one of her screen antecedents, Katharine Hepburn.

If the redolence of *My Night at Maud's* is like the intriguing aftertaste of a fine cognac savored through a conversation with friends, *Claire's Knee* scrutinizes our delight in this pleasure. Jean-Claude Brialy, Rohmer's hero, is a man of letters who in the first and last scene rationalizes about the intricacies of his desires and who tests himself to a degree Trintignant would think damnation itself. But, like Trintignant, he remains an intellectual sensualist who delights in the play of ideas by infusing the most ordinary conversations with his provocative rebuttals. In his relationship with the precocious girl who matches her wit and charm against Brialy and who is clearly more exciting than her sister Claire, Brialy seems to admit a weakness in declining her favors while choosing to satisfy his penchant for Claire's modish looks by stroking her knee. It is not that he is a hypocrite, but that his faith in language, ideas, and beauty is displaced by the weaknesses that are supposedly mastered by the man of culture.

After the stimulating exchanges and limpid psychological insights of *Claire's Knee*, *Chloe in the Afternoon* proves considerably less engaging. Rohmer's protagonist lacks Brialy's guile and inquisitiveness; unlike Trintignant, he does not win our respect even as one regrets his choices. His romantic dalliance seems all too familiar, as if the question of his sleeping with Chloe merely rested on his libidinal impulse. It is the softest of the moral tales, in which the pleasures of Rohmer's dialogue, as much for the fellowship it generates as for the ideas that are stimulated, have dissipated. Rohmer is far too sympathetic to his hero, whose married life takes on a cocoonlike quality: an excuse is always provided to avoid the perilous disrobing of Chloe. In the hero's final reunion with his wife, as they cuddle up to each other in the manner of teenage lovers, Rohmer honors the sanctity of marriage in too rigorous and simplistic a fashion; this man has returned simply because he is weak.

Rohmer's *The Marquise of O ...* is a faithful, literal translation of the novella, in which the emotionally repressed style of Von Kleist's tale matches well with that of Rohmer. But Rohmer's straighforward narrative undercuts the tensions between Von Kleist's distant, reflective point of view and the near surreal dramatic delineation. The allure of Von Kleist's prose is in the matter-of-factness with which he relates the most bizarre actions; in Rohmer's films, there is not enough ambiguity between the simplicity of his style and the unlikely circumstances. A shorter, more episodic work, Jean-Marie Straub's *Chronicle of Anna Magdalena Bach*, conveys a more precise, historical fidelity to the icy depths of the baroque through a compressed, resplendent staging.

With films like *The Lovers* and *A Very Private Affair*, Louis Malle seemed the least complex, the most securely melodramatic of the new breed of French directors. *The Lovers* retains its interest because of Moreau's erotic presence and Malle's mimicking, though crudely done, of the characters' expressions of love and their final, ironic destiny. Perhaps of all the major films associated with the New Wave, it is the most leaden and didactic in suggesting the romantic and aesthetic esprit of the New Wave. *A Very Private Affair* shows Malle's unquestionable roots in soap opera, shrewdly inverting the genre's basic formulas as Brigitte Bardot's heroine searches for the tranquillity housewives have sought to escape.

In *The Thief of Paris* Malle's pictorial framing explores the oppressive, stultifying nature of Parisian society in the late nineteenth century through its expressive decor. Henri Decaë's dark-hued colors imbue the settings with a languorous, musty quality, but Belmondo's exploits as the thief fail to identify the social and emotional antagonisms unique to the period. Since Malle does not undertake the grandiose operatic treatment in Visconti's films, Belmondo's inexorably dehumanized thief lacks an essential tragic dimension, exemplified in the scene in which he hands the stolen goods to the porter without any fear of detection. *Viva Maria* gives the strongest indication of Malle's inclination to the leisurely entertainments that were once standard Hollywood fare. The overall conception is heavy-handed, but Moreau's vivacity and Bardot's surprising good humor more than sustain our interest. One remembers with pleasure the daring striptease they perform in front of their good-natured audience or the final uprising that combines the rousing heroics of an Errol Flynn adventure with the rowdiness of the Marx Brothers. Like numerous epics of Hollywood's golden age, *Viva Maria* is an amusingly disconnected exercise in production over-kill; the flippancy the two stars bring to the dusty myths of the West immerses the filmgoer in the melodramatic parodies as if the art of the movies were an invitation to a costume drama narrated by a cross-eyed storyteller. *Murmur of the Heart* shows Malle's modest development as a film director in his mirthful treatment of an inherently aberrant tale. It may be that Malle's droll point of view is too fanciful for the subject of incest, but he sensitively balances the casual gaiety of the family with the youngest son's more shy manner. *Agostino, Viva la muerte*, or even Mai Zetterling's dreadful *Night Games* strike the properly morbid tone that accompanies incestuous thoughts, but as a devious treatment of a deviant protagonist, Malle's film broadens the literary imagination of the movies.

The bits and pieces of cinematic ingenuity in Malle's filmography in no way prepare one for the dramatic sweep of *Lacombe, Lucien*. One of the most accomplished of a growing number of films about the Holocaust, it rediscovers the subsurface of ideas in its subject without abstracting their dramatic embodiment. In his story of the primitive Lucien who aids the Nazis, Malle pursues the question of guilt through Lucien's relationship with the Jewish girl. At first, Lucien seems to personify the anonymous followers of a reign of terror who do not question the service they perform. When he encounters the Jewish family, he uses his power like a child given toy guns and a cowboy outfit; he is attracted to the girl but appears confused by her father's ironic, tragic detachment. They finally escape, as the girl scorns her Jewish identity in favor of Lucien's instinctive emotionalism. In the last scene Malle's naïfs. alone in a forest, appear to question their isolated existence. The ending is too pat, but one applauds Malle's diligent exploration of the paradoxical nature of his protagonists and how the fulfillment of their instincts leaves them in a state of ignorance similar to Lucien's condition at the beginning of the film. The question of his country's guilt during the Nazi occupation is redrawn through Lucien's withdrawal from the social realities of war into the ephemeral pleasures of ignorant innocence. What, then, began as one of the least auspicious of careers has, through the eclecticism of his projects, embraced a part of the movies that was in abeyance during the sixties. It is a style of filmmaking that renews both the escapist and humanist scope of the movies —a combination crucial to the reassertion of the movies as a primary medium of entertainment and ideas.

# 22
# The Italian Film

## Roberto Rossellini

Roberto Rossellini's emergence as the voice of the Italian humanist cinema marked a new era for the movies at a most critical time. The search for moral regeneration in Rossellini's postwar films alerted audiences that the movies would examine the human condition in a most fundamental way. The awkward, almost shoddy quality of large segments of *Open City, Paisan,* or *Flowers of St. Francis* does not undercut the validity of Rossellini's achievement. Rossellini is concerned with characters who are purposely set in a barren, disheveled universe, seeking a sign of their humanity from God or their fellow man. The importance of these films as documents of intellectual history rather than as independent works of art derives from Rossellini's interest in turning our attention to a facet of the film experience largely overlooked since the apotheosis of the Russian silent film.

Considering the undeniable humanistic scope of his films, Rossellini's place in film history was secure. But in the late sixties, beginning with *The Rise of Louis XIV,* Rossellini renews his interest in a cinema of humanism while incorporating a completely different set of aesthetic priorities than those featured from *Paisan* through *General Della Rovere.* The humanism of his earlier films lies in his realization of a moral awakening in the most stark, impoverished backgrounds; these movies are journals of self-discovery, examples of a medium adopting a documentary format in recording man's spiritual rebirth. Unlike the troubled soldiers and underground fighters of *Paisan* and *Open City* or St. Francis and his followers who are treated as acquiescent, romantic figures impervious to the rubble of their makeshift society, his later films evoke a more historical, stylistic aspect of humanism in a manner wholly antithetical to his first efforts.

Rossellini, however, avoids both De Mille's ponderous reconstructions and Dreyer's style of poetic introspection. When reading Plato's dialogues, one undoubtedly imagines encounters filled with the scintillating intellectual counterpoints of great theater and history. But Rossellini conceives them from a considerably modified epic viewpoint. When Socrates gathers with his disciples to engage in a dialogue, it has the appearance of a casual meeting of friends and is not treated either in the solemn, pseudohistorical style of Hollywood epics or the austere manner of Dreyer and Bresson, whose conflicts are charged with a symbolic, transcendent meaning. There are no awesome long shots of Athens or vivid reaction shots of Socrates as he addresses his followers. During the trial of Socrates, Rossellini does not visually augment this battle of life and death, nor does he underscore the intellectual crisis. The case against Socrates is presented in a straightforward manner; when Socrates defends himself, Rossellini moves to close-up and only cuts when Socrates turns his head to address a different section of the audience. Rossellini's rigorous attention to Socrates' face and words results in one of the most fascinating fifteen-minute close-ups in film history; the scene is inspired by Rossellini's awareness that the history and truth of this moment lie in our seeing his pathos and intensity and in listening to his rhetoric. The humanism, then, of *Socrates* consists of Rossellini's moral fidelity to his material. One believes in the action and speech of his characters as the most simple, direct, and profound expression of the intellectual foundations of our culture. It is not the epic cinema of Griffith, Gance, or Eisenstein, or the romantic recreation of the past in the films of Ophüls and Mizoguchi. Rossellini sees the past in terms of the ideas that were expounded, as if he were a scribe who realizes that one's first task is to penetrate the spiritual climate of ancient Greece. It does not then become a question of asking whether Rossellini's more didactic interpretations rival the work of other epic filmmakers, but of sharing in his embrace an examination of our intellectual heritage.

*The Rise of Louis XIV* and *Blaise Pascal* are not as effective as *Socrates*, but for different reasons. In *The Rise of Louis XIV*, the king does not possess the moral stature of Socrates. Rossellini places greater emphasis on the social ambience of the court, for example, in the scene in which the king's friends and advisors patiently await his return from a romp in the bushes. It is the type of narrative that a historian rather than a dramatist would construe; the opening and closing scenes concerning the death of Mazarin and the king's realization of his destiny are suggestive motifs that are not fully realized in the major sections of the film. If the film had no other virtues, it would work as a tonic to the fussy, grandiloquent treatment usually given to French court life on film. But Rossellini is a great deal more than a theoretician; the king's eventual realization of the revolutionary impact of his demands is stylistically paralleled through his increasing self-consciousness. What the audience misses is a clarification of the king's most precise feelings about his destiny as the Sun King, but in his attention to the etiquette of court society Rossellini defines both the pedantry and magnificence of the period.

The intellectual character of Pascal's life would seem to invite a treatment similar to that used in *Socrates*, but the film assumes the form of historical biography in the manner of *The Rise of Louis XIV*. It is comprised in equal parts of the solitary nature of Pascal's rustic existence, his articulation of mathematical and metaphysical theories, and his lifelong battle against physical ailments. Unlike *Socrates*, in which there is an incipient realization of the primacy of Socrates' face and words, Pascal's reclusiveness leads to a less personal statement about his life and writings. The film's medium-shot framework effectively absorbs one in Pascal's daily routines; his confrontation with Descartes, however, is handled in such a repressed manner as to become hyperbole. At the end of the film, Rossellini attempts a more pictorial dramatization of Pascal's suffering, as images resonate a Rembrandt-like truth concerning the artist's faltering condition.

*The Age of the Medici* sustains Rossellini's study of history through its major controversies and personalities. One again notes his reluctance to create a grandiose historical superstructure, choosing instead to highlight the period through medium-shot and close-up encounters. Yet the manners and politics of the Renaissance are manifested in the characters' methodical speeches and in their recognition that their social and political decisions represent an idea for the future. The meaning of their society is expressed in the way the diplomat Cosimo or the scientist Alberti meditate on their plans: Rossellini's rigorous attention to their reflective facial expressions and prolonged monologues scrutinizes the period's social fabric to discover its prosaic ideology.

It seems only natural that Rossellini's last efforts should have been made for television, imbuing the most accessible and least polemic of media with a sense of the art and history of the past it has so successfully resisted. It will be the responsibility of Rossellini's successors to further the humanistic and aesthetic claims he made for television in such a forthright, intelligent manner. Only then, perhaps, will his last achievements be understood in the light of his entire contribution to film and intellectual history over the last thirty-five years.

## Luchino Visconti

Of the major Italian directors, Luchino Visconti seems the most removed from the debilitating moral climate and harsh economic truths of postwar Italy. There is, however, some evidence of the coercive nature of materialsim in his films from the pile of dishes and proletariat lowlife that the wife faces daily in *Ossessione* to the cluttered, baroque circumference of Ludwig's castle. But whereas his contemporaries adhere to a rigid cause-and-effect pattern between the oppressive nature of their settings and their characters' stultified personal expressiveness, Visconti favors a less schematic approach. In Visconti's first films, the protagonists are presented as heroic, romantic adventurers whose passions are overshadowed by their poverty. In *La terra trema*, a major statement from the Italian humanist cinema, the fishermen become archetypal figures engulfed in an unending cycle of triumph and devastation; in *Ossessione*, there are fragments of a more vibrant romanticism that will pervade his later films, but he seems hesitant to explore the sensual intimacy of his lovers.

*Senso* asserts the preeminent operatic design for which Visconti became famous. Although the film fails to fulfill its exuberant melodrama, it bears favorable comparison both to *The Damned* and to *Ludwig*. Visconti maintains a handsome symmetry between the romantic presence of Alida Valli and the elaborate but ultimately repressed nature of the Italian aristocracy. In *The Leopard* he takes a more impassive view of the moral rigor and physical splendor of the aristocracy. In *Senso* Valli's tremulous heroine, though conscious of the depth of the mores of her hierarchical society, appears to test its resiliency through her adulterous affair. In *The Leopard* Visconti identifies his players as part of an imperious social order, whether in his encompassing long shots of Burt Lancaster's estate—which reveal Visconti's powers as a landscape painter who overlooks no single detail in denoting the historical permanency of the family's estate—or in his sumptuous interior scenes, personified by the ball. Unlike Ophüls whose characters exaggerate the romantic luster of his backdrops, the characters in *The Leopard* do not challenge their society. Lancaster lacks the truly magisterial authority his role demands, but, in retrospect, one's admiration grows for Visconti's recreation of the style of the aristocracy. *The Leopard* is his least problematical, least original film, but he convinces us of the sanctity of his museum.

In *Rocco and His Brothers* Visconti immerses himself in the chaotic adventures of a lower-class family. The treatment remains inherently operatic in his emotional absorption in the characters' conflicts, whether among themselves or with society. The film lacks the patience for a psychological probe of their wayward behavior—to follow the characters in their less volatile moments and to broaden the canvas in order for the rattle and misery of city life to transform the work from melodrama into a romantic vivisection of Italian society. Yet it works quite well as melodrama. Renato Salvatori has the gruffness and the brutality of the streets, while Annie Girardot suggests both its poverty and sensuality. If Visconti's treatment is too visceral, the film's emotional climaxes support a way of looking at the world that met with continued opposition in the cinema of the sixties.

Visconti's two least operatic films, *Sandra* and *The Stranger*, show some unexpected strengths and several predictable weaknesses. *Sandra* has the texture of a modest psychological novel, in which Visconti's abrupt camera movements punctuate the oblique, incestuous love of Jean Sorel for Claudia Cardinale. Unlike Bolognini whose indolent point of view distances the viewer from the drama in *Agostino*, Visconti empathizes with the characters' ephemeral grasp of the redolent mysteries of time and place. However, there are weaknesses in the film representative of Visconti's preference for romantic abstraction. The role of the townspeople is obscured; he suggests their choruslike function but in such a murky way that we are never sure if they feel simply removed from the aristocratic family's personal problems. While the characters of Sorel and Cardinale are enveloped by the musty aura of their estate, her husband is a peripheral figure. Again one notes Visconti's mastery of the sweet cadences of sensuality. Now if he could only feel the pain.

*The Stranger* demands a different kind of literacy. In adapting Camus's celebrated novel to the screen, Visconti dwells on the torpor, the harsh, sultry humidity of Meursault's environment. But even as his narrative evokes Mastroianni's phlegmatism, he fails to capture the inherently tragic aspects of his character. Meursault is not simply an uninteresting, apathetic figure, but one who recognizes his precarious grip on reality. Visconti, however, seems fearful of deviating from his matter-of-fact point of view, as if he would be accused of romanticizing his material. Mastroianni gives a restrained portrayal of Meursault, but because of Visconti's reliance on the scorched features of his tropical setting, we never understand the peculiarities of Mastroianni's character. The place and mood are unsettling but not the protagonist.

In *The Damned, Death in Venice,* and *Ludwig* Visconti undertakes a more radical dramatization of history as opera. Unlike *Senso* in which Alida Valli found herself drawn into the operatic matrix of romance and revolution, and unlike *The Leopard,* in which Visconti pictures the aristocracy as a family mosaic threatened by the social upheaval, his characters' larger-than-life passions in these films are seen as emblematic of a profound historical force. But in *The Damned* his German family of arms manufacturers does not so much participate in German history as they exemplify it. Visconti has moved from the epic social framework of *Senso* and *The Leopard* and even *Rocco and His Brothers* to *verismo,* in which his characters' emotional vicissitudes function as the film's narrative fulcrum. To work as an example of cinematic *verismo,* the characters must appear as historically flawed figures, but Visconti is unable to achieve this personal-historical parallel except for Helmut Berger's debauched heir. Dirk Bogarde is both linguistically and dramatically alienated from the other family members, and Ingrid Thulin seems to play the role of the decadent in her sleep. Visconti's camerawork and staging are static, refractory; they fail to distinguish the historical underpinnings of the characters' corrupt behavior; one noteworthy exception is the S.S. raid on the S.A., in which his fluid camerawork underscores the perversely sexual killings. The very wickedness of his characters' actions then serves as a self-referential commentary on their society: Visconti has replaced the sweeping, historical canvas in his earlier epics with a taut, expressionistic veneer; yet the film's erotic entanglements do not enlighten us about the singular destiny of Visconti's family of arms merchants. They only seem pathetic creatures who could not more foment the Third Reich than they could sustain their family fortune.

*Death in Venice* adopts a different point of view, even though there are similarities between this work and *The Damned* that go beyond the period and characters. The visual style can, I think, be best described as one of mannerism and is closest to *The Leopard* in Visconti's sensitivity to the sepulchral luster of Venice. In *The Leopard* the characters are independent, heroic defenders of the aristocracy; in *Death in Venice* the society is more severely structured, the characters' stolid, studied persona symptomatic of the film's pictorially designed social tensions. The drama originates in the more anxious, self-conscious rhetoric of mannerism; it not only affects the backgrounds, but also the characters' precise, choreographed movements. For this reason the andante movement of Mahler's Fifth Symphony is superfluous; the music superimposes a romantic element that is not visible in Visconti's staging. The dialogue is purposely repressed, whereby its dramatic potential does not intrude into his ornate, ritualized configurations. It is Visconti's most sincere film, though without the seductive, romantic decrescendos of his earlier epics. *Death in Venice* shows Visconti as a craftsman who never fully understood how characters are brought to life in his historical pageants; yet with its pictorial transformation of Mann's evocative characters into sleepwalkers, it may also be his most cogent work.

*Ludwig* is a muddled film, and, as is the case with many truncated works, the problem seems to lie with the director and not the distributor. One cannot fault Visconti for his choice of Berger as Ludwig, considering Berger's masterly portrayal in *The Damned*. Although Trevor Howard does not lend any insight into his characterization of Wagner, Visconti is the chief culprit. Ludwig's decline into madness is not treated in the manner of Berger's ravenous erotic appetite in *The Damned*, but as a soporific interlude in the life of a dandy. Berger is shown in various stages of inebriation, but there is no complementary intellectual thread to magnify or crystallize his self-decline. It would appear to be Visconti's most abstract work, but one in which his fascination for the artifacts and decor of a society as signs of spiritual optimism or pessimism had yet to be resolved.

In his last films Visconti's collaborations with scriptwriter Suso de'Amico Cecchi (*Bellissima, Senso, White Nights, The Stranger, Ludwig, Rocco and His Brothers, The Leopard*) resulted in more conventional literary treatments. Like *The Leopard*, *The Innocent* shows Visconti's transcendent attention to the architecture of time and space as a means of discovering the voice of his characters. The settings are not simply pretty to look at, but transform the aristocracy into ornaments of culture. Their handsome, sensual dress and theatrical mannerisms delineate a drama of elaborate fussiness in which chairs and tables, couches and curtains are arranged so meticulously as to suffocate the characters' emotionalism. The drama is coexpressive with their labyrinthian physical emblems of social identification; the characters' outbursts lose their emotional intensity when played against the film's fastidious design. Giannini makes an earnest effort as the cavalier aristocrat, but his overly expressive eyes and strident gestures were more effective in Lina Wertmuller's comic melodramas. While he abuses Laura Antonelli's saturnalian figure, he, too, is a victim of Visconti's coiffed interiors, unable to escape from the redolence of the past in the clothes he wears or in the sensual, severe composition of his settings.

*Conversation Piece* is a more ironic meditation. The resonance of culture is identified in the museum of books and art in Burt Lancaster's home. He is the curator of our indelible past who is intrigued by the silly romantic escapades of Silvana Mangano, her daughter, and their mutual lover played by Berger. Visconti has fashioned a pardoxical polemic, but we are not sure to what depths he intended to pursue the abuses Lancaster suffers at the hands of these decadents or, perhaps in a contrary manner, to show Lancaster's desire to rediscover himself through his new tenants. Few directors have given us such a sure-handed sense of culture, but owing to the uncertainty of Lancaster's characterization as its contemporary curator, Visconti leaves one with an inconclusive image of culture awaiting its final onslaught.

## Federico Fellini

Federico Fellini's career began as auspiciously as that of any Italian film-maker, and through *8½*, with little more than ten years of work as a director, Fellini seemed well on the way to earning recognition as one of the most stylish of artists the movies have known. His first efforts, *Variety Lights* and *The White Sheik*, are original examples of Fellini's comic temperament, his appreciation for the buoyant innocence and daring of his protagonists whose fantasies are threatened by the equally implausible quirks of modern city life. Like Preston Sturges, he celebrates the unwielding comic force in his characters' rustic, folk humor; but unlike Sturges who introduces an element of self-doubt about the innocence and energy of his country protagonists, Fellini imposes a less morally antagonistic view. His characters have learned to accept their unsettled existence, realizing that there is more than enough humor and happiness to be gained from their pleasure in one another's company to offset the money and success that will never be theirs. It is joyously manifest in *Variety Lights* when members of the circus troupe are invited to dinner by a landowner who fancies one of the entertainers. Fellini's camera does not caricature their uncouth table manners but seems to share in their ravenous appetite, their comic energy, and their loquacity. They are mischievous, wholly unidealized figures, a collection of tramps who have learned that there is nothing in this world to compare with the blissful disorderliness of the circus.

*The White Sheik* is a more pointed satire in which Fellini's anarchic instincts are filtered through the antic charm of the newlyweds who arrive in the city, particularly the bride who fantasizes about a pop-culture adventurer known as the "White Sheik." Fellini is most adept in counterbalancing their ubiquitous awkwardness with the more hidden ticks of the bureaucrats and charlatans they encounter. The film's satiric tone draws heavily on the conventions of slapstick comedy while adopting a more genteel approach to its comic nihilism. The bride's discovery of the White Sheik and her participation in the filming of the serial achieves its comic flavor as a result of Fellini's generous treatment of the frivolity common to each character: they are caught up in a fantasy in which normality is viewed as a stigma to be avoided at all costs. How else could the wife hope to survive her dreary prospects if her husband were not envisioned in the last scene as her new White Sheik?

*I Vitelloni* is an acute departure from the comic, chaotic thrust of *Variety Lights* and *The White Sheik*. Fellini's focus turns to a different social sphere, the middle class, where his characters cannot casually dismiss the aftereffects of their comically disruptive adventures. It shows Fellini at a stylistic crossroad; although he does not accentuate the comic vitality of his performers in the manner of his two previous films, he is unwilling to adopt the distant, cerebral tone of *La dolce vita* or *8½*. He is still too close to his characters, too enamored of their gaiety and humor to castigate their moral decrepitude. In a manner similar to *The Nights of Cabiria*, Fellini sustains the comic interplay throughout a major section of the film; however, unlike *The Nights of Cabiria*, one detects an undercurrent of tension and indecisiveness about his characters' glib manner. After the party, when in masks they decry their mournful condition, the film's symbolism seems arbitrary, heavy-handed; the moralist has supplanted the humorist in Fellini. Their discovery of the porpoise is a fake, pretentious symbol better suited to Bergman's allegorical style than to Fellini's naturalism. *I Vitelloni* leads one to surmise that Fellini is uncertain about his status as a comic director, that he has yet to find a subject and tone which will allow the viewer to see the characters as the symbols Fellini self-consciously draws them as at the end of the film.

In *La strada* and *Il bidone* Fellini completes one phase of his stylistic evolution from a rousing comic artist who cherishes the commedia dell'arte attributes of his low-life protagonists to the expressionist who penetrates the grim underside of postwar Italy. *La strada* is the more ambitious film; he transforms the innocent spirit of misadventure in *Variety Lights* and *The White Sheik* into poetic allegory. Through the extraordinary pathos of Masina's innocent and the taut characterizations of Anthony Quinn and Richard Basehart, he achieves an artful expansion of the commedia dell'arte by pinpointing the characters' fate as social misfits as mirror images to their roles as theatrical performers. The film's emotionalism, like that of *Il bidone*, is its most impressive feature; Fellini diminishes the importance of their impoverished rural backgrounds by responding to their fragile, poetic mask as a natural expression of both their social and dramatic identity. Fellini's attraction for the fabrications of the theater has led him away from the romantic embellishments of Chaplin's *City Lights* and *The Circus* to the expressionism of Rouault: he is no longr attracted to the lyrical gradations of his characters' fantasies, but to the expressive contortions and painful subjectivity surrounding their destinies as socially flawed theatrical protagonists.

*Il bidone* is the most overlooked work in Fellini's filmography, perhaps because it has neither the comic effects for which his early films are remembered nor the overpowering symbolism that characterizes his work since *La dolce vita*. It remains one of the most riveting films of the Italian humanist cinema, imbued with a grittiness rare even for a national cinema honored for its realism. Fellini is not interested in presenting his con men, led by Broderick Crawford, as anti-heroes superior to the society they swindle. They are cruel, pernicious figures who feel no remorse in deceiving ignorant farmers. At first, Fellini exposes their self-disgust and the mechanical nature of their routines; it is only a matter of time before the cops will apprehend them or an outraged victim will kill them. Fellini's moral pessimism is effectively understated, for example, in the scene at a party where Crawford stares at another man for only a moment, and without exchanging a word, the audience realizes that they will join forces in a swindle. This leads to the film's most dramatic encounter and one of the most emotionally explosive in the history of the cinema. Crawford, disguised as a priest, is confronted by a crippled girl to whom he sold purportedly medicinal pills. He appears to weaken and admit the deceit, but he is unable to tell her the truth. Fellini is to be credited with creating this most harrowing picture of the

scum of the earth without the crude cynicism that often creeps into such projects. His triumph is to have exposed the precarious humanism of the postwar
Italian cinema while pointing to the rising notes of alienation and abstraction in
the Italian and international cinema of the sixties.

*The Nights of Cabiria* again features Giulietta Masina, and what an amusing,
puckish figure she cuts, from her garrulous exchanges with the other prostitutes
to her escapade with a matinee idol, which leads to her spending a night in his
closet when his girl friend suddenly appears. Unlike the protagonists in Fellini's
other comedies, Masina is more aware of the depressing nature of her existence;
she attacks it with a romantic ferocity that results, however, in a more didactic
conclusion. From the time she meets the man at the carnival, we know that he is
out to trick her, to abuse her feelings by appearing as forlorn as Masina. Fellini
attempts to blend in the comic naturalism of *Variety Lights* with the stylized
conventions of theatrical comedy by having Masina believe that her desire for
the amenities of marriage has a chance of success. While recalling the comedic
spirit of his first films, *The Nights of Cabiria* suffers from Fellini's imposing the
glum ambience in *La strada* and *Il bidone*.

*La dolce vita* marks Fellini's entrance into modernism, in which the rural,
makeshift backgrounds of his earlier films are replaced by the glitter of city life.
In his previous films, the settings reflected the nature of his characters' identity
and desires, from the giddy circus world of *Variety Lights* to the microcosmic
theater troupe of *La strada*. The moral vacuum at the heart of *I Vitelloni* is probably most similar to *La dolce vita*, but the characters' decline is partly attributable to the film's small-town setting and to their failure to escape to the city. In
*La dolce vita*, his canvas is not limited to any one segment of society but denotes
the sensationalism surrounding the exploits of Mastroianni's scandal-sheet
journalist. Fellini must then convince the audience of his protagonist's descent
into the abyss through the vicissitudes of empathy and estrangement that Mastroianni experiences within Fellini's spectacular apocalypses of social enervation. This is a recognized feature of epic, yet as much as the viewer is titillated
by Mastroianni's infatuation with Anita Ekberg during the party, in their
ascent of the tower, and in their dalliance in the fountain, one is hard put to
discover their personal and moral residue. What is immediately apparent is that
the grandeur of these scenes underscores the characters' complete immersion in
their amoral society. Mastroianni's other major encounters—with his unstable
girl friend, with his father enraptured by the festivities and foppery, with his
friend who commits suicide, and with the children's rumored sighting of the
Virgin Mary—provide further examples of Fellini's fluidity in uncovering a
portentous sense of unease and self-disgust. But how well do these episodes
dramatize the alluring, destructive power of the sweet, easy life? Does Mastroianni's excursion through the nightlife of Rome faithfully encompass the full
meaning of its decrepitude? Are Fellini's characters representative of modern
man's slothful nature or that of only a select group of people? Do his engrossing
scenic arrangements—in which he shows the utmost care in casting the
homosexual seated in the background of a party next to an androgyny—convey

a profound note of emptiness? The answer is both yes and no, for what Fellini fails to capture is a sense of aesthetic distance from his spectacle. Its problematic point of view is personified by the supine nature of Mastroianni's journalist; his indolent character allows Fellini to glibly explore the awesome decadence of modern Rome but without the accompanying quality of self-awareness that would question its origins. Fellini has given new significance to epic filmmaking, but his elaborate paean to those who participate in this absurdist landscape lacks the tension necessary to express his characters' self-negation.

In *8½* Fellini circumvents the encompassing theme and style of alienation in *La dolce vita* by casting Mastroianni as a film director. This makes for a more intuitive conflict because Mastroianni and the other scandal-sheet journalists never extricate themselves from the gaudy proceedings. Mastroianni's Guido Anselmi, however, is at once the creator and the victim of Fellini's three-ring circus; his memories of the past are characterized by an element of fantasy and the grotesque similar to his surreal encounters at the health spa, where he is besieged by his producer, wife, and mistress. The film concerns the uncertainty an artist faces when he recognizes the impossibility of creating some order out of the vast rumblings of his subconscious—who finds his everyday world inundated with the humor and horror of his phantomesque past. Visually sweeping scenes, such as young Guido's dance on the beach with "Big Mama," the sauna in which the characters appear submerged in a Dante-like waiting room, and Guido's amphitheater bordello, where he must tame his restless concubines, are examples of a daydreaming poet who idealizes the dreamlike qualities of his work as a film director by situating his most esoteric fantasies alongside the equally bizarre creatures that surround him at the health spa. For Fellini, fantasy has not become a romantic haven, a style of cinematic prolixity; it is the most succinct and sincere manner of understanding his identity as a filmmaker and the symbolic nature of his art.

Although *Juliet of the Spirits* presents an inquiry into his wife's personal fears and fantasies, Fellini loses the dramatic edge that made Mastroianni's Guido such a sympathetic guide. Masina's Juliet, wearing less makeup than her husband, lacks Guido's humor in experiencing the erotic and religious specters of her past and her dreams. Unlike other voyages through a make-believe world, her fantasies neither illuminate the nature of her neurosis nor evoke a particularly harmonious, self-referential dreamscape. The voices that communicate with Masina offer a dramatic alternative for Fellini and Masina, but they become a receding motif in traveling through her unconscious. It is Fellini's most self-indulgent film and proves of less interest than *La dolce vita* because one never believes that Masina can challenge or accentuate the autonomy of her baroque inner visions. In such scenes as the outing on the beach, Fellini's garish colors imitate the surrealist's premise of hyperbole; his picture-book evocation of Masina's estate seems the work of a rococo designer who has transgressed the delicate line of extravagance and excrescence. Fellini's visual style from *Variety Lights* through *8½* has led him to adopt a more tentative approach to his characters; by moving from the comic, lyric naturalism in his first films to the epic format of *La dolce vita*, *8½*, and *Juliet of the Spirits*, he has undertaken a delineation of the archetypal anxieties and the fantasies of the modern age. But in *Juliet of the Spirits* the interplay and displacement between reality and fantasy do not lead toward any definite understanding of Masina's housewife; the film glistens with the transparency of a fashion layout, with no particular point of view other than celebrating the submission of its alienated heroine to the tedious sensuality of a bacchanal.

*Fellini Satyricon*, like *La dolce vita*, is a clear departure for Fellini. In earlier collaborations with scriptwriters Tullio Pinelli and Ennio Flaiano and with cinematographers Otello Martelli and Gianni Di Venanzo, Fellini explored a style of film drama that mixed elements of the rustic humor of theater folk with the slapstick farces of silent-film comedy. In *La strada*, his initial attraction for the pathos and artifices of vaudeville humor achieves a more poetic treatment, yet it is one whose psychological intensity, combined with its rural, folkloristic backgrounds, reflects the voice of an expressionist searching for a more expansive symbolist terrain. In his other films of this period, it is only in *Il bidone* that the psychological realism of *La strada* is successfully adapted to the social realism of the postwar Italian school. In *Il bidone* Fellini matches Antonioni's *Il grido* and its physical absorption in a countryside marked by postwar devastation and the junk pile homes of refugees with the brutality and unrelenting self-destructiveness of Broderick Crawford's gang of ghetto degenerates. In *I Vitelloni* and *The Nights of Cabiria*, Fellini's moral pessimism flirts with literary and theatrical symbolism in divorcing his protagonists from the familiar backgrounds of his contemporaries. But his cynical, estranged, middle-class drifters in *I vitelloni* lack an authority in their dismissal of society; their final self-confessions do not express any distinct strains of misery that would distinguish their fate from other symbolic wanderers in postwar literature, theater, and film. *The Nights of Cabiria* is more successful if only because of Masina's heartfelt portrayal of a street gamine, but her final comic-tragic escapade is a less natural resolution of her dramatic persona than that of Fellini's trio of ill-fated circus performers in *La strada*.

With *La dolce vita*, Fellini once again delves into his cultural and stylistic origins. He turns to the epic as a symbolic social narrative, as a painting genre dramatizing great moments of history, and as a style of filmmaking that was most prolifically featured in the Italian cinema during the formative years of the silent film. The one area of film production in which Italian filmmakers most securely challenged Griffith and the more kinetic sagas of the American silent film was in their design. If the focus in the American film was to discover the idealistic resources of the individual and family, the Italian epic came alive in its interiors. The opulence of Italy's film pioneers was lavished on temples, coliseums, fortresses, and the final eruption of thousands of actors running through massive columns, statuaries, and diligently constructed, three-dimensional backgrounds. The inclination of Griffith and his American contemporaries was to sustain a more dynamic action drama and to use the backgrounds, not so much as the central metaphor, but as a complementary physical and historical motif. The permanent, classical heritage of Italian producers, writers, directors, cinematographers, and art directors may have brought about a more cautious attitude in their film treatments, but their interest in the theatrical grandeur of their settings underlined a major preoccupation of filmmakers in the silent era. It also, however, was the most strikingly original evidence of the tendency to dramatic imperviousness among filmmakers, both silent and sound, because of the predisposition of many film craftsmen to compose their stories for the set and not the camera. This interpretation of a film drama as a transposition or transfiguration of painting styles has been an important objective for many filmmakers; during different periods and for different reasons, the film medium has been used to mesmerize its audience by treating the actors as iconographic or coloristic emblems in a painting. We see history remade in the style of great painters, with one extravagant and often stillborn composition following another. Beginning with *La dolce vita*, Fellini's interest in using the medium as a painter's canvas is of the most ambitious scope. The origins of Fellini's symbolically drawn narratives lie in the unicellular circus microcosm of *Variety Lights* and *The White Sheik*; in *La dolce vita*, *8½*, and *Juliet of the Spirits*, his three-ring circus mirrors the isolation and the fantasies of his protagonists. Yet only in *8½* does Fellini's flamboyance seem inspired by the whimsy and demons of his hero. Guido's subconscious functions as the cognitive orchestrator of the film's fluid visions; he seems to step in and out of his fantasies, usually returning to his childhood to rediscover those lustful dreams that have led to his middle-aged traumas. In *8½* Fellini has artfully sidestepped the blankness of *La dolce vita*—with its dirgelike celebration of decadence and lethargy, and its florid sequences of social nullification—and the pictorial excesses of *Juliet of the Spirits*—with Masina's acquiescence to the wistful memories of childhood and to her fantasies of erotic rejuvenation. In *8½* there is an underlying recognition of the creative and fatalistic nature of Guido's dream life; the audience shares with him the comic-tragic uniformity of his conscious and unconscious lives.

In discussing the design of *Fellini Satyricon* with cinematographer Giuseppe Rotunno, set and costume designer Danilo Donati, and architect Luigi Scaccianoce, Fellini refers to the tactile textures of fresco painting. The pictorial foreshortening and predominant rectilinear design of fresco painting are well-suited to the wide screen. Rotunno worked as an assistant to Leon Shamroy and is an admirer of Shamroy's liberal use of color filters and his style of lighting with color. Yet there is no inherent dynamic to *Fellini Satyricon*. The cutting does not suggest the parodic excesses of the story, but the encompassing dimensions of Fellini's modernist abstractions. The colors are among the most brightly mordant ever used in a film, but there is no continuity or logic to their application. The half-dozen examples of process photography have the metallic sheen of De Chirico; the confrontation in the arena with the Minotaur or the orgy after the sexual revitalization of its hero recalls the airy expansiveness of Dali. Other scenes make more explicit references to the depersonalized, formalist rhetoric of mannerist painting. Fellini, however, seems to return to the underlying themes of anxiety and illusion in surrealist art. In *Roma* after the underground frescoes are discovered, Fellini cuts to a lyrical interlude involving the hippie decadents of Rome; *Fellini Satyricon* fulfills this suggestive analogy by selecting for his leads two actors who are used as votive offerings in a pagan ceremony. Fellini shows some interest in treating the different stages through which his protagonists pass as part of a mythological, underworld arena but only to establish a more acute autonomy about their adventures in abasement. The classical sources and modern textures of *Fellini Satyricon* are examples of Fellini's fulfillment of filmmaking as fantasy, as an apotheosis of those motifs of self-absorption that have characterized most of his heroes. Fellini's aesthetic gambit has removed the murky elements of alienation surrounding his wife's flight into fantasy in *Juliet of the Spirits*, but with an escalation of production excess. The tranquil, implicitly catatonic spirit of self-reverie in *Fellini Satyricon*, in which fantasy is conceived as both a social condition and an artistic ideal, will figure in both his successes and failures of the seventies.

*The Clowns*, part documentary, part autobiography, is an affectionate work, but one suspects that Fellini is uncertain of his direction at this stage of his career. The film takes an impressionistic look at Fellini's memories of the circus, but just as he is about to immerse himself in his essaylike study, his autobiographical digressions undercut the integrity of his subject. It is as if the predominant surreal style of his work since *8½* has prevented him from pursuing the linear, compassionate point of view that is necessary in *The Clowns*. Fellini's apparent self-mockery is more conspicuous in *Roma*, in which he satirizes the droll nature of autobiography. There is no reason to think that autobiography can no longer work for Fellini, but he lacks an essential self-criticism. Since he is not engaged in the elaborate narrative experiment of *8½*, his reminiscences seem painless, romantically ephemeral. Some of the scenes are amusing, but they are most likely to titillate those viewers who have not experienced the lyrical comic ploys of his first films or the more complex twists of his later works. In the latter part of the film, when he turns the camera on himself and his friends, *Roma* becomes not only striking evidence of the stasis of the artist, but also of his self-contempt; Gore Vidal pontificating on Rome, for example, belongs as a minor image in *8½*. Fellini has assumed the easygoing manner of a tour guide, espousing the fanciful clichés about the imperial majesty of the city.

In *Amarcord* Fellini explores his adolescence with greater feeling. He is not so quick to underline the farcical elements of his rural upbringing, but seeks to convey the joyous, pranksterish spirit of his boyhood adventures. The film benefits from staying with its young innocents instead of assuming the disparate, comical style of *Roma*. It is a gentler, less intricate work than his early or middle-period films; he is not as interested in discovering the painful intermingling of reality and fantasy as he is in picturing his adolescence as a fabulist who has never abandoned the infectious high spirits of his youth. Several scenes are slight indeed when compared with previous excursions into his past, but Fellini retains our interest through such sympathetic treatments as that of the town's single, attractive woman whose marriage ends the film on the note of romance that Fellini seems to see as representative of all of our boyhood peregrinations.

The film has the texture of a Rousseau painting, asking the audience to interpret its characters and their adventures as intrinsically phantasmagorical. It is most happily expressed when the natives go out to sea, and Fellini uses a scenic backdrop as a symbol of their wonderment. Fellini has made more adventurous films, but the nostalgic echoes of adolescent adventure in *Amarcord* find Fellini engaged in the myths with which he is most comfortable.

*Casanova*, however, suggests that *Amarcord* was only a momentary diversion; the densely pictorial style which was most severely used in *Fellini Satyricon* is featured once again. The film, however, lacks the theoretical validity of *Fellini Satyricon*; Fellini disdains the anecdotal pleasures of Casanova's autobiography for a fragmented, callous picture of eighteenth-century manners and morals. Casanova's romantic encounters make little sense because Fellini chooses to evoke only the vulgarization of courtship and romance. In *Fellini Satyricon* his provocative design at least showed an artist conceptualizing the monstrous gluttony of Petronius's world. But in *Casanova* Fellini's antipathy for the period is not conveyed through the paradoxical nature of his protagonist, but through his dissipated visual style. Donald Sutherland does an earnest job in the title role, but Fellini fails to respond to his dandyism as a way of dramatizing his meretricious society. In the last segments of the film, when Casanova is more acutely alienated from his society, Fellini begins to sketch out surreal metaphors for its decline. But the absence of plot or a resonant visual format suggests that the origin of the degeneracy of morals in eighteenth-century Europe lies in Fellini's script and not with Casanova and his contemporaries.

*Orchestra Rehearsal* offers another vantage point to Fellini's work after *Fellini Satyricon*. The film's simple design—its white-shirted, informally attired performers haphazardly seated or moving about their classical settings—creates an effective dramatic and pictorial counterpoint to the drawings and colors that have faded but which still grace the walls of the cave in which they perform. Fellini's stylistic control in leading up to the farcical outbursts of the performers points to an inherent stylistic uniformity between the dangling, hyphenated figures that cover the cave's walls and the conviviality and high spirits of the orchestra. His original instincts for the primitive folk humor of theater and film are rediscovered in what would seem to be an incongruous setting but one which Fellini shows contains elements of timelessness and time—the memory of man's iconoclastic signature in history and his recurrent instinct for playful improvisation. Sentiment happily coalesces with style, and the vagaries of personal creation overrule the critic's pedantic generalizations.

## Michelangelo Antonioni

From *Story of a Love Affair* through *Blow-Up*, Michelangelo Antonioni advanced to the top ranks of directors through his study of our increasingly anonymous, abstracted postwar environment. In *Story of a Love Affair*, a much underrated work, Antonioni introduces the precarious romantic triangle that is most incisively explored in *Il grido* and his love trilogy. His first feature film concerns a wealthy Milanese industrialist who decides to investigate his wife, whose past hinges on the death of her closest friend, the fiancée of her former lover, who is reunited with her in Milan. The dilemma facing the lovers is simply stated: who was responsible for the girl's death, and what will occur when the husband finds out about the "accident" and his wife's present liaison?

Antonioni's probing of the girl's death prefigures the role of the third person in his later films (Alida Valli's husband who is never seen in *Il grido* and that of Lea Massari in *L'avventura*). From the moment the viewer learns of the girl's accident, we realize that the married woman and her lover were equally guilty. Although neither one pushed the girl, who fell down an elevator shaft, they could have warned or rescued her. Thus, their previous affair, which resulted in their failure to save the girl, establishes the moral paradox for the duration of their relationship. The film then projects a more acute sense of melodrama than Antonioni's succeeding work. In the private meetings of the lovers and in those scenes in which they are separated by her husband or girl friends, Antonioni shows their indecisiveness in failing to resolve a renewed love affair. In his later films, he will not draw our attention to the denouement as he does in *Story of a Love Affair*; throughout the film one awaits the husband's reaction to their relationship. This may make it a minor film, but, nonetheless, a shrewd, telltale work in discerning the failure of romance in modern society.

*La signora senza Camelie*, set against the backdrop of film and theater production, concerns the chicanery of entrepreneurs who control the destiny of a rising starlet. Antonioni sees her perilous identity as trapped by the melodramatic action surrounding both her stage and real life roles; his camera setups continually superimpose a baroque, theatrical angle in her scenes outside the theater while sustaining an intensive, emotional drama through his close-ups of the actress in her dressing room or in rehearsal. The interpenetration of film and theater in *La signora senza Camelie* becomes a metaphor for the abstraction of the heroine's desires—for her alienation in a social landscape that will undergo a more geometric, dehumanizing form in Antonioni's succeeding films.

In *Il grido* Antonioni isolates Steve Cochran's love for Alida Valli as the cause of his frustration and pain. In one brief, deeply moving scene, Cochran, carrying a piece of paper with the name of a person he is to see about a job, walks on the outskirts of the town. He begins to examine the paper but suddenly rolls it up and throws it away. Cochran has expressed the dissatisfaction and emptiness from which he knows he can never escape because of his unfulfilled love for Valli. But Cochran's harrowing portrayal of a man in search of love but doomed to failure is not the only reason *Il grido* captures our interest. Unlike Antonioni's other films, it does not transpire against the background of the middle- and upper-class parties and the spiraling abstract forms that crowd our cityscapes; the wasteland is not spiritual, but uncompromisingly physical in a way that few films have explored poverty and wreckage. It is not the destitute physical universe of Rossellini's early films, and although one might think of Von Stroheim's *Greed*, Antonioni does not duplicate Von Stroheim's close-up, penetrating camera angles. He favors long tracking shots, for example, in the scene in which Cochran and his girl friend, enjoying a picnic, are found resting in what seems to be a garbage dump. It is Antonioni's bleakest film, in which the humanism of the first postwar Italian filmmakers faces its most severe test and in which that humanism is found to be wanting.

In his love trilogy—*L'avventura, La notte, L'eclisse*—Antonioni returns to the romantic entanglements of *Story of a Love Affair*. *L'avventura*, along with Fellini's *La dolce vita*, underscores the changes in their society and filmmaking styles from a country beset by everyday necessities to one flourising and floundering in its economic resurgence. Unlike *L'eclisse*, in which the abstracted cityscape reflects the characters' emotional isolation, *L'avventura*, with its greater fluidity, remains the most accessible, though perhaps not the best film of the trilogy. The most engrossing sequence—the search on the island—works as an interminable tracking shot around a surface whose meaning remains impenetrable and yet which yields unexpected parallels to the film's central theme of unrequited love. But there are also scenes in the films—stretches might be a better term—in which his characters' listlessness indecisively dramatizes their alienation.

Though much has been written of Monica Vitti's character, little effort has been made to study the methodlike qualities of her performance. Her easygoing, impetuous nature makes her the focal point in understanding the changes each of the characters undergoes in their search for Massari; Vitti's character also determines the audience's awareness of the meaning of Antonioni's sprawling landscape. Vitti's open character; her unattached existence, as if she alone among those invited on the cruise were not a social stereotype; her awareness of her growing attraction for Ferzetti—these give her the freedom to experience the film's shifting emotional currents more intuitively than Ferzetti can. The beauty of her performance is not in what is commonly associated with bravura acting or even the more acknowledged glories of the Stanislavski method: it is slow to take shape, its meaning largely expressed in the way she moves around a room, for example, in the scene in which she awakes and swings with the music on the radio while putting on her stockings. There are scenes, however, that obscure her dramatic identity, in which she functions as a diminishing figure of human communication in Antonioni's amorphous backgrounds. But the film remains a noble, pioneering study of the individual suddenly discovering his invisibility in society. Antonioni confronts one of the most difficult of all dramatic viewpoints: how to convey a sense of temporal evolution and dramatic metamorphosis during the two and a half hours in which the film unfolds. He has brilliantly redrawn the romantic triangle of *Story of a Love Affair*, but he has yet to achieve the precise narrative-pictorial balance to change the emphasis of the Italian cinema from humanism to abstraction.

*La notte* is a less conclusive work, its characters unaware of the degree of solitude in their surroundings. This is not to imply that Antonioni is solely interested in clarifying the spheres of darkness that threaten the marriage of Mastroianni and Moreau, but he seems unsure of their congruity within his rigidly abstracted canvas. For example, the imposing, high-rise architecture of the hospital where Marcello Mastroianni and Jeanne Moreau visit a friend undercuts the impact of their conversation and leads to Mastroianni taking advantage of a female patient. But does Antonioni really want to show Mastroianni as such an abhorrent figure? Or has he simply exaggerated the degree to which he feels our environment makes neurotics of us all? An equally problematic scene, and one more central to the film's dramatic cogency, concerns the businessman's offer to Mastroianni's writer. One does not feel that this would be literature's loss; the viewer is left to question how the businessman could have any faith in Mastroianni.

During Moreau's excursion in the city early into the film, in which she breaks up a fight among some teenagers and then watches the lighting of fireworks, which so delights her that she calls Mastroianni and asks him to join her, Antonioni seems to strive for a burgeoning emotional impressionism. But since he has not made Mastroianni's writer a believable character, his attraction to Vitti's existentialist-on-the-prowl fails to evoke the despair of a failed marriage. Antonioni has led his audience to recognize a large part of city life as a new wilderness, full of inanimate terrors that have replaced the wild animals of primitive cultures. But for Antonioni to have Moreau read Mastroianni a few sentences from his own writings, which he is unable to identify, and then to show them falling into each other's arms as the camera tracks along the garden of the estate is not simply implausible, but dishonest. The romanticist in Antonioni momentarily denies the profoundly dehumanizing features of our society. He has sketched out the significant configurations of his canvas; now he must find the right characters and dramatic tone to expose the tragic paradoxes of postwar urban life.

*L'eclisse* makes that essential dramatic and stylistic leap. The note of alienation that haunted the romance of Vitti and Ferzetti and that dissipated the marriage of Moreau and Mastroianni becomes the film's most visible, and surprisingly vibrant theme. In the opening scene which transpires in the apartment of Vitti's boyfriend from whom she is separating, Antonioni uses a minimum of cuts as she walks around the room while her lover questions her decision. After ten minutes elapse, Antonioni uses his first establishing shot as Vitti looks across the room at her lover, who is seen as a receding figure amid the numerous possessions that fill the room. When she then draws the blinds, the most prominent object outside the apartment is a lone, vertical structure resembling a primitive obelisk as well as suggesting a phallic emblem of modern architecture. By restricting his drama to the city, Antonioni does not merely envision its abstract design and artifacts as visual correlatives of desperation, but as the very forms that determine the way individuals communicate and live. He is not, however, presenting a bleak picture of the transiency of human emotions and the intransiency of man-made landscapes. The streetlights that clatter in the wind as Vitti walks home are both frightening and beautiful—frightening in that their elongated form denotes the loneliness of this nocturnal setting and beautiful because they imbue this deserted area with an exquisite primitive sound. Antonioni develops the impression that as anonymous as we have become in our daily routines, there is much to delight the eye. As Vitti walks with her lover, played by Alain Delon, they pass a man; Vitti then turns and runs after him, remarking on his handsome features. The scenes that feature a nun wheeling a baby carriage and the cigarette in the water barrel are further examples of the sights that color and give meaning to everyday life. Antonioni draws one's attention to commonplace objects and actions, leaving us with a residue of their beauty and isolation, for example, the flight on the plane and the ensuing drink in the bar, one of several motifs from his earlier films that will undergo their most extreme fragmentation in *Zabriskie Point*.

Antonioni's paradox is most astutely realized in the stock-market sequence. In depicting its energy and cacophony, Antonioni takes a comic-tragic approach to the ultimately Byzantine world of finance. After the frenzy, Vitti follows a man, who having lost ten million lire, walks to a café, orders and finishes a drink, draws a bird on a napkin, and quietly leaves. The mood inevitably, is one of trepidation as Vitti acknowledges the desperation of a man who recklessly drives by and whose body is recovered the following morning with his hand sticking out of the car as if reaching for help. In the stunning final scene, Antonioni intercuts between several images spotted earlier by Vitti. With the final, conclusive image of the lamppost, which seems to duplicate the febrile intensity of the sun, Antonioni suggests that his characters are engaged in a losing battle to retain their individuality. It is one of the grimmest films ever made and all the more remarkable for his sensitivity to those ephemeral notes of light and lyricism that Vitti cherishes.

In *L'eclisse* Antonioni avoids the blank pessimism of *La notte* through a less didactic, invariably more tragic picture of how human relationships are eclipsed by the awesome design of modern cities. In *Red Desert* he attempts a simplified yet problematic picture of man's relationship to his environment. His canvas is not as cluttered as it was in the trilogy, while Vitti's neurosis stems from her dislocation amid the obscure sounds and disturbing visual outlines in her industrial town. Carlo Di Palma's colors are unusually evocative, from the washed out gray of the store Vitti hopes to open to the reddish brown tints that seem to hang suspended over the town. In one scene Vitti and her husband entertain two couples in a shack colored in bright red by the sea; a steamship passes, treated with the dimness of a dream image. Vitti is startled by what she says is a scream, but her declaration is supported by only one of the guests; Antonioni underlines the undetectable origins of the hidden, mysterious sights and sounds that result from the intrusion of model, anonymous new-world cities in barren, isolated settings. He is not making a film that indulges his schematic pictorial style; through Vitti's emotional incongruity, he discovers a miasma of fear and pain in her apprehension of the social anonymity of modern urban and rural planners.

Vitti's neurosis, however, lacks sufficient dramatic credibility. Her tense, jagged movements are like the vertiginous lines in a drawing by an abstract expressionist, but these lines never coalesce to explain her trauma. Her most deviant actions, for example, her asking to eat a laborer's half-eaten sandwich, fail to explain the demons with which she lives, while the other characters lack the slightest sensitivity to her predicament. One questions Richard Harris's failure to recognize Vitti's anxiety in his hotel room with its stark, antiseptic design. Antonioni seeks to create a parallel between his abstracted exteriors and interiors and the characters' behavior; his occasional jump cuts, like Vitti's precarious movements, are reactions to the implications of his design. But he dogmatically accepts the modernist's premise of the inexplicability of his symbols; it is this element of ambiguity that he will directly confront in *Blow-Up*.

Since his first films Antonioni has worked with his cinematographers and set designers to personify the motif of isolation as a dominant physical reality. In *La signora senza Camelie* the heroine's everyday studio backdrops are often superimposed against natural exteriors; Antonioni exaggerates the illusions practiced by the scene painter to suggest the encompassing nature of her identity as an actress. In his trilogy and in *Red Desert*, his protagonists discover that the designs of modern architects, painters, and decorators have transformed their homes and cities into abstract friezes. The action and dialogue embody these expressive, obtruding emblems of danger—the superannuation of human communication through the symbolic redefinition of cities and homes as artful fabrications with no supporting humanist imprint.

*Blow-Up* finds Di Palma translating Antonioni's flair for theatrically baroque backgrounds into the multicolored stages of David Hemmings's studio and into exterior compositions that, like *La signora senza Camelie*, show narrow streets and paths offering an escape into the background. Hemmings drives through London with stretches of buildings painted in a bright blue and red; these fanciful motifs provide an element of imaginative parody and colorful contemplation. In *Red Desert*, Antonioni leaves one with the impression that the autonomous color configurations have resulted in the neurotic behavior of Vitti's housewife. She is unable to relate to her role as wife, mother, or adulteress because whichever way she turns, Vitti, like a primitive traveling through an unexplored terrain, is frightened by its images and sounds; she lives in an abstract canvas, unable to accept its singular forms as mere decorations. In *Blow-Up* Antonioni correlates this theme of abstraction to the identity of David Hemmings's photographer and the relativity underlying the apparent objectivity of the film image. Hemmings interprets his craft in terms of its isolated imagery, from the model's simulation of desire to the distraught faces of the elderly that are to be featured in a book of his photographs. When he walks into an antique shop and buys a propeller, Antonioni deftly emphasizes how the film's seemingly random symbols, from the hippies in whiteface, who first identify the film's theme, to the propeller's dual identity as part of a plane or ship and as the mathematical sign of infinity, contribute to the irrevocably symbolic shadings of his protagonist's mod, carefree world. This motif is most profoundly developed as Hemmings blows up his pictures of the park and finds that what he thought was an innocent rendezvous was a cover for murder.

Hemmings's life is suddenly fraught with mystery. During lunch with his publisher, he sees a person looking at his car. He runs after the man but is unsuccessful in his pursuit; the viewer wonders whether the man was a car thief or was involved in the murder. After Hemmings returns to the park and finds the body, he spots Vanessa Redgrave, the mysterious woman involved in the murder. Hemmings loses her, stumbles into a loft, and, like the other crazed fans attending the rock concert, makes a mad rush for the broken guitar; out in the street, he cannot understand why he wanted it. His cool, indolent manner has begun to erode. He arrives at a party and asks one of his models why she has delayed her trip to Paris; she—high on pot—responds that she is in Paris, a natural expression of the frivolous behavior of London's hip underworld.

Hemmings returns to his studio and finds all the photographs except one are missing; when he shows it to a neighbor, played by Sarah Miles, she can make no sense of it. Like her boyfriend's pointillist painting which fascinated Hemmings, the photograph is made up of many little dots, which suggest various forms but cannot be definitely interpreted to represent any one object. The subjectivity underlying modernism becomes the film's pervasive motif both through Hemmings's inability to prove the murder with his photographs and through the fantasy-ridden nature of London's hippie subculture. Antonioni crystallizes this theme in the final scene as Hemmings returns to the park and encounters the mimes in whiteface. They simulate a game of tennis without the physical accoutrements of a racket or a ball. When they first begin their pantomime, there is a slight surface grating on the sound track; after Hemmings retrieves their imaginary ball, and with the camera facing Hemmings, their tennis game is clearly audible on the sound track. Just as Hemmings had asked his publisher to conclude his book, containing harrowing photographs of poverty, with the tranquillity of his park scenes, the moody, murky nature of Hemmings's voyage of self-discovery ends with a high-angle shot of Hemmings's isolation and a quixotic dissolve marking the end and Hemmings's invisibility. Antonioni has refuted the viability of Hemmings's attempt to prove or objectify the murder while equating the tenuousness that surrounds Hemmings's adventure with the filmgoer's belief in the objectivity of the film image. He has taken a minor, pretentious story about self-negation and has created a perfect parable about the elusiveness of truth either as a form of self-assertion or artistic interpretation. The aesthetics and metaphysics of *Blow-Up* are masterly intertwined, revealing the subjective nature of truth through the subjectivity underlying the aesthetic realism of the cinema.

From *Story of a Love Affair* through *Red Desert* Antonioni has recorded the increasing abstraction of his postwar Italian landscapes. In *Zabriskie Point* the vast, open spaces of the American Southwest offer yet another distinct background, but one that proves less evocative than those in any of his previous films. A comparison between a sequence from *L'avventura* and a strikingly similar one from *Zabriskie Point* exemplifies the fatalistic nature of Antonioni's pursuit of the individual in America.

In *L'avventura* Monica Vitti and Gabriele Ferzetti arrive in a small town; while he inquires about Lea Massari's whereabouts, Vitti is left alone in the deserted town square. A group of men appear and begin to encircle her; the camera slowly draws back, showing her surrounded by some twenty men. Antonioni poetically suggests the uncertainty that marks the voyage of self-discovery of Vitti and Ferzetti; within a quasi-realist framework, he strikes a note of psychological terror. In *Zabriskie Point* Daria, traveling in the desert, meets a group of children and asks if they know the whereabouts of their school director. They suround Daria and threaten her, but she escapes unharmed. The scene, however, fails to clarify any aspect of Daria's or Mark's trek along the desert; after their lovemaking at Zabriskie Point, during which Daria fantasizes about a troupe of hippies engaged in playful, primitive intercourse, the film becomes an extension of their fantasies about freedom and revolution, culminating in Mark's return in the brightly repainted airplane and Daria's vision of America's consumer icons exploding in the desert.

Antonioni remains an intuitive film painter, and though the desert sequences become tedious celebrations of his hippie anti-heroes, many of the compositions, for example, Mark's flight over the mazelike highways of Los Angeles, fulfill Antonioni's original work in the Italian cinema in distinguishing the physical forms and symbols endemic to a culture and period of history. Rod Taylor's executive office, with its television monitors and imposing three-dimensional backgrounds, is one masterly example of how the expressive bric-a-brac of Antonioni's Italian bourgeoisie has become the dominant emblem of his American interiors. However, Antonioni regresses to a drawback common to many wide-screen film artists: several of his compositions, especially in the first part in Los Angeles, use the Panavision lens in a doctrinaire manner. Antonioni seems to purposely accentuate the fuzziness in background images through his penchant for tight, close-up camera angles; the baroque gradations of his Italian films have led to the foreground fragmentations of *Zabriskie Point* through his simplistic use of the zoom lens on billboards and neon-lit stores. His increasingly tenuous treatment of social alienation and fantasy finds him empathizing with his folk heroes while obscuring Mark's involvement in the shooting of the policeman or Daria's affair with Rod Taylor. The last primitive image to which he turns, that of the sunset, underscores the lack of tension in his treatment of the counterculture. In *Blow-Up* David Hemmings's acceptance of the illusory premise of the mimes is a shattering symbol of self-negation; in *Zabriskie Point* Antonioni simply asks us to accept the frivolous verities of hippiedom.

*The Passenger*, though a more craftsmanlike work, marks a more precipitous decline. In his story of a journalist who assumes the identity of a gunrunner, Antonioni seems tentative in exploring its numerous parallels to classic literary themes. If the film is to embody a variation on the motif of the double, one needs to know more about Jack Nicholson's previous life as a journalist and about that of the gunrunner; in Nicholson's affair with Maria Schneider, there is a nagging, unexplored allusion to the story of Odysseus and Circe as Schneider asks him to give up his dual identity. Antonioni is obviously uncomfortable with the script's overladen symbolism, and Nicholson, one of the few individual stylists of nonconformity to appear in the American cinema over the last twenty years, is indecisive in his newfound identity as a smuggler. Adding to the apparent incongruity between Antonioni's opaque style and the overt symbolism of Peter Woolen's script lies the impression that Antonioni seems removed from the singular paradoxes of romance and revolution in the seventies. Along with Yasujiro Ozu and Jean-Luc Godard, he has made the modern cinema a dramatic, intellectual extension of the silent and early sound film. That his style suddenly appears wooden and anachronistic does not so much reflect the loss of his powers as a director, but how our understanding of art and society have moved beyond the realities that Antonioni made so very clear and meaningful only a few years ago.

## The Italian Cinema

The Italian humanist cinema of Rossellini, De Sica, and Visconti exists as a landmark period in the history of the cinema; it also nourished the sensibilities of Fellini and Antonioni in leading to the more introspective, metaphysical style of the sixties. Its meaning, however, is not restricted to these celebrated figures, but is as visible in the aggressive journalism of Francesco Rosi as it is in the rousing primitive dialectic of *Padre, Padrone*. Although a producer like Dino De Laurentiis, a star like Vittorio Gassman, and a perverse subgenre like the spaghetti western are evidence of the diverse social and cultural forces that have contributed to the popularity of the postwar Italian cinema of the sixties and seventies, its unique intensity derives from the rigorous humanist themes of its founders. A case has been made for the early, silent Italian epics as the precursor of, if not superior to, Griffith's first major efforts; on the evidence of *Assunta spina*, *Cabiria*, and *Quo Vadis?*, this does not seem to be a valid argument. They are ornate melodramas, suggesting that one of the most enduring traits of the Italian cinema has been its pictorial legacy, first celebrated in the lavish though static interiors of its silent epics and renewed in the sensual, empty-headed muscle and macho fantasies of ancient Rome and the American West. Alessandro Blasetti, a key figure in the Italian cinema of the thirties, makes a valid, heroic use of the moving camera and natural exteriors in *1860* and *Terra madre*. Yet we need to see more of his work and that of his contemporaries to more fully understand the evolution of Rossellini, De Sica, and Visconti. There is a rich comic legacy to be savored in the films of Fellini, Pietro Germi, Dino Risi, Marco Ferreri, Ettore Scola, and Lina Wertmuller, and in the caricatures of Vittorio Gassman, Alberto Sordi, Sophia Loren, Marcello Mastroianni, Giancarlo Giannini, Ugo Tognazzi, Stefanià Sandrelli, Mariangela Melato, and Laura Antonelli; but their most incisive parodies draw on the protagonists and backgrounds in the films of Rossellini, De Sica, and Visconti.

Of the four Mauro Bolognini films I have seen, their handsome varnish seems most reminiscent of Visconti. Unlike Visconti, however, whose epics are infused with a transcendent note of ritual, Bolognini is a passive observer of social mores. There are several impressive long shots of the town square in *La viaccia* and of the country estate in *Il bell'Antonio*, but for the most part the films come alive in the decorative interiors of the whorehouse in *La viaccia* and in the home of Mastroianni's parents in *Il bell'Antonio*. Bolognini rarely separates his characters from their surroundings; the medium-shot range unravels their dilemma in the context of their sensual backgrounds. His films lack the romantic intensity of Visconti's epics or the chemistry of period detail and personal discords in some of Hollywood's more stirring melodramas. In *La giornata balorda* Bolognini's literalism in adapting Moravia's and Pasolini's story about twenty-four hours in the life of Jean Sorel's street urchin develops as a wry commentary on Sorel's pursuit of love and money. Sorel is surprisingly moving in a role that recalls James Dean; the difference between Dean and such similar European actors as Sorel and Alain Delon is that Sorel does not evoke Dean's psychological traumas while Delon is more of a gritty Machiavellian. In *La giornata balorda* Sorel's remorseless panhandler does not feel that he deceives his sweetheart by pursuing other women. His lack of chagrin is stylishly reflected in Bolognini's simple, almost transparent direction. In *Agostino* Bolognini's directorial restraint admirably articulates the boy's exploration of his dependence on his mother. But the style seems bland in comparison to Visconti's *Sandra*; it is too civilized, too detached, as if the boy were looking back at his adolescence and was not experiencing it firsthand.

Elio Petri is a more schematic director whose florid design and baroque camerawork embody a mood of fear and violence. In *The Tenth Victim*, he scores many direct hits on murder as the primary entertainment spectacle of the future. The film is particularly adept in its gaudy pop-art design and with the deadpan humor of Marcello Mastroianni and Ursula Andress as they try to kill each other. But it is a callous satire, debunking the popularity of the spy genre in a facile manner. In *Investigation of a Citizen above Suspicion*, Petri's feverishly energetic tracking shots reflect the crazed, psychotic mentality of Gian Maria Volonté's police superintendent. Volonté is a bravura actor who brings an aura of fanaticism to whatever role he plays: the crazed desperado in *For a Few Dollars More*, the malevolent Lucky Luciano, or the wily financier of *The Mattei Affair*. The problem with his characterization in *Investigation of a Citizen above Suspicion* is that there is little nuance to his role; his psychopathic nature is evident from the start, leaving little to be discovered about his character in his confrontations with his mistress and the leftist demonstrators. It is *verismo* cinema whose appeal is encompassed by Volonté's two-dimensional portrayal of police dementia.

Among the directors discussed in this chapter, the strongest case can be made for Francesco Rosi as worthy of consideration as a major artist. His position in the Italian cinema is similar to that of Claude Charbol in France in that his acutely melodramatic themes seem removed from the more modernist treatments of his contemporaries. *Salvatore Giuliano* shows a quasi-journalistic style, which is less prominently featured in *Hands Over the City*, *The Mattei Affair*, and *Illustrious Corpses*. It is by far the best of these films and appears to have been overlooked by film historians because of its ill-fated premiere at a time when Fellini and Antonioni changed the direction of the contemporary cinema from its centrifugal social structure to the centripetal themes of abstraction and alienation. Like the earlier works of Fellini and Antonioni, his films are a clear, lineal descendent of the Italian humanist cinema. The film medium is used for its documentarylike effects in exploring the historical antecedents of the Mafia, the etiolated social structure of Sicily, and Giuliano's singular identity as outcast and hero. Rosi's aggressive camerawork blends elements of reportage and poetry; the Mafia is defined in both a historical context and as a classic example of the dramatic villain, while Giuliano becomes the archetypal fighter of reform and justice. *Hands Over the City* is a more expressionistic stylization. However, an incongruity arises between Rosi's refractory image of nameless civil servants meeting to fill their pockets and the harsh immediacy of urban decay: the sensitive journalist in Rosi appears at odds with the modernist. But the explosive scene centered on the debate at city hall is one of the most exciting expressions of fiction as history in the making. Not since the sequences in the assembly in Gance's *Napoleon* does one find such strong evidence for the medium's ability to capture the intensity and paradoxes of an erupting social controversy without seeming affected or contrived. His camera swings back and forth from the furious debates and the reaction of the public to the brief, furtive glances which are more likely to determine the course of history.

The *Mattei Affair* and *Illustrious Corpses* are less conclusive films. Several scenes in *The Mattei Affair* depict an arresting element of heroism in Volonté's maverick industrialist's probing of the frontier of modern technology and the Third World. But the information regarding Volonté's rise and sudden, mysterious death, drawn as it is from the tabloids, is sketchy: Rosi has failed to explain Volonté's motivation for his surreptitious alliances. *Illustrious Corpses* is Rosi's most devious attempt to expose a social cancer, that of political assassination. Lino Ventura's police detective, however, does not bring any particular outlook to solving the murders. Rosi's treatment is inherently baroque, but his distancing camera angles do not enhance our appreciation of corruption; he has gravitated to the style of Petri's *Investigation of a Citizen above Suspicion* without delineating the neurotic underpinnings of police work.

Some of Rosi's other films are also marred by his indecisive, eclectic viewpoint. *La sfida* is notable for the extraordinary sensuality of Rosanna Schiaffino as she seems to glide on the roof of her apartment when confronting her husband about their failing marriage. One is sure Visconti would have praised and might have learned something from Rosi's handling of Schiaffino, but her husband's fight against the criminals involved in Naples's fruit and vegetable market is treated in a perfunctory manner. *Uomini contro* is a costume drama wholly incongruous to Rosi's style, but *The Moment of Truth* remains, some fifteen years after its premiere, one of the jewels of poetic narrative in the movies. By adopting a distant point of view toward his protagonist, Rosi transcends the quaintness of his tale of an illiterate country boy who becomes a national hero as a bullfighter only to die when he reaches the top. The simplicity of his story and his precise visual parallels, like the hero's early encounter with a prostitute and his later seduction by an attractive aristocrat, possess the harmony and inevitability of classic storytelling.

Of the three major humanist directors of the forties and early fifties, Vittorio De Sica, whose passionate social voice was the most traditional and whose relevance seemed the most secure, suffered the most severe decline. His involvement in several films advertised as comedies can be passed over, but his last two efforts, *The Garden of the Finzi-Continis* and *A Brief Vacation*, are noteworthy in evaluating his filmography. *The Garden of the Finzi-Continis* is a mawkish addition to films concerning the Holocaust; De Sica's affected lyricism functions as a hackneyed metaphor for the aristocratic manners and moral apathy of the Finzi-Continis. The romantic interlude is as poorly sketched out as in any number of tedious films of adolescent love, except that his story purports to concern the decline of civilization. Dominique Sanda's sensuality has withstood the test of several bad films; in De Sica's film, she is the only living presence.

*A Brief Vacation* is a pleasant surprise, though a minor one. What is most striking about the film is not the melodramatic nature of the story about a poor, ailing woman and her recovery and romance at a sanitarium, but De Sica's limpid direction of the woman's suddenly awakened romantic impulse. Florinda Bolkan is a majestic, regal figure who does not appear miscast in De Sica's stylish soap opera. Rather than abbreviating her romanticism into a ponderous tract about the failure of love among the poor, De Sica explicitly draws out her stay at the clinic as a dream come true, of love once realized in the most alien surroundings. It may not be the film for which De Sica wanted to be remembered, but it has a delicacy and dramatic vibrancy that De Sica could have utilized in future works.

Whereas recent French comedies are charged by a traditional romantic flavor, the films of Dino Risi, Marco Ferreri, and Ettore Scola show the imprint of Italy's humanist directors. Risi's *The Easy Life* is a social satire that takes an ambivalent attitude to the buffoonery and energy of its star, Vittorio Gassman. Some of Gassman's other films with Risi are straightforward farces, in which Gassman exploits his mimetic talent in poking fun at the stiff mannerisms of the middle class. The films are largely a tour de force by Gassman, who like a well-to-do tramp upsets the tedium of everyday society; he has some of the manic charm of the silent-film tramps but is less ethereal in his desires. In *The Easy Life* Gassman's education of the young innocent played by Jean-Louis Trintignant does not emphasize the raucous antics in Risi's other films with Gassman. At first, Gassman's callous behavior is amusing, but he is then seen as a villainous rake, a crude hipster who seduces Trintignant's aunt. We laugh at his pranks but are left with a feeling of unease because there is no truly heroic side to his outlandishness. Gassman has soured on society, but not to the degree that his chagrin denotes its amorality. Trintignant's death then appears as a superfluous, didactic touch, as if to reprove the viewer for enjoying Gassman's cleverness. In their most recent collaboration, *Scent of a Woman*, Gassman's ingenuity lacks the sparkle of his earlier film misdeeds; the revelation that, because of his blindness, he plans a double suicide with a friend seems incongruous to his sardonic nature.

Marco Ferreri directed Ugo Tognazzi in several films that recall the rustic spirit of Fellini's *Variety Lights* and *The White Sheik* with mixed results. *The Conjugal Bed* is perhaps the best of these. Tognazzi restrains his desire to make love to his fiancée, entertaining her family of dullards and dimwits only to be overcome by her insatiable appetite for lovemaking once they are married. The film is reminiscent of Billy Wilder's brittle comedies, but Ferreri's sensitivity to Tognazzi's predicament avoids the self-conscious note of ridicule in Wilder's humor. *The Ape Woman* is a more questionable work. Tognazzi plays a huckster who discovers a bearded woman, played by Annie Girardot, living in a convent. He becomes her guardian and markets her alienated condition in various enterprises. She forces him to marry her and in the original script, was to have died from an abortion. In the film, she loses her facial hair while Tognazzi struggles as a laborer with Girardot as his pretty, faithful wife. There are several wickedly funny moments, for example, the striptease and the scene in which Girardot demands that Tognazzi make love to her. But, like Wilder, Ferreri proves very clever in humiliating his characters without exploring the truly pathetic nature of their self-degradation. Had he spent more time juxtaposing Girardot's emotionalism with Tognazzi's con man, the quaintly middle-class overtures of the ending would have worked. Ferreri's compromise is not in shelving his original ending, but in the treatment of his outcasts.

Ettore Scola works with a more devious canvas than either Risi or Ferreri. Unlike the amorphous, middle-class backgrounds surrounding the characterizations of Gassman and Tognazzi, Giancarlo Giannini and Marcello Mastroianni in *The Pizza Triangle*, and the three male friends of *We All Loved Each Other So Much* are working-class figures whose comic entanglements arise from their impoverished condition. In *The Pizza Triangle* Mastroianni's obese wife leads him to Monica Vitti's punkish character, but she then turns to Giannini's more romantic laborer. Some of Scola's effects are mannered, for example, in his florid treatment of their encounters in the amusement park or in the market sequences; they lack the more hyperbolic operatic overtones of Wertmuller's *The Seduction of Mimi*. But he conveys an infectious buoyancy in depicting Mastroianni's increasingly neurotic behavior and the reckless lovemaking of Vitti and Giannini. *We All Loved Each Other So Much* is a more ambitious film; the three friends who become lovers of Stefanià Sandrelli reflect different sides of a working-class mentality. Nino Manfredi remains the unsophisticated proletarian, fated to a life as a latrine attendant in a hospital; Stefano Satta Flores becomes a film critic, enacting scenes from famous movies only to be fooled by an ambiguously worded question about De Sica's *The Bicycle Thief* on a game show; Vittorio Gassman marries into money, but his life is found wanting as he fails to respond to his wife's loneliness. The style is more eclectic than *The Pizza Triangle*, but for all of its slapstick reminiscences and the energy of its performers, the film lacks a point of view. Sandrelli evinces a poignant humanism in trying to satisfy her three admirers, but she achieves a far greater comic and erotic resonance with her hallucinatory cries of sexual liberation in *Alfredo Alfredo*.

The humanism of the Italian cinema has undergone numerous tests and transformations. One anxiously awaits to learn if the treacherous lower-class characterizations of Lina Wertmuller and Giancarlo Giannini are the final products of the classical heritage of Italian filmmakers or if the remarkable poetic grace of *The Meadow* by the Taviani brothers signals its rebirth.

# 23
## Three Independents

### Luis Buñuel

Luis Buñuel's filmography is an uneven, often daring example of the pertinence of surrealism in twentieth-century art. In his first film shorts he uses the extremely fast editing favored by the French avant-garde to attack conventional behavior and the visual and cognitive keys on which we rely to make sense of the everyday world. The images in *An Andalusian Dog* and *L'Age d'Or* reverberate with the tension between the literal and the symbolic; their cumulative effect is that of a populace storming a palace, in which the arsenal of the artist's inner consciousness replaces the standard weapons of the downtrodden. Surrealism is a subjective, frequently didactic modern style. The relevance, however, of *An Andalusian Dog* and *L'Age d'Or* does not lie in their heavy-handed symbolism, but in their visually aggressive punctuation. Buñuel's work in the Mexican and Spanish film industry shows a further exploration of the basic tenets of surrealism as he balances a wry, mocking point of view with the anguish of the expressionist writers and painters of the nineteenth century. Yet his two greatest films of this period, *Los olvidados* and *Viridiana*, make only subliminal references to the surrealism of his earliest projects in depicting a desolate countryside and the characters' erotic immaturity. In *Los olvidados* the surrealist ethic is most visible in the dream sequence and in the gross behavior of the blind beggar. It is a film that suggests the dramatic limitations of surrealism in that Buñuel's moral pessimism derives from the unrelenting psychological realism of his study of a youth at bay. In *Viridiana* Fernando Rey's deviously inspired suicide shows the sly touch of the ironist who, in distancing his feelings toward his players, creates a more engrossing, tragic mood. It is a profound study of the loss of faith, whose impact stems from the clarity with which Buñuel depicts the folly of Viridiana's altruistic venture.

Though many of his Mexican and Spanish films are encumbered by the raw quality of his backgrounds and scripts, they are invariably characterized by Buñuel's blending of realism and surrealism. In *The Illusion Travels by Streetcar*, the anonymous collection of ecclesiastics, laborers, and businessmen is transformed into a cartoonlike travesty of Mexican society. Buñuel undercuts the skeletal nature of his story by his pointed ridicule of the characters' absurdist mannerisms, as in the bus sequence with the carcass that is hung on the strap, the collection undertaken by the nuns, and the businessmen's aloofness. His more personal films—*The Criminal Life of Archibaldo de la Cruz* and *El*—are marred by tentative characterizations and awkward transitions, but there are many shrewd insights into his confused aristocrats and their erotic misadventures. *The River and Death* is less typical of Buñuel; the tale of murder and revenge between two families is treated in a straightforward manner. By refusing to inject this study of machismo with the satiric tone in his other Mexican films, Buñuel approaches the confrontation between the two feuding families in the impassive manner of an ethnologist who refuses to impose a theme or structure foreign to the story. Several scenes, especially those involving the protagonist's futility in explaining to his mother the inconsequentiality of the killings, suggest the inherent absurdity surrounding the adherence to a primitive cycle of revenge. The film lacks the subtlety of *Viridiana* or the tragic inevitability of *Los olvidados*, but as a study of Mexican folklore it is not without its corollaries in other countries. *Death in the Garden* is one of Buñuel's more highly regarded works. But the oblique touches used in his other films of this period are missing in this story about an escape from a tyrannical government. He is not concerned with low-life figures or sexually innocent aristocrats, but with a more complex mixture of social and personal discontent; the survivors' trek through the jungle, however, uneasily veers to allegory, wherein he tries to incorporate the moralism of *Robinsón Crusoe* into an inherently incongruous dramatic setting.

In two of Buñuel's last black-and-white films, *The Exterminating Angel* and *Diary of a Chambermaid*, the surrealist touches are more pronounced than they are in the ribald humor of his other Mexican productions. They do not emphasize the violence or the vigorous assault on our conception of the everyday world in the manner of *An Andalusian Dog* or *L'Age d'Or*. Buñuel chooses instead to confuse us like a father who freely improvises in reading a fable to his children. But these distancing elements only underscore the disdain of the surrealist, as in the opening scene of *The Exterminating Angel*, in which the servants announce their departure, and which is repeated after the arrival of the guests. Several questions are purposely unresolved. For example, why does he cut off this scene with the entrance of guests? Why does he choose to replay only this scene? The answer, I suggest, lies in the basic premise of surrealism: that an irrational image or action can be introduced at any moment, without any justification. Buñuel's elliptical variations in the dialogue between the guests, particularly in the relationship involving the homosexual and the character with the least sympathetic attitude toward him who uses the homosexual's electric shaver to remove his leg hairs, underline the stasis common to both *The Exterminating Angel* and surrealism. Buñuel's more rhetorical images force one to question the degree to which his offbeat situations elucidate the conventions and conundrums of social gatherings. One concludes the surrealist artist—when he is not engaged in a prolonged joke on the viewer's need for a logical story—is satisfied with a vague attack on social mores.

Like *The Exterminating Angel*, the action in *Diary of a Chambermaid* is resolved by the actions of an ambivalent female character, that of Jeanne Moreau's chambermaid. Though she is a more paradoxical figure than Silvia Pinal's virago in *The Exterminating Angel*, her role is obscured by the standard Buñuel miscreants, from the foot fetishist to the violent groundkeeper. Moreau shows a genuine affection for the little girl who is attacked, while also conveying qualities of both imperviousness and anonymous acquiescence. But Buñuel fails to explore the possible effect of her character in the manner of Paulette Goddard's naïf in Renoir's adaptation of the Mirbeau novel. He combines elements of Marxist social commentary and Freudian unrest in exposing the gentry's fascistic social order and its underlying erotic neurosis. Buñuel sustains this ambiguity with Moreau's marriage to the elderly neighbor, but it seems an extraneous epilogue with its implications of the obliquities of social justice and personal behavior. The film closes with a coda, three jump cuts on a military parade, followed by a shot of the clouds. Since it does not refer to an earlier stylistic nuance, the ending only serves to remind the audience that Buñuel is the sole architect of the fiction it has witnessed.

In *Belle de jour* and *Tristana* Buñuel creates a more elaborate setting to reveal the social permanence of surrealism. There are several motifs in *Belle de jour*, however, that detract from the film's psychological acuity, most critically in that Buñuel allows the viewer to interpret the film either as Catherine Deneuve's fantasy or that of her husband played by Jean Sorel. But Buñuel's fascination with the subconscious shows the dreamlike intruding into his characters' lives with a deft irony. The first sequence, in which Sorel orders the coachman to rape Deneuve and then shows her awakening, suggests that the film will serve as an exploration of Deneuve's fantasies and sexual maturity. Early in the film, Deneuve's childhood is twice recalled: first, her being pawed by an elderly man and second, her receiving communion during a church service. The one solipsistic scene has Sorel and Michel Piccoli eating soup in a field and throwing dung at Deneuve who is tied to a tree.

During Deneuve's activities as a prostitute, Buñuel explores her incipient independence and sexual satisfaction. She becomes attracted to a petty hoodlum, who shoots Sorel and who is later killed by the police. Had the film, then, ended with Deneuve tending her ailing husband, it would have depicted the irresolvable tension between an adherence to socially acceptable behavior and the need to gratify our antisocial, erotic instincts. In the final scene, however, Sorel, who has been informed of Deneuve's dual life, rises out of his wheelchair. Deneuve tells him that since his accident she no longer dreams, as the coach from the opening scene passes in front of their home. Buñuel now intimates that the film can be interpreted as Sorel's reverie—that he has fantasized about his wife as a prostitute to compensate for their frigid lovemaking. Such touches as Sorel's wheelchair being the same one which had intrigued him prior to his being wounded by the gangster, create a coherent thread of ambiguity about the film, hinting at the endless similarities between reality and our dreams. Beneath the genteel, civilized facade of his characters' comfortable middle-class existence there exists a mysterious dreamworld that, as Buñuel cleverly shows, obtrudes directly into their most innocent routines.

In *Tristana* Buñuel adds to his own and other studies of Deneuve's romantic mask, a bewitching combination of virago and siren. It is not as whimsical as *Belle de jour*, its tone more disquieting in observing the relationship of Fernando Rey and Deneuve, who plays Rey's ward. The film's surrealist impact does not derive from its few disconnected images of subconscious terror, but from Buñuel's reticence in explaining the initial attraction and subsequent marriage of Rey and Deneuve. Paradox is paramount, for example, in the scene where Deneuve discusses the differences in each pea with her maid. Her decision to eat one parallels her asking the maid which street they should follow, as the one she does take leads to her affair with Franco Nero's painter. Buñuel seems to say that if we try to grasp the reasons underlying our motivation, we will discover the absence of logic or reason.

The film's most severe shortcoming lies in Buñuel's unwillingness to clarify Deneuve's feelings for Rey. She is neither a fallen maiden nor a seducing virgin, while her refusal to marry Nero's virile painter suggests that she has been tragically marked by her relationship to Rey. There are several amusing moments depicting Rey's quixotic behavior and one breathtaking scene in which Deneuve motions a deaf-mute boy to stand outside her window while she disrobes. But the film lacks the understated terror of *Viridiana*'s loss of faith; Buñuel chooses to conceive their relationship as impenetrable, one in which the viewer only receives the slightest clues as to the neurosis that binds them together. He has entered the baroque world of love and sexual dependence, but because of the surrealist's reverence for enigma, he refuses to unlock the door to their ambiguous, lifelong affair.

In his more recent collaborations with scriptwriter Jean-Claude Carrière, Buñuel seems equally removed from the revolutionary poetics of *An Andalusian Dog* and from the impassioned social rhetoric of *Los olvidados*. Carrière's *The Discreet Charm of the Bourgeoisie* and *That Obscure Object of Desire* recall the devious parodies of *El* and *Simon of the Desert*. In the earlier works Buñuel joked about man's innocence in sexual matters and lambasted the duplicity of religious beliefs. What is most surprising, however, about the disdainful, theatrical facade of *The Discreet Charm of the Bourgeoisie* and the elliptical moral twists of *That Obscure Object of Desire* is the softening of Buñuel's surrealism. Buñuel assumes the stance of an eighteenth-century classicist who in ridiculing our naiveté is more interested in challenging the audience's grasp of reality than that of his characters. Carrière combines the sardonic exegesis of *The Milky Way* with the more elusive psychological twists of *Belle de jour*, yet the film is betrayed by Buñuel's training and commitment to the surrealist riddle. He shows little patience in developing any gag or theme with the result that his actors' broad self-mockery diffuses the film's literacy; instead of emphasizing the alienating nature of their adventures or their intrinsically idiosyncratic behavior, he suddenly, inconclusively terminates the story. The film is not as heavy-handed as *The Exterminating Angel* or as opaque as *The Milky Way*, but his cosmic voyagers are too removed from our world to invite the multilevel comedy of manners with which Carrière and Buñuel flirt. Although Buñuel seems naturally sympathetic to the numerous twists and paradoxes of this hoary theatrical genre, he is unwilling to compromise the surrealist's enduring belief in irrationality. The enlightened moralists of the theater also recognized the decisive interplay of reality and illusion, but they showed more patience and dexterity in exploiting man's frivolous nature.

*That Obscure Object of Desire* is similar to *Tristana* but proves a less satisfying work. *Tristana* holds one's interest owing to Buñuel's cool, understated handling of the neurotic relationship of Rey and Deneuve. In *That Obscure Object of Desire*, however, the antipodal features and feelings of the two actresses playing the part of Rey's love object are treated in a blithe manner. One seems aristocratic and ethereal, the other coarse and sensual, but Rey's erotic debasement fails to clarify the paradoxical nature of his attraction. He simply appears as a hopelessly confused protagonist whose erotic appetite is crudely, inexplicably transformed into masochism. The references to the terrorist group can only whet the appetite of the filmgoer who believes that the movies should not enlighten us, while the backgrounds never come alive as a reflection either of Rey's neurosis or of Buñuel's impression of the real world as fantasy.

In his first films Buñuel attacked the visual conventions underlying the film experience with a refreshing sense of outrage; in *That Obscure Object of Desire* he dogmatically revives the surrealist conceit that the world is a sham. His career has never been without interest, but because of his allegiance to surrealism his pessimism and dramatic irony, which have made for many fine films, have suffered from the elusive, illusory spirit of surrealism. The surrealistic shadings of *Los olvidados*, *Viridiana*, *Simon of the Desert*, *Belle de jour*, and *Tristana* enrich their psychological proximity; because of the more substantial surrealistic textures of *The Discreet Charm of the Bourgeoisie* and *That Obscure Object of Desire*, Buñuel's wit and despair are marked by the very quality surrealism initially attacked: the blandness of the artistic conceit.

## Orson Welles

From *Citizen Kane* through *F for Fake*, Orson Welles's career has been surrounded by—if not engulfed in—controversy. But regardless of the documentation of his supporters and critics, the films remain the primary evidence. His first efforts, *Citizen Kane* and *The Magnificent Ambersons*, are among the most evanescent works in film history. *Citizen Kane* is a magnificent feast for the eyes and ears and mind, charged with the lightning bolt of inspiration and insouciance of a young artist fresh from victories in other art forms; *The Magnificent Ambersons* is a response to the outrageous inventiveness of the preceding film. It is a graceful, masterly work, imbued with the authority and asceticism with which the Ambersons isolate themselves from society. The startling differences in the two films—in subject matter, tone, and dramatic cogency—originate in the antinomy Welles discovers in America's past. He shows himself equally sympathetic to the destiny of the Ambersons, to Joseph Cotten's inventor, and to Kane's empire builder. Although *The Magnificent Ambersons* is marred by an incongruous ending, the shimmering solemnity of its patrician interiors and the grandeur and decline of its aristocratic progatonists are captured with an objectivity that reflects their magnificence while acknowledging their impermanence.

Welles's mysteries—*The Lady from Shanghai*, *The Stranger*, *Mr. Arkadin*, *Touch of Evil*—provide some of the most breathtaking examples of film expressionism. Their familiar melodramatic themes of danger and deceit are punctuated by a stylistic perference for wide-angle-lens and floor shots, and by a general presentation of space and time as irrevocably altered by the vagaries of personal victimization. If the art of the German silent film resonates a style of subconscious self-destruction, Welles reenters its murky terrain like a mythic warrior with far greater confidence about his destiny within its expressionist maze. *The Lady from Shanghai* is the most abstracted of these films, wherein his creepy settings and poisonous character relationships seem appropriately resolved in the hall of mirrors. He has bewitched us with his freak show, with his theatrical sense of trompe l'oeil: the trick has been executed with flair, even though we recognize the transparency of the hoax. In *Touch of Evil* Welles's raucous, dazzling camera angles present a fatalistic picture of Charlton Heston's pursuit of justice. In changing his setting from the vacation resort of *The Lady from Shanghai* to a Mexican border town, the grim social environment serves as a defense of Hank Quinlan's murderous maverick of a police inspector. The mischievous excitement of these films suggests that despite his difficulties with producers, Welles was unwilling to reembrace the epic, heroic scope of his earliest achievements. Chaplin's tramp survives some forty years until his death in *Limelight*; in Welles's very first film, however, his admiration and identification with Kane lead to his demise.

In the past two decades Welles has returned to a more humanistic, historical framework in *The Trial*, *Falstaff*, *The Immortal Story*, and *F for Fake*. Welles's adaptation of *The Trial* is the most interesting of these four films. One glaring weakness in this and in his other recent works is a cavalier attitude in casting; his years of playing legendary tyrants and mystics with equal strains of playfulness and braggadocio seem to have carried over in the characterizations in his own films. Anthony Perkins is miscast, Welles is embarrassing as the prosecutor, and Akim Tamiroff and Elsa Martinelli act their roles as if *The Trial* were a spoof. It is on this account that Welles's credibility as an artist is most suspect; yet with all of its playful excesses in acting and design, *The Trial* is not without merit. Welles transcribes Kafka's hallucinatory prose through his nervy, fast cuts and the isolated, alienating backgrounds, showing Joseph K. as trapped in a spider's web. The film is much nastier than the novel in that Welles's liberties with Kafka create a more self-conscious showcase of terror. Some of the effects in the courtroom exaggerate Kafka's immersion in a disjointed universe; the film lacks a focus other than its racing through the novel's most frightening images of paranoia. Welles is unable to establish a unifying theme to make sense of the excesses and irreverence in the style of *Citizen Kane*; it has some of the energy of his first film, but its explosive theatricality becomes mannered, redundant.

*Falstaff* has much less to recommend it. The beginning is marred by Welles's reliance on sharp, dynamic cuts that disrupt Gielgud's speeches as the ailing king; they are altogether incongruous to the rich, baroque tapestry of the language and period, creating an unduly precarious atmosphere. The tavern sequence with Welles's Falstaff fails to enliven either Shakespeare's wit or the profound break that is about to ensue between Hal and Falstaff. Unlike the excessive rhythms in the first scenes, it is sluggishly played, with Welles's Falstaff as the dominant foreground image and the wenches and jolly boys in the background. Welles shows some sensitivity in highlighting the ritualistic elements of medieval society, augmenting the musical and plastic features of court life; the extreme close-up camera range during the battle creates a moving, truncated Gothic image of pain and terror juxtaposed to the comic picture of Falstaff trapped in his armor.

*The Immortal Story*, a short telefilm, has many splendid images, especially in Welles's impressionistic picture of the town square where the viewer seems to be inside a canvas. Welles counterpoises the bulk and torpor of his aged, arthritic recluse with the sensual, musty elegance of his estate while the lovemaking of the sailor and prostitute explodes across the screen in a flurry of translucent colors and briefly remembered objects. Yet these touches are fleeting memories whose redolence is only briefly experienced and which is further undercut by a muted sound track and the absence of a telling romantic vibrancy in the performances. The film's shortcomings are typical of his most recent films, as if his pictorial conception of Dinesen's story presented a ready-made movie. There is an element of both artifice and artificiality in the transition from the exterior to interior scenes and in the players' lack of symmetry to the fully realized chiaroscuro of Welles's compositions.

*F for Fake* is an enjoyable, often intriguing study of fakery in art, focusing on the career of a celebrated art forger and a brief but not fully explored analogy to the illusions practiced by the filmmaker. The story involving Picasso, however, simply shows bad taste, while Welles concludes the film on a note of disdain for both the viewer and himself. There have been bad boys in film history and those whose careers have been cruelly and tragically shortened by various financiers and studios. It is therefore somewhat perverse to find the most celebrated enfant terrible of the cinema so casually dismissing a theme that has been a pivotal feature of his films. His career has led to the wreckage of a great talent, and one suspects while viewing *F for Fake* that Welles seems indifferent to his fate as the successive target of Johnny Carson's barbs.

## Ingmar Bergman

Ingmar Bergman's filmography—ranging from the realism of *Port of Call* through the lyricism of *Summer Interlude*, the metaphysical abstractions of *Persona*, and the impassioned self-analysis of *Scenes from a Marriage*—is one of the most prodigious in film history. It is also one of the most problematic.

To the general public, Bergman is probably the most revered figure in the modern cinema. His films provide exhaustive examples of the artist grappling with the major traumas of his age; yet with few exceptions, his work prior to *Persona* reflects Bergman's difficulty in articulating his arresting themes on film. His narratives are replete with psychological conflicts and philosophical paradoxes, but their tones of pessimism and alienation are presented in such generalized symbols of social and personal turmoil that they function as thinly veiled autobiographical digressions. The more tedious and obtuse of his early films—*Brink of Life, Dreams, Secrets of Women*—employ a variety of dramatic formulas with a minimum of stylistic gracefulness. *Brink of Life* is a hospital drama with none of the symbolic figures in his period films. There are innumerable passive close-ups of the fallen woman and the mother who fears she is losing her attractiveness. But what distinguishes this film from the standard hospital teledrama is his highly gifted ensemble of actresses. The struggle of Eva Dahlbeck in delivering her child, the sensuality of Bibi Andersson's wayward teenager, and Ingrid Thulin's mask of alienation transcend the wooden script and show Bergman's potential as an artist through his absorbtion in his characters' humanity.

*Dreams* and *Secrets of Women* project the straightforward style of theatrical melodrama, but as films they lack the fluidity to make the characters seem as real on the screen as they would on the stage. The one original sequence in *Dreams* transpires in a suddenly inoperative elevator, in which the prim behavior of Gunnar Björnstrand and Eva Dahlbeck gives way to an outpouring of love. The less satisfying scenes in the two films evoke a strained, psychological ambience, for example in Björnstrand's momentary dalliance with Harriet Andersson in *Dreams* or in the empty-headed, true-confession melodrama of Dahlbeck's confrontation with her lover and his wife in *Secrets of Women*. Only in *Summer Interlude*—through his use of the flashback and the background of the young heroine's ballet training—does Bergman's probing study of love sustain an independent quality on film. The characters are fresher, his picture of their retreat more personal, and the mood less forced. His one unequivocal success of this period, *Smiles of a Summer Night*, possesses the theatrical flair one associates with directors like Ernst Lubitsch and Sacha Guitry. Bergman is wholly enamored of the buoyant theatrical juxtaposition of sophistication and naiveté; his actors' aggressive playacting and larger-than-life erotic appetites are joyously pinpointed through his direction.

Two of his more expressionistic films, *Monika* and *The Naked Night*, show an obtrusive technical awkwardness. In his early bittersweet romances he searches for the most direct, naturalistic means to convey the warmth and fragility of his players. But in *Monika* and *The Naked Night* he moves through a darker, symbolic landscape in which his camerawork must effect a more poetic tone. The squalor and sexual tension of *Monika*, from her home to the sailboat in which she escapes with her lover, are depicted with little subtlety, but Harriet Andersson's lubricious, amoral character is so palpably realized that Bergman's heavy-handedness seems almost extraneous. His insensitivity to the way the camera can reflect her erotic presence is characteristic of the shortcomings in many of his films and will be most deliriously exposed in *Hour of the Wolf* and *The Ritual*. In *Monika* after Andersson and her lover arrive on the island, Bergman begins a scene in long shot; the audience watches Monika walk by the water and enter a thicket. By shooting the scene in long shot, her figure is obscured; since he has not previously used this camera setup, it fails either to establish an analogy with a previous scene or to prepare us for what follows. Had Bergman shown her lover looking at Monika from this distance, it would have served as a valid expression of the boy's fascination and frustration. One of the few moments in the film that matches technique to story occurs when the boy visits Monika in the hospital after her delivery. A nurse asks him if he would like to see the child, and he walks uncertainly to the glass partition. Bergman's camera slowly follows the boy, and instead of placing the camera behind the boy's shoulder for a technically distancing effect, the camera moves in on his perplexed expression.

*The Naked Night*, however, makes the symbolism of Bergman's religious trilogy seem slight indeed. Its bombast is perhaps without rival in film history; his pedantic, contrived melodrama and heavy-handed technique give new meaning to pretentiousness. The film begins with one of the stagecoach drivers telling the present circus owner about an incident involving two of the performers. The story is shot in a dreamlike haze, augmented by dissolves, sharp cuts and an overloaded, psychologically palpitating sound track. These effects are integrated in such a shrill, sloppy manner that one is likely to overlook what Bergman is trying to say. The wife of the circus clown teases a group of soldiers, who then bathe with her; her husband, with a copious amount of white paint on his face then comes to retrieve her and discovers that her clothes are hidden. Carrying her on his back, Bergman's clown, unlike Chaplin's or Keaton's, carries such a symbolic weight that the film becomes an allegory. His sudden, tragic alienation—unlike the revelatory moments of doubt that the tramps of film and art history have experienced—is only representative of Bergman's dramatic overkill.

The ensuing seventy minutes function as a brutal transcription of the prologue, but what Bergman says and how he says it is as superficial and self-evident as the hospital threnody, *Brink of Life*. The circus owner experiences personal and managerial difficulties, and when he asks a theater company manager whether he can borrow some costumes, the symbolic implications of their encounter are likely to provide an ecstatic moment for sleuthing symbolists in the audience. The different roles the characters assume in addition to their identities as circus performers are reenforced without the slightest nuance. Bergman's dramatic allegory climaxes during a fight between the circus owner and an actor who has spent an afternoon with the owner's wife. The actor's violent triumph exemplifies the theater director's previous statement that the circus performer only plays with his life, whereas the actor assumes a role and thus holds circus entertainers in contempt. For the filmgoer who seeks the slightest opportunity to be overcome with self-disgust, *The Naked Night*, among other Bergman entropies, is the true modern elixir.

If *The Naked Night* marks a low point in Bergman's search for a cinematic and narrative style to perpetuate his self-despair, *Wild Strawberries* and *The Magician* are his most impressive works since *Summer Interlude* and *Smiles of a Summer Night*. Although *Wild Strawberries* comes perilously close to the perfunctory pessimism of *The Silence*, Bergman is more adept in his use of the cinema's vast technical resources. We are never sure whether it is Bergman or the elderly doctor who is telling the story, but Bergman's sensitivity to his actors' humanity, particularly in Victor Sjöström's performance as the doctor, establishes a more naturalistic stage for his excursions into the past. In several scenes Bergman is unable to differentiate the past and present and adopts a distant point of view, for example, in the scene in which Sjöström observes his wife's infidelity. This stylistic incongruity is most damaging to two scenes in the last part of the film. In the first Sjöström is on trial before a judge, who is played by one of the people Sjöström has picked up during his drive into the city. If Sjöström is examining his failings as a young man and doctor during this excursion, why does the young man become his judge? The second, more disturbing scene concerns Sjöström's conversation with his childhood fiancée, played by Bibi Andersson, who has run off with Sjöström's brother; why, when Sjöström's physical obtrusion into the past has not been previously acknowledged, should he now be seen as an eighty-year-old doctor talking to his twenty-year-old sweetheart? Is this remembrance a rearrangement? Since Bergman appears to conceive it as a blending of the two, Sjöström's reminiscences suffer an unnecessary dilution. But Bergman's immersion in Sjöström's psychological self-examination overshadows his interest in the blatant symbolism in his other projects of the early sixties.

*The Magician* may be Bergman's most personal and honest cinematic reverie. Unlike his other experiments in metaphysical cinema, the exaggerated, lurid compositions and the grotesqueness of the effects, especially during Björnstrand's autopsy of Von Sydow, work to his advantage in illuminating the precarious identity of his actors' roles as stage performers. There is an underlying mocking tone, notably in the illusions performed by Von Sydow, and in the paradoxical declarations of discontent and disdain by members of the host's party and perhaps most ironically conveyed in the performance of Bibi Andersson as the fickle housemaid who sees through the boasting of the performers' stagecoach driver. The film is a Chinese box of illusions; its manipulative mordancy superimposes a note of irreverence surrounding his actors' self-doubts and those of Bergman in visualizing the interchangeability of reality and illusion on film.

In *Persona* Bergman undertakes his most severe analysis of the relevance of the film medium by intertwining his own pursuit of truth—through his references to the cutting room and the flickering light of the camera—with the transitory grip on reality of his two central characters, the actress (Liv Ullmann) and her nurse (Bibi Andersson). Many of Sven Nykvist's images—the boy who wakes up groping for the camera lens and then fondles the dual image of Andersson and Ullmann and that of the alienated Ullmann in her room, staring at the image of the Buddhist monk on television who sets himself on fire— are not only powerful in their own right, but create a viable expressionist framework for the abstruse psychological interpenetration of Andersson and Ullmann during their stay at the doctor's country retreat. Bergman's film expressionism is not equivalent to the baroque camera movements of a Murnau or Welles; as his earliest work has shown, it derives from the profound expressiveness of his actors and from his shading them through Nykvist's close-up portraiture in a revealing chiaroscuro of emotional anxiety. Like Rossellini and Kurosawa—but utilizing a more contrived, ascetic, symbolic landscape— Bergman creates a drama in which action and technique are subordinated to the immediacy and poignancy of his performers.

Once they are settled in the doctor's home, these two gifted actresses communicate Bergman's original contribution to film art. The lengthy middle section of the film is almost exclusively a study of Andersson's face and words—for example, when she recounts a painful sexual episode, which inspires Ullmann's first words, refuted, however, the following morning. Andersson is experiencing the frustration, the uncertainty, the loneliness that one imagines has led to Ullmann's silence during a performance of *Electra*. The final breakdown in their relationship appears to begin with the scene in which Andersson places a piece of glass on the pavement which Ullmann will walk across. This fails to elicit a response from Ullmann; Andersson then picks up a pot of boiling water, which she aims at Ullmann. Again, Ullmann does not respond, but their fragile bond has reached its breaking point. The setting remains naturalistic, yet the concluding scenes are more emphatically dreamlike; too many questions are left dangling, as if their stark emotional self-realization precluded a clear resolution of Andersson's apparent neurosis and Ullmann's return to society. Why, for example, does Bergman only replay the scene in which their two faces become one? Is it the culminating expression of their personality transference or the definitive picture of their fate as schizophrenic modern women? Bergman relies on images of alienation to signify the ineffable boundaries of madness that have first trapped Ullmann and that now threaten to close in on Andersson. It is more effective than the literary symbolism of his earlier films, but he has compromised the one principle—the immeasurable, corporeal expressiveness of the human face—that has enabled the viewer to recognize the barely discernible line that separates sanity from madness.

There are fewer inconclusive moments in *Shame*. One questions Bergman's decision to place the camera over the shoulders of Ullmann and Von Sydow as they sit at the kitchen table and then make love only because it detracts from his steadfast interest in his characters' humanism. *Shame* is certainly one of Bergman's exemplary works in which his handsome, rustic couple of Ullmann and Von Sydow undergoes a severe testing of its grip on civilization. Von Sydow's hypochondria is a bit overplayed; Ullmann becomes the savior not only of a broken man but of a torn, disheveled world. During the last scene, however,

Bergman shows his maturing film sense by using a technique to enhance the meaning of his somber tale. With Von Sydow, Ullmann, and several other persons adrift in the ocean, he uses a fade to black four times to convey an indefinite passage of time. From Von Sydow's apathy as he watches a man drown himself to the dream Ullmann relates, Bergman underscores the cinema's pervasive note of illusion while alluding to Von Sydow's first words in the film that also concern a dream. In her hallucination Ullmann holds a baby in her arms by a river while trees are being set on fire, and she knows she must remember something but forgets exactly what it is. The self-revulsion and, inevitably, the self-negation at the heart of Bergman's films have gained their maximum expression in the breakdown of human communication.

The grueling self-devastation of *Shame*—the idea that the concern for one's fellow man is a pretense—suggests that Bergman can no longer take comfort in the dramatic ploys of humanism. This is borne out in a most cruel manner in *Hour of the Wolf*, in which Bergman's loathing for the world is directed toward his actors. He tries to support the film's surreal framework by incorporating various absurdist effects, but they fail to provide a cogent picture of Von Sydow's character or of the helplessness that overcomes Ullmann. In one representative scene Von Sydow tells Ullmann how slowly time goes by and asks her to consider the length of a minute; for one minute the camera becomes a passive observer of Von Sydow's desperation and Ullmann's duress. When Ullmann meets an old woman, she is first seen in extreme close-up, followed by an extreme close-up of Ullmann looking at the woman. Bergman then uses a jump cut to show the woman in an entirely different position; the treatment is arbitrary, the scribblings of an artist who disdains the idea that madness can be articulated. Bergman's increasingly ludicrous stylization of despair leads to a climactic evening at the castle of Von Sydow's neighbors; Bergman features several alienating touches, such as extremely rapid tracking shots and cuts and a nightmarish sound track; it concludes with Von Sydow thanking his hosts for "breaking the mirror." Bergman's capacity for self-disgust is seemingly infinite, yet his reckless, apocalyptic treatment forces one to question the depth of his estrangement. The dread luminously depicted in *Persona* through the loquacity of Bibi Andersson's nurse and the reticence of Ullmann's actress becomes a most dismal cry of anguish in *Hour of the Wolf*.

If *Hour of the Wolf* finds the artist unable to rationalize the chaos around him, *The Ritual*, a telefilm with its sophomoric images of despair, plays as a caricature of the metaphysical cinema of which Bergman is the patron saint. During the film's nine segments, Bergman's acting troupe is interrogated, indulges in abusive actions toward one another, and finally performs the ritual for the investigating bureaucrat. The bureaucrat tells them he understands it, a confession as absurd as that of Von Sydow thanking his hosts for breaking the mirror in *Hour of the Wolf*. That the bureaucrat can find a theme of self-ridicule in such a pseudoritual as Bergman has concocted damns the bureaucrat along with the actors as purely plastic protagonists.

In *The Passion of Anna* Bergman reembraces the underlying humanism that he has shattered in *Hour of the Wolf*. The dramatic formulas are the least complex he has used since *Winter Light*. There is little originality in his story of the pain and duplicity of a marriage, but his faith in the extraordinary intensity of his actors conveys the anxiety surrounding the decline of their marriage. One is not simply applauding Bergman's direction of actors, but how his camera, pressed up against the confused terrain of the human face, discovers a naked truth about human behavior in a manner unique to film. Yet as sincere and direct as it is, one senses that Bergman's decision to return to the conventional narrative and symbolic design of *The Passion of Anna*, after such radical experiments as *Persona, Hour of the Wolf,* and *The Ritual,* is something of a compromise. The artist's struggling humanism needs a new, perhaps simpler focus, and it is boldly undertaken in *The Touch, Cries and Whispers,* and *Scenes from a Marriage*.

Many scenes in *The Touch* are awkward and derivative, and the casting of Elliott Gould raises more questions than it solves. Its most striking feature is Bergman's willingness to explore an aspect of human relationships that he has subordinated since *Wild Strawberries*. Bibi Andersson's visit to her ailing mother connotes an overpowering emotionalism as she is struck by the numbness of her feelings. When she visits Gould's sister, who suffers from palsy, the white walls and barren apartment are presented in such a straightforward manner that it is as if we were watching a diligent student of Bergman's trying to reconstruct the dimensions of a world his master has disavowed. What is most unusual about the film's dramatic nuances is Bergman's handling of his three major stars. Gould simply lacks the range to suggest the uncertainty an artist faces, but in Gould's brutal rape of Andersson, Bergman exposes both Gould and Andersson as weak, helpless victims of their emotions. There are no symbolic overtones in this harrowing scene; one observes a man showing his failure to communicate with a woman who has shown him patience and love and who refuses to scream because of her desire to help him at whatever the cost. Von Sydow has a minor role, yet his polite, retiring husband is handled with such charm that one senses his aplomb as an actor in this appropriately bland, supporting role.

*Cries and Whispers* is a thoughtful distillation of the complex drama and shadow play in the earlier expressionistic collaborations of Bergman and Nykvist. The story introduces the familiar Bergman terrain of reality and dream in which two sisters are troubled by the voices of the past, resulting in their imagining episodes of fantasized self-degradation. The color of the film is red, and it becomes a symbolic barometer of their humanity—Ullmann's sensuality, Thulin's guilt, and, perhaps most vividly, the decline of the third sister, played by Harriet Andersson. The red backdrop becomes a psychological expression of their different but unified memories and fantasies. Nykvist's portraiture, presenting them in shoulder or head shots, has a purity that personifies, rather than reflects, their traumas. The cries and whispers are the voices of their past combined with their own subconscious fears; the unexpected, concluding motif of resolution, if not happiness, is provided by an entry from Andersson's diary. The film does not possess the intensely personal ambiguities of *Persona*, but it shows a compassion and sublimity that one would have thought all but dismissed by Bergman since *Persona*.

*Scenes from a Marriage* extends the dramatic simplicity and moral optimism of *The Touch* and *Cries and Whispers*. Bergman utilizes the simplest of cinematic and narrative devices: the naturalism of the documentary film and its interview format. In adopting this conventional style Bergman has made one of the major films of the seventies by identifying the commonplace dramatic tensions of *Scenes from a Marriage* as a theme fundamental to human communication and to the communicability of technology. One might argue that it is only one example of Bergman's diverse interests, that its refreshing directness results from his working in television. But the reason *Scenes from a Marriage* remains a high point in the movies of the seventies is that its tight 16-millimeter format, its journalistic premises, and diagnostic severity renew the humanistic themes that his more expressionist works repressed. Bergman is not returning to the primitive cinema of Rossellini, but is using his middle-class characters and their commonly experienced traumas to turn back the pages of film history. It also reveals why Bergman has survived the sixties, while directors like Antonioni and Godard have been unable to adapt their styles to the conservative instincts of the past decade.

# 24
## The Japanese Film

One of the major tasks awaiting film historians is the inclusion of the contemporary Japanese cinema in the mainstream of world cinema. The early masterworks of the Japanese film from Teinosuke Kinugasa's *A Page of Madness* through the first films of Yasujiro Ozu, Kenji Mizoguchi, Keisuke Kinoshita, Mikio Naruse, and Heinosuke Gosho were discovered in the West at the same time their major postwar works were screened. While we have yet to fully integrate the silent and early sound films of the Japanese cinema into film history, we have fewer excuses in regard to their major filmmakers of the sixties and seventies. There are enough film festivals and retrospectives for one to keep in touch with the Japanese film; clearly, we are at a much greater advantage than our predecessors in the thirties and forties. Our task is made immeasurably simpler by the impression that there seems to be a radical difference in the works of the "elders" of the Japanese cinema—who either in period dramas or contemporary settings identified the permanency of the past, its paramount ideals of self-acquiescence and social transcendence—and modern directors with their self-doubt and misanthropy. But the anxiety of the postwar generation of Japanese filmmakers is of such a peculiar shading that we are led to see that even in such an eclectic, "international" medium as the movies, the folklore and intellectual fabric of each country is invariably translated on film.

Tadashi Imai's *Muddy Waters*, one of the celebrated examples of Japanese neorealism, is a striking example of how the Japanese filmmaker, even as he reflects the humanism of the postwar cinema, also redefines the ineradicable differences between East and West. Imai, like De Sica, undertakes an unrelenting study of a family's economic hardships as the father lines up to secure employment in the early morning hours, and like De Sica, Imai shows how the lack of economic security leads to the breakdown of social relationships. But unlike De Sica or other humanist directors in the European and American cinema, Imai suggests the spiritual transcendence of the family. After working for thieves, the father orders his children to commit suicide but then realizes that the family bond can never be destroyed. The film is not so much a bitter tract against poverty as it is about the reaffirmation of the Japanese family in a period when its existence seemed least tenable.

Two directors who develop the theme of the breakdown of Japanese values and the decline of the family are Kon Ichikawa and Masaki Kobayashi. Both directors strike notes of alienation and terror that reverberate throughout the films of Kurosawa. Some of Ichikawa's lesser known films, like *Punishment Room*, *The Men of Tohoku*, and *Kokoro*, sustain Kurosawa's aggressive journalism in studying his protagonists' fatalistic nature and the meretriciousness of Japan's most revered symbols of social unity. They lack the interplay of violence and humanism in Kurosawa's work but are significant examples of how a style of postwar despair was perceived by Japanese directors. The most penetrating relationship in *Punishment Room* is not between the boy and the other gang members or even with the girl he rapes and to whom he apologizes by crushing a piece of glass against his leg; it is with his father, who lends his son's friend some money and who is savagely ridiculed by Ichikawa when the money is returned. *The Men of Tohoku* documents the mistreatment of an outcast, a theme common to Kinoshita's *Apostasy*. Kinoshita's classical moralism features the extended self-confessions and violent harangues by Raizo Ichikawa's pariah. Although the outcast's problem in *The Men of Tohoku* is comical in spirit—he is rejected by his fellow outcasts because of his body odor—the film attempts a similar moral slap at Japanese bigotry. The outcast journeys to a remote village that he is told is inhabited by maidens and whose illusory utopia is rendered as a drawing. Yet Ichikawa's crude comic ploys and the contrived nature of the final scene reflect the differences in the idealism underlying Kinoshita's treatment and Ichikawa's contemporary voice of disenchantment. Ichikawa's tentativeness in imbuing classic controversies with a modernist's sense of disillusion also characterizes his adaptation of Natsume Soseki's classic Japanese novel, *Kokoro*. Soseki's novel is an extended meditation on guilt developed through the master-student relationship. Yet the novel's straightforward discursiveness is translated into melodramatic expressions of remorse. Whereas the master's hara-kiri in the novel offers a traditional Japanese resolution of his earlier misdeed, in the film it comes across as a mundane example of postwar depression.

Ichikawa is an eclectic filmmaker and proves least rewarding when he dabbles in oblique themes, for example, in *Odd Obsession*, a shabby film version of Junichiro Tanizaki's *The Key*. He is most effective in his adaptation of *Fires on the Plain*, a devastating study of war, and *An Actor's Revenge*, a high-spirited, stylized romp through eighteenth-century Japanese theater. *An Actor's Revenge*, photographed by Setsuo Kobayashi—who was behind the camera for *Hoodlum Soldier* and *The Red Angel*, two of Masumura's most evocative films—is an especially engaging work, delighting in the illusory nature of playacting while joyously elaborating these theatrical tricks on film. It is a magical translation of a work and style wholly of the theater, whose enigmas are enhanced by the multiple stages in a film.

Masaki Kobayashi's *The Human Condition* is one of the most ambitious undertakings in epic cinema since Eisenstein's *Ivan the Terrible*. A nine-hour drama that follows Tatsuya Nakadai from his work as an engineer in a prisoner of war camp through his induction into military service, his capture, and his death, the film strives for a Zolaesque study of the triumph of pain and corruption over innocence and idealism. Much of this three-part epic, especially the middle section involving the drafting of Nakadai and the soldiers' loss of faith, is handled in a ponderous, heavy-handed manner. There is, however, a final, drawn-out barrage of tanks and shelling in the second part that brutally underscores the nihilism that overwhelms the soldiers. But it is the first and third parts that best represent Kobayashi's virtues as an epic filmmaker. Like Kurosawa, he attacks his social history with the immediacy of a journalist, without exaggerating his inherently gruesome story. The prisoners' pilfering of the grain and the suicide on the electric wire fence move us through their credibility and poignancy. Kobayashi's Zolaesque treatment is first manifested in Nakadai's frustration as he fights to improve the conditions of the labor camp, in the rumblings of communism among the prisoners, and in Kobayashi's more epic concern with the decline of humanism through the war years. The third part lacks the progressive dramatic scope of the first section; the social contract has broken down in the cesspool of the internment camps, leading to a recognition that absurdity has become the way of the world. This engrossing study of the loss of faith misses Kurosawa's thematic and compositional rigor; there is a pronounced socialist ethic in the first part that is obscured by Kobayashi's more universal expression of the oppressiveness of war. Yet the earnestness in his study of Japan's guilt during the war, by comparison, diminishes the power of such respected American films as *All Quiet on the Western Front* and *Paths of Glory*.

Kobayashi's *Samurai Rebellion* is another example of his interest in the moral paradoxes underlying history. The camerawork and lighting impressively pinpoint the austere nature of the antiquated feudal order, but once introduced to Toshiro Mifune's samurai warrior, the audience knows it will only be a matter of time before he will avenge his lord's pernicious treatment of his family. Kobayashi lacks the irony of Okamoto's *Kill*, which in turn misses the more refined and savage humor of Kurosawa or Leone. A more moving work in this genre is Imai's *Night Drum*. The repressive rule of the shogun is exemplified in the characters' stiff, formal movements and in the vibrantly realized mood of treachery and deceit involving the husband, wife, and music teacher. Kobayashi's *Kwaidan* is one of his least satisfying works because his style does not seem suited to the dreamlike nimbus of Japanese fairy tales. Some of his effects, for example, during the naval encounter, embody the exquisite craftsmanship of Japanese art, but he lacks the mordant humor in the first story or the aesthetic control in the last part to fully embrace the somnolent splendor of the medieval world in the manner of Mizoguchi's *Princess Yang Kwei Fei*.

*Kaseki*, however, shows Kobayashi's considerable development as a dramatist and filmmaker. He no longer works with an unwieldy, expressionistic canvas, but strives for a romantic, impressionistic picture of his protagonists' voyage of discovery in Europe. Informed by his doctors that he has less than a year to live, Kobayashi's hardworking, circumspect businessman, played with discerning subtlety by Shin Saburi, goes to Europe and attempts to infiltrate a culture and way of life he has never experienced. There is an astute, handsome rendering of the protagonist's sensitivity to the beauties of his European sojourn and his paradoxical feelings for the attractive Japanese woman he first spots outside a museum in Paris. The film is most memorable for Kobayashi's deliberate, poetic camerawork; Saburi's promenades through the streets reflect his joyful yet distant appreciation for the different colors and forms around him. He remains emotionally withdrawn in his relationships, unable to resolve his ambivalence to the abundance of sensual faces and vistas. When he is informed that the prognosis was wrong—that, in fact, he enjoys excellent health—one realizes how Saburi's romantic self-enlightenment will be forgotten with little or no effort, as he refuses to answer an inquiry from the woman he has met during his travels. What a marvelous sequel to *Ikiru*! In the Kurosawa film the dying Takashi Shimura fights against the apathy of Japan's bureaucracy to build a playground and voices a triumphant note of humanism. In *Kaseki*, however, Kobayashi intimates that even the specter of death cannot overcome the reserve, the immeasurable depth of probity in the Japanese character.

Among the newer faces in the Japanese cinema, there has been a greater willingness to experiment with techniques and themes made popular in the West. One example is Susumu Hani's use of *cinéma vérité* in *A Full Life*, *Bride of the Andes*, and *Bwana Toshi*. *A Full Life* concerns the trials of a woman following the death of her husband. At first the film has the look of a splintered documentary, full of bits and pieces that fail to establish the necessary links to immerse the audience in her precarious adventures and to clarify her awakening as an independent woman. But, similar to Hani's other films, once he feels he has defined the central issue facing his protagonist, his use of *cinéma vérité* becomes less dogmatic. He breaks away from a claustrophobic view of her isolated struggle, elaborating the larger, humanistic sweep of her fight to assert her independence. In *Bride of the Andes* his estranged heroine journeys to Peru with her infant son after the death of her husband. Here *cinéma vérité* proves a more obtrusive technique because the viewer needs to understand the peculiarly unsettling nature of the remote village in which she has settled. Hani gravitates to this more compassionate viewpoint once she is accepted by the villagers. There are several impressive scenes in which Hani follows his heroine at work or as she is introduced to an ancient village ritual that simultaneously expresses her identity as a foreigner and the unique luminosity of this primitive culture. *Bwana Toshi* is not as successful because the central figure is not engaged in the truly Herculean self-discovery that his wife and star, Sachiko Hidari, underwent in *A Full Life* and *Bride of the Andes*. The tone is more comical, and, although there are a few amusing scenes involving Toshi and his African friend, Hani is too flippant in his treatment of the barriers Toshi tries to cross.

Hiroshi Teshigahara directed *Woman in the Dunes*, one of the few contemporary Japanese films that has been integrated into the repertory of the postwar cinema. His direction is a model for translating a novel to film; the protagonist's subterranean existence with the woman of the dunes, his initial resistance to his entrapment, his fight against the elements, his doomed plans for escape, and his gradual acceptance of life in the sand pit are treated with a classic awareness of human psychology. The film becomes a metaphor for man's acquiescence to nature, not through any devious symbolism, but by making the viewer feel the suppression of a man's rebellious spirit. *The Pitfall*, however, is a case study in how not to translate an absurdist tale to film. The story of two drifters pursued by a man on a motorcycle slumbers along an existential maze; Teshigahara's garish double exposures and elliptical editing rhythms invariably depersonalize the drifters' tragic destiny.

In Tadashi Imai's *A Story from Echigo*, in Akio Jissoji's *This Transient Life*, and in the films of Shohei Imamura, Yasuzo Masumura, Nagisa Oshima, and Masahiro Shinoda, eroticism is explored both as a self-fulfilling romanticism and as a metaphor for social turbulence. No other national cinema displays such a fascination with this subject. In Europe there are, among others, Losey, Chabrol, and Bertolucci, while there are sundry examples of disrobement in the American cinema; but there is a poignancy and detail in the Japanese film that is unmatched in the West. Imai's *A Story from Echigo* uses the story of the rape of a woman to portray the dehumanization of Japanese society between the two wars. The film's most startling quality is that none of the three major characters is seen in a favorable light. The rapist, played by Rentaro Mikuni, the husband in Imai's *Night Drum*, is a virile, powerful actor who plays his role as an indolent blue-collar worker. The wife is seen as a silly, naive heroine, while the husband is shown to be a dull, stupid man, who believes his wife his having an affair with Mikuni. He kills her in a paddy field, tries to revive her by sleeping with her corpse, and finally kills Mikuni and himself. The morbid ambience surrounding their isolated coastal town and physically demanding jobs negates any hope of social or personal redemption. They are locked in a gray netherworld of emotional passivity in which Mikuni's violent, cynical behavior seems to be the first sign of the sleepwalker's regaining consciousness. In a manner similar to the sexual excesses in the films of Imamura and Masumura, Imai uses the rape to dramatize the ominous breakdown of society in the period between the two world wars.

Akio Jissoji's *This Transient Life* concerns the incestuous relationship between a brother and a sister. The sister becomes pregnant and, following her brother's instructions, seduces her house servant, who marries her. He then discovers the brother and sister engaged in sex and commits suicide. The brother serves as an apprentice to a sculptor of religious objects, who is stimulated by the brother's lovemaking sessions with his wife. The son of the artist then sleeps with his stepmother, while Jissoji attempts to absolve himself of the brother's hedonism by killing him in a dreamlike coda. The film's major shortcoming—the reason it fails to expand its sensual frictions—lies with the protagonist's complete lack of paradox. He sees himself as intrinsically superior to the other characters, telling a priest that he, too, would like to sleep with his sister. He is no perverse hoodlum, but in his devotion to his craft—an extension of his love of physical beauty—he refuses to recognize any form of sinful damnation. Sex, to him, is an aesthetic experience, and Jissoji's camera is undeniably alluring in depicting the pleasure and self-fulfillment of those who disdain any feelings of guilt. It is a film from which pornographers could learn, one of the few successful studies of an uninhibited sensuality on film.

Imamura's *Legends from a Southern Island* is set in a remote island whose tragic folklore is identified through the erotic destiny of one family. But like other contemporary filmmakers, Imamura abuses the tense relationship between the villagers and the outcast family by inundating his film with enough neurotics to fill an asylum. His film is awash with coarse, sensual images, from his close-ups of lizards to the repeated seizures of the demented daughter. The one credible family member functions as a priestess for the village ceremonies. She wants to resign her post, but she is dissuaded by the village chieftain, with whom she has an affair. The chilling effect created by the masks that they wear while making love and that the natives don in the tribal killing of her brother and sister is fragmented by Imamura's preference for sharp cuts and grotesque behavior, reducing the mysterious veneer of the island's past to a Freudian concoction of circuslike proportions. The one scene in which Imamura does not accentuate the sordid configurations of his story involves a brief excursion by the father and the son to a neighboring island. As they converse by the edge of a cliff, a group of birds begins to gather; by the end of this ten-minute scene, the screen is engulfed by a colony of exotic, winged forms. The fate of his characters as mythological protagonists is communicated through Imamura's understated treatment of their affinity with nature and not through the modernist's expanding chords of dissonance.

*Intentions of Murder* and *Vengeance Is Mine* feature highly expressionistic tableaux that veer uneasily from parody to perversity. *Intentions of Murder* is one of the most overheated *film noir* exercises in the postwar cinema. Imamura's story concerns an anomalous sexual encounter between a maid, who, like her mother, lacks a viable social identity in her employer's home, and her rapist. Imamura exaggerates their forlorn social standing; he shows the maid as a good-natured, ultimately acquiescent figure in the lower depths of human passion. The rapist is not a solitary, symbolic figure of evil, but a lugubrious Dostoevskian exile caught between his losing battle with drug addiction and the ephemeral freedom obtained in his assaults on the maid. Imamura's penchant for oblique angles and oppressively low-key lighting juxtaposed to the characters' intermittent soliloquies in the grip of sexual upheaval creates a baroque but uneven black comedy. *Vengeance Is Mine* is not as paradoxical in recounting the true story of a laborer's multiple murders. Unlike the outcast family in *Legends from a Southern Island* and the pitiful characters of the maid and criminal in *Intentions of Murder*, the murderer in *Vengeance Is Mine* does not suffer the sordid strains of repressed yet recurrent feudal traditions. Though several references are made to his father's corrupt sensuality, Imamura's anti-hero presents a faceless mask of evil, a glib pragmatist who forfeits his life for the pleasures of his savage, momentary triumphs. In *Eijanaika*, a period drama, Imamura's blatant theatricality —overhead shots, shock cuts, compositions of lurid, lewd sexual romps— interprets the social tension between the ruling class and the stage actors as a freak show. He does not attempt the ironic characterizations or comic-tragic interplay in the manner of Ichikawa's *An Actor's Revenge* or Shinoda's *The Scandalous Adventures of Buraikan*. Whereas the films of Ichikawa and Shinoda utilize the expansive realism of the film medium to enrich the theatrical textures of their stories, Imamura's decadence is peculiar to his interpretation.

Masumura takes a more introspective approach to eroticism in *Hoodlum Soldier*, *The Red Angel*, and *Naomi*. *Hoodlum Soldier* follows the unlikely relationship between a thug and a student during training camp in World War II. The thug continually gets into scraps from which he is bailed out by the student. Masumura, however, is not as interested in exploring the reasons for their friendship as he is in having the audience experience the exhaustive physical hardships of training camp, from the numerous fights involving the thug to the arduous twenty-mile hike during which he collapses. Masumura sees the army as a Darwinian struggle for survival, one whose moral and intellectual undercurrents are quelled by the brute force of one man subduing another. His treatment of this theme is hyperbolic; like Jissoji's simple espousal of sensuality, Masumura interprets the question of war in terms of the awesome physical demands it makes on the psyche and in the way this usurpation of physical power transforms men into beasts.

*The Red Angel* is a more humane study of the debilitating effects of war. Masumura focuses on the grotesque consequences of war, in which legs and arms are amputated and piled up as if the doctors were collecting firewood. Masumura's protagonist is a nurse who is drawn to a soldier who has lost his arms. She finally accedes to his desire to make love, after which he commits suicide; in a confused epilogue, the nurse joins the fighting and is killed. Masumura seems to conclude that the horror of war has led to the nurse's self-awareness—that her only form of salvation can come through participating in combat. Like the coda in *This Transient Life*, it is superfluous because Masumura's humanism lies in his refusal to compromise the physical hardships of war. In *Naomi* Masumura's setting is present-day Japan and the relationship of a businessman to the ward he has raised. The film, however, misses the element of abnormal behavior that so forcefully pervades *Hoodlum Soldier* and *The Red Angel*. *Love Suicide at Sonezaki* is a departure from Masumura's frontal attacks on Japanese society. In his adaptation of a classic Chikamatsu puppet play, his approach is theatrical, sardonic. The humor is generated not by extravagant cross-references between film and theater in the manner of Ichikawa's *An Actor's Revenge*, but by his concise editing and close-ups, complementing the performer's artful excesses with the play's contemporaneousness.

If one detects a movement away from the appreciation of the intransigence of nature and the rigid, hierarchical nature of Japan's history in their postwar cinema, the films of Nagisa Oshima and Masahiro Shinoda reveal this break with the past in a more radical manner. In their equally distinct modernist styles, their films underline the idea that the legacy of Ozu and Mizoguchi, at least for the present, has little meaning for them, while Kurosawa's bleak social consciousness is identified as a critical turning point for the Japanese film.

Oshima is both the more eclectic and experimental of the two. In *Boy, Death by Hanging*, and *Diary of a Shinjuku Burglar* he incorporates elements of natural-ism, Brechtian theater, and avant-garde polemic. In *Boy* he uses the realism of *cinéma vérité* to detail the grim situation in which the child is placed by faking car accidents. But instead of condensing his material, he attempts to cover too many aspects of the characters' family life, from the estrangement of the hus-band and wife to the boy's personal fantasies. He wants the audience to recog-nize the family's dire straits as a social cancer but refuses to question its origin.

This thematic and stylistic ambiguity also mars *Death by Hanging*. The failure to kill the doomed protagonist enables Oshima to ridicule the officials' confu-sion. The victim's fantasies, however, do not personify his role as one of soci-ety's outcasts, while the bickering of the bureaucrats seems only a conventional interpretation of their protofascist mentality. The tension between the real and surreal is never clearly articulated because Oshima seems unsure of the manner in which he wants to attack Japanese bureaucracy—whether with the intensity of a journalist or with the poetic disengagement of a surrealist. In *Diary of a Shinjuku Burglar* two college students dramatize their revolutionary activities, citing examples from literary history in the manner of Godardian rebels. The shinjuku thief is a rock 'n' roll star whose involvement in a kabuki drama is similar to the numerous associations between Godard's adventurers and the commedia dell'arte in *Pierrot le fou*. Whereas Godard's interest in abstraction is explicitly manifested in his analogies to social and art history, Oshima's pro-tagonists, without taking the risks of Godard's anti-heroes, never resolve their identity. *The Pleasures of the Flesh* and *The Man Who Left His Will on Film* are two of Oshima's most static, didactic films. In the former, the young man's sexual misanthropy leads to a superficial sermon on the delinquency of Japan's youth. In the latter film his student rebels and filmmakers lack the aggressive indi-vidualism of young artists in the West who turn to the movies as a form both of personal expression and social protest. They are not as frivolous in recording their nihilistic activities on film while their bitterness seems to reach for a dramatic forcefulness that the avant-garde aesthetic cannot fulfill. Not surpri-singly Oshima's most successful films—the ones in which his humanism most acutely infiltrates his picture of the turmoil in Japanese society—are his least experimental.

A measure of Kurosawa's influence in Oshima's work was conspicuous early in his career in several *cinéma vérité* shorts about war veterans and displaced children. But the dominant effect of Kurosawa's legacy is his intense, nihilistic exposés of Japanese institutions whose foundations have begun to crack. One thinks of the party sequence in *The Idiot*, the bureaucratic chicanery of *Ikiru*, the diseased family life of *The Bad Sleep Well*—examples of Kurosawa's integrating the terror and treachery of his period studies to modern life. It is this explosive spirit that makes for the most rewarding moments in Oshima's work.

The most formidable technique Oshima borrows from Kurosawa in *The Catch* is his use of the enclosed setting of Rentaro Mikuni's manor to reflect Mikuni's feudal rule. Oshima suggests the doom that awaits postwar Japan in maintaining such antiquated social groupings as exist on Mikuni's estate. The servants sit around, inebriated by Mikuni's sake, lunging at one another as if they were convicts on death row celebrating their last hours. There is a similar feeling of claustrophobia in several East European filmmakers, but in the contemporary Japanese film the stasis denotes a diseased erotic atmosphere that is invariably linked to the feudal origins of the society; in the East European cinema, the constricted economy is seen as the decisive threat to personal fulfillment.

Oshima's attraction to and attack on traditional symbols of social orthodoxy undergo a more problematic stylization in *The Ceremony*. Oshima's theme is the self-destructive nature of an aristocratic family. His ornate design, however, seems extraneous; the family's tenuous stability is analyzed in a tedious tal-kathon with few of the humanistic insights in such an exemplary work as *Ikiru*. During the wedding of the protagonist, the tension finally erupts when his bride fails to appear. The family gathers in a room, but they no longer sit and converse in the stiff, formal manner that is their custom. The bastard hero begins to treat his wealthy guardian as the bride that had been selected for him. While the other family members crowd around this confrontation, the eldest son, the bridegroom's closest friend and the one family member conscious of its duplicity, pushes the father into his friend's arms, saying that he must play the bride who has failed to appear. The father finally extricates himself, but the hero then goes to a chamber where his cousin, a police officer accidentally killed in a car accident earlier in the day, has been placed. He removes the bandaged body, and enters the coffin with his female cousin. This bizarre action marks the death knell for the family which, during the bridegroom's absurdist playacting, is forced to realize that its acquiescence to the father's directives is no longer tenable. But Oshima lacks the sensitivity to empathize with the family's tragic destiny; Oshima is a modernist, possessing a greater affinity with the unrest facing Japan's younger generation. This is why *The Sun's Burial* more successfully evokes a predominant tone of nihilism than the social and psychological traumas of *The Ceremony*. *The Sun's Burial* is also the strongest proof of Kurosawa's influence; Oshima adapts several of Kurosawa's premises and in the process creates an explosive study of a modern purgatory. The acting, as in most of Oshima's films, is flawed. But it is less relevant in *The Sun's Burial*; unlike the gallery of family portraits of *The Ceremony*, *The Sun's Burial* is a sprawling canvas of the darkest, most mordant colors. Like the most frenetic sequences in Kurosawa's *Drunken Angel*, *I Live in Fear*, and *The Bad Sleep Well*, the coercive, volatile nature of Oshima's story of the miscreants and dregs of society derives its bleakness from his lack of distance in entering a netherworld of squalor and violence. His excessive touches, highlighted by the harsh, burned-out colors of the deserted lots and back streets of Tokyo and the bloodred faces of his adolescent hoods, underscore the idea that the lower depths of Japanese society now encompass present-day Tokyo. The film also exemplifies the differences in the modernism of, for example, Godard and that of Oshima and the Japanese cinema. Unlike Godard who translates his intellectual discontent through various modernist techniques, Oshima, like Kurosawa, immerses the viewer into his social reality until one is overwhelmed by the raucous sounds and raw under-belly of lower-class discontent. This theme is explicitly exploited in the film's conclusion. Oshima's anti-hero meets a friend in a lot and asks him to leave the gang with him. He replies that he wants to be left alone, and pointing a knife in the direction of the protagonist, walks away. Suddenly the two begin to fight; Oshima moves to long shot, encircling the combatants, augmenting the violence with an unsettling jazz score. The fight is a hypnotic example of his characters' self-destructiveness in which Oshima's devious orchestration of the camera and music embellishes his picture of the nihilism surrounding them.

Masahiro Shinoda's affinity with Kurosawa is both more simple and more complex. In his samurai film, *Assassination*, a sly masterless warrior plays two camps against each other. Shinoda uses fewer images of violence than Kurosa-wa, and unlike Mifune, the warrior does not act as moral agent. The tone is less comic than in Kurosawa or Okamoto; Shinoda emphasizes the political double-dealing that concludes with the death of the samurai. The film lacks the more incisive thematic ironies of *Yojimbo*, but one senses that Shinoda's moral ambiguity would work well in a modern setting. This is confirmed by *Pale Flower*. Unlike a majority of contemporary thrillers that abstract the essential chemistry of the thriller or private eye genre, *Pale Flower* uncovers a peculiarly Japanese mood of disenchantment in its magnified baroque shading of the gambling dens and the doomed romance of the gangster and gambler.

A less successful, inherently incongruous work is *Double Suicide*. Shinoda does not use any natural exteriors, restricting his characters to a world of painted, artificial backdrops. His cloying design only serves to remind the viewer of the delicate, yet impassioned essays of Mizoguchi. Shinoda's lovers rebel against their severely structured society in various sexually liberating performances. While illustrating the exuberance in the portrayal of eroticism in the Japanese cinema, they are expressions of a sensibility that Mizoguchi never would have envisioned.

In two of his best films, *Punishment Island* and *The Scandalous Adventures of Buraikan*, Shinoda returns to the theme of anarchy that made *Assassination* and *Pale Flower* valid variations on Kurosawa's misanthropy. *Punishment Island* util-izes the selective and rack focus techniques he introduced in *Assassination*, by which the characters and objects in the background are purposely obscured until the protagonist in the foreground turns to look at them. The story concerns a young man who returns to the island from which he was exiled as a child. He seeks to find the two people who tortured him and left him for dead; he learns that his chief tormentor, played too pompously by Rentaro Mikuni, also killed his parents for the honor of Japan. The film, then, becomes a study in the nature of violence—of one generation forcing expiation on another. During the climac-tic ending at Mikuni's home, Shinoda drenches the set in blackness, dimming the figures of the two actors. Mikuni is threatened with his life, but he cannot remember killing the man's parents; their few, barely visible movements seem to transpire in a dark underworld, symbolic of the nihilism that first Mikuni and now the protagonist represent. The ending is arbitrary: after Mikuni's daughter pleads for the life of her father, the protagonist cuts off one of Mikuni's fingers and in a series of jump cuts is seen leaving the island. *Punishment Island* and *The Sun's Burial* present very different but equally valid interpretations of the despair and violence that haunted postwar art in Europe and America.

*The Scandalous Adventures of Buraikan*, Shinoda's best film and one of the genuine neoclassical triumphs of the cinema of the seventies, turns to a different source. Like Ichikawa's brilliant tour de force, *An Actor's Revenge*, Shinoda's theme is the illusory nature of Japanese drama, exaggerating the motif, "the play's the thing." The film is set during a festival at the turn of the century and involves a mysterious political schemer named Buraikan, an acting troupe, and a would-be actor played with customary expertise by Tatsuya Nakadai. Numerous stylistic analogies are drawn, from commedia dell'arte to Brecht, but the spirit of *The Scandalous Adventures of Buraikan*, like *An Actor's Revenge*, is uniquely Japanese, notably in the treatment of the film as a series of mesmerizing screen paintings brought to life.

Nakadai finds himself in the midst of a confrontation involving a war lord who is against freedom in the arts and Buraikan who hopes to infest Japan with his whimsical, good-natured playacting. Again, Shinoda features the selective and rack focus techniques to reinforce the main theme of the story: the integration of all the characters and backgrounds as part of a scintillating panel painting. It is a story whose pictorial lushness could only be realized on film, instilling the original beauty of the visual arts in Japan with a black humor unique to Shinoda and his contemporaries.

*The Ballad of Orin* is executed in a more classical style. His picture of feudal Japan—centering on the story of a blind balladeer who longs for the companionship of a man denied her by law—exudes the feeling and craftsmanship of a scholar reimagining the spiritual permanence of the past. Kazuo Miyagawa's shots of the blind singers walking through the countryside convey both their privation and their role as surreal inhabitants of Japanese history. Orin's closed eyes and expression of sensual serenity show Shinoda's sympathy with outsiders, encasing her figure at various ceremonies in a light both cherubic and sexual. Orin is seen by her companion as a reincarnation of the Buddha, an acknowledgment by Shinoda that the hieratic nature of medieval Japan gave its outsiders a sense of dignity and otherworldliness that could not be effaced by social strictures. The triumphant moderism of *The Scandalous Adventures of Buraikan* and *The Ballad of Orin* is not equivalent to refuting the past, but to its enrichment.

# 25
# The Contemporary Cinema

In *Before the Revolution* one of the characters tells Bertolucci's protagonist, "Remember, Fabrizio, one cannot live without Rossellini." This salutation to the Italian humanist underlines a theme unique to the contemporary cinema: the permeance of film history. For Bertolucci, among other writers and directors in the vanguard of the contemporary cinema, the awareness and application of history and aesthetics derive from the films with which he grew up; the identity of contemporary filmmakers as artists with a heritage distinct from other art forms originates with the masters of the silent film and those artists who developed the poetics of a sound film. It was fifties and sixties film-critics-turned-directors in Italy, England, and France who became the first group of filmmakers to fashion their work on the theoretical and stylistic assumptions of artists from Griffith through Rossellini. This does not mean that they refer to the tremulous romanticism of Griffith or the pregnant moralism of Rossellini as supporting motifs in their films. Instead they turn to their predecessors to determine how the world is to be imagined; they formulate their ideas of time and space not from historians and philosophers but from the way in which filmmakers from Griffith through Rossellini imagined the world on film. Jean-Luc Godard's controversial identity as the modernist par excellence rests on the premise that film history is a viable, living organism. In his films one finds the juxtaposition of past and present, the emphasis and often the overemphasis on the techniques, themes, morals, and icons of film history as the enduring legacy of this twentieth-century art form.

One of the more felicitous examples of the permeance of the past in the contemporary cinema is Dušan Makavejev's *Innocence Unprotected*. Makavejev's first film, *Man Is Not a Bird*, evinces a satirical camera eye, delighting in his rustic adventurers and their struggle to reconcile their libido and social consciousness. It is a rough, uneven work, but one that embraces the dichotomies of personal happiness in Eastern Europe without the mannered intellectualism of a Wajda or Skolimowski. In *Innocence Unprotected* he employs an ingenious dramatic point of view. His narrative is an irreverent interpolation of the first Serbo-Croatian talkie, a maudlin tale about an ingenue hounded by her parents and rescued by a circus strong man. Makavejev breaks up the film by intercutting documentary footage of prewar Yugoslavia and interviews with the actors, focusing on the muscleman who offers several amusing insights into his routines. Makavejev further abstracts the proximity of the antique talkie by hand-tinting numerous scenes, superimposing a collage effect in his consideration of the mystique of this dusty epic and the role of the movies in his country's social history. It is a work whose cleverness never reduces its players to Brechtian automatons; he injects new meaning into the past by suggesting that the original film, the historical footage, the interviews, and his own whimsical touches amiably coexist within a film universe. Makavejev later directed the dismal *Mysteries of the Organism*, in which there is none of the antic humor of *Man Is Not a Bird* or the more sophisticated stylistic assemblage of *Innocence Unprotected*. But if he never directs anything on the level of *Innocence Unprotected*, Makavejev has secured a place in film history and furthered the cause of modernism by exposing the relativity underlying film and social history.

The interrelationship of past and present among the newest faces in the contemporary cinema—the growing realization that film has created its own language and mythology—is predominant in the contemporary cinema. Younger filmmakers, however, are retreating into a private universe that often disengages the audience their predecessors worked so hard to win. No better example of this trend exists than in the films of Bernardo Bertolucci.

Bertolucci's *Before the Revolution* is a paradoxical treatment of the tensions existing in directors torn between the classic virtues film enjoys with other art forms and its unique potential for political activization and modern abstraction. This conflict is poetically articulated at the beginning of *Before the Revolution* through the numerous dissolves; they work as a reflection of the hero, Fabrizio, played by Francesco Barilli, and his changing feeling toward his environment. The film's central relationship concerns Fabrizio, a classic protagonist from the country and his affair, prior to his marriage, with Gina, the seductive city temptress played by Adriana Asti. In the course of their affair, Bertolucci surprisingly changes his focus from Fabrizio's rural innocent to Gina's erotic presence.

Gina takes a lover for the afternoon, and, after parting from him, she is confronted by Fabrizio. As Fabrizio walks away, Bertolucci visualizes Gina's predicament by shooting the background of the separate streets crossed by Fabrizio and Gina's lover out of focus. It is only Gina's face that remains in focus, as if the romantic spark she brings to the film is far more empathetic than Fabrizio's intellectual self-doubt. Shortly thereafter they meet again, and Gina reproaches Fabrizio for not hitting her or her lover, adding that the man almost struck her when she refused to give him her address.

The concluding scenes underscore the change in Bertolucci's sympathies. In a conversation, first with an elderly intellectual, Fabrizio's criticism of the man's passive existence expresses his own fears for his future political commitment. When Fabrizio then meets with his former teacher, Bertolucci undercuts their discussion of social activism by numerous cutaways, perhaps the most telling one to a woman who laments the death of Marilyn. Bertolucci continues this emotionally frenetic pacing in the final sequence at the Rome Opera, where

Fabrizio and his bride talk to Gina. Gina then kisses her youngest nephew, intimating a future romance. The ending may be too abrupt as an epilogue to Fabrizio's romantic education. But Bertolucci's decision to identify with Gina's sensuality instead of Fabrizio's intellectual indecisiveness is all the more remarkable when one considers the prevalence of pessimism and alienation in the contemporary cinema.

The first part of Bertolucci's *Partner*, starring Pierre Clementi, is a stylish, offbeat study of a dandy whose existence is given over to making sense of nonsense. Clementi's ironic interplay with his manservant suggests a modern, iconoclastic variation on the comic banter between Cary Grant and Edward Everett Horton. But in the second part of the film, Clementi's outlandish behavior results in a potpourri of modernist effects. The slight but charming humor of Clementi's outsider is displaced by the modernist's fateful attraction to abstraction. The film, then, not only prefigures Bertolucci's own predicament as a filmmaker attempting to extend the stylistic experiments of a Godard or an Antonioni, but it points to a paradox unique to those directors caught between the aesthetics of film and the tenuous, chaotic imprint of modern history.

Bertolucci's gambit—one that usually appears in the work of directors with strong ties to the avant-garde—faces a number of contemporary directors. The only period in film history revealing a similar degree of tension between abstraction as a style of social expressiveness and abstraction as a style of artistic self-consciousness occurred in the twenties when both Russian and French filmmakers experimented with a montage-oriented cinema. Whereas Russian directors used montage to duplicate the dynamics of revolution, the French film avant-garde exploited film's intuitive affinity with fantasy. The abstruse metaphysics in the films of Bergman and Antonioni and Godard's radical political and poetical sensibility, however, create a different legacy for their successors. Film historians have argued that the sound film offered a logical technological extension of the silent film, but no such awesome change awaited directors who began their careers in the sixties and seventies. Instead of a profound technological development, modern directors are faced with the extreme forms of alienation and politicization that characterize the most recent works of Bergman, Antonioni, and Godard. In *Partner* this artistic paradox is resolved, however unsuccessfully, by conceiving Clementi's split personality as a study first in Apollonian humor and then in the fragmented Dionysian rhetoric of Clementi's revolutionary.

*The Conformist*, Bertolucci's handsome, expressionistic study of fascism, is marked by a baroque camera eye that recalls Welles's fascination with the spiraling forms of power and darkness surrounding Kane's private empire. But the film fails to engross the viewer in the manner of *Citizen Kane* or in the style of Welles's more shrill films like *The Lady from Shanghai* and *Touch of Evil*. The problem lies with Jean-Louis Trintignant's protagonist; his paranoia, his self-doubts and sexual innocence sustain the theatrical fireworks without isolating any one theme. Bertolucci suggests elements of fascism through the florid architecture and rapid editing. However, he is unwilling to correlate these motifs to Trintignant's character, a decision that might have made Trintignant's abject figure a devastating metaphor for Italy in the thirties. He prefers to sketch in a half-dozen riveting themes without resolving any one of them. For example, during Trintignant's visit to his former professor, whom Trintignant will soon kill, they discuss Plato's theory of the caves and man's phantomesque existence. Bertolucci photographs the room and their figures in an encompassing shadow, breaking up their conversation with a series of fade-outs; it is a brilliant scene, but one that titillates instead of enlightening the viewer. *The Spider's Stratagem*, Bertolucci's most neoclassical film, avoids both the romantic exuberance of *Before the Revolution* and the self-conscious flourishes of *The Conformist*. During his protagonist's encounters with his father's mistress and friends, Bertolucci penetrates the town's romantic luster through distancing camera setups and movements that denote the inescapable subjectivity of the hero's investigation into his father's murder. The meetings with his father's friends combine the mystery of his father's assassination during a performance of *Rigoletto* and the elusiveness of their memories and intentions. It is Bertolucci's most cogent work because the lingering, linear tracks of Vittorio Storaro's camera visualize the protagonist and those natives he queries as equally enveloped by the undiluted classical resonance of their backgrounds. The extended depth of field finds its hero, like the impassive residents of the town, absorbed by their classical compositions—the fragrance of an expansive field or the distant image of a man on his bicycle subjecting the hero's investigation to the timeless mysteries of man in nature. The precision with which Bertolucci and Storaro study their resplendent backgrounds intimates that the most formidable qualities of the past are not its sudden, historical permutations but the ever present sunlight and uniform, geometric patina of the town and its inhabitants.

Bertolucci completed only two major films during the seventies, *Last Tango in Paris* and *1900*. Both inspired a great deal of controversy but both, unhappily, fail to deliver on the promise of *Before the Revolution* or on the classicism of *The Spider's Stratagem*. Bertolucci captures the chagrin of Brando's character in his initial sexual encounter with Maria Schneider, but their ensuing erotic relationship, Brando's poisoned memories of his deceased wife, and Jean-Pierre Léaud's self-caricature present a tame picture of self-abnegation. Brando has a few chilling moments, but Bertolucci seems content to glamorize the radicalism of their sexual encounters. Brando and Schneider lack the sweet, glistening sensuality of Chabrol's outcast lovers; their affair unwittingly exposes the very traumas that first drew them together. Lacking hubris either in their humanity or passion, their last tango becomes a Fannie Hurst melodrama updated to the seventies, suggesting that the audience for soap opera has broadened to encompass the shabbier parameters of sexual liberation.

A sweeping sociosexual history of a landed-gentry family and their farmers, *1900* is one of the most ambitious historical dramas undertaken in the contemporary cinema. Like *The Conformist*, it confirms Bertolucci's greater affinity with classic literary, dramatic, and pictorial styles than with the ambiguity and abstraction of the modernists. Yet, like *Last Tango in Paris*, it finds this gifted director experimenting with various operatic subplots that are a poor substitute for the old-fashioned literary formulas that would have held our interest in the characters while clarifying his epic intellectual drama. There are elements of Visconti but without Visconti's faith in his protagonists' romantic passions; Burt Lancaster's suicide, as he decries the loss of his virility to the pretty peasant girl in a cowshed, plays as a self-parody. The episodes involving De Niro, Depardieu, and the epileptic and Donald Sutherland's murder of the boy during a sexual spree are among the dumbest, most callous portrayals of eroticism in the modern cinema. Regardless of the problems of reediting and dubbing that mar *1900* Bertolucci never pinpoints the historical or personal identity of his aristocrats and peasants; the film is comprised of numerous melodramatic confrontations meant to shock the viewer, but the essential link between his characters and history is diffused. De Niro is wasted, while the alluring Dominique Sanda mawkishly replays her role as the decadent. Suprisingly, Donald Sutherland, through the very excess of his characterization, from his lycanthropic smirk to his gritty self-abasement, remains the one engrossing figure. It may be that *1900* did not provoke the rage it deserved because so few filmmakers have attempted this type of project in recent years. But its messy, awkward narrative, its puerile political rhetoric, and its crude sexual polemic should be cited as a major example of the failed classicism of the movies of the seventies. Bertolucci seemed to offer much promise for the future of the movies in the context of Godard's modernism and the metaphysical dread of Bergman and Antonioni; *1900*, however, shows that we are as far from rediscovering the styles and ideas of classical humanism as we were in the sixties.

It is important to remember that *Before the Revolution* appeared at a time when the humanist doctrines of Rossellini and De Sica were under siege. While the most recent films of Antonioni and Fellini questioned the basic premises of the postwar Italian cinema, their dramatic potential was not exhausted. There is strong evidence of the continuity of the humanist tradition in the films of Ermanno Olmi; his poetic studies of Italy's increasing industralization seem to usher in a reappreciation of the basic tenets of humanism. In *The Sound of Trumpets*, he diligently recaptures the young man's awe of the modern city, where he eventually finds a job. The cadence is slower and softer than in the films of Rossellini and De Sica; the theme is no longer one of survival, as in the early works of the humanist cinema, but a recognition of the ominous social dehumanization in a new rebuilt society.

*The Fiances* is a more convincing work. The opening sequence—in which a deserted hall is transformed into a joyous, overcrowded dance celebration—shows the incandescent magic of a director in full control of and in sympathy with his medium and his characters. Carlo Cabrini's performance stands out as one of understated strength and humanity, a laborer who senses the disturbing nature of his job and environment but who does not surrender his natural instincts for fun and camaraderie. In the last fifteen-minute sequence Olmi's camera lyrically delights in the natural wonders of the countryside. However, one feels that his optimism is superimposed and that Antonioni, with greater rigor, has uncovered the impact of our industrial environment in the ending of *L'eclisse*. In *The Scavengers* Olmi abandons the straightforward narrative of *The Sound of Trumpets* and *The Fiances* for a more oblique style. He intercuts between isolated long shots and abrupt close-ups, while his moving camera evokes a more disquieting mood than was evident in his earlier films. His scavengers fail to come alive as individuals or as metaphors for the lethargy resulting from the cancerous effects of poverty. There is no longer the faith in the simple ideals of human dignity and communication that characterized Rossellini's studies of a ruined, desolate country and that was renewed with genuine poetic nuance in *The Sound of Trumpets* and *The Fiances*.

After several years of commercial and stylistic invisibility, Olmi enjoyed a resounding comeback with *The Tree of Wooden Clogs*. A stylistic antidote to Bertolucci's *1900*, Olmi's epic is infused with an appreciation for the land and its workers that reconfirms the pathos in the first films of Rossellini and De Sica. Olmi avoids the polemical stance of these early masters of Italian humanism, showing his laborers as steeped in an interminable replenishing of the land; their few, simple moments of social interaction around a fire reconfirm their solidarity and their underlying bond with nature. His camera picks up those traveling on the road to their communal home the way the sun illuminates a previously invisible stretch of the countryside. The different episodes involving the ailing cow or the father who cuts down a tree to make a new pair of clogs for his son are presented as part of the ebb and flow of nature. The peasants are united by their common dependence on the land and their pleasure in achieving the most meager emblems of social respectability. Olmi's triumph is to have painted the land as the original source of their humanity, suggesting that their creative involvement in the forms and moods of nature is the basis of our civilization—a moral exemplified during the married couple's boat trip to the city. His farmers achieve an almost miraculous simplicity as an act of faith; the tremors of Rossellini's original protagonists have disappeared in the emotional continuum of Olmi's peasants and nature.

The films of Jean-Marie Straub, Jerzy Skolimowski, and Glauber Rocha offer a different perspective as to the direction of the contemporary cinema. *Chronicle of Anna Magdalena Bach* is probably Straub's best-known work, a cogent, even stirring example of how a repressed narrative can enrich its subject. With a minimum of sets and cuts and the use of prints to introduce his historical backgrounds, the splendor of the baroque age is simply, magically animated on film. The film's understated elegance—the selection of the simplest detail to denote the grandeur of the baroque—makes this form of minimalist cinema seem the farthest removed, yet an important addition to the epics of Griffith, Gance, Eisenstein, and Mizoguchi.

In his adaptations of *Billiards at Half-Past Nine* and *Othon*, Straub's asceticism, when combined with the absurdist elements of the avant-garde of the sixties, makes for an inherently solipsistic treatment. *Unreconciled* subverts the argument of Heinrich Böll's novella; people and places are defined in a subjective light, threadbare examples of the agnosticism of the avant-garde. In *Othon* he uses Corneille's drama as a subtext, situating his characters against the background of modern Rome. The film is a philosophic experiment rather than an aesthetic one; his static, extensive long shots and the wooden characterizations refute the passion and heroism of epic drama. Straub's minimalism is best exemplified in a short film that has no title; its characters and images have little meaning other than their lack of meaning; the short concludes with Straub telling the viewer that it was all part of a dream. Once again the reductionist elements of experimentalism are underscored; film is used as a metaphor for the elusiveness of truth—the ultimate example of the art of irrationality.

The films of Jerzy Skolimowski are less schematic than those of Straub but are plagued by equally lethal doses of the poetics of the absurd. Two short films, *Identification Marks: None* and *Barrier*, display a keen graphic eye, but, similar to the work of Miloš Forman, his characters seem trapped by the grim tedium of their surroundings. He is not as sophomoric as Forman, but his characters lack the ingenuity to challenge their society. *Le Départ*, made in France and starring Jean-Pierre Léaud, finds Skolimowski as derivative in his reliance on the bluesy nonchalance of the New Wave as he was in his dependence on the theater of the absurd in his work in Poland. Léaud's skittish behavior as he asks a friend to punch him in the nose, his falling asleep in a car at an automobile exposition, Skolimowski's glib montage of the fashion show, and Léaud's drive through the country are textbook examples of artiness hopelessly lost in its pursuit of art.

Skolimowski's *Deep End*, his first English language film, is an even more negligible effort. The film centers on a shy adolescent and his relationship with a perverse co-worker in a health club. Skolimowski has little interest in explaining the young man's sexual frustration and gradual descent into madness, treating us instead to garish scenes that become, unintentionally, a parody of erotic drama. There is one amusing scene involving Diana Dors as she swarms over the young man while playing out a sexual fantasy. Skolimowski relies on the most precarious elements of experimentalism, particularly in his failing to question his protagonist's absurdist condition. Skolimowski later directed Nabokov's *King Queen Knave*, a film of such unmitigated tastelessness and vapidity that it seems more the work of a Hollywood hack rather than that of a struggling modernist.

Glauber Rocha, a Brazilian director, is one of the few well-known Third World filmmakers. *Antonio das mortes*, *Earth Entranced*, and *Black God—White Devil* are rough-hewn, shoddy dramatic works that assume the form of a wandering balladeer's fables about the war between imperialists and the poor. He spices the films with elements of Brechtian theater but only to the degree that the audience acknowledges that the film it is watching is a document expressly committed to the revolt against the oppressors. *Antonio das mortes* could be interpreted as a poor man's saga of the West, but its importance lies in the use of the movies to dramatize a crude folk poetry. *Earth Entranced* is more typical of the absence of a harmonious interplay of form and content in his anti-West films. *Black God—White Devil* is the one Rocha film I have seen in which Rocha attempts to distinguish the moral and thematic entanglements in his symbolic tales of oppression and rebellion. His use of jazz and the more fluid integration of action scenes show how the movies might one day serve as the folk poetry of the Third World.

With the exception of *The Harder They Come*, which largely derives its antisocial rhetoric from one of the most vibrant music scores ever used on film, the Third World has had little impact on film history. Tomás Gutiérrez Alea's *Memories of Underdevelopment* is a moody, ambivalent study of a sensualist during the first years of the Castro regime. Humberto Solas's *Lucia*, however, with its operatic flourishes, its melodrama, and its final raucous story of a young married couple, which surprisingly recalls the Italian comedies of the sixties, may be more representative of the films that will be produced in Cuba and other Third World countries.

Although Cuban films provide some insight into the evolution of movies during the last decades of the twentieth century, it is the West German cinema that gives one a most detailed reading on the relevance of the contemporary cinema. It is possible that other countries may have made more significant advances that have gone unrecognized because of distribution problems. However, based on the evidence of several movie retrospectives in New York, the films of Rainer Werner Fassbinder, Wim Wenders, and Werner Herzog best articulate the strengths and weaknesses of the movies in the vanguard of modern intellectual history.

Fassbinder was one of the most prolific directors in film history, and this fact alone defines a decisive aspect of movie modernism. Like Godard, Fassbinder's interest in experimenting with numerous effects and themes reenforces the idea that no one style has been accepted as the most valid or incisive way to interpret our social history. Though it would be foolhardy to make any generalization about his disparate corpus of over thirty films, Fassbinder, like Bertolucci, seems most effective in his experiments with classic narratives. Several of his films, for example, *Beware of a Holy Whore*, are characteristic of the cul-de-sac facing the contemporary cinema as he exploits the tentativeness of the film image in this film about a stranded movie company. Unlike, however, Godard's *La Chinoise*, in which the references to Godard's shooting the film enhance its radical point of view, *Beware of a Holy Whore* is marked by prolix self-confessions that lack the lean, sharp cutting edge of Godard's polemic. There is a more acute element of parody in Fassbinder's film, but the amorous interplay among members of the film crew lacks the stylistic irony to make the film work as an example of self-referential cinema.

Fassbinder's experimentalism is, then, of a considerably modified nature. *The American Soldier* is a self-indulgent essay on the gangster film with none of the breezy, wily misanthropy of Godard's *Breathless*. *Why Does Herr H. Run Amok?* is an effective, yet limited study of a man who goes over the brink; its roots are in the psychological novel and not the radical, antisocial poetics one associates with the avant-garde. The problem with *Mother Küsters Goes to Heaven* and *Fox and His Friends* is in Fassbinder's attempt to humanize the feelings of an out-

sider in a straightforward manner. In *Mother Küsters Goes to Heaven* he distorts
Brigitte Mira's desperation through the character of her sluttish daughter. The
daughter uses her father's suicide to secure a job in a nightclub; the raffishness
of her character and the dreadfulness of her cabaret act are juxtaposed in a
heavy-handed, absurd manner to her mother's anxiety. Mira's relationship
with the communist couple and the fairy-tale ending evidence Fassbinder's
tentative tone. In *Fox and His Friends* the theme is the mistreatment of a poor,
homosexual circus laborer, played by Fassbinder, by other homosexuals. The
problem with the film is not so much Fassbinder's minimal acting talent but its
contrived, soap-opera trimmings. One cannot only forecast the downfall of
Fassbinder's character, but the other characters lack the intellectual or physical
beauty to make one care about their callous behavior: Fassbinder's humanism
is undercut by the sappiness of his feelings.

   In his best films—*The Merchant of Four Seasons, Ali: Fear Eats the Soul, The Bitter
Tears of Petra von Kant*—Fassbinder continually surprises one with his sensitivity to the forlorn nature of his protagonists. In *The Merchant of Four Seasons* Fassbinder shows his uncompromising humanism in his portrayal of the pessimism
that haunts the married couple who try to give meaning to their tedious, un-
eventful lives. The two lead performers brilliantly dramatize the fatalism
with which they must live: the wife supports the family while the husband's
moroseness, because of his tubercular condition, leads to his self-destruction.
The story is a conventional one, but it is the freshness and compassion with
which Fassbinder views his characters that create a style of emotionalism that is
altogether fascinating.

   The failure of two ordinary people to sustain a relationship is also the subject
of *Ali: Fear Eats the Soul.* The film concerns Brigitte Mira as an elderly washerwoman and a young, handsome Tunisian who, inexplicably, are drawn to each
other. Mira is self-conscious about her age and dumpy features; the Tunisian, of
his color and his ulcerous stomach condition. She is ridiculed by her neighbors,
while the Tunisian, suffering from the unexpressed stigma of his color, is drawn
to a voluptuous cocktail waitress. Their need for each other is not visualized in
melodramatic expressions of love, but derives from their miserable existence
and their failure to explain their compatibility to their friends. In *Ali: Fear Eats
the Soul* Fassbinder's tendency to the poetics of absurdity is rendered in a far
more intelligent manner than in *Mother Küsters Goes to Heaven* or in *Fox and His
Friends.* The camera seems to be pressed up against the players' faces in the way
a child acquaints himself with strangers or unusual situations; by suddenly cutting back to a reaction or establishing shot of them in a narrow hallway or
sitting against the walls of their freshly painted kitchen, Fassbinder simply abstracts their distraught condition. Fassbinder concludes that because of their
identity as social outcasts their love will never be fully resolved: one is left cher-
ishing Mira's pathos, crying by Ali's bedside in a hospital room after he has
suffered a relapse. Like Handke's *A Sorrow Beyond Dreams* the simplicity and
straightforwardness of the narrative make for an original understanding of
loneliness in the modern world.

*The Bitter Tears of Petra von Kant* is another stirring example of Fassbinder's interest in depicting the commonplace emotional needs of uncommon relationships. His lesbian protagonists, however, are not troubled by the merchant's harrowing self-pity or by the desire for social acceptance of Ali and the washerwoman. The entire film transpires in the home of Petra von Kant, where the characters' lesbianism, like the merchant's terminal illness or Ali's blackness, is implicitly seen as the one factor that draws them together, and, ultimately, that drives them apart. One of the film's virtues, like that of Wolfgang Petersen's *The Consequence*, is Fassbinder's ability to make one empathize with his characters without suggesting that any special consideration is needed to understand their condition. Their glances of affection or suspicion, their outbursts of resentment or longing are wholly inspired by their emotional and sexual dependence on one another. But, unlike *The Consequence*—a moving study of two people who love each other and happen to be homosexuals—Fassbinder's lesbians are not hounded by society nor do they seek its approval in the manner of Ali and the washerwoman; instead he exposes the sophistication and decadence of these women of high fashion as the most fragile of masks. Petra von Kant becomes a lovesick protagonist whose affection for the model, played by Hanna Schygulla, is no less valid or tragic than the great loves of romantic literature. She is an aesthete who discovers the inherent corruptibility of love; though her love object is a woman, Petra von Kant is forced to acknowledge the potential for deceit in every relationship.

Wim Wenders is a less original stylist than Fassbinder. Among West German filmmakers he seems closest in spirit to the brilliant Austrian novelist and playwright Peter Handke, whose *The Goalie's Anxiety at the Penalty Kick* he adapted to the screen. Handke has studied his Kafka well, and his work is an evocative treatment of the vertigo that awaits those who suddenly deviate from their everyday routines. The film lacks the precise, elliptical cadence of the novel, but there is an underlying recognition of how the protagonist's languor places him on the same precipice between control and chaos that he faced as a goalkeeper. Wenders's *Alice in the Cities* is similar to Handke's *Short Letter, Long Farewell*, a journal of the author's travels in America and his observations about our music and movies. While Handke's diary indecisively juxtaposes the author's search for his wife to his increasingly staid comments on American culture, Wenders's film is so enamored of pop music that he does not bother to explain either the character of his traveler or his relationship with the young girl he befriends. The protagonist, in both Handke and Wenders, becomes an obscure catalyst who is more attuned to disjointed reflection than an in-depth study of person and place. This is also true of Wenders's *Summer in the City*, a prototypical avant-garde work in which Wenders uses American rhythm and blues to denote his protagonist's lassitude. There is little interest in making sense of his adventures, in explaining his background or his motivation. Wenders continually fragments our interest in a particular encounter by inexplicably changing the scene; though he seems a more intuitive modernist than Fassbinder, *Summer in the City* is stuck in the avant-garde quagmire of alienation.

*Kings of the Road* is a more committed examination of life on the road than *Alice in the Cities*. But if the earlier film was too sketchy in its character delineation, in *Kings of the Road* Wenders is fearful of omitting any detail in the life of his protagonist who travels from town to town repairing broken film equipment. Since the character is naturally taciturn, it is only when he picks up another drifter and they discuss their feelings of alienation and their underlying need for love that the film begins to get inside the meaning of life on the road. *The American Friend* shows Wenders's development as a film director; he is not as confined by his text as he was in his adaptation of Handke's novel. This is also the problem with the film since Patricia Highsmith's Ripley novels, especially *Ripley's Game* on which *The American Friend* is based, are baroque studies of crime that demand editing rather than elaboration. Tom Ripley and Jonathan Trevanny are two of the most intriguing characters in crime fiction; they are not so much prototypes of the genre as terribly real individuals trapped in a poisonous web of murder. *The American Friend* is an exciting, expressionistic adventure, a collective entry by Dennis Hopper's Ripley and Bruno Ganz's Trevanny into an international underworld punctuated by their bizarre friendship. The editing, especially in the first part of the film, moving from Hamburg to Paris and New York, is almost surreal in its beauty; it uncovers abstracted images of menacing although common origin that reflect the dangerous scheming of Ripley's art forgeries and the fatalism surrounding Trevanny's inescapable identity as a victim of disease. Highsmith's novel takes a traditional, psychologically introspective approach—the violent murders become a terrifying realization of the desperation of both Ripley and Trevanny. The film presents a more ambient study of social dislocation, one whose textual rhythms suggest that Wenders's roots are in the complexities of narrative cinema.

Werner Herzog is the primitive of the West German cinema. In *Even Dwarfs Started Small*, his primitivism derives from his attempt to humanize the dwarfs' condition and their intuitively deviant actions. His direction, however, is too schematic; Herzog's sympathy for his subject is diffused by a quasi-Brechtian staging of life among the dwarfs, awkwardly moving between a naturalistic and expressionistic format. *Land of Silence and Darkness* also concerns an alienated community, in this case the blind and deaf. But unlike *Even Dwarfs Started Small* in which Herzog's tentative dramatic ploys diminish one's interest in his characters, in *Land of Silence and Darkness* he does not obscure his subjects' humanism with extraneous or unfocused stylistic effects. He simply listens to these extraordinary people, as their physical interaction reconfirms the strengths of *cinéma vérité*. In two other documentary shorts, *The Great Ecstasy of the Sculptor Steiner* and *La Soufrière*, Herzog's avowed radicalism is overshadowed by the naturalistic terrain of the documentary film. The films draw on the strengths of television sports and *National Geographic* specials, celebrating the breathtaking physical and aesthetic dimensions of ski flying in the former and entering, with the viewer, into the unsettling physical presence of Guadeloupe in the latter. Herzog seems to admit, at least in these documentary shorts, that the camera's ability to record the most specialized activity or its ability to immerse the viewer in a remote landscape negates the need for any abstraction on the part of the director. But he is unwilling to adopt such an impersonal, objective point of view in his other films.

With the exception of the opening trek across a mountain pass, *Aguirre, the Wrath of God* fails to capture the visually unsettling qualities of the search for El Dorado. Herzog is more interested in dramatizing the discordant effect of a primitive environment on the soldiers. But Klaus Kinski's Aguirre acts no differently in this role than in the numerous German crime thrillers in which he has been featured. His psychopathic facade remains the most visible proof of Herzog's shrill attack on the explorers of the New World. The other actors seem perfunctory, somewhat mechanical, leading one to conclude that for Herzog, time, place, and motivation are secondary, if not superfluous. The actors' dramatic incongruity is paralleled by the sudden dramatic twists, beginning with the mutiny and ending with the slaughter.

*Stroszek* and *The Mystery of Kaspar Hauser* feature Bruno S., and his performances create an inherently dispossessing relationship between audience and film. In real life Bruno S. was hospitalized for schizophrenia; in *Stroszek* he plays a released inmate who decides to journey with an elderly musician and a fallen girl to Wisconsin. But his slow, accented facial contortions and generally quirky behavior do not establish a distinct framework for Herzog's penetration of America. Herzog isolates the disconcerting clichés of American life, for example, the mobile homes and the truckers with their CBs; however, Bruno S. and his two companions seem as lost in America as they were in Germany. As outsiders they are impervious to the special qualities of their environment; the absurdity of their condition reverberates with little tension other than as an encounter session comprised of neurotics and malcontents. Bruno S.'s suicide in the amusement park underlines this theme, reacting to the girl's departure and the incarceration of his musician friend in a final act of despair. *The Mystery of Kaspar Hauser* is a more problematic and deeply flawed film because the ideas Herzog hopes to abstract and ends up dissipating possess an inherent philosophical depth. Karl Jakob Wassermann's novel is a magnificent treatment of the social corruption of innocence; Herzog, however, is not interested in the novel's profound interplay between religious and scientific ideas. The film also avoids Handke's linguistic, gestalt interpretation of the myth of the wild child, choosing instead to absorb the camera in Bruno S.'s debilitated appearance and retarded motor responses. With the exception of a dream Bruno S. relates, little effort is made to see how this naïf visualizes the world or how the different sectors of the community respond to his appearance. Herzog's approach is more emotional, and although Bruno S. makes a determined effort to express the boy's development as a member of society, the subject remains too intellectual for Herzog's intuitive direction.

While undertaking a brief survey of the contemporary cinema to better understand the artistic alternatives available for its future development, an attempt must also be made to see how the artistic resources of the movies are affected by the medium's social and technological evolution. One of the earliest voiced criticisms of the movies was that its development was contingent on finance and technology; a general feeling prevailed that the vision of a script-writer or director could not flourish in the way a painter, musician, or writer perfected his work. Yet even as film has gained a modest acceptance among academics, its future development may be dependent on the very idea that gave birth to motion pictures: scientific, technological progress.

The principle of progress is infinite. Scientific advances in the nineteenth century created more powerful instruments for penetrating the mysteries of the human mind and body and for controlling the forces of nature. The initial mastery of capturing motion on film seemed an innocent yet potentially revolutionary invention, a primitive form of entertainment whose absence of speaking voices led filmmakers to pursue abstract styles of visual communication. Griffith offered one alternative for epic filmmakers by searching for poetic archetypes of space and time through his idealized pictures of nature and the individual and the dynamic abbreviation of his dramatic conflicts. Slapstick comedians established an underlying equation between the dizzying technology of modern life and the cinema's facility for accentuating its disconcerting scope. The German film industry, expanding Méliès original experiments in theatrical trompe l'oeil, explored the sensory potential of the silent-film experience through their psychologically stylized settings of social oppression and personal strife. Russian filmmakers and the French avant-garde emphasized the rhythmic dynamics of the film drama through symbolic equivalents to Marx's dialectic of historical conflict and to the Freudian schema of repression and revolt.

The increasing simplification and diversification of film technology—lighter, more mobile cameras, coated lenses, incandescent lighting, panchromatic film, optically recorded sound—led to a greater fluidity in the film drama; filmmakers were achieving a technological independence in imagining the world on film. The eventual application of wide-screen filmmaking, however, revealed that technological advance was not synonymous with an increase in the medium's dramatic potential. While producers would eventually adopt Henri Chrétien's anamorphic lens and a wide film in meeting the challenge of television, the style of their productions became increasingly archaic, duplicating the masterpieces of Western art.

The introduction of television in the late forties offers an intriguing corollary to the development of wide-screen technology. With its small screen and silent-film aspect ratio, the structural properties of the television medium enabled it to explore the very qualities film was renouncing. Because of its heightened powers of social unification and its unique affinity with the ever present news event—whether in its coverage of an ongoing war, in its close-up interviews with those who govern, in its corresponding man-in-the-street profiles, or through its expanding the audience for a sporting event or an opera telecast—television transforms world history into an entertaining social mosaic.

The reason for the repeated analogies drawn between the video image and the mosaic lies in the predominant foreground space common to both. As the eye is wholly absorbed by the compressed foreground stylization of the video image, the inability of the viewer to establish a spatial interplay with three-dimensional space lends a far greater cognitive and spatial authority to the foreground images. The featured close-ups of newscasters or talk-show hosts, among two of the most popular and paradigmatic of television personalities, reassert the primacy of a one-to-one dialogue, divorced from the spatial depth that we observe in everyday society. The ubiquitousness of space in medieval art denotes the omnipresence of God; the ubiquitousness of space on the television screen substitutes the iconography of the church and the ideal of transcendence with popular cultural heroes and the ideal of immediate, constant energy.

Yet the original resources of television to span time and space in making the spectacle of history an immediately perceived phenomenon must be considered against the conventional entertainment quotients that fill the viewer's day. Whereas early-morning and late-evening talk shows make a shrewd though superficial use of the medium as the intermediary between the individual and society, a majority of television time is comprised of outdated forms of social mimesis and entertainment. Daytime programming with its game shows and soap operas and prime-time television with its slick action shows and its bland situation comedies turn to the Hollywood studio system of the thirties and its double-bill fare as a blueprint. Prime-time television in particular has tried to revitalize the mythmaking potential of film studio production of the thirties and in the process has increased the susceptibility of the movies to its demographic formulas. Television continues to adhere to a shopworn notion of entertainment because of the social and economic makeup of its audience. Television is a great unifier, and, therefore, it must search for the most common threads of experience to achieve a reading in the collective Nielsen unconscious. A country which promotes ideals of freedom and privacy remains cautious if not fearful of renouncing the faceless, middle-of-the-road identity that is fulfilled by the three major networks. A change in the concept of television as entertainment will only emerge when a fundamental change has occurred in the aspirations of its public—both in the idea of the society it desires and in the role of television in making us more passive or active members of our society.

While a term like "popular art" is used to designate the influence of film, it assumes a new meaning through television. The eclecticism of a popular art like film undergoes a further transformation on television owing to television's role as a neutral archive of various cultural forms while making them a part of the home experience. It is this synthesis of hoary cultural styles and primitive forms of entertainment and communication that makes television a more pure exemplar of popular culture. The outer spaces of television's satellites become our immediate, uniform reality; we live in this space, our individuality and consciousness submerged into a collective physical and cognitive reality.

McLuhan's "medium is the message" erroneously argued that technology exists as an autonomous force; yet his intellectual daring as one of the prophets of technology cannot be dismissed when we consider his characterization of television transforming movies into art. McLuhan understood that movies on television would assume a venerable patina of culture. How ironic, then, that film, originally attacked for its lack of culture, should become on television one of our most treasured symbols of the past.

# Works Cited

Bergson, Henri. *Creative Evolution*. Translated by Arthur Mitchell. New York: The Modern Library, 1944.

Dickens, Charles. *Martin Chuzzlewit*. New York: Dodd, Mead & Co., 1945.

Eisenstein, Sergei. *Film Form*. New York: Harcourt, Brace & World, 1949.

Hall, Ben. *The Best Remaining Seats*. New York: Clarkson N. Potter, 1961.

Hartman, Geoffrey H. *The Unmediated Vision*. New Haven: Yale University Press, 1954.

Hoffman, Daniel. *Poe Poe Poe Poe Poe Poe Poe*. New York: Doubleday, 1972.

Kahnweiler, Daniel-Henry. *The Rise of Cubism*. Translated by Henry Aronson. New York: Wittenborn, Schultz, 1949.

Leyda, Jay. *Kino*. London; Winchester, Mass.: Allen & Unwin, 1960.

Malevich, Kasimir. *The Non-Objective World*. Translated by Howard Dearstyne. Chicago: Paul Theobald, 1959.

Mallarmé, Stéphane. *Selected Prose Poems, Essays, and Letters*. Baltimore: Johns Hopkins University Press, 1956.

Mumford, Lewis. *The Brown Decades*. New York: Dover Publications, 1971.

Orsini, G. N. G. *Coleridge and German Idealism*. Carbondale: Southern Illinois University Press, 1969.

Rosenfeld, Paul. *Musical Impressions: Selections from Paul Rosenfeld's Criticism*. Edited by Herbert A. Leibowitz. New York: Hill and Wang, 1969.

Wilenski, R. H. *The Meaning of Modern Sculpture*. London: Faber & Faber, 1932.

Wittgenstein, Ludwig. *The Blue and Brown Books*. Oxford: Basil Blackwell, 1958.

# Index